KU-222-392

Real Time UML
Third Edition

The Addison-Wesley Object Technology Series

Grady Booch, Ivar Jacobson, and James Rumbaugh, Series Editors
For more information, check out the series web site at www.awprofessional.com/otseries.

Ahmed/Umrysh, *Developing Enterprise Java Applications with J2EE™ and UML*

Arlow/Neustadt, *Enterprise Patterns and MDA: Building Better Software with Archetype Patterns and UML*

Arlow/Neustadt, *UML and the Unified Process: Practical Object-Oriented Analysis and Design*

Armour/Miller, *Advanced Use Case Modeling: Software Systems*

Bellin/Simone, *The CRC Card Book*

Bergström/Råberg, *Adopting the Rational Unified Process: Success with the RUP*

Binder, *Testing Object-Oriented Systems: Models, Patterns, and Tools*

Bittner/Spence, *Use Case Modeling*

Booch, *Object Solutions: Managing the Object-Oriented Project*

Booch, *Object-Oriented Analysis and Design with Applications, 2E*

Booch/Bryan, *Software Engineering with ADA, 3E*

Booch/Rumbaugh/Jacobson, *The Unified Modeling Language User Guide*

Box/Brown/Ewald/Sells, *Effective COM: 50 Ways to Improve Your COM and MTS-based Applications*

Carlson, *Modeling XML Applications with UML: Practical e-Business Applications*

Collins, *Designing Object-Oriented User Interfaces*

Conallen, *Building Web Applications with UML, 2E*

D'Souza/Wills, *Objects, Components, and Frameworks with UML: The Catalysis(SM) Approach*

Douglass, *Doing Hard Time: Developing Real-Time Systems with UML, Objects, Frameworks, and Patterns*

Douglass, *Real-Time Design Patterns: Robust Scalable Architecture for Real-Time Systems*

Douglass, *Real Time UML, 3E: Advances in The UML for Real-Time Systems*

Eeles et al., *Building J2EE™ Applications with the Rational Unified Process*

Fontoura/Pree/Rumpe, *The UML Profile for Framework Architectures*

Fowler, *Analysis Patterns: Reusable Object Models*

Fowler et al., *Refactoring: Improving the Design of Existing Code*

Fowler, *UML Distilled, 3E: A Brief Guide to the Standard Object Modeling Language*

Gomaa, *Designing Concurrent, Distributed, and Real-Time Applications with UML*

Graham, *Object-Oriented Methods, 3E: Principles and Practice*

Heinckiens, *Building Scalable Database Applications: Object-Oriented Design, Architectures, and Implementations*

Hofmeister/Nord/Dilip, *Applied Software Architecture*

Jacobson/Booch/Rumbaugh, *The Unified Software Development Process*

Jordan, *C++ Object Databases: Programming with the ODMG Standard*

Kleppe/Warmer/Bast, *MDA Explained: The Model Driven Architecture™: Practice and Promise*

Kroll/Kruchten, *The Rational Unified Process Made Easy: A Practitioner's Guide to the RUP*

Kruchten, *The Rational Unified Process, 3E: An Introduction*

Lau, *The Art of Objects: Object-Oriented Design and Architecture*

Leffingwell/Widrig, *Managing Software Requirements, 2E: A Use Case Approach*

Manassis, *Practical Software Engineering: Analysis and Design for the .NET Platform*

Marshall, *Enterprise Modeling with UML: Designing Successful Software through Business Analysis*

McGregor/Sykes, *A Practical Guide to Testing Object-Oriented Software*

Mellor/Balcer, *Executable UML: A Foundation for Model-Driven Architecture*

Mellor et al., *MDA Distilled: Principles of Model-Driven Architecture*

Naiburg/Maksimchuk, *UML for Database Design*

Oestereich, *Developing Software with UML, 2E: Object-Oriented Analysis and Design in Practice*

Page-Jones, *Fundamentals of Object-Oriented Design in UML*

Pohl, *Object-Oriented Programming Using C++, 2E*

Pollice et al. *Software Development for Small Teams: A RUP-Centric Approach*

Quatrani, *Visual Modeling with Rational Rose 2002 and UML*

Rector/Sells, *ATL Internals*

Reed, *Developing Applications with Visual Basic and UML*

Rosenberg/Scott, *Applying Use Case Driven Object Modeling with UML: An Annotated e-Commerce Example*

Rosenberg/Scott, *Use Case Driven Object Modeling with UML: A Practical Approach*

Royce, *Software Project Management: A Unified Framework*

Rumbaugh/Jacobson/Booch, *The Unified Modeling Language Reference Manual*

Schneider/Winters, *Applying Use Cases, 2E: A Practical Guide*

Smith/Williams, *Performance Solutions: A Practical Guide to Creating Responsive, Scalable Software*

Stevens/Pooley, *Using UML, Updated Edition: Software Engineering with Objects and Components*

Unhelkar, *Process Quality Assurance for UML-Based Projects*

van Harmelen, *Object Modeling and User Interface Design: Designing Interactive Systems*

Wake, *Refactoring Workbook*

Warmer/Kleppe, *The Object Constraint Language, 2E: Getting Your Models Ready for MDA*

White, *Software Configuration Management Strategies and Rational ClearCase®: A Practical Introduction*

The Component Software Series

Clemens Szyperski, Series Editor
For more information, check out the series web site at www.awprofessional.com/csseries.

Allen, *Realizing eBusiness with Components*

Apperly et al., *Service- and Component-based Development: Using the Select Perspective™ and UML*

Atkinson et al., *Component-Based Product Line Engineering with UML*

Cheesman/Daniels, *UML Components: A Simple Process for Specifying Component-Based Software*

Szyperski, *Component Software, 2E: Beyond Object-Oriented Programming*

Whitehead, *Component-Based Development: Principles and Planning for Business Systems*

Real Time UML
Third Edition

Advances in The UML
for Real-Time Systems

Bruce Powel Douglass

Addison-Wesley

Boston • San Francisco • New York • Toronto • Montreal
London • Munich • Paris • Madrid
Capetown • Sydney • Tokyo • Singapore • Mexico City

Many of the designations used by manufacturers and sellers to distinguish their products are claimed as trademarks. Where those designations appear in this book, and Addison-Wesley was aware of a trademark claim, the designations have been printed with initial capital letters or in all capitals.

The author and publisher have taken care in the preparation of this book, but make no expressed or implied warranty of any kind and assume no responsibility for errors or omissions. No liability is assumed for incidental or consequential damages in connection with or arising out of the use of the information or programs contained herein.

The publisher offers discounts on this book when ordered in quantity bulk purchases and special sales. For more information, please contact:

> U.S. Corporate and Government Sales
> (800) 382-3419
> corpsales@pearsontechgroup.com

For sales outside of the U.S., please contact:

> International Sales
> (317) 581-3793
> international@pearsontechgroup.com

Visit Addison-Wesley on the Web: www.awprofessional.com

Library of Congress Cataloging-in-Publication Data

Douglass, Bruce Powel.
    Real time UML : advances in the UML for real-time systems / Bruce Powell
Douglass.—3rd ed.
      p.   cm.—(The Addison-Wesley object technology series)
  Includes bibliographical references and index.
    ISBN 0-321-16076-2 (alk. paper)
    1. Embedded computer systems—Programming.   2. Real-time data processing.
  3. Object-oriented methods (Computer science) I. Title. II. Series.

QA76.6D658 2004
005.1'17—dc22   2003022902

Copyright © 2004 by Pearson Education, Inc.

All rights reserved. No part of this publication may be reproduced, stored in a retrieval system, or transmitted, in any form, or by any means, electronic, mechanical, photocopying, recording, or otherwise, without the prior consent of the publisher. Printed in the United States of America. Published simultaneously in Canada.

For information on obtaining permission for use of material from this work, please submit a written request to:

> Pearson Education, Inc.
> Rights and Contracts Department
> 75 Arlington Street, Suite 300
> Boston, MA 02116
> Fax: (617) 848-7047

ISBN: 0-321-16076-2
Text printed on recycled paper
1 2 3 4 5 6 7 8 9 10—CRS—0807060504
First printing, February 2004

This book is dedicated to my family—Scott and Blake, my two wonderful sons—of whom I am extremely proud—and Sarah, the most beautiful, sexy, wonderful, and geeky woman in the world. :-x

Contents

Figure List xix
About the Author xxvii
Foreword to the Third Edition xxix
Foreword to the Previous Editions xxxi
Preface to the Third Edition.. xxxvii
Preface to the Second Edition xli
Preface to the First Edition xlv
Acknowledgments xlix

Chapter 1: **Introduction to the World of Real-Time and
            Embedded Systems** 1
   1.1 What Is Special about Real-Time Systems? 2
   1.2 Time, Performance, and Quality of Service 7
        1.2.1 Modeling Actions and Concurrency 8
        1.2.2 Modeling Resources 15
        1.2.3 Modeling Time 16
        1.2.4 Modeling Schedulability 17
        1.2.5 Modeling Performance 28
   1.3 Systems Engineering vs. Software Engineering 29
   1.4 What Do We Mean by *Architecture*? 30
   1.5 The Rapid Object-Oriented Process for
        Embedded Systems (ROPES) Process 31
        1.5.1 Model-Driven Development (MDD) 33
        1.5.2 The ROPES Spiral in More Detail 36
   1.6 MDA and Platform-Independent Models 43
   1.7 Scheduling Model-Based Projects 46
        1.7.1 Why Schedule? 46
        1.7.2 Estimation 48
        1.7.3 BERT and ERNIE 48
        1.7.4 Scheduling 51

1.8   Model Organization Principles 55
       1.8.1   Why Model Organization? 55
       1.8.2   Specific Model Organization Patterns 60
1.9   Working with Model-Based Projects 65
1.10 Looking Ahead 73
1.11 Exercises 74
1.12 References 75

**Chapter 2:   Object Orientation with
UML 2.0—Structural Aspects** 77
2.1   Object Orientation with UML 78
2.2   Small Things: Objects, Classes, and Interfaces 80
       2.2.1   Objects 80
       2.2.2   Classes 83
       2.2.3   Notation 87
       2.2.4   Interfaces 89
       2.2.5   Messaging 92
2.3   Relations 94
       2.3.1   Associations 95
       2.3.2   Aggregation 98
       2.3.3   Composition 100
       2.3.4   Generalization 103
       2.3.5   Dependency 106
       2.3.6   Structural Diagrams 108
       2.3.7   Mapping Objects to Code 110
2.4   Big Things: Packages, Components, and
       Subsystems 113
       2.4.1   Model Organization: Packages 114
       2.4.2   Structured Classes: Composites, Parts,
                Ports, and Connectors 116
       2.4.3   Components 120
       2.4.4   Subsystems 123
       2.4.5   Deployments: Nodes and Nonesuch 125
       2.4.6   So, Nodes or Classes? 127
       2.4.7   Architectural Hierarchy 129
2.5   Advanced: UML Metamodel of Structural
       Elements (for the Advanced Modeler) 131
2.6   Additional Notations and Semantics 133

2.7   Looking Ahead 136
2.8   Exercises 136
2.9   References 137

Chapter 3:   **Object Orientation with UML 2.0—**
Dynamic Aspects 139
3.1   Behavior and the UML 140
3.2   Types of Behavior 141
      3.2.1   Simple Behavior 141
      3.2.2   State Behavior 142
      3.2.3   Continuous Behavior 143
3.3   Behavior Primitives: Actions and Activities 144
3.4   Behavior and the Single Object 148
      3.4.1   Basic Statechart Elements 148
      3.4.2   And-States 156
      3.4.3   Pseudostates 158
      3.4.4   Inherited State Models 167
      3.4.5   Ill-Formed Statecharts 169
      3.4.6   Cardiac Pacemaker Example 172
      3.4.7   Protocol State Machines 182
      3.4.8   Activity Diagrams 184
3.5   Interactions 189
      3.5.1   Sequence Diagrams 190
      3.5.2   Timing Diagrams 204
3.6   Summary 212
3.7   Exercises 212
3.8   References 214

Chapter 4:   **UML Profile for Schedulability, Performance,**
and Time 215
4.1   UML Profiles 216
      4.1.1   Stereotypes 217
      4.1.2   Tagged Values 219
      4.1.3   Profiles 220
4.2   "RT UML" Profile 222
      4.2.1   General Resource Model Subprofile 227
      4.2.2   Time Modeling Subprofile 232
      4.2.3   Concurrency Modeling Subprofile 240

        4.2.4   Schedulability Modeling Subprofile 242
        4.2.5   Performance Modeling Subprofile 256
        4.2.6   Real-Time CORBA Subprofile 268
    4.3   Looking Ahead 273
    4.4   Exercises 273
    4.5   References 275

Chapter 5:   Requirements Analysis of Real-Time Systems 277
    5.1   Requirements 278
    5.2   Use Cases 280
        5.2.1   Actors 282
        5.2.2   Use Cases and Text 297
        5.2.3   Use Case Relations 299
        5.2.4   Using Use Cases 301
        5.2.5   Identifying Use Cases 301
    5.3   Detailing the Use Cases 305
        5.3.1   Scenarios for Use Cases 306
        5.3.2   Statecharts 317
        5.3.3   Activity Diagrams 322
        5.3.4   Timing Diagrams 325
    5.4   Looking Ahead 327
    5.5   Exercises 328
    5.6   References 329

Chapter 6:   Analysis: Object Domain Analysis 331
    6.1   The Object Discovery Process 332
    6.2   Connecting the Object Model with
           the Use Case Model 334
    6.3   Key Strategies for Object Identification 339
        6.3.1   Underline the Noun Strategy 339
        6.3.2   Identify the Causal Objects 343
        6.3.3   Identify Services (Passive Contributors) ... 345
        6.3.4   Identify Messages and Information
                 Flows 346
        6.3.5   Identify Real-World Items 346
        6.3.6   Identify Physical Devices 348
        6.3.7   Identify Key Concepts 349
        6.3.8   Identify Transactions 349
        6.3.9   Identify Persistent Information 351

	6.3.10	Identify Visual Elements	351
	6.3.11	Identify Control Elements	355
	6.3.12	Apply Scenarios	356
6.4	Identify Object Associations		358
6.5	Object Attributes		362
6.6	Discovering Candidate Classes		364
6.7	Class Diagrams		365
	6.7.1	Associative Classes	367
	6.7.2	Generalization Relationships	370
6.8	Looking Ahead		396
6.9	Exercises		396
6.10	References		398

Chapter 7: Analysis: Defining Object Behavior 399
7.1	Object Behavior		400
	7.1.1	Simple Behavior	400
	7.1.2	State Behavior	402
	7.1.3	Continuous Behavior	403
7.2	Defining Object State Behavior		404
	7.2.1	Cardiac Pacemaker Example	409
	7.2.2	Calculator Example	422
	7.2.3	Event Hierarchies	441
7.3	Interactions		443
	7.3.1	Sequence Diagrams	444
7.4	Defining Operations		463
	7.4.1	Types of Operations	465
	7.4.2	Strategies for Defining Operations	468
7.5	Looking Ahead		471
7.6	Exercises		472
7.7	References		472

Chapter 8: Architectural Design 473
8.1	Overview of Design		474
8.2	What Is Architectural Design?		477
	8.2.1	Logical Architecture	478
	8.2.2	Physical Architecture	482
	8.2.3	Subsystem and Component View	486
	8.2.4	Concurrency and Resource View	488
	8.2.5	Distribution View	492

8.2.6   Safety and Reliability View 497

8.2.7   Deployment View 499

8.2.8   Physical Architecture Issues 501

8.2.9   Software Architecture Issues 503

8.3   Software Meets Hardware:
Deployment Architecture in UML 509

8.4   Concurrency and Resource Design 512

8.4.1   Representing Threads 512

8.4.2   System Task Diagram 513

8.4.3   Concurrent State Diagrams 515

8.4.4   Defining Threads 516

8.4.5   Identifying Threads 518

8.4.6   Assigning Objects to Threads 520

8.4.7   Defining Thread Rendezvous 520

8.4.8   Sharing Resources 522

8.4.9   Assigning Priorities 523

8.5   Looking Ahead 523

8.6   Exercises 524

8.7   References 525

Chapter 9:   **Mechanistic Design** 527

9.1   What Is Mechanistic Design? 528

9.2   Mechanistic Design Patterns 530

9.3   The Observer Pattern 533

9.3.1   Abstract 533

9.3.2   Problem 533

9.3.3   Pattern Structure 534

9.3.4   Collaboration Roles 535

9.3.5   Consequences 536

9.3.6   Implementation Strategies 536

9.3.7   Sample Model 537

9.4   The Proxy Pattern 538

9.4.1   Abstract 538

9.4.2   Problem 538

9.4.3   Pattern Structure 540

9.4.4   Collaboration Roles 540

9.4.5   Consequences 543

9.4.6   Implementation Strategies 543

9.4.7   Sample Model 544

9.5   Reliable Transaction Pattern 547
       9.5.1   Abstract 548
       9.5.2   Problem 548
       9.5.3   Pattern Structure 548
       9.5.4   Collaboration Roles 551
       9.5.5   Consequences 553
       9.5.6   Implementation Strategies 553
       9.5.7   Sample Model 553
9.6   Smart Pointer Pattern 555
       9.6.1   Abstract 555
       9.6.2   Problem 556
       9.6.3   Pattern Structure 557
       9.6.4   Collaboration Roles 557
       9.6.5   Consequences 558
       9.6.6   Implementation Strategies 560
       9.6.7   Related Patterns 560
       9.6.8   Sample Model 560
9.7   Guarded Call Pattern 562
       9.7.1   Abstract 562
       9.7.2   Problem 562
       9.7.3   Pattern Structure 563
       9.7.4   Collaboration Roles 563
       9.7.5   Consequences 564
       9.7.6   Implementation Strategies 565
       9.7.7   Sample Model 565
9.8   Container Pattern 567
       9.8.1   Abstract 568
       9.8.2   Problem 568
       9.8.3   Pattern Structure 569
       9.8.4   Collaboration Roles 570
       9.8.5   Consequences 570
       9.8.6   Implementation Strategies 570
       9.8.7   Sample Model 570
9.9   The Rendezvous Pattern 579
       9.9.1   Abstract 580
       9.9.2   Problem 580
       9.9.3   Pattern Structure 580
       9.9.4   Collaboration Roles 581
       9.9.5   Consequences 582

9.9.6   Implementation Strategies 582

9.9.7   Related Patterns 583

9.9.8   Sample Model 583

9.10   Looking Ahead 585

9.11   Exercises 585

9.12   References 586

Chapter 10: Detailed Design 589

10.1   What Is Detailed Design? 590

10.2   Data Structure 591

10.3   Associations 597

10.4   Operations 600

10.5   Visibility 602

10.6   Algorithms 604

10.7   Exceptions 610

10.8   Summary 614

10.9   Exercises 615

10.10 References 616

Chapter 11: Special Topic: C⁴ISR Architecture and the UML 617

11.1   Introduction 618

11.2   What is C⁴ISR? 618

11.3   Required Products of C⁴ISR 625

11.3.1 AV-1 Overview and
            Summary Information 626

11.3.2 The AV-2 Integrated Dictionary 626

11.3.3 OV-1 High-Level Operational
            Concept Graphic 626

11.3.4 OV-2 Operational Node Connectivity
            Description 631

11.3.5 OV-3 Operational Information
            Exchange Matrix 632

11.3.6 SV-1 System Interface Description 633

11.3.7 TV-1 Technical Architecture Profile 635

11.4   Supporting Products 635

11.4.1 OV-4 Command Relationships Chart 635

11.4.2 OV-5 Operational Activity Model 635

11.4.3 OV-6a Operational Rules Model,
            SV-10a Systems Rules Model 638

	11.4.4	OV-6b Operational State Transition Description, SV-10b Systems State Transition Description	640
	11.4.5	OV-6c Operational Event-Trace Description, SV-10c Systems Event Trace Description	640
	11.4.6	OV-7 Logical Data Model	641
	11.4.7	SV-3 Systems-Systems Matrix	641
	11.4.8	SV-4 Systems Functionality Description	644
	11.4.9	SV-5 Operational Activity to Systems Function Traceability Matrix	645
	11.4.10	SV-6 Systems Data Exchange Matrix	646
	11.4.11	SV-7 Systems Performance Parameters Matrix	646
	11.4.12	SV-8 Systems Evolution Description	648
	11.4.13	SV-9 Systems Technology Forecast	649
	11.4.14	SV-11 Physical Schema	649
11.5	Summary		652
11.6	Acknowledgments		652
11.7	References		652
Appendix: Notational Summary			653
Index			675

Figure List

Figure 1-1: Synchronization Patterns 13
Figure 1-2: ‹‹active›› Objects and Threads 14
Figure 1-3: Required and Offered Quality of Service 15
Figure 1-4: Priority Inversion Model 24
Figure 1-5: Priority Inversion Scenario 25
Figure 1-6: ROPES Spiral Macrocycle 32
Figure 1-7: ROPES SemiSpiral Lifecycle 34
Figure 1-8: ROPES Spiral 37
Figure 1-9: ROPES Process Artifacts 39
Figure 1-10: MDA Overview 44
Figure 1-11: The MDA Approach 45
Figure 1-12: Sample Schedule 53
Figure 1-13: Resource Histogram 54
Figure 1-14: Use Case-Based Model of Organization 60
Figure 1-15: Framework-Based Model Organization 61
Figure 1-16: Logical Model-Based Model Organization 63
Figure 1-17: Physical Model-Based Model Organization 65
Figure 1-18: Model Execution 69

Figure 2-1: Object Abstraction 83
Figure 2-2: Objects and Classes 87
Figure 2-3: Objects and Classes in Use 89
Figure 2-4: Interfaces 91
Figure 2-5: Sending Messages 93
Figure 2-6: Simple Association 96
Figure 2-7: Association, Aggregation, and Composition 99
Figure 2-8: Composition and Parts 101
Figure 2-9: Generalization 104
Figure 2-10: Dependency 108

Figure 2-11: Packages 115
Figure 2-12: Structured Classes 117
Figure 2-13: Interfaces, Connections, and Ports 121
Figure 2-14: Components 122
Figure 2-15: Subsystems 124
Figure 2-16: Subsystem Example 126
Figure 2-17: Nodes and Deployment 128
Figure 2-18: Levels of Abstraction in Architecture 130
Figure 2-19: Subset of UML Metamodel for Structural Elements 132
Figure 2-20: Constraints in Action 135

Figure 3-1: State Machine for an Object 143
Figure 3-2: Telephone Statechart 149
Figure 3-3: State Internal Features 151
Figure 3-4: Statechart of Object with And-States 157
Figure 3-5: UML Pseudostates 159
Figure 3-6: Branches and Junctions 162
Figure 3-7: History 165
Figure 3-8: Forks and Joins 166
Figure 3-9: Referencing State Machine; OnHook
            and OffHook Submachines 168
Figure 3-10: Inherited Statecharts 170
Figure 3-11: Ill-Formed Statechart 171
Figure 3-12: Pacemaker Class Diagram 175
Figure 3-13: Communications Subsystem 176
Figure 3-14: Pacing Engine Subsystem 177
Figure 3-15: ReedSwitch State Model 178
Figure 3-16: CoilDriver State Model 179
Figure 3-17: Communications Manager State Model 180
Figure 3-18: Processing Statechart 181
Figure 3-19: Chamber Model State Model 182
Figure 3-20: Atrial Model State Model 183
Figure 3-21: Ventricular Model State Model 184
Figure 3-22: Protocol State Machine Context and Machines 185
Figure 3-23: Activity Chart 187
Figure 3-24: Additional Activity Diagram Notations 188
Figure 3-25: Sequence Diagram 191
Figure 3-26: Additional Sequence Diagram Annotations 193
Figure 3-27: Partial Ordering 194

Figure 3-28: Loops and Branches 198
Figure 3-29: Parallel Regions 200
Figure 3-30: Assert, Consider, Ignore? 202
Figure 3-31: Referencing Sequence Diagram 203
Figure 3-32: Lifeline Decomposition 204
Figure 3-33: Referenced Interaction Fragment 205
Figure 3-34: Simple State Timing Diagram 207
Figure 3-35: Timing Diagram with Multiple Lifelines 208
Figure 3-36: Simple Task Timing Diagram 209
Figure 3-37: Task Timing Diagram with Shading 210
Figure 3-38: Timing Diagram with Continuous Values 211

Figure 4-1: UML Stereotypes 218
Figure 4-2: Tagged Values and Constraints 220
Figure 4-3: Representing Tagged Values 221
Figure 4-4: RT UML Profile Use Cases 224
Figure 4-5: Usage Paradigm for the RT Profile 225
Figure 4-6: RT UML Profile Organization 226
Figure 4-7: Client-Server Basis of the GRM 228
Figure 4-8: Core Resource Model 228
Figure 4-9: Static Resource Usage Model 229
Figure 4-10: Causality Loop 230
Figure 4-11: Dynamic Resource Usage Model 230
Figure 4-12: Timing Marks 239
Figure 4-13: Concurrency Subprofile Domain Model 240
Figure 4-14: Concurrency Subprofile Stereotypes Example 244
Figure 4-15: Schedulability Domain Model 245
Figure 4-16: Schedulability Subprofile Example (Global RMA) 253
Figure 4-17: Schedulability Subprofile Example
                (Scenario Analysis) 255
Figure 4-18: Performance Domain Model 258
Figure 4-19: Performance Model Example (Structure) 264
Figure 4-20: Performance Model Example (Deployment) 265
Figure 4-21: Performance Model Example (Scenario) 267
Figure 4-22: Broker Pattern 269
Figure 4-23 Real-Time CORBA Domain Model 270

Figure 5-1: Requirements Taxomomy 279
Figure 5-2: Use Case Diagram 281

Figure 5-3: Air Traffic Control System Use Cases 283

Figure 5-4: Anesthesia Machine Use Cases 284

Figure 5-5: Anesthesia Subsystems 285

Figure 5-6: Decomposition of Deliver Anesthesia Use Case 287

Figure 5-7: Use Case Activity Breakdown 288

Figure 5-8: Ventilator Use Cases 289

Figure 5-9: User Interface Use Cases 290

Figure 5-10: Vaporizer Use Cases 291

Figure 5-11: SPO2 Monitor Use Cases 292

Figure 5-12: CO2 Monitor Use Cases 293

Figure 5-13: Agent Monitor Use Cases 294

Figure 5-14: Breathing Circuit Use Cases 295

Figure 5-15: Bad Use Case Modeling 296

Figure 5-16: Textual Characterization of Use Cases 298

Figure 5-17: Use Case Relations 300

Figure 5-18: ECG Use Cases 303

Figure 5-19: Use Cases in Development 304

Figure 5-20: Relating Text and Scenarios 309

Figure 5-21: Use Case Sequence Diagram 311

Figure 5-22: Deliver Anesthesia Collaboration 313

Figure 5-23: Elaborated Scenario Part 1 314

Figure 5-24: Elaborated Scenario Part 2 315

Figure 5-25: Alarm On Critical Event Requirements 319

Figure 5-26: Alarm On Critical Event Statechart 320

Figure 5-27: Statecharts and Text 321

Figure 5-28: Statecharts and Sequence Diagrams 323

Figure 5-29: Display Waveform Activity Diagram 324

Figure 5-30: Use Case Timing Diagram 327

Figure 6-1: ROPES Nanocycle for Domain Analysis 333

Figure 6-2: Use Cases, Collaborations, and Objects 335

Figure 6-3: Domains 337

Figure 6-4: Information Flows 347

Figure 6-5: Elevator Central Station Main View 353

Figure 6-6: Elevator Central Station Menu View 354

Figure 6-7: Elevator Central Station Zoom View 355

Figure 6-8: Pace the Heart in AAI Mode (Use Case Level) 356

Figure 6-9: Pacemaker Object Collaboration 357

Figure 6-10: Pace the Heart in AAI Mode (Object Level) 358

Figure 6-11: First-Cut Elevator Object Diagram 361
Figure 6-12: Modeling Nonprimitive Attributes 363
Figure 6-13: Session Associative Class 369
Figure 6-14: Button Subclasses 371
Figure 6-15: Generalization and Constraints 376
Figure 6-16: Extending and Specializing 378
Figure 6-17: Positioning Attributes in the Generalization
            Hierarchy 394
Figure 6-18: Repositioned Attributes 395

Figure 7-1: Token-Flow Semantics 402
Figure 7-2: Retriggerable One-Shot Timer FSM 405
Figure 7-3: Message Transaction Structure 407
Figure 7-4: Message Transaction Behavior 408
Figure 7-5: Pacemaker Use Cases 413
Figure 7-6: Pacemaker Class Diagram 414
Figure 7-7: ReedSwitch State Model 417
Figure 7-8: CoilDriver State Model 418
Figure 7-9: Communications Gnome State Model 418
Figure 7-10: Chamber Model State Model 420
Figure 7-11: Chamber Model SelfInhibited Statechart 421
Figure 7-12: Chamber Model SelfTriggered Statechart 421
Figure 7-13: AtrialModel Dual Mode Statechart 422
Figure 7-14: VentricularModel Dual Mode Statechart 423
Figure 7-15: Calculator Use Cases 423
Figure 7-16: Calculator Classes 425
Figure 7-17: CharParser Statechart 429
Figure 7-18: Tokenizer Statechart 432
Figure 7-19: Evaluator Statechart 433
Figure 7-20: Stimulator Statechart 441
Figure 7-21: Event Hieracrchy/Reception 442
Figure 7-22: HeartChamber Actor Statechart 445
Figure 7-23: Inserting Events 448
Figure 7-24: Debugging with a Web Browser 449
Figure 7-25: Debugging View 450
Figure 7-26: CardioNada Sequence 1—Creation and
            Initialization 451
Figure 7-27: CardioNada Sequence 2—Pacing 452
Figure 7-28: CardioNada Sequence 3—Inhibiting 453

Figure 7-29: Debug Configuration 455
Figure 7-30: Calculator Scenario 2* (3+4) page 1 457
Figure 7-31: Calculator Scenario 2* (3+4) page 2 459
Figure 7-32: Calculator Scenario 2* (3+4) page 3 460
Figure 7-33: Calculator Scenario 2* (3+4) page 4 461
Figure 7-34: Calculator Scenario 2* (3+4) page 5 462

Figure 8-1: Three Levels of Design 475
Figure 8-2: Logical and Physical Architecture 477
Figure 8-3: Logical Domain Architecture 480
Figure 8-4: Relating Logical and Physical Architecture 481
Figure 8-5: Levels of Architectural Abstraction 483
Figure 8-6: The Five Views of Architecture 485
Figure 8-7: System View 486
Figure 8-8: Subsystem View 487
Figure 8-9: Component View 489
Figure 8-10: Concurrency and Resource View 490
Figure 8-11: Distribution View 493
Figure 8-12: Safety and Reliability View 498
Figure 8-13: Deployment View 500
Figure 8-14: Elevator Architecture 504
Figure 8-15: OSI Model Layered Architecture 505
Figure 8-16: Vertical Slices 506
Figure 8-17: Deployment Diagram Notation 510
Figure 8-18: Telescope Position Controller
                      Deployment Diagram 511
Figure 8-19: Elevator Task Diagram 514
Figure 8-20: Concurrency in Active Objects 516

Figure 9-1: Observer Pattern 534
Figure 9-2: Observer Pattern Example Structure/Scenario 539
Figure 9-3: Proxy Pattern 541
Figure 9-4: Proxy Example Structure 545
Figure 9-5: Proxy Example Scenario 546
Figure 9-6: Transaction Pattern 549
Figure 9-7: Sender/Receiver Transaction Statechart 550
Figure 9-8: Reliable Transaction Example Structure/Scenario 554
Figure 9-9: Basic Smart Pointer Pattern/Wrapper Variant 558
Figure 9-10: Smart Pointer Cycles 559

Figure 9-11: Smart Pointer Pattern Structure/Scenario 561
Figure 9-12: Guarded Call Pattern Structure 563
Figure 9-13: Guarded Call Pattern Structure/Scenario 566
Figure 9-14: Container Pattern 569
Figure 9-15: Container Pattern Example 571
Figure 9-16: Rendezvous Pattern Structure 581
Figure 9-17: Thread Barrier Synch Policy Statechart 583
Figure 9-18: Rendezvous Pattern Scenario Example 584

Figure 10-1 Role Constraints and Qualified Associations 597
Figure 10-2: Detailed Design of Multivalued Roles 599
Figure 10-3: Balanced In-Order Tree 606
Figure 10-4: Unbalanced Tree after Adding Node 9 607
Figure 10-5: Rebalanced Tree 607
Figure 10-6: Left Rotation 609
Figure 10-7: Activity Diagram for Add Node Operation 610

Figure 11-1: Report on Model for AV-1 Overview 627
Figure 11-2: AV-2 Integrated Dictionary 628
Figure 11-3: OV-1 Operation Concept Diagram with
                Standard Notation 629
Figure 11-4: OV-1 Operational Concept Diagram in
                Rhapsody with Icons 630
Figure 11-5: OV-2 Operational Node Connectivity
                with Classes 631
Figure 11-6: OV-2 Operational Node Connectivity with
                Deployment Diagram 632
Figure 11-7: OV-3 Data Information Exchange 633
Figure 11-8: SV-1 System Interface Description 634
Figure 11-9: SV-1 Intrasystem Perspective 634
Figure 11-10: OV-4 Command Relationship Chart 636
Figure 11-11: OV-5 Operational Activity Model 636
Figure 11-12: OV-5 Operational Activity Mode with
                Swim Lanes 637
Figure 11-13: OV-5 Operational Activity Model with
                Two Agencies 638
Figure 11-14: OV-6a Logical Data Model for Operational Rules 639
Figure 11-15: OV-6b Statechart for Operation State Transition
                Description 641

Figure 11-16: OV-6c Event-Trace Description with
             Sequence Diagram 642
Figure 11-17: OV-7 Logical Data Model 643
Figure 11-18: SV-3 Systems-Systems Matrix with
             Class Diagram 644
Figure 11-19: SV-4 Systems Functionality Description 645
Figure 11-20: SV-6 Data Flow on Class Diagram 647
Figure 11-21: SV-7 Systems Performance on Class Diagram 647
Figure 11-22: SV-7 Systems Performance in Reports
             and Browser 648
Figure 11-23: SV-8 Systems Evolution Description 649
Figure 11-24: SV-11 Physical Schema with Deployment 650
Figure 11-25: SV-11 Physical Schema with Components 651

Additional figures appear in the Appendix.

About the Author

Bruce was raised by wolves in the Oregon wilderness. He taught himself to read at age 3 and calculus before age 12. He dropped out of school when he was 14 and traveled around the US for a few years before entering the University of Oregon as a mathematics major. He eventually received his M.S. in exercise physiology from the University of Oregon and his Ph.D. in neurophysiology from the USD Medical School, where he developed a branch  of mathematics called autocorrelative factor analysis for studying information processing in multicellular biological neural systems.

Bruce has worked as a software developer in real-time systems well in excess of 20 years and is a well-known speaker and author in the area of real-time embedded systems. He is on the Advisory Board of the *Embedded Systems* and *UML World* conferences where he has taught courses in software estimation and scheduling, project management, object-oriented analysis and design, communications protocols, finite state machines, design patterns, and safety-critical systems design. He has developed and taught courses in real-time object-oriented analysis and design for many years. He has authored articles for a number of journals and periodicals in the real-time domain.

He is the Chief Evangelist[1] for i-Logix, a leading producer of tools for real-time systems development. Bruce worked with Rational and the other UML partners on the specification of the UML. He is one of the co-chairs of the Object Management Group's Real-Time Analysis and Design Working Group, which is currently examining the UML for possible future real-time extensions. He also consults, trains, and mentors a number of companies building large-scale real-time safety-critical systems. He is the author of several other books on software, including *Doing Hard Time: Developing Real-Time Systems with UML, Objects, Frameworks, and Patterns* (Addison-Wesley, 1999) and *Real-Time Design Patterns: Robust Scalable Architecture for Real-Time Systems* (Addison-Wesley, 2002), as well as a short textbook on table tennis.

Bruce enjoys classical music and has played classical guitar professionally. He has competed in several sports, including table tennis, bicycle racing, running, and full-contact Tae Kwon Do, although he currently only fights inanimate objects that don't hit back. He and his two sons contemplate epistemology in the Frozen North. He can be reached at *bpd@ilogix.com.*

---

[1] Being a Chief Evangelist is much like being a Chief Scientist, except for the burning bushes and stone tablets.

Foreword to the Third Edition

Bruce Douglass' book has only improved with time. The main change, of course, is that it now caters to the new version of the the language, UML 2.0. As with the first edition, this edition too is one of the clearest and most valuable texts for engineers who want to model and specify systems using the UML, especially reactive and real-time ones. Hence, I applaud Bruce for updating the text and presenting to the public another valuable product of his prolific pen (keyboard? . . .).

Still, I should say a few words about the UML itself, especially relating to the following two passages from the earlier foreword—one a prediction and one an opinion:

> *The recent wave of popularity that the UML is enjoying will bring with it not only the official UML books written by Rational Corporation authors, but a true flood of books, papers, reports, seminars, and tools, describing, utilizing, and elaborating upon the UML, or purporting to do so. Readers will have to be extra careful in finding the really worthy trees in this messy forest. I have no doubt that Bruce's book will remain one of those. . . .*
>
> *Despite all of this, one must remember that right now UML is a little too massive. We understand well only parts of it; the definition of other parts has yet to be carried out in sufficient depth to make crystal clear their relationships with the constructive core of UML (the class diagrams and the statecharts). . . .*

As to the first of these quotes, it wasn't too hard to predict the flood, which has materialized above all expectations. Here is one small statistic: A search at amazon.com for books with "UML" in the title results in 213 items, and the same search limited to 1998 and on yields 198 items. That is, there were 15 UML books when the first edition of this book was published, and there are some 200 more now! Nevertheless, I maintain that Bruce's book indeed remains one of the few really worthy ones.

As to the second remark, about the UML being a little too massive, things have not really improved much. With version 2.0 almost ready to be launched, a fact that is doubtless a milestone in the development of the UML, we may ask ourselves whether it has become leaner and meaner, or larger and messier. Many people hoped that a new version of of something that was so multifaceted and complex, but which had been adopted as a standard to be used worldwide, would concentrate on its most important aspects. It would improve and sharpen them and narrow down or discard those things that turned out to be inessential or less well-defined. This could have resulted in a language that was easier to learn, easier to use, easier to implement responsibly, and thus would carry a lot more "punch." While UML 2.0 contains several exciting new features, especially for the realm relevant to this book—real-time and reactive systems—the new version of UML is larger and more complex.

As mentioned in the 1997 foreword, object-orientation is here to stay and so is the UML, probably in a big way. Let us thus hope that version 3.0 of the language will remove, intergrate, clarify, and solidify more than it adds. In any case, good books about a language are almost as important as the language itself, and in this respect the present book is one of only a handful that can be heartily recommended.

David Harel
The Weizmann Institute of Science
Rehovot, Israel
November 2003

Foreword to the Previous Editions

Embedded computerized systems are here to stay. Reactive and real-time systems likewise. As this book aptly points out, one can see embedded systems everywhere; there are more computers hidden in the guts of things than there are conventional desktops or laptops.

Wherever there are computers and computerized systems, there has to be software to drive them—and software doesn't just happen. People have to write it, people have to understand and analyze it, people have to use it, and people have to maintain and update it for future versions. It is this human aspect of programming that calls for modeling complex systems on levels of abstraction that are higher than that of "normal" programming languages. From this also comes the need for methodologies to guide software engineers and programmers in coping with the modeling process itself.

There is broad agreement that one of the things to strive for in devising a high-level modeling approach is good diagrammatics. All other things being equal, pictures are usually better understood than text or symbols. But we are not interested just in pictures or diagrams, since constructing complex software is not an exclusively human activity. We are interested in *languages* of diagrams, and these languages require computerized support for validation and analysis. Just as high-level programming languages require not only editors and version control utilities but also—and predominantly!—compilers and debugging tools, so do modeling languages require not only pretty graphics, document generation utilities, and project management aids, but also means for executing models and for synthesizing code. This means that we need *visual formalisms* that come complete with a syntax to determine what is allowed and semantics to determine what the allowed things mean. Such formalisms should be as visual as possible (obviously, some things do not lend themselves to natural visualization) with the main emphasis placed on topological relationships between diagrammatic entities, and then, as next-best options, geometry, metrics, and perhaps iconics, too.

Over the years, the main approaches to high-level modeling have been *structured analysis* (SA), and *object orientation* (OO). The two are about a decade apart in initial conception and evolution. SA started in the late 1970s by DeMarco, Yourdon, and others, and is based on "lifting" classical, procedural programming concepts up to the modeling level. The result calls for modeling system structure by functional decomposition and flow of information, depicted by (hierarchical) data-flow diagrams. As to system behavior, the early- and mid-1980s saw several methodology teams (such as Ward/Mellor, Hatley/Pirbhai, and the STATEMATE team from i-Logix) making detailed recommendations that enriched the basic SA model with means for capturing behavior based on state diagrams or the richer language of statecharts. Carefully defined behavioral modeling is especially crucial for embedded, reactive, and real-time systems.

OO modeling started in the late 1980s, and, in a way, its history is very similar. The basic idea for system structure was to "lift" concepts from object-oriented programming up to the modeling level. Thus, the basic structural model for objects in Booch's method, in the OMT and ROOM methods, and in many others, deals with classes and instances, relationships and roles, operations and events, and aggregation and inheritance. Visuality is achieved by basing this model on an embellished and enriched form of entity-relationship diagrams. As to system behavior, most OO modeling approaches adopted the statecharts language for this (I cannot claim to be too upset about that decision). A statechart is associated with each class, and its role is to describe the behavior of the instance objects. The subtle and complicated connections between structure and behavior—that is, between object models and statecharts—were treated by OO methodologists in a broad spectrum of degrees of detail—from vastly insufficient to adequate. The test, of course, is whether the languages for structure and behavior and their interlinks are defined sufficiently well to allow the "interpretation" and "compilation" of high-level models—full model execution and code synthesis. This has been achieved only in a couple of cases, namely in the ObjecTime tool (based on the ROOM method of Selic, Gullekson, and Ward), and the Rhapsody® tool (from i-Logix, based on the Executable Object Modeling method of Gery and the undersigned).

In a remarkable departure from the similarity in evolution between the SA and OO paradigms for system modeling, the last two or three years have seen OO methodologists working together. They have compared notes, debated the issues, and finally cooperated in formulating a general Unified Modeling Language (UML) in the hope of bringing together the best of the various OO modeling approaches. This sweeping effort, which in its teamwork is reminiscent of the Algol60 and Ada efforts, is taking place under the auspices of Rational Corporation, spearheaded by G. Booch (of the Booch method), J. Rumbaugh (codeveloper of the OMT method), and I. Jacobson (czar of use cases). Version 0.8 of the UML was released in 1996 and was rather open-ended, vague, and not nearly as well defined as some expected. For about a year, the UML team went into overdrive, with a lot of help from methodologists and language designers from outside Rational Corporation (the undersigned contributing his 10 cents worth, too), and version 1.1, whose defining documents were released in early 1997, is much tighter and more solid. The UML has very recently been adopted as a standard by the object management group (OMG), and with more work there is a good chance that it will become not just an officially approved, if somewhat dryly documented, standard, but the main modeling mechanism for the software that is constructed according to the object-oriented doctrine. And this is no small matter, as more software engineers are now claiming that more kinds of software are best developed in an OO fashion.

For capturing system structure, the UML indeed adopts an entity-relationship-like diagrammatic language for classes and objects. For early-stage behavioral thinking it recommends use cases and utilizes sequence diagrams (often called message sequence charts or MSCs). For the full constructive specification of behavior it adopts statecharts.

In this book, Bruce Douglass does an excellent job of dishing out engineering wisdom to people who have to construct complex software—especially real-time, embedded, reactive software. Moreover, it does this with UML as the main underlying vehicle, a fact which, given the recent standardization of the UML and its fast-spreading usage, makes the book valuable to anyone whose daily worry is the expeditious and smooth development of such systems. Moreover, Bruce's book is clear and very well written, and it gives the reader the confidence boost that stems from the fact that the author is not writing from the ivy-clouded heights of an academic institution or the religiously-tainted vantage point of a professional methodologist, but that he has extensive experience in engineering the very kinds of systems the book discusses.

The recent wave of popularity that the UML is enjoying will bring with it not only the official UML books written by Rational Corporation authors, but a true flood of books, papers, reports, seminars, and tools, describing, utilizing, and elaborating upon the UML, or purporting to do so. Readers will have to be extra careful in finding the really worthy trees in this messy forest. I have no doubt that Bruce's book will remain one of those.

Despite all of this, one must remember that right now UML is a little too massive. We understand well only parts of it; the definition of other parts has yet to be carried out in sufficient depth to make crystal clear their relationships with the constructive core of UML (the class diagrams and the statecharts). For example, use cases and their associated sequence and collaboration diagrams are invaluable to users and requirements engineers trying to work out the system's desired behavior in terms of scenarios. In the use case world we describe a single scenario (or a single cluster of closely related scenarios) for all relevant objects—we might call it *interobject behavior*. In contrast, a statechart describes all the behavior for a single object—*intraobject behavior*. I would like to term this stark difference as *the grand duality of system behavior*. We are far from having a good algorithmic understanding of this duality. We don't know yet how to derive one view from the other, or even how to efficiently test whether descriptions presented in the two are mutually consistent.

Other serious challenges remain, for which only the surface has been scratched. Examples include true formal verification of object-oriented software modeled using the high-level means afforded by the UML, automatic eye-pleasing and structure-enhancing layout of UML diagrams, satisfactory ways of dealing with hybrid systems that involve discrete as well as continuous parts, and much more.

As a general means for dealing with complex software, OO is also here to stay, and hence, so is the UML. OO is a powerful and wise way to think about systems and to program them, and will for a long time to come be part and parcel of the body of knowledge required by any self-respecting software engineer. This book will greatly help in that. On the other hand, OO doesn't solve *all* problems, and hence, neither does the UML. There is still much work to be done. In fact, it is probably no great exaggeration to say that there is a lot more that we *don't* know and *can't* achieve yet in this business than what we do and can. Still, what we have is tremendously more than we would have hoped for five years ago, and for this we should be thankful and humble.

David Harel
The Weizmann Institute of Science
Rehovot, Israel
October 1997

Preface to the Third Edition

The UML is an evolving standard. This has, of course, both pros and cons. One of the cons is that it keeps changing, but I believe this is more than offset by the primary pro—that the standard continues to improve. Since the second edition of *Real-Time UML*, some important changes to the UML have taken place.

The most important of these is the UML 2.0. At the time of this writing (summer 2003), the UML 2.0 specification has been "voted to adopt." This means that the UML 2.0 has been accepted by the Object Management Group and, pending a couple of more votes, is ready to begin the finalization process to make it into a released standard. This finalization process may take a year or more but hopefully a bit less. The UML 2.0 is an incremental improvement to the UML 1.x standards, improving the clarity of the UML for capturing architectures and improving its scalability. Because the UML 2.0 still must undergo the finalization process to remove defects and make it more consistent, the released standard may differ somewhat from what is described in this book. Nevertheless, I believe such differences will be small and relatively insignificant.

The other improvement for the real-time community at least, is the adoption of the UML Profile for Schedulability, Performance, and Time (the so-called Real-Time Profile [RPT]). This profile uses the standard lightweight extension mechanisms of UML 1.x to provide a standard set of tags for capturing schedulability and performance constraints of systems. Although the profile doesn't add any new capabilities to the UML, it does provide a standard way of capturing the timeliness quality of services aspects so that tools can exchange models and understand the timeliness constraints when they do so. This means that schedulability and performance analysis tools can read UML models (compliant with the profile) and then perform mathematical analysis of these models.

The UML continues to gain momentum in the world of real-time and embedded systems, particularly complex ones. For this reason, I have included a Special Topics chapter at the end that shows how to represent C4ISR (Command, Control, Communications, Computers, Intelligence and Reconnaissance) architectures with the UML. C4ISR systems are among the most complex software systems on the planet but the C4ISR standard was released about the same time as the original UML standard, so they have not been previously discussed together.

Audience

The book is oriented toward the practicing professional software developer and the computer science major, in the junior or senior year. This book could also serve as an undergraduate or graduate level text, but the focus is on practical development rather than a theoretical introduction. Very few equations will be found in this book, but more theoretical and mathematical approaches are referenced where appropriate. The book assumes a reasonable proficiency in at least one programming language and at least a cursory exposure to the fundamental concepts of both object orientation and real-time systems.

Goals

The goals for the second edition remain goals for this edition as well. This book is still meant to be an easy-to-read introduction to the UML and how to apply its notation and semantics to the development of real-time and embedded systems. At the time of this writing, it is one of a few books on the UML and real-time systems. I am also the author of two others: *Doing Hard Time: Developing Real-Time Systems using UML, Objects, Frameworks, and Patterns* (Addison-Wesley, 1999) and *Real-Time Design Patterns: Robust Scalable Architecture for Real-Time Systems*

(Addison-Wesley, 2002). *Doing Hard Time* is a more in-depth look at the fundamentals and vagaries of real-time systems, with emphasis on analysis of object schedulability, the use of behavioral patterns in the construction of statechart models, and how to use real-time frameworks effectively. *Doing Hard Time* is a deeper exploration of real-time systems that happens to use the UML to express these concepts. My other book, *Real-Time Design Patterns: Robust Scalable Architecture for Real-Time Systems* is a book about architecture and the application of design patterns to the development of architecture using the Five Views of architecture defined in the ROPES process: Subsystem and Component View, Concurrency and Resource View, Distribution View, Safety and Reliability View, and the Deployment View. This book is more specialized than Doing Hard Time, focusing almost exclusively on software and systems architectures. In contrast, *Real-Time UML* is primarily an introduction to the UML and its use in capturing the requirements, structure, and behavior of real-time systems.

In addition to these original goals for the first and second editions, the third edition adds two more: (1) bring the book in conformance with the recent changes in the UML standard (especially the soon-to-be-released UML 2.0 and the UML Profile for Schedulability, Performance, and Time), and (2) enhance the book's effectiveness based on feedback from the first two editions.

Interested readers visit the I-Logix Web site, *www.ilogix.com*. There you will find a number of papers on related topics, written by myself and others, as well as the UML specifications, tool descriptions, and links to relevant sites. I also moderate a Yahoo group (*www.groups.yahoo.com/RTUML*) for discussions and papers relevant to the UML and its application to real-time and embedded systems.

Bruce Powel Douglass, Ph.D.
Summer 2003

Preface to the Second Edition

I have been both pleased and gratified by the success of the first edition of *Real-Time UML: Developing Efficient Objects for Embedded Systems.* I think the popularity of the first edition is due to both its timeliness and appropriateness of object technology (in general) and the UML (in particular) to the development of real-time and embedded systems. At the time of the publication of the first edition, it was clear that the UML would be a major force in the development of object-oriented systems. However, even its strongest supporters have been surprised by the rapidity and near totality of its acceptance by developers. As one methodologist supporting a different modeling approach expressed it to me, "I ignored the UML and then got hit with a freight train." The UML is wildly successful in the Darwinian sense of the term as well in its technical superiority and has become the most dominant life form in the object ecosphere.

As embedded systems gain in complexity, the old hack-and-ship approaches fail utterly and completely, and occasionally, spectacularly. The complexity of today's systems is driving developers to construct models of the system from different viewpoints, in order to understand and plan the various system aspects. These views include the physical or deployment view, and the logical, or essential, view. Both views must support structural and behavioral aspects. This is what the UML is about and this is why it has been so successful.

Audience

The book is oriented towards the practicing professional software developer and the computer science major, in the junior or senior year. This book could also serve as an undergraduate or graduate level text, but the focus is on practical development rather than a theoretical introduction. Very few equations will be found in this book, but more theoretical and mathematical approaches are referenced where appropriate. The book assumes a reasonable proficiency in at least one programming language and at least a cursory exposure to the fundamental concepts of both object orientation and real-time systems.

Goals

The goals for the first edition remain goals for this edition as well. This book is still meant to be an easy-to-read introduction to the UML and how to apply its notation and semantics to the development of real-time and embedded systems. At the time of this writing, it is one of two books on the UML and real-time systems. I am also the author of the other, *Doing Hard Time: Developing Real-Time Systems with UML, Objects, Frameworks, and Patterns* (Addison-Wesley, 1999). *Doing Hard Time* is a more in-depth look at the fundamentals and vagaries of real-time systems, with emphasis on analysis of object schedulability, the use of behavioral patterns in the construction of statechart models, and how to use real-time frameworks effectively. *Doing Hard Time* is a deeper exploration of real-time systems that happens to use the UML to express these concepts. In contrast, *Real-Time UML* is primarily about the UML and secondarily about capturing the requirements, structure, and behavior of real-time systems using the UML.

In addition to these original goals for the first edition, the second edition adds two more: (1) bring the book in conformance with the recent changes in the UML standard, and (2) enhance the book's effectiveness based on feedback from the first edition.

The UML has undergone a couple of revisions. The first revision, 1.2, as almost exclusively editorial, with no significant modification. The UML revision 1.3, on the other hand, is a significant improvement in a variety of ways. For example, the «uses» stereotype of generalization of use cases has now been replaced with the «includes» stereotype of dependency, which makes a great deal more sense.

Similarly, the notion of an action in UML 1.1, relied heavily on the use of "uninterpreted text" to capture its details. The UML 1.3 has elaborated the metamodel to encompass a number of different kinds of actions, making behavioral modeling more complete. The action semantics metamodel, and how it relates to object messaging, is discussed in Chapter 2 and 4.

There have been a number of changes to the statechart model in the 1.3 revision as well. The first edition of *Real-Time UML* devoted a lot of space to statecharts, and this second edition expends even more effort in the coverage of behavioral modeling with statecharts. Much of this space is used for the new features of statecharts—synch pseudostates, stub states, and so on. This resulted in a significant rewrite of Chapter 4, which deals with object behavioral modeling.

Recent consulting experience in fields ranging from advanced medical imaging to the next generation of intelligent autonomous spacecraft, in addition to reader feedback from the first edition, is reflected in this second edition. For example, numerous consulting efforts have convinced me that many developers have a great deal of difficulty with understanding and applying use cases to capture requirements for real-time and embedded systems. To address this need, I developed a one-day course called *Effective Use Cases,* which I have given at NASA and elsewhere. Those principles that have proven their effectiveness in the field are captured here, in Chapter 2. Similarly, the techniques and strategies that have worked well for capturing object models or state behavior, have wound up expressed in this book as well.

Another change in this book is the elaboration of an effective process for using the UML in product development. I call this process Rapid Object-oriented Process for Embedded Systems (ROPES). The most common questions I have been asked since publication of the first book have been about the successful deployment of the UML in project teams developing real-time and embedded systems. Thus, Chapter 1 has explains this process, and identifies the work activities and artifacts produced during different parts of the iterative lifecycle. In fact, the ROPES process forms the basis for the organization of the book itself from Chapters 2 through 7[1].

Despite the goals of the UML in terms of providing a standard, there has been some fractionalization as vendors try to differentiate themselves in the marketplace. While progress will naturally involve vendors providing new and potentially valuable model constructs above and beyond those provided by the UML, several vendors have claimed that their new features will be part of some new yet-to-be-announced UML for Real-Time. Interestingly, some of these vendors don't even participate in the OMG while others provide mutually incompatible "enhancements." By spreading this FUD (Fear, Uncertainty, and Doubt) among the developer community, I feel these vendors have done a grand disservice to their constituency. Developers should understand both the benefits *and* risks of using single-source modeling concepts. These features may make the system easier to model (although in many cases these so-called "enhancements" fail in that regard), but it also locks the product development to a single vendor's tool. Another risk is the inability to use model interchange between tools when the models no longer adhere to the UML standard. This can greatly decrease the benefits to the developer that the use of the UML was developed to provide. In an effort to dispel some of the FUD, I've added Appendix B to outline what it means to make changes to the standard, why *no* single vendor can claim they own the UML standard (it is, after all, owned by the OMG), and what changes are likely to be made to the UML over the next several years.

Finally, I would suggest that interested readers visit the I-Logix Web site, *www.ilogix.com.* There you will find a number of papers on related topics, written by myself and others, as well as the UML specifications, tool descriptions, and links to relevant sites.

Bruce Powel Douglass, Ph.D.
Spring, 1999

---

[1] More information on the ROPES process can be had from the I-Logix Web site, *www.ilogix.com,* as well in another book, *Doing Hard Time: Developing Real-Time Systems with UML, Objects, Frameworks, and Patterns* (Addison-Wesley, 1999).

Preface to the First Edition

Goals

Real-Time UML: Developing Efficient Objects for Embedded Systems is an introduction to object-oriented analysis and design for hard real-time systems using the Unified Modified Language (UML). UML is a third-generation modeling language that rigorously defines the semantics of the object metamodel and provides a notation for capturing and communicating object structure and behavior. Many methodologists—including Grady Booch (Booch Method), Jim Rumbaugh (Object Modeling Technique [OMT]), Ivar Jacobson (Object-Oriented Software Engineering [OOSE]), and David Harel (Statecharts)—collaborated to achieve UML. Many more participated, myself included, in the specification of the UML, and we believe that it is the leading edge in modeling for complex systems.

There are very few books on the use of objects in real-time systems and even fewer on UML. Virtually all object-oriented books focus primarily on business or database application domains and do not mention real-time aspects at all. On the other hand, texts on real-time systems have largely ignored object-oriented methods. For the most part, they fall into two primary camps: those that bypass methodological considerations altogether and focus solely on "bare metal" programming, and those that are highly theoretical with little advice for actually implementing workable systems. *Real-Time UML: Developing Efficient Objects for Embedded Systems* is meant to be a concise and timely bridge for these technologies, presenting the development of deployable real-time systems using the object semantics and notation of the UML. This has many advantages, including focusing the development process of real-time systems into logical, concrete steps that progress in an orderly fashion with a standardized notation.

Audience

The book is oriented toward the practicing professional software developer and the computer science major, in the junior or senior year. This book could also serve as an undergraduate or graduate level text, but the focus is on practical development rather than a theoretical introduction. Very few equations will be found in this book, but more theoretical and mathematical approaches are referenced where appropriate. The book assumes a reasonable proficiency in at least one programming language and at least a cursory exposure to the fundamental concepts of both object orientation and real-time systems.

Organization

The book follows the normal analysis "design" implementation approach followed by most development projects. The first chapter identifies the fundamental concepts of objects and real-time systems. The next two discuss analysis—the identification and specification of the problem to be solved. Analysis is divided into two portions: black-box requirements analysis using context diagrams, use cases and scenarios (Chapter 2), and capturing the key concepts and their relationships from the problem domain (Chapter 3).

Design follows analysis and adds details as to how the analysis model should be implemented. Design is broken up into three parts, each taken up in a separate chapter—Architectural, Mechanistic, and Detailed design. The parts differ in the scope of their concerns. Architectural design deals with very broad scope strategic decisions, such as tasking models and inter-processor design. Mechanistic design focuses on how groups of object collaborate together to achieve common purposes. Both architectural and mechanistic design chapters include a number of patterns that have been found generally applicable in real-time systems. Finally, detailed design specifies the internal structure and function of individual objects.

Throughout the book, the UML notation is introduced where and as needed. However, a notational summary is provided in the appendix so that this book can continue to serve as a reference guide as your projects evolve.

Examples

Two different approaches to examples are used in different texts. Some authors (and readers) prefer a single example taken throughout the entire book to illustrate the various concepts. The other approach is to use many different examples with the idea being that it is more useful to see the concepts used in a wide variety of applications. This book uses a compromise approach. A variety of real-time examples illustrate the concepts and notation of UML in the several different real-time application domains, but they reappear in different chapters of the book. This approach reinforces the concepts by showing how they apply in various situations. Special care has been taken to select real-time examples with rich behavioral semantics, however examples which are not strictly real-time are used where appropriate.

Bruce Powel Douglass, Ph.D.
Summer 1997

Acknowledgments

A book like this is always a joint effort, but not only of the direct contributors, such as the editorial staff of Addison-Wesley (and I'd especially like to thank my editorial helpers Kathy Glidden and Carol Noble) but of many others who in their own way have raised the bar for all of us. The core team members working on the UML—Cris Kobryn, Eran Gery, Jim Rumbaugh, Bran Selic and many many others are certainly among those that should be acknowledged in bringing forth a useful standard language for capturing and manipulating models of systems. Thanks to David Harel, inventor of Statecharts (the basis for the behavioral model of the UML) for writing the Foreword, and to my reviewers: Therese Smith, Soma Chatterjee, Sandy Friedenthal, Scott Niemann, Ben Watson, and Gary Evan for keeping me honest and helping to catch errors . . . ummm, I mean *features*, before the book went to press.

Chapter 1

Introduction to the World of Real-Time and Embedded Systems

Real-time applications vary in ubiquity, cost, size, and performance-sensitivity—from wristwatches and microwave ovens to factory automation and nuclear power plant control systems. Applying a general development methodology to the development of real-time systems requires that such a process must scale from small 4-bit and 8-bit controller-based systems up to networked arrays of powerful processors coordinating their activities to achieve a common purpose.

Real-time systems are ones in which timeliness, performance, and schedulability are essential to correctness. Model-driven approaches are a natural fit because they allow different aspects of the system—structural, behavioral, functional, and quality of service—to be specified, analyzed, designed, simulated, and/or executed.

Notation and Concepts Discussed:

What Is Special about Real-Time Systems	ROPES Process	Working with Models
Systems Engineering	Time, Performance, and Quality of Service	
Organizing Models	Model-Based Development	

1.1 What Is Special about Real-Time Systems?

If you read the popular computer press, you would come away with the impression that most computers sit on a desktop (or lap) and run Windows. In terms of the numbers of deployed systems, embedded real-time systems are orders of magnitude more common than their more visible desktop cousins. A tour of the average affluent American home might find one or even two standard desktop computers but literally dozens of smart consumer devices, each containing one or more processors. From the washing machine and microwave oven to the telephone, stereo, television, and automobile, embedded computers are everywhere. They help us evenly toast our muffins and identify mothers-in-law calling on the phone. Embedded computers are even more prevalent in industry. Trains, switching systems, aircraft, chemical process control, and nuclear power plants all use computers to safely and conveniently improve our productivity and quality of life.[1]

The software for these embedded computers is more difficult to construct than software for the desktop. Real-time systems have all the problems of desktop applications plus many more. Systems that are not real-time do not concern themselves with timelines, robustness, or safety—at least not to nearly the same extent as real-time systems. Real-time systems often do not have a conventional computer display or keyboard, but lie at the heart of some apparently noncomputerized device. The user of these devices may never be aware of the CPU

---

[1] Not to mention that they also keep a significant number of us gainfully employed.

embedded within, making decisions about how and when the system should act. The user is not intimately involved with such a device as a computer per se, but rather as an electrical or mechanical appliance that provides services. Such systems must often operate for days or even years without stopping, in the most hostile environments. The services and controls provided must be autonomous and timely. Frequently, these devices have the potential to do great harm if they fail.

Real-time systems encompass all devices with performance constraints. *Hard deadlines* are performance requirements that absolutely must be met. A missed deadline constitutes an erroneous computation and a system failure. In these systems, *late* data is *bad* data. *Soft* real-time systems are characterized by time constraints which can (a) be missed occasionally, (b) be missed by small time deviations, or (c) occasionally skipped altogether. Normally, these permissible variations are stochastically characterized. Another common definition for soft real-time systems is that they are constrained only by average time constraints (examples include on-line databases and flight reservation systems), although such constraints actually refer to throughput requirements rather than the timeliness of specific actions. In soft real-time systems, *late* data may still be *good* data, depending on some measure of the severity of the lateness. The methods presented in this text may be applied to the development of all performance-constrained systems, hard and soft alike. When we use the term *real-time* alone, we are specifically referring to hard real-time systems. In actuality, most real-time systems are a mixture of hard and soft real-time constraints, together with some requirements that have no timeliness requirements whatsoever. It is common to treat these different aspects separately, although when present, the hard real-time constraints tend to dominate the design.

An *embedded system* contains a computer as part of a larger system and does not exist primarily to provide standard computing services to a user. A desktop PC is not an embedded system, unless it is within a tomographical imaging scanner or some other device. A computerized microwave oven or VCR is an embedded system because it does no standard computing. In both cases, the embedded computer is part of a larger system that provides some noncomputing feature to the user, such as popping corn or showing Schwarzenegger ripping telephone booths from the floor.[2]

---

[2] *Commando,* a heart-warming tale if ever there was one.

Most real-time systems interact directly with electrical devices and indirectly with mechanical ones. Frequently, custom software, written specifically for the application, must control or access the device. This is why real-time programmers have the reputation of being "bare metal code pounders." You cannot buy a standard device driver or Windows VxD to talk to custom hardware components. Programming these device drivers requires very low-level manipulation. This kind of programming requires intimate knowledge of the electrical properties and timing characteristics of the actual devices.

Virtually all real-time systems either monitor or control hardware, or both. Sensors provide information to the system about the state of its external environment. Medical monitoring devices, such as electrocardiography (ECG) machines, use sensors to monitor patient and machine status. Air speed, engine thrust, attitude, and altitude sensors provide aircraft information for proper execution of flight control plans. Linear and angular position sensors sense a robot's arm position and adjust it via DC or stepper motors.

Many real-time systems use actuators to control their external environment or to guide some external processes. Flight control computers command engine thrust and wing and tail control surface orientation so that the aircraft follows the intended flight path. Chemical process control systems control when, what kind, and the amounts of different reagents are added to mixing vats. Pacemakers make the heart beat at appropriate intervals with electrical leads attached to the walls inside the (right-side) heart chambers.

Naturally, most systems containing actuators also contain sensors. While there are some open loop control systems,[3] the majority of control systems use environmental feedback to ensure that control loop is acting properly.

Standard computing systems react almost entirely to users and little else.[4] Real-time systems, on the other hand, may interact with the user, but have more concern for interactions with their sensors and actuators.

---

[3] An *open loop system* is one in which feedback about the success of the performed action is not used to control the action. A *closed loop system* is one in which the action is monitored and that sensory data is used to modify future actions.

[4] It is true that behind the scenes even desktop computers must interface with printers, mice, keyboards, and networks. The point is that they do this only to facilitate the user's whim.

One of the problems that arise with environmental interaction is that the universe has an annoying habit of disregarding our opinions of how and when it ought to behave. The order and arrival times of external events are frequently unpredictable. The system must react to events when they occur rather than when it might be convenient. An ECG monitor must alarm quickly following the cessation of cardiac activity if it is to be of value. The system cannot delay alarm processing until later that evening when the processor load is lower. Many hard real-time systems are *reactive* in nature, and their responses to external events must be tightly bounded in time. Control loops, as we shall see later, are very sensitive to time delays. Delayed actuations destabilize control loops.

Most real-time systems do one or a small set of high-level tasks. The actual execution of those high-level tasks requires many simultaneous lower-level activities. This is called *concurrency*. Since single processor systems can only do a single thing at a time, they implement a *scheduling policy* that controls when tasks execute. In multiple processor systems, true concurrency is achievable since the processors execute asynchronously. Individual processors within such systems schedule many threads pseudoconcurrently (executing a single thread at a time, but switching among them according to some scheduling policy) as well.

Embedded systems are usually constructed with the least expensive (and therefore less powerful) computers able to meet the functional and performance requirements. Real-time systems ship the hardware along with the software as part of a complete system package. Because many products are extremely cost sensitive, marketing and sales concerns push for using smaller processors and less memory. Providing smaller CPUs with less memory lowers the manufacturing cost. This per-shipped-item cost is called *recurring cost*, because it recurs with each manufactured device. Software has no significant recurring cost—all the costs are bound up in development, maintenance, and support activities, making it appear to be free.[5] This means that most often choices are made that decrease hardware costs while increasing software development costs.

Under UNIX, a developer needing a big array might just allocate space for 1 million floats with little thought for the consequences. If the

---

[5] Unfortunately, many companies opt for decreasing (primarily hardware) recurring costs without considering all of the development cost ramifications, but that's fodder for another book.

program doesn't use all that space—who cares? The workstation has hundreds of megabytes of RAM and gigabytes of virtual memory in the form of hard disk storage. The embedded systems developer cannot make these simplifying assumptions. He or she must do more with less, resulting in convoluted algorithms and extensive performance optimization. Naturally, this makes the real-time software more complex and expensive to develop and maintain.

Real-time developers often use tools hosted on PCs and workstations, but targeted to smaller, less capable computer platforms. This means that they must use cross-compiler tools, which are often more temperamental (i.e., buggy) than the more widely used desktop tools. Additionally, the hardware facilities available on the target platform—such as timers, A/D converters, and sensors—cannot be easily simulated accurately on a workstation. The discrepancy between the development and the target environments adds time and effort for the developer wanting to execute and test his or her code. The lack of sophisticated debugging tools on most small targets complicates testing as well. Small embedded targets often do not even have a display on which to view error and diagnostic messages.

Frequently, real-time developers must design and write software for hardware that does not yet exist. This creates very real challenges since developers cannot validate their understanding of how the hardware functions, even though, according to my experience, the hardware never functions exactly as specified. Integration and validation testing become more difficult and time consuming.

Embedded real-time systems must often run continuously for long periods of time. It would be awkward to have to reset your flight control computer because of a GPF[6] while in the air above Newark. The same applies to cardiac pacemakers, which last up to *10 years* after implantation. Unmanned space probes must function properly for years on nuclear or solar power supplies. This is different from desktop computers that may be frequently reset at least daily. It may be acceptable to have to reboot your desktop PC when an application crashes the operating system, but it is much less acceptable to have to reboot a life support ventilator or the control avionics of a commercial passenger jet.

---

[6] *General Protection Fault*, a term that was introduced to tens of millions of people with Microsoft's release of Windows 3.1.

Embedded system environments are often adverse and computer-hostile. In surgical operating rooms, electrosurgical units create intense electrical arcs to cauterize incisions. These produce extremely high EMI (electromagnetic interference) and can physically damage unprotected computer electronics. Even if the damage is not permanent, it is possible to corrupt memory storage, degrading performance or inducing a systems failure.

Apart from increased reliability concerns, software is finding its way ever more frequently into safety systems. Medical devices are perhaps the most obvious safety related computing devices, but computers control many kinds of vehicles such as aircraft, spacecraft, trains, and even automobiles. Software controls weapons systems and ensures the safety of nuclear power and chemical plants. There is compelling evidence that the scope of industrial and transportation accidents is increasing [1,2].[7]

For all these reasons, developing real-time software is generally much more difficult than developing other software. The development environments traditionally have had fewer tools, and the ones that exist are often less capable than those for desktop environments or for "Big Iron" mainframes. Embedded targets are slower and have less memory, yet must still perform within tight timing and performance constraints. These additional concerns translate into more complexity for the developer, which means more time, more effort, and (unless we're careful indeed) more defects than standard desktop software of the same size. Fortunately, advances have been made in the development tools, approaches, and processes, which is what this book is all about.

1.2 Time, Performance, and Quality of Service

In 2002, the Object Management Group (OMG) adopted the *Unified Modeling Language*™ (UML) profile that provided a standardized means for specifying timeliness, performance, and schedulability aspects of systems and parts of systems, the so-called Real-Time Profile (RTP) [7]. In the same year, an initial submission was made for a UML profile that

---

[7] It is not a question of whether or not developers of safety-critical software are paranoid. The real question is "Are they paranoid enough?"

detailed a generalized framework for Quality of Service (QoS) aspects—of which timeliness, performance, and schedulability are common examples—as well as a specific profile for fault tolerance mechanisms [8]. To be sure, these profiles are clearly not *necessary* for modeling the QoS aspects—developers have been doing this for as long as UML has been around (OK, even longer!); however, codifying what the best developers were already *doing* and defining specific names for the aspects, allows models to be easily exchanged among different kinds of tools, such as UML design and schedulability analysis tools.

These profiles provide a minutely specialized form of UML dealing with the issues important to some domain of concern. In this case, of course, the domain of concern is real-time, high-reliability, and safety-critical systems. These specializations take the form of representation of domain concepts as stereotypes of standard UML elements, with additional tag values for the QoS aspects, whose values can be specified in constraints. The details of the profiles will be discussed later. For now, let's limit our concern to the domain concepts themselves and not to how they are presented in the profiles.

1.2.1 Modeling Actions and Concurrency

Two critical aspects of real-time systems are how time is handled and the execution of actions with respect to time. The design of a real-time system must identify the timing requirements of the system and ensure that the system performance is both logically correct *and* timely.

Most developers concerned with timeliness of behavior express it in terms of actual execution time relative to a fixed budget called a *time constraint*. Often, the constraint is specified as a deadline, a single time value (specified from the onset of an initiating stimulus) by which the resulting action must complete. The two types of time constraints commonly used are *hard* and *soft*:

- Hard   The correctness of an action includes a description of timeliness. A late completion of an action is incorrect and constitutes a system failure. For example, a cardiac pacemaker must pace outside specific periods of time following a contraction or fibrillation.[8]

---

[8] Uncoordinated contraction of random myocardial cells. This is a *bad* thing.

- Soft   For the most part, software requirements are placed on a set of instance executions rather than on each specific execution. *Average deadline* and *average throughput* are common terms in soft real-time systems. Sometimes, missing an entire action execution may be acceptable. Soft real-time requirements are most often specified in probabilistic or stochastic terms so that they apply to a population of executions rather than to a single instance of an action execution. It is common to specify but not validate soft real-time requirements. An example of a soft real-time specification might be that the system must process 1200 events per second on average, or that the average processing time of an incoming event is 0.8 ms.

Usually a timing constraint is specified as a deadline, a milestone in time that somehow constrains the action execution.

In the RTP, actions may have the time-related properties shown in Table 1-1.

As Table 1-1 suggests, the basic concepts of timeliness in real-time systems are straightforward even if their analysis is not. Most time requirements come from bounds on the performance of reactive systems. The system must react in a timely way to external events. The reaction may be a simple digital actuation, such as turning on a light, or a complicated loop controlling dozens of actuators simultaneously. Typically, many subroutines or tasks must execute between the causative event and the resulting system action. External requirements bound the overall performance of the control path. Each of the processing activities in the control path is assigned a portion of the overall time budget. The sum[9] of the time budgets for any path must be less than or equal to the overall performance constraint.

Because of the ease of analysis of hard deadlines, most timeliness analysis is done assuming hard deadlines and worst-case completion times. However, this can lead to overdesign of the hardware at a potentially much greater recurring cost than if a more detailed analysis were done.

In the design of real-time systems several time-related concepts must be identified and tracked. An action may be initiated by an external

---

[9] Although due to blocking and preemption, it is not generally just a simple arithmetic sum.

Table 1-1: *Timeliness Properties of Actions*

Attribute	Description
Priority	The priority of the action from a scheduling perspective. It may be set as a result of static analysis or by dynamic scheduling software.
Blocking Time	The length of time that the action is blocked waiting for resources.
Ready Time	The effective Release Time expressed as the length of time since the beginning of a period; in effect a delay between the time an entity is eligible for execution and the actual beginning of execution.
Delay Time	The length of time an action that is eligible for execution waits while acquiring and releasing resources.
Release Time	The instant of time at which a scheduling job becomes eligible for execution.
Preempted Time	The length of time the action is preempted, when runable, to make way for a higher-priority action.
Worst-Case Completion Time	The overall time taken to execute the action, including overheads.
Laxity	Specifies the type of deadline, hard or soft.
Absolute Deadline	Specifies the final instant by which the action must be complete. This may be either a hard or a soft deadline.
Relative Deadline	For soft deadlines, specifies the desired time by which the action should be complete.
start	The start time of the action.
end	The completion time of the action.
duration	The total duration of the action (not used if start and end times are defined).
isAtomic	Identifies whether the action can be pre-empted or not.

event. Real-time actions identify a concept of *timely*—usually in terms of a deadline specified in terms of a completion time following the initiating event. An action that completes prior to that deadline is said to be timely; one completing after that deadline is said to be late.

Actions are ultimately initiated by events associated with the reception of messages arising from objects outside the scope of the system. These messages have various *arrival patterns* that govern how the various instances of the messages arrive over time. The two most common classifications of arrival patterns are *periodic* and *aperiodic* (i.e., episodic). Periodic messages may vary from their defined pattern in a (small) random way. This is known as *jitter*.

Aperiodic arrivals are further classified into bounded, bursty, irregular, and stochastic (unbounded). In bounded arrival times a subsequent arrival is bounded between a *minimum interarrival time* and a *maximum interarrival time*. A *bursty* message arrival pattern indicates that the messages tend to clump together in time (statistically speaking, there is a positive correlation in time between the arrival of one message and the near arrival of the next).[10] Bursty arrival patterns are characterized by a *maximum burst length* occurring within a specified *burst interval*. For example, a bouncy button might be characterized as giving up to 10 events within a 20ms burst interval. The maximum burst length is also sometimes specified with a probability density function (PDF) giving a likely distribution or frequency within the burst interval. Lastly, if the events arrivals are truly uncorrelated with each other, they may be modeled as arising randomly from a *probability density function* (PDF). This is the stochastic arrival pattern.

Knowing the arrival pattern of the messages leading to the execution of system actions is not enough to calculate schedulability, however. It is also important to know how long the action takes to execute. Here, too, a number of different measures are used in practice. It is very common to use a worst-case execution time in the analysis. This approach allows us to make very strong statements about absolute schedulability, but has disadvantages for the analysis of systems in which occasional lateness is either rare or tolerable. In the analysis of so-called *soft real-time systems*, it is more common to use average execution time to determine a statistic called *mean lateness*.

---

[10] Bursty message arrival patterns are characterized by a Poisson distribution and so do not have a standard deviation but do have an average interarrival time.

Actions often execute at the same time as other actions. We call this *concurrency*. Due to the complexity of systems, objects executing actions must send messages to communicate with objects executing other actions. In object terminology, a *message* is an abstraction of the communication between two objects. This may be realized in a variety of different ways. *Synchronization patterns* describe how different concurrent actions rendezvous and exchange messages. It is common to identify means for synchronizing an action initiated by a message sent between objects.

In modern real-time systems it cannot be assumed that the sender of a message and the receiver of that message are located in the same address space. They may be executing on the same processor, in the same thread, on the same processor but different threads, or on separate processors. This has implications for the ways in which the sender and receiver can exchange messages. The transmission of a message *m* may be thought of as having two events of interest—a send event followed by a receive event. Each of these events may be processed in either a synchronous or an asynchronous fashion, leading to four fundamental synchronization patterns, as shown in Figure 1-1. The sending of an event is synchronous if the sender waits until the message is sent before continuing and asynchronous if not.[11] The reception of an event is synchronous if the receiver immediately processes it and asynchronous if that processing is delayed. An example of synch-synch pattern (synchronous send–synchronous receive) is a standard function or operation call. A message sent and received through a TCP/IP protocol stack is an example of an asynch-asynch transfer, because the message is typically queued to send and then queued during reception as well. A remote procedure call (RPC) is an example of a synch-asynch pattern; the sender waits until the receiver is ready and processes the message (and returns a result), but the receiver may not be ready when the message is sent.

In addition to these basic types, a *balking* rendezvous is a synch-synch rendezvous that aborts the message transfer if the receiver is not immediately ready to receive it, while a *timed wait* rendezvous is a balking rendezvous in which the sender waits for a specified duration for the receiver to receive and process the message before aborting. A *blocking*

---

[11] Note that some people consider an invocation synchronous if the caller waits until the receiver returns a response. This is what we would call the blocking kind of synch-synch rendezvous.

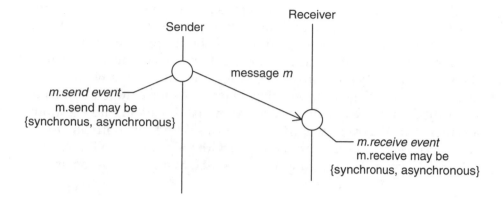

Figure 1-1: *Synchronization Patterns*

rendezvous is a synch-synch rendezvous in which the sender will wait (forever if need be) until the receiver accepts and processes the message.

In lay terms, concurrency is doing more than one thing at once. When concurrent actions are independent, life is easy. Life is, however, hard when the actions must share information or rendezvous with other concurrent actions. This is where concurrency modeling becomes complex.

Programmers and models typically think of the units of concurrency as threads, tasks, or processes. These are OS concepts, and as such available as primitive services in the operating system. It is interesting that the RTP does not discuss these concepts directly. Instead, the RTP talks about an *active resource* (a resource that is capable of generating its own stimuli asynchronously from other activities). A *concurrent Unit* is a kind of active resource that associates with a scenario (a sequenced set of actions that it executes) and owns at least one queue for holding incoming stimuli that are waiting to be accepted and processed. Sounds like a thread to me ;-)

As a practical matter, «active» objects contain such *concurrentUnits*, have the responsibility to start and stop their execution, and, just as important, delegate incoming stimuli to objects contained within the «active» objects via the composition relationship. What this means is that we will create an «active» object for each thread we want to run, and we will add passive (nonactive) objects to it via composition when we want them to execute in the context of that thread. Figure 1-2 shows a typical task diagram in UML.[12] The boxes with thick borders are the «active» objects. The resource is shown with the annotation «resource», called a *stereotype*. In the figure, an icon is used to indicate the semaphore

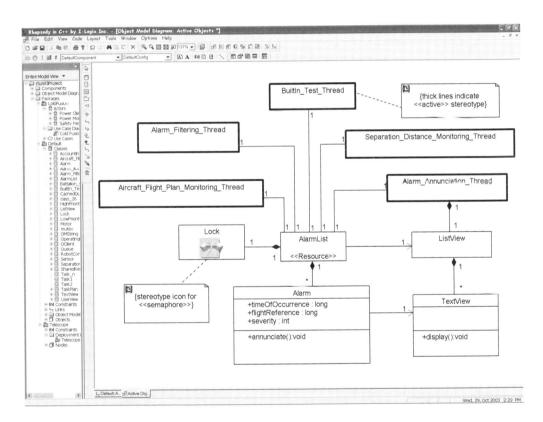

Figure 1-2: *«active» Objects and Threads*

---

[12] A task diagram is just a class diagram (see Chapter 2) whose mission is to show the classes related to the concurrency of the system.

rather than the alternative «stereotype» annotation. We will discuss the UML notions of objects and relations in much more detail in the next chapter.

1.2.2 Modeling Resources

A simple analysis of execution times is usually inadequate to determine schedulability (the ability of an action to always meet its timing constraints). Most timeliness analysis is based, explicitly or implicitly, on a client-resource model in which a client *requires* a specified QoS from a resource and a resource *offers* a QoS. Assuming the offered and required values are correct, schedulability analysis is primarily a job of ensuring that offered QoS is always at least as good as required. See Figure 1-3.

A resource from [7] is defined to be "an element whose service capacity is limited, directly or indirectly, by the finite capacities of the underlying physical computing environment." *Resource* is a fundamental concept, one that appears many times in real-time systems. Much of the design of a real-time system is devoted to ensuring that resources act in accordance with their preconditional invariant assumptions about exclusivity of access and quality of service.

The execution times used in the analysis must take into account the blocking time, that is, the length of time an action of a specific priority is blocked from completion by a lower-priority action owning a required resource.

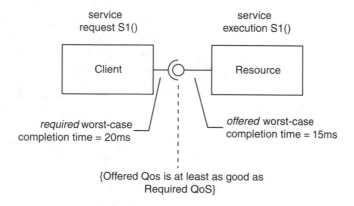

Figure 1-3: *Required and Offered Quality of Service*

1.2.3 Modeling Time

At the best of, uh, times, *time* itself is an elusive concept. While we lay folks talk about it *passing,* with concepts like past, present, and future, most philosophers reject the notion. There seem to be two schools of thought on the issue. The first holds that time is a landscape with a fixed past and future. Others feel it is a relationship between system (world) states as causal rules play out. Whatever it may be,[13] with respect to real-time systems, we are concerned with capturing the passage of time using milestones (usually deadlines) and measuring time. So we will treat time as if it flowed and we could measure it.

The RTP treats time as an ordered series of time instants. A *timeValue* corresponds to such a physical instant of time and may be either dense (meaning that a timeValue exists between any two timeValues) or discrete (meaning there exist timeValue pairs that do not have another timeValue between them). A timeValue measures one or more physical instants. A *duration* is the interval between two physical instants; that is, it has both starting and ending physical instants. A *timeInterval* may be either absolute (same as a duration) or relative. So what's the difference between a duration and a timeInterval? A duration has a start and end physical instant, while a timeInterval has a start and end timeValue. Confusing? You bet!

Fortunately, the concepts are not as difficult to use in practice as they are to define precisely. In models, you'll always refer to timeValues because that's what you measure, so timeIntervals will be used more than durations.

Speaking of measuring time. . . . We use two mechanisms to measure time: clocks and timers. All time is with reference to some clock that has a starting origin. It might be the standard calendar clock, or it might be time since reboot. If there are multiple clocks, they will be slightly different, so in distributed systems we have to worry about synchronizing them. Clocks can differ in a couple of ways. They can have a different reference point and be out of synch for that reason— this is called clock *offset*. They may also progress at different rates, which is known as *skew*. Skew, of course can change over time, and that is known as clock *drift*. Offset, skew, and drift of a timing mechanism

---

[13] And I, for one, feel like St. Augustine of Hippo who said he knew what time was until someone asked him to explain it.

are all with respect to a reference clock. Clocks can be read, set, or reset (to an initial state), but mostly they must march merrily along. Timers, on the other hand, have an origin (as do clocks) but they also generate timeout events. The current time of a timer is the amount of time that must elapse before a timeout occurs. A timer is always associated with a particular clock. A retriggerable timer resets after a timeout event and starts again from its nominal timeout value, while a nonretriggerable timer generates a single timeout event and then stops.

There are two kinds of time events: a timeout event and a clock interrupt. A clock interrupt is a periodic event generated by the clock representing the fundamental timing frequency. A timeout event is the result of achieving a specified time from the start of the timer.

1.2.4 Modeling Schedulability

It might seem odd at first, but the concepts of concurrency are not the same as the concepts of scheduling. Scheduling is a more detailed view with the responsibility of executing the mechanisms necessary to make concurrency happen. A scheduling context includes an execution engine (scheduler) that executes a scheduling policy, such as round robin, cyclic executive, or preemptive. In addition, the execution engine owns a number of resources, some of which are scheduled in accordance with the policy in force. These resources have actions, and the actions execute at some priority with respect to other actions in the same or other resources.

Operating systems, of course, provide the execution engine and the policies from which we select the one(s) we want to execute. The developer provides the schedulable resources in the forms of tasks («active» objects) and resources that may or may not be protected from simultaneous access via mechanisms such as monitors or semaphores. Such systems are fairly easy to put together, but there is (or should be!) concern about the schedulability of the system, that is, whether or not the system can be guaranteed to meet its timeliness requirements.

Determining a scheduling strategy is crucial for efficient scheduling of real-time systems. Systems no more loaded than 30% have failed because of poorly chosen scheduling policies.[14] Scheduling policies

---

[14] Doug Locke, Chief Scientist for TimeSys, private communication.

may be *stable, optimal, responsive,* and / or *robust.* A stable policy is one in which, in an overload situation, it is possible to a priori predict which task(s) will miss their timeliness requirements. Policies may also be *optimal.*[15] A *responsive* policy is one in which incoming events are handled in a timely way. Lastly, by *robust,* we mean that the timeliness of one task is not affected by the misbehavior of another. For example, in a round robin scheduling policy, a single misbehaving task can prevent any other task in the system from running.

Many different kinds of scheduling policies are used. Scheduling policies can be divided into two categories: *fair* policies and *priority* policies. The first category schedules things in such a way that all tasks progress more or less evenly. Examples of fair policies are shown in Table 1-2.

In contrast, priority-driven policies are *unfair* because some tasks (those of higher priority) are scheduled preferentially to others. In a priority schedule, the priority is used to select which task will run when more than one task is ready to run. In a preemptive priority schedule, when a ready task has a priority higher than that of the running task, the scheduler preempts the running task (and places it in a queue of tasks ready to run, commonly known as the "ready queue") and runs the highest-priority ready task. Priority schedulers are responsive to incoming events as long as the priority of the task triggered by the event is a higher priority than the currently running tasks. In such systems, interrupts are usually given the highest priority.

Two competing concepts are *importance* and *urgency. Importance* refers to the value of a specific action's completion to correct system performance. Certainly, correctly adjusting the control surface of an aircraft in a timely manner is of greater importance than providing flicker-free video on a cabin DVD display. The *urgency* of an action refers to the nearness of its deadline for that action without regard to its importance. The urgency of displaying the next video frame might be much higher than the moment-by-moment actuation control of the control surfaces, for example. It is possible to have highly important, yet not urgent actions, and highly urgent but not important ones mixed freely within a single system. Most scheduling executives, however, provide only a single means for scheduling actions—priority. Priority is an

---

[15] An optimal policy is one that can schedule a task set if it is possible for any other policy to do so.

Table 1-2: *Fair Scheduling Policies*

Scheduling Policy	Description	Pros	Cons
Cyclic Executive	The scheduler runs a set of tasks (each to completion) in a never-ending cycle. Task set is fixed at startup.	• Fair • Very simple • Highly predictable	• Unresponsive • Unstable • Nonoptimal • Nonrobust • Requires tuning • Short tasks[16]
Time-Triggered Cyclic Executive	Same as cyclic executive except that the start of a cyclic is begun in response to a time event so that the system pauses between cycles.	• Fair • Very simple • Highly predictable • Resynchronizes cycle with reference clock	• Unresponsive • Unstable • Nonoptimal • Nonrobust • Requires tuning • Short tasks
Round Robin	A task, once started, runs until it voluntarily relinquishes control to the scheduler. Tasks may be spawned or killed during the run.	• Fair • More flexible than cyclic executive • Simple	• Unresponsive • Unstable • Nonoptimal • Nonrobust • Short tasks
Time-Division Round Robin	A round robin in which each task, if it does not relinquish control voluntarily, is interrupted within a specified time period, called a *time slice*.	• Fair • More flexible than cyclic executive or round robin • Simple • Robust	• Unresponsive • Unstable • Nonoptimal

---

[16] By *short tasks* we mean that for the policy to be fair, each task must execute for a relatively short period of time. Often a task that takes a long time to run must be divided by the developer into shorter blocks to achieve fairness. This places an additional burden on the developer.

implementation-level solution offered to manage both importance and urgency.

All of the priority-based scheduling schemes in Table 1-3 are based on urgency. It is possible to also weight them by importance by multiplying them by an importance factor w_j and then set the task priority

Table 1-3: *Priority Scheduling Policies*

Scheduling Policy	Description	Pros	Cons
Rate Monotonic Scheduling (RMS)	All tasks are assumed periodic, with their deadline at the end of the period. Priorities are assigned as design time so that tasks with the shortest periods have the highest priority.	• Stable • Optimal • Robust	• Unfair • May not scale up to highly complex systems
Deadline Monotonic Scheduling (DMS)	Same as RMS except it is not assumed that the deadline is at the end of the period, and priorities are assigned at design time, based on the shortness of the task's deadline.	• Stable • Optimal • Robust	• Unfair • Handles tasks more flexibly
Maximum Urgency First (MUF)	Priorities are assigned at run-time when the task becomes ready to run, based on the nearness of the task deadlines—the nearer the deadline, the higher the priority.	• Optimal • Scales up better than RMS or DMS • Robust	• Unstable • Unfair • Lack of RTOS support

Table 1-3: *(cont.)*

Scheduling Policy	Description	Pros	Cons
Earliest Deadline Scheduling (EDS)	Laxity is defined to be the time-to-deadline minus the remaining task-execution-time. LL scheduling assigns higher priorities to lower laxity values.	• Robust • Optimal	• In naïve implementation, causes thrashing • Unstable • Unfair • Even less RTOS support than EDS • More complex
Least Laxity (LL)	MUF is a hybrid of LL and RMS. A *critical task set* is run using the highest set of priorities under an RMS schedule, and the remaining (less critical) tasks run at lower priorities, scheduled using LL.	• Robust • Optimal	• Critical task set runs preferentially to other tasks, to some stability is achieved, although not for the LL task set • In naïve implementation, causes thrashing • Unstable • Unfair • Even less RTOS support than EDS • More complex

equal to the product of the unweighted priority and the importance factor. For example, in RMS scheduling the task priority would be set to

$$[DISEQ]p_j = w_j/C_j$$

Equation 1-1: *Importance-Weighted Priority*

Where p_j is the priority of task j, w_j is some measure of the importance of the completion of the task, and C_j is the period of task j. [10] provides a reasonably rigorous treatment of weighted scheduling policies for generalized scheduling algorithms. Note that some operating systems use ascending priority values to indicate higher priority while others use descending priorities to indicate higher priority.

Since essentially all real-time systems running multiple tasks must coordinate those tasks and share resources, the manner in which those resources are managed is crucial not only to the correct operation of the system but also to its schedulability. The fundamental issue is the protection of the resource from corruption due to interleaved writing of the values or from a reader getting an incorrect value because it read partway through an update from another task. Of course, for physical resources, there may be other integrity concerns as well, due to the nature of the physical process being managed. The most common basic solution is to serialize the access to the resource and prevent simultaneous access. There are a number of technical means to accomplish this. For example, access can be made *atomic*—that is, no other task is allowed to run when one task owns a resource. Such accesses are made during what is called a *critical section*. This approach completely prevents simultaneous access but is best suited when the access times for the resource are very short relative to the action completion and deadline times [11]. Atomic access also breaks the priority-based scheduling assumption of infinite preemptibility (that is, when a task will run as soon as it is ready to run and the highest priority ready task in the system). However, if the critical section isn't too long, then a mild violation of the assumption won't affect schedulability appreciably. When a resource must be used for longer periods of time, the use of critical sections is not recommended.

Another common approach to access serialization is to queue the requests. That is useful when the running task doesn't have to precisely synchronize with the resource, but wants to send it a message. Queuing a message is a "send-and-forget" kind of rendezvous that works well for some problems and not for others, depending on whether the resource (typically running in its own thread in this case) and the client must be tightly coupled with respect to time. For example, sending a time-stamped log entry to a logging database via a queue allows the sending task to send the message and go on about its business, knowing that eventually the database will handle the log entry. This would not be appropriate in a real-time control algorithm in which a sensor value is being used to control a medical laser, however.

A third common approach to access serialization is protect the resource with a mutual exclusion (mutex) semaphore. The semaphore is an OS object that protects a resource. When access is made to an unlocked resource, the semaphore allows the access and locks it. Should another task come along and attempt to access the resource, the semaphore detects it and blocks the second task from accessing the resource—the OS suspends the task allowing the original resource client to complete. Once complete, the resource is unlocked, and the OS then allows the highest-priority task waiting on that resource to access it, while preventing other tasks from accessing that resource. When a task is allowed to run (because it owns a needed resource) even though a higher-priority task is ready to run, the higher-priority task is said to be *blocked*.

While this approach works very well, it presents a problem for schedulability called *unbounded priority inversion*. When a task is blocked, the system is said to be in a condition of priority inversion because a lower-priority task is running even though a higher-priority task is ready to run. In Figure 1-4, we see two tasks sharing a resource,[17] HighPriorityTask and the LowPriorityTask. In the model presented here, a low-priority value means the task is a high priority. Note that there is a set of tasks on intermediate priority, Task1 through Task_n, and that these tasks do not require the resource. Therefore, if LowPriorityTask runs and locks the resource, and then HighPriorityTask wants to run, it must block to allow LowPriorityTask to complete its use of the resource and release it. However, the *other* tasks in the system are of higher priority than LowPriorityTask and then can (and will) preempt LowPriority Task when they become ready to run. This, in effect, means that the highest priority task in the system is blocked not only by the LowPriority Task, but potentially by *every other task* in the system. Because there is no bound on the number of these intermediate priority tasks, this is called *unbounded priority inversion*. There are strategies for bounding the priority inversion and most of these are based on the temporary elevation of the priority of the blocking task (in this case, LowPriority Task). Figure 1-5 illustrates the problem in the simple implementation of semaphore-based blocking.

---

[17] The notations will be covered in the next chapter. For now, the boxes represent "things" such as tasks, resources, and semaphores, and the lines mean that connected things can exchange messages. The notes in curly braces, called *constraints*, provide additional information or annotations.

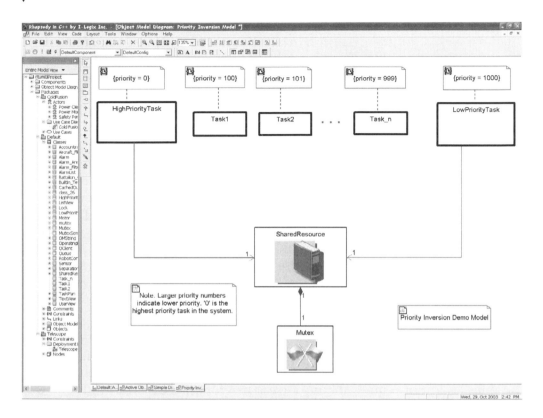

Figure 1-4: *Priority Inversion Model*

As mentioned, there are a number of solutions to the unbounded priority inversion problem. In one of them, the *Highest Locker Pattern* of [11] (see also [9,12]), each resource has an additional attribute—its priority ceiling. This is the priority *just above* that of the highest-priority task that can ever access the resource. The priority ceiling for each resource is determined at design time. When the resource is locked, the priority of the locking task is temporarily elevated to the priority ceiling of the resource. This prevents intermediate priority tasks from preempting the locking task as long as it owns the resource. When the resource is released, the locking task's priority is reduced to either its nominal priority or to the highest priority ceiling of any resources that remain locked by that task. There are other solutions with different pros and cons that the interested reader can review.

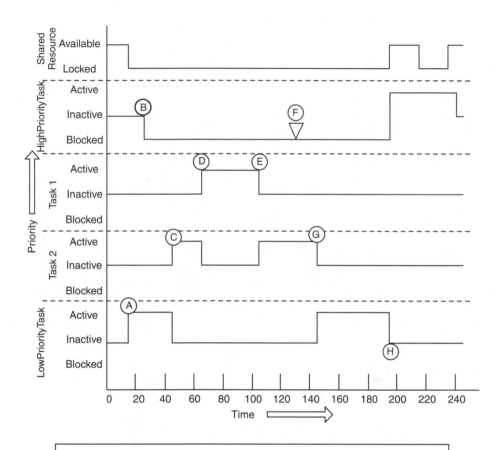

Legend:
Priorities: HighPriorityTask (HPT) > Task 1 > Task 2 > LowPriorityTask (LPT)
A: LPT is ready to run and starts and during execution, locks the shared resource (SR).
B: HPT is ready to run, but needs the resource. It is blocked and must allow Task 1 to complete.
C: Task 2, which is a higher priority than LPT, is ready to run. Since it doesn't need the resource, it preempts LPT. HPT is now effectively blocked by both LPT and Task 2.
D: Task 1, which is a higher priority than Task 2, is ready to run. Since it doesn't need the resource, it reempts Task 2. HPT is now effectively blocked by three tasks.
E: Task 1 completes, allowing Task 2 to resume.
F. HPT's deadline is missed even though it was long enough to allow the execution of both HPT and LPT. It was not long enough to allow all the other tasks to run, however.
G. Task 2 completes, allowing LPT to resume.
H. LPT (finally) completes and releases the resource, allowing Task 1 to access the resource.

Figure 1-5: *Priority Inversion Scenario*

An important aspect of schedulability is determining whether or not a particular task set can be scheduled, that is, can it be *guaranteed* to always meet its timeliness requirements? Because timeliness requirements are usually expressed as deadlines, that is the case we will consider here.

When a task set is scheduled using RMS, then certain assumptions are made. First, the tasks are time-driven (i.e., periodic). If the tasks are not periodic, it is common to model the aperiodic tasks using the minimum interarrival time as the period. While this works, it is often an overly strong condition—that is, systems that fail this test may nonetheless be schedulable and always meet their deadlines, depending on the frequency with which the minimum arrival time actually occurs. The other assumptions include infinite preemptibility (meaning that a task will run immediately if it is now the highest-priority task ready to run) and the deadline occurs at the end of the period. In addition, the tasks are independent—that is, there is no blocking. When these things are true, then Equation 1-2 provides a strong condition for schedulability. By *strong*, we mean that if the inequality is true, then the system is schedulable; however, just because it's not true does not imply necessarily that the system is not schedulable. More detailed analysis might be warranted for those cases.

$$\sum_n \frac{C_j}{T_j} \le n \left(2^{\frac{1}{n}} - 1 \right)$$

Equation 1-2: *Basic Rate Monotonic Analysis*

In Equation 1-2, C_j is the execution time for the task. In a worst-case analysis, this must be the worst-case execution time (i.e., worst-case completion time). T_j is the period of the task, and n is the number of tasks. The ratio C_j/T_j is called the *utilization* of the task. The expression on the right side of the inequality is called the *utilization bound* for the task set (note that 2 is raised to the power of $(1/n)$). The utilization bound converges to about 0.69 as the number of tasks grows. It is less than 1.0 because in the worst case, the periods of the tasks are prime with respect to each other. If the task periods are all multiples of each other (for example, periods of 10, 100, 500), then a utilization bound of 100% can be used for this special case (also for the case of dynamic priority

Table 1-4: *Sample Task Set*

Task	Execution Time (ms)	Period (ms)	Cj/Tj
Task 1	10	100	0.1
Task 2	30	150	0.2
Task 3	50	250	0.2
Task 4	100	500	0.2

policies, such as EDS). As an example, consider the case in which we have four tasks, as described in Table 1-4.

The sum of the utilizations from the table is 0.7. The utilization bound for four tasks is 0.757; therefore, we can guarantee that this set of tasks will always meet its deadlines.

The most common serious violation of the assumptions for Equation 1-2 is the independence of tasks. When one task can block another (resource sharing being the most common reason for that), then blocking must be incorporated into the calculation, as shown in Equation 1-3.

In this equation, B_j is the worst-case blocking for task j. Note that there is no blocking term for the lowest-priority task (task n). This is because the lowest-priority task can never be blocked (since it is normally preempted by every other task in the system).

$$\sum_j \frac{C_j}{T_j} + \max\left(\frac{B_1}{T_1}, ..., \frac{B_{n-1}}{T_{n-1}}\right) \leq n\left(2^{\frac{1}{n}} - 1\right)$$

Equation 1-3: *Rate Monotonic Analysis with Blocking*

As mentioned above, it is necessary to take into account any chained blocking in the blocking term. That is, if one task can preempt a blocking task then the blocking term for the blocking task must take this into account. For example, in the model shown in Figure 1-5, the blocking term for HighPriorityTask must include the time that Low PriorityTask locks the resource *plus* the sum of the worst-case execution time for all the intermediate-priority tasks (because they can preempt LowPriorityTask while it owns the resource), unless some special measure is used to bound the priority inversion.

Detailed treatment of the analysis of schedulability is beyond the scope of this book. The interested reader is referred to [5,9,12], for a more detailed discussion of timeliness and schedulability analysis.

1.2.5 Modeling Performance

Performance modeling is similar to modeling schedulability. However, our concerns are not meeting specific timeliness requirements but capturing performance requirements and ensuring that performance is adequate. Performance modeling is important for specifying performance requirements, such as bandwidth, throughput, or resource utilization, as well as estimating performance of design solutions. The measures of performance commonly employed are resource utilization, waiting times, execution demands on the hardware infrastructure, response times, and average or burst throughput—often expressed as statistical or stochastic parameters. Performance modeling is often done by examining scenarios (system responses in specific circumstances such as a specific load with specified arrival times) and estimating or calculating the system response properties. Performance analysis is done either by application of queuing models to compute average utilization and throughput or via simulation. This often requires modeling the underlying computational hardware and communications media as well.

One key concept for performance modeling is *workload*. The workload is a measure of the demand for the execution of a particular scenario on available resources, including computational resources (including properties such as context switch time, some measure of processing rate, and whether the resource is preemptible). The priority, importance, and response times of each scenario are required for this kind of analysis. The properties of the resources used by the scenarios that must be modeled are capacity, utilization (percentage of usage of total available capacity), access time, response time, throughput, and how the resources are scheduled or arbitrated. Chapter 4 discusses the UML Profile for Schedulability, Performance, and Time, and its application for modeling performance aspects.

1.3 Systems Engineering vs. Software Engineering

In many, if not most, real-time and embedded systems development, it is crucial to consider not only the software aspects, but also the *system* aspects. By *systems aspects,* we mean those aspects that affect the system as a whole, independent of the implementation technologies (e.g., software, electronic, mechanical, or chemical), as well as how these different design aspects collaborate. By *systems engineering* we mean the definition, specification, and high-level architecture of a system that is to be realized with multiple disciplines, typically including electrical, mechanical, software, and possibly chemical engineering. The primary activities encompassed by systems engineering include

- Capturing, specifying and validating the requirements of the system as a whole
- Specification of the high-level subsystem architecture
- Definition of the subsystem interfaces and functionality
- Mapping the system requirements onto the various subsystems
- Decomposing the subsystems into the various disciplines— electronic, mechanical, software, and chemical—and defining the abstract interfaces between those aspects

In all these activities, systems engineers are not concerned with the design of the discipline-specific aspects of the software or the electronics, but *are* concerned with the specification of what those design aspects must achieve and how they will collaborate.

The use of UML in systems engineering is increasing. A number of papers have been written on the topic (for examples, see [13,14]). The OMG has recently released a request for proposal (RFP) called "UML for Systems Engineering: Request for Proposal" [15]. At the time of this writing, work is underway creating a UML variant for this purpose.[18] The current schedule calls for adoption of this language variant in mid-2004.

1.4 What Do We Mean by *Architecture*?

In the ROPES process (described later in this chapter) *architecture* is defined as the set of strategic design decisions that affect the structure, behavior, or functionality of the system as a whole. The ROPES process goes on to discuss five primary aspects of architecture:

- *Subsystem/Component Architecture*—The large-scale pieces of the system that can be done prior to the decomposition of the system into hardware and software aspects, or may refer to the large-scale software pieces, as appropriate for the project.

- *Resource and Concurrency Architecture*—The identification of the concurrent tasks, how the primitive semantic objects map into those threads, the scheduling policies, and policies for synchronization and resource management. Note that in the UML, the primary unit of concurrency is the «active» object, which creates and owns the thread in which it executes. Note also that this is primarily a software architecture concern and has a relatively minor impact on system engineering and hardware architectures. However, it does impact the selection of processors and connection media such as networks and busses.

- *Distribution Architecture*—The identification of how objects map into different address spaces, and how they will communicate across those address space boundaries, including distribution patterns (such as Publish/Subscribe, Broker, etc.) and communication protocols.

- *Safety and Reliability Architecture*—The specification of how faults will be identified, isolated, and managed during runtime. This typically includes the redundant architectural substructures and their management in the event of faults.

- *Deployment Architecture*—The specification of how the different architectural aspects relate to each other, specifically the software, mechanical, electronic, and chemical aspects. This can be done asymmetrically, where each piece of software is assigned at design time to run on a particular hardware target, or symmetrically where runtime

---

[18] The author is a member of the SysML consortium working on this submission at the time of this writing.

locale decisions are made dynamically at runtime to permit load-balancing.

We call these architectural *aspects* because there is a single system that in fact contains all of these. Therefore the system model must likewise have an architecture that contains *all* of these different aspects in a coherent and consistent way. Systems engineers are responsible for the subsystem and component architecture, the safety and reliability architecture, and the deployment architecture. They also may heavily influence, although not completely design, the other architectural aspects—distribution and concurrency and resource architectures. Software engineers may be responsible for the subsystem and component architectures for the software, most of the concurrency and resource management architecture, and parts of the distribution, deployment, and safety and reliability architectures. In the next chapter, we'll talk about how to represent these different architectural views using the UML.

1.5 The Rapid Object-Oriented Process for Embedded Systems (ROPES) Process[19]

The ROPES process exists on three time scales simultaneously:

- *Macro*—The entire length of the project, typically one to several years
- *Micro*—The time required to produce a single increment or version of the system that achieves some targeted functionality—typically four to six weeks
- *Nano*—The time needed to produce, compile, execute, and/or test some very small portion of the system—typically 30 minutes to an hour

You can see that the macrocycle is divided up into four overlapping macrophases:

- Key concepts
- Secondary concepts

---

[19] Rapid Object Oriented Process for Embedded Systems. For more information see reference [5].

- • Design concepts
- • Optimization and deployment concepts

In each macrophase, there are usually several incremental proto-types produced. For example, if the macrocycle is 18 months long, you would expect the key concept macrophase to be on the order of four to five months long. This would encompass anywhere from three to five microcycles. Each microcycle results in a single prototype, so in this example, there would be three to five versions of the system incrementally produced that primarily focused on identification, specification, and elaboration of key concepts, whether these concepts are requirements, architecture, or technological concepts. Later prototypes would spend less effort on these key concepts but add more concern on the secondary and tertiary concepts. Still later prototypes would focus more on design and implementation issues, while the last set would tend to focus on optimization and deployment issues. Each prototype has a testable *mission*—its purpose—which tends evolve over time.

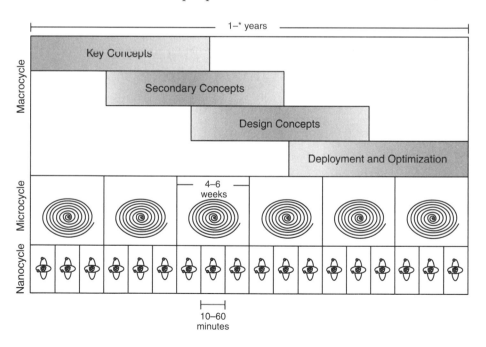

Figure 1-6: *ROPES Spiral Macrocycle*

The ROPES process defines an alternative lifecycle used when there is significant codesign and some of the hardware components have a long lead time—the *SemiSpiral* lifecycle shown in Figure 1-7. This macrocycle at first proceeds like a waterfall—a complete requirements capture phase is followed by a complete systems engineering phase. This allows the specification of all the requirements and all the high-level architecture. Thus the long-lead-time hardware devices can be designed with a complete knowledge of all the requirements, with the downside being that if there are *strategic defects* in either the requirements or the high-level architecture, they will be costly to correct (similar to the waterfall lifecycle). Nevertheless, the design continues in a multidisciplinary spiral, so that early and frequent testing still results in a higher-quality product than a waterfall lifecycle.

The nanocycle[20] is the constant design-execution-debug cycle that is most successful designers' preferred style of working. The idea is that you should *constantly* ask *and answer* the question "Is this *right*?" never being more than minutes away from being able to demonstrate that it *is* right. The use of executable UML tools, such as Rhapsody®, allows you do accomplish this easily and with less effort, because Rhapsody can execute your UML models almost immediately.

1.5.1 Model-Driven Development (MDD)

The current state-of-the-art in software development process relies on a small number of important principles:

- *Iterative Development*—Iterative development is based on the concept of incremental construction; that is, building a large-scale product by constructing it as a series of smaller products of increasing completeness. Because the prerelease versions of the system are smaller, they are easier to "get right" by testing, and this testing can come much earlier than in a waterfall lifecycle. To be effective, the rapid prototypes must be production-quality software, be small focused pieces of the overall application, and address identified or perceived risks.

---

[20] The nanocycle workflow is very similar to the workflow in the XP (extreme programming) or Agile methods processes. That is, constant execution and constant test throughput development.

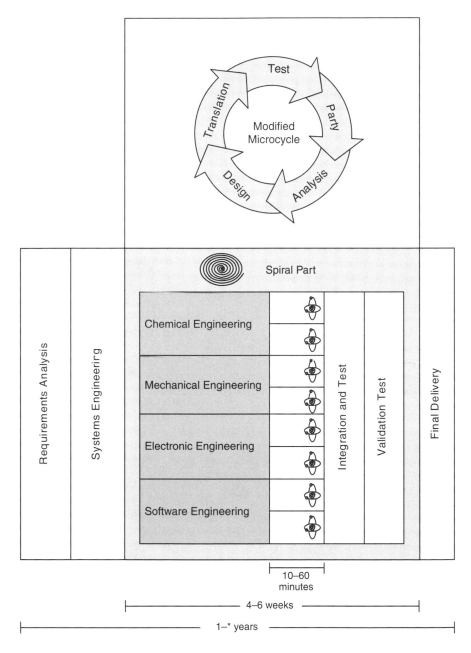

Figure 1-7: *ROPES SemiSpiral Lifecycle*

- *Use of Models*—Large, complex systems can't be effectively constructed using only source-code-level constructs. Abstract models permit the developers to capture the important characteristics of the application and how they interrelate. Models provide us with a way of thinking about the application domain by representing domain concepts as model elements. This enables us to structure the application around the concepts and properties of the application domain, which is much easier to prove correct because domain experts are available in our domain areas.

- *Model-Code Bidirectional Associativity*—For model-based systems, it is absolutely crucial that the code and the diagrams are different views of the very same underlying model. If the code is allowed to deviate from the design model, then the separate maintenance of the code and model becomes burdensome, and the system ultimately becomes code-based. As such, system complexity can no longer be effectively managed.

- *Executable Models*—You can only test things that execute—therefore, build primarily executable things, both *early* and *often*. The key to this is model-based translation of designs so that transforming a design into something that executes takes on the order of seconds to minutes, rather than weeks to months using traditional hand-implementation approaches.

- *Debug and Test at the Design Level of Abstraction*—Because today's applications are extremely complex, we use abstract design models to help us understand and create them. We also need to debug and test them at the same level. We need to be able to ask "Should I put the control rod into the reactor core?" rather than merely "Should I be jumping on C or NZ?"

- *Test What You Fly and Fly What You Test*—Simulation has its place, but the purpose of building and testing executable models is to quickly develop defect-free applications that meet all of their functional and performance requirements. Using appropriate technology, you can get all the benefits of rapid iterative development and deployment, model-level debugging, and executable models using generated production-level software so that the *formal testing only needs to be done once.*

Using these six principles, even the most demanding and complex real-time and embedded system can be effectively developed. Most development methodologies in practice today utilize these principles—some more effectively than others, mind you—and the approach I recommend is no different.

1.5.2 The ROPES Spiral in More Detail

The microcycle is the "spiral" portion of the process, lasting usually four to six weeks (although if it's somewhat shorter or longer than this, it really doesn't matter) and resulting in a single incremental version of the system (called a *prototype*) that meets a specific mission. The prototype mission is usually a combination of some set of use cases (capabilities or coherent sets of requirements), reduction of some specific risks, and/or the addition of some set of technologies.

The microcycle, or spiral, shown in Figure 1-8, is divided into five primary microphases:

- *Party*—devoted to project planning, project assessment, and process improvement
- *Analysis*—devoted to identifying the essential properties required of the prototype, that is, properties without which the system would be considered "wrong"
- *Design*—devoted to identifying a specific optimal solution consistent with the analysis model
- *Translation*—devoted to the production of high-quality, defect-free components of the prototype, completely unit-tested and inspected
- *Testing*—devoted to ensuring that the architecture is properly met (integration) and that the prototype meets its mission (validation), including required performance

We can see that there is a systems engineering subphase in the analysis microphase. This does not mean or imply that it is only during this period that system engineers are doing useful work. Rather, it defines a particular set of activities resulting in a particular set of artifacts released at the end of the subphase. The workflow of the systems engineer is discussed in more detail later in this book.

The spiral approach is a depth-first approach of system development. Although in the first party phase, the expected use cases are named and

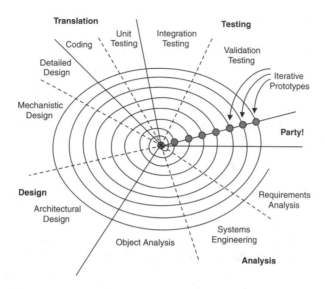

Figure 1-8: *ROPES Spiral*

roughly scoped, they are not detailed until the project matures to that point in the schedule. Thus, development proceeds without a detailed understanding of *all* of the requirements; instead, the focus is on the higher-risk issues and requirements, so that they are completely understood before those of lesser risk and significance are detailed. The early testing of the high-risk and high-importance aspects of the system reduces risk optimally, and the early and frequent testing ensures that the system produced is of high quality.

The major activities in the ROPES spiral are:

- *Analysis*—defines the essential application properties that must be true of all possible, acceptable solutions, leaving all other characteristics free to vary. Analysis consists of three parts:

    ▾ *Requirements analysis*—Requirements analysis identifies in detail the black-box[21] requirements, both functional and performance, of the system without revealing the internal structure (design).

    ▾ *Systems engineering*—In multidisciplinary systems development— that is, those that include software, electronic, mechanics, and

---

[21] By *black box* I mean that the requirements are visible to objects interacting with the system not requiring knowledge of the systems internal structure.

possible chemical aspects—the system architecture is constructed early and system-level requirements are mapped down onto the various aspects of the architecture.

▼ *Object (domain) analysis*—In object analysis, the various concepts inherent in the various domains of concern are identified, along with their relations to each other. This is normally done one use case at a time. There are two primary aspects of object analysis: structural and behavioral.

- *Object structural analysis*—identifies the key abstractions of the application that are required for correctness, as well as the relation that links them together. The black box functional pieces are realized by collaborations of objects working together.

- *Object behavioral analysis*—identifies how the key abstractions behave in response to environmental and internal stimuli, and how they dynamically collaborate together to achieve system-level functionality.

- *Design*—Design defines a particular solution that optimizes the application in accordance with the project objectives while remaining consistent with the analysis model. Design is *always* about optimization. Design also consists of three parts:

  ▼ *Architectural design*—Architectural design identifies the strategic design decisions that affect most or all of the application, including the mapping to the physical deployment model, the identification of runtime artifacts, and the concurrency model. This is typically accomplished through the application of architectural design patterns.

  ▼ *Mechanistic design*—Mechanistic design adds to the collaborations to optimize their behavior according to some system optimization criteria. This is typically done through the application of mechanistic design patterns.

  ▼ *Detailed design*—Detailed design adds low-level information necessary to optimize the final system.

- *Translation*—Translation creates an executable application from a design model. Translation normally includes not only the development of executable code but also the unit-level (i.e., individual object) testing of that translation.

- *Testing*—Testing applies correctness criteria against the executable application to either identify defects or to show a minimal level of conformance to the requirements and/or design. Testing includes, at minimum, integration and validation testing.

These activities may be arranged in many different ways. Such an arrangement defines the *development process* used for the project. The iterative development process looks like Figure 1-8.

The iterative development process model shown in Figure 1-8 is known as ROPES, for *rapid object-oriented process for embedded systems* (see [5] for a more complete description). Each iteration produces work products, known as *artifacts*. A single iteration pass, along with the generated artifacts, is shown in Figure 1-9. This model is somewhat simplified in that it doesn't show the subphases of analysis and design, but does capture the important project artifacts, how they are created and used.

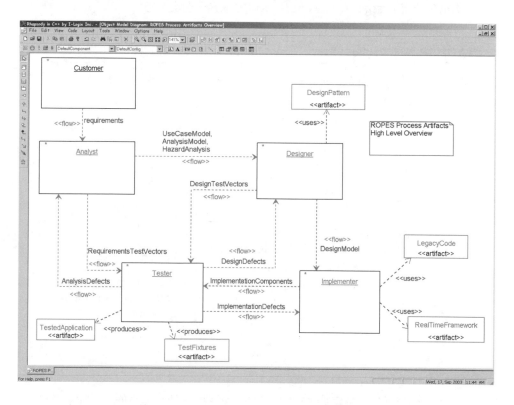

Figure 1-9: *ROPES Process Artifacts*

Rhapsody from I-Logix[22] is an advanced model creation tool with integrated product-quality code generation and design-level testing capabilities built in. Rhapsody was developed specifically to aid in the development of real-time and embedded systems, and integrates smoothly into the ROPES process model. Fully constructive tools, such as Rhapsody assist by providing support for all of the precepts mentioned at the beginning of this section. Although the UML in general and the ROPES process in particular can be applied using manual means for translation of models into code and debugging and testing that code, the use of such powerful automated tools greatly enhances their effectiveness. shows how a fully constructive tool can aid in the generation of development phase artifacts. Table 1-5 shows which artifacts are created in the various phases of the ROPES process.

Table 1-5: *Phased Artifacts in the ROPES Process*

Activity	Process Step	Generated Artifacts	Tool Generated Artifacts
Analysis	Requirements Analysis	Use case model Use case scenarios	Use case diagrams Use case descriptions Message sequence diagrams Use case statecharts and/or activity diagrams Report generation
	Object Structural Analysis	Structural object model	Class diagrams Object diagrams Reverse engineering creates models from legacy source code Report generation

---

[22] See *www.ilogix.com* for more information about the Rhapsody tool. Several white papers on the development of real-time systems are also available on the I-Logix Web site.

Table 1-5: (*cont.*)

Activity	Process Step	Generated Artifacts	Tool Generated Artifacts
Analysis (*continued*)	Object Behavioral Analysis	Behavioral object model	Message sequence diagrams Statecharts Activity diagrams Report generation
Design	Architectural Design	Subsystem model Concurrency model Distribution model Safety/reliability model Deployment model	Architectural class and object diagrams Architectural design patterns Active objects Component model (file mapping) Framework provides OS-tasking model Use of existing legacy code and components
	Mechanistic Design	Collaboration model	Class diagrams Message sequence diagrams Framework provides design patterns Framework provides state execution model
	Detailed Design	Class details	Browser access to • attributes • operations • user-defined types • package-wide members Round-trip engineering updates model from modified source code (*continued*)

Table 1-5: (*cont.*)

Activity	Process Step	Generated Artifacts	Tool Generated Artifacts
Translation		Executable application	Fully-executable code generated from structural and behavioral models including • object and class diagrams • sequence diagrams • statecharts • activity diagrams
Testing	Unit Testing Integration Testing Validation Testing	Design defects Analysis defects	Design level debugging and testing on *either* host or remote target, including • animate multithreaded applications • animated sequence diagrams • animated statecharts • animated attributes in Browser • breakpoints on • operation execution • state entry or exit • transition • event insertion • execution control scripts Simultaneous debugging with other design-level tools (such as Rhapsody from I-Logix) and source-level debuggers

1.6 MDA and Platform-Independent Models

A *model* is an integrated set of abstractions and their internal relations. Models are expressed in a *modeling language* that consists of two parts: a set of abstract elements (called *metaclasses*), which is a syntax for representing and viewing these elements and their relations, and a semantic framework that specifies the precise meaning of these abstract elements.

A model may support any number of different views. A UML class diagram may show a number of classes interacting together to realize a use case, for example. Another class diagram may show the same class in a generalization taxonomy. Still another class diagram may show how the class fits within its domain of interest. The behavioral constraints of a class may be represented as a statechart that shows how it responds to different events in different circumstances. Source code representing the implementation of the class can be viewed as text.

None of these views is, by itself, the model. Each is a narrow, restricted view of the model, using a particular graphical syntax to represent a particular point of view. The *model* is, in fact, the logical conjugation of the information shown in *all* views of the model. A class diagram is no more (or less) a model of a system than the source code. Both are important views of the model that concentrate on different aspects. This distinction between *model* and *view* is very important, as it turns out, in system development and maintenance, as we shall explore.

An *executable model* is a model that is defined with a rich enough set of semantics that its execution behavior is predictable. One can argue that any model that can be represented ultimately as executable machine code is, in fact, an executable model. At least two distinct views of an executable model must be constructed. The first is the structural view. What is the information manipulated by the model and how is it logically represented? What are the relationships among these structural elements? In the UML, for example, the structural view is represented by class diagrams (for logical elements) and object, deployment, and component diagrams (for physical elements). Secondly, what are the operations permitted to be done on that information and what constraints apply to the execution of those operations? The UML provides sequence, communication, and timing diagrams to show how model elements collaborate together and statecharts and activity diagrams to show how the behavior individually. Given these two views of a model, it is possible, in every important sense, to execute the model.

MDA is an approach that separates aspects of a model that are independent of underlying technologies from those that are dependent upon those aspects. The platform-independent model (PIM) is constructed to be independent of the processor(s) on which it runs, the communication infrastructure (such as Ethernet and TCP/IP), middleware (such as COM or CORBA), and even the implementation language (such as C or Ada). From the PIM, the platform-specific model (PSM) is constructed, either by translation or by elaboration (although the literature focuses primarily on the former). The PSM incorporates these aspects of the physical realization of the system. Of course, this can be done in stages, resulting in a succession of increasingly detailed PSMs until all the physical details of the system have been completely specified. Figure 1-10 shows this process schematically.

What does this mean in practice? Different tools support MDA to different degrees. Most tools are completely nonconstructive and nongenerative, and do not execute in any way. In such tools, the user must maintain two different models, performing the translation from the PIM to the PSM manually. Constructive tools handle more or less of this translation for you. Figure 1-11 shows how the Rhapsody® tool from I-Logix approaches MDA.

The Rhapsody tool can be thought of as consisting of several parts. The most visible to the user are the graphic editors used to perform model entry and manipulation and the report generator. Behind the

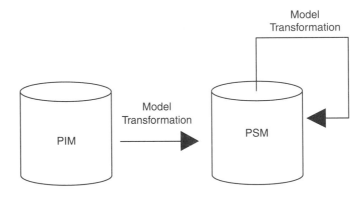

Figure 1-10: *MDA Overview*

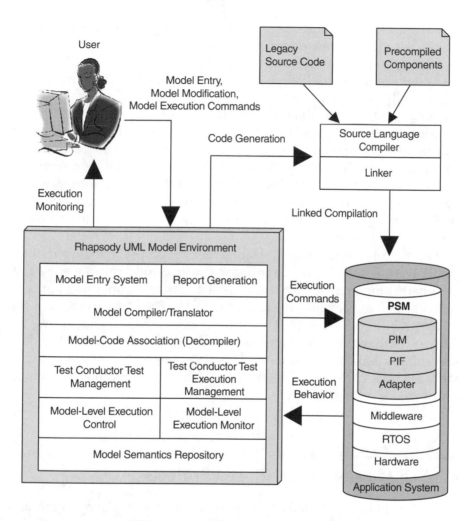

Figure 1-11: *The MDA Approach*

scenes, however, there is an elaborate system that compiles your model and can control and monitor the execution of the model. The model compiler takes the model semantics entered by the user via the diagrams and compiles it into source code that can be fed into a standard compiler for language such as C, C++, Java, and Ada. The model-code association component maintains the model and the code "in sync," whether the user modifies the model or the source code directly, eliminating the very pervasive problem of what to do when the model and the code disagree.

The model execution aspects of Rhapsody allow you to insert events, set breakpoints, and step and run the application. The model monitoring aspects of the tool allows the user to see the execution of the system at the model level—that is, see sequence diagrams drawn dynamically as the system runs, view the execution of the state machines and activity diagrams of the various objects of the system, examine the attributes, and so on. These tools allow the user to control and monitor the application execution on the user's desktop or on the actual target hardware. The Rhapsody Test Conductor® is a scenario-based test environment built on top of that debugging infrastructure that constructs (and applies) test vectors from the requirements scenarios. Of course, all of this uses the underlying model semantics stored in the model repository.

The compiler and linker work together to compile the output of the model compiler and compile in legacy source-code components. Precompiled components, such as third-party libraries, are linked in with the compiled application to create the PSM. The PSM consists of the PIM with bindings (links) into platform-specific aspects, including the PIM, the platform-independent framework (PIF), and the RTOS Adaptor, and any linked components. This PSM sits on top of any middleware, such as COM or CORBA, the RTOS, and, of course, the target hardware.

1.7 Scheduling Model-Based Projects

While this is not intended to be a book on project management and scheduling, I think it is an important enough topic to share what the ROPES process has to say on the subject. In my experience, lack of good scheduling is a leading cause of project failure, so while it might be a bit tangential, I will offer a few thoughts on the topic.

1.7.1 Why Schedule?

There are two primary reasons projects are estimated and scheduled. These two reasons are incompatible and mutually exclusive. Nevertheless, they are often combined—with disastrous results.

The primary reason for estimating and scheduling projects is to *plan*—and this requires the understanding of the cost and resource and time-based properties of the project. For example:

- When will the project be done?
- How much will it cost?
- Is this project likely to provide a good return on investment (ROI)?
- Should I invest in this project or another project?
- How many resources must I apply to it?
- Do I need to hire people and if so, with what skills?
- When should I begin ancillary activities, such as gearing up manufacturing, starting the marketing campaign, beginning the next project?

These are legitimate business questions and can only be answered with accurate schedules constructed from reasonable estimates.

The other primary use for schedules is *motivation*. Motivational (i.e., optimistic) schedules are used to inspire workers to apply their lazy selves to the project at hand and not goof off. Also to donate their non-work time (i.e., professional time) to the project. To accomplish this motivation, the project requires a sense of urgency, and this is instilled by constructing a schedule that is unachievable without Herculean efforts, if at all. An accurate schedule is actually an impediment to this motivational goal, so that the two primary uses for schedules are in fact at odds with each other.

The real difficulty arises when a schedule is used for both purposes. The schedule is constructed to be optimistic but then used as if it were an accurate planning tool. The first step to estimating and scheduling projects is to select for which of these purposes the schedule is to be used. If it is to be used to *plan*, then the goal should be an accurate schedule. If it is to *motivate*, then an urgent schedule should be created. If both are needed, then you need to create two different schedules.

In reality, the only really appropriate use for schedules is for planning. In my experience, the vast majority of engineers are highly motivated, hardworking professionals[23] who respond best to being treated as if they were. For this reason, we will assume that our goal is the first purpose—the creation of schedules that are accurate and reasonable so

---

[23] The only exception that comes to mind was an individual who quit to go into marketing.

that they are useful tools for planning. We will relegate the use of motivational schedules to the Dilbertesque business environments where they belong.

1.7.2 Estimation

As a group, we engineers *fail miserably* at accurately estimating how long things will take. Studies of just how bad we are at this abound in the literature. In one 1995 study, 53% of all projects were almost 200% over budget and 31% were cancelled after being started. Other and more recent studies confirm these results. In a more recent study, 87% of the projects missed functionality expectations, 73% were delivered late, and a full 18% of the projects were so off the mark that they were cancelled *after development had completed.*

There are many reasons why this is true. The primary reason for such incredibly poor estimation success, in my experience, is because engineers are actively encouraged not to be accurate. For example, one manager told me, in response to my estimate for a project, "That's the wrong number. Go do it again." Of course, this anti-accuracy bias is based in the desire for motivational, rather than accurate, schedules While the desire itself may be well meant (such as maximizing fourth-quarter revenue), one cannot ignore the facts without consequence.

Even if being done with the best of intentions, estimation is *hard!* Estimation is inherently more inaccurate than observation for obvious reasons. Good estimation is possible, but it will never be as accurate as hindsight *in principle.* A good estimate must come to embrace uncertainty as a way of life but understand that the more you know the more accurate your estimates will be. *The further along you are in the project, the more accurate your estimates will be.* Schedule management must in principle include refinement of estimates and the schedule over time, resulting in ever-increasing accurate forecasts. In practice, few engineers are trained in estimation or even rewarded for accuracy; in fact, far too often, engineers are actively encouraged to give inaccurately low estimates.

1.7.3 BERT and ERNIE

The ROPES process provides means for both constructing estimates and for improving one's ability to estimate. These (sub)processes are known as BERT and ERNIE.

1.7.3.1 Constructing Estimates: The BERT Approach

Bruce's Evaluation and Review Technique (BERT) is the ROPES way of constructing estimates. Estimates are always applied to estimable work units (EWUs). EWUs are small, atomic tasks typically no more than 80 hours in duration.[24] The engineer estimating the work provides three estimates:

- The mean (50%) estimate
- The optimistic (20%) estimate
- The pessimistic (80%) estimate

Of these, the most important is the 50% estimate. This estimate *is the one that the engineer will beat half of the time.* The central limit theorem of statistics states that if all of the estimates are truly 50% estimates, then overall the project will come in on time. However, this estimate alone does not provide all necessary information. You would also like a measure of the perceived risk associated with the estimate. This is provided by the 20% and 80% estimates. The former is the time that the engineer will beat only 20% of the time, while the latter will be beat 80% of the time. The difference between these two estimates is a measure of the confidence the engineer has in the estimate. The more the engineer knows, the smaller that difference will be.

These estimates are then combined to come up with the estimate actually used in the schedule using equation 1-4.

$$\frac{Low + 4 * Mean + High}{6} * EC$$

Equation 1-4: *Computing Used Estimate for Scheduling*

The estimate confidence (EC) factor is based on the particular engineer's accuracy history. An ideal estimator would have an EC value of 1.00. Typical EC values range from 1.5 to 5.0. As an estimator's ability to estimate improves, that number gets smaller over time, (hopefully) approaching 1.00.

---

[24] Although it can be used for larger units early before the decomposition to smaller units has been made.

1.7.3.2 Improving Estimation Capability: The ERNIE Method

We also want engineers to improve their ability to estimate. As Tom DeMarco notes, "If you don't track it, you can't control it." The approach in the ROPES process for estimation improvement is called Effect Review for Nanocycle Iteration Estimation (ERNIE). It consists of tracking estimated versus actual and recording these. From this, the EC factor used in Equation 1-4 is computed.

A sample from an estimation tracking spreadsheet is shown in Table 1-6.

To construct a new EC value, use the formula

$$EC_{n+1} = \Sigma(\text{deviations using } EC_n)/(\text{\# of estimates}) + 1.00$$

For example, to construct a new EC value from Table 1-6, you would compute

$$EC_2 = (0.425 + 0.56 + 0.842 + 0.1)/4 + 1.00 = 1.48$$

In this example, the engineer went from an EC factor of 1.75 to and EC factor of 1.48 (a significant improvement). This EC value will be used to adjust the "unadjusted used" computed estimate for insertion in the schedule. It is important to track estimation success in order to improve it. In order to improve a thing, it is necessary to track it.

Table 1-6: *Sample from Estimation Tracking Spreadsheet*

Date	Task	Low	Mean	High	Unad- justed Used	EC	Used	Actual	Dev.	% Diff.
9/15/04	User Interface	21	40	80	43.5	1.75	76.1	57	17	0.425
9/17/04	Database	15	75	200	85.8	1.75	150.2	117	42	0.56
9/18/04	Database Conversion	30	38	42	37.3	1.75	65.3	60	32	0.842
9/20/04	User Manual	15	20	22	19.5	1.75	34.1	22	2	0.1

1.7.4 Scheduling

A schedule is a sequenced arrangement of EWUs taking into account which can be run in parallel and which must be serialized. Further, the schedule must take into account inherent dependencies, level of risk, and the availability of personnel.

The waterfall lifecycle scheduling is often considered more accurate by naïve managers because schedules are constructed early and may be tracked against for the remainder of the project. However, this ignores the fundamental rule of scheduling: *The more you know, the more accurate you can be.* Early schedules are *inherently* inaccurate because you know less than you do one third, one half, or even seven eights of the way through a project than you do at the end. So it is ridiculous *in principle* to state at the outset of a project that it will be done in 18 months, 3 days, 6 hours, 42 minutes, and 13 seconds. Nevertheless, managers often act as if they can dictate the passage of time and the invention of software.

The BERT and ERNIE approach can be applied to waterfall or spiral projects. In either approach, though, early estimates will be less accurate than later refinements, when later refinements take into account information gleaned from observing the progress of the project. In principle, I believe the following accuracies for a waterfall lifecycle are achievable:[25]

- Concept ± 50%
- Requirements ± 25%
- Systems analysis ± 20%
- Design ± 15%
- Implementation ± 10%
- Validation testing ± 5%

When schedules are first constructed, in the concept phase, "10 person-years" means, in fact, anywhere from 5 to 15 person-years. If you need a hard number, then go with 15, but if your estimation process is fairly good, then 10 will be the most accurate single number you can provide.

In the spiral approach, the milestones are not the end of these waterfall phases, but instead planned prototypes. If you plan for 10 prototypes, then your first working schedule will have 10 primary

---

[25] The astute reader will note that these far exceed the accuracies of most project schedules.

milestones, one for each prototype. On average, these will usually be four to six weeks apart, but some may be longer or shorter, depending on their scope. If you want to construct larger-scale milestones, similar to preliminary design review (PDR) and critical design review (CDR) called out by some development methodologies, then you (somewhat arbitrarily) say that one prototype (say 3) will form the basis of the PDR and a later one (say 6) will form the basis of the CDR.

The ROPES scheduling approach uses the Central Limit Theorem from statistics, which states that if you take enough samples from a population, your accumulated samples will form a Gaussian distribution. What that means is that if you have enough estimates of the pieces and they are *in fact* 50% estimates, then half of them will be early, half of them will be late, and overall, your project will be on time.

That having been said, schedules must be not only tracked against, but also managed and maintained. Assessment and realignment of the schedule is one of the primary activities done in the so-called party phase of the ROPES microcycle.

Figure 1-12 shows a constructed schedule using prototypes as the primary scheduling points on a Gantt chart. Each prototype has a mission, defined to be a set of requirements (normally one to a small number of use cases) to be developed and a set of risks to be reduced. In the figure, the first such prototype, called "Hello World," is subdivided into the microcycle phases, each with some time attached to it. We see that in this particular example, PDR, CDR, and customer review activities are specifically scheduled. This schedule is tracked against on a daily, or at least weekly, basis, and modified to incorporate new information as it becomes available. The net result is a self-correcting schedule that improves over time.

Other scheduling views are important as well—especially the resource view that shows how your people are mapped against the schedule. Special care must be taken to ensure that they are neither over- nor underutilized in your schedule.

Figure 1-13 is a *resource histogram* showing the loading of a resource over time.[26] In the example, you want to be sure to neither over- nor underutilize the resource. This means that for a typical eight-hour

---

[26] You *never ever* want to *schedule overtime*. If you are in the position of scheduling overtime, you will never meet your plan. At that point, you should take some corrective measures on your schedule to adjust it rather than schedule overtime.

workday, you should not assume more than four to six hours of productive work effort per day, the actual value of which varies according
to the business environment. You should also not assume that a work
year is more than 45 weeks, to account for sick and vacation time,[27]
training, and other business activities that may be not directly related
to your project.

Figure 1-12 shows a highly serial set of prototypes. It is possible to
run some prototypes in parallel and merge them together in a future
prototype. This makes the schedule a bit more complex, but it may be
more optimal. The important thing is to come up with a plan that you
actually intend to follow. This allows you to be more accurate and to
effectively track against the plan to see how you're doing.

Tracking against the schedule is crucial. In virtually all things, the
earlier you try to correct something, the cheaper and easier it is. This
is especially true with schedules. This means that you must schedule
what actually is supposed to happen and must identify deviations

Task Name	Duration	Start	Finish	Predecessors
⊟ Hello World Prototype	43 days	Wed 12/26/01	Fri 2/22/02	
Analysis	20 days	Wed 12/26/01	Tue 1/22/02	
Design	10 days	Wed 1/23/02	Tue 2/5/02	2
Translation	5 days	Wed 2/6/02	Tue 2/12/02	3
Testing	8 days	Wed 2/13/02	Fri 2/22/02	4
⊟ Party	0 days	Fri 2/22/02	Fri 2/22/02	5
Prototype Delivery	0 days	Fri 2/22/02	Fri 2/22/02	
⊞ Primary Monitoring	44 days	Mon 2/25/02	Thu 4/25/02	1
⊞ Primary Control	37 days	Fri 4/26/02	Mon 6/17/02	8
⊞ Closed Loop Control	46 days	Tue 6/18/02	Tue 8/20/02	15
PDR	2 days	Wed 8/21/02	Thu 8/22/02	22
⊞ Distribution Architecture	40 days	Fri 8/23/02	Thu 10/17/02	29
⊞ Built-In Testing	41 days	Fri 10/18/02	Fri 12/13/02	30
⊞ Hardware Test Functions	45 days	Mon 12/16/02	Fri 2/14/03	37
CDR	2 days	Mon 2/17/03	Tue 2/18/03	44
⊞ Primary Functions	30 days	Wed 2/19/03	Tue 4/1/03	51
Customer Evaluation	15 days	Wed 4/2/03	Tue 4/22/03	52
⊟ Reliability Management Prototype	41 days	Wed 4/23/03	Wed 6/18/03	59
Analysis	18 days	Wed 4/23/03	Fri 5/16/03	
Design	10 days	Mon 5/19/03	Fri 5/30/03	61
Translation	8 days	Mon 6/2/03	Wed 6/11/03	62
Testing	4 days	Thu 6/12/03	Tue 6/17/03	63
Party	1 day	Wed 6/18/03	Wed 6/18/03	64
Prototype Delivery	0 days	Wed 6/18/03	Wed 6/18/03	65

Figure 1-12: *Sample Schedule*

---

[27] Yes, in some environments, engineers actually get vacation time!

from that plan. If you have a schedule but it does not reflect how the work is being done, you cannot track against it. The work against the EWUs (such as the "Design Phase of Prototype 3") must be tracked if you want to be able to make adjustments, either to take advantage of the fact that it is coming in early or to adjust for the fact that it appears to be coming in late. The earlier you have this information, the easier that adjustment process will be.

Adjusting the schedule may involve

- Adding or removing manpower to an activity
- Outsourcing a component
- Dropping a feature
- Replanning subsequent scheduled items

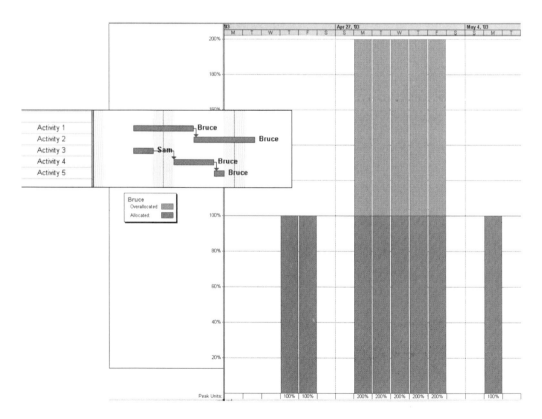

Figure 1-13: *Resource Histogram*

Schedules are dynamic entities that change over time. They are never completely accurate, except perhaps in hindsight, but a good scheduler can take advantage of the elasticity of a schedule and use it to guide the management of the project to a successful conclusion.

1.8 Model Organization Principles

In simple-enough systems, you can pretty much do anything you like and still succeed. Once you have a system complex enough to require *more than one person,* then it begins to matter what you do and how you do it. Once there are *teams* of people in place, it matters a great deal how the work is organized for the teams to effectively work together.

1.8.1. Why Model Organization?

The reasons for worrying about model organization are to

- Allow team members to contribute to the model without losing changes made by those or other team members, or in some other way corrupting your model
- Allow team members to use parts of the model they are not responsible for developing
- Provide for an efficient build process so that it is easy to construct the system
- Be able to locate and work on various model elements
- Allow the pieces of the system to be effectively reused in other models and systems

At first blush, it might appear that the first two issues—contributing and using aspects of a common model—are dealt with by configuration management (CM). This is only partially true. CM *does* provide locks and checks such that only one worker can own the "write token" to a particular model element and other users can only have a "read token." However, this is a little like saying that C solves all your programming problems because it provides basic programmatic elements such as assignment, branching, looping, and so on. CM does not say anything about what model elements ought to be configuration items (CIs), only that if a model element is a CI, then certain policies of usage apply. Effective model organization uses the CM infrastructure but provides a higher-level set of principles that allow the model to be used effectively.

For example, it would be awkward in the extreme if the entire model were the only CI. Then only a single worker could update the model at a time. This is clearly unacceptable in a team environment. The other extreme would be to make *every* model element at CI—for example, every class and use case would be a separate CI. Again, in simple systems, this can work because there are only a few dozen total model elements, so it is not too onerous to explicitly check out each element on which you need to work. However, this does not work well on even medium-scale systems. You would hate to have to individually list 30 or 40 classes when you wanted to work on a large collaboration realizing a use case.

The UML provides an obvious organizational unit for a CI—the *package.* A UML package is a model element that contains other model elements. It is essentially a bag into which we can throw elements that have some real semantic meaning in our model, such as use cases, classes, objects, diagrams, and so on. However, UML does not provide any criteria for what should go into one package versus another. So while we might want to make packages CIs in our CM system, this begs the question as to what policies and criteria we should use to decide how to organize our packages—what model elements should go into one package versus another.

A simple solution would be to assign one package per worker. Everything that Sam works on is in SamPackage, everything that Julie works on is in JuliePackage, and so on. For very small project teams, this is in fact a viable policy. But again, this begs the question of what Sam should work on versus Julie. It can also be problematic if Susan wants to update a few classes of Sam's while Sam is working on some others in SamPackage. Further, this adds artificial dependencies of the model structure on the project team organization. This will make it more difficult to make changes to the project team (say to add or remove workers) and will really limit the reusability of the model.

It makes sense to examine the user workflow when modeling or manipulating model elements in order to decide how best to organize the model. After all, we would like to optimize the workflow of the users as much as possible, decoupling the model organization from irrelevant concerns. The specific set of workflows depends, of course, on the development process used, but there are a number of common workflows:

- Requirements
  - ▾ Working on related requirements and use cases
  - ▾ Detailing a use case
    - Create set of scenarios
    - Create specification of a use case via statechart or activity diagram
  - ▾ Mapping requirements (e.g., use cases) to realizing model elements (e.g., classes)
- Realizing requirements with analysis and design elements
  - ▾ Elaborating a collaboration realizing a use case
  - ▾ Refining collaborations in design
  - ▾ Detailing an individual class
- Designing the architecture
  - ▾ Logical architecture—working on a set of related concepts (classes) from a single domain
  - ▾ Physical architecture—working on a set of objects in a single runtime subsystem or component
- Construction and testing
  - ▾ Translation of requirements into tests against design elements
  - ▾ Execution of tests
  - ▾ Constructing the iterative prototypes from model elements at various stages in the project development
- Planning
  - ▾ Project scheduling, including work products from the model

When working on related requirements and use cases, the worker typically needs to work on one or more related use cases and actors. When detailing a use case, a worker will work on a single use case and detailed views—a set of scenarios and often either an activity diagram or a statechart (or some other formal specification language). When elaborating a collaboration, the user will need to create a set of classes related to a single use case, as well as refining the scenarios bound to that use case. These workflows suggest that one way to organize the requirements and analysis model is around the use cases. Use packages to divide up the use cases into coherent sets (such as those related by generalization, «includes», or «extends» relations, or by associating with a common set of actors). In this case, a package would contain a use case and the detailing model elements—actors, activity diagrams, state-charts, and sequence diagrams.

The next set of workflows (realizing requirements) focus on classes, which may be used in either analysis or design. A *domain,* in the ROPES process, is a subject area with a common vocabulary, such as User Inter-face, Device I/O, or Alarm Management. Each domain contains many classes, and system-level use case collaborations will contain classes from several different domains. Many domains require rather special-ized expertise, such as low-level device drivers, aircraft navigation and guidance, or communication protocols. It makes sense from a work-flow standpoint (as well as a logical standpoint) to group such ele-ments together because a single worker or set of workers will develop and manipulate them. Grouping classes by domains and making the domains CIs may make sense for many projects.

Architectural workflows also require effective access to the model. Here, the architecture is broken up into the logical architecture (organi-zation of types, classes, and other design-time model elements) and physical architecture (organization of instances, objects, subsystems, and other runtime elements). It is common for the logical architecture to be organized by domains and the physical architecture to be orga-nized around components or subsystems. If the model is structured this way, then a domain, subsystem, or component is made a CI and assigned to a single worker or team. If the element is large enough, then it may be further subdivided into subpackages of finer granularity based on subtopic within a domain, subcomponents, or some other cri-terion such as team organization.

Testing workflows are often neglected in the model organization, usually to the detriment of the project. Testing teams need only read-only access to the model elements under test, but nevertheless they do need to manage test plans, test procedures, test results, test scripts, and test fixtures, often at multiple levels of abstraction. Testing is often done at many different levels of abstraction but can be categorized into three primary levels: unit testing (often done by the worker responsible for the model element under test), integration (internal interface testing), and validation (black-box system level testing). Unit-level testing is usually accomplished by the owner of the model element under test or a "testing buddy" (a peer in the development organization). The tests are primarily white-box, design, or code-level tests and often use additional model elements constructed as test fixtures. It is important to retain these testing fixture model elements so that as the system evolves, we can continue to test the model elements. Since these elements are white box and tightly coupled with the implementation of the model elements, it makes the most sense to colocate them with the model elements they test. So, if a class myClass has some testing support classes, such as myClass_tester and myClass_stub, they should be located close together. If the same worker is responsible for all, then perhaps they should be located within the same package (or another package in the same scope). If a testing buddy is responsible, then it is better to have it in another package but make sure that it is in the same CI as the model elements under test.

Integration and validation tests are not so tightly coupled as at the unit level, but clearly the testing team may construct model elements and other artifacts to assist in the execution of those tests. These tests are typically performed by *different workers* than the creators of the model elements they test. Thus, independent access is required and they should be in different CIs.

It is important to be able to efficiently construct and test prototypes during the development process. This involves both tests against the architecture (the integration and testing activities) and against the entire prototype's requirements (validation testing activities). There may be any number of model elements specifically constructed for a particular prototype that need not be used anywhere else. It makes sense to include these in a locale specific to that build or prototype. Other artifacts, such as test fixtures that are going to be reused or evolved and apply to many or all prototypes should be stored in a locale that allows them to be accessed independently from a specific prototype. Tools such as I-Logix iNotion™ provide company-wide repositories, access, and control over the complete sets of management, development, marketing, and manufacturing artifacts.

1.8.2 Specific Model Organization Patterns

In the preceding discussion, we see that a number of factors influence how we organize our models: the project team organization, system size, architecture, how we test our software, and our project lifecycle. Let us now consider some common ways to organize models and see where they fit well and where they fit poorly.

The model organization shown in Figure 1-14 is the simplest organization we will consider. The system is broken down by use cases, of which there are only three in the example. The model is organized into four high-level packages: one for the system level and one per use case. For a simple system with three to 10 use cases, and perhaps one to six developers, this model can be used with little difficulty. The advantages

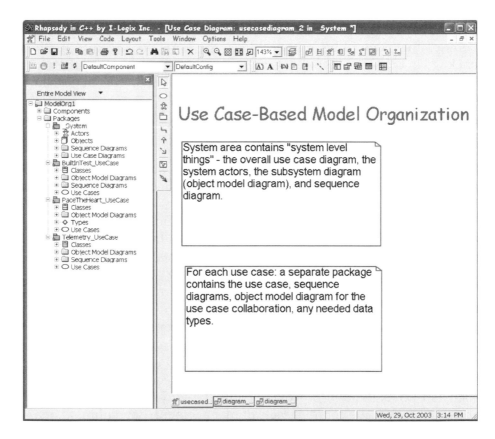

Figure 1-14: *Use Case-Based Model Organization*

of this organization are its simplicity and the ease with which requirements can be traced from the high level through the realizing elements. The primary disadvantages of this approach are that it doesn't scale up to medium- or large-scale systems. Other disadvantages include difficulty in reuse of model elements and that there is no place to put elements common to multiple use case collaborations, hence a tendency to reinvent similar objects. Finally, there is no place to put larger-scale architectural organizations in the model, and this further limits its scalability to large systems.

The model organization shown in Figure 1-15 is meant to address some of the limitations of the use case-based approach. It is still targeted

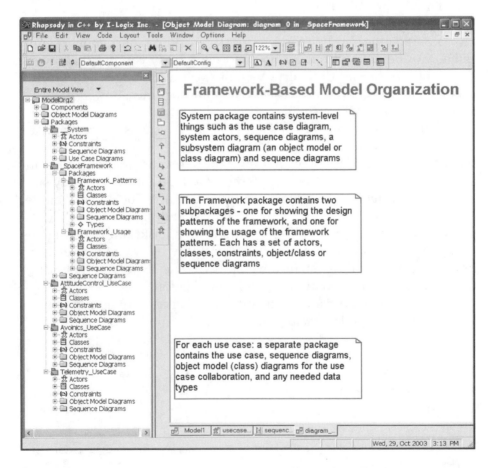

Figure 1-15: *Framework-Based Model Organization*

toward small systems, but adds a Framework package for shared and common elements. The Framework package has subpackages for usage points (classes that will be used to provide services for the targeted application environment) and extension points (classes that will be subclassed by classes in the use case packages). It should be noted that there are other ways to organize the Framework area that work well too. For example, Frameworks often consist of sets of coherent patterns—the subpackaging of the Framework can be organized around those patterns. This organization is particularly apt when constructing small applications against a common Framework. This organization does have some of the same problems with respect to reuse as the use case-based model organization.

As mentioned early on, if the system is simple enough, virtually any organization can be made to work. Workflow and collaboration issues can be worked out ad hoc and everybody can get their work done without serious difficulty. A small application might be 10 to 100 classes realizing 3 to 10 use cases. Using another measure, it might be on the order of 10,000 or so lines of code.

One of the characteristics of successful large systems (more than, say, 300 classes) is that they are architecture-centric. That is, architectural schemes and principles play an important role in organizing and managing the application. In the ROPES process, there are two primary subdivisions of architecture—logical and physical.[28] The logical model organizes types and classes (things that exist at design time), while the physical model organizes objects, components, tasks, and subsystems (things that exist at runtime). When reusability of design classes is an important goal of the system development, it is extremely helpful to maintain this distinction in the model organization.

The next model organization, shown in Figure 1-16, is suitable for large-scale systems. The major packages for the model are

- System
- Logical model
- Subsystem model
- Builds

---

[28] "Components: Logical and Physical Models" by Bruce Douglass, *Software Development Magazine*, December 1999.

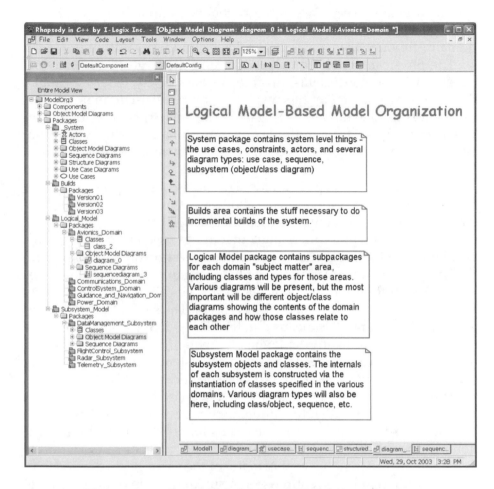

Figure 1-16: *Logical Model-Based Model Organization*

The system package contains elements common to the overall system—system level use cases, subsystem organization (shown as an object diagram), and system-level actors. The logical model is organized into subpackages called *domains*. Each domain contains classes and types organized around a single subject matter, such as User Interface, Alarms, Hardware Interfaces, Bus Communication, and so on. Domains have domain owners—those workers responsible for the content of a specific domain. Every class in the system ends up in a single domain. Class generalization hierarchies almost always remain within a single domain, although they may cross package boundaries within a domain.

The physical model is organized around the largest-scale pieces of the system—the subsystems. In large systems, subsystems are usually developed by independent teams, thus it makes sense to maintain this distinction in the model. Subsystems are constructed primarily of instances of classes from multiple domains. Put another way, each subsystem contains (by composition) objects instantiated from different domains in the system.

The last major package is builds. This area is decomposed into subpackages, one per prototype. This allows easy management of the different incremental prototypes. Also included in this area are the test fixtures, test plans, procedures, and other things used to test each specific build for both the integration and validation testing of that prototype.

The primary advantage of this model organization is that it scales up to very large systems very nicely because it can be used recursively to as many levels of abstraction as necessary. The separation of the logical and physical models means that the classes in the domains may be reused in many different deployments, while the use of the physical model area allows the decomposition of system use cases to smaller subsystem-level use cases and interface specifications.

The primary disadvantage that I have seen in the application of this model organization is that the difference between the logical and physical models seems tenuous for some developers. The model organization may be overly complex when reuse is not a major concern for the system. It also often happens that many of the subsystems depend very heavily (although never entirely) on a single domain, and this model organization requires the subsystem team to own two different pieces of the model. For example, guidance and navigation is a domain rich with classes, but it is usually also one or more subsystems.

The last model organization to be presented, shown in Figure 1-17, is similar to the previous one, except that it blurs the distinction between the logical and physical models. This can be appropriate when most or all subsystems are each dominated by a single domain. In this case, the domain package is decomposed into one package for each domain, and each of these is further decomposed into the subsystems that it dominates. For common classes, such as bus communication and other

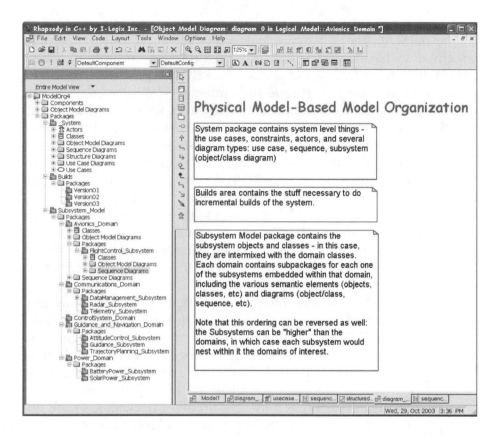

Figure 1-17: *Physical Model-Based Model Organization*

infrastructure classes, a separate shared Framework package is provided to organize them, similar to the Framework-based model organization shown in Figure 1-15.

1.9 Working with Model-Based Projects

Given that your team has selected and implemented a reasonable model organizational structure, the question remains as to how to do the daily work of analysis, design, translation, and testing. These questions should be answered by your company's (or project's) *software development plan* (SDP). The SDP documents how the team is to work together effectively, what standards of work must be met, and other process details. In Section 1.5.2, we introduced the ROPES process. This can be used, as it has in many real-time and embedded projects, or your own favorite process may be used instead. However, for the teams to work together, it is crucial that all the team members understand their roles and expectation on their deliverable products [16].

One of the key activities in the daily workings of a project is configuration management. In a model-based project, the primary artifact being configured with the CM system is *the model.* If you are using a full-generative tool, such as Rhapsody, then you might be able to get away with CMing the model and not the generated code because you can always produce the code from the model automatically. Nevertheless, many projects, especially those with high safety requirements, CM both the mode *and* the generated code.

Ideally the CM tool will interface directly with the modeling tool and most UML modeling tools do exactly that. Most also allow a great deal of configurability as to the level and number of configuration items (CIs). The default behavior should be that a package and all its contents, form a single CI, so there will be approximately the same number of CIs from the model as there are packages. However, for large-scale systems, packages may contain other packages, so the default should probably be the number of bottom-level packages. Packages, in the UML, may contain any model element, and will, of course, reflect your model organization. It may be desirable to have finer-level control over CIs, in which case you may want to go as far down as the individual class or function, but in large-scale systems, that level of control can be very tedious to manipulate. For the purpose of this discussion, we will assume you use the package as the primary CI for manipulation.

You will mostly likely want to use a locking mechanism on your CIs—that is, when one developer checks out a CI for updating, no one else can check it out except for reference. Because classes must collaborate across package boundaries, it is important that clients of a CIs can be referenced. However, this *does* create a problem. As we will see when we discuss classes in the next chapter, associations are normally bi-directional. When you add such an association, you must have write access to *both classes* in order to add the association. If one of these classes is checked out read-only, then you don't have write privileges to it and cannot add the bi-directional association. One possible solution for is to add unidirectional associations to classes for which you have only read access. As long as you're sending messages *to* objects of such a class, you don't need write access to create the association. Another solution is to get write access for that small change.

Still another option is to allow multiple developers to work on the same CIs and merge the changes when they are finished. This is often done with code using text-based diff and merge tools. Some tools (such as Rhapsody) can perform these functions on models and identify when changes are in conflict, allowing the developers to decide what to do should the changes made to the CIs be mutually incompatible.

A *generative tool* is one that can take the structural and behavioral semantics specified in the model diagrams and use them to generate executable code. As mentioned, it is common to CM the code in addition to the models, but in many cases, this may not be necessary.

Normal work in the presence of a CM infrastructure proceeds as the engineer checks out the model CIs on which he or she wishes to work, as well as getting read-only locks on the CIs containing elements they wish to reference. They make the design changes, additions, or updates and check the CIs back in. In some cases, a two-tiered CM system is used—local CM for the individual worker at the desktop and project CM for the entire team. This approach allows the team member to work with CIs without breaking anyone else's work. Once the CIs are in a stable configuration, they may be checked back in to the project CM. The ROPES process recommends that before any CI can be used in a team build, the CI be unit-tested and reviewed. In my experience, this eliminates many work stoppages due to simple and easily correctable (and all too frequent) errors.

Another important aspect is requirements management (RM). This is particularly important in high-reliability (hi-rel) systems development in which the cost of system failure is high. The concept of requirements management is a simple one, very similar to that of configuration management. Requirements are identified in an RM system and then their design, implementation, and testing are tracked to the individual requirement. Forward RM allows the developer to track from the specific requirement to where the requirement is met in the design and code, and to its test status. This allows for queries such as "Where is this requirement met," "How many requirements have been implemented," and "How many requirements have been successfully tested?" Backward tracability allows the developer to look at some portion of the design or some set of tests and identify which requirements they meet. RM is best accomplished with tools design for that specific purpose and there are several available that interface with modeling tools.

The executability of a model is, in my opinion, very important. Whenever you do some portion of a model, you must be able to answer the question "Is this right?" Experience has shown that asking—and answering—this question throughout the development lifecycle has enormous impact on the quality of the system at the end. Indeed, the spiral development lifecycle is an attempt to ensure that the system is constructed using relatively small increments (called prototypes) that are each tested to be correct *before* moving on and adding more functionality. This is done not only at the level of the microcycle (four to six weeks is a typical timeframe) but also at the level of the nanocycle (every few minutes to hours). So if you are designing a collaboration of 50 classes to realize a use case, rather than create all 50 classes, generate them, and hope that they're right, you might create three classes and execute and test that portion of the collaboration. Once you're convinced that much is right, you might add one or two more and get *that* to work. Then add another class and some more behavior to two of the existing classes. And so on. This is a highly effective way in which to create complex systems. This approach is made even more productive when the modeling tool used is executable—that is, it can execute and debug portions of or the entire model. There exist UML tools that do this, Rhapsody being a prime example.

Executable tools come in two flavors: simulation tools and generative tools. Simulators pretend they are the real system and allow the system to execute in a simulated environment. Simulators have a good deal of merit, particular for proving logical correctness, but they suffer from a few flaws as well. First, because you're not testing the real system or the real code, you must test twice, once on the simulated version and once on the final code. Second, the simulation cannot easily run on the actual target environment nor in anything close to real time, so they are once removed from the true execution environment.

The other approach to executability is to use a generative tool. By *generative tool,* I mean that the tool can take the semantics of your model, by far most commonly entered using structural and behavioral

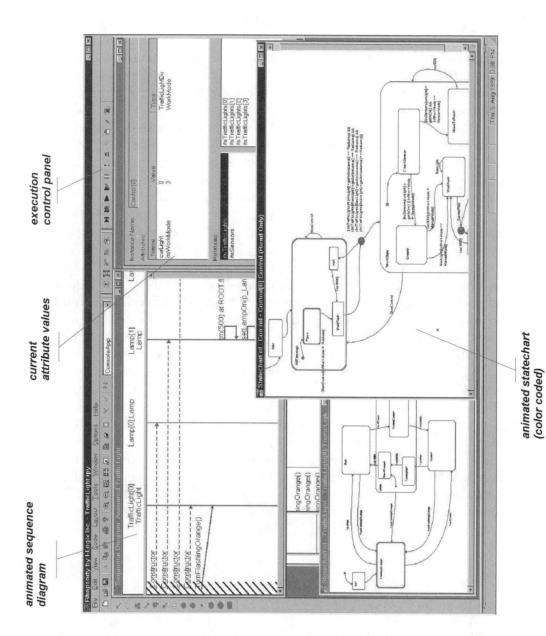

Figure 1-18: *Model Execution*

diagrams, and generate code in the desired target source code language, such as C++, C, Java, or Ada. Since the code generated is the same as that which will be ultimately deployed, it is usually only necessary to test it once, saving valuable time and effort. Also, because true source code is generated, it can be run on the desktop debugging environment or, with nothing more than a recompile, also on the target hardware environment. For this reason, generative tools are considered by most to be "stronger" in terms of their executability.

In either case, the execution and debugging of models should be done at the *model level* rather than the level of the source code. If the developer is using class diagrams to show structure, and statecharts and sequence diagrams to specify behavior, then those are, in fact, the very views that should be used to examine the executing system.

Of course, standard debugging concepts should be supported at this model level—single step, step-over, step-into, set breakpoints, and so on—but they should be using design-level concepts, such as setting a breakpoint when a state is entered or an operation is invoked. Most of the system debugging should be done at this level of abstraction, although it may be necessary sometimes to drill down to the source-code level (and use a source-code-level debugger) or even to the assembly or logic analyzer level. Nevertheless, most of the debugging of a model should be done at the level of abstraction at which the model was created.

Debugging may be thought of as testing by roaming around. It is usually highly informal and unstructured. Debugging at the model level allows us to much more easily ensure that the system is behaving as expected than if we were limited to debugging the code resulting from the models. Beyond debugging, there is testing. By *testing*, I mean a structured and repeatable execution of the system or some portion thereof, with well-defined test conditions and a set of expected results with clear and unambiguous pass/fail criteria. Testing should also be done primarily at the model level as well.

In the ROPES process, there are three identified levels of testing:

- Unit testing
- Integration testing
- Validation testing

Unit-level testing is done primarily white box and at the class or component level. Such testing ensures the detailed design of the primitive building blocks of the system is correct, that preconditional invariants (such as "pointers are valid" and "enumerated values are ensured to be in range") are checked. The consistent application of good unit-level testing is, in my experience, where the biggest improvements in overall system quality may be made.

Integration testing is a test of the architecture. Specifically it tests that the large-scale pieces of the system—typically components or subsystems—fit together properly and collaborate as expected. Failure to adhere to interface requirements, especially those that are more subtle than simple operation parameter list types, is a leading cause of large-system failure. Interfaces are more than simple collections of operations that may be called from other architectural components. They have many assumptions about value ranges, the order in which operations may be invoked, and so on, that may not be caught by simple visual inspection. By putting together these architectural pieces and demonstrating that they do all the right things *and* catch violations of the preconditional invariants, we can alleviate many of the failures we see.

The last level of testing is validation testing. This is done primarily black box. Validation testing means that a system (or prototype of a system) properly executes its requirements in the real or simulated target environment. In an iterative development lifecycle, the primary artifacts produced at the end of each spiral constitute a version of the system that realizes some coherent set of requirements. Each prototype in the ROPES spiral is tested against that set of requirements, normally represented as a small set of use cases. In subsequent spirals, old requirements are validated using a set of regression tests to ensure that the new functionality hasn't broken the old.

As stated, the primary artifact of each spiral is the prototype—a tested, working version of the system, which may be incomplete. Another artifact is a *defect report,* identifying the defects that weren't fixed in the previous spiral. The next spiral typically adds new requirements as well as fixing previously identified minor defects (major defects must be repaired before the spiral may end). Often, as new functionality is added and known defects are removed, the model must be internally reorganized in minor ways. This is called *refactoring.* Refactoring is a normal outcome of the iterative lifecycle and is not to be feared. In the spiral approach, early design decisions are made with incomplete knowledge, after all, and even though an attempt is made to ensure that future additional functionality won't radically affect the architecture, sometimes it will. Usually these are small changes that must be made. But working with a spiral model means that you expect some refactoring to be necessary. It is only a concern if you find major architectural changes are necessary in a number of prototypes. Should this occur, then it would be useful to step back and consider the architectural selection with a greater scrutiny.

The last aspect of model-based development I would like to consider is that of reviews or inspections, as they are sometimes called. Inspections serve two primary purposes: to improve the quality of the portion of the model being inspected and to disseminate knowledge of some portion of the model to various team members.

The ROPES process has particular notions of what constitutes good models. One of the common problems made by neophyte modelers is that of too much information in one place. While in books, problems are simplified to make concrete points (and this book is no exception), in the real world, problems are complex. It simply isn't possible to put every aspect of a system in a single diagram. What is needed is a good rule for how to break up a model into the diagrams so that they aid in model creation and understanding. The ROPES rule for diagrams revolves around the notion of a "mission." Each diagram should have a single mission and include only those elements necessary to perform that mission, but should include all of those elements. So rather than create a class diagram that has every class in the system (requiring "E" size plotter paper and a 2-point font), a class only appears on diagrams when it is relevant to its mission. Likewise, given that a class is relevant to the diagram's mission, only the aspects of the class that are relevant are shown—operations, attributes, associations, and so on that are not relevant to the particular diagram are not shown on this diagram, although they may very well appear on a different one. This means that it is common for a class to appear on more than one diagram.

Common diagrammatic missions include

- A single collaboration (set of classes working together for a common purpose, such as realizing a use case)
- A class taxonomy (i.e., generalization)
- An architectural view
    - ▼ Subsystem and/or component architecture
    - ▼ Distribution of elements across multiple address spaces

- ▼ Safety and/or reliability management
- ▼ Concurrency and/or resource management (e.g., task diagram)
- ▼ Deployment of elements on processors
- ▼ Organization of processors and buses
- The organization of the model (package diagram)
- A scenario of a collaboration
- A coherent set of requirements
- Behavior of a structural element (e.g., statechart or activity diagram)

And these missions may occur at multiple levels of abstraction.

1.10 Looking Ahead

So far, we have only touched on the defining characteristics of real-time systems and the very basic aspects of the model-based development. In the subsequent chapters of this book, we'll examine the basic concepts of the UML (Chapters 2 and 3) and apply these ideas to the process of creating real-time embedded applications. The process is broken into the overall analysis and design steps, as called out in Section 1.5.1. Analysis is subdivided into specification of external requirements and the identification of inherent classes and objects. Design is divided into three parts—architectural, mechanistic, and detailed levels of abstraction. Architectural design specifies the strategic decisions for the overall organization of the system, such as the design of the processor and concurrency models. Mechanistic design is concerned with the medium level of organization—the collaboration of objects to achieve common goals. Detailed design defines the internal algorithms and primitive data structures within classes. All the process steps are required to create efficient, correct designs that meet the system requirements. In the next chapter, we'll focus on using the UML to capture the structural aspects of systems.

1.11 Exercises

1. Define the term *real-time*. What is the difference between hard and soft real-time?

2. Define the following terms: *priority, blocking time, worst-case completion time, laxity, absolute deadline,* and *relative deadline.*

3. What are the four fundamental types of message synchronization? How to they differ?

4. What is the OMG and why should we care?

5. What does *QoS* mean? Provide five examples of QoS characteristics.

6. What is an *action*? What is a *message*?

7. What are the types of aperiodic arrival times? How do they differ?

8. What is the downside of assuming hard deadlines when the timeliness requirements may be soft?

9. Define what is meant by a *resource*. How do resources relate to concurrency units?

10. What is the difference between RMS and EDS?

11. What is *priority inversion* and what conditions are necessary for it to arise?

12. What are the three timescales on which the ROPES process may be viewed? What are the approximate timeframes for each?

13. What does the acronym ROPES stand for?

14. Explain the BERT process of estimation.

15. What are the five important views or aspects of architecture in the ROPES process?

16. What are PIM and PSM and how do they differ?

17. What is the primary unit of organization in a model?

1.12 References

[1] Leveson, Nancy G. *Safeware: System Safety and Computers, SPHIGS Software*. Reading, MA: Addison-Wesley, 1995.

[2] Neumann, Peter G. *Computer Related Risks*. Reading, MA: Addison-Wesley, 1995.

[3] Ellis, John R. *Objectifying Real-Time Systems*. New York: SIGS Books, 1994.

[4] Rumbaugh, James, Michael Blaha, William Premerlani, Frederick Eddy, and William Lorensen. *Object-Oriented Modeling and Design*. Englewood Cliffs, NJ: Prentice Hall, 1991.

[5] Douglass, Bruce. *Doing Hard Time: Developing Real-Time Systems with UML, Objects, Frameworks, and Patterns*. Reading, MA: Addison-Wesley, 1999.

[6] Rumbaugh, James, Grady Booch, and Ivar Jacobson. *The UML Reference Guide*. Reading, MA: Addison-Wesley, 1999.

[7] *UML Profile for Schedulability, Performance, and Time Specification*. ptc/2003-03-02. Needham, MA: OMG, 2002, *www.omg.org*.

[8] *UML Profile for Modeling Quality of Service and Fault Tolerance Characteristics and Mechanisms: Initial Submission*. ptc/TBD. Needham, MA: OMG, 2002, *www.omg.org*.

[9] Klein, M.; Ralya, T.; Pollak, B.; Obenza, R.; and Harbour, M. *A Practitioner's Guide for Real-Time Analysis: Guide to Rate Monotonic Analysis for Real-Time Systems*. Norwell, MA: Kluwer Academic Publishers, 1993.

[10] Pinedo, Michael. *Scheduling: Theory, Algorithms, and Systems*. Englewood Cliffs, NJ: Prentice Hall, 1995.

[11] Douglass, Bruce Powel. *Real-Time Design Patterns: Robust Scalable Architecture for Real-Time Systems*. Reading, MA: Addison-Wesley, 2002.

[12] Briand, L. and Roy, D. *Meeting Deadlines in Hard Real-Time Systems: The Rate Monotonic Approach*. Los Alamitos, CA: IEEE Computer Society Press, 1999.

[13] Douglass, Bruce Powel. *Dr. Douglass's Guided Tour Through the Wonderland of Systems Engineering, UML, and Rhapsody*. Andover, MA: I-Logix, 2002, *www.ilogix.com*.

[14] Friedenthal, S., H. Lykins, and A. Meilich. "Adapting UML for an Object-Oriented Systems Engineering Method (OOSEM)," in *Proceedings of Tenth Annual International Symposium INCOSE*. Minneapolis, MN, 2000.

[15] *UML for Systems Engineering: Request for Proposal OMG Document*. ad03-03-41. Needham, MA: OMG, 2003.

[16] *Information Technology—Software Life Cycle Processes ISO/IEC 12207:1995*. Geneva, Switzerland: International Organization for Standardization (ISO), 1995, *www.iso.org*.

Chapter 2

Object Orientation with UML 2.0— Structural Aspects

The first primary aspect of the UML involves the specification of structure; that is, the organization of elements that exist at runtime, their internal organization, and the organization of elements in interactions. Additionally, the structural aspects of the UML allow you to identify the design-time types of these elements that exist at runtime and the relations among both the type and the instances of those types.

Notation and Concepts Discussed

Advantages of Objects	Structured Classes	Packages
Interfaces and Ports	Stereotypes	Components
Architecture	Classes and Objects	Constraints
Subsystems	Relations	Tags

2.1 Object Orientation with UML

The Unified Modeling Language™ (UML) is used to express the constructs and relationships of complex systems. It was created in response to a request for proposal (RFP) issued by the Object Management Group (OMG), the organization that owns the UML standard. Dozens of people from many different companies worked on the UML and several calendar years went into its creation. The OMG accepted it as a standard in November 1997. The success of the UML is unprecedented; it has been widely adopted and used in the creation of all kinds of systems, including real-time and embedded systems. These systems range from the small (e.g., cardiac pacemakers) to the large (e.g., fighter aircraft) and from the mundane (e.g., printers) to the exotic (e.g., spacecraft frameworks). Systems in many vertical markets, including telecom, office automation, factory automation, robotics, avionics, military, medical, and automotive, have been modeled in the UML and implemented. I have consulted with companies building widely different systems *all* created with the UML and found that with the proper and intelligent application of the UML, they have been able to make significant (30% to 80%) improvements in time-to-market, quality, and reusability of corporate intellectual property (IP). All done with the UML, as it is specified in the standard, without modification or extension.[1]

That having been said, there exist a number of extensions to the UML. Some are proprietary extensions, claiming to offer some improvement in this way or that. Others are standardized extensions, in the form of a UML "profile"—a specialized version of the UML that is extended in only small ways to make it more applicable to some particular subject domain. In my role as cochair of the Real-Time Analysis and Design Working Group (RTAD) within the OMG, I have even participated in the creation of some of these extensions. Nevertheless, I stand by my assertion that the UML is completely sufficient for the modeling and creation of real-time and embedded systems. What the profiles have done is simply to codify a particular way in which the UML has been used. For example, the UML Profile for Schedulability,

---

[1] I don't mean to imply that merely the adoption of UML will improve productivity. There have been some notable failures in the adoption of UML. The successful adoption of any new technology requires willingness, thoughtfulness, and perseverance on the part of the adopter.

Performance and Time (also called the Real-Time Profile, or RTP) [3], does little more than codify what developers were already doing in UML to capture real-time and performance aspects of the systems they were creating. Profiles like the RTP enable better exchange of models, particularly between modeling creation tools, such as Rhapsody®, and schedulability analysis tools, such as RapidRMA™.[2] The RTP is the subject of Chapter 4.

As of this writing the UML standard is 1.5 [1].[3] However, work is almost completed for a major revision to the UML, version 2.0 [2]. A submission from the U2P consortium, of which I-Logix was a key contributor, was adopted in the spring of 2003. The submission is now undergoing finalization. At this time, the expectation is that the new version will be released in the spring of 2004. The metamodel and notations for the UML 2.0 submissions are fairly stable at this time, although there may be small deviations from what is ultimately released as the new standard.

UML is more complete than other methods in its support for modeling complex systems and is particularly well suited for real-time embedded systems. Its major features include

- Well-defined object model for defining system structure
- Strong dynamic modeling with modeling of both collaborative and individual behavior
- Support for different model organizations
- Straightforward representation of concurrency aspects
- Models of physical topology (deployment)
- Support for object-oriented patterns to facilitate design reuse

Throughout this book, these features will be described in more detail and their use shown by examples. This chapter explores the structural aspects of the UML at the fine- and coarse-grained abstraction level.

---

[2] RapidRMA is a schedulability analysis tool available from Tri-Pacific Corporation, www.tripac.com.

[3] The management of "point" releases of the UML is done by a revision task force (RTF) whose mandate is to fix defects and which is not allowed to introduce fundamentally new concepts to the UML. Thus, UML 1.x versions are all highly similar and have no significant semantic differences.

LIVERPOOL
JOHN MOORES UNIVERSITY
AVRIL ROBARTS LRC
TEL. 0151 231 4022

2.2 Small Things: Objects, Classes, and Interfaces

The UML has a rather rich set of structural elements and provides diagrammatic views for related sets of them. The UML is intentionally, recursively self-similar in its structural and dynamic concepts. That is, the same set of concepts may be used at different levels of abstraction, from the largest system and subsystems down to small, simple objects. Nevertheless, some concepts are used more at the smaller scale and others more at the larger scale.

A number of elementary structural concepts in the UML show up in user models: object, class, data type, and interface. These structural elements form the basis of the structural design of the user model. In its simplest form, an *object* is a data structure bound together with operations that act on that data. An object only exists at runtime; that is, while the system is executing, an object may occupy some location in memory at some specific time. The data known to an object are stored in *attributes*—simple, primitive variables local to that object. The behaviors that act on that data are called *methods*; these are the services invoked by clients of that object (typically other objects) or by other methods existing within the object.

2.2.1 Objects

Structured methods look at a system as a collection of functions decomposed into more primitive functions. Data is secondary in the structured view and concurrency isn't dealt with at all. The object perspective is different in that the fundamental decompositional unit is the *object*. So what is an object?

The short form:
> *An object is a cohesive entity that has attributes, behavior, and (optionally) state.*

The long form:
Objects represent things that have both data and behavior. Objects may represent real-world things, like dogs, airfoil control surfaces, sensors, or engines. They may represent purely conceptual entities, like bank accounts, trademarks, marriages, or lists. They can be visual things,

like fonts, letters, ideographs, histograms, polygons, lines, or circles. All these things have various features, such as

- Attributes (data)
- Behavior (operations or methods)
- State (memory)
- Identity
- Responsibilities

For example, a real-world thing might be a sensor that can detect and report both a linear value and its rate of change.

Sensor Object

Attributes	Behavior	State	Identity	Responsibility
• Linear value • Rate of change (RoC)	• Acquire • Report • Reset • Zero • Enable • Disable	• Last value • Last RoC	Instance for robot arm joint	• Provide information for the precise location of the end of the robot arm with respect to some reference coordinate frame

The sensor object contains two attributes: the monitored sensor value and its computed rate of change (RoC). The behaviors support data acquisition and reporting. They also permit configuration of the sensor. The object state consists of the last acquired/computed values. The identity specifies exactly which object instance is under discussion. The responsibility of the sensor is defined to be how it contributes to the overall system functionality. Its attributes and behaviors must collaborate to help the object achieve its responsibilities

An airline flight is a conceptual thing, but is nonetheless an important object as well.

Airline Flight Object

Attributes	Behavior	State	Identity	Responsibility
• Flight number • Departure time • Arrival time • Flight plan	• Depart • Arrive • Adjust course	Current location (x, y, z, t)	• Today's flight NW394 to Minneapolis	• Transfer luggage and passengers to destination • File flight plan • Adhere to flight plan

Certain of these characteristics (i.e., attributes, behaviors, or state) may be more important for some objects than for others. One could envision a sensor class that had no state—whenever you asked it for information, it sampled the data and returned it, rather than storing it internally. An array of numbers is an object that may have interesting information but doesn't have any really interesting behaviors.

The key idea of objects is that they combine these properties into a single cohesive entity. The structured approach to software design deals with data and functions as totally separate entities. Data flow diagrams show both data flow and data processes. Data can be decomposed if necessary. Independently, structure charts show the static call tree to decompose functions (somewhat loosely related to the data processes). Objects, on the other hand, fuse related data and functions together. The *object* is the fundamental unit of decomposition in object-oriented programming.

Abstraction is the process of identifying the key aspects of something and ignoring the rest. A chair is an abstraction defined as "a piece of furniture with at least one leg, a back, and a flat surface for sitting." That some chairs are made of wood while others may be plastic or metal is inessential to the abstraction of "chair." When we abstract objects we select only those aspects that are important relative to our point of view. For example, as a runner, my abstraction of dogs is that they are "high-speed teeth delivery systems." The fact that they may have a pancreas or a tail is immaterial to my modeling domain. In Figure 2-1, we see a number of concrete instances of sensors being abstracted in a common concept.

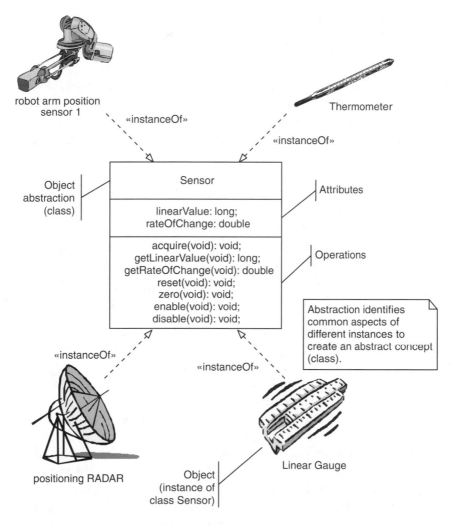

Figure 2-1: *Object Abstraction*

2.2.2 Classes

Objects exist at *runtime*; at some point in time, objects (at least software objects) occupy a memory address located in a computer. A class is the specification for a set of objects. Classes exist at *design time*. A class is the "type" of some set of objects, in the same way that "int" is the "type" of a variable x that may assume different values at runtime, such as 3 and –17, or "double" is the "type" of a variable y that may assume the value 45.5 during runtime. A *class* specifies both the structure and the defined behavior of the objects instantiated from it. All objects of a class have their own copies of the very *same* set of typed attributes. Thus, if a thermometer is an instance of class Sensor, then it will have an attribute named *linearValue,* of type long, and another attribute called *rateOfChange,* of type double. Each object, in fact, has its own copy of these attributes with which it is free to manipulate and manage, but structurally the objects are all identical.

Similarly, each object has the same set of methods (functions) defined by the class. However, the objects "share" the code for these, so you don't end up replicating identical code when you have many instances of the same class. The methods are provided the information as to which object is being manipulated when the method is called— usually invisibly to the programmer.

In their simplest expression, classes are nothing more than abstract data types (ADTs) bound together with operators that manipulate that information. This is a low-level perspective and doesn't capture all of the richness available in the object paradigm. Software developers use such ADTs and operators as low-level mechanisms all the time— stacks, queues, trees, and all the other basic data structures are nothing more than objects with specific operations defined. Consider these common ADTs that appear in the table on page 85.

At a low level of abstraction, these are merely ADTs bound together with separate functions to provide the services. Because the concept of a stack is meaningless without both the operations and the data, it makes the most sense to bind these things tightly together—they are different aspects of a single concept. This is called *strong cohesion*—the appropriate binding together of inherently tightly coupled properties.

Classes have two important *features.* Classes may (and usually do) contain attributes. These structural features hold the data or information known to the object. Also, classes have methods—behavioral features that provide services that usually manipulate the object's attributes. Classes may also have state machines, a topic that will be discussed in Chapter 3.

2.2.2.1 Attributes

Attributes, in OO-speak, refer to the data encapsulated within an object or specified within a class. It might be the balance of a bank account, the current picture number in an electronic camera, the color of a font, or the owner of a trademark. Some objects may have just one or a small number of simple attributes. Others may be quite rich. In some object-oriented languages, all instances of data types are objects, from the smallest integer type to the most complex aggregate. In C++, in deference to minimizing the differences between C and C++, variables of the elementary data types, such as int and float, are not really objects. Programmers may treat them as if they are objects[4] but C++ does not require it.

Data Structure	Attributes	Operations
Stack	TopOfStack: int	Push
	Size: int	Pop
	Element: DATA	Full
		Empty
Queue	Head: int	Insert
	Tail: int	Remove
	Size: int	Full
	Element: DATA	Empty
Linked List	Next: Node pointer	Insert
	Previous: Node pointer	Remove
	Element: DATA	Next
		Previous
Tree	Left: Node pointer	Insert
	Right: Node pointer	Remove
	Element: DATA	Next
		Previous

---

[4] Well, almost anyway—but that's a programming, rather than a modeling, issue.

2.2.2.2 Methods and Operations

As mentioned, a class is a union of the specification of an abstract data type with the operations that act on that data. Strictly speaking, a class contains *methods*—the implementation of operations. An operation is defined in the UML as "a service that an instance of the class may be requested to perform." Operations have a formal parameter list (a typed list of named values passed to and/or from the operation) and a return value. The parameters and return value are optional. A method is said to be the implementation of an operation; reflexively, an operation specifies a method.

All instantiable classes have two special operations defined: a *constructor*, which knows how to properly make an instance of the class, and a *destructor*, which knows how to properly remove an instance of that class. Constructors may be parameterless—the so-called default constructor—and will use default values of any creational parameters, including the allocation of memory and creation of links to other objects. It is not uncommon to have a number of parameterized constructors as well, which bypass one or more defaults. Constructors are invoked whenever an object is created. A common example is if the "++" operator is defined for a class, then X++ (post increment) actually creates a new instance of the class (of which object X is an instance), although this may be optimized away in some cases. Destructors are parameterless and properly destroy the object, including removing allocated memory when necessary. Improperly written destructors are a common cause of memory leaks and care should be taken to ensure that they properly deallocate any memory that the object exclusively owns.

Not all classes are instantiable. *Abstract classes* are not instantiated because their specification is not complete. That is, they define an operation but not a corresponding method. In order to create an instance of such a class, the abstract class must be subclassed (see Generalization, later in this chapter) and the subclass must provide a method. In C++ terms, abstract classes contain at least one *pure virtual* operation shown with the unlikely syntax of assigning the operation the value of zero. For example,

$$\text{void resetDevice(s: initialValue)} = 0$$

Abstract classes and abstract (i.e., "pure virtual") operations are identified by italics.

2.2.3 Notation

Figure 2-2 shows the relationship between classes (the template, or "cookie cutter") and objects (the instance, or "cookie"). The class defines the features, both structural and behavioral, for all instances of objects for which it is the type. Classes can be shown as a simple named rectangle (called "canonical form") or in a more detailed form. In the

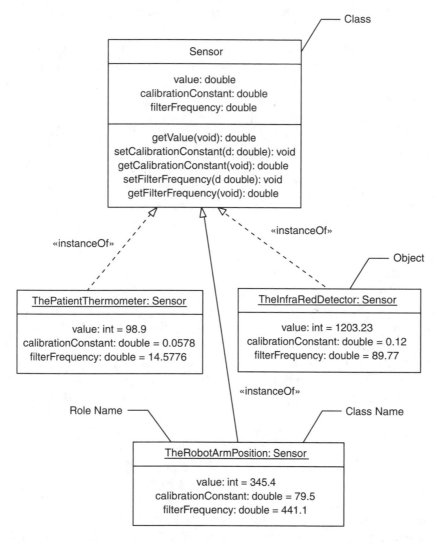

Figure 2-2: *Objects and Classes*

detailed form, attributes and methods may be listed in separate compartments, as they are in the figure. The objects are instances of the class and, when shown, depict a "snapshot" of the system at some point in time. This allows us to identify particular values of the attributes at the instant the snapshot was taken. Note that the object name is underlined, but all that is really necessary is to observe the presence of the colon (:), which separates the name of the object, called the *role name* (such as *ThePatientThermometer*) from the class that specifies it (such as *Sensor*).

Figure 2-3 is similar to a diagram you'd find in the design of a system. The figure shows both classes (e.g., *TaskPlan*) and object (e.g., Elbow: Motor) as well as associations (relations between classes). Both canonical (simple) and detailed forms of classes are shown.

It isn't necessary to show any of the features of a class or object on a diagram, or if shown, it isn't necessary (or usually wise) to include *all* of the attributes or operations. Figure 2-3 shows some of the attributes and methods of the classes. Note that the attributes include their types and the methods include their parameters and return types. The marks by the class features indicate the visibility of those aspects.

The UML provides notation to indicate four levels of visibility. When a feature (attribute, method, or operation) is public, it may be proceeded by a "+", as they are in the figure. *Public visibility* means that the feature may be accessed by anyone. *Protected visibility* (indicated by a preceding hash mark, #) means that the feature may be accessed by subclasses (see Generalization in the section on Relations, later in this chapter) but not by clients of the class. Clients may be able to gain access to the data, but must go through a public method do to so. Private visibility is even more restricted than protected—only methods inside the same class may access the feature. The last level of visibility, *package,* is rarely used. It is indicated with a tilde ("~") and means the feature is visible to any element in the same package.

The lines connecting the classes and objects in the figure are called *associations* and allow the objects to collaborate, that is, to send and receive messages. This will be discussed in more detail later.

Usually diagrams are constructed exclusively with classes rather than by mixing in objects. Because classes are *universal,* class diagrams define sets of possible object configurations. An object may come and go during the execution of the system, so an object diagram is always a snapshot of the system at some specific point in time. Object diagrams,

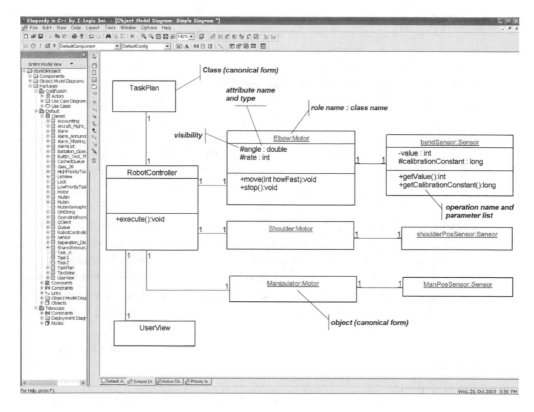

Figure 2-3: *Objects and Classes in Use*

part of what is known as a system's *instance model,* may be useful, but class diagrams are far more common.

2.2.4 Interfaces

An *interface* is a specification of a named contract offered by a class. It primarily consists of a collection of operations, but in UML 2.0, interfaces may also include attributes and a special form of a state machine called a *protocol state machine.* While not required, interfaces allow you to separate out the specification of a set of services from the implementation of those services. As we've seen, a class contains *methods,* which include the lines of code that implement the service. An operation is a specification of the service that does not include this implementation.

To be well formed, the operation should define the signature for invoking the service, including the required parameters and return value (if any), plus the preconditional and postconditional invariants of the operation. Preconditional invariants are things that must be true prior to the invocation of the service, while postconditional invariants are things that the operation guarantees are true upon its completion.

In UML 1.x, interfaces could only have operations (specifications of methods) but not any implementation; neither could they have attributes or state machines. In UML 2.0, interfaces may have attributes but they are *virtualized*, meaning that any realizing class must provide an attribute of that type. A class is said to *realize* an interface if it provides a method for every operation specified in the interface, and an attribute for every virtualized attribute in the interface. The class methods must have the same names, parameters, return values, preconditions, and postconditions of the corresponding operations in the interface. In UML 2.0, interfaces may also have protocol state machines for the specification of the allowed set of sequences of operation invocation for realizing classes. Protocol state machines will be discussed in the next chapter.

Interfaces may be shown in two forms. One looks like a class except for the key word interface placed inside guillemots, as in «interface». This form, called a *stereotype* in UML, is used when you want to show the operations of the interface. The other form, commonly referred to as the "lollipop" notation, is a small named circle on the side of the class. Both forms are shown in Figure 2-4. When the lollipop is used, only the name of the interface is apparent. When the stereotyped form is used, a list of operations of the interface may be shown. In the figure, the *Sensor* class is said to *depend* on the interface *iFilter,* while the *Filter* class *realizes* that interface. In UML 2.0, interfaces may be specified from either "end." The UML 1.x interface (the lollipop end in Figure 2-4) specified *provided interfaces,* that is, features that the realizing class agrees to provide to its client. The other end (the socket in the figure) is a *required* interface. This allows consistency checking between what is expected and what is provided in the interfaces.

Interfaces are used to ensure interface compliance, that is, the client class can consistently and correctly invoke the services of a server class. There is another means to ensure interface compliance that uses the generalization relation from what is called *abstract classes* (classes that may

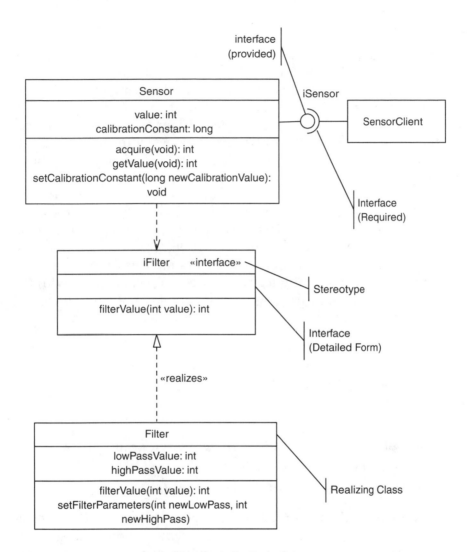

Figure 2-4: *Interfaces*

not be directly instantiated). Abstract classes define operations but not methods, just as an interface does, and so may be used to ensure interface compliance. Either (or both, for that matter) approach can be used to ensure that the clients and servers connect correctly at runtime. Generalization and other class relations are discussed in the Section 2.3.4.

2.2.5 Messaging

The low-level unit of behavior of an object is an action. There are several kinds of actions defined within the UML. The most common one, called a *CallAction,* invokes a method defined in the receiving object. Actions may appear in methods (they also appear in state machines, as we will see in the next chapter). Activities, discussed later, are types of behaviors that may be methods. In structured software development, explicit calls were shown on structure charts. While this has the advantage of showing the set of invoked services, it has a number of serious disadvantages, including that the order of calls isn't shown in structure charts, nor are conditional branches, nor is there any way to show other, possibly asynchronous communications. This last is the most serious limitation because much of the communication between objects in real-time systems takes place using techniques other than simple function calls.

In the UML, the logical interface between objects is done with the passing of *messages*. A message is an abstraction of data and or control information passed from one object to another. Different implementations are possible, such as

- A function call
- Mail via a real-time operating system (RTOS)
- An event via a RTOS
- An interrupt
- A semaphore-protected shared resource service call
- An Ada rendezvous
- A remote procedure call (RPC) in a distributed system

Early analysis identifies the key messages between objects that collaborate. Later, design elaborates an implementation strategy that defines the synchronization and timing requirements for each message. Internally, the object translates the messages into method calls, event receptions, commands, or data to munch on, as appropriate. Messages generally only occur between object pairs that share a link (an instance of an association that is defined between the classes of those objects). Figure 2-5 illustrates how messages flow between objects in a running system.

Logically, an object's interface is the facade that it presents to the world and is defined by the set of protocols within which the object

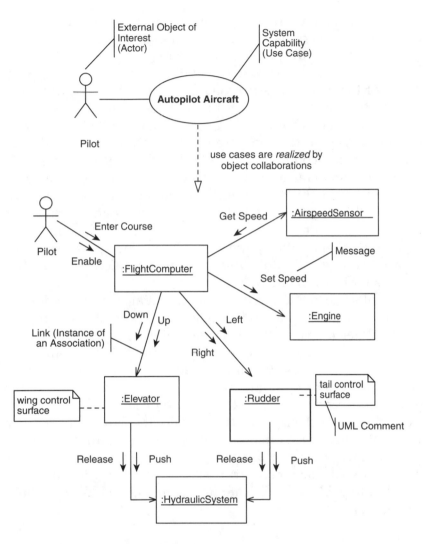

Figure 2-5 *Sending Messages*

participates. An interface protocol consists of invariants, which include three things:

- Preconditions
- Signature
- Postconditions

The preconditions are the conditions guaranteed to be true before the message is sent or received. For example, if a parameter is an enumerated type *Color,* the possible values are preconditions. If a parameter is a pointer that is expected to point to a valid object, then the validity of the pointer is a precondition. Ensuring that preconditions are met is normally the responsibility of the object sending the message. Postconditions are the things guaranteed to be true by the time the message is processed and are the responsibility of the receiver of the message. Postconditions include that the return values are well formed and within range, and the service is properly completed. Other postconditions might be that only a certain set of exceptions will be thrown in the presence of a fault. The message signature is the exact mechanism used for message transfer. This can be a function call with the parameters and return type or RTOS message post/pend pair, or bus message protocol. Most invariants are specified using UML constraints, a topic covered in Section 2.6.

The interface should reflect the essential characteristics of the object that require visibility to other objects. Objects should hide inessential details, especially their internal design. The reasons for this are obvious—if a client knows how a server object is structured, client class developers will use that information. As soon as that information is used, the server object structure is no longer free to vary without breaking its clients. This is nothing more or less than the concept of "data hiding," which has been around since the dawn of time.[5] By publishing only enough information to properly use the provided services, objects enforce strong encapsulation. In C++, for example, common practice is to hide data members (making the private or protected visibility), but to publish the operations that manipulate the data (making them public).

2.3 Relations

Most classes, objects, and interfaces are small things. To do anything system-wide, many of these small things need to work together. And to work together, they must relate in some way. The UML provides

---

[5] Which occurred sometime in the late sixties, I believe ;-).

three primary kinds of relations—association, generalization, and dependency—to link together your model elements so that they may collaborate, share information, and so on. The most fundamental of these is association, because associations enable collaborations of objects to invoke services, and will be considered first.

2.3.1 Associations

The most fundamental kind of relation between classes in the UML is the *association*. An association is a design-time relation between classes that specifies that, at runtime, instance of those classes may have a *link* and be able to request services of one another.

The UML defines three distinct kinds of associations: association, aggregation, and composition. An association between classes means simply that at some time during the execution of the system objects instantiated from those classes may have a link that enables them to call or somehow invoke services of the other. Nothing is stated about how that is accomplished, or even whether it is a synchronous method call (although this is most common) or some kind of distributed or asynchronous message transfer. Think of associations as conduits that allow objects to find each other at runtime and exchange messages. Associations are shown as lines connecting classes on class diagrams.

The direction of navigability of the association may be specified by adding an (open) arrowhead. A normal line with no arrowheads (or showing an arrowhead at both ends) means that the association is bi-directional; that is, an object at either end of the association may send a message to an object at the other end. If only one of the objects can send a message to the other and not vice versa, then we add an *open arrowhead* (we'll see later that the type of arrowhead matters) pointing in the direction of the message flow. Thus we see that an *AlarmingObject* object can send a message to an *AlarmManager* object, but not vice versa. This does not imply that the *AlarmingObject* object cannot retrieve a value from an *AlarmManager* object because it can call a method that returns such a value. It means, however, that an object of type *Alarming Manager* cannot spontaneously send a message to an *AlarmingObject* object because it doesn't know, *by design,* how to find it.

Every association has two or more ends; these ends may have *role names.* These name the instances with respect to the class at the other end of the association. It is common practice to give the role name on the opposite end of the association to the pointer that points to that instance. For example, in Figure 2-6, the *Alarm* class might contain a pointer named *myView* to an instance of type *TextView*. To invoke a service on the linked instance of *TextView* an action in an operation in the *Alarm* class would deference the pointer, as in

myView->setText("Help!")

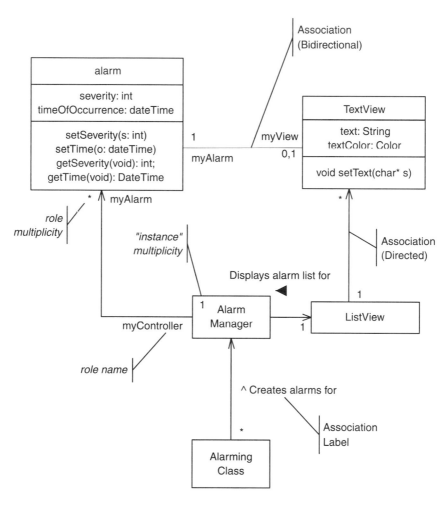

Figure 2-6: *Simple Association*

Although somewhat less common, *association labels* may also be used, such as between the *AlarmingClass* and *AlarmManager* classes. The label is normally used to help explain why the association exists between the two classes. In this case, the label "Creates alarms for" indicates that is how the *AlarmingClass* intends to use the *AlarmManager*. To get the directionality of the label you can add an arrowhead next to the label to show the speaking perspective. The UML specification calls out an arrowhead with no associated arrow (as shown between the *Alarm Manager* and *ListView* classes), but more commonly tools use the characters "^", ">", "<", and "V" in the label itself to indicate speaking perspective. Note also that the speaking perspective of the label is unrelated to the association direction. In the association between *Alarm Manager* and *ListView* messages flow from the *AlarmManager* only, but the association label speaks from the *ListView* perspective.

The *multiplicity* is probably the most important property of an association end. The multiplicity of an association end indicates the possible numbers of instances that can participate in the association role at runtime. This may be

- A fixed number, such as "1" or "3"
- A comma separated list, such as "0,1" or "3,5,7"
- A range, such as "1..10"
- A combination of a list and a range, such as "1..10, 25", which means "one to 10, inclusive, or 25"
- An asterisk, which means "zero or more"
- An asterisk with an endpoint, such as "1..*" which means "one or more"

In Figure 2-6, we see multiplicities on all the associations. Multiplicity is shown at the role end of the class to which it applies. Thus each *Alarm* object associates with zero or one *TextView* objects, and each *ListView* object associates with exactly zero or more *TextView* objects. The *AlarmManager* uses *instance multiplicity* to show that there is exactly one instance in the context of the shown collaboration. Since there is only one, it isn't necessary to show a 1 on all the association ends that attach to it. All of these adornments, except for perhaps multiplicity, are optional and may be added as desired to further clarify the relation between the respective classes.

An association between classes means that at some point during the lifecycle of instances of the associated classes, there *may be* a link that enables them to exchange messages. Nothing is stated or implied about which of these objects comes into existence first, which other object creates them, or how the link is formed.

In UML 1.x, an associative class was a special kind of class that was used when the association itself had features of interest. Perhaps the most common example is the association between a Man class and a Woman class called "Marriage." The marriage has attributes, such as date, duration, and location, and operations such as *createPrenuptial Agreement(),* which are not really features of the collaborating objects themselves. In UML 2.0, associative classes were discarded, and all associations may have these features, as desired. Figure 2-7 shows such an associative class notation where the *Charging* association has attributes of the connection between the *Battery* and *Charger.*

2.3.2 Aggregation

An aggregation is a specialized kind of association that indicates a "whole-part" relation exists between two classes. The "whole" end is marked with a white diamond, as in Figure 2-7. For example, consider, the classes *Message List* and *Message*. The *Message List* class is clearly a "whole" that aggregates possibly many *Message* elements. The diamond on the aggregation relation shows that the *Message List* is the "whole." The asterisk (*) on the *myMsg* association end indicates that the list may contain zero or more *Message* elements. If we desired to constrain this to be no more than 100 messages we could have made the multiplicity "0..100."

Since aggregation is a specialized form of association, all of the properties and adornments that apply to associations also apply to aggregations, including navigation, multiplicity, role names, and association labels.

Aggregation is a relatively weak form of "whole-part," as we'll see in a moment. No statement is made about lifecycle dependency or creation/destruction responsibility. Indeed, aggregation is normally treated in design and implementation identically to association. Nevertheless, it can be useful to aid in understanding the model structure and the relations among the conceptual elements from the problem domain.

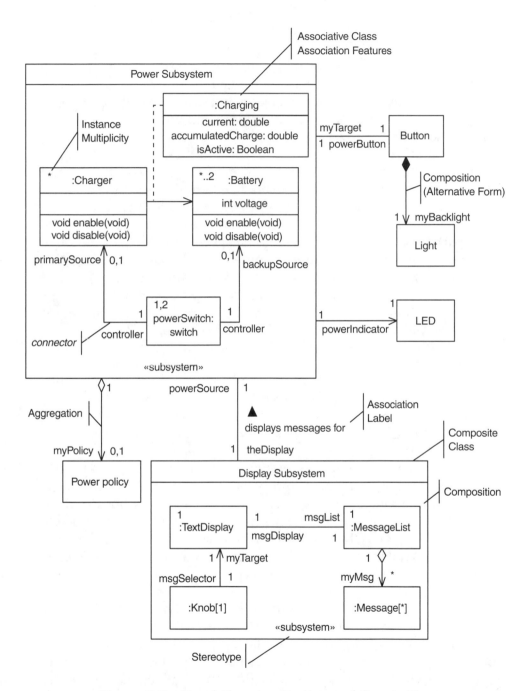

Figure 2-7: *Association, Aggregation, and Composition*

2.3.3 Composition

Composition is a strong form of aggregation in which the "whole" (also known as the "composite") has the explicit responsibility for the creation and destruction of the part objects. Because of this, the composite exists before the parts come into existence and continues to exist (although sometimes not for very long) after they are destroyed. If the parts have a fixed multiplicity with respect to the composite, then it is common for the composite to create those parts in its constructor and destroy them in its destructor. With nonfixed multiplicities, the composite dynamically creates and destroys the part objects during its execution. Because the composite has creation and destruction responsibility, each part object can only be owned by a *single* composite object, although the part objects may participate in other association and aggregation relations. Composition is also a kind of association so it can likewise have all of the adornments available to ordinary associations.

Composition has two common presentations: nested class boxes and a filled-in diamond. Figure 2-7 shows both forms. The *Power Subsystem*, for example, is a composite class that contains parts of type *Charger*, *Battery*, and *Switch*. The *Button* class is also a composite that contains a single *Light* part. These parts are not objects exactly—they are *object roles*. These roles are played by objects executing in the system at runtime but may be played by different objects at different times. Similarly, the lines connecting the parts are not links (which occur between objects) but *connectors* that occur between roles.

With the containment presentation, there is an issue as to how to show the multiplicity of the part (by definition, the multiplicity on the whole end of a composition is exactly 1). Since there is no line on which to place the multiplicity, it is common to put the multiplicity in one of the upper corners of the part class or in square brackets after the part name. This is called *instance multiplicity*. We see that the *Power Subsystem* contains either one or two objects of type *Switch*, zero or more objects of type *Charger*, and zero to two objects of type *Battery*. The *Display Subsystem* has exactly one *Knob* but an unspecified number of *Messages*.

The two forms of composition are subtly different. The filled-in diamond shows relations between classes, but when these classes are nested within the composite class they need to be objects, or more precisely, object roles (called "parts"). In addition to making the classes into parts, the composite class environment may add additional constraints, often in terms of more precisely specifying multiplicity. Figure 2-8 shows an example of this, a set of composition relations with the filled diamond at the top and a representation of the very same system with the nested notation below. Notice that the composition role names in the

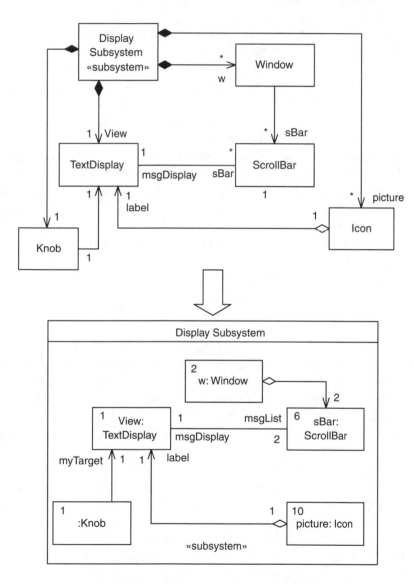

Figure 2-8: *Composition and Parts*

upper part of the figure become the part names in the lower part. Also note that the multiplicity of the parts is, in this case, more precisely specified—for example, "*" Windows becomes "2" window parts in the lower figure. The refinement of multiplicities is optional—"*" could have remained "*" had we desired.

The most common implementation of an association, as we will see later in Code Listing 2-4, is an object pointer (in C++) or an object reference (in Java). This is true regardless of which kind of association it is—an ordinary association, an aggregation, or a composition. There are many other ways of implementing an association—including nested class declaration, object identifier reference (as in a MS Windows handle or a CORBA object ID), an operating system task ID, and so on—but using a pointer is the most common.

Composition plays a very important role in the scalability of the UML by enabling objects to be defined in terms of parts, which are defined to be roles played by objects in the running system. These (part) objects themselves are typed by their class, of course, and those classes may themselves have parts. Thus, in UML we have the ability nest composite structures arbitrarily deeply—a crucial feature for scalability of the UML to very large systems. This important topic will be discussed soon in Section 2.4.2.

2.3.3.1 Stereotypes

In a couple of places in Figure 2-7 notice that a class has a special adornment called a *stereotype*. Stereotypes are used in several ways. In one sense, a stereotype simply "metatypes" the role of a commonly used icon, such as the rectangle in Figure 2-7. A subsystem is special kind of class but we still use a class box to show it. To indicate that we mean a subsystem and not an ordinary class, we add the stereotypes. Subsystems are discussed later in this chapter, in Section 2.4.

The other usage of a stereotype is to tailor the UML to meet a specific need or purpose. It is part of the lightweight extension mechanism defined within the UML. A stereotype is a user-defined kind of element that is based on some already-defined element in the UML, such as *Class, Operation, Association,* and so on. You can create your own stereotypes if you wish, adding your problem-domain vocabulary to the UML. Stereotypes must always "subtype" an existing metaclass, such as Class, Component, Package, Association, and so on already defined in the

UML specification. Stereotypes are usually shown by attaching the stereotype name in guillemots with the stereotyped element or shown using a user-defined icon.

2.3.4 Generalization

The generalization relation in the UML means that one class defines a set of features, which are either specialized or extended in another. Generalization may be thought of as an "is a type of" relation and therefore only as having a design-time impact, rather than a runtime impact.

Generalization has many uses in class models. First, generalization is used as a means to ensure interface compliance, much in the same way that interfaces are used. Indeed, it is the most common way to implement interfaces in languages that do not have interfaces as a native concept, such as in C++. Also, generalization can simplify your class models because you can abstract a set of features common to a number of classes into a single superclass, rather than redefining the same structure independently in many different classes. In addition, generalization allows for different realizations to be used interchangeably; for example, one realization subclass might optimize worst-case performance while another optimizes memory size and yet another optimizes reliability because of internal redundancy.

Generalization in the UML means two things. First, it means *inheritance*—that subclasses have (at least) the same attributes, operations, methods, and relations as the superclasses they specialize. Of course, if the subclasses were *identical* with their superclasses, that would be boring, so subclasses can differ from their superclasses in either or both of two ways—by specialization or by extension.

Subclasses can *specialize* operations or state machines of their superclasses. Specializing means that the same operation (or action list on the statechart) is implemented differently than in the superclass. This is commonly called *polymorphism*. In order for this to work, when a class has an association with another which is a superclass, at runtime an instance of the first can invoke an operation declared in the second, and if the link is actually to an subclass instance, the operation of the subclass is invoked rather than that of the superclass.

This is much easier to see in the example presented in Figure 2-9. The class *MsgQueue* is a superclass and defines standard queue-like behavior, storing *Message* objects in a FIFO fashion with operations

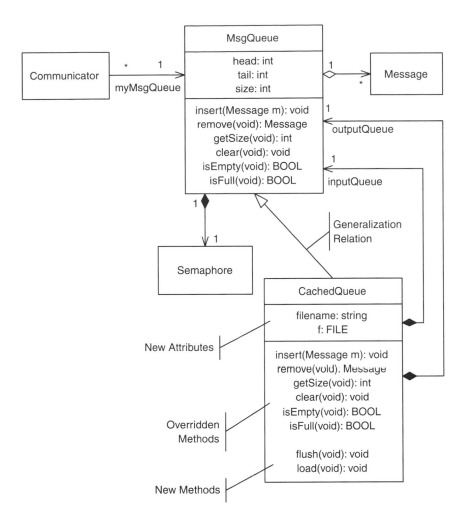

Figure 2-9: *Generalization*

such as *insert()* and *remove()*. *CachedQueue* specializes and extends *MsgQueue* (the closed arrowhead on the generalization line points to the more general class). *The Communicator* class associates with the base class *MsgQueue*. If it needs to store only a few messages, a standard in-memory queue, that is, an instance of *MsgQueue,* works fine. But what if some particular instance of *Communicator* needs to store millions of messages? In that case, the instance can link to an instance of the *Cached Queue* subclass. Whether *Communicator* actually links to an instance of

MsgQueue or one of its subclasses is unknown to the instance of *Communicator*. It calls the *insert()* or *remove()* operations as necessary. If the connected instance is of class *MsgQueue*, then the correct operations for that class are called; if the connected instance is of class *CachedQueue*, then the operations for that class are invoked instead, but the client of the queue doesn't know (or care) which is invoked.

It is common not to show methods in the subclass unless they override (redefine) methods inherited from the superclass, but this is merely a stylistic convention. Remember that a *CachedQueue is a MsgQueue*, so that everything that is true about the latter is also true of the former, including the attributes, operations, and relations. For example, *CachedQueue* aggregates zero or more *Message* objects and has a composition relation to the class *Semaphore* because its superclass does. However, in this case, the operations for insert and remove are likely to work differently.

For example, *MsgQueue::insert()* might be written as shown in Code Listing 2-1:

```
void MsgQueue::insert(Message m) {
        if (isFull())
                throw OVERFLOW;
        else {
                head = (head + 1) % size;
                list[head] = m;
                };
        };
```

Code Listing 2-1: *MsgQueue::insert() Operation*

However, the code for the insert operation in the subclass must be more complex. First, note that the subclass contains (via composition) two *MsgQueues,* one for input buffering and one for output buffering. The *CachedQueue::insert()* operation only uses the *MsgQueue* instance playing the *inputQueue* role. If this is full, then it must write the buffer out to disk and zero out the buffer. The code to do this is shown in Code Listing 2-2.

```
void CachedQueue::insert(Message m) {
        if (inputQueue->isFull()) {
                // flush the full queue to disk and then
                // clear it
```

```
                    flush();
                    inputQueue->clear();
                    };
                inputQueue->insert(m);
                };
```

Code Listing 2-2: *CachedQueue::insert() Operation*

Similarly, the operations for *remove()*, *getSize()*, *clear()*, *isEmpty()*, and *isFull()* need to be overridden as well to take into account the use of two internal queues and a disk file.

Note that in the UML attributes cannot be specialized. If the superclass defines an attribute of time *sensedValue* and it has a type int, then all subclasses also have that attribute and it is of the same type. If you need to change the type of an attribute, you should use the «bind» stereotype of dependency, a topic discussed in Section 2.3.5. Subclasses can also *extend* the superclass—that is, they can have new attributes, operations, states, transitions, relations, and so on. In Figure 2-9, *CachedQueue* extends its base class by adding attributes *filename* and *f* and by adding operations *flush()* and *load()*.

The other thing that generalization means in the UML is *substitutability*; this means that any place an instance of the superclass was used, an instance of the subclass can also be used without breaking the system in any overt way. Substitutability is what makes generalization immensely useful in designs.

2.3.5 Dependency

Association, in its various forms, and generalization are the key relations defined within the UML. Nevertheless, there are several more relations that are useful. They are put under the umbrella of *dependency*. The UML defines four different primary kinds of dependency—abstraction, binding, usage, and permission, each of which may be further stereotyped. For example, «refine» and «realize» are both stereotypes of the abstraction relationship, and «friend» is a stereotype of permission. All of these special forms of dependency are shown as a stereotyped dependency (a dashed line with an open arrowhead).

Arguably, the most useful stereotypes of dependency are «bind», «usage», and «friend». Certainly, they are the most commonly seen, but there are others. The reader is referred to [2] for the complete list of "official" stereotypes.

The «bind» stereotype binds a set of actual parameters to a formal parameter list. This is used to specify parameterized classes (templates in C++-speak or generics in Ada-speak). This is particularly important in patterns because patterns themselves are parameterized collaborations, and they are often defined in terms of parameterized classes.

A parameterized class is a class that is defined in terms of more primitive elements, which are referred to symbolically without the inclusion of the actual element that will be used. The symbolic name is called a *formal parameter* and the actual element, when bound, is called an *actual parameter.* In Figure 2-10, *Queue* is a parameterized class that is defined in terms of two symbolic elements—a class called *Element* and an int called *Size.* Because the exact elements that these parameters refer to are not provided in the definition of *Queue, Queue* is not an instantiable class—those undefined elements must be given definitions before an instance can be created. The «bind» dependency does exactly that, binding a list of actual elements to the formal parameter list. In the case of *MsgQueue, Element* is replaced by the class *Message* and the int *Size* is replaced by the literal constant 1000. Now that the actual parameters are specified and bound, *MsgQueue* is an instantiable class, meaning that we can create objects of this class at runtime.

The diagram shows three common forms for the «bind» dependency. Form 1 is the most common, but the other forms are prevalent as well.

The usage relation indicates some element requires the presence of another for its correct operation. The UML provides a number of specific forms such as «call» (between two operations), «create» (between classifiers, e.g. classes), «instantiate» (between classifiers), and «send» (between an operation and a signal). Of these, «call» is common, as well as an unspecified «usage» between components, indicating that one component needs another because some of the services in one invoke some set of services in the other.

The permission relation grants permission for a model element to access elements in another. The «friend» stereotype is a common one between classes, modeling the *friend* keyword in C++. «access» is similar to Ada's *use* keyword, granting access of a namespace of one Ada package to another. The «import» relation adds the public elements of one namespace (such as a UML package) into another.

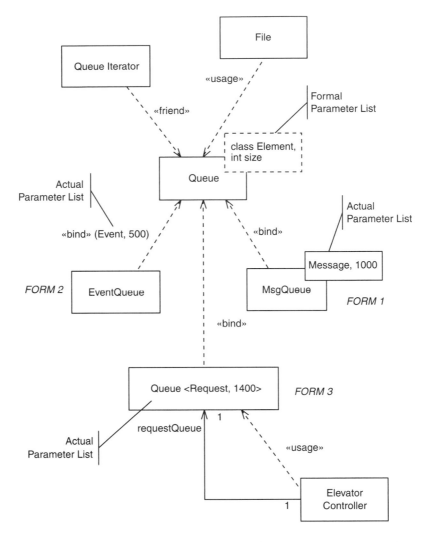

Figure 2-10: *Dependency*

2.3.6 Structural Diagrams

UML is a graphical modeling language, although, perhaps surprisingly, the notation is less important than the semantics of the language. Nevertheless, there is a common set of graphical icons and idioms for creating these views of the underlying model. We call these views "diagrams."

UML has been unjustly criticized for having too many diagram types—class diagrams, package diagrams, object diagrams, component diagrams, and so on. The fact is that these are all *really the same diagram type*—a structural diagram. Each of these diagrams emphasizes a different aspect of the model but they may each contain all of the elements in the others. A package diagram may contain classes and a class diagram may contain objects, while a component diagram might have objects, classes, and packages. In truth, the UML has one *structural* diagram, which we call by different names to indicate the primary purpose of the diagram.

We use diagrams for a number of purposes: as a data entry mechanism, as a means to understand the contents of the model, and as a means to discuss and review the model. The model itself is the totality of the concepts in your system and their relations to one another. When we use diagrams as a data entry mechanism, we add, modify, or remove elements to the underlying model as we draw and manipulate the diagrams.

The most common diagrams you'll draw are the class diagrams. These diagrams emphasize the organization of classes and their relations. The other aspects are used as needed, but class diagrams provide the primary structural view.

In real systems, you cannot draw the entire system in a single diagram, even if you use E-size plotter paper and a 4-point font. As a practical matter, you must divide up your system into different structural views (behavioral views will be described later). How, then, can we effectively do this? What criteria should we use to decide how many diagrams we need and what should go on them?

In the ROPES process, we use a simple criterion for decomposing the views of the system into multiple diagrams. The ROPES process introduces the concept of a *mission* of an artifact—its "purpose for existence." For diagrams, the mission is straightforward—each diagram should show a *single important concept*. This might be to show the elements in a collaboration of objects or classes realizing a use case, or a generalization taxonomy, or the contents of a package. Usually, every element of your model appears in some diagram somewhere, but it is perfectly reasonable for it to appear in several diagrams. For example, a class might be involved in the realization of three use cases (resulting in three different diagrams), be a part of a generalization taxonomy, and also be contained in a package of your model. In this case, you might expect it to appear in five different diagrams. It is also not necessary for all aspects of the class to be shown in all views. For example, in the class diagrams showing collaborations, only the operations and attributes directly involved in the mission of that collaboration would be shown; in a diagram showing generalization, only the features added or modified by that class would be shown; in a diagram showing the contents of the package that owns the class, you probably wouldn't show any attributes or operations.

Which of the views is right? The answer is *all of them*. Just because a feature of a class or some other element isn't shown doesn't mean or imply that the feature doesn't exist or is wrong. The semantics of the class or model element is the sum of the semantic statements made in *all* diagrams in which it appears. Indeed, you can define model elements without explicitly drawing them on diagrams at all but instead adding them to the model repository directly. One of the most valuable things that modeling tools provide, over simple drawing tools, is the maintenance of the semantic information about the structure and behavior of your system.

Normally, you don't draw object diagrams directly. Most often, classes and class relations are drawn and these *imply* the possible sets of objects and their relations. If for some reason you want to depict particular configurations of the runtime system the object diagrams are the appropriate venue. A case in which you do is the composite structure diagram. This is a diagram that shows a composite class and its parts (as object roles). This diagram is used as the primary view for showing the hierarchical structure of a system, as we will see in Section 2.4.2.

2.3.7 Mapping Objects to Code

Of course, the UML model must ultimately map to source code. In Java and C++, the mapping is straightforward. The source code for such the class diagram in Figure 2-4 (in Java) is the most straightforward because Java contains interfaces as a native concept. The Java source code would look like Code Listing 2-3.

```
public class SensorClient {
    protected myISensor iSensor;
    public void displayValue(void) {
        int sensedValue = iSensor.getValue();
        System.out.println(value);
```

```
        };
}; // end class SensorClient

interface iSensor {
        int acquire(void);
        int getValue(void);
        void setCalibrationConstant(long
                newCalibrationConstant);
}; // end interface iSensor

public class Sensor implements iSensor {
        protected iFilter myIFilter;
        int value;
        long calibrationConstant;
        public int acquire(void){ /* method here */ };
        public int getValue(void) {
                return myIFilter.filter(value); };
        public void setCalibrationConstant(long
                newCalibrationConstant) {
                calibrationConstant =
newCalibrationConstant;
                };
}; // end class Sensor

interface iFilter {
        public int filterValue(int value);
}; // end interface iFilter
public class Filter implements iFilter {
        int lowPass;
        int highPass;
        public int filtervalue(int value) {
                /* method here */
        };
        public setFilterParameters(int newLowPass,
                int newHighPass) {
                lowPass = newLowPass;
                highPass = newHighPass;
        };
}; // end class Filter
```

Code Listing 2-3: *Class Diagram in Java*

In C++, the code is almost as straightforward as the Java code, but not quite, because an interface is not a native concept in C++. There are two common approaches to implement interfaces in C++. The first, shown in

Code Listing 2-4, is to create an *abstract base class* by declaring the interface operations as pure virtual. The other common approach is to use the
Interface or *Façade* pattern. This involves creating the interface class as an
instantiable class that associates to a separate implementation class.

```
class SensorClient {
protected:
      iSensor* myISensor;
public:
      void displayValue(void) {
            int sensedValue = iSensor.getValue();
            cout << value << endl;
      };
};
class iSensor { // abstract class

public :
      virtual int acquire(void)=0; // pure virtual
      virtual int getValue(void)=0; // pure virtual
      virtual void setCalibrationConstant(long
            newCalibrationConstant)=0;
};

class Sensor : public iSensor {
protected :
      iFilter* myIFilter;
      int value;
      long calibrationConstant;
      public :
      int acquire(void);
      int getValue(void){
            return myIFilter->filterValue(value);
      };
      void setCalibrationConstant(long
            newCalibrationConstant) {
            calibrationConstant = newCalibrationConstant;
      };
};

class iFilter {
public :
      virtual int filterValue(int value)=0; // pure
virtual
};
class Filter : public iFilter {
```

```
public :
     int filterValue(int value) {
             lowPass = newLowPass;
             highPass = newHighPass;
     };
};
```

Code Listing 2-4: *Class Diagram in C++*

In summary, an object is one of many possible *instances* of a class. A class has two notable features—attributes (which store data values) and methods (which provide services to clients of the class). Interfaces are named collections of operations that are *realized* by classes. Interfaces need not be explicitly modeled. Many useful systems have been designed solely with classes, but there are times when the addition level of abstraction is useful, particularly when more than a single implementation of an interface will be provided.

2.4 Big Things: Packages, Components, and Subsystems

Classes, objects, and interfaces are usually little things. It takes collaborations of many of them to achieve system-wide behavior. Because of the complexity of today's systems, it is unusual to find a system that can be effectively developed and managed without thinking about larger-scale structures. The UML does provide a number of concepts to manage systems in the large scale (all based on the concept of a class), although most of the literature has not effectively explained or demonstrated the use of these features.

"Big things" come in two primary flavors to reflect the two common scalability problems in building real systems. The first is the issue of organizing a model, keeping track of hundreds or thousands of classes, and effectively sharing the work among many different developers, possibly geographically separated. The model management question is primarily addressed with the UML concept of packages, as we will see in the next section.

The other scalability concept is for large runtime things. If I'm building a spacecraft, I need to think at many different levels of abstraction. I might have a use case (system capability) like "Go get a rock on Mars" and this will involve potentially *millions* of things at the most primitive scale. I would like to think about the roles of the deep space network, the launch vehicle, the orbiter, the lander, Mission Control, and so on. These elements are BIG, each containing thousands of parts. In the design of the space-craft, I may want to consider large-scale things such as the navigation system, attitude control, the communications system, hydraulics, power control, life support, thermal management, and so on. Each of these things is likewise BIG (although only a piece of the largest-scale things in the system to be considered), also containing potentially thousands of simple parts. And so on until we get down to the level of simple individual sensors, switches, messages, waypoints, batteries, and the like. We need some way to think about large-scale elements that exist at runtime that are composed of parts, which may themselves contain smaller parts. The UML 2.0 specification refines the concepts of component and subsystem, and even class, for this purpose. These concepts will be discussed after we discuss the easier issue of packages and model management.

2.4.1 Model Organization: Packages

Packages are (design-time) model elements that can contain other model elements, including other packages. Packages are used to subdivide models to permit teams of developers to manipulate and work effectively together. Packages cannot be instantiated and can only be used to organize models. They do define a namespace for the model elements that they contain, but no other semantics. The UML does not provide any criterion as to whether a class should go in this package or that—it merely provides packages as model-building blocks to aid in whatever organizational purpose the developer desires.

The ROPES process recommends that packages be used with a specific criterion—"common subject matter or common vocabulary." This is similar to the Shaler and Mellor concept of a *domain,* and the ROPES process uses the stereotype «domain» to indicate this particular usage of packages. However, packages can be used to organize the application model in just about any desired way.

A package normally contains elements that exist only at design-time—classes and data types—but may also contain use cases and various diagrams, such as sequence and class diagrams. These design pieces are then used to construct collaborations that realize system-wide functionality. Packages are normally the basic configuration items for a configuration management tool, rather than the individual classes. Figure 2-11

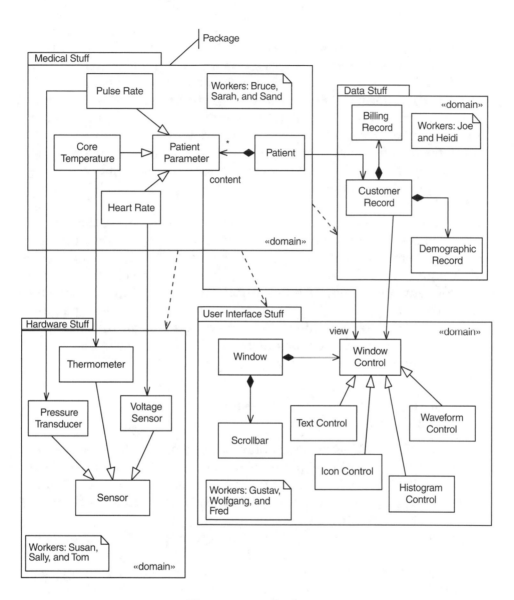

Figure 2-11: *Packages*

shows that packages are drawn to look like a tabbed folder and may optionally show elements that they semantically contain. In this figure, there are four packages—Medical Stuff, Data Stuff, User Interface Stuff, and Hardware Stuff. Each class in the system resides in a single package, although it may be referenced by elements of other packages. In fact, we see many associations from elements in one package to elements in another, such as *PatientParameter* associating with *WindowControl*. This association allows the two classes to collaborate so that a *WindowControl* may display information held within the *PatientParameter*. A domain is organized around a single subject matter and vocabulary, such as user interface or hardware. All the classes that are within that subject matter are defined in the appropriate domain. Generalization taxonomies almost always fall within a single domain (a subclass of a window class is always a kind of window). If a class seems to fit in multiple domains, then it has too broad a scope and should be broken down into a set of collaborating classes, each of which fits in a single domain. Other strategies use packages with different rules about the elements they contain. Several different strategies are given in Chapter 1.

It is important to remember that packages have very little in the way of semantics. They define an enclosing namespace for the elements contained within them but that's all. They are not instantiable—you can't point to a running system and point to an instance of a package. Packages are used to organize models for model management and are, therefore, design-time organizational concepts only.

2.4.2 Structured Classes: Composites, Parts, Ports, and Connectors

So far, we've considered classes only at the small end of the scale—simple, primitive, and easy to implement. If only life could be so easy! However, it is necessary to concern ourselves as well with "designing in the large" and construct and manipulate classes that are not simple, primitive, and directly implemented.

When we talk about nonprimitive things, we mean things that are defined in terms of smaller pieces. Structured classes (or more properly *structured classifiers*) are exactly that—classes that contain an internal collaboration structure of *Parts*. Parts are instance roles linked together with *Connectors* (similar to links, but connect parts rather than objects). Structured classes are not any different than ordinary classes really, it's just that classes may be specified in terms of smaller, contained parts which themselves are typed by classes. There are a couple of special kinds of structured classifiers—components and subsystems—that carry particular meaning, but really it's all just classes.

The concept of a structured class is based on both *decomposition* and *encapsulation*. The decomposition aspect is provided by the part objects contained within the structured class. In this case, we mean that the *Smart Arm* in Figure 2-12 is "rich" in the sense that it is internally implemented by the collaboration of its internal parts, including instances of *CommandQueue, CommandController, ForceSensors, PositionSensors, Lamps,* and so on. The structured class is not relegated to be a simple runtime container of these parts. Not only does it have the responsibility to create and destroy the part instances, it may also coordinate the activities and collaboration of these various part objects; when this is done, a statechart is normally created for the structured class to control and mediate the interaction of the parts.

The structured class itself is a class that owns its parts via the composition relation already discussed. For example, Figure 2-12 presents a structured class called *Smart Arm*. This robotic arm provides some set of services via the collaboration of its internal parts, such as instances of

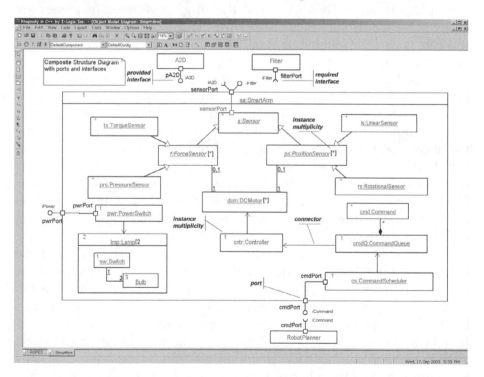

Figure 2-12: *Structured Classes*

classes *Controller, DCMotor,* or *Lamp.* This use of the composition relation between the structured class and its parts implies several things. First, only a single structured class may own a specific part (instance of a contained class). Further, the structured class is responsible for the creation, destruction, and linking together of its parts. The number of instances of a Part held within a structured class is specified by its *instance multiplicity.*

Instance multiplicity is the number of instances for a part within its context. There may be other instances that are parts of other structured classes (or even other instances of the same structured class), but they aren't considered in the multiplicity of a part within another class. There are two common forms for showing instance multiplicity. The first is to put the multiplicity in square brackets following the name of the class, as was done in Figure 2-12 for the *DCMotor* class. The other notation is to put the multiplicity in a corner of the part class as was done for the *Controller* class. If the multiplicity of a part is fixed, then those parts are made in the constructor of the structured class. For example, the seven *DCMotors* and the single *Controller* instances are made in the constructor of the *SmartArm* class. When the multiplicity of the part is variable (such as 0..4 or *) then the structured class typically does not create the parts in the structured class's constructor, but rather on as-needed basis during the execution of the structured class. Examples are the *Command* objects owned by the *Command Queue.*

The parts within a structured class are linked together with *connectors.* A connector is a link, owned not by the part objects (which is the usual case with association instances), but rather, owned by the structured class. Each connector has two or more connector ends, each terminating on a part. The actual location of the connector end points forms the part topology of the structured class. The connectors are created by the structured class and link together the parts so that they can collaborate in the context of the structured class.

The other key concept of structured classes is *encapsulation* of the class away from its environment. This is done through the use of ports, and offered and required interfaces. A structured class offers a set of services to its clients and in turn may levy requirements on its servers in the form of required interfaces. Some of these services are commands that can be sent to the *Smart Arm* via the *iCommand* interface, such as *acceptCommand(c: Command)* or *reset(void).* The *acceptCommand (c: Command)* operation is really defined on the part class called *Command Scheduler.* We would like this interface published across the encapsulation boundary defined by the *Smart Arm*, and we do this by defining a *port* to present that interface across this encapsulation boundary. Figure 2-12 provides a port that associates with an interface called *iCommand*. Note the use of the ball-and-socket notation for offered (ball) and required (socket) interfaces. This means that the client, *Robot Planner*, requires a specific set of services defined by *iCommand* to be met by a class, while the *Smart Arm* offers that same set of services. One can think of a port as a window placed on the boundary of a structured object to some specific internal feature that you want to make visible. The port delegates the operation on the edge of the structured class and redirects any message coming in to the internal part, or from that part out to an external object attached to the structured class via the port.

Most commonly, a port is associated with either an offered or required interface, but a port is more general than that. Ports may be associated with either, neither, or both offered and required interfaces. Ports are said to be typed by their interfaces.

It should be noted that ports, and even interfaces for that matter, are *not* required to build systems with structured classes. Using ports will usually introduce some runtime overhead and require additional memory. Since ports are not required, an operation of an internal part may be used directly by an external object (we call the structured class *transparent* in that case), although that tends to tightly couple the structured class internal structure with its environment. Ports and interfaces provide a convenient notation for specifying how a service offered from an internal part is published across the boundary of its enclosing structured class. As we will see in the next chapter, ports and interfaces may specify their behavior and sequencing constraints in protocol state machines so that we have the power to specify exactly how we want the operations published via the interfaces to work.

The real power of structured classes is to enable the containment hierarchy of systems. That is, classes may contain internal parts, each of which may be decomposed into smaller parts, ad infinitum. This is necessary to model and manipulate models of large-scale real-time and embedded systems, from medical devices and aircraft to C[4]ISR[6] systems.

---

[6] Command, Control, Communication, Computers and Intelligence, Surveillance, and Reconnaissance systems, such as the C[4]ISR Architecture Framework developed by the U.S. Department of Defense and in use in the Future Combat Systems (FCS) and similar projects. A C[4]ISR-UML mapping is provided in Chapter 11.

LIVERPOOL JOHN MOORES UNIVERSITY
LEARNING SERVICES

2.4.2.1 Ports: Connecting Outside the Box

Ports are different than interfaces in one important aspect—ports are instantiable while interfaces are not. A port instance is a connection slot into an instance of a class that either relays a message to a part internal to the class (called a *relay* port) or accepts the message and hands it off to the object for handling (called an *end* or *behavioral* port). Since ports are instantiable, they have identity so that the class can tell which port provided the message. Since ports themselves may have behavior, they can mediate the handling of messages in a state-based way.

An interface is a named collection of operations, but those operations are provided elsewhere. Interfaces *have* no behavior in and of themselves, they just allow a collection of services to be given a name. The required and offered aspects of the interface form a contract to which the client and server agree adhere. To get behavior, a class must realize the operations of the interface by providing matching methods that actually provide the services. An interface is like a phone book in that it names the services, while a port is like a telephone switchboard that handles the incoming messages and patches them through to where they need to go.

Figure 2-13a shows metaphorically how I, at least, think of ports, interfaces, and connections. The interface is the contract, the rules by which you agree to abide, while the ports actually connect the plays (client and server) to invoke the services specified in the contract. In the example, the server is in fact a part of a larger service organization so that services requests are mediated by a relay port (our metaphorical secretary) but ultimately services requests are sent via the end port to the server. The connection is the infrastructure used to convey the messages (the phone lines in the metaphor). Figure 2-13b shows the UML notational equivalent for the metaphor.

2.4.3 Components

Now we understand the basic concepts of a structured class as having parts connected, publishing services via interfaces, and providing runtime connections via ports. Any class can do this in the UML 2.0, but these notions relate very significantly to the concept of a UML component.

In some sense, a UML component is merely a structured class with aspirations—it is meant to be the primary *replaceable unit* of

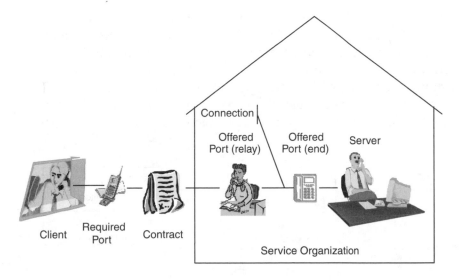

Figure 2-13a: *Interfaces, Connections, and Ports (Semantic Metaphor)*

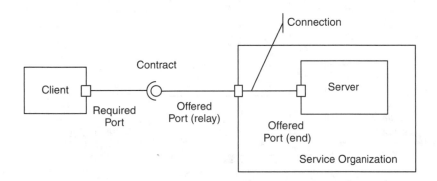

Figure 2-13b: *Interfaces, Connections, and Ports (UML Notation)*

software—a well-encapsulated piece of software that provides a coherent set of services, normally used and replaced together. There have been long and strenuous debates within the UML community over what constitutes a component versus a class, and how the specifically differ. The answer is that they don't, not really, but the term is so commonly used that relating concepts of structured classes to components used in the literature (and programming frameworks) is very helpful.

As structured classes, components usually (but needn't necessarily) have interfaces and ports. To optimize a component for replaceability, encapsulating them away from their external environment is important and ports and interface help in this. In the UML 2.0 the notation for a component changed slightly, as shown in Figure 2-14. In UML 2.0, a component uses a box, just like a class, but can use either the stereotype «component» or the component icon inside the box.

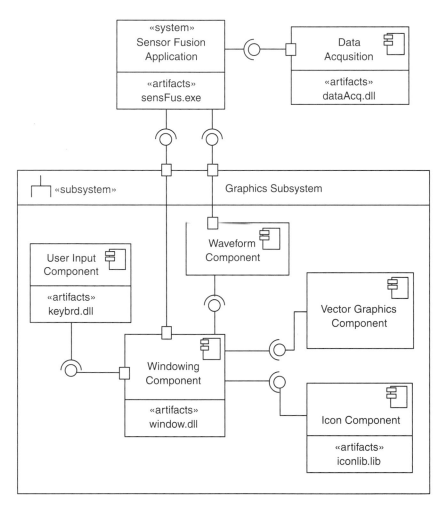

Figure 2-14: *Components*

Note that some of the components have an «artifact» section. In UML 2.0, an artifact represents a piece of work created to deploy or represent information used in the systems or software development process. Documents, defect reports, Microsoft® Word documents, and computer files are all examples of artifacts. With components and other software entities on UML diagrams, the most common use for artifacts is to specify the unit of deployment of the software unit—usually, although not limited to, a disk file. The identification of the implementing artifact is optional.

In the example shown in Figure 2-14, the sensor fusion application consists of three primary pieces: the system (with the artifact *senfus.exe*), a data acquisition component (deployed in the artifact *dataAcq.dll*), and a graphics subsystem, which is further decomposed into several components. These components (and the subsystem) are all elements of the system structural architecture. These elements are each not primitive, but are internally decomposed into smaller pieces, and some of those may themselves be decomposed as well. In fact, it is common for components to contain (i.e., be composed of) smaller components just as structured classes may contain parts which are themselves structured classes. Just as a component is really nothing more than a class at the architectural level, this component diagram is nothing more than a class diagram that emphasizes the component architecture of the system.

Frequently, component-based systems are built on a commercial or at least standardized component framework, such as Enterprise Java Beans (EJB), COM+, .NET, or the CORBA Component Model (CCM). Such component frameworks provide a standardized set of services (such as COM+ *iUnknown* interface for component identification) and the ability to load, unload, and otherwise manage components at runtime. This is not required to use the UML component concept, but the UML is consistent with those infrastructures. It is also common to construct real-time and embedded systems with custom component frameworks.

2.4.4 Subsystems

Subsystems are used to decompose the physical organization of large-scale systems at the highest level of abstraction. Figure 2-14 included an example of a subsystem, shown using both the stereotype «subsystem» and the icon (an inverted two-pronged fork). Like components, subsystems are architectural-level structured classes, and as such may have ports, and interfaces, and are decomposed into smaller parts. In the UML 2.0, in fact, a subsystem is a specialized kind of component (formally speaking, a stereotype), one that also includes a packaging namespace. In actual usage, there is little to distinguish subsystems from components.

Various notations for subsystems are shown in Figure 2-15. The *Power Subsystem* is shown with a stereotype and two subdivisions, one for specification (containing the specifying use cases) and one for real-ization (containing the parts that implement the subsystem specifica-tion). Either or both of these compartments may be suppressed as desired. The *Power Source* subsystem uses a subsystem stereotype icon

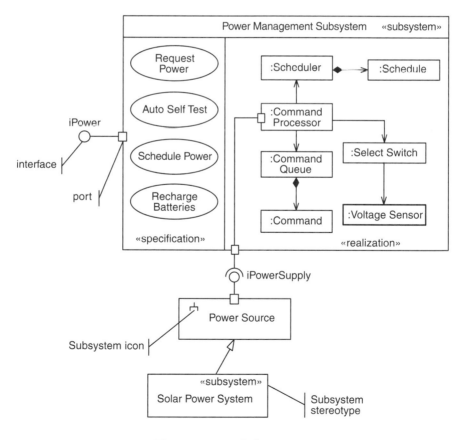

Figure 2-15: *Subsystems*

(the inverted fork) rather than the textual stereotype and doesn't show any of its contents. In the figure, subsystems have both ports and interfaces, and while the use of interfaces is strongly encouraged, they are not required.

The next figure, Figure 2-16, provides an example of a subsystem diagram. In this diagram, a system object (the spacecraft) is shown with its internal subsystem parts. Of course, these subsystems are large and complex and are, no doubt, decomposed at least one or two more levels, if not more. In addition, exposed interfaces and ports are shown, along with the actors that interact with the system. However, this diagram shows the high-level system architecture. The connections among the subsystems support their collaboration to collectively realize the system's use cases.

Subsystems need not be constrained to be only composed of software elements. In systems engineering environments, it is common to use the UML notion of subsystem to represent things that are internally decomposed into parts of various kinds, including software, electronic, mechanical and chemical.

2.4.5 Deployments: Nodes and Nonesuch

As mentioned earlier, artifacts such as files implement software elements such as components, subsystems, and classes. Artifacts are useful for describing processes, and the UML can be used to model development processes and document flow, but primarily we'll be concerned here about artifacts that deploy executable software elements. While we don't normally think of executing documents, we do think of executing .exe, .dll, and .lib files, and we think of these artifacts as being the implementation of components and other objects. In the UML, the thing onto which an artifact is deployed is called a *node*. A node executes the implementation of these software elements. So it is with UML 2.0. While in UML 1.x, it was common to nest a component within a node, in UML 2.0, we nest artifacts that implement them instead.

In UML 2.0, the two primary kinds of nodes are devices and execution environments. Devices are commonly further stereotyped into «processors» and «simple devices», a «processor» being a device that executes the software that you write, while a «simple device» is one that does not (such as a printer, display, keyboard, or sensor). It is very common to use iconic stereotypes for various kinds of «simple

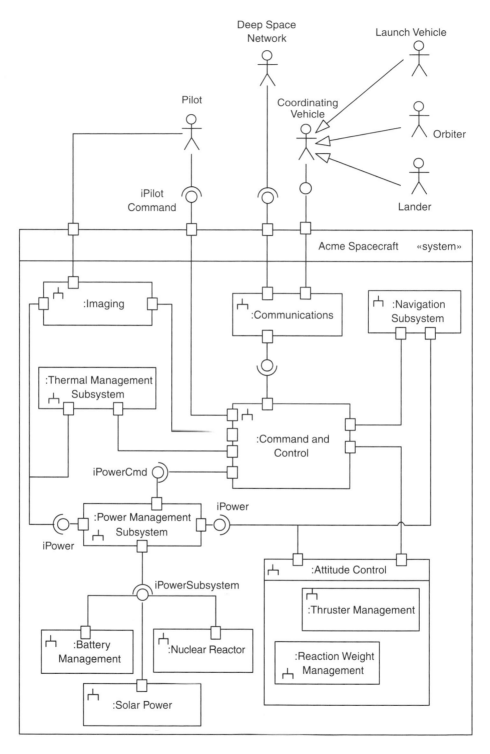

Figure 2-16: *Subsystem Example*

devices» such as DC motors, stepper motors, IR sensors, thermometers, force sensors, pressure transducers, and so on. The other kind of node, an execution environment, is a kind of virtualized device, such as the Java Virtual Machine.

Nodes connect to other nodes via *connections*, which represent the physical media through which the artifacts executing on the nodes send and receive messages. As with UML 1.x, a node is the only three-dimensional icon used, and artifacts may optionally be shown on them. While perhaps not strictly proper, it is still nevertheless perfectly reasonable to nest components in the nodes as well with the understanding that we are, in fact, executing the implementing artifact on the node.

Figure 2-17 shows a typical deployment diagram. The three-dimensional boxes are nodes—you can see that both textual stereotypes are used as well as icons, so you may use whichever you prefer. Several kinds of connections are shown, including Ethernet, RS485, RS232, and a digital line of exchanging messages and control information as well as a power bus. The artifacts inside the nodes may be indicated with the textual stereotype «artifact», or they may be shown with the more common artifact stereotype icon (a rectangle with a folded corner). These artifacts implement components which may also be shown within a constraint, as is done for a number of the artifacts. The artifacts shown are java files, .jar Java repositories, dynamic link libraries, and executable .exe files.

2.4.6 So, Nodes or Classes?

A node is a kind of structured class in the UML 2.0, so it has all the richness of classes—it may have behavior and state machines. This is important in systems engineering when these software and hardware elements must be executed, simulated, and/or analyzed for performance. This work can be done by representing all the elements—both hardware and software—as classes and then generating VHDL or SystemC for the ones that are realized in hardware and C, C++, or Ada for the ones that are realized in software. It is most likely more work to manually change nodes to classes and vice versa within design tools, so when different hardware/software breakdowns are to be evaluated, it probably is less work to just model everything as classes. Note that this applies for systems engineering (rather than software engineering) work primarily. If your project uses COTS (commercial off-the-shelf)

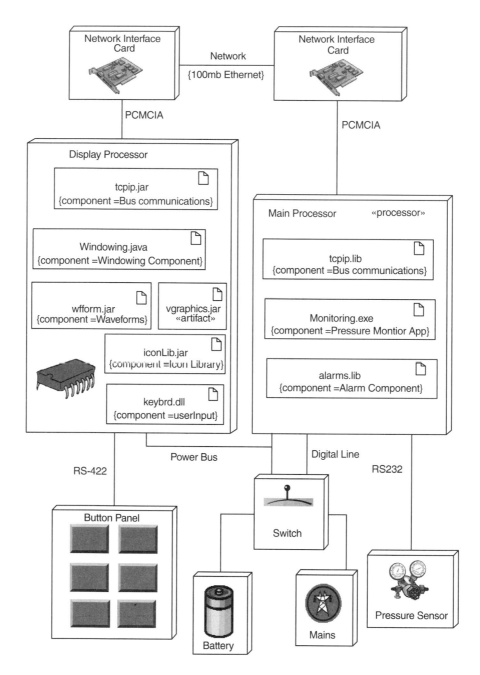

Figure 2-17: *Nodes and Deployments*

hardware or the hardware is not being codesigned, the decomposition of the system can be made more obvious by making the hardware pieces nodes and the software pieces classes. However, it really can be done either way.

2.4.7 Architectural Hierarchy

While the concepts of system, subsystem, and component are sufficiently flexible to support most any runtime organizational schema you would like to employ, I generally find it useful to use these concepts in a particular way. The system (shown with the «system» class stereotype) represents the entire system under development. The largest scale pieces of the system are «subsystem» objects (which, in systems engineering environments may contain hardware and software elements). Subsystems may in turn contain software (and other kinds of) components. Components may contain multiple threads, modeled with «active» objects. And the passive or semantic objects, which do the real work of the system, run within the «active» objects. For really large projects, you may have all of these levels and perhaps even multiples at one or more levels—for example, a large system might have subsystems decomposed into subsubsystems before you get to the component level. For simpler systems, you may not require all of these levels—you might skip the subsystem level and just have components. You may even find that, for very simple systems, you only need the system, «active» objects, and semantic objects. Your mileage may vary in terms of how you apply these concepts, but I have found this a useful way to use the organizational concepts in practice. This size hierarchy is shown in Figure 2-18.

This set of levels is a recommendation only and is not mandated (or even discussed) in the UML specification. In my experience, using the UML concepts in this way maps well to engineers' expectations.

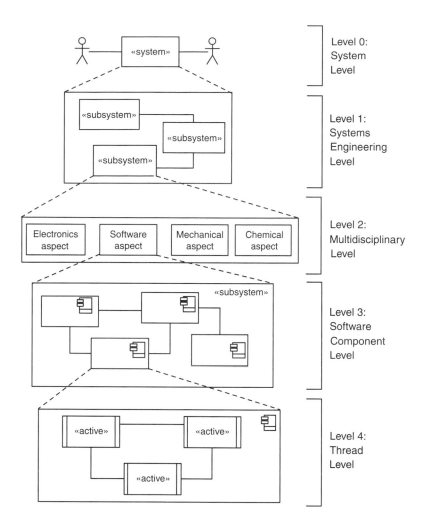

Figure 2-18: *Levels of Abstraction in Architecture*

2.5 Advanced: UML Metamodel of Structural Elements (for the Advanced Modeler)

Note: Here be dragons. . . .[7]

We've talked about the UML concepts quite a bit in this chapter. In this section, we discuss the UML internals in just a bit more detail. Models done in UML are done in what is called a four-layer metamodel architecture, as shown in Table 2-1.

The idea is that each layer is built using the elements specified in the layer above. The UML at the M2 level is constructed from a basis defined by the meta-metamodel at level M3, while user model elements (M1) are constructed using UML elements, such as classes, associations, and so on. The runtime model (M0) executes instances of the classes defined in the user model.

Table 2-1: *Metamodel Language Architecture*

Layer	Description	Examples
M3 Meta-metamodel	Provides a language for specifying metamodels, such as UML	Metaclass, meta-attribute, meta-association, meta-operation
M2 Metamodel	An instance of a modeling language, such as UML	Class, interface, attribute, association, operation, state, component
M1 User Model	Model of the user application or system done in the metamodel language	Sensor, DC motor, Gaussian filter, window, direction, speed, inertia, waveform, text display
M0 User Objects	Instances of the specification elements of the user model	Sensor [1], myMotor:Motor, MAF:Filter, mainWindow:Window

---

[7] These particular dragons are the most likely thing in this book to be wrong as the internals of the metamodel are reworked during the finalization process of the UML 2.0. However, their semantic meaning will be stable even if the details of the metarelations change, so for the average UML modeler, such changes will be largely irrelevant.

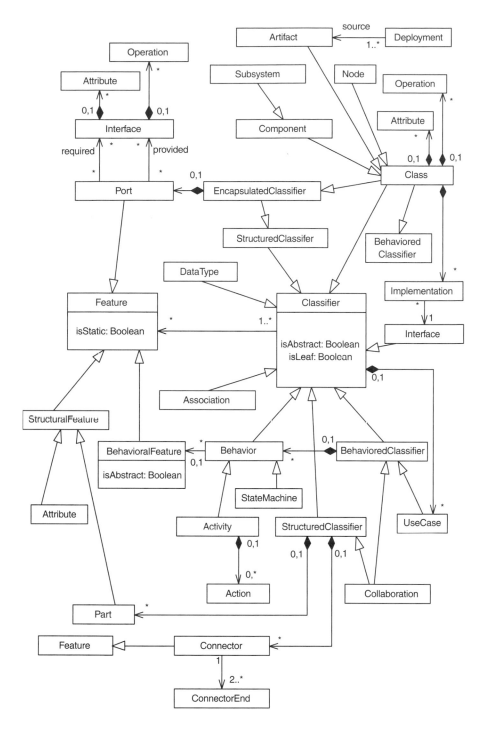

Figure 2-19: *Subset of UML Metamodel for Structural Elements*

That having been said, we've thrown around some UML metamodel elements such as classifier, class, component, subsystem, interface, and so on. The UML 2.0 specification is the ultimate arbitrator of what is or is not UML, and is a maintained (i.e., managed, updated, and revised) standard, so the particulars at any point in time might differ slightly from what is presented here. Nevertheless, it is useful to understand the metarelations between the meta-elements in the UML. Figure 2-19 shows the relation of the primary structural elements in the UML that we have discussed in this chapter.

The UML metamodel is, of course, (far) more complex than this. I have not shown all the relations among the elements, nor all the more abstract metasuperclasses, the most central metaclass being *Classifier*. Common *Classifiers* include *Class, DataType, Association, StructuredClassifier, Component, Subsystem, Node,* and *Use Case.* The fact that they have a common ancestry allows the common aspects to be captured in a single place. *Classifiers* associate with *Features*, which may be either *BehavioralFeatures* (such as operations) or *StructuralFeatures.* In addition, *BehavioredClassifiers* may have *Behaviors*, such as *Statemachines* or *Activities.*

2.6 Additional Notations and Semantics

UML is has a rich set of notations and semantics. This richness makes it applicable to a wide set of modeling applications and domains. In this chapter, we have only discussed the primary structural modeling facilities of UML. In the coming chapters, new notations within UML will be presented when the context requires them. A concise overview of the notation is provided in Appendix A. Some notational elements we wish to present here include the text note, the constraint, and the stereotype because they will be used in a variety of places throughout the book.

A text note is a diagrammatic element with no semantic impact. It is visually represented as a rectangle with the upper righthand corner folded down (similar to the icon used to indicate an artifact). Text notes are used to provide textual annotations to diagrams in order to improve understanding.

A constraint is some additional restriction (above the normal UML well-formedness rules) applied against a modeling element. Timing and other QoS constraints can be shown on any kind of diagram, but are commonly used in both structural and behavioral diagrams. Constraints are usually shown inside curly brackets, and may appear inside of text notes.

Figure 2-20 shows text notes and constraints used together in a class diagram. In the model shown in the figure, two active classes (i.e., classes that own the threads in which they execute) collaborate via a *Waveform* class resource. The *Sensor* class monitors the external environment and executes periodically at a rate of 100Hz (10 ms period), with a worst-case execution time of 3 ms. These quantitative properties of the *Sensor* class are captured in the curly braces commonly used to identify constraints. The constraints themselves are put into a note. As can be seen in the ordering constraint on the *WaveformSample* class, constraints don't have to be put inside of notes, but since it helps to visually set such annotations off, it is common to do so. The active classes are shown by the double-bordered box indicating that they are classes of the «active» stereotype (the text indication could have been used just as easily). The active classes are further stereotyped; specifically, they are stereotyped «SASchedulable» and «SAAction» from the *UML Profile for Schedulability, Performance, and Time,* the so-called "Real-Time Profile"[3]. These stereotypes define the specific tags that are used in the constraints, such as *isPeriodic, SAPriority,* and so on. The tags are called *tagged values* in the UML and their values are commonly specified inside constraints, just as they are here.

A stereotype is a particular kind of a standard modeling element, such as an «active» class, a «SAAction» kind of action (which is also applied to «active» classes in this model). A «SAResource» is a kind of classifier but has some additional properties, captured as tags, assigned to it. In this case, the capacity of the resource—the number of clients it can simultaneously service—is set to 1. The tags defined for a stereotype are assigned particular values in constraints. This allows developers to annotate quantitative, schedulability, and performance properties of their models. This is such an important topic, we will devote Chapter 4 to how to use these stereotypes, tagged values, and constraints effectively to model the concurrency and performance aspects of systems later in this book.

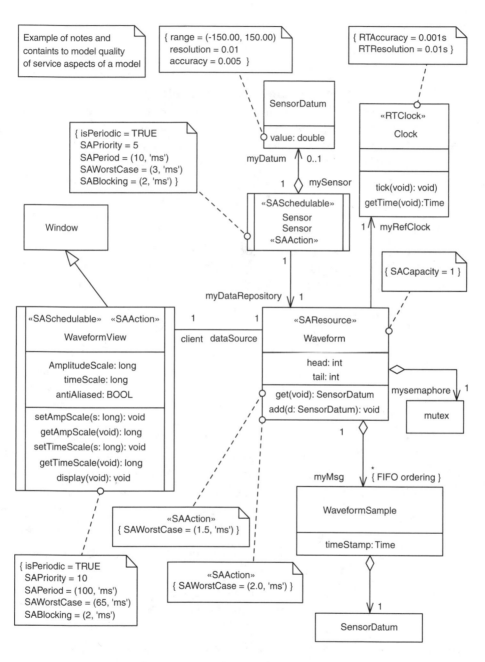

Figure 2-20: *Constraints in Action*

2.7 Looking Ahead

In this chapter, we've discussed the elements (metaclasses) available within UML for modeling system and software structure—things like classes, interfaces, ports, and objects at the small scale, and packages, components, subsystems, and nodes at the large scale. We've also identified the ways in which these elements may be linked together to form collaborations. What we have not yet discussed is how to model the behavior of these elements. The UML allows us to model the behavior of individual elements as well as to model the emergent behavior of interacting collaborations of elements. That is the subject of Chapter 3.

Chapter 4 focuses on concurrency and resource modeling, and techniques that are commonly used to model them. Special attention will be given to the "RT Profile" and how to apply it.

2.8 Exercises

1. What is the difference between a class and an object? When do they each exist?

2. What are the three essential features of an object?

3. What is an interface? How does it relate to a class?

4. Define precondition, postcondition, and signature. To what elements of an interface do they apply?

5. There are four types of visibility defined in UML. What are they and how are they indicated?

6. What does the term *abstract* mean in terms of class and operation? How is this visually denoted?

7. What are the three primary kinds of association in the UML? How are they shown diagrammatically and what is the semantic difference among them?

8. Name two ways of implementing interfaces in C++.

9. What is the key difference between a package and a subsystem?

10. What are the differences between a structured class, component, and subsystem?

11. What element *types* a port?

12. What are the two kinds of ports?

13. What is a node? What kind of diagram does it go on?

14. Identify, describe, and give two examples of each of the four metalevels.

15. Name four metaclasses that relate in some way to the classifier metaclass and describe their relationship.

16. Define the term *constraint* as it is used in UML.

17. What is a stereotype?

2.9 References

[1] *Unified Modeling Language Specification formal.* 01-09-67. Needham, MA: OMG, 2001 *www.omg.org.*

[2] *Unified Modeling Language: Superstructure Version 2.0.* ptc/03-08-02. Needham, MA: OMG, 2003. *www.omg.org.*

[3] *UML™ Profile for Schedulability, Performance, and Time Specification,* ptc/ 02-09-06. Needham, MA: OMG, 2002, *www.omg.org.*

[4] *UML Profile for Modeling Quality of Service and Fault Tolerance Characteristics and Mechanisms Revised Submission realtime.* 03-08-06. Needham, MA: OMG, 2003 *www.omg.org.*

[5] *UML Testing Profile Revised Submission ad* 03-03-26. Needham, MA: OMG, 2003 *www.omg.org.*

[6] Douglass, Bruce, *Doing Hard Time: Developing Real-Time Systems with UML, Objects, Frameworks, and Patterns.* Reading, MA: Addison-Wesley, 1999.

[7] Rumbaugh, James, Grady Booch, and Ivar Jacobson, *The UML Reference Guide.* Reading, MA: Addison-Wesley, 1999.

Chapter 3

Object Orientation with UML 2.0— Dynamic Aspects

Dynamics is the second primary aspect of the UML. Dynamics has to do with how values or states of objects change over time. The UML allows you to model both the specification of behaviors of individual objects (including systems, subsystems, and components) and the capturing traces of interactions among many objects working together. The former behavior is usually captured in statecharts or activity diagrams, while the latter is normally captured in sequence or timing diagrams.

Notation and Concepts Discussed

Types of Behavior	States	Interactions
Actions	Protocol State Machines	Sequence Diagrams
Activities		
Statecharts	Activity Diagrams	Timing Diagrams

3.1 Behavior and the UML

The previous chapter presented the structural elements defined within the UML—things like classes, objects, interfaces, ports, subsystems, and components—and how structural views of the system could be constructed from assemblies of these elements. The other pillar of object-oriented modeling is the specification of *dynamic behavior.* Behavior binds the structure of objects with their attributes and relationships so that objects can meet their responsibilities. Ultimately, actions implement an object's behavior, and the UML provides several approaches for linking action executions. One approach is to put the actions in the methods of classes, and the invocation of these actions takes place using the normal rules of the implementation action language. Common action languages are C, C++, Java, and Ada. Another approach for constraining these primitive actions into permissible sequences is through the use of activity diagrams—a generalized kind of flowchart that allows us to specify action execution, branching, looping, concurrency, and so on. The last primary facility in the UML for specifying action sequences is with state machines, especially when the object is "reactive," that is, its behavior is executed in response to received events. This chapter discusses these concepts in some detail.

The behavioral specification approach defines the behavior of individual elements (Classifiers). We must also concern ourselves with collaborative behavior—that is, behavior of collections of instances that work together to achieve a common, higher-level purpose, such as the realization of a use case. We model the behaviors of collaborations using *interactions.* Such interactions may be completely synchronous, relying on method calls, completely asynchronous, using various message-queuing schemes, or a combination of the two. The UML uses interaction diagrams such as sequence, collaboration, and timing diagrams to capture and represent interactions. Additionally, activity diagrams, with activities bound to swim lanes, may also specify interactions among objects represented by those swim lanes.

3.2 Types of Behavior

In the previous chapter we discussed the definition of structural elements of the system—classes and objects (in the small), and systems, subsystems, and components (in the large). As developers, we are usually even more concerned about how these structural elements behave dynamically as the system runs. Behavior can be divided up into two distinct perspectives—how structural elements act in isolation and how they act in collaboration.

In the UML metamodel, *Elements* are the primary structural elements that have behavior. *Classifiers* (which are types of *Elements*) also have *BehavioralFeatures*, such as *Operations*, and their realization, *Methods.* In practice, we are primarily concerned with the specification of the reactive behavior of only certain *Classifiers* (classes, objects, systems, subsystems, components, and use cases) and certain other *Elements (Actions, Operations, Methods, States, Events, Signals, and Transitions).*

Logically, behavior of single elements or groups of elements can be modeled as one of three distinct types: simple, stateful, and continuous. All three are important, although the second has a particular importance in real-time systems.

3.2.1 Simple Behavior

The most common kind of behavior is called *simple.* The object performs services on request and keeps no memory of previous services. Each action is atomic and complete, at least from an external perspective. A simple object may maintain a collection of primitive data types and operations defined to act on them. A binary tree object, for instance, shows simple behavior. Another example is a cos(x) function. cos($\pi/2$) always returns the same value, regardless of what value it was invoked with before. It retains no memory of previous invocations. This kind of object is also called *primitive* because it adds no additional constraints on the use of its operations.

An object exhibiting simple behavior always responds to a given input in exactly the same way, regardless of its history. Some examples of simple behaviors are

- Simple mathematical functions, such as cosine or square root

- A search operation of a static data structure that always starts from the same point, such as the search of a static binary tree
- Sort operations
- A knob that returns the number of clicks for a given user action

Note that simple behavior is also known as *functional* behavior, meaning that it defines simple behavior to be a mathematical function. Simple behavior is often modeled using activity diagrams, a topic covered in Section 3.4.8. Simple behavior is composable in the sense that if $g(c) = a$ and $f(a) = b$, then $f(g(c)) = b$.

3.2.2 State Behavior

The second type of object behavior treats the object as a particular type of machine, called a *finite state automaton* or *finite state machine* (FSM). This kind of object possesses a bounded (finite) set of conditions of existence (state). It must be in one and only one state at a time. An automaton exhibits modal behavior, each mode constituting a state. A state is defined to be a mutually exclusive condition of existence defined by the set of events it processes and the actions it performs. Because objects with state machines react to events in well-defined ways, they are also called *reactive objects*.

Incoming events can induce transitions between object states in some predefined manner.

A sample-and-hold A/D converter is such an object (see Figure 3-1). It shows the states of

- *Disabled:* In this state, the object is not acquiring data and the hardware inverters are turned off.
- *Enabled:* In this state, the hardware inverters are turned on and the object may be in one of the following states: ready to acquire data, actively acquiring data, or holding data that has been acquired.
- *Ready:* The object is enabled but has not yet begun to capture data.
- *Sampling:* The object is actively acquiring data.
- *Holding:* The object is holding data that it previously acquired.

The statechart semantics and notation are discussed in more detail later in this chapter. Nevertheless, we can see that the state machine

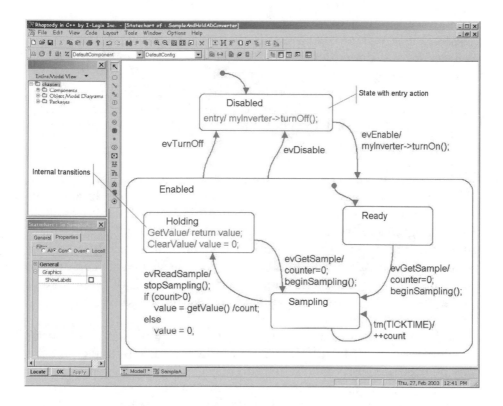

Figure 3-1: *State Machine for an Object*

controls the sequence of the execution of the actions defined within the statechart. For example, when the object is in the state of Ready and it receives a GetSample event, it initializes a counter attribute to zero and begins the sampling process. When in the Holding state, the object responds to the receipt of a GetValue request event by returning the value held in the object's attribute "value."

3.2.3 Continuous Behavior

The third kind of object behavior is called *continuous*. An object with continuous behavior is one with an infinite, or at least unbounded, set of existence conditions. One example is the so-called *algorithmic object*. This is an object that executes some algorithm on a possibly infinite data stream. A moving average filter performs a smoothing function over an incoming data stream. Objects with continuous behavior are objects whose current behavior is dependent on past behavior and inputs, but the dependency is of a continuous, rather than discrete nature. Fuzzy systems, PID[1] control loops, and digital filters are examples of objects exhibiting continuous behavior. Their current behavior depends on past history but in a quantitative not qualitative way.

All that is required for continuous behavior is that the current output depends on the previous history in a mathematically smooth way.

Although the UML is very expressly a discrete modeling language, it is possible to model continuous behavior by specifying actions on activity diagrams or statecharts. Since the UML doesn't define an action language (although it does define the things that an action language must be able to do), the continuous aspects are, strictly speaking, outside of the auspices of the UML.[2] Nevertheless, people can and do build systems that perform continuous behavior with differential and partial differential equations. This process is discussed in Chapter 10, which covers detailed design.

It is even sometimes appropriate to mix state and continuous behavior. For example, different sets of trajectory differential equations may be used, depending on whether a spacecraft is undergoing launch, achieving orbit, in orbit, or in cruise. Such systems are called *piece-wise continuous*. The way in which this is normally done is to define a different set of equations (or activity diagram) for each state of the object.

3.3 Behavior Primitives: Actions and Activities

In the UML, Classifiers (specifically *BehavioredClassifiers*) have behaviors, and one kind of behavior is called an *Activity*. Activities contain actions, the elemental quanta of UML behavior. Activities provide an

---

[1] PID, proportional integral-differential, is a common type of control theoretic system that uses feedback, integration, and differentiation to smoothly control continuous systems.

[2] As of this writing, work is under way on the "UML for Systems Engineering" specification. This work defines a means for modeling truly continuous behavior via extensions to activity diagrams. This UML extension is expected to be adopted by the OMG as a separate specification in late 2004 or 2005.

execution context for actions, including scope of values (e.g., variables) manipulated by a common set of actions. Activities may be represented textually by an action language or graphically in an activity diagram.

An action takes a (possibly empty) set of inputs and produces a (possibly empty) set of outputs. That is, it is a primitive, simple statement similar in scope to a single statement in a standard source-level language, such as "++X" or "a=b+sin(c*π)." Formally speaking, each input value enters the action on an Input Pin and each output value is sent to an Output Pin; however, for virtually all real modeling, the notions of pins can be safely ignored. It is enough to say that actions take input values and computationally produce a set of output values.

The UML specification identifies a number of kinds of actions, such as the following:

- CallOperationAction—an action that results in the synchronous invocation of an Operation or Method

- SendSignalAction—an action that results in the asynchronous transmission of an event

- BroadcastSignalAction—an action that results in the broadcast of a signal to all target objects in the system

- SendObjectAction— an action that sends a copy of a signal object to a target object

- PrimitiveAction—an action that cannot be decomposed into smaller subactions, such as simple mathematical functions

   Some types of PrimitiveActions include

- CreateObjectAction

- DestroyObjectAction

- TestIdentityAction

- ReadSelfAction

- ReadStructuralFeatureAction

- WriteStructuralFeatureAction

- ClearStructuralFeatureAction

- AddStructuralFeatureValueAction

- RemoveStructuralFeatureValueAction

- LinkAction (e.g., read, write, create, destroy)

- VariableAction (e.g., read, write, create, destroy)
- AcceptEventAction
- LoopAction
- ConditionalAction

This all may seem confusing (mostly because *it is*), but if you just remember that actions are meant to describe the kinds of statements you find in standard programming languages, you'll be all right. Actions are normally computationally simple things and, by far, are most commonly represented using an *action language*. The UML does not define an action language,[3] because most developers want to use the implementation source-level language for the action language in their models. That is, almost all of the time, actions in a UML model are specified in the implementation language of that system. A more abstract action language could be used, allowing the developer to generate code in multiple target languages, but the UML does not define one. There are advantages to using abstract language—independence of the model from the implementation being the primary one—but there are disadvantages as well, such as making the testing and debugging of the system more difficult. Whether the best action language is the implementation language or abstract action language depends on the nature of the application. If the application has a very long lifecycle or will be ported to multiple environments, then an abstract action language is arguably the best choice. If the application will remain on a single platform, if the difficulty of test and debugging the system is high, if it is clear that a single source language will be used in the implementation, or if you'd like be able to work in either the source language or the model, then using the implementation language to specify the actions will be preferred.

Actions are normally specified in one of three places: First, and most common, actions are simply entered into the bodies of methods defined within classes. This enables the generation of both simple and continuous behaviors, although in most action languages continuous behaviors are "discretized" and differential equations are represented using difference equations. Another common place for actions is in

---

[3] Although it does define the semantics for an action language, the UML does not define a syntax, a necessary aspect of any language.

statecharts. In statecharts, activities may be specified for execution when a state is entered or exited, when a particular transition is taken, or when special "do activities" are done after the entry activities are executed. Figure 3-1 shows examples of state entry and transition activities that are executed as the object moves from state to state. These activities may be simple textual lists of actions in the action language, or they may refer to activity diagrams for graphical representation.

Actions have "run-to-completion" semantics, meaning that once an action is started it will run until it is done. This does not mean that an action cannot be preempted by another action running in a higher-priority thread, merely what when the context executing that action returns from preemption, it will continue executing that action until it is complete before doing anything else. This means that if an object is executing an action, the action will run to completion even if that object receives events directing it to do something else. The object will not accept the incoming events until the action has completed. For this reason, actions are usually, although not always, short in duration.

Activities do not have run-to-completion semantics. Activities may be interruptible between their contained actions.[4] An object executing a "do activity" may receive an event that triggers a transition in its state machine, exiting the state and terminating the activity. Thus, the UML allows the modeling, at a primitive level, of both interruptible and non-interruptible behaviors. Activities are most often represented on activity diagrams and are composed of sequences of action executions that proceed largely through completion (i.e., they progress by completing actions as opposed to waiting for events of interest).

An *operation* is a specification of an invocable behavior of a Classifier, whereas a Method is the implementation of an Operation. That is, an Operation is a specification of a Method. Operations are synchronously invoked with CallActions and are logically associated with CallEvents in the UML metamodel. Operations have typed parameter lists, as you might expect, and can return typed values. It is common to use an operation call as an action on a state behavior.

Modeling of the behavior of an operation is done primarily in two ways. First, and most common, is to simply list, in a textual fashion, all

---

[4] Entry, exit, and transition activities have run-to-completion (i.e., noninterruptible) semantics, while do activities are interruptible.

of the actions comprising the internals of the operation or method, such as "write the code" for the method. The second, which will be described shortly, is to model the operation with a synchronous state machine or with an activity diagram.

3.4 Behavior and the Single Object

In state machines designed by traditional structured methods, the portion of the system exhibiting the state behavior is not clearly defined. Some set of functions and data collaborate together in a way that lends itself to finite state modeling, but generally this set is only vaguely defined. In object-oriented methods, the programmatic unit exhibiting state behavior is clear—only *Classifiers,* such as systems, subsystems, components, classes, and use cases, can define state models, and only instances of those Classifiers can execute state machines.

The two fundamental concepts of statecharts are *State* and *Transition.* A State is a condition of existence of an instance that is distinguishable from other such conditions. States that are disjoint are called *or-states* because the object must be in one such state or another.

Figure 3-2 shows a simple class diagram for a PBX telephone system. We see that *Telephones* associate with *Lines,* which in turn associate with *Connections* and *Call Routers.* The lower part of the figure shows the statechart for the relatively simple class *Telephone.*

3.4.1 Basic Statechart Elements

States are shown as rounded rectangles. As mentioned earlier, states are conditions of existence of the class they define. In this case, the instances of the Telephone class may be in the or-state of "On Hook" or "Off Hook." These are or-states because the Telephone *must* be in one of them but cannot be in both of them. While the Telephone is in the On Hook state, it may be either in an Idle state or in a Incoming Ringing state (because a remote caller is calling). These are also or-states but are nested within the composite state On Hook. When the Telephone is in the On Hook state, it *must* be in one of these nested substates, and so these nested states are also or-states, but their context is the enclosing composite state.

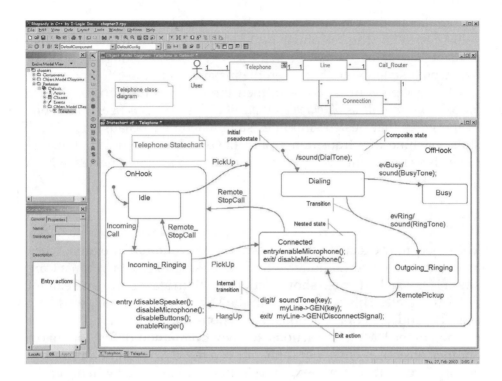

Figure 3-2: *Telephone Statechart*

Nesting of states is a very straightforward idea. If you were at the Embedded Systems Conference[5] in San Francisco and I called you and asked you if you were in California, you'd say "Yes" because you *are* in the state of California. If I ask if you were in San Francisco, you might say "Yes, but next week I'll be in LA, so I'll still be in California." What you're saying is that you're in the nested state "San Francisco" now but later you'll be in the nested state "LA." In both cases you'll be in the state of California. Statecharts have a built-in operator IN() (sometimes called IS_IN()) that you can apply to a stateful object, and it will return TRUE if the object is in that state when the operation is invoked. Thus, if the Telephone is in the state of Incoming Ringing, IN(Incoming Ringing) will return TRUE, but so will IN(On Hook). IN(Idle) and IN(Off Hook) will both return FALSE in this case.

---

[5] A highly recommended state to be in!

Similar to the On Hook state, the Off Hook state also has nested substates. While the Telephone is Off Hook, it can be in one (at a time) of its nested states—it may be in a Dialing, Outgoing Ringing, Busy, or Connected state. Note that when the instance is in the Off Hook state, if a Hang Up event is received, then the object transitions to the On Hook state *regardless of which substate of Off Hook was active.* This is one of the ways that nested simplifies state machines, because in a "flat" state machine this transition would have to be drawn four times to have the same semantics, one from each of the states nested within Off Hook.

3.4.1.1 State Features

The object may execute actions when a state is entered or exited, when an event is received (although a transition isn't taken), or when a transition is taken. Figure 3-3 shows actions on both state entry and exit for the *Ready* state. This is shown with the key word *entry,* followed by a slash (/) and a list of the actions. The actions may be any kind of action defined in the UML—call actions (to invoke a method defined in this or another object), event generation, or even the execution of a primitive action statement such as ++x. Entry actions are executed whenever the *Ready* state is entered, regardless of which transition path was taken to get there, whether it is the transition invoked by the event *evToReady* or the transition-to-self invoked by the event *evRedo.* The *Ready* state also has exit actions that are executed whenever the object leaves this state regardless of which transition path is taken to exit the state. The syntax is the same as for entry actions except for the key word *exit.*

Notice in Figure 3-2 that the associated *Line* object is notified when the phone transitions from the Off Hook to the On Hook state by the generation of a *DisconnectSignal* event. This action is executed whenever the object leaves the Off Hook state regardless of which transition path is taken. Note that transitions among the internal nested states of Off Hook don't cause this action to execute because the object doesn't leave the enclosing composite state Off Hook until it transitions to the On Hook state.

Internal transitions are similar to "transitions to self"—that is, transitions that begin and end on the same state. However, with a transition to self, both the exit and entry actions are performed in addition to the actions specified on the transition itself. In the case of the transition to self initiated by the event *evRedo* in Figure 3-3, the order of execution of actions is

- Exit actions, such as $--x$; $y = \cos(\mathrm{sqrt}(x))$
- Transition actions, such as cout << "redoing . . ." << endl
- Entry actions, such as $++x$; $y = \mathrm{foo}(x\^{}2)$

An internal transition executes neither the exit nor the entry actions of the state; in response to the specified event, it executes only the particular actions identified for the internal transition. In Figure 3-3, state *Ready* has two internal transitions, one of the event *keyPress* and another on the event *knobTurn*. If either of these events occur when the object is in that state, then only their respective actions are performed, not the entry and exit actions for the state.

The activities (and their nested actions) defined for state entry or exit, or specified on transitions, are simple run-to-completion behaviors. States may also specify do activities, as discussed in the previous section. Such activities are not run-to completion; in fact, when such an activity is executing in a state and the object receives an incoming event

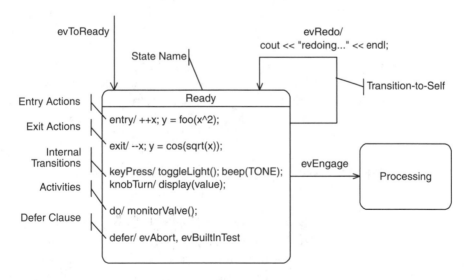

Figure 3-3: *State Internal Features*

that is processed while in that state, the activity aborts and the specified transition is taken. Do activities are specified with the syntax

do activity-name

where *activity-name* is the name of the activity to be executed. Such activities may be only specified within states and begin after the completion of that state's entry actions. In practice, activities are only rarely used in statecharts, and most of the primitive behavior executed by a statechart is expressed in various actions.

Sometimes an object may be in a state where processing an event would be inappropriate, but you'd like that object to remember that the event occurred and process once it transitions to the next state. The *defer* clause allows you to specify exactly that. Following the key word *defer* is a list of events to be deferred. The semantics of the defer clause are that, should one of the deferred events occur, it will not be processed but it will be remembered. As long as the object transitions to states where that event is in a defer clause, the event will continue to be remembered. As soon as the object transitions to state where the event is no longer deferred then it will be processed; that is, it will either fire a transition, fire an internal transition, or be discarded.

3.4.1.2 Transitions

Transitions are directed arcs beginning at the starting state and finishing at the target state. Transitions usually have named event triggers optionally followed by actions (i.e., executable statements or operations) that are executed when the transition is taken. The *event signature* for a transition is of the form

event-name '(' parameter-list ')' '[' guard-expression ']'
'/' action-list

All of these fields are optional. A transition without an event signature fires as soon as the state is entered (i.e., its entry actions have completed) or, if there are do activities defined within the state, as soon as those activities complete. That having been said, most transitions do specify at least the event-name. Table 3-1 details the fields of the event signature.

Table 3-1: *Transition Syntax*

Field	Description
Event-name	The name of the event triggering the transition.
Parameters	A comma-separated list containing the names of data parameters passed with the event signal.
Guard	A Boolean expression that must evaluate to TRUE for the transition to be taken. The expression should not have side effects such as assigning values.
Action list	A list of operations executed as a result of the transition being taken. These operations may be of this or another object.

3.4.1.3 Events

The UML defines four kinds of events:

- *SignalEvent:* An event associated with a Signal. A Signal is a specification of an asynchronous communication, so a SignalEvent is an event associated with an asynchronously received signal.

- *CallEvent:* An event associated with a Call. A Call is a specification of a synchronous communication, so a CallEvent allows one object to affect the state of another by invoking one of its methods directly.

- *TimeEvent:* An event associated with the passage of time, usually indicated with either tm(<duration>) or after(<duration>). Almost all TimeEvents are relative time; that is, they specify that the event will occur after the object has been in the specified state for at least <duration> time units. If the object leaves that state before the timeout has elapsed, then the logical timer associated with that duration disappears without creating the timeout event.

- *ChangeEvent:* An event associated with the change in value for an attribute. It is rarely used in software applications; however, when a state attribute is memory mapped onto a piece of hardware, it can be used to indicate that the memory address changed value.

Events may specify formal parameter lists, meaning that events may carry actual parameters. In Figure 3-2, for example, we could have show the *digit* event pass a value indicating which key was pressed, such as 0 or #, by using the transition

digit(key: keyType) / show(key)

Some tools use alternative notations, such as not referring explicitly to the parameter in the parameter list but using a special pointer called *params* to point to the passed parameters. In this case, the full transition might be something like this:

digit / show(params->key)

In either case, the action *show* accepts the parameter *key* and displays it on the screen. In order to generate this event from another object, you might use a helper macro in a tool such as Rhapsody with

GEN(digit(EnterKey))

where EnterKey is of the same type as params->key. Alternatively, if the event is synchronous, you might just a method on the object to send a CallEvent, as in

myTelephone->digit(key)

which dereferences a pointer called myTelephone to an instance of class Telephone, and calls a method called *digit* passing the appropriate parameter.

Sometimes a transition will appear without a named event in its signature. This is called an *anonymous transition* or a *completion event*. Such a transition fires when the predecessor state is entered; that is, when the state's entry actions have completed and the activities, if any, have completed. If there are no activities defined within the state, then the anonymous transition fires as soon as the state's entry actions have completed. If there are activities, and another event that fires another transition comes in before the activities complete, then the activities are aborted and the named transition is taken. This is the primary difference between actions (which are run-to-completion) and activities (which are interruptible).

Some examples of legal transitions are

1. E1
2. E1 [x < mySensor->Value)]
3. E1 (x: float) / y = filter(x*100)
4. E1 (x: float, y:long) [abs(x) > abs(y^2) > 0] / result = x / y
5. [mySensor->IS_IN(Has_Data)] / value =filter(mySensor->get Value())
6. / y = sqrt(x^2 + y^2); z = 2*y - 3

The first transition specifies only an event. The second specifies an event with a guard. The third passes a parameter and then uses the value of that parameter in an assignment computation. The fourth combines a named event with two passed parameters, a guard, and an action. The fifth has no named event trigger but does have a guard and an action. The sixth just specifies an action list (containing two actions) but not a named event or a guard.

3.4.1.4 Guards

The guard expression is a Boolean expression, enclosed between square brackets, that must evaluate to either true or false. Care must be taken to ensure that guards do not have any side effects, such as changing an attribute's value. Typical guards will specify invariants that should be true before a transition is taken, such as [x>0] (returning TRUE that the object's attribute x has a value of greater than zero) or [myLine->IS_IN(Idle)] (TRUE when the associated object referred to via the myLine pointer is currently in the Idle state). Guards are a very simple way to ensure preconditions are met, such as that the door is closed before powering the emitter in a microwave oven (an important consideration for repeat business!).

3.4.1.5 Action Execution Order

Actions do the real work of a state machine. The state machine is important because it defines the possible set of sequences of action executions under a (possible large) set of circumstances. Nevertheless, the actions are where the object actually does something interesting in the real world.

The order of execution of actions is important. The basic rule is exit-transition-entry. That is, the exit action of the predecessor state is executed first, followed by the actions on the transition, followed by the entry actions of the subsequent state. In the presence of nesting, exit actions are executed in an inner-to-outer fashion, while entry actions are executed from outer-to-inner. In the example of Figure 3-2, when taking the transition "pick up" while the object is in the state *Incoming Ringing* the order of action execution would be

1. IncomingRinging exit actions
2. On Hook exit actions
3. Pick up transition actions
4. Off Hook entry actions
5. Connected entry actions

3.4.2 And-States

We have already discussed the semantics of or-states; if A and B define the set of possible or-states of a specific context, then the object must be either A or B at all times. It cannot be in both and it cannot be in neither. The UML also has the notion of and-states to model conditions that must be simultaneously true and independent.

Statecharts provide a very clear yet succinct representation of and-states, as shown in the simple Microwave Oven object example in Figure 3-4. This object exhibits four independent state aspects—cooking, timing, display, and door monitoring. Obviously, for safe and effective operation, all these activities must go on simultaneously. These independent state aspects are called *and-states* and are separated with dashed lines. The and-states are often referred to as *regions,* or *orthogonal regions.* And-states are always substates of an enclosing composite state.

Each of the and-states is named and operates independently of the others, as if they are concurrent—and in an important sense they are. What do we mean by *concurrent* in this case? Basically the same as in other cases—that the processing within an and-state proceeds independently from processing in other, peer and-states, and you cannot *in*

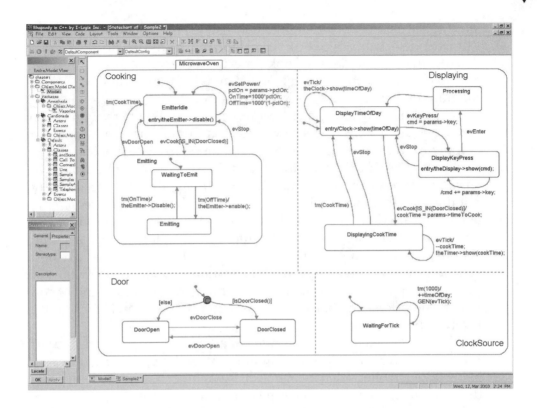

Figure 3-4: *Statechart of Object with And-States*

principle predict which and-state will process an event first. Each active and-state basically receives its own personal copy of any event received by the object and is free to independently process or discard that event, as appropriate. This means (and we'll see why this is important in a moment), that multiple and-states may process the same event when an event is received by the object.

The complete "state" of the object is the cross-product of all of its currently active and-states. The Microwave Oven may be, for example, in the state of [Emitting, DisplayingCookTime, DoorClosed, and Waiting ForTick], or it may be in the state of [EmitterIdle, DisplayingTimeOf Day, DoorOpen, and WaitingForTick]. And-states make the specification of independent aspects of a stateful object much more parsimonious as compared with normally Mealy-Moore (M&M) state machines. M&Ms don't have the notion of and-states and so must display the state space as an explicit enumerated list, giving rise to states named "Emitting-DisplayingCookTime-DoorClosed-WaitingForTick," "NotEmitting-DisplayingCookTime-DoorClosed-WaitingForTick," and so on. This is obviously a long list, making the creation of the state diagram in Figure 3-4 with M&Ms a daunting task.[6]

The addition of and-states to your state-modeling paradigm is very powerful, but it also creates new questions. For example, how do I synchronize and communicate among peer and-states when necessary?

There are four primary ways that and-states can communicate, synchronize, and collaborate. Remember, first of all, that it is the *object* and not the state that receives incoming events. When an object receives an event, it is acted upon by *all* of its active and-states and that action may be to take a transition, execute an "internal transition" (execute a set of actions without changing state), or discard it. It is as if each active and-state receives its own copy of the incoming event to do with as it pleases, independently of all the other and-states. This is a kind of contained "broadcast" in that all active and-states receive each event as it is received by the object.

The second means for and-state collaboration are *propagated events.* Propagated events are events that are sent as the result of a transition being taken in one and-state or object. Remember, the UML defines two different kinds of actions that can be used to create such events—Send Actions (resulting in SignalEvents) and CallActions (resulting in CallEvents). Call actions must be used carefully as propagated events as they execute in the same run-to-completion step as the initiating event.

Another means for and-state collaboration is with the IS_IN( ),[7] which returns TRUE if another and-state is currently in the specified nested state. This allows for and-state coordination. In Figure 3-4, we see the IS_IN() operator used in guards; for example in the Cooking region the evCook transition is protected with an IS_IN(DoorClosed) guard to ensure that we don't cook the chiefs!

3.4.3 Pseudostates

The UML defines a number of different pseudostates, as shown in Figure 3-5. Pseudostates indicate the use of special semantics; they are not

---

[6] Exercise left to the reader.

[7] IN( ) is another common form for this operator.

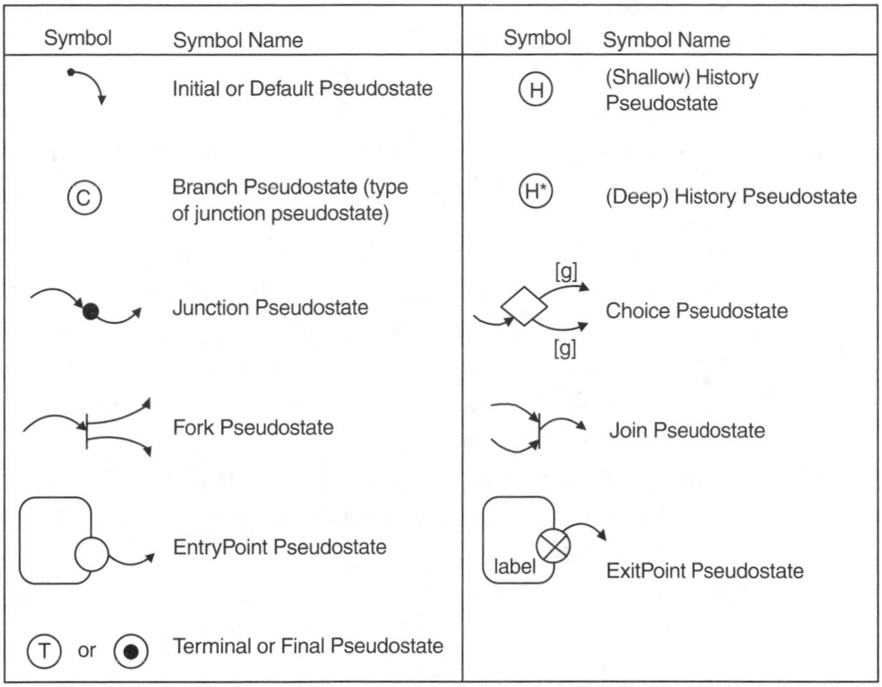

Symbol	Symbol Name	Symbol	Symbol Name
	Initial or Default Pseudostate	(H)	(Shallow) History Pseudostate
(C)	Branch Pseudostate (type of junction pseudostate)	(H*)	(Deep) History Pseudostate
	Junction Pseudostate	[g] [g]	Choice Pseudostate
	Fork Pseudostate		Join Pseudostate
	EntryPoint Pseudostate	label	ExitPoint Pseudostate
(T) or (●)	Terminal or Final Pseudostate		

Figure 3-5: *UML Pseudostates*

in any way states, but they are used as annotations of some defined special state chart behaviors. The UML 2.0 has removed a few of the lesser used pseudostates, such as the synch pseudostate, and replaced the stub pseudostate with the entry point and exit point pseudostates.

Briefly, these pseudostates are as follows:

- *Initial or default:* Within a composite state context, the initial pseudo-state indicates which substate is initially entered as a default. The initial pseudostate may be overridden, either by transitioning directly to a different nested state or with the history pseudostate.

- *Terminal or final:* The final state indicates that the enclosing composite state is terminated. If the final state appears in the outermost level of nesting, it indicates that the object no longer accepts any event, usually because it is about to be destroyed.

- *Junction:* Vertices used to join together multiple transitions, or to divide a transition into a set of sequential transition segments.

Regardless of the number of transition segments connected, they all execute in a single run-to-completion step.

- *Branch or conditional:*[8] The branch pseudostate indicates a set of possible target or-states, one of which will be selected on the basis of a guarding condition. The branch pseudostate is nothing more than a junction with guards on exiting transition segments. However, it was called out in previous versions of the UML with a special icon (usually a ©) and is still indicated using an independent icon by many modeling tools so it is separately identified here.

- *Choice point:* A choice point is a kind of junction that executes its action list before going on to the next transition segment. This allows actions bound to the first transition segment to execute prior to the evaluation of subsequent guards.

- *Shallow history:* This pseudostate indicates that the default state of a composite state is the last state visited of that composite state, *not* including nested substates.

- *Deep history:* This pseudostate indicates that the default state of a composite is the last state visited of that composite state, including substates nested arbitrarily deeply.

- *Join:* A connector that joins multiple incoming transitions from peer and-states into a single transition. This is not the same as a junction. (And-states are discussed in Section 3.4.2.)

- *Fork:* A connector that branches into multiple transitions, each entering a different and-state, from a single input transition. This is not the same as a branch because in a branch only a single transition activates; in a fork, all outgoing transition segments activate.

- *Entry point:* An entry point is used in conjunction with a composite state to serve as a connector between its nested states and its peer states. It is usually not used unless the nested states are hidden and put on a separate state diagram.

- *Exit point:* An entry point is used in conjunction with a composite state to serve as a connector between its nested states and its peer

---

[8] This pseudostate was removed in the 1.3 revision of the UML, after it was noted to be just a kind of the junction pseudostate. However, since it is still widely used in tools, I have continued to use it here.

states. It is usually not used unless the nested states are hidden and put on a separate state diagram.

3.4.3.1 Initial Pseudostate

Whenever a class defines a statechart there is always the question of what state the object starts in when it is created. This is indicated with the initial (or default) pseudostates. This special annotation is a transition with a ball at one end. In Figure 3-2, the Telephone enters the state On Hook when it is first created. Because composite states have states nested inside, it must also contain an indication as to which nested state is the default (Idle, in this case; Dialing, in the case of the Off Hook state). When a transition terminates on the composite state, the default pseudostates inside the composite state indicate which nested state is entered initially. The default nested state can be bypassed by drawing a transition directly to a different nested state if desired, as illustrated by the transition from the Incoming_Ringing state to the Connected state.

To be well formed, a statechart must have an initial pseudostate to specify the starting state when an object is created. Additionally, each composite state must indicate the initial pseudostate for its nested states, and each and-state region must have an initial pseudostate as well.

3.4.3.2 Branches and Junctions

Transitions may be broken up into segments with the junction pseudostate. A complete transition path may have only a single event associated with triggering it, but they may join, to share actions. Junctions may have multiple incoming transitions as illustrated in junction pseudostate 1 in Figure 3-6. Both transitions share the common branch of the exiting transition. Junction pseudostates may also have multiple exiting transitions, provided they are all guarded, as shown with junction pseudostate 2 in the same figure. The guard selects which transition path will be taken. It is important to note that if all the guards evaluate to FALSE, then no transition will be taken from the originating state—the state machine must have a complete, valid path to a subsequent state before an event may trigger a transition. Note that in the figure, if state 1 is the current state and the event ev2 occurs, at least one of the guards exiting junction pseudostate 2 *must* evaluate to TRUE or

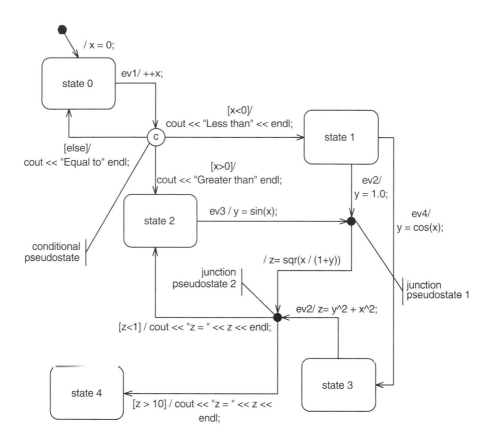

Figure 3-6: *Branches and Junctions*

the event will be discarded without executing any action; that is, before any actions will be taken, z must either be greater than 10 or less than 1.

Older UML use the conditional pseudostate (©) to indicate conditional branching; however, in later revisions of the UML, the junction pseudostate included the conditional pseudostate because any junction may have multiple guarded exiting transitions. The figure shows a typical use of the conditional pseudostate as well as a semantic trap. Can you spot it?

The question is, starting in state 0, when the event ev1 is received, to what state will the object transition? Most people think (incorrectly) that the object will transition to state 2 because of the preincrement of x in the event signature action list. However, the guard is evaluated prior to the execution of any actions; therefore the else clause (which evaluates to TRUE when all the other exiting branches all evaluate to FALSE) is taken because at the time of evaluation of the guards, the value of the attribute x is zero.

Another interesting question is what happens if multiple guards evaluate to true. The UML specifies that one of the true branches will be taken, but which one is indeterminate? After all, whichever branch is taken will have a TRUE guard condition. Normally, when multiple exiting transitions fire, it indicates a modeling error, and the model is said to be ill-formed. Don't let this happen to you![9]

3.4.3.3 Choice Points

Because actions are only executed if a transition is taken, they are *not* executed before the guards are evaluated. This is because the guards must be evaluated *prior* to the execution of the actions. Sometimes this is an inconvenient thing to do. In these cases, you should use choice points instead. A *choice point* is a specialized form of junction used when the result of an action executed during a transition is to be used in a guard. In this case, the actions on the initial segment of a compound transition are executed *before* checking the guard. The notation for a choice point is a diamond, but otherwise it looks like a conditional pseudostate.

Choice points are dangerous in use because the actions are executed before the guards are evaluated. If the guards should all evaluate to FALSE, then the object is no longer in a valid state. Because of the likelihood of this happening, I recommend that you not use choice points, but use junctions (or conditionals) instead. If you stick with junctions, then the object will always remain in a valid state when the guards evaluate to FALSE.

3.4.3.4 History

As we have seen, composite states are decomposed into nested states. The default nested state for a composite state is indicated with an initial pseudostate. When the composite state is exited and later reentered,

---

[9] In the general case, this is very difficult to automatically check for, because the guards may invoke operations that have nested operations. Therefore, modeling tools don't usually check for this kind of error.

the same nested state is again reentered. But what if the semantics you want are not to reenter the same nested state but to instead reenter the *last active* nested state?

The statechart answer is *history.* The history pseudostate is a letter "H" in a circle. Figure 3-7 shows the different aspects of the history pseudostate. To be activated, the transition must terminate on it, as with the transition from state 0, labeled e1, and the transition labeled e2 from state 1. Both of these transitions terminate on the history pseudostate. The transition labeled e0 from state 0 does not, so the normal default (to nested state a1) is activated whenever that transition is taken. However, if the active state is state a2 when transition e1 is taken, followed by transition labeled e2, then, the object reenters state a2. Of course, when the object is in state a2, it must also be in one of its nested states. Because of the kind of history used for composite state A, the default nested state for state a2 will always be reentered even if the last active nested state was state a24.

There is another kind of history as well—deep history. Deep history differs in that while shallow history only applies to the immediate level of nested and no deeper, deep history applies through all levels of nesting no matter how deep. Deep history is indicated with a circumscribed H*, and is shown in composite state B. When the current state is state b23, and the object receives an event f1 (taking it to the default state of composite state A) followed by an event f0, the object reenters the state b23. As before, transitions that do not terminate on the history pseudostate don't activate the history semantics.

3.4.3.5 Forks and Joins

When a composite state with and-state regions is entered, the default state for each of the regions is entered. But what if you want to bypass those default states under some circumstances? As with many of the other pseudostates, there are special pseudostates for explicitly doing nondefault behavior. In the case of and-states, these are the *fork and join* pseudostates.

If you want to bypass the default for a normal (or-) composite state you simply draw the transition directly to the desired nested state. However, in the case of entering and-state regions you have multiple branches you'd need to specify. That is exactly what the fork pseudostate does. Unlike with or-states, where multiple branches indicate

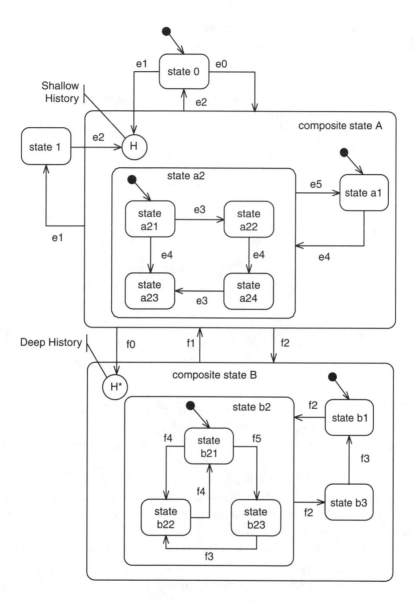

Figure 3-7: *History*

selection (since only one branch can be taken), the multiple transitions exiting a fork indicate *concurrency*, at least in the logical sense, because *all* branches are taken, essentially at the same time. Figure 3-8 shows a fork in use. The default nested states are the InitTool and the InitArm

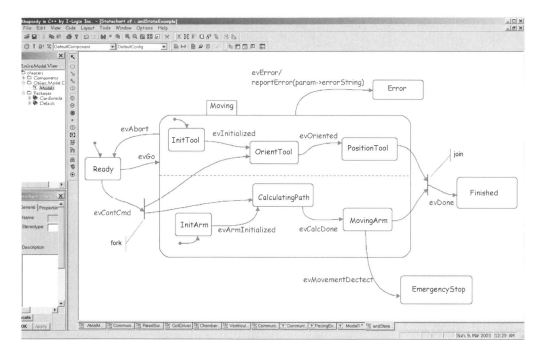

Figure 3-8: *Forks and Joins*

states, and these states are entered when the transition labeled evGo is taken. However, when the transition labeled evContCmd is taken, then these defaults are bypassed and the states orientTool and calculating-Path are taken instead.

Conversely, the evError transition exits the Moving state, regardless of which of the states nested within the and-state regions are active. If you want to specify a single nested state in one and-state and the other and-states are "don't cares," then you can initiate a transition from the (single) desired substate, as is done with the evMovementDetect transition leaving the moveArm state; it doesn't matter what nested state is active in the other and-state, when moveArm is active and the object receives the evMovementDetect event, the transition is taken. When you want to specify multiple predecessor states, then you must specify which ones you mean—this means joining multiple branches. That is the purpose of the join pseudostate. In the figure, both positionTool and MoveArm must be active for the transition labeled evDone to be taken. If either of those states is not active when that event is received, then the event is simply discarded. The join can only be initiated by a single event; that is, you cannot join transitions resulting from the receipt of multiple events.

3.4.3.6 Submachines, Entry, and Exit Points

Previously, we've seen that or-states and and-states can be nested within other states. In most cases, the entire state machine will be specified on a single statechart, using whatever level of nesting is called for. In large, complex statecharts, this can lead to diagrams that are difficult to decipher. For this reason, the internal state decomposition of a superstate can be defined on a separate statechart called a *submachine*. Figure 3-9a shows the same state machine from Figure 3-2, now hiding the internal structures of the OnHook and OffHook composite states. As long as transitions initiate or terminate on the border of the composite state, the defaults are used. For transitions terminating on the composite state, the initial state will be entered; for transitions initiating on the composite state, the transition will be taken regardless of what nested state of the composite is currently active. But what if a transition initiates only from a specific nested or terminates on a nondefault state? How can this be shown?

The answer is to use entry and exit points. These are the circles on the state boundaries shown in Figure 3-9. The empty circles are entry points—they indicate that a transition terminating (from outside the composite state) on the entry point will be delegated to a specific, but not-shown state inside the composite. The circles containing a cross are called *exit points.* A transition originating from that pseudostate arises from some specific, but not-shown nested state inside the composite.

Figures 3-9b and 3-9c show the internals of the composite states from Figure 9-9a. The entry and exit points are explicitly named so they can clearly specify which transition paths they define. I have used the name of the initiating or terminating state in the name of the entry and exit point labels, but any meaningful label may be used.

3.4.4 Inherited State Models

UML 1.x was a bit vague on how to interpret the inheritance of state machines when a stateful class was specialized. UML 2.0 is more precise on this matter. In order to ensure compliance with the Liskov Substitution

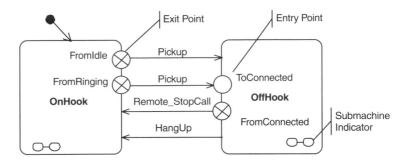

Figure 3-9a: *Referencing State Machine*

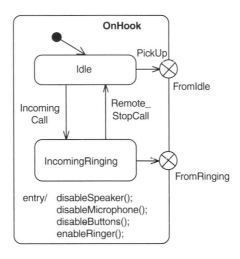

Figure 3-9b: *OnHook Submachine*

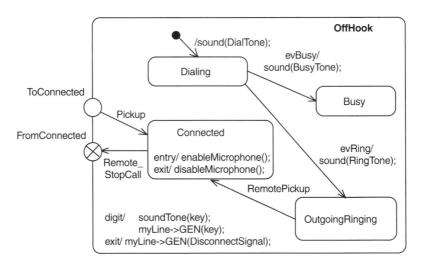

Figure 3-9c: *OffHook Submachine*

Principle (that instances of subclasses must be freely substitutable for instances of their superclass) some rules must govern the modifications that can be made to an inherited state model:

- New states and transitions may be freely added in the child class.
- States and transitions defined by the parent cannot be deleted (the subclass must accept all events and messages that can be accepted by the parent).
- Action and activity lists may be changed (actions and activities may be added or removed) for each transition and state.
- Actions and activities may be specialized in the subclass (i.e., actions may be polymorphic).
- Substates may not alter their enclosing superstate (including adding a new one).
- Transitions may be retargeted to different states.
- Orthogonal components may be added to inherited states.

A simple example of inherited state models is provided in Figure 3-10. The class model is shown at the upper left of the figure. The class *Blower* has a simple on-off state model (shown at the upper right). The *evSwitch On* transition has a single action in its action list, the function powerMotor(). The *Dual Speed Blower* class extends the *Blower* class by adding *Low* and *High* speed substates to the On state. Note that the action for the *evSwitchOn* transition is now changed to the execution of the functions LED(ON) and setPower(LOW). Additionally, the Off state now has an entry action and the action for the *evSwitchOff* transition has been changed. The *Dual Speed Multiheat Blower* class continues the specialization by adding three heat settings as an orthogonal component to the *Low* and *High* states added by the previous subclass. Also action lists have been changed. Nevertheless, the generalization taxonomy is clear from the statecharts that a Dual Speed Multiheat Blower is still a kind of Dual Speed Blower, and a Dual Speed Blower is, in fact, a kind of Blower.

3.4.5 Ill-Formed Statecharts

A wise man once said that any language rich enough to say all the things you want also provides the ability to state nonsense.[10] Statecharts

---

[10] It's one of Douglass's Laws. See [2].

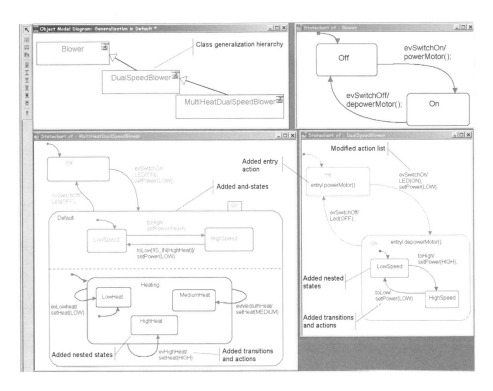

Figure 3-10: *Inherited Statecharts*

are certainly no exception. When a statechart makes a nonsensical statement, we say that it is *ill-formed.* Figure 3-11 shows some ways in which we can use statecharts to say things we probably didn't mean to say.

The first thing to notice about the statechart in the figure is that we didn't define the default state for the class. Is it state_0? State_10? Maybe state_7? We also didn't identify the default state in the lower and-state region of state_0.

Less obvious are the two race conditions specified in the and-states. The first is activated by the event e1. In one and-state, the action modifies the attribute x by augmenting it by one; the second multiplies it by three. The answer we get after the event is processed by the object depends on the order of execution of these actions but it is not possible, *in principle,* to determine what that order is. This is the classic definition of a race condition—a situation in which a computational result depends on an execution order, which is inherently unknowable. Not that using the same event in more than one and-state is inappropriate—in fact, it is a common way for synchronization of and-states when required. However, care must be taken that race conditions are avoided.

The second race condition is perhaps a bit more obvious. The e6 event causes two things to occur which are mutually exclusive. In the upper and-state region, it causes a transition to the state_1 nested state, while in the lower and-state region it leaves the composite state altogether. While this is obvious bad and not "computable," there are more subtle versions of this. Suppose event evSub is a subclass of event e6 and it is this event that appears on the transition to state_10 in the figure. If an evSub6 occurs, then the state machine is *still* ill-formed because evSub *is a kind of* e6; therefore, when evSub6 occurs, all active transitions with e6 event triggers also fire.

At the bottom of the figure we see overlapping guard conditions. In this case, it is obvious that if x has the value 25, that both guards evaluate to TRUE. One could conceive of a tool that would find such overlapping conditions. Nevertheless, finding the general case of overlapping

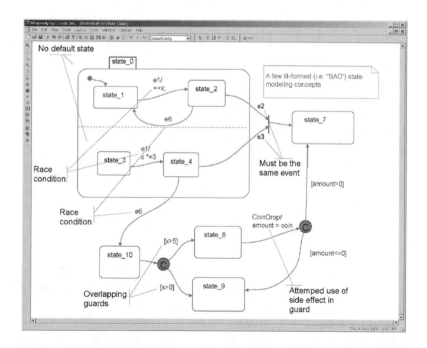

Figure 3-11: *Ill-Formed Statechart*

guards is NP-hard. Using simple guards will allow you to detect these conditions more easily.

On the right side of the figure we see a reasonable-looking transition: CoinDrop with an action to add the value of the coin to an attribute called "amount." The problem lies in that the guards subsequent to that event signature use the amount attribute in the guard. What is probably meant is that the updated value of amount should be used in the guard execution; however, what is actually done is that guards are evaluated before any actions are taken. Therefore the value of amount examined is prior to adding in the value of the coin. There are a couple of common solutions to this. One is to use a choice point, although I personally don't recommend it for the reasons discussed previously. Another solution is to use more elaborate guard expressions such as [amount + coin>0], taking into account that it has not yet been augmented. Another solution is to add a state between the CoinDrop transition segment and the guards. This will force the completion of the action before the guards (now exiting the new state) are evaluated.

The last error on the diagram is that transitions with different events enter into a join. A join brings together transition segments from different and-states and must be triggered by a *single* event. Event responses are handled one at a time, in a run-to-completion fashion. Different events cannot be joined together.

3.4.6 Cardiac Pacemaker Example

A cardiac pacemaker is an excellent example of a system in which most objects use finite state machines. The problem statement below will be developed into a class model that will allow us to see how the various statechart features can be used in a real system.

Problem Statement: A Cardiac Pacemaker

A cardiac pacemaker is an implanted device that assists cardiac function when underlying pathologies make the intrinsic heart rate too low or absent (bradycardia). Pacemakers operate in different behavioral modes, indicated by a three-letter acronym. The first letter is either A, V, or D, depending on whether the atrium or the ventricle or both (dual) is being paced (electrically stimulated). The second letter is also A, V, or D, depending on which heart chamber is being monitored (electrically monitored). The last letter is I, T, or D, indicating inhibited, triggered, or dual pacing modes. In an inhibited mode, a sensed heart event (e.g., a detected cardiac contraction) within the appropriate timeframe will inhibit the delivery of a pace from the pacemaker. In triggered mode, a sensed heart event will immediately trigger a pace from the pacemaker. For example, VVI mode means that the ventricle is paced (the first V) if a ventricular sense (the second V) does not occur. If a ventricular sense does occur, then the pace is inhibited (the I). Dual modes are more complex and will not be discussed here.

Most of the time, a pacemaker waits for a sense event. When it decides to pace, the pacemaker conducts an electric current of a programmable voltage (called the *pulse amplitude*) for a programmable period of time (called the *pulse width*). Following a pace, the pacemaker is put into a refractory state for a set period of time, during which all cardiac activity is ignored. Following the refractory period the pacemaker resumes monitoring for the next cardiac event. The rate of pacing is determined by the programmable pacing rate. The length of the waiting state is computed based on the pacing rate and the pulse width. The refractory period is fixed, but the time waiting for a sense + the pulse width + the refractory time = pacing rate. For example, for a pacing rate of 70 beats per minute (0.857 seconds per beat), if the refractory time is 50 ms and the pulse width is 15 ms, then the length of time the pacemaker will wait for a pace is 792 ms. The refractory period is fixed. This particular pacemaker operates in VVI, AAI, VVT, AAT, and AVI pacing modes as programmed by the physician.

Pacemaker parameters are programmed via a telemetric interface to an external programmer device. Telemetry is sent by pulsing an electromagnetic coil a certain number of times (15 +/− 2) to indicate a "0" bit and a different number of times (8 +/2) to indicate a "1" bit. The pulse On and Off time periods are identical (i.e., the pulse stream is a square wave), with each pulse taking 1.0 ms.

(continued)

> ### *Problem Statement: A Cardiac Pacemaker* (cont.)
>
> There is a period of 5 ms between bits in the same byte; 10 ms between bytes in the same message and at least 100 ms between messages. To avoid inadvertent programming by electrical noise, a reed switch must be closed with an external magnet before telemetry is enabled. The commands constructed from the bits must be checked prior to acting on them.
>
> Pacing and communications must occur in parallel—i.e. the pacing of the heart cannot stop because the device is communicating via telemetry.

This short problem statement can be represented by a simple class model, as in Figure 3-12. The pacemaker itself is shown as a structured class containing the three subsystems—Communications, PacingEngine, and Power. These subsystems contain the objects that collaborate to do meet the required functionality required of the subsystems.

The Communications subsystem, shown in Figure 3-13, contains instances of various classes that enable it to do its primary communications functionality. The ReedSwitch, CoilDriver, and Communications Manager and associated MessageQueues and Messages form the Communications subsystem. Note that the Communications Manager associates with two MessageQueues—one to hold messages waiting to be transmitted, and one to hold messages received via telemetry. The Communications Manager has an association with the PacingEngine subsystem to enable it to send the commands that change the pacing parameters, such as pulse width, pulse amplitude, pacing rate, and operational mode.

The PacingEngine subsystem internal structure is shown in Figure 3-14. This subsystem is straightforward. The Chamber Model defines the basic behavior for pacing a heart chamber, including associations to a PaceOutput object (providing an interface to the stimulation hardware) and a VoltageSensor object (providing an interface to the monitoring hardware). As an aside, the operations shown for the Pace Output and VoltageSensor classes are standard method calls, while the operation shown for the pacing classes (Chamber Model, Atrial Model,

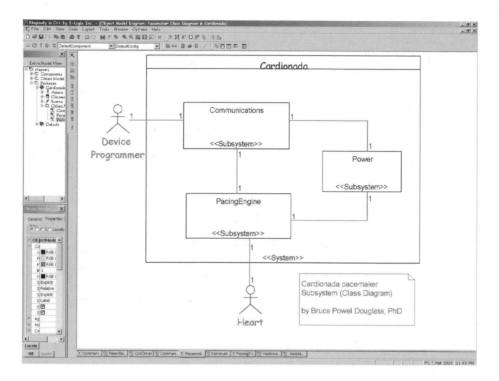

Figure 3-12: *Pacemaker Class Diagram*

and Ventricular Model) are event receptors that show which events are received and processed by instances of the class. This is a bit more obvious on the state machines than on the class diagrams. Note also that the class diagram follows the common idiom of only showing the new operations (or events receptions) defined in the subclass and not those inherited from the superclass. These inherited operations *are* defined (in the superclass), but not shown in the subclass on the diagram.

A statement about the generalization relationships in the pacing subsystem is in order. The Chamber Model class defines the basic behavioral model for pacing a cardiac chamber so it seems as though the Atrial Model and Ventricular Model ought to be instances of the Chamber Model class rather than different subclasses. If, in fact, the behavior of the two chambers differed only in their context, then a single class Chamber Model would be appropriate. However, we are going to specialize the Chamber Model class in how the two cardiac

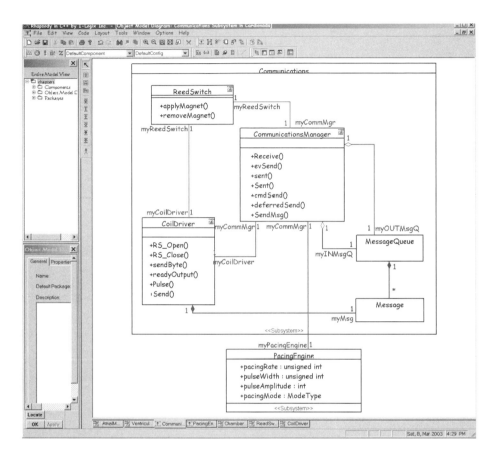

Figure 3-13: *Communications Subsystem*

chambers define their behavior in AVI mode. This will allow us to define the basic behavior in the superclass and specialize it for the two subclasses.

Now that we have seen the structure of the Cardionada pacemaker, let's look at the behavioral model defined with the statecharts. The classes on the class diagram that have a state machine have a small icon in their upper righthand corner. Starting with the Communications Subsystem, we see that the reactive classes are the ReedSwitch, CoilDriver, and CommunicationsManager.

The ReedSwitch has simple on-off state behavior, as we see in Figure 3-15. It propagates events to other classes communication subsystem to enable and disable communications via the GEN() macro—specifically the *ReedSwitch* sends the RS_Close and RS_Open events to both the CoilDriver and CommunicationsGnome.

The *CoilDriver* class has more elaborate behavior (see Figure 3-16). The default initial state is *Disabled.* When the *Reed Switch* closes, it propagates an *RS_Close* event to the CoilDriver and the CoilDriver enters the *Idle* substate. The CoilDriver supports half-duplex operation—that is, it can either send or receive at any given time, but not both at the same time. In the Idle state, if an incoming pulse on the coil is detected, then it enters the ReceivingMsg state. The CoilDriver starts counting the pulses until it gets a timeout [shown as tm(BIT_TM)]. The number of pulses receives is then decoded into a bit value with the decode() action and then the next bit is retrieved. Once we receive all the bits in a byte, we add the byte into the message we are constructing and we wait for the next byte. At some point, we have received all the bytes [as

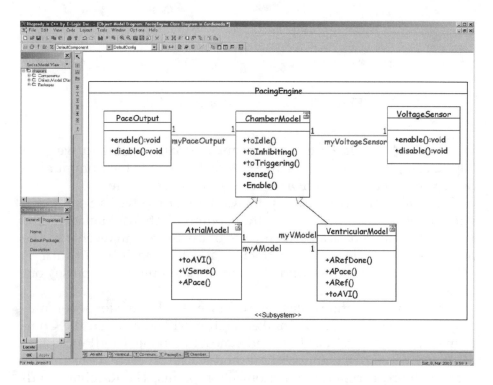

Figure 3-14: *Pacing Engine Subsystem*

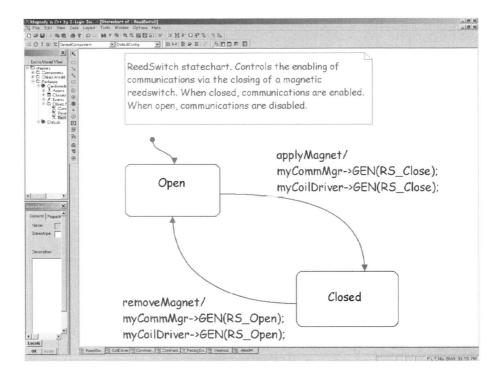

Figure 3-15: *ReedSwitch State Model*

indicated by the elapse of the timeout tm(MSG_TM)], and we now have a complete message. The message is then sent to the Communications Manager and the CoilDriver returns to the Idle state.

Transmission is begun when the CoilDriver receives a Send event with a message to send from the Communications Manager. The process to send is basically the reverse of the process to receive it. The first byte of the message is extracted, and then each bit, in turn, is extracted and is used to send the appropriate number of pulses out through the Coil.

The Communications Manager oversees the bidirectional communication process for the pacemaker. Figure 3-17 shows that the Communications Manager has four and-states: Receiving, CmdProcessing, MsgSending, and Queuing. These and-states proceed more or less independently except for synchronization points. The Receiving and-state validates messages that it receives from the CoilDriver and then

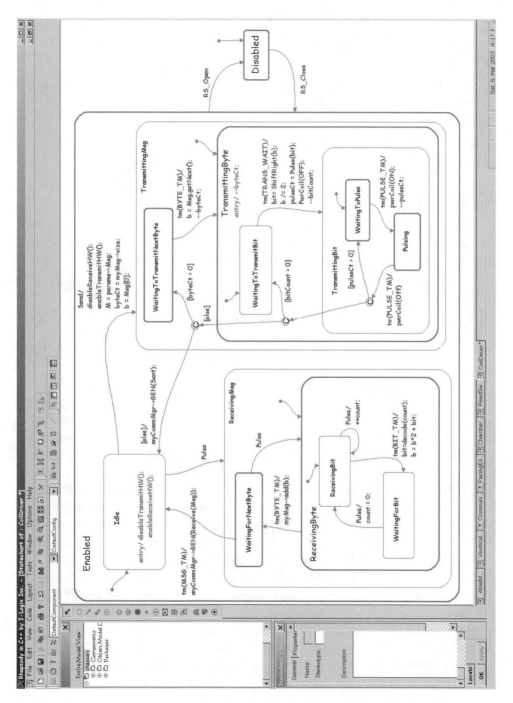

Figure 3-16: *CoilDriver State Model*

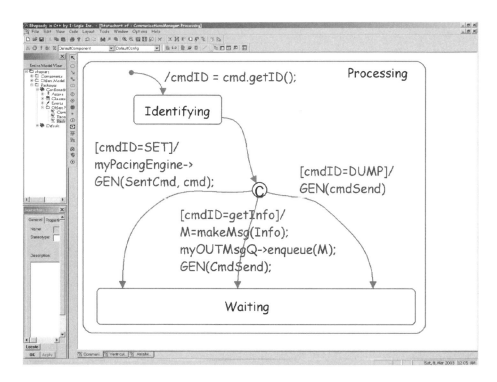

Figure 3-17: *Communications Manager State Model*

either enqueues it from processing and responds to the programming device with an ACK message (if valid) or discards it and sends a NAK message if not. Validation is done via the isValid operation, which presumably checks the command ID, the message length, and a CRC.

The cmdProcessing state is decomposed into a submachine, which is shown in Figure 3-17. The Dump command tells the pacemaker to start sending the queued messages, while the Set command sets the parameters or mode for the pacing engine.

The PacingEngine is where the pacing behavior occurs (see Figure 3-18). It changes mode only when commanded by the external programmer. When the Communication Manager receives a command to set the pacing mode, it validates the command and, if valid, processes it. The PacingEngine decides how to deal with these Set commands. For example, when a Set command that commands the pacemaker into VVI mode is received, the PacingEngine must send a ToIdle event to

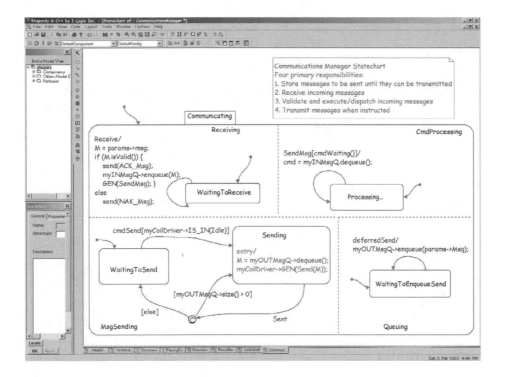

Figure 3-18: *Processing Statechart*

the Atrial Model instance and a ToInhibiting event to the Ventricular Model. To enter the AVI mode, the PacingEngine must send toAVI events to both the Atrial Model and Ventricular Model objects.

Most of the pacing behavior is defined in the Chamber Model statechart in Figure 3-19. If the Atrial Model is in the SelfInhibiting state and the Ventricular Model is in the Idle state, the pacemaker is said to be in AAI mode; if the Atrial Model is in the Idle State and the Ventricular model is in the Triggering mode, then the pacemaker is said to be in VVT mode. And if both objects are in the AVI state, then the pacemaker is in the AVI mode.

The next two figures (Figures 3-20 and 3-21) specialize the AVI state using the inherited state model rules given previously. By comparing the two specialized versions of the AVI state, you can see how the two objects communicate to coordinate their state machines. The Atrial Model and the Ventricular Model coordinate their activities by propagating events back and forth to ensure the behavior is correct in the AVI

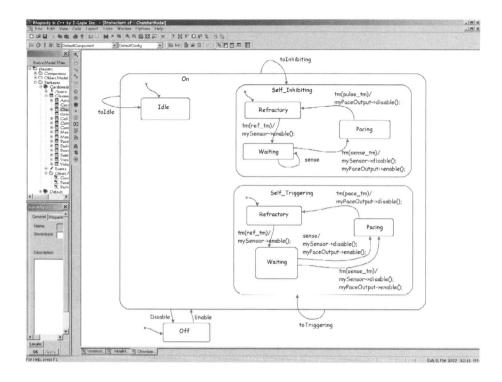

Figure 3-19: *Chamber Model State Model*

mode. The AVI mode is defined to be when the electrical activity in the ventricle is used to determine whether or not pacing should occur; the pacing is actually performed by stimulating the atrium of the heart. Further, if the ventricle beats on its own fast enough, then the pacing of the atrium should be inhibited.

3.4.7 Protocol State Machines

The state machines we dealt with in the previous section are called *behavioral* state machines because they specify how instances of a classifier respond to incoming events. There is another use of state machines, which is to define usage protocols for interfaces and ports; such state machines are called *protocol state machines* because they define the events and allowed sequences of events in usage protocols for classifiers. A protocol state machine defines which operations of a classifier

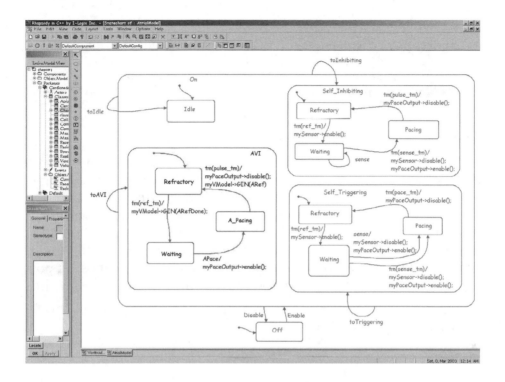

Figure 3-20: *Atrial Model State Model*

may be called in which state and the pre- and postconditions for the execution of the operations.

As with behavioral state machines, protocol state machines must be "complete" in the sense that all the transitions that can result in the change of state and execution of operations must be captured. On the other hand, operations that do not affect the state machine are not represented on the protocol state machine. The purpose of the protocol state machine, once again, is to formalize the protocol of interaction (i.e., preconditions having to do with sequencing) for the classifier.

Protocol state machines differ from behavioral state machines in the following ways:

- The key word "protocol" is used in the statechart.

- Preconditions and postconditions are shown on the transitions as guards.

- Actions are not permitted.
- States may not have entry or exit actions or activities.

Figure 3-22 shows two examples of protocol state machines for the door management of an elevator.

3.4.8 Activity Diagrams

Activity diagrams in UML 1.x were semantically equivalent to state-charts and shared a common metamodel. In UML 2.0, activity diagrams are given their own semantic basis independent from statecharts. In UML 2.0, there are multiple levels of activity diagrams: basic, intermediate, complete, and so on. The UML 2.0 activity diagrams are (mostly) compatible with the UML 1.x activity diagrams. In practice, the use of activity diagrams as "concurrent flowcharts" remains its most important usage in the real-time and embedded domains. Activity diagrams

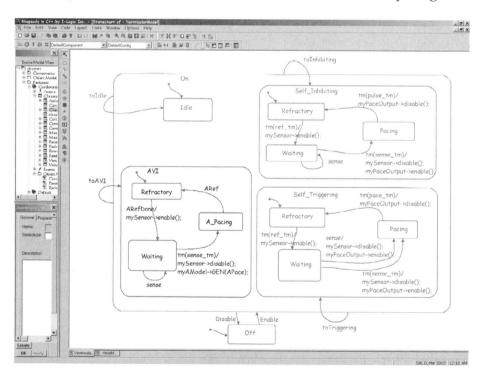

Figure 3-21: *Ventricular Model State Model*

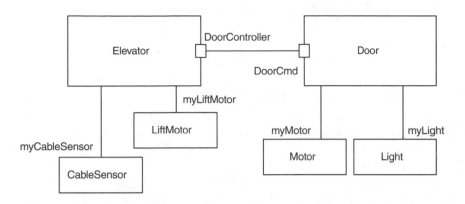

Figure 3-22a: *Protocol State Machine Context*

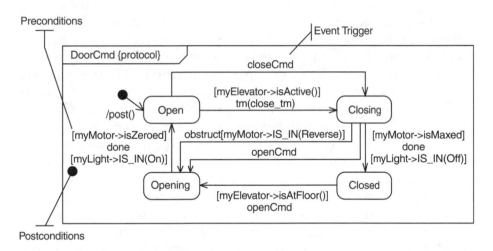

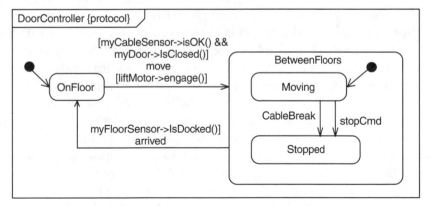

Figure 3-22b: *Protocol State Machines*

185

are usually used to specify the behaviors of operations and use cases and other classifiers. In usage, the difference between activity diagrams and statecharts is that statecharts are used when the classifier progresses primarily from state to state upon receipt of events of interest, whereas activity diagrams are used when the classifier progresses from state to state primarily when the actions done in the predecessor state have completed.

This is primarily because activity diagram semantics are based on the notion of *token flow,* from Petri nets, where a token contains an object, datum, or locus of control. The activity diagram is said to be in a state (or "node") when that state contains a token. Tokens flow from node to node when the input edges connect to nodes that contain tokens. In the case of simple sequence flow, the transition between them fires when the predecessor node (activity) has completed its work. In the case of a join, there must be tokens in *all* the predecessor nodes before the subsequent node becomes active. Conversely, with a fork, when the incoming transition fires, a token is placed in all subsequent nodes.

In practice, statecharts are used to model the reactive behavior of classes and use cases, when they proceed via the reception of events. Activity charts are used to model control flow behavior of operations, activities on states (entry, exit, transition, and do activities) and use cases, and less often, classes. Note that entry, exit, and transition activities run according to run-to-completion semantics—that is, the object providing the context for these actions will not accept or process any event until those activities, and their nested actions have completed. Do activities are not run-to-completion and may accept events to terminate their execution. The common use of activity diagrams in the real-time and embedded domain is to show computational algorithms.

The model shown in Figure 3-23 shows how an activity diagram can model the behavior of an operation. In this case, the activity receives incoming data—SourceID—and processes the data into two concurrent flows, emanating from the fork pseudostate. The input data "appears" to the activity diagram on an input activity parameter node (a kind of object node, analogous to an input pin on an action). The computation result appears on an output activity parameter node (analogous to an output pin on an action). One of the concurrent flows initializes the sensor and acquires the data. The other readies the filter. Once this is done, the join then brings together the concurrent flows and filters the data and returns it. Remember that the output flow from

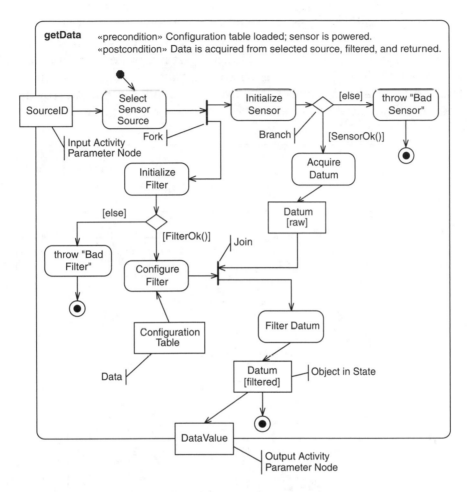

Figure 3-23: *Activity Chart*

the join fires only when control tokens appear on *all* of its predecessor nodes. This is just a fancy way of saying that it fires only when both threads feeding into it have completed their processing.

Note the use of a "class box" to represent data, whether it is a class or just an ADT (abstract data type). The Datum is shown using the "object in state" notation (the name of the current state shown inside square brackets), making the state of the Datum visible as that datum is processed in the activity. Note also the use of preconditions and post-conditions to clarify the processing requirements of the activity.

There are some additional notations available for activity diagrams. In Figure 3-24 we see special symbols that can be shown for event reception. In the example, a Proximity Alert might be created when a beam of light is broken (such as when a human arm crosses its path). In the activity diagram, this event causes the behavior in the interruptible segment (indicated with the dashed rounded rectangle) to abort, and

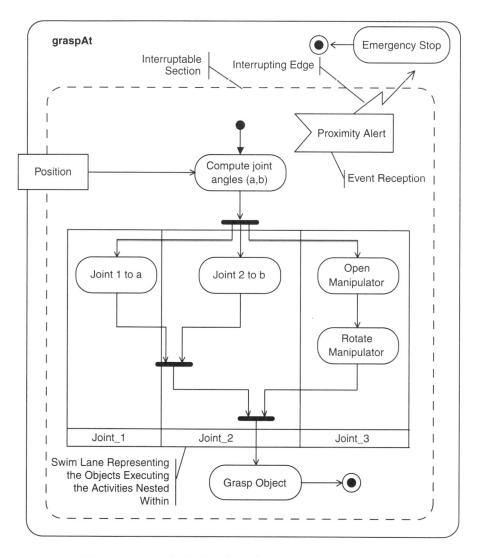

Figure 3-24: *Additional Activity Diagram Notations*

the control path to the Emergency Stop activity is taken. The use of explicit "interrupting edges" is an important departure from UML 1.x activity diagrams; in its earlier incarnation, UML allowed a flow on an activity diagram to be triggered by an event.

Swim lanes define partitions in the activity diagram that can be bound to objects or object roles. This provides activity diagrams with the ability to represent interactions of objects during the execution of the activity flow. Swim lanes enable the depiction of interactions of multiple objects during the execution of an algorithm. In addition, activity states themselves can also be decomposed on the same or on different diagrams. This is crucial for the scalability of the notation to model complex algorithms. The official notation used to indicate that an activity is decomposed on a separate diagram is an inverted three-pronged fork.

3.5 Interactions

In the previous section, we saw how the behavior of individual classifiers, such as classes and use cases, can be modeled using statecharts and their close cousins, activity charts. In this section, we will see how the UML models the collaborative behavior of multiple entities working together.[11] Collective behavior, or *interactions,* concerns itself with the (partially) sequenced exchange of messages (which may be events, operation calls, or instance creation/destruction actions) among a possible large set of interacting objects.

There are three primary diagrammatic forms in the UML for depicting interaction scenarios—communication diagrams,[12] sequence diagrams, and timing diagrams. Communication diagrams are basically object diagrams with messages shown, each with a sequence number. Because communication diagrams are relatively little used as compared with their cousin, the sequence diagram, they won't be discussed

---

[11] As noted in the previous section, activity diagrams with swim lanes can be used to *specify* interactions; sequence diagrams are used to show specific scenarios, which are, in some sense, instances of those specifications. However, the elaborations of sequence diagrams in UML 2.0 make that distinction fuzzier.

[12] In UML 1.x these were known as *collaboration diagrams.*

here. Timing diagrams emphasize the changes in value or state over time for either single or multiple classifiers roles. Timing diagrams are discussed in Section 3.5.2.

3.5.1 Sequence Diagrams

Figure 3-25 shows the basic elements of a sequence diagram. The five-sided box at the upper lefthand corner names the sequence diagram. In general, a sequence diagram contains one or more interaction fragments, each of which is enclosed in a frame and one or more operators. As previously mentioned, sequence diagrams are more commonly used than communication diagrams even though they show basically the same information. The reason is that sequence diagrams emphasize sequence over structure, so it is very easy to find the "next" message—it is the message following the current one in the diagram. Time goes down the page, but not normally linearly; that is, further down implies later in time, but 2 cm at one place in the diagram does not imply the same amount of time as 2 cm somewhere else on the diagram. Further, because messages on sequence diagrams are only partially ordered (a topic discussed shortly), in many cases the relative timing between messages is not specified. Since timing diagrams are shown against a common clock (depicted with the time ruler on the diagram), timing diagrams messages are fully ordered. When time, rather than sequence, is the primary focus, I recommend that timing diagrams be used instead.

The vertical lines, called *lifelines*, represent the roles (i.e., parts of a composite class or a object roles in a collaboration) the instances play during a scenario. These roles may be parts of a collaboration and/or internal parts of a structured class, component, or subsystem. Objects roles can send and receive messages during the execution of a scenario. Messages are represented by the arrowed lines going from one lifeline to another. These messages can be synchronous or asynchronous, calls or signals.

The frame enclosing the diagram encapsulates an interaction fragment. Each interaction fragment has at least one operator, held in the five-sided box at the upper left corner of the interaction fragment. Section 3.5.1.2 details the standard operators available.

The sequence diagram in the figure has other elements that could be found in the sequence diagrams in UML 1.x: constraints, states, messages, and so on. One of the most important differences between UML

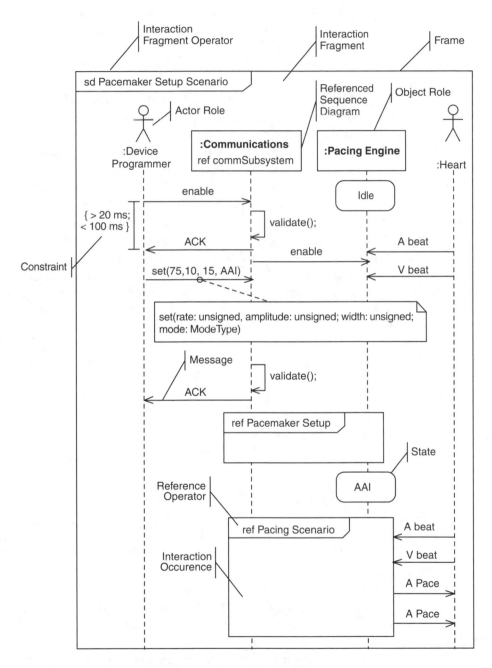

Figure 3-25: *Sequence Diagram*

2.0 sequence diagrams and UML 1.x sequence diagrams is the ability to decompose interaction fragments into nested interaction fragments. Figure 3-25 has three interaction fragments. The sd operator names the primary interaction fragment, but there are also two nested interaction fragments. The ref operator identifies the name of the sequence diagram that is being referenced, but not shown in the current diagram. Each of these features will be discussed in more detail shortly.

There are more annotations available, as shown in Figure 3-26. Messages can be either lost or found. Lost messages are pretty obvious—a message is sent, but due to some error or failure, it fails to arrive at its destination. The notation for that is to have the message terminate in a circle. Conversely, a found message arrives from an unknown or unspecified source; this is shown with a message starting from a circle.

As with UML 1.x, activation of an instance can be shown, although the UML 2.0 specification refers to this as an *execution instance*. This is shown with the shaded rectangle placed onto an instance line to show that the instance is actively executing behavior in response to receiving a message. This annotation is really only useful for completely synchronous calls among instances, and I personally tend not to use the notation for that reason.

The kind of message may be shown as well. Open arrowheads denote asynchronous messages, while a filled arrowhead indicates a synchronous call. The open arrowhead with a dashed line is optionally used with the call message to show a reply. Replies may also be shown as a return value on the original message, as in

    goto(4, UP): TRUE;

which indicates that TRUE is returned.

A large X at the terminal end of a lifeline indicates that the instance has been destroyed. In the figure, we see the Elevator lifeline destroys the request lifeline when the request has been fulfilled.

We've already seen that states on the lifelines show the state of the instance playing the role of the lifeline in the interaction. We can use any testable condition, such as the value of an attribute. In the figure, we show how the value of the floor attribute can be shown on the Elevator lifeline.

The last new thing shown in the figure is the *coregion*, an area on the lifeline between square brackets. In a coregion, we do not care

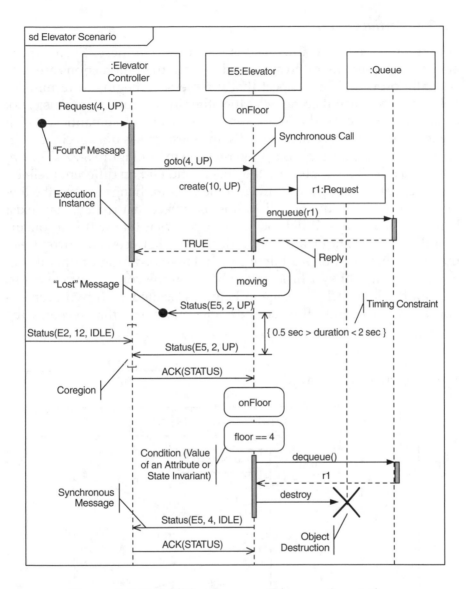

Figure 3-26: *Addition Sequence Diagram Annotations*

about, and do not specify, the order of the messages. This violates the normal partial ordering rules discussed in the next section. A more general way of showing coregions is to use the par operator, as discussed in Section 3.5.1.2.2.

3.5.1.1 Partial Ordering

A note on ordering in interactions is appropriate here. Even experienced UML users are often surprised to learn that interactions are only partially ordered. They expect that if a message begins or terminates below another then it comes *after* the other in absolute time. This is not quite true. Sequence diagrams support concurrent semantics, which means that the relative ordering of some messages is not specified.

For example, does message m0 precede m1 in Figure 3-27? The answer is, *we don't know,* because they begin and end on different lifelines. A sequence diagram shows a trace of message exchange among the lifelines of interest. Sequence diagrams assume concurrency may exist between the lifelines. What concurrency means is that within a concurrent thread, operations are fully ordered, but between concurrent elements, nothing can be said about the relative ordering of operations, except at points of synchronization between the concurrent elements. We can think of each message as being associated with two events— one event that sends the message and one event that receives the

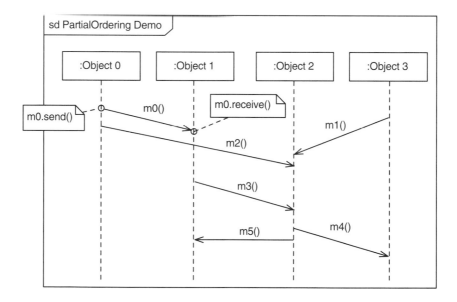

Figure 3-27: *Partial Ordering*

message, as shown with the constraints for m0.send() and m0.receive() in the figure. The two kinds of sequences that are fully ordered are the events that occur on a single lifeline and the receive() events that follow the corresponding send() events.

This means that in the figure, m0.send() precedes m0.receive(); m1.send() precedes m1.receive() and so on. Further, the events on the Object1 lifeline are fully ordered; m0.receive() precedes m3.send(), which precedes m5.receive(). However, you can't tell from the sequence diagram whether m0.send or even m0.receive() follows m1.send() or m1.receive().

In the sequence diagram shown in Figure 3-27 the following orders can be determined:

- m0.send()->m0.receive()
- m1.send()->m1.receive()
- m2.send()->m2.receive()
- m3.send()->m3.receive()
- m4.send()->m4.receive()
- m5.send()->m5.receive()
- m1.receive->m2.receive()->m3.receive()->m4.send()->m5.send()
- m0.receive()->m3.receive()->m5.receive()

But we cannot assume that even messages that are sent in a particular sequence are received in the same sequence, if they terminate on different lifelines. For example, it is clear that m0.send() precedes m2.send() because they initiate from the same lifeline. However, they terminate on different lifelines so one cannot assume that m2.receive() occurs after m1.receive(). If m2.receive() arrives prior to m0.receive(), this is called *message overtaking*. How can this occur? Imagine that Object 0 and Object 1 both reside on a computer in Mission Control, while Object 2 resides on a probe orbiting Europa. Obviously, message transmission time on the same computer requires orders of magnitude less time that transmission across hundreds of light minutes. Even in more mundane applications, the priorities of different threads can mean that messages sent earlier may still be received later. The problem is further exacerbated with distribution of objects across multiple processors and physical locations.

3.5.1.2 Interaction Operators

We have seen that the interaction fragments on sequence diagrams have operators. So far, we've only seen the sd (interaction fragment name) and ref (interaction fragment reference) operators but there are quite a number. The predefined operators are shown in Table 3-2.

The most important of the operators are discussed in more detail in the text that follows.

Table 3-2: *Interaction Operators*

Operator	Description
sd	Names an interaction fragment.
ref	References an interaction fragment, which appears in a different diagram.
alt	Provides alternatives, only one of which will be taken. The branches are evaluated on the basis of guards, similar to statecharts. An else guard is provided that evaluates to TRUE if and only if all other branch alternatives evaluate to FALSE.
opt	Defines an optional interaction segment; that is, one that may or may not occur depending on the runtime evaluation of some guard.
break	Break is a shorthand for an alt operator where one operand is given and the other is the rest of the enclosing interaction fragment. A sequence diagram analogue to the C++ statement.
loop	Specifies that an interaction fragment shall be repeated some number of times.
seq	Weak sequencing (default). Specifies the normal weak sequencing rules are in force in the fragment.
strict	Specifies that the messages in the interaction fragment are fully ordered—that is, only a single execution trace is consistent with the fragment.
neg	Specifies a negative, or "not" condition. Useful for capturing negative requirements.

Table 3-2: *(cont.)*

Operator	Description
par	Defines parallel or concurrent regions in an interaction fragment. This is similar to alt in that subfragments are identified, but differs in that *all* such subfragments execute rather than just a single one.
criticalRegion	Identifies that the interaction fragment must be treated as atomic and cannot be interleaved with other event occurrences. It is useful in combination with the par operator.
ignore/consider	The ignore operator specifies that some message types are not shown within the interaction fragment, but can be ignored for the purpose of the diagram. The consider operator specifies which messages should be considered in the fragment.
assert	Specifies that the interaction fragment represents an assertion.

3.5.1.2.1 ALTERNATIVES, BRANCHES, OPTIONS, AND LOOPS

There are several operators devoted to branching: alt, break, opt, and loop. All (except break) are shown in Figure 3-28. For those readers who remember the (admittedly pathetic) branching capability of UML 1.x sequence diagrams, the alt operator for interaction fragments will be a very welcome addition to the UML. With the alt operator, the fragment (called a *compound fragment* in this case) is broken up into multiple sections, separated by an operand separator—a dashed line crossing the width of the fragment. Guards control which of the alternative branches will be taken. Remember, this is branching, rather than concurrency, so that at most only a single operand fragment will execute. The fragment being operated on by the alt operator in the figure has three operands, each with a separate guard. The [else] guard is TRUE if and only if the other guards are all FALSE. If all the guards of an alt operator are FALSE, then none of the operands will execute; if multiple guards are true, then one of the operands guarded by a true guard will execute but you cannot predict which one it will be (normally an undesirable situation).

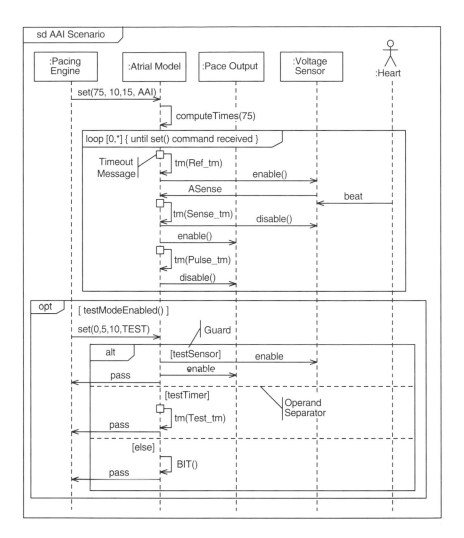

Figure 3-28: *Loops and Branches*

The opt operator is like an alt with a single operand—it designates its fragment as being optional.

Loops are shown with the loop operator. The loop operator may specify the minimum number of iterations as well as the maximum number of iterations inside square brackets. If no numbers are specified, then [0, *] is assumed, where the asterisk (*) is indeterminate. If only the first number is given, then the fragment will iterate a fixed number of times. By adding a constraint, we can limit the number of times the fragment will execute. In the figure, we indicate that the specified fragment will iterate until a set() command is received by the pacing engine.

Note also the special notation used for a timeout message. While not officially part of the standard, it is often useful to indicate timeouts as special. They are shown as a "message to self" initiating from a small square. A cancelled timeout (not shown) has the same notation, except that the message arrow is dashed.

3.5.1.2.2 Parallel and Critical Regions

If alternatives were painful to show in UML 1.x sequence diagrams, parallel regions were well nigh impossible. UML 2.0, however, makes specifying parallel regions on sequence diagrams easy. The par operator indicates two or more parallel regions, but otherwise looks much like the alt operator. In Figure 3-29, two parallel regions are shown for the microwave oven. The consider operator (discussed in the next section) indicates that these messages have special meaning and should not be ignored should they occur. Inside each of parallel regions is a loop; the first specifies an unlimited number of iterations but is constrained to terminate when the attribute timeToCook reaches zero. The second doesn't specify a terminating condition. The par operator is a more general (and useful) form of the coregion operator shown in Figure 3-26.

Also notice the critical region in one of the parallel regions. This has the same meaning as a critical section in normal concurrency programming—that is, traces of execution of this fragment cannot be interleaved with other possible concurrent fragments. Normally, a critical Region fragment is nested within one of the parallel regions as it is in the figure.

The assert operator indicates that this *must* be true for the trace to be considered valid. This essentially adds causality to sequence diagrams and allows them to be used to specify test vectors. The assert operator is discussed more in the next section.

3.5.1.2.3 Assert, Consider, Ignore?

UML 1.x sequence diagrams really don't have any notion of causality—they are merely traces of what happened or what could happen during

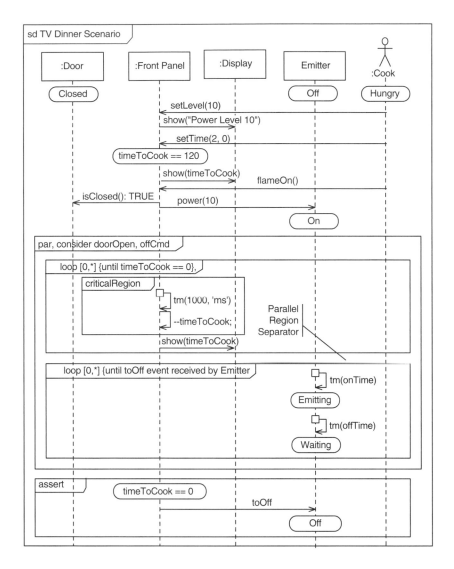

Figure 3-29: *Parallel Regions*

an interaction. They don't specify what *must* happen. David Harel and Werner Damm [5] have done some work on adding the notions of causality to sequence diagrams. These notions have been added, although in a somewhat different form, to the UML 2.0 sequence diagrams with the consider, ignore, and assert operators.

The ignore operator lists messages, as parameters, that are outside of the causal stream and may be ignored. For example, consider the ignore operator in Figure 3-30. It says that while the Door is opening, presses to the open button (resulting an OpenCmd) are ignored, which is behavior you would expect.

Also note that the sd and ignore operators are combined in the primary fragment shown in the diagram. This indicates that pressing the CloseButton has no effect on the scenario.[13]

In the lower part of the figure, the consider operation is used. Consider is the opposite of ignore. It considers the specified messages (in this case, stopCmd, arrived, and cableBreak) are the important ones, and all other messages may be ignored.

Finally, the assert operator is used inside the consider fragment. The proper interpretation of this fragment is that an openCmd *must follow* the arrived message.

3.5.1.3 *Sequence Diagram Decomposition*

Probably the most significant improvement in sequence diagrams with UML 2.0 is the ability to decompose the diagram into subparts. UML has always had the ability to do this with class diagrams and statecharts, but sequence diagrams lacked a standard way to do such decomposition. This feature is crucial for effective large-scale systems development because such interactions become complex in at least two ways.

First, many more interacting elements become added to interactions as designs evolve and are elaborated. In class diagrams, this is handled by using structured classes and composition relationships and by showing only the internal structure of the larger-scale objects. The second way that sequence diagrams become more complex is that more messages, more alternatives, and more variants are added.

The addition of operators, such as alt and par, help this problem tremendously, but there is still a need to move all the details of an interaction and show it on a separate diagram. This might be done to manage a complex scenario as well as when the same sequence may be referenced from more than one interaction fragment. UML 2.0 sequence diagrams allow this kind of decomposition in two ways: referencing interaction fragments and decomposing lifelines.

---

[13] You always suspected as much didn't you?

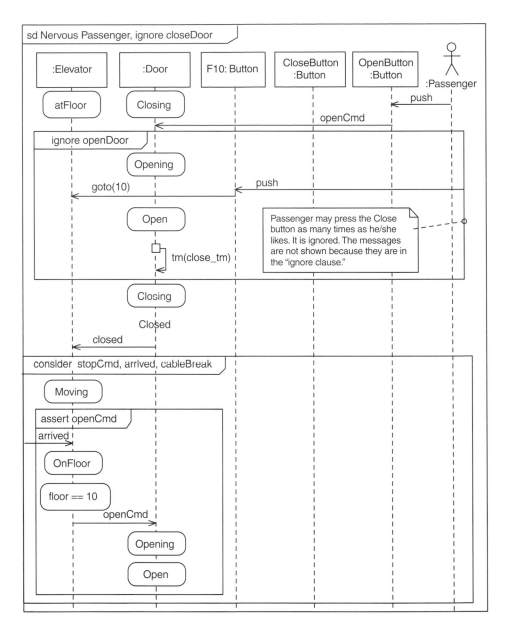

Figure 3-30: *Assert, Consider, Ignore?*

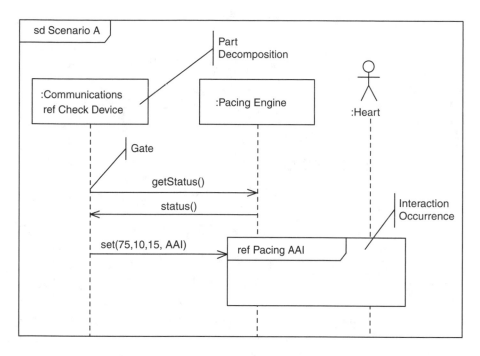

Figure 3-31: *Referencing Sequence Diagram*

Figure 3-31 illustrates both means of decomposing sequence diagrams. The lifeline Communications is decomposed in the interaction fragment called *Check Device*. The decomposed interaction is shown in Figure 3-32. The decomposed lifeline includes more lifelines than the first. This is one of the advantages of such decomposition—it allows us to manage the burgeoning complexity of our sequence diagrams as more and more lifelines are added. In addition, the Check Device fragment itself includes interaction occurrences that reference interaction fragments shown elsewhere. This allows us to hide the details of the "bit banging" done during the actual transmission and reception of the bits with the CoilDriver. Lastly, we see that message enter and leave this interaction fragment. Each point on the frame where a message enters or leaves is called a *gate*. To be well formed, the referenced fragment must a corresponding gate for every gate that appears in the interaction occurrence, and the message type and parameters must be consistent as well.

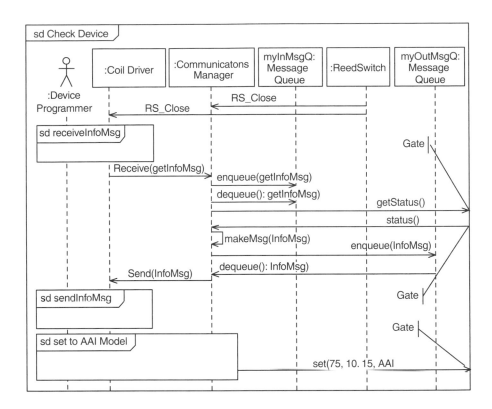

Figure 3-32: *Lifeline Decomposition*

The other kind of decomposition is to have an interaction occurrence that references a separately defined interaction fragment. In Figure 3-31, this is the nested fragment called Pacing AAI. The internal structure of that interaction appears in Figure 3-33. Just as in the previous decomposition, this fragment details the internal structure of the interaction and may add additional lifelines as necessary.

Clearly, these means for decomposing sequence diagrams allow us to construct and understand complex interactions far better than the sequence diagrams from UML 1.x.

3.5.2 Timing Diagrams

Electrical engineers have used timing diagrams for a long time in the design of electronic state machines. A timing diagram is a simple

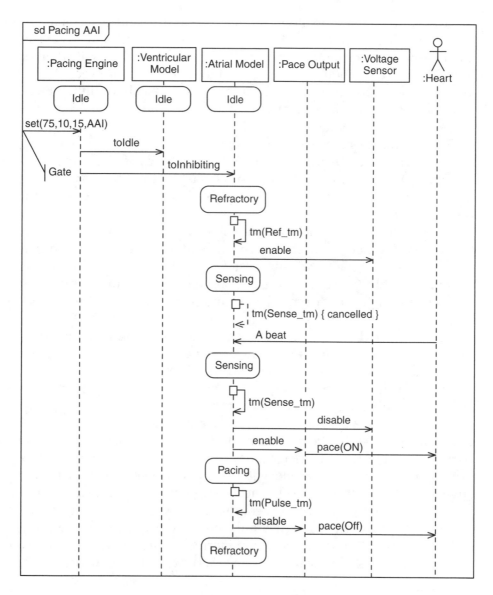

Figure 3-33: *Referenced Interaction Fragment*

LIVERPOOL
JOHN MOORES UNIVERSITY
AVRIL ROBARTS LRC
TEL. 0151 231 4022

representation with time along the horizontal axis and object state or attribute value along the vertical axis. Of course, electrical engineers usually only concern themselves with a small number of states for an individual circuit node, such as low, high, or high impedance.[14] Software engineers can use timing diagrams just as easily on much more elaborate state machines or many-valued attributes to show how the values change over time.

Timing diagrams are similar to sequence diagrams in that they show traces, or scenarios, of collaborations. Many different traces are possible with the same collaboration. This is different than statecharts in that statecharts specify all of the reactive behavior of the classifier it is specifying.

Timing diagrams depict state (or value) as a horizontal band across the diagram. When the system is in that state, a line is drawn in that band for the duration of time the system is in the state. The time axis is linear, although special notations are sometimes used to indicate long uninteresting periods of time. The simple form of a state timing diagram is shown in Figure 3-34.

This timing diagram shows a particular path through the *Atrial Model* state machine. It begins in the Idle state and remains there until it receives a command to enter begin pacing (To Inhibiting). At this point, it jumps to the sensing state. The vertical line segments connecting states show that the time used for the transition is (approximately) zero relative to the scale of the timing diagram. Later, an atrial sense is detected (as shown by the transition annotation on the diagram) and the Atrial Model returns to the sensing state. Sometime later, the sense time-out occurs and the Atrial Model enters the pacing state. In this state, the engine is actively putting an electrical charge through the heart muscle. When the pacing pulse width is complete, the object transitions to the refractory state. Once this times out, the system reenters the sensing state. The timing diagram view is preferred to the sequence diagram view when time is of critical importance, as opposed to sequence.

---

[14] In some cases, electrical engineers will be concerned with a somewhat larger set of states, such as strongly but consistently driven (transistor driver) high and low, strongly and inconsistently driven (conflict), weakly driven (resistively driven) high and low, floating and undriven (high impedance, all outputs tri-stated) high, low and in the transition region, unknown transistor driven, unknown resistively driven, transitioning monotonically, transitioning with oscillation, and so on. But usually not ;-)

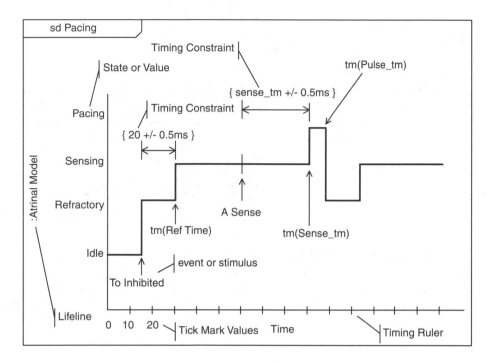

Figure 3-34: *Simple State Timing Diagram*

We see constraints and other annotations on the timing diagram. Constraints are useful to help specify the timing requirements. For example, the timing for the transition from the refractory state in Figure 3-34 might be 19.6 ms, in this particular scenario, but this is within the required time window of 20 +/- 0.5 ms.

In this simple form, only a single object (or system) is represented. It is possible to show multiple objects on the same diagram. Separating these objects with operand separator lines clearly delineates the different (and possibly concurrent) objects. Propagated transitions can be marked with directed lines showing event dependency. Figure 3-35 shows just such a diagram depicting a scenario of collaboration among three objects involved in the transmission of telemetry. We see the collaboration unfold as they exchange messages. When it is inconvenient to draw the message from one lifeline directly to another, labels can be used, as with the case of the send(value) message.

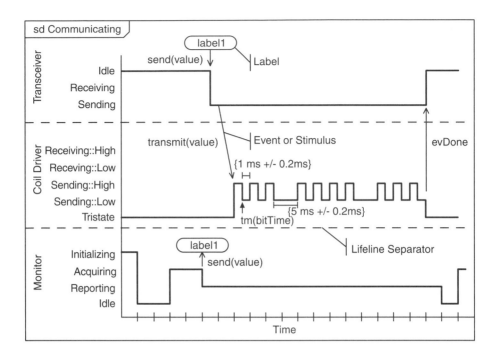

Figure 3-35: *Timing Diagram with Multiple Lifelines*

Timing diagrams are very good at showing precise timing behavior and are often used to closely analyze the timing of periodic and aperiodic tasks. When used in this way, some common elements are shown in Table 3-3.

When there are many tasks to be shown on a single diagram, a common simplified form of the timing diagram shows only which task is executing at any point in time (see Figure 3-36).[15] If desired, more details of the task state can be shown with pattern shading, as in Figure 3-37. Although timing diagrams show no information beyond that available in annotated sequence diagrams, the absolute timing of events and state changes and the relative timing among objects is much clearer and more obvious than on sequence diagrams, even when explicit timing constraints are added.

---

[15] This is a notational extension to what is currently defined in the adopted specification [1].

Table 3-3: *Commonly Shown Timing Information*

Period	The time between initiations for the same state.
Deadline	The time by which the state must be exited and a new state entered.
Initiation time	The time required to completely enter the state (i.e., execute state entry actions).
Execute time	The time required to execute the entry and exit actions and the required activities of the state.
Dwell time	The time the object remains in the state after the execute time before the state is exited. Includes time for exit actions.
Slack time	The time between the end of actions and activities and the deadline.
Transition time	The time required for the transition into the state to complete. This includes the time necessary to execute the transition actions.
Jitter	Variations in the start time for a periodic transition or event.

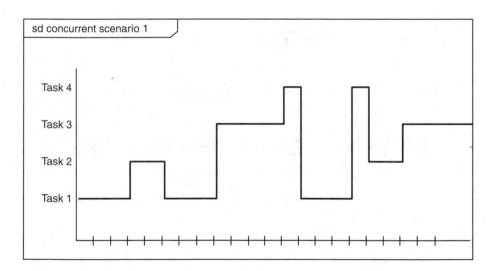

Figure 3-36a: *Simple Task Timing Diagram (standard)*

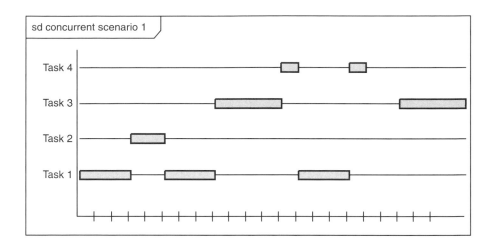

Figure 3-36b: *Simple Task Timing Diagram (alternative)*

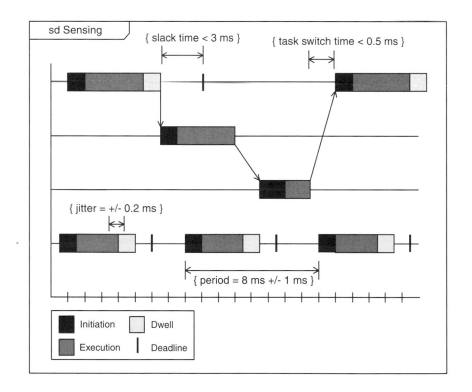

Figure 3-37: *Task Timing Diagram with Shading*

Lastly, timing diagrams can be used to show the values of attributes. Commonly, timing diagrams are used to show the changes in values of discrete enumerable attribute values, but they can also be used for continuous values, as shown in Figure 3-38. The "preferred" form, shown at the bottom of the figure, is appropriate when a value is changed in respond to a change event at some specific point in time. The attribute holds the value until the message is received and the value is (discontinuously) modified. For systems or continuous modeling, this format may not be very helpful, so a second notation is recommended in these cases, shown in the upper part of the figure.[16]

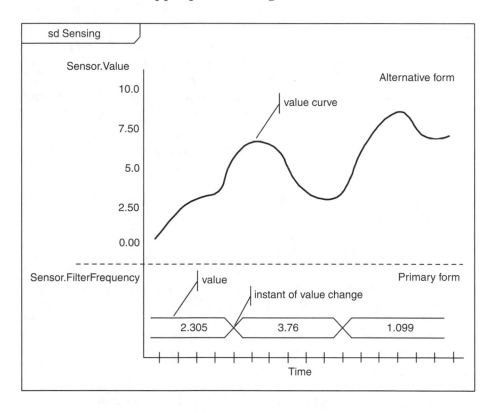

Figure 3-38: *Timing Diagram with Continuous Values*

---

[16] This is, likewise, an extension to the current adopted specification. It is being used in the work being done for the "UML for Systems Engineering" specification—an effort with which the author collaborates.

3.6 Summary

We have seen in this chapter the richness of the UML's behavioral modeling capabilities. Actions provide the most primitive units of behavior. Activities bind actions together into sequences connected via logical operators, such as branching and forking, as well as providing execution connections for them. Statecharts and activity diagrams allow us to depict the set of allowable sequences for the execution of these actions. Protocol state machines allow us to define the protocols of interaction among various classifiers. On the other hand, interactions cannot be conveniently represented by a state machine, since a state machine is bound to an individual classifier. For interactions, we model traces of event or message exchange among the instance roles participating in the interaction. Sequence diagrams are the most common means to capture such interactions. The UML 2.0 has introduced ways to manage the complexity of interactions with interaction fragments, operators, and the ability to decompose interactions into smaller interaction fragments. For those concerned especially with time, timing diagrams provide an expressive means to detail change in value or state of classifiers and attributes.

In the next chapter, we focus on the specification of time and modeling of timing constraints. There is an adopted standard for this, the "UML Profile for Schedulability, Performance, and Time," which captures the most common ways in which this was done in the past and abstracts them, then codifies them into a standard. While you are certainly free to use your own tags and constraints for capturing timing and performance requirements, the existence of a standard will facilitate the exchange of models among different tools.

3.7 Exercises

1. What are the three kinds of behavior? What are the characteristics of each?

2. What is the basic unit of primitive behavior in the UML?

3. What is the primary compositional unit of the elements named in question 2?

4. Name four kinds of actions.

5. Which aspects of an action language are defined in the UML and which aspects are not?

6. Define the terms *state* and *transition*.

7. When can an activity (set of actions) be executed on a state machine? Which are interruptible?

8. What is meant by *run-to-completion semantics*?

9. What is the symbol for the default (initial) pseudostate?

10. What is the difference between deep and shallow history? How are they indicated?

11. What is the difference between and-states and or-states? How are and-states denoted?

12. What is the difference between a conditional connector and a fork? Under what circumstances would you use each?

13. What is the difference between a conditional connector and a choice point?

14. What are the four kinds of events defined in the UML?

15. What are the special semantics of guards? Where do they appear in a statechart?

16. What is the order of execution of actions in a state machine?

17. When are explicit entry and exit points used in statecharts?

18. What are the rules governing how you can specialize or extend an inherited state machine?

19. What is special about a protocol state machine?

20. Explain what is meant by *token-flow semantics* as it is used in activity diagrams.

21. What are the three primary views in UML of interaction scenarios?

22. What are the vertical lines on a sequence diagram called?

23. How do the alt, opt, loop, and par operators in sequence diagrams differ?

24. Explain the rules used to determine partial ordering in sequence diagrams.

25. What are the two ways that a sequence diagram can be decomposed?

26. What is the semantic difference between timing and sequence diagrams in terms of ordering?
27. What kinds of values are typically shown on the left edge of a timing diagram?

3.8 References

[1] *Unified Modeling Language: Superstructure, Version 2.0.* ptc/03-08-02. Needham, MA: OMG, 2003. *www.omg.org.*

[2] Douglass, Bruce Powel. *Doing Hard Time: Developing Real-Time Systems with UML, Objects, Frameworks, and Patterns.* Reading, MA: Addison-Wesley, 1999.

[3] Gamma, E., R. Helm, R. Johnson, and J. Vlissides. *Design Patterns: Elements of Reusable Object-Oriented Software.* Reading, MA: Addison-Wesley, 1995.

[4] Buschmann, F., R. Meunier, H. Rohnert, P. Sommerlad, and M. Stal. *A System of Patterns: Pattern-Oriented Software Architecture.* New York: John Wiley and Sons, 1996.

[5] Damn, W. and D. Harel "LSCs: Breathing Life into Message Sequence Charts", *Formal Methods in System Design* 19:1 (2001), 45-80.

Chapter 4

UML Profile for Schedulability, Performance, and Time

The OMG has adopted a standard way to capture timeliness, performance, and schedulability properties of real-time systems. This profile doesn't invent any new techniques, but rather codifies what people were already doing when capturing timeliness and related properties. The profile uses stereotypes, tagged values, and constraints with specific names. The primary benefit is the ability to exchange timeliness properties among different tools, such as UML modeling tools and schedulability analysis tools.

Notations and Concepts Discussed

UML Profiles	General Resource Subprofile	Real-Time CORBA Subprofile
Time Subprofile		
Schedulability Subprofile	Concurrency Subprofile	

4.1 UML Profiles

A UML profile is a variant of the UML that is specialized in some minor ways. A UML profile is allowed to contain specialized versions (called *stereotypes*) of the metamodel elements defined in the UML metamodel, user-defined values (properties or tags) attached to these elements, and additional well-formedness rules (constraints). A profile is not allowed to break existing UML semantics, although it is allowed to specialize them. A profile may additionally provide new graphical icons and diagrams and domain-specific model libraries. The purpose of a profile is to provide UML that is tailored for a particular vertical market domain or technology area. Thus, it is possible to have a profile for testing, for modeling quality of service, for modeling business processes, and so on. Each of these is, at its core, vanilla UML, but with some (very) minor extensions and specializations to allow it to apply in a more obvious way to the specific domain.

Because a profile is not allowed to change the semantics of the modeling language in any important or fundamental way, what are the advantages of profiling? The primary advantages are creating profiles that allow us to standardize idioms and design patterns common in a particular domain, and that allow tools to exchange models that use the profile. We shall see later that these are precisely the advantages provided for the UML Profile for Schedulability, Performance, and Time (also called the RT UML profile, or RTP) and the other profiles discussed in this chapter. As a variant of the standard, it has all the disadvantages of a standard—lack of tool support, lack of trained staff, lack of reference materials, and so on. Standardizing the profile mitigates such effects but does not remove them—since they appeal to a subset of the UML user community, tools may offer only limited support.

Nevertheless, profiles *can* be useful in modeling specific domains, especially when the members of the domain can agree on the contents and notations for the domain. A profile is simply a coherent set of specialized metamodel elements (stereotypes), named values (properties or tagged values), and rules (constraints). Once defined, a profile allows us to use these stereotypes as a part of our basic language in which to express user models, and if done well, the profile provides a richer vocabulary that is more closely aligned with the problem domain to which it is being applied.

4.1.1 Stereotypes

The UML uses stereotypes for a couple of purposes. First, and most common, is to indicate which metamodel element is typing a model element on a diagram. For example, a *class box* shows you the operations within the interface, and the stereotype *interface* identifies that this is an interface and not a class. The second primary use for a stereotype is to indicate a specialized kind of metamodel element defined within a profile.[1] Note that you are not allowed to add fundamentally new metamodel elements to a profile—they must be specializations of existing metaclasses in the metamodel.

Stereotypes are shown in one of two ways. Either a textual annotation is attached to the metaclass being stereotyped, such as a class, relation, or node, or the default icon for the metaclass is replaced with a special icon. Figure 4-1 shows both approaches being used. Several stereotypes are used. The first is for the «active» class. An «active» class owns the root of a thread and is how the concurrency model for a system is constructed with UML; instances "contained" via the composition relation (such as the instances of the MQueue class in the figure) run in the context of the thread owned by the instance of the composite active class. The UML 1.x used a class with a heavy boarder as the icon for this kind of class, while in UML 2.0 the icon is a class box with a double line border on the left and right ends. Both forms are shown in Figure 4-1.

---

[1] Stereotypes were originally specified as they are so that tools wouldn't have to provide extensible schemas for their repositories while still enabling some limited extensions by users. In the four-level meta-architecture described in Chapter 2, they are approximately metalevel 1.5. Alternatively, we can specialize the UML at the level of M2 by defining new classes using the language in which the UML itself is defined—the MetaObject Facility (MOF).

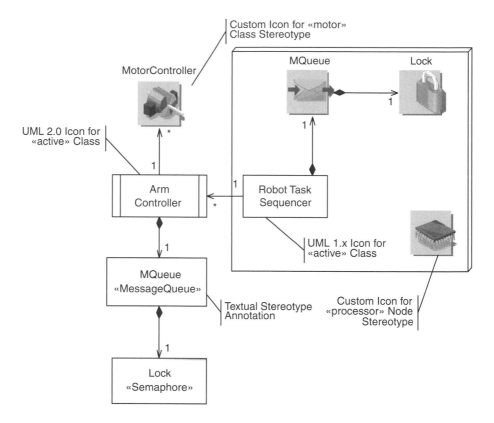

Figure 4-1: *UML Stereotypes*

The MQueue class is stereotyped—it is a "special" kind of class called a «MessageQueue». The MQueue class also contains, via composition, a Lock class, which is likewise stereotyped to be a «Semaphore». The same stereotypes, using the textual notation option, are also shown on the figure. The MotorController class is also stereotyped to be a «motor». Last, any metaclass can be stereotyped—the node shown in the figure is stereotyped to be a «Processor», but they can be applied to any kind of metaclass in the UML.

Stereotypes exist so users (and people building profiles) can add their domain's specific concepts to their modeling language in an easy, lightweight way.

4.1.2 Tagged Values

To some degree, just stereotyping something may be useful because it indicates that it is in a class of entity in your domain's conceptual landscape. Using such stereotypes may clarify the model to domain experts trying to construct or understand your system. However, stereotypes are more useful when they contain special values that apply (only) to that kind of stereotype. The first way in which stereotypes are customized is by adding what is called a *tagged value* or *property*. A tagged value is a property name–value pair. It is common to identify special kinds of values that apply to this stereotype and not others, and to capture these in the model.

The tagged value provides the definition of the kind of information added to the stereotype. The actual values for particular instantiations of the stereotype (e.g., user classes based on the stereotype) are added by assigning or using the tagged values in constraints anchored to the stereotype).

A constraint is a user-defined rule or rule of correctness. The UML has many constraints in its metamodel defining the legal uses for classes, associations, and other model elements. However, these are necessarily highly generalized because the UML can be used to model systems in many domains. A *constraint* is a way in which a user can express a restriction that makes sense in the particular domain from which a model element is drawn. Figure 4-2 shows a typical use of constraints, combining tagged values that are defined for the stereotype.

For example, a stereotype «Semaphore» might have a tagged value called "capacity," which indicates the number of active users of a resource. In the figure, the tagged value is explicitly set to 1. Similarly, a «MessageQueue» might have a maxSize tagged value, an «active» class might have tags such as IsPeriodic, period, and so on. A «processor» node might have tagged values such as memory size, CPU speed, and endian orientation. A constraint is the classic way to specify specific values for the tags that are valid for a stereotype. Constraints, as can be seen in the figure, are normally shown inside of note boxes and within curly braces to set them off from semantic-free comments.

Given that we can use constraints to specify the values associated with the tags, how do we define the tags themselves? There are two common ways. The first, shown in Figure 4-3a, is to use a property sheet

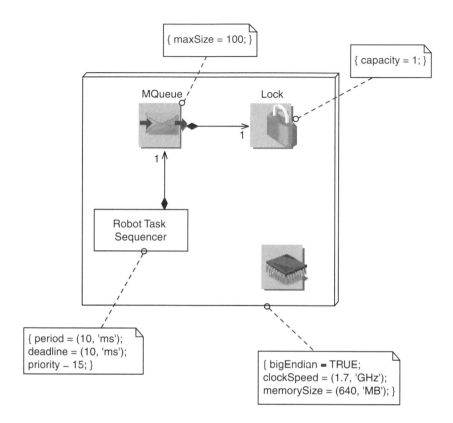

Figure 4-2: *Tagged Values and Constraints*

that shows in a context-sensitive way what tags are available for a particular stereotype. The second, shown in Figure 4-3b, is to show the relevant tags in a compartment labeled «tags». Either can be used, depending on your particular UML design tool and personal preference.

4.1.3 Profiles

A profile is a metamodel of some particular domain of interest, expressed using a coherent set of UML stereotypes with associated tagged values that are used via constraints, possibly accompanied by a model library specific to the domain(s) of interest. The constraint on this definition is that all of the elements of this domain metamodel must be expressed as

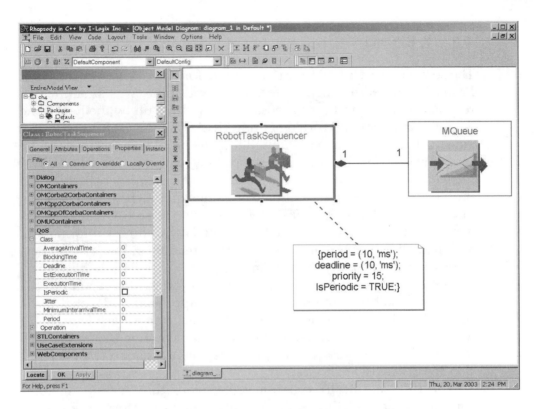

Figure 4-3a: *Representing Tagged Values in Property Sheets*

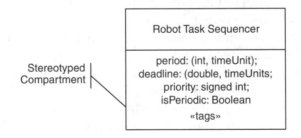

Figure 4-3b: *Representing Tagged Values with Specialized Compartments*

stereotypes of predefined UML metaclasses, such as class, association, node, component, and so on. A profile is not allowed to "break" normal UML semantics, but it is permitted to subset them, specialize them, and extend them, as well as add notations as needed.

4.2 "RT UML" Profile

The so-called RT UML Profile (RTP), more formally known as the UML Profile for Schedulability, Performance, and Time, was submitted in response to a Request for Proposal (RFP) written up by the Real-Time Analysis and Design Working Group (RTAD) of the OMG, of which I am a cochair, as well as a co-submitter of the profile. The purpose of the profile was to define a common, standard way in which timeliness and related properties could be specified, and the primary benefit of the profile was seen to be the ability to exchange quantitative properties of models among tools. Specifically, we wanted to be able to define a standard way for users to annotate their models with timely information, and then allow performance analysis tools read those models and perform quantitative analysis on them.

A consortium of several companies was formed to respond to the RFP. The result was the profile as it was approved and voted to be adopted in 2001. Following the voting, the Finalization Task Force (FTF) was formed to remove defects and resolve outstanding issues. The FTF has completed its work and the profile is now maintained by the Revision Task Force (RTF).

The RFP specifically calls for submissions that "define standard paradigms for modeling of time-, schedule- and performance-related aspects of real-time systems." This does *not* in any way mean that these things cannot be modeled in the UML without this profile. Indeed, the approach the submissions team took was to codify the methods already in use to model time, schedulability, and performance, and then define a standard set of stereotypes and tags. Thus, the tag SApriority allows the user to specify the priority of an active class in a way that a performance analysis tool knows how to interpret.

Several guiding principles were adhered to during the creation of the proposal. First and foremost, the existing UML cannot be changed in a profile. We also did not want to limit how users might want to model their systems. We all felt that there is no one right way to model a system, and we wanted to allow the users freedom to choose the modeling approach that best suited their needs. We did not want to require the user to understand the detailed mathematics of the analytic methods to be applied, and we wanted the approach used to be scalable. By *scalable*, we meant that for a simple analysis, adding the quantitative information should be simple and easy, but for more complex models it was all right to require additional effort. In general, if the analysis or the model were 10 times more complex, then one might reasonably expect 10 times the effort in entering the information. We wanted to provide good support for the common analytical methods such as rate monotonic analysis (RMA) and deadline monotonic analysis (DMA), but we did not want to limit the profile to only such methods. We did not want to specify the analytic methods at all, but concentrate instead on how to annotate user models so that such analysis could easily be done. And finally, we wanted to support the notion that analytic tools could synthesize models and modify the user models to improve performance or schedulability, if appropriate.

Figure 4-4 shows the use cases for the profile.[2] The analysis method providers are actors[3] that define the mathematical techniques for analysis and provide tools and models to execute the analysis of user models. The infrastructure providers are actors that provide infrastructures, such as real-time operating systems, distribution middleware such as CORBA ORBs, or other kinds of frameworks or libraries that might be incorporated into user systems. These use cases are important because the performance of these infrastructures can greatly affect the performance of the overall system. If such an infrastructure provider supplies a quantitative model of their infrastructure, this would allow the modeler to better analyze their system. Finally we have the modelers (you guys) that build user models. The Modelers actor represents the people constructing models and wanting to annotate and analyze them. It is the use cases associated with this actor on which I will focus.

The Modeler use cases are used to create the user models, to perform the quantitative analysis on these models, and to implement the analyzed models. The expected usage paradigm for the profile is shown in Figure 4-5.

In this figure, the user enters the model into a UML modeling tool, such as Rhapsody from I-Logix, as well as entering the quality of service properties of the elements. A modeling analysis tool, such as Rapid RMA from Tri-Pacific Corporation, inputs the model (most likely via XMI), converts it as necessary into a quantitative model appropriate for

---

[2] Use cases are discussed in more detail in the next chapter. For now, just think of uses cases as specifying coherent clumps of requirements, focused around a particular usage of the system.
[3] Objects outside the scope of the system that interact with the system in important ways.

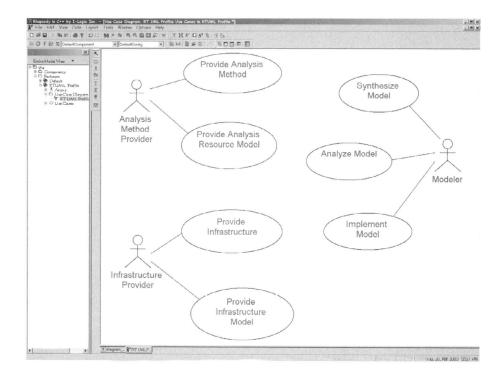

Figure 4-4: *RT UML Profile Use Cases*

the analysis, and applies the mathematical techniques used to analyze the model. Once the analysis is complete, the modeling analysis tool updates the user model—perhaps just to mark it as schedulable or perhaps to reorder task priorities to improve performance. Once the model is adequate and validated, the application system is generated from the updated UML model.

Because the profile is quite large it is divided into subprofiles for improved understandability and usage. Figure 4-6 shows the organization of the profile. It is possible, for example, that some user might want to use one or a smaller number of parts of the profile but not other parts. By segmenting the profile into subprofile packages, the user isn't burdened with all of aspects of the entire profile unless he or she actually needs them.

The three primary packages of the profile are shown in Figure 4-6. The general resource modeling framework contains the basic concepts

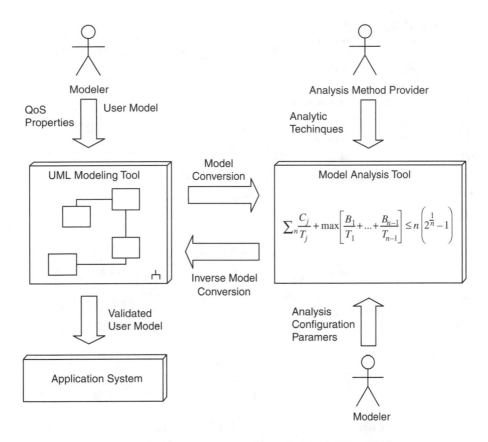

Figure 4-5: *Usage Paradigm for the RT Profile*

of real-time systems and will generally be used by all systems using the framework. This package is subdivided into three smaller subprofiles: RT Resource Modeling, RT Concurrency, and RT Time Modeling. The first of these defines what is meant by a resource—a fundamental concept in real-time systems. The second of these defines a more detailed concurrency model than we see in the general UML metamodel. The last specifies the important aspects of time for real-time systems, time, durations, and time sources, such as timers and clocks.

The second main package of the profile is called *analysis models*. In this package, we provide subpackages for different kinds of analytic methods. The Schedulability Analysis (SA) package defines the stereotypes, tags, and constraints for common forms of schedulability analysis.

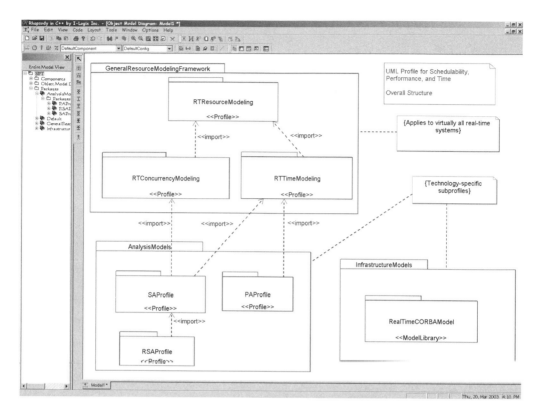

Figure 4-6: *RT UML Profile Organization*

Likewise, the Performance Analysis (PA) package does the same thing for common performance analysis methods. These packages use the concepts defined in the resource, concurrency, and time subprofiles mentioned earlier. The RSA profile specializes the SA profile. As new analytic methods are added, it is anticipated that they would be added as subprofiles in the analysis models package.

The last primary package is the infrastructure package. In this package, infrastructure models are added. The RFP specifically called for a real-time CORBA infrastructure model, but it is anticipated that other infrastructure vendors would add their own packages here if they wish to support the profile.

In the specification of the profile, each of these packages supplies a conceptual metamodel modeling the fundamental concepts of the specific domain, followed by a set of stereotypes and their associated tagged values and constraints. We will discuss each of these subprofiles in turn and finally provide a more complete example of using the overall profile to provide a user model ready for schedulability analysis.

To aid in understanding and tracking down where tags and stereotypes are defined, each tag or stereotype is preceded with a code identifying which subprofile defined the item. Thus, things beginning with "GRM" are defined in the general resource model subprofile, things beginning with PA are to be found in the performance analysis subprofile, and so on.

Because UML is undergoing a major internal reorganization as a result of the UML 2.0 effort, the RTP will need to undergo a similar level of revision to make it consistent with the new UML standard. The RTAD as a group has decided (rightly, I believe) that this cannot be done within the confines of the Revision Task Force (RTF) that maintains the profile but will require a new request for proposal (RFP) with new submissions. As of this writing, the new RFP is scheduled to be written in the coming months.

4.2.1 General Resource Model Subprofile

As you might guess, the most important concepts in the GRM subprofile are *resource* and *quality of service*. A resource is defined to be a model element with finite properties, such as capacity, time, availability, and safety. A quality of service is a quantitative specification of a limitation on one or more services offered by a resource.

The general resource model is built on a classic client-server model. The client requests services to be executed by the server. This service request is called a *resource usage* and may be accompanied by one more qualities of service (QoS) parameters. QoS parameters come in two flavors—offered and required. The client may require some performance QoS from the service during the execution of the service, while the server may provide a QoS parameter. If the offered QoS is at least as good as required, then the QoS parameters are said to be consistent. Figure 4-7 shows this relation schematically.

The basic domain model of resources is shown in Figure 4-8 and the model for static resource usage is shown in Figure 4-9. We see that a descriptor "types" an instance. These classes are subclassed so that a resource (a kind of descriptor) likewise types a ResourceInstance. Resources provide ResourceServices (which type corresponding Resource

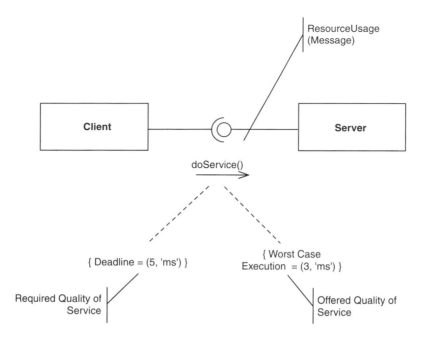

Figure 4-7: *Client-Server Basis of the GRM*

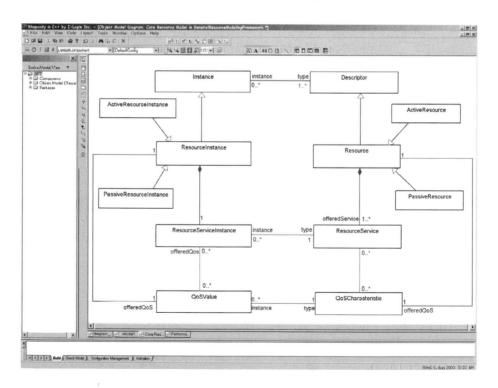

Figure 4-8: *Core Resource Model*

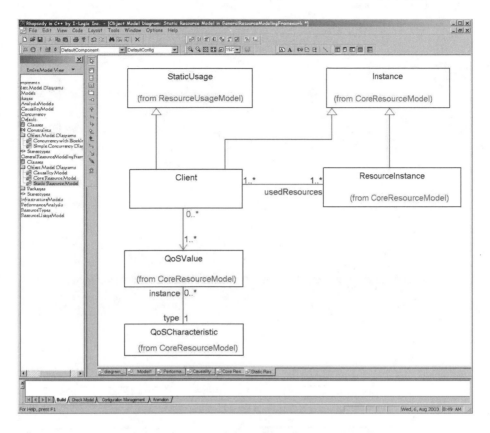

Figure 4-9: *Static Resource Usage Model*

ServiceInstances), each of which can have an associated quality of service characteristic (and corresponding QoS values on the instance side). This strong separation of specifications and instances allows us to perform either static analysis on the specifications or dynamic analysis on the instances of those specifications.

An important basis for dynamic models, the causality loop relates the notion of an event occurrence with the execution of a scenario. An event describes a change in state and may be (among others) a stimulus generation or a stimulus reception. A stimulus, from the UML specification, is an instance of communication between objects. This causality loop is shown in Figure 4-10. In it, we see that a scenario associates with a set on instances that receive stimuli. Each stimulus is created by a stimulus generation and results in a stimulus reception.

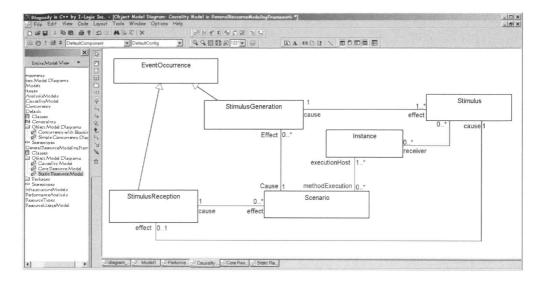

Figure 4-10: *Causality Loop*

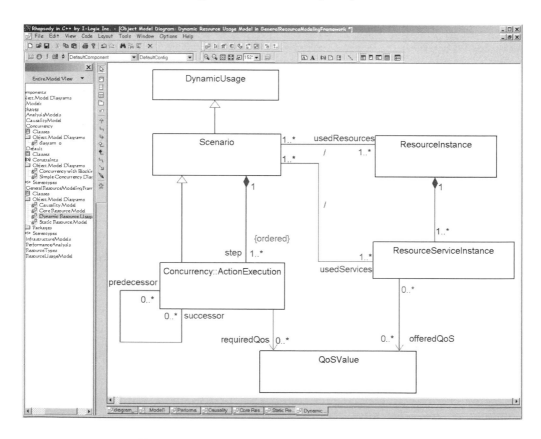

Figure 4-11: *Dynamic Resource Usage Model*

The dynamic resource usage model is used to analyze more complex situations than the much simpler static resource usage model. The static model assumes that properties can be assigned to types and the details of the scenarios need not be characterized. In the dynamic usage model, the internal instances of the executing scenarios are given precise QoS values for analysis. We see in Figure 4-11 that a scenario is composed to an ordered set of ActionExecutions, each of which can have required QoS values. The scenario can also have one or more ResourceServiceInstances, each of which can have an offered QoS value. The ResourceServiceInstances belong to ResourceInstances used in the scenario. Tables 4-1 to 4-6 list the stereotypes defined in this subprofile, along with the applicable metaclasses, tags, and descriptions.

Table 4-1: *General Resource Model Stereotypes*

Stereotype	Applies to (metaclasses)	Tags	Description
«GRMacquire»	Stimulus, Message, Action, ActionExecution, Operation, Reception, Method, ActionState, Transition, SubactivityState	GRMblocking, GRMexclServ	An operation or invocation that acquires access rights to an exclusive resource
«GRMcode» (subclass of «GRMrealize»)	Abstraction	GRMmapping	Relates a logical element model to the component that contains its code
«GRMdeploys» (subclass of «GRMrealize»)	Abstraction	GRMmapping	Identifies where logical model elements are deployed
«GRMrealize»	Abstraction	GRMmapping	A realization mapping
«GRMrelease»	Stimulus, Message, ActionExecution, Action, Operation, Reception, Method, ActionState, Transition, SubactivityState	GRMexclServ	An operation or invocation that releases and exclusive resource acquired previously

(continued)

Table 4-1: *(cont.)*

Stereotype	Applies to (metaclasses)	Tags	Description
«GRMrequires» (subclass of «GRMrealize»)	Abstraction	GRMmapping	A specification of a requirement environment for one or more logical elements

Table 4-2: *General Resource Model Tag Type Definitions*

Tag	Type	Multiplicity	Description
GRMblocking	Boolean	[0..1]	AcquireService::isBlocking
GRMexclServ	Reference to an Action, Action Execution, Operation, Method, ActionState, or SubactivityState	[0..1]	
GRMmapping	GRMMappingString	[0..1]	This tag value should be used only if the mapping details are not fully specified by the realization relationship itself.

4.2.2 Time Modeling Subprofile

The time modeling subprofile specifies the stereotypes and tags for modeling time and related concepts. These are detailed in Table 4-3.

Table 4-3: *Time Subprofile Stereotypes*

Stereotype	Applies to (metaclasses)	Tags	Description
«RTaction»	Action, Action Execution, Stimulus, Message, Method, ActionSequence, ActionState, SubactivityState, Transition, State	RTstart RT end RTduration	An action that takes time

Table 4-3: (*cont.*)

Stereotype	Applies to (metaclasses)	Tags	Description
«RTclkInterrupt» (subclass of «RTstimulus»)	Stimulus, Message	RTtimeStamp	A clock interrupt
«RTclock» (subclass of «RTtiming Mechanism»)	Instance, DataType, Classifier, ClassifierRole, Object, DataValue	RTclockId	A clock mechanism
«RTdelay» (subclass of «RTaction»)	Action, ActionExecution, Stimulus, Message, Method, ActionSequence, ActionState, SubactivityState, Transition, State	RTduration	A pure delay activity
«RTevent»	Action, ActionExecution, Stimulus, Message, Method, ActionSequence, ActionState, SubactivityState, Transition, State	RTat	An event that occurs at a known time instant
«RTinterval»	Instance, Object, Classifier, DataType, DataValue	RTintStart, RTintEnd, RTintDuration	A time interval
«RTnewClock»	Operation		An operation that creates a new clock mechanism[4]
«RTnewTimer»	Operation	RTtimerPar	An operation that creates a new timer[4]

(continued)

---

[4] The stereotype can only used on operations that are declared for a model element that is stereotyped «RTtimeService».

Table 4-3: *(cont.)*

Stereotype	Applies to (metaclasses)	Tags	Description
«RTpause»	Operation		A pause operation on a timing mechanism[5]
«RTreset»	Operation		An operation that resets a timing mechanism[5]
«RTset»	Operation	RTtimePar	An operation that sets the current value of a timing mechanism[5]
«RTstart»	Operation		An operation that starts a timing mechanism[5]
«RTstimulus»	Stimulus, ActionExecution, Action, ActionSequence, Method	RTstart, RTend	A timed stimulus
«RTtime»	DataValue, Instance, Object, DataType, Classifier	RTkind, RTrefClk	A time value or object
«RTtimeout» (subclass of «RTstimulus»)	Stimulus, ActionExecution, Action, ActionSequence, Method	RTtimestamp (inherited)	A timeout signal or a timeout action
«RTtimer» (subclass of «RTtiming Mechanism»)	DataValue, Instance, Object, ClassifierRole, Classifier, DataType	RTduration, RTperiodic	A timer mechanism
«RTtimeService»	Instance, Object, ClassifierRole, Classifier		A time service

---

[5] The stereotype can only be used operations that are declared for a model element that is stereotyped as «RTtimingMechanism» or one of its subclasses.

Table 4-3: *(cont.)*

Stereotype	Applies to (metaclasses)	Tags	Description
«RTtiming Mechanism»	DataValue, Instance, Object, ClassifierRole, Classifier, DataType	RTstability, RTdrift, RTskew, RTmaxValue, RTorigin, RTresolution, RTaccuracy, RTcurrentVal, RToffset, RTrefClk	A timing mechanism

Table 4-4: *Time Subprofile Tag Definitions*

Tag	Type	Multiplicity	Description
RTstart	RTtimeValue	[0..1]	A starting time
RTend	RTtimeValue	[0..1]	An ending time
RTduration	RTtimeValue	[0..1]	The length of time for the referenced stereotype
RTclockID	String	[0..1]	Name of a clock
RTat	RTtimeValue	[0..1]	Time of event occurrence
RTintStart	RTtimeValue	[0..1]	Start of a time interval
RTintEnd	RTtimeValue	[0..1]	End of a time interval
RTintDuration	RTtimeValue	[0..1]	Duration of a time interval
RTtimerPar	RTtimeValue	[0..1]	The time parameter
RTkind	Enumeration of ('dense', 'discrete')	[0..1]	Discrete or continuous time
RTrefClk	Reference to a model element stereotyped as «RTclock», or String	[0..1]	Reference clock; must point to or name a model element that is stereotyped «RTclock» *(continued)*

Table 4-4: (*cont.*)

Tag	Type	Multiplicity	Description
RTperiodic	Boolean	[0..1]	Identifies whether the timer is periodic
RTstability	Real	[0..1]	The ability of the mechanism to measure the progress of time at a consistent rate (an offered QoS characteristic)
RTdrift	Real	[0..1]	The rate of change of the skew (an offered QoS characteristic)
RTskew	Real	[0..1]	Identifies how well the mechanism tracks the reference clock (an offered QoS characteristic)
RTmaxValue	RTtimeValue	[0..1]	The current value cannot be exceeded (an offered QoS characteristic)
RTorigin	String	[0..1]	A clearly identified timed event from which it proceeds to measure time
RTresolution	RTtimeValue	[0..1]	The minimal time interval that can be recognized by the mechanism (an offered QoS characteristic)
RToffset	RTtimeValue	[0..1]	The difference between two clocks
RTaccuracy	RTtimeValue	[0..1]	The maximal offset of a clock over time
RTcurrentVal	RTtimeValue	[0..1]	The current value of a timing mechanism

Tagged values hold values that are taken from its type. TimeValues can be expressed in a number of forms:

- time string   hr ":" min ":" sec
- date string   year "/" month "/" day
- day string   Mon, Tues, etc.
- metric timer string   <number> PDF <time unit>
  - ▾ PDF   specifies a probability density function
  - ▾ time unit   ns, ms, us, s, min, hr, days, wks, mos, yrs

Arrival patterns are specified with the RTArrivalPattern tag. There are several kinds: bounded, bursty, irregular, periodic, and unbounded. Formally, the syntax is

```
RTArrivalPattern ::= <bounded-string> | <bursty-
string> | <irregular-string> | <periodic-string> |
  <unbounded-string>
bounded-string ::= " 'bounded' ," <time-value> ","
  <time-value>
<bursty-string> ::= " 'bursty' ," <time-value> ","
  <integer>
<irregular-string> ::= " 'irregular' ," <time-value>
  [ '," <time-value> ]*
<periodic-string> ::= " 'periodic' ," <time-value>
  [ "," <time-value>]
<unbounded-string> ::= " 'unbounded' ," <PDF-string>
```

Bound arrival patterns are specified with the keyword *bounded,* followed by a lower and upper bound, as in "bounded, (0, 'ms'), (15, 'ms')." A bursty arrival pattern means that the arrival of events is correlated in time, that is, the arrival of one event makes it more likely that another event will arrive soon after. Bursty arrival patterns are specified with the *bursty* key word followed by a time value (indicating the burst interval) and an integer value (indicating the maximum number of events in that interval, as in "bursty, (20, 'ms'), 100)." An irregular arrival pattern describes a series of arrival times. It is specified using the keyword *irregular,* followed by a list of time values, as in "irregular, (10, 'ms'), (15, 'ms'), (5, 'ms')." The asterisk (*) in the grammar means that the term can be repeated an arbitrarily number of times. Periodic arrival patterns are very common. They are indicated with the keyword *period* and a time value indicating the period. The period value may optionally be followed by another time value that indicates the maximal deviation from the period (sometimes called *jitter*), as in "periodic, (100, 'ms'), (500, 'us')." Finally, an unbounded arrival pattern is one in which the arrival times are drawn as a renewal process from an underlying probability density function, as described below. An example would be "unbounded, normal (100, 'ms'), (15, 'ms')" to specify a normal (Gaussian) distribution with a mean of 100 ms and a standard deviation of 15 ms.

The time subprofile identifies the most common probability density functions (PDFs) used with event time distributions—Bernoulli, binominal, exponential, gamma, histogram, normal, Poisson, and uniform. Each of these has one or more parameters qualifying the mathematical properties of the distribution. Bernoulli distribution has a single real parameter specifying the probability (in the range of 0 to 1). Binomial distributions have two parameters, a real (the probability) and an integer (the number of trials). Exponential distributions have a single real parameter, the mean, as in "exponential 100." Gamma distributions have two parameters; the first is an integer k, and the mean from the formula in Equation 4-1.

$$\frac{x^{k-1} \cdot e^{-(x/mean)}}{mean^{k} \cdot (k-1)!}$$

Equation 4-1: *Gamma Distribution*

A histogram distribution is a set of real number pairs, followed by a single real number. Each number pair indicates the start of an interval and the probability of occurrence within that interval. The last single number defines the ending point for the last interval, as in "histogram, 10, 0.10, 20, 0.50, 30, 0.30, 40, 0.1, 50." A normal distribution is characterized by a mean and standard deviation, as in "normal, 90.5, 8.5." A Poisson distribution has a mean, as in "poisson, 80.5." Lastly, a uniform distribution is characterized by a starting and ending points, as in "uniform 50.0, 150.0."

Timing information can be applied to action executions using a set of defined "timing marks," including

- *RTstart:* The time the action begins or the stimulus is sent.
- *RTend:* The time the action ends or the stimulus response has completed
- *RTduration:* The length of time the of an action execution or the stimulus response, that is, RTduration = RTend - RTstart for the same action execution or stimulus

These timing marks are used in timing expressions captured in constraints applied against the actions or stimuli, as in

$$\{ RTend - RTstart < (10, \text{'ms'}) \}$$

which specifies that the time that a stimulus is received until the initiated action completes is less than 10 ms.

Such timing specifications are often made on sequence diagrams, such as that in Figure 4-12. We see some of the messages stereotyped as

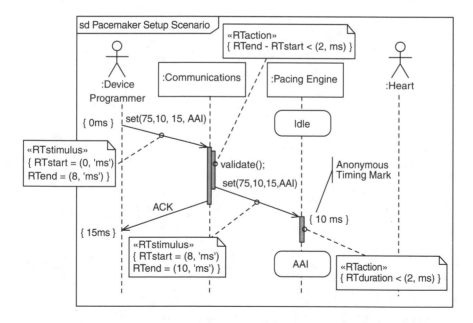

Figure 4-12: *Timing Marks*

«RTstimulus» and the actions stereotyped as «RTaction». Timing information is added as tags associated with the stereotypes. In addition, there are some "anonymous timing marks" that allow the annotation of the progress of time during the execution of the scenario.

4.2.3 Concurrency Modeling Subprofile

The concurrency subprofile refines the core UML's somewhat vague notions of concurrency. The domain model for the profile's concurrency subprofile is shown in Figure 4-13. The most central concept is that of ConcurrentUnit. A ConcurrentUnit is a kind of ActiveResource,

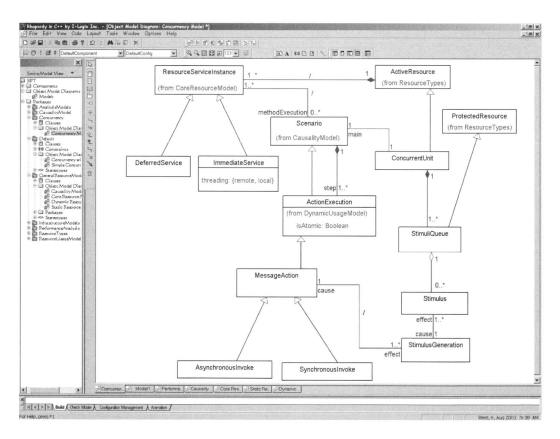

Figure 4-13: *Concurrency Subprofile Domain Model*

which in turn is a kind of ResourceInstance, a domain concept discussed in Section 4.2.1. An ActiveResource is a resource instance that is able to generate its own stimuli concurrently, that is, independent from other activities. A ConcurrentUnit runs a main scenario and may have one or more StimuliQueues. Because it is a subclass of ResourceInstance, it may also own (via composition) an unbounded number of Resource-ServiceInstances (instances of services provided by resources). This is what most closely corresponds to the notions of thread, task, and process found in the operating systems literature.

ConcurrentUnits then have a main() operation that invokes the main scenario, which in turn is composed of a set of ActionExecutions and associates with one or more resource service instances. These resource service instances may be either deferred or immediate, and if immediate, they may be either local or remote. An immediate service instance handles incoming requests immediately, spawning new threads to do so if required (local threading) or assumes an existing thread will handle it (the remote threading). When a service instance is deferred, the request or stimulus waits until the receiving server is ready to process it. The ConcurrentUnits may collaborate by sending stimuli to each other—this is done via the execution of either synchronous or asynchronous message actions.

This domain model is cast into the UML standard as a set of stereotypes and tags, as shown in Tables 4-5 and 4-6.

The scenario shown in Figure 4-14 illustrates how the concurrency subprofile tags can be used to indicate relevant quality of service properties. The Atrial Timer and the AtrialModel instances are both active and own their own thread of execution ("ConcurrentUnit," in the profile's parlance). In addition, the Atrial Timer is also an «RTtimer» stereotype. Various messages are stereotyped to allow the appropriate tags to be attached to the message to specify their qualities of service. For example, the toInhibiting message is stereotyped to be a «RTevent» with the RTat tag specified: {RTat = (0, 'ms') }. The set() operation that sets the value and starts the timer is stereotyped to be a «RTstart» kind. Some of the action executions are stereotyped to be either «CRSynch» or «CRAsynch» depending on whether they execute in the thread of the caller («CRSynch») or not («CRAsynch»). Some are also stereotyped to be «RTAction» so that the tag RTDuration can specify the execution time QoS for the action.

Table 4-5: *Concurrency Subprofile Stereotypes*

Stereotype	Applies to (metaclasses)	Tags	Description
«CRaction»	Action, ActionExecution, Stimulus, Message, Method, ActionState, SubactivityState, Transition, State	CRatomic	An action execution
«CRasynch»	Action, ActionExecution		An asynchronous invocation
«CRconcurrent»	Node, Component, Artifact, Class, Instance	CRmain	A concurrent unit concept
«CRcontains»	Usage		A generalized usage concept
«CRceferred»	Operation, Reception, Message, Stimulus		A deferred receive
«CRimmediate»	Operation, Reception, Message, Stimulus	{remote, local}	An instance of an immediate service
«CRmsgQ»	Instance, Object, Class, ClassifierRole		A stimulus queue
«CRSynch»	Action, ActionExecution		A synchronous invocation

4.2.4 Schedulability Modeling Subprofile

The previous subprofiles, the general resource model, time, and concurrency subprofiles, do provide useful stereotypes and tags for the specification of important qualities of service, but the schedulability subprofile is where the concepts come together for the most common types of schedulability analysis.

Table 4-6: *Concurrency Tags*

Tag	Type	Multiplicity	Description
CRatomicRTend	Boolean	[0..1]	Whether an «CRAction» is interruptible or atomic.
CRmain	A reference to a method, or a string that contains a path to a method	[0..1]	Identifies the main method of a concurrent unit, such as a thread.
CRthreading	enumeration of {'remote', 'local'}	[0..1]	Identifies whether the invocation of «CRImmediate» stereotype of an operation, method, or reception or the sending of a stimulus is remote or local.

The core domain model for the schedulability subprofile is shown in Figure 4-15. This domain model connects to the other domain models in that many of the domain classes are subclasses of classes in the previous subprofiles. For example, SAction is a subclass of Timed Action (from the TimedEvents package in the time subprofile), Trigger is a subclass of UsageDemand (from the ResourceUsageModel of the general resource model subprofile), RealTimeSituation is a subclass of AnalysisContext (from the ResourceUsageModel of the general resource model subprofile), an ExecutionEngine is a subtype of ActiveResource, Processor, and ProtectedResource (all from the ResourceTypes package of the general resource model subprofile), an SResource is a subclass of ProtectedResource (ibid), and SchedulableResource is a subclass of both SResource and ActiveResource.

An SAction, or *schedulable action,* may contain nested actions. The QoS properties of an SAction may be derived, if necessary, from the QoS properties of its subordinate parts. SActions have a large number of tags that can be used for schedulability analysis, such as SApriority, SAblocking, SAworstCase (worst-case completion time), and so on, as well as those inherited from its superclass TimedAction. These actions engine may be a CPU, operating system, or virtual machine running the scheduling job. A scheduling job is associated with a trigger that starts it off and a response—a sequence of actions that is separately

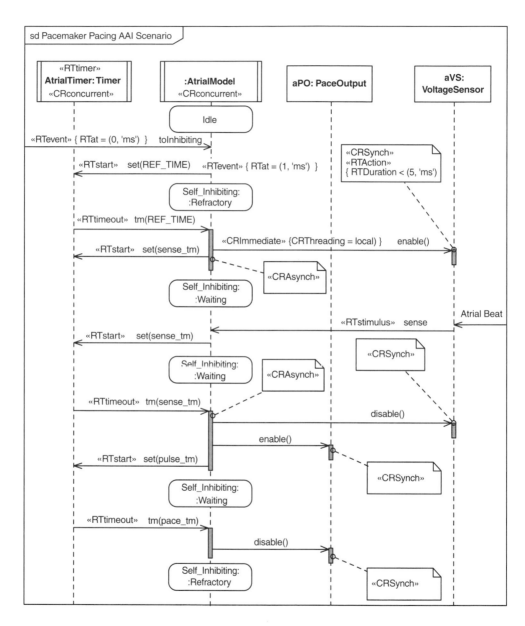

Figure 4-14: *Concurrency Subprofile Stereotypes Example*

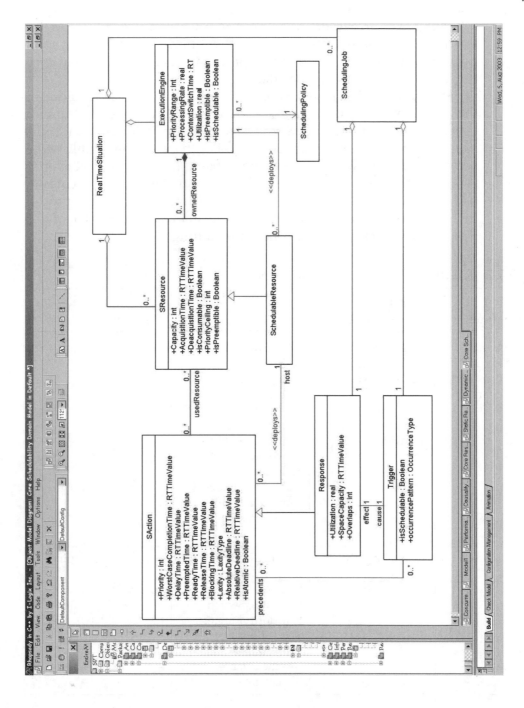

Figure 4-15: *Schedulability Domain Model*

schedulable on an execution engine. A response is a subclass of SAction but adds a few more QoS aspects, such as utilization, slack time, spare capacity, and how many instances of the response may overlap their execution in the case of missed deadlines.

An SResource is a kind of protected resource that is accessed during the execution of a scheduling job. Because it may be shared among concurrently executing actions, it must be protected with a mutual exclusion lock such as a semaphore or by a policy that prevents simultaneous access. Examples of an SResource are a shared queue or A/D converter. A SchedulableResource is a kind of SResource that is used to execute one or a set of actions. This domain class represents a task, thread, or process in the OS world. These domain concepts are mapped into the stereotypes and tagged values identified in Tables 4-7 through 4-12.

Table 4-7: *Schedulability Subprofile Stereotypes*

Stereotype	Applies to (metaclasses)	Tags	Description
«SAaction» (subclass of «RTaction» and «CRAction»)	Action, ActionExecution, Stimulus, Message, Method, ActionState, SubactivityState, Transition	SApriority, SAbctualPty, SAblocking, SAbeady, SAdelay, SArelease, SApreempted, SAworstCase, SAlaxity, SAabsDeadline, SAaelDeadline, SAusedResource, SAhost	A schedulable action
«SAengine»	Node, Instance, Object, Classifier, ClassifierRole	SAschedulingPolicy, SAaccessPolicy, SArate, SAcontextSwitch, SApriorityRangc, SApreemptible, SAutilization, SAschedulable, SAresources	An execution engine

Table 4-7: *(cont.)*

Stereotype	Applies to (metaclasses)	Tags	Description
«SAowns» (subclass of «GRMrealize»)	Abstraction		Identifies ownership of resources.
«SAprecedes»	Usage		
«SAresource»	Classifier, ClassifierRole, Instance, Object, Node	SAaccessControl, SAconsumable SAcapacity, SAacquisition, SAdeacquisition, SAptyCeiling, SApreemptible	A resource
«SAresponse» (subclass of «SAAction»)	Action, ActionExecution, Stimulus, Message, Method	SAutilization, SAspare, SAslack, SAoverlaps	A response to a stimulus or action
«SAschedulable» (subclass of «SAResource»)	Classifier, ClassifierRole, Instance, Object, Node		A schedulable resource
«SAscheduler»	Classifier, ClassifierRole, Instance, Object	SAschedulingPolicy, SAexecutionEngine	A scheduler
«SAprecedes»	Usage		A precedence relationship between actions and triggers
«SAsituation»	Collaboration, Collaboration Instance, ActivityGraph		A schedulability analysis context
«SAtrigger» (subclass of «SAaction»)	Message, Stimulus	SAschedulable, SAprecedents	A trigger
«SAusedHost»	Usage		Identifies schedulable resources used for execution of actions.
«SAuses»	Usage		Identifies sharable resources.

Table 4-8: *SAAction Tagged Values*

Tag	Type	Multiplicity	Description
SApriority	integer	[0..1]	Maps to operating system priority
SAblocking	RTtimeValue	[0..1]	Time that the action may be prevented from execution by a lower-priority task that owns a required resource
SAdelay	RTtimeValue	[0..1]	The length of time that an action that is ready to run must wait while acquiring and releasing resources
SApreempted	RTtimeValue	[0..1]	The length of time a ready-to-run action is prevented from running by a higher-priority task
SAready	RTtimeValue	[0..1]	The length of time between when an action is ready to run until it begins execution
SArelease	RTtimeValue	[0..1]	The instant of time at which an action becomes ready to run
SAworstCase	RTtimeValue	[0..1]	The longest period of time required for an action to complete its execution, including all the overheads (blocking, delay, preemption, etc.)
SAabs Deadline	RTtimeValue	[0..1]	The final instant of time by which an action must be complete
SAlaxity	Enumeration of {"Hard," "Soft"}	[0..1]	Specifies the kind of deadline, hard or soft
SArel Deadline	RTtimeValue	[0..1]	For soft deadlines, specifies the desired time by which the action is complete
SAused Resource	Reference to a model element that is stereotyped «SAResource»	[0..*]	Identifies a set of resources this action may use during execution

Table 4-8: (*cont.*)

Tag	Type	Multiplicity	Description
SAhost	Reference of a model element that is stereotyped «SASchedulable»	[0..1]	Identifies the schedulable resource on which the action executions, in effect, a deployment relation
start time (inherited from TimedAction)	RTtimeValue	[0..1]	The start time of the action
end time (inherited from TimedAction)	RTtimeValue	[0..1]	The ending time of the action
duration (inherited from TimedAction)	RTtimeValue	[0..1]	The total duration of the action (not used if start and end times are specified)
isAtomic (inherited from Concurrent Action)	Boolean	[0..1]	Identifies whether or not the action may be preempted

Table 4-9: *SAEngine Tagged Values*

Tag	Type	Multiplicity	Description
SAaccess Policy	Enumeration: {'FIFO', 'Priority Inheritance', 'NoPreemption', 'HighestLocker', 'PriorityCeiling'}	[0..]	Access control policy to arbitrate simultaneous access requests
SArate	Float	[0..1]	A relative speed factor for the execution engine, expressed as a percentage (*continued*)

Table 4-9: *(cont.)*

Tag	Type	Multiplicity	Description
SAcontext Switch	Time function	[0..1]	The length of time (overhead) required to switch scheduling jobs
SApriority Range	integer range	[0..1]	A set of valid priorities for the execution engine (OS dependent)
SApreemptible	Boolean	[0..1]	Indicates whether or not the execution engine may be preempted once it begins the execution of an action
SAutilization	Percentage (Real)	[0..1]	A computed result indicating the percentage of usage of the execution engine
SAscheduling Policy	Enumeration: {'RateMonotonic', 'Deadline Monotonic', 'HKL', 'FixedPriority', 'Minimum LaxityFirst', 'Maximum AccurredUtility', 'MinimumSlack Time' }	[0..1]	A set of scheduler that schedule jobs on this execution engine
SAschedulable	Boolean	[0..1]	A computed result indicating whether or not the jobs executing on the execution engine can be guaranteed to meet their timeliness requirements
SAresources	Reference to an element stereotyped «SAResource»	[0..*]	Resources owned by the execution engine

Table 4-10: *SAResponse Tagged Values*

Tag	Type	Multiplicity	Description
SAutilization	Percentage (Real)	[0..1]	The percentage of the period of the trigger during which the response is using the schedulable resource
SAslack	RTtimeValue	[0..1]	The difference between the amount of time required to complete the work and the amount of time remaining in the period
SAspare	RTtimeValue	[0..1]	The amount of execution time that can be added to a scheduling job without affecting the schedulability of low-priority scheduling jobs in the system
SAoverlaps	Integer	[0..1]	In the case of soft deadlines, the number of instances that may overlap their execution because of missed deadlines

Table 4-11: *SAResource Tagged Values*

Tag	Type	Multiplicity	Description
SAaccess Control (inherited from Protected Resource)	Enumeration: { 'FIFO', 'Priority Inheritance', 'NoPreemption', 'HighestLockers', 'Distributed PriorityCeiling' }	[0..1]	Access control policy for handling requests from scheduling jobs, such as FIFO, Priority Ceiling, etc.
SAcapacity	Integer	[0..1]	The number of permissible concurrent users (e.g., as in counting semaphore)
SAacqusition	RTtimeValue	[0..1]	The time delay of an action between the request to access a resource and the granting of that access *(continued)*

Table 4-11: *(cont.)*

Tag	Type	Multiplicity	Description
SA deacquisition	RTtimeValue	[0..1]	The time delay of an action between the request to release a resource and the action being able to continue
SA Consumable	Boolean	[0..1]	Indicates that the resource is consumed by the use
SAPtyCeiling	Integer	[0..1]	The priority of the highest-priority scheduling job that can ever access the resource
SA preemptible	Boolean	[0..1]	Indicates whether the resource can be preempted while in use

Table 4-12: *SATrigger Tagged Values*

Tag	Type	Multiplicity	Description
SA schedulable	Boolean	[0..1]	A computed value when the trigger is schedulable
SAprecedents	Reference to a model element stereotyped as «SAAction»	[0..1]	Actions that execute prior to the trigger
SAoccurrence	RTArrival Pattern	[0..1]	How often the trigger occurs, such as periodically

All this probably seems confusing, more from the plethora of stereotypes and tags than from their inherent complexity. In actual fact, you will most likely use a small subset of the stereotypes and tags in any given analysis of schedulability. Different kinds of analysis will tend to use different stereotypes and tags.

For example, look at the model in Figure 4-16. It contains five active objects, each of which owns a thread. The properties of these threads, such as the occurrence pattern ("periodic"), the period, worst-case execution time, and so on are all provided as tagged values in the

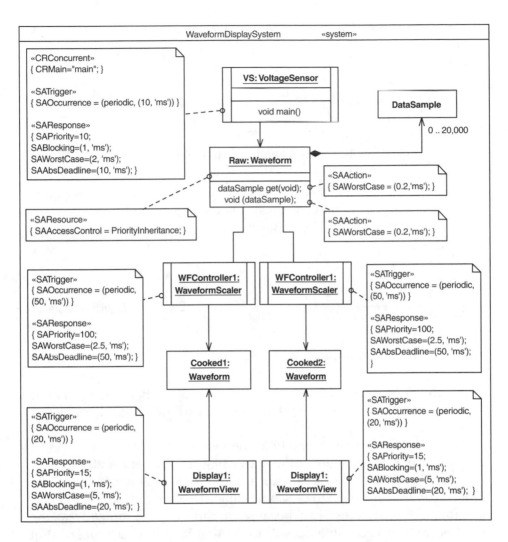

Figure 4-16: *Schedulability Subprofile Example (Global RMA)*

constraints. In this case, the higher the value of the priority, the lower the priority; in the model; the classes with priority 100 are the lowest priority threads. Note that the lowest priority threads have no blocking term because, by definition, they cannot be blocked, only preempted. There are also three resources (waveform queues), different instances of the same class, Waveform. To perform schedulability analysis on this model is straightforward.

First, remember the global RMA analysis inequality shown in Equation 4-2.

$$\sum_j \frac{C_j}{T_j} + \max\left(\frac{B_1}{T_1}, \ldots, \frac{B_{n-1}}{T_{n-1}}\right) \leq utilization(n) = n\left(2^{\frac{1}{n}} - 1\right)$$

Equation 4-2: *Rate Monotonic Analysis with Blocking*

in which C_j is the worst-case execution time for task j, T_j is the period of task j, B_j is the blocking time for task j, and n is the number of tasks.

Inserting the information from the tags into the inequality, we get Equation 4-3.

$$\frac{2}{10} + \frac{3}{20} + \frac{3}{20} + \frac{2.5}{50} + \frac{2.5}{50} + \max\left(\frac{0.2}{10}, \frac{0.2}{20}\right) = 0.62 < utilization(5) = 0.743$$

Equation 4-3: *Analysis of Static Model*

Since the inequality is true, we can guarantee that the system is schedulable; that is, it will always meet its deadlines, regardless of task phasings.

More detailed analysis can be done by looking at the sequences of actions rather than merely at the active objects. This is usually done if the global RMA analysis fails, indicating that the system can't be guaranteed (by that analysis) to be schedulable. The global analysis method is often overly strong—just because it can't be guaranteed by the method to be schedulable doesn't mean that it isn't. It just means that the analytic method can't guarantee it. However, a more detailed analysis may be able to guarantee it.

A more detailed analysis might analyze a specific scenario, or class of scenarios. Such a scenario is shown in Figure 4-17. This sequence diagram uses both the sd and the par operators, so that the interaction subfragments (separated by operand separators) are running concurrently. The scenario is schedulable if it can be demonstrated that all of its concurrent parts can meet their deadlines, including any preemption due to the execution of peer concurrent interactions.

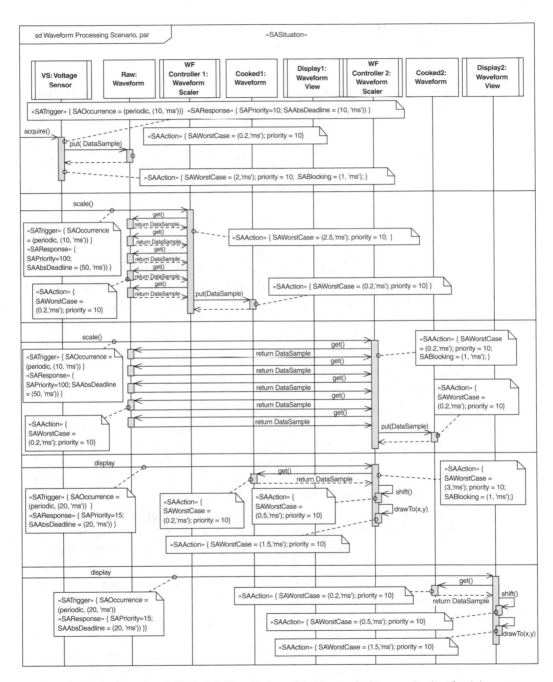

Figure 4-17: *Schedulability Subprofile Example (Scenario Analysis)*

In this scenario, the timing and scheduling information is provided in a more detailed view from which the global summary may be constructed. For example, in the first parallel interaction fragment, the acquire() method is stereotyped to be both an SAtrigger (so it can have an occurrence pattern and period) and an SAresponse (so it can have a priority and a deadline). The timing properties of each of the call actions are defined. Since priority inheritance is used to limit priority inversion, an action may be blocked by, at most, a single lower-priority action. The blocking time for the overall sequential thread of execution is the largest blocking term for any of its subactions.

4.2.5 Performance Modeling Subprofile

The performance analysis (PA) subprofile is concerned with annotating a model for computation of system performance. Specifically, this profile uses the concepts and tags defined in the resource, concurrency, and time subprofiles to create stereotypes and tags that are useful for adding quantitative measures of performance, so that overall system performance analysis may be performed. Note that is this different from schedulability analysis, which analyzes a system to ensure whether it can meet its schedulability requirements.

Performance analysis is inherently instance-based (as opposed to class- or type-based). Scenarios, sequences of steps for which at least the first and last steps are visible, are associated with a workload or a response time. Open workloads are defined by streams of service requests that have stochastically characterized arrival patterns, such as from a Poisson or Gaussian distribution. Closed workloads are defined by a fixed number of users or clients cycling among the clients for service requests.

Scenarios, as we have seen, are composed of scenario steps, which are sequences of actions connected by operators such as decision branches, loops, forks, and joins. Scenario steps may themselves be composed of smaller steps. Scenario steps may use resources via resource demands, and most of the interesting parts of performance analysis have to do with how a finite set of resource capabilities are shared among their clients. Resources themselves are modeled as servers.

Performance measures are usually modeled in terms of these resources, such as the percentage of resource utilization or the response time of a resource to a client request. Within those broad guidelines, these measures may be worst case, average case, estimated case, or measured case.

Performance analysis is normally done either with queuing models or via simulation. Queuing models assume that requests may wait in a FIFO queue until the system is ready to process them. This waiting time is a function of the workload placed on the resources as well as the time (or effort) required by the system to fulfill the request once started. In simple analysis, it may only require the arrival rates of the requests and the response time or system utilization required to respond. More detailed analyses may require distributions of the request occurrences as well. Simulation analysis logically "executes" the system under different loads. A request *in process* is represented as a logical token and the capacity of the system is the number of such tokens the may be *in process* at one time. Because of bottlenecks, blocking, and queuing, it is possible to compute the stochastic properties of the system responses.

The domain model for performance modeling is shown in Figure 4-18. As discussed earlier, a scenario is associated with a workload, the latter being characterized in terms of a response time and a priority. Scenarios use resources and are composed of scenario steps. Resources may be passive or active processors resources. The elements of this domain model which are subclasses of elements in other profiles are shown with the base elements colored and the packages from whence they are defined are shown using the scope dereference operator "::".

These domain concepts are used to identify stereotypes of UML elements, and the domain concept attributes are defined as tags in the performance analysis profile. Tables 4-13 through 4-18 give the stereotypes, the applicable UML metaclasses, the associated tags, and a brief description.

There are a few special types used in the tag definitions above. Specifically, SchedulingEnumeration, PAperfType, and PAextOpValue. The SchedulingEnumeration type specifies various scheduling policies that may be in use. These are commonly exclusive. The PA profile defines the following types of scheduling policies:

- FIFO: First-in-first-out scheduling
- HeadOfLine: Cyclic executive scheduling
- PreemptResume: Preemptive multitasking scheduling
- ProcSharing: Processor sharing, or round-round scheduling
- PrioProcSharing: Priority round-round scheduling
- LIFO: Last-in-first-out scheduling

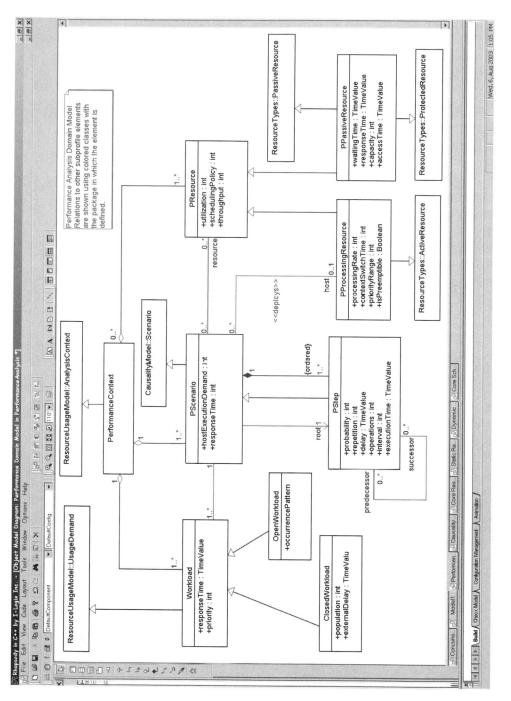

Figure 4-18: *Performance Domain Model*

Table 4-13: *Performance Subprofile Stereotypes*

Stereotype	Applies to (metaclasses)	Tags	Description
«PAclosedLoad»	Action, ActionExecution, ActionState, SubactivityState, Stimulus, Message, Method, Operation, Reception	PArespTime, PApriority, PApopulation, PAextDelay	A closed workload
«PAcontext»	Collaboration, Collaboration InstanceSet, ActivityGraph		A performance analysis context
«PAhost»	Classifier, Node, ClassifierRole, Instance, Partition	PAutilization, PAschdPolicy, PArate, PActxtSwT, PAprioRange, PApreemptible, PAthroughput	An execution engine that hosts the scenario
«PAopenLoad»	Action, ActionExecution, ActionState, SubactivityState, Stimulus, Message, Method, Operation, Reception	PArespTime [0..*,] PApriority, PAoccurrence	An open workload
«PAresource»	Classifier, Node, ClassifierRole, Instance, Partition	PAutilization, PAschdPolicy, PAschdParam, PAcapacity, PAaxTime, PArespTime, PAwaitTime, PAthroughput	A passive resource

(continued)

Table 4-13: *(cont.)*

Stereotype	Applies to (metaclasses)	Tags	Description
«PAstep»	Messasge, ActionState, Stimulus, SubactivityState	PAdemand, PArespTime, PAprob, PArep, PAdelay, PAextOp, PAinterval	A step in a scenario

Table 4-14: *PAclosedWorkload Tagged Values*

Tag	Type	Multiplicity	Description
PArespTime	PAperfValue	[0..*]	Time required for completion of the scenario from the start of the scenario
PApriority	Integer	[0..1]	Priority of workload
PApopulation	Integer	[0..1]	The size of the workload (i.e., the number of system users)
PAextDelay	PAperfValue	[0..1]	The delay between the completion of one response and the start of the next for each member of the population of system users

Table 4-15: *PAhost Tagged Values*

Tag	Type	Multiplicity	Description
PAutilization	Real	[0..*]	The mean number of concurrent users
PSschdPolicy	Scheduling Enumeration	[0..1]	Policy by which host schedules workloads
PArate	Real	[0..1]	Processing rate of the scenario execution
PActxtSwT	PAperfValue	[0..1]	Context switch time

Table 4-15: *(cont.)*

Tag	Type	Multiplicity	Description
PAprioRange	Integer range	[0..1]	Valid range for priorities of workloads
PA preemptable	Boolean	[0..1]	Whether scheduled workloads may be preempted
PA throughput	Real	[0..1]	Number of workloads completed per unit time

Table 4-16: *PAopenLoad Tagged Values*

Tag	Type	Multiplicity	Description
PArespTime	PAperfValue	[0..*]	Time required for completion of the scenario from the start of the scenario
PApriority	Integer	[0..1]	The priority of workload
PAoccurrence	RTarrivalPattern	[0..1]	The arrival pattern of the workload

Table 4-17: *PAresource Tagged Values*

Tag	Type	Multiplicity	Description
PAutilization	Real	[0..*]	The mean number of concurrent users
PAschdPolicy	Scheduling Enumeration	[0..1]	Policy by which host schedules workloads
PAcapacity	Integer	[0..1]	Number of workloads that can be handled simultaneously, i.e. the maximum number of concurrent users of the system
PAaxTime	PAperfValue	[0..1]	Resource access time, that is, the time required to acquire or release the resource
PArespTime	PAperfValue	[0..1]	Time required for the resource to complete its response *(continued)*

Table 4-17: *(cont.)*

Tag	Type	Multiplicity	Description
PAwaitTime	PAperfValue	[0..1]	The time between when a resource access is requested and when it is granted
PAthroughput	Real	[0..1]	Number of workloads that can be completed per unit time

Table 4-18: *PAstep Tagged Values*

Tag	Type	Multiplicity	Description
PAdemand	PAperfValue	[0..*]	The total demand of the step on its processing resource
PArespTime	PAperfValue	[0..*]	The total time to execute the step, including the time to access and release any resources
PAprob	Real	[0..1]	In stochastic models, the probability that this step will be executed (as opposed to alternative steps)
PArep	Integer	[0..1]	The number of times the step is repeated
PAdelay	PAperfValue	[0..*]	Delay between step execution
PAextOp	PAextOpValue	[0..*]	The set of operations of resources used in the execution of the step
PAinterval	PAperfValue	[0..*]	The time interval between successive executions of a step when the step is repeated within a scenario

The PAperfValue is a performance value type of the form

"(" <source-modifier> "," <type-modifier> "," <time-value> ")"

The source modifier is a string that may be any of the following:

- 'req' (for required)
- 'assm' (for assumed)

- 'pred' (for predicted)
- 'msr' (for measured)

The type modifier may be any of the following expressions:

- 'mean' <integer>, for average
- 'sigma' <integer>, for variance
- 'kth mom' <integer>, for kth moment
- 'max' <real>, for maximum
- 'percentile' <real>, for percentage value
- 'dist', for probability distribution

The time value is defined by the specification of RTtimeValue provided in the section of schedulability.

For example:

- { PAdemand = 'msr', 'mean', (20, 'ms')) }
- { PAdelay = 'req', 'max', (500, 'us')) }
- { PArespTime = 'mean, 'sigma', (100, 'ms')) }

PAestOpValue is a string used to identify an external operation and either the number of repetitions of the operation or a performance time value. The format is of the form

```
"(" <String> "," <integer> | <time-value> ")"
```

where the string names the external operation and the integer specifies the number of times the operation is invoked. The time value is of type PAperValue and specifies a performance property of the external operation.

The three figures that follow, Figures 4-19 through 4-21, provide an example model that can be analyzed for performance. Figure 4-19 shows the object structure of the system to be analyzed—an engine control system that includes a Doppler sensor for detecting train velocity, an object that holds current speed (and uses a filtering object to smooth out high-frequency artifacts), and an engine controller that uses this information to adjust engine speed—plus two views for the train operator, a textual view of the current speed (after smoothing) and a histogram view that shows the recent history of speed.

Figure 4-20 shows how these objects are deployed. In this case, there are four distinct processing environments. A low-power acquisition module reads the emitted light after it has been reflected off the train track and computes an instantaneous velocity from this, accounting for angle and at least in a gross way for reflection artifacts. This process runs at a relative rate of 10. Since the reference is the 1MBit bus, this can be

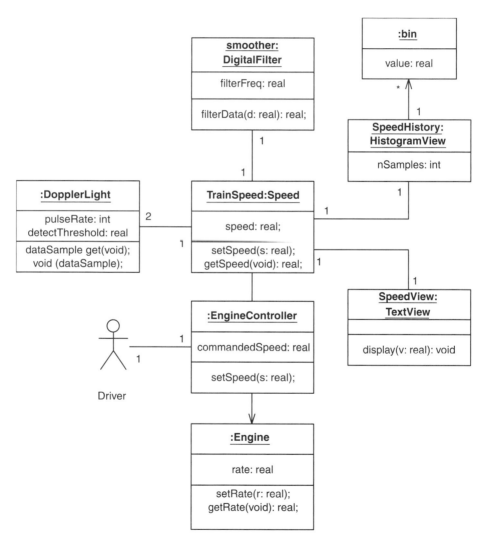

Figure 4-19: *Performance Model Example (Structure)*

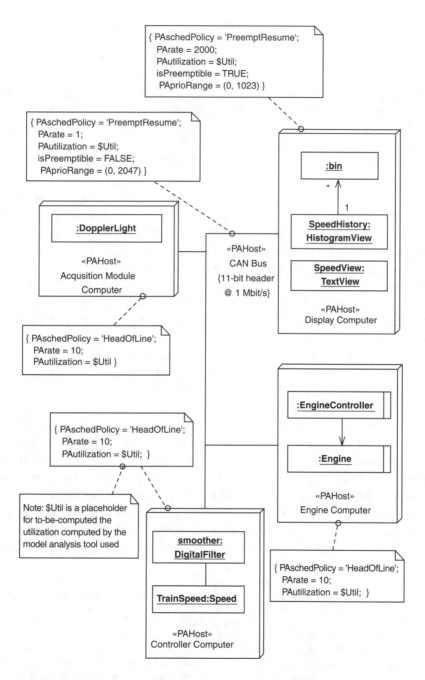

Figure 4-20: *Performance Model Example (Deployment)*

considered to be 10MHz. Note the "$Util" in the constraint attached to the processor—this is where a performance analysis tool would insert the computed utilization once it has performed the mathematical analysis.

As with all the processors, this computer links to the others over a 1Mbit CAN bus link. The CAN bus uses its 11-bit header (the CAN bus also comes in a 29-bit header variety) to arbitrate message transmission using a "bit dominance" protocol,[6] a priority protocol in which each message header has a different priority.

The controller computer runs the TrainSpeed object and its associated data filter. It runs at the same rate as the acquisition module. The EngineController and Engine objects run on the Engine computer, which also runs at the 10MHz rate. The last computer is much faster, running at 2,000 times the rate of the bus, 2GHz. It runs the display software for showing the current speed (via the SpeedView object) and the histogram of the speed (via the SpeedHistory object).

Lastly, Figure 4-21 shows an example of execution. Note that the execution on the different processors is modeled in parallel regions in the sequence diagram (the interaction fragments within the par operator scope), and within each the execution is sequential. Messages are sent among the objects residing on different processors, as you would expect, and the time necessary to construct the message, fragment it (if necessary—the CAN bus messages are limited to 8 bytes of data), transmit it, reassemble the message on the target side, do the required computational service, and then repeat the process to return the result is all subsumed within the execution time of the operation. A more detailed view is possible that includes these actions, (construct, fragment, transmit, receive, reconstruct, invoke the desired service, construct the response message, fragment it, transmit it, reassemble it on the client side, extract the required value, and return it to the client object). However, in this example, all those smaller actions are considered to be executed within the context of the invoked service, so that calls to TrainSpeed.getSpeed()

---

[6] A bit dominance protocol works like this: Any node on the bus can transmit during a specified begin-transmit interval. When it transmits, it also independently listens to what actually appears on the bus. Bits can be either dominant or passive, meaning that if two nodes try to write different bits to the bus in the same interval, the dominant will "win" and actually appear on the bus, while the passive will lose. If a node detects that it has put out a passive bit but a dominant bit occurs on the bus, then it loses (that message has a lower priority) and drops off to try again later. In this way, the message header determines the priority of the message to be transmitted, and 2^{11} messages of different priority are possible.

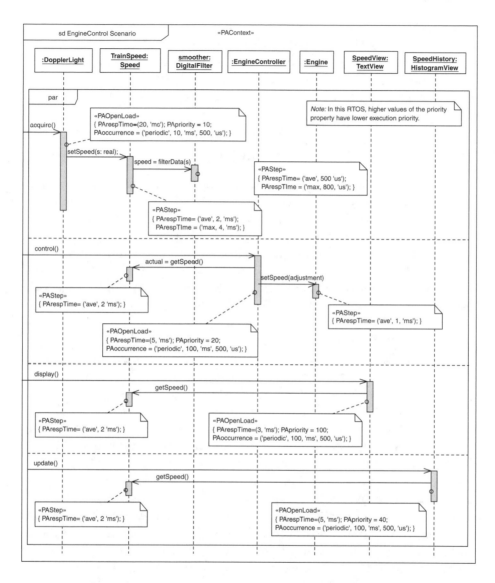

Figure 4-21: *Performance Model Example (Scenario)*

are assumed to include all those actions. For an operation invoked across the bus that requires 1 ms to execute, the bus transmission alone (both ways) would require on the something a bit less than 200 us, assuming that a full 8 bytes of data (indicating the object and service to be executed) are sent. There will be a bit more overhead to parse the message and pass it off to the appropriate target object. Thus, the time overhead for using the CAN bus shouldn't be, in general, more than 500 us to 1 ms unless large messages are sent (requiring message fragmentation) or unless the message is of low priority and the bus is busy. This does depend on the application protocol used to send the messages and the efficiency of the upper layers of the protocol stack.

4.2.6 Real-Time CORBA Subprofile

The RFP for the RTP requires that submissions include the ability to analyze real-time CORBA (RT CORBA) models. CORBA stands for Common Request Broker Architecture and is a middleware standard also owned by the Object Management Group. A detailed discussion of CORBA is beyond the scope of this book but a short description is in order.

CORBA supports systems distributed across multiple processor environments. The basic design pattern is provided in [4]:

> *The Broker Pattern extends the Proxy Pattern through the inclusion of the* Broker—*an "object reference repository" globally visible to both the clients and the servers. This broker facilitates the location of the servers for the clients, so that their respective locations need not be known at design time. This means that more complex systems that can use symmetric deployment architecture, such as required for dynamic load balancing, can be employed.*

The domain model for real-time CORBA is shown in Figure 4-23. Note that the RTCorb (Real-Time CORBA Orb) is a processing environment and the domain models contain RTCclients and RTCservers as expected. All the domain concepts are prefaced with RTC, while the profile stereotypes and tags are prefaced with RSA (*real-time CORBA schedulability analysis*). The following tables show the defined stereotypes.

An RSAschedulingPolicy is one of the following enumerated values: {'FIFO', 'RateMonotonic', 'DeadlineMonotonic', 'HKL', 'FixedPriority', 'MinimumLaxityFirst', 'MaximizeAccruedUtility', 'MinimumSlackTime'}.

An SAschedulingPolicy is one of the following enumerated values: {'FIFO', 'PriorityInheritance', 'NoPreemption', 'HighestLockers', 'PriorityCeiling'}.

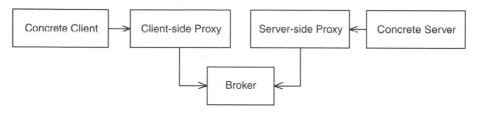

Figure 4-22a: *Broker Pattern (Simplified).* From [4]

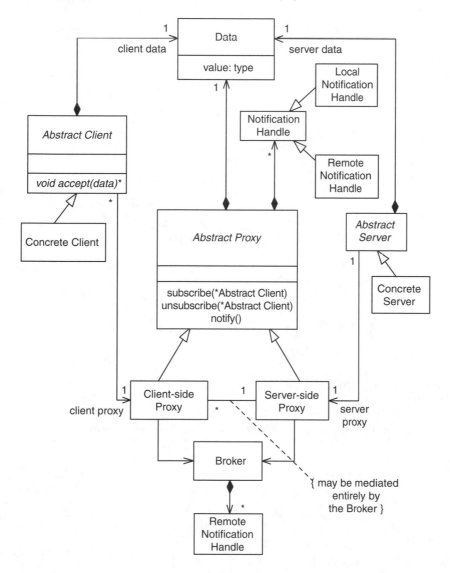

Figure 4-22b: *Broker Pattern (Elaborated).* From [4].

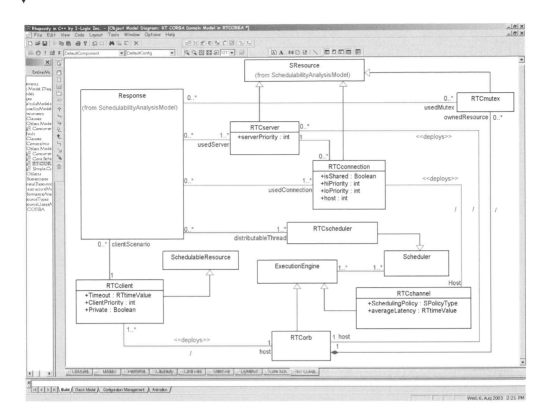

Figure 4-23: *Real-Time CORBA Domain Model*

Table 4-19: *Real-Time CORBA Stereotypes*

Stereotype	Applies to (metaclasses)	Tags	Description
«RSAchannel»	Classifier, ClassifierRole, Instance, Object, Node	RSAscheduling Policy, RSAaverage Latency	An instance of a communication channel between RT CORBA ORBs
«RSAclient» (subclass of «SAschedRes»)	Classifier, ClassifierRole, Instance, Object, Node	RSAtimeout, RSAclPrio, RSAprivate, RSAhost	An RT CORBA client

Table 4-19: *(cont.)*

Stereotype	Applies to (metaclasses)	Tags	Description
«RSAconnection» (subclass of «SAschedRe» and «SAResource»)	Classifier, ClassifierRole, Instance, Object, Node	SAAccessControl, RSAshared, RSAhiPrio, RSAloPrio, RSAhost, RSAserver	An RT CORBA connection
«RSAmutex» (subclass of «SAResource»)	Classifier, ClassifierRole, Instance, Object, Node	SAAccessControl, RSAhost	An RT CORBA mutex
«RSAorb» (subclass of «SAEngine»)	Classifier, ClassifierRole, Instance, Object, Node	SAscheduling Policy	An RT CORBA ORB
«RSAserver» (subclass of «SAResource»)	Classifier, ClassifierRole, Instance, Object, Node	RSAsrvPrio, SACapacity	An RT CORBA server

Table 4-20: *RSAchannel Tags*

Tag	Type	Multiplicity	Description
RSA Scheduling Policy	Enumeration	[0,1]	Policy by which an RSAchannel is scheduled
RSAaverage Latency	RTtimeValue	[0,1]	Latency of the channel

Table 4-21: *RSAclient Tagged Values*

Tag	Type	Multiplicity	Description
RSAtimeout	RTtimeValue	[0,1]	Timeout
RSAclPrio	Integer	[0,1]	Client priority
RSAprivate	Boolean	[0,1]	Accessibility of client
RSAhost	Reference to an element stereotyped as «RSAorb»	[0,1]	Hosting ORB

Table 4-22: *RSAconnection Tagged Values*

Tag	Type	Multiplicity	Description
SAAccess Control	Enumeration of {Priority Inheritance, Distributed PriorityCeiling}	[0,1]	Access control for the resource
RSAshared	Boolean	[0,1]	If the resource is shared among clients
RSAhiPrio	Integer	[0,1]	Highest priority for connection
RSAloPrio	Integer	[0,1]	Lowest priority for the connection
RSAhost	Reference to an element stereotyped as «RSAchannel»	[0,1]	Hosting channel
RSAserver	Reference to an element stereotyped as «RSAserver»	[0,1]	Server of connection

Table 4-23: *RSAmutex Tagged Values*

Tag	Type	Multiplicity	Description
SAAccess Control	Enumeration of {Priority Inheritance, Distributed PriorityCeiling}	[0,1]	Access control for the resource
RSA Host	Reference to an element stereotyped as «RSAorb»	[0,1]	Hosting ORB

Table 4-24: *RSAorb Tagged Values*

Tag	Type	Multiplicity	Description
SAscheduling Policy	Enumeration	[0,1]	Policy by which an SAEngine is scheduled

Table 4-25: *RSAserver Tagged Values*

Tag	Type	Multiplicity	Description
RSAsrvPrio	Integer	[0,1]	Server priority
SACapacity	Integer	[0,1]	Capacity

4.3 Looking Ahead

The UML Profile for Schedulabilty, Performance, and Time defines semantic model of real-time concepts. These are divided up into several subprofiles—the general resource model, the time model, the concurrency model, the schedulability model, the performance model, and the CORBA infrastructure model. Each of these models has a set of related concepts, represented by stereotypes and properties (tagged values). To use the profile, select (or create) the appropriate classes in your user model and apply the stereotypes. Once these stereotypes are applied, the tagged values may be specific assigned values. Such annotated models can then be analyzed for schedulability. The next several chapters focus on the utilization of the elements of the UML (and RTP) to specify, design, and construct systems.

4.4 Exercises

1. What is a profile?
2. What is the advantage of profiles in general and of the UML profile for schedulability, performance, and time (real-time profile or RTP) in particular?

3. What four things does one typically find in a profile specification?

4. What are the two primary ways that a stereotype is visually indicated on a diagram?

5. How are constraints and tagged values related? How are constraints commonly denoted on diagrams?

6. Name three primary packages of the RTP and the subprofiles that are nested within them.

7. What are the two most important concepts in the general resource model subprofile?

8. How does the general resource model relate to the classic client-server model?

9. What is the difference between a QoSValue and a QoSCharacteristic?

10. To what metaclasses does the RTaction apply?

11. What is the difference between a time value and a timing mechanism. Give two examples of each.

12. Compare and contrast clock stability, drift, skew, accuracy, and offset.

13. What is an arrival pattern? What are the kinds of arrival pattern provided in the RTP?

14. What is the difference between *bounded* and *bursty*?

15. What is the basic element of concurrency in the RTP? What UML element is used to represent this?

16. Of what elements are scenarios in the RTP resource model composed?

17. If we define a *rendezvous* as a service request across thread boundaries, how many types of rendezvous are defined in the RTP concurrency model?

18. How do the concerns of schedulability differ from the concerns of performance?

19. To what metaclasses does the «SAaction» stereotype apply? Name and define the 13 tags defined for this stereotype.

20. What is the difference between *preemption* and *blocking?*

21. What is *slack time* and how does it relate to *deadline?*

22. Contrast *open* and *closed workload* as defined in the performance analysis subprofile.

23. What UML model element and stereotype does one typically use to model the performance of a CPU running our software?

24. What is meant by the word *utilization?*

25. For what does the acronym CORBA stand?

26. Why does the RTP contain a Real-Time CORBA subprofile?

4.5 References

[1] *Unified Modeling Language: Superstructure, Version 2.0.* ptc/03-08-02. Needham, MA: OMG, 2003, *www.omg.org.*

[2] *OMG Unified Modeling Language Specification (draft) Version 1.3 beta R1, April 1999.* Needham, MA, 1999.

[3] Douglass, Bruce Powel. *Doing Hard Time: Developing Real-Time Systems Using UML, Objects, Frameworks, and Patterns.* Reading, MA; Addison-Wesley, 1999.

[4] Douglass, Bruce Powel. *Real-Time Design Patterns: Robust Scalable Architecture for Real-Time Systems.* Reading, MA: Addison-Wesley, 2002.

Chapter 5

Requirements Analysis of Real-Time Systems

Real-time systems interact with their external environment. The set of external objects of significance and their interactions with the system form the basis for the requirements analysis of the system. In the UML, this is captured by the use case model. A use case is a system capability that is detailed with accompanying text, examples (scenarios) or state models. The use case model decomposes the primary functionality of the system and the protocols necessary to meet these functional requirements.

Notations and Concepts Discussed

Actors	State	Statechart
Events	Use Case Diagrams	
Scenarios	Sequence Diagram	

5.1 Requirements

Requirements are specifications of what a system must do independently of how the system is designed. Requirements are not first-order elements defined in the UML; however, they are specified to be in the upcoming UML Profile for Systems Engineering [1]. A taxonomy of requirements is shown in Figure 5-1. A set of requirements specifies one or more systems, while in turn a system realizes a set of requirements. Use cases organize sets of requirements. Requirements are validated by tests applied to the system. Tests are part of test suites. Test fixtures optionally drive the system under test according to the specific test. Requirements relate to other requirements in a couple of ways. Requirements may contain nested, or sub, requirements. This allows us to view requirements at various levels of abstraction, such as "Get a rock on Mars" and "Attain Mars Orbit." This is shown as the aggregation of requirement by requirement. A slightly different relation is the association with the role end "derivedRequirement." In this case, design constraints may interact with requirements to result in more specific forms of a requirement.

At the high level of the requirements taxonomy are three requirements: operational, functional, and quality of service (QoS).[1] Operational requirements have two primary subtypes: interaction requirements and interface requirements. Interaction requirements have a system representation as a scenario, modeled as a sequence, timing, or communication, or possibly an activity diagram. Functional requirements are met by collaborations (sets of interacting object roles). QoS requirements are typically modeled as constraints and come in a variety of types: performance and timeliness; safety; reliability; security; and a variety of quality requirements. Quality requirements may include reusability, portability, adherence to standards and guidelines, and meeting objective quality metrics.

This requirements taxonomy helps us understand the relation of requirements to the system and its test, as well as understand how requirements tend to be represented.

---

[1] The currently ongoing work for UML for Systems Engineering identifies several more requirements: operational, design constraint, functional, interface, performance, physical, storage, stakeholder need, and specialized. These can easily be mapped to the taxonomy used here.

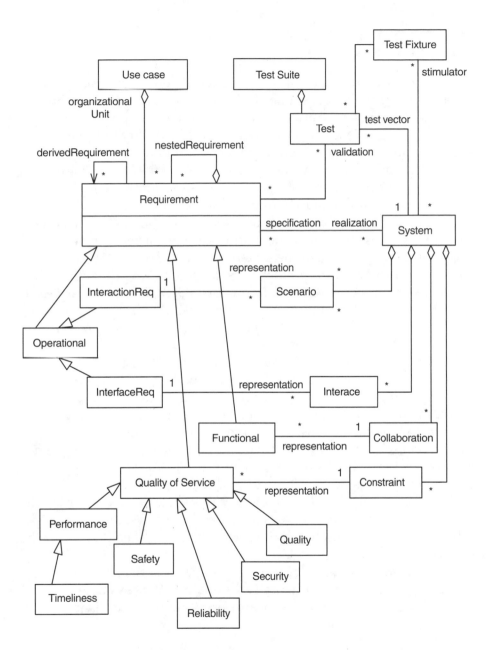

Figure 5-1: *Requirements Taxonomy*

5.2 Use Cases

A *use case* is a named capability of a structural entity in a model. Most often, use case analysis is applied only to the system as a whole, but use cases can be applied to any structural entity, including subsystems[2] or even classes. Use cases define a system-level capability without revealing or implying any particular implementation or even design of that capability. That is to say that use cases are part of the functional view of the system. As we will see shortly, use cases are implemented (*realized* in UML-speak) by collaborations of classes.

Use cases exist within a structural context. In the case of the system, this context consists of the system and associated *actors*. An actor is an object outside the scope of the system under discussion, which nevertheless interacts with it. In order to be a use case, the capability must return a result visible to one or more actors. If a capability of a system is invisible from the outside, then it is not a use case and should not be captured during requirements analysis (since it is a design concern). Figure 5-2 shows a simple use case diagram.

The ovals in Figure 5-2 are the use cases and the stick figures are the actors. The lines connecting the use cases with the actors are associations, meaning that the actor interacts with the system as it executes the use case; that is, messages are either sent to the actor or received from the actor while the use case is executed. The large square is called the *system boundary* and is optional. The diagram also shows dependency relations between the use cases, generalization of use cases, constraints (the statements inside curly braces), and comments.

Used primarily in early analysis, the *use case diagram* shows the black-box functional capabilities provided by the system. These capabilities manifest themselves as interactions among the system and the external objects.

One of the advantages of use case diagrams is their ability to capture a broad view of the primary functionality of the system in a manner easily grasped by nontechnical users. The use case diagrams can

---

[2] In the UML, a *subsystem* is a component, which is in turn a kind of structured class; therefore a subsystem is a class that is composed of parts represented by object roles.

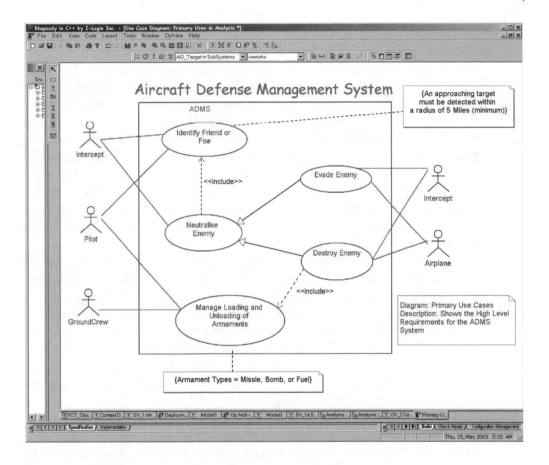

Figure 5-2: *Use Case Diagram*

become a centralized roadmap of the system usage scenarios for people specifying the requirements of the system.

It is important to note that use cases are not themselves requirements. Rather, they organize requirements into chunks, based on the organizational principle of common operational capability. This principle can be used regardless of the more detailed representation of the requirements themselves, whether it is text, sequence diagrams, state machines, or activity diagrams. It is common for a use case to represent and organize many pages of textual requirements or dozens of usage scenarios.

5.2.1 Actors

As mentioned earlier, an *actor* is an object outside that scope of the system under consideration that has significant interactions with it. The icon for an actor, as shown in Figure 5-2, is a stick figure. Many people misconstrue this to mean that actors must therefore be human users of the system. An actor is *any* object that interacts directly with the system in ways that important to be modeled—this means that they either provide information (or control inputs) to the system or receive information (or control outputs) from the system. Some writers have mistakenly stated that all use cases must be initiated from an actor or that each use case should have a single primary actor. As a matter of fact, use cases can initiate themselves (usually based on the passage of time) and often interact with many actors.

Actors should be named with singular nouns[3] and represent objects outside the scope of the system under consideration that have important interactions with the system. If the use cases are being applied to a piece of a large system, such as a component or subsystem, then some of the actors will be outside the overall system while other, "internal," actors will be peer architectural pieces of the system such as other components or subsystems. From the perspective of the unit of concern, these peer architectural units are actors even though they are parts of the entire system being constructed.

Figure 5-3 shows some of the use cases for an air traffic control system. Note that of the several actors identified, only one of them (the *Controller*) is a human user. All the rest are legacy systems, or devices to which the system must integrate or interface. Packages are used to group the use cases into broad categories of concern, Execution_Use-Cases and Management_UseCases. Packages may be used to organize systems with many use cases as appropriate.

In general, not all actors participate in all use cases. The two radar actors in Figure 5-3, for example, interact with the Locate Tracks use case, but not with the other use cases. The use cases with which the actor interacts are indicated by the association drawn between the actor and the related use case. Of course, an actor can participate in more than a single use case, just as a use case may interact with multiple actors.

---

[3] As the multiplicity on the associations to the use cases can indicate when multiple actors of the same type are involved in a use case.

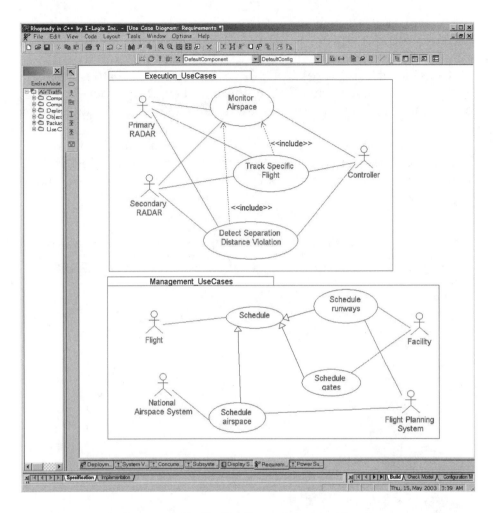

Figure 5-3: *Air Traffic Control System Use Cases*

Associations among actors are not drawn (since they are outside the scope of the system of concern), but sometimes actor generalization is shown. For example, a user in a library may participate in a Check Out Book use case, but only a certain type of user, called Librarian, may add new books to the library system or register a new user. Generalization is therefore sometimes shown among the actors.

At the system level, the actors for use cases are objects outside the entire system. However, if the use case is applied to an internal subsystem or class, then the actors will be truly external actors (as in the system case) plus the peer-level subsystems or classes with which that the element under analysis associates.

Consider the use cases in Figure 5-4. Here, the anesthesia system interfaces with an external ECG monitor and chart recorder. The other two actors are human users of the system—the physician and the patient.

Now, consider a breakdown of the anesthesia machine into some large-scale subsystems, as shown in the class diagram in Figure 5-5.[4] This diagram shows the anesthesia system as a structured class containing the various subsystems as parts. Note that the subsystem stereotype is shown using two notations—the iconic form for a subsystem

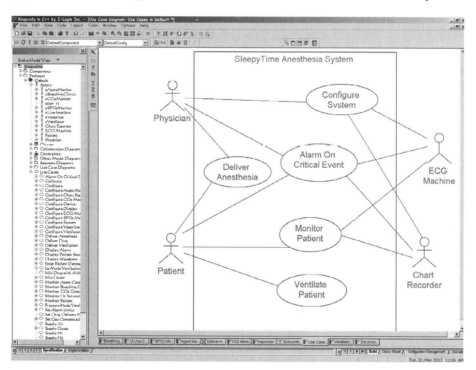

Figure 5-4: *Anesthesia Machine Use Cases*

---

[4] The use of heavier lines for the association to external actors has no semantic meaning—they are just normal associations—but it does allow the interfaces that cross the system border to be easily identified.

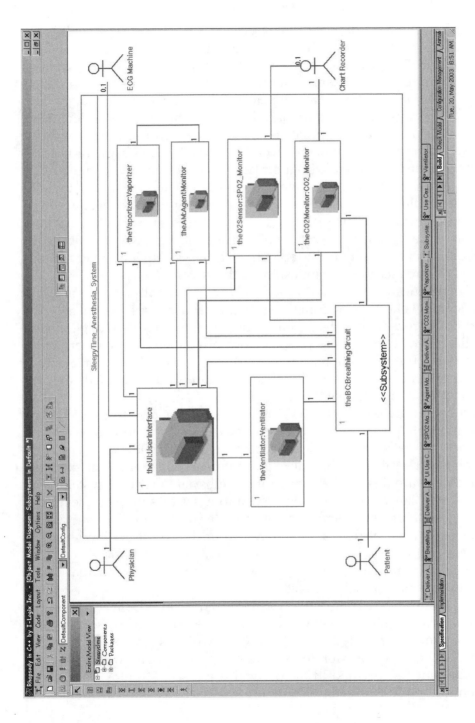

Figure 5-5: *Anesthesia Subsystems*

(using a custom icon inside the object rectangle) and text. Usually only one form will be shown, but the diagram illustrates how both look.

Figure 5-4 shows the use cases for the entire system. Use case analysis may be applied recursively to these subsystems as well—that is, it is useful to define a set of use cases for each of the subsystems so that the subsystem teams clearly understand the responsibilities and requirements for their subsystem. In principle, these subsystem use cases should be derived from two distinct sources. First of all, the subsystem requirements must be derived from system-level requirements; they are, in essence, a project of the portion of the system requirements that the subsystem fulfills. The second source is the subsystem architecture. Even though architecture is really part of design, it groups the functionality into these large architectural units called *subsystems*. The subsystem requirements must take into account both the system level requirements and the architecture decomposition of the system.

The question is, how do I formally (or informally) derive my subsystem-level use cases from the system-level use cases? Technically, the ROPES process does this via the «include» stereotype of dependency. This means that one use case includes or contains the smaller "part" use case, but for some reason the part use case has been extracted out and given a name. Typically, this extraction of an included use case might be done because the same "part" use case is used in more than one larger use case and extraction allows the use case to be referenced in multiple places rather than replicated. However, in this usage, the «include» relation is used to decompose a system-level use case into part use cases that will be realized by different subsystems. The extracted use cases are then realized by a single subsystem each. A system-level use case can then be decomposed into a set of subsystem-level use cases, each of which is realized by a single subsystem. Each subsystem then has a set of use cases, derived from the set of system-level use cases that define the requirements for that particular subsystem. The subsystem design and development team then has a coherent set of requirements for their subsystem.

Figure 5-6 takes one of the system-level use cases, Deliver Anesthesia and performs this decomposition. This system-level use case is decomposed into 12 included use cases, each of which is realized by one subsystem. The Agent Monitor subsystem, for example, will realize the requirements specified in the derived use cases: Monitor Agent Concentration, Calibrate, and Configure. Similarly, most of the remaining

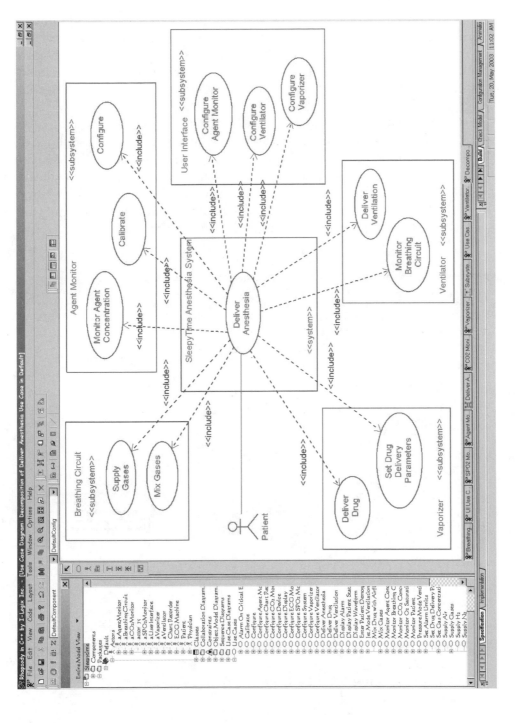

Figure 5-6: *Decomposition of Deliver Anesthesia Use Case*

subsystems must realize some other requirements for the system to meet the Deliver Anesthesia use case, including the User Interface, Ventilator, Vaporizer, and Breathing Circuit subsystems. For simplicity, the subsystem-level use cases in Figure 5-6 don't show their associated actors. Instead the actors appear on the more detailed, subsystem diagrams , Figures 5-8 through 5-14.

An assistive approach to constructing the decomposition is to decompose a system-level use case into a partially ordered sequence of activities on an activity diagram, mapping the activities to the subsystems with swim lanes. Figure 5-7 does this for the Deliver Anesthesia use case. Note the forks and joins among some of the activities—this indicates that we really don't care which of these is performed first (the fork), only that they are all completed before the next step (the join).

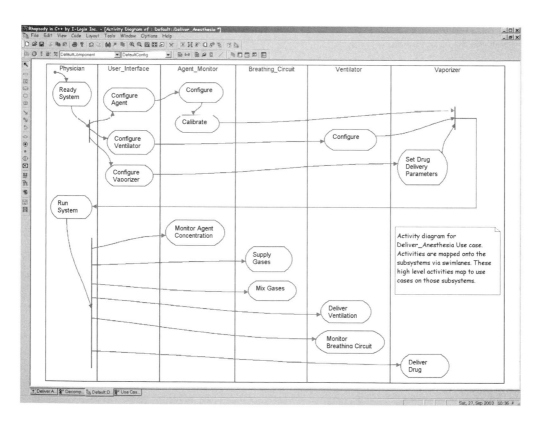

Figure 5-7: *Use Case Activity Breakdown*

These subsystem-level activities can be represented or mapped onto subsystem-level use cases.

Note that the actors for the subsystem use cases may be actors that exist outside the entire system; they may also be other peer architectural subsystems. For convenience, we stereotype these actors with «internal» to indicate that they are inside the scope of the entire system but outside the current scope of concern. In addition, I have prefaced the name of the subsystem with an "a" to indicate that this in an internal piece of the system in an actor role in this context, such as aVentilator and aUserInterface. This is shown in the next several figures.

Figure 5-8 is a use case diagram for the Ventilator subsystem. The primary use cases are to deliver ventilation (of which there are three specialized forms for different modes or kinds of ventilation) and to monitor the output of the breathing circuit. Of course, we still need to

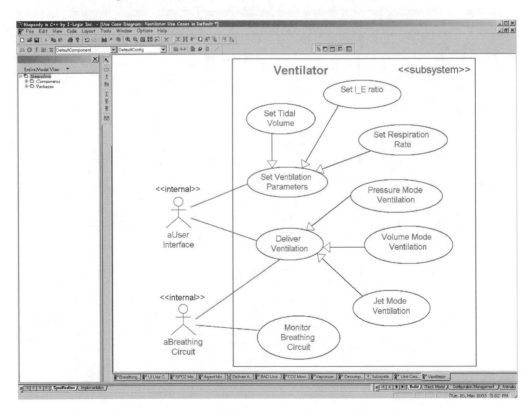

Figure 5-8: *Ventilator Use Cases*

detail all the dozens or hundreds of requirements of those use cases, but that will be discussed later in this chapter.

The user interface subsystem use cases are defined in Figure 5-9. Because the user interface is the means by which the physician controls and monitors the execution of the system, there are many smaller use cases (mostly specialized use cases of the Configure Device use case).

The Vaporizer subsystem's use cases are shown in Figure 5-10. We see that the Deliver Drug use case is decomposed into Vaporize Drug and Mix Drug with Airflow use cases. The SPO2 Monitor and CO2 Monitor use cases (Figures 5-11 and 5-12) look similar, but the details of how they operate and how they are set up will differ. Figure 5-13 for the Agent Monitor subsystem use cases is similar, but it also includes a constraint showing what agents may be monitored with this device.

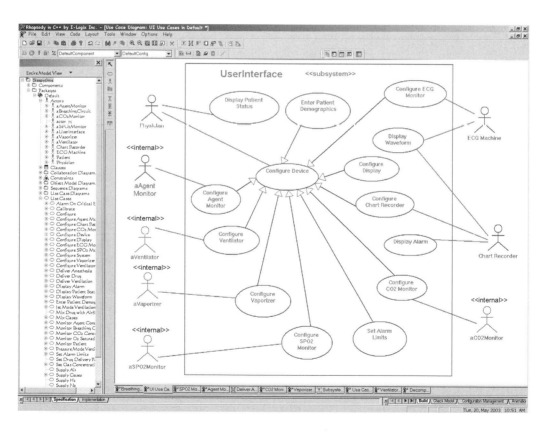

Figure 5-9: *User Interface Use Cases*

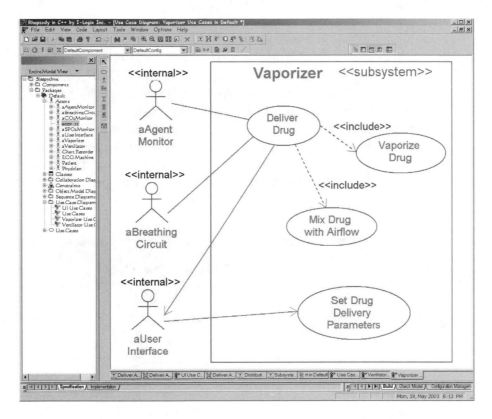

Figure 5-10: *Vaporizer Use Cases*

The Breathing Circuit use cases in Figure 5-14 deal with setting the gas concentration and flows, the actual delivery of the gas flows with the set concentrations and the mixing of the gases.

Use cases are interactions between the system and some set of associated actors. It is important to understand what use cases are not, as it is common to waste time during use case analysis either capturing design details or functionally decomposing the internals of a system. A use case is *not* any of the following:

- *A single message or event:* The details of a use case are represented with scenarios, consisting of many, potentially dozens of messages flowing back and forth between the system and the actors. If you identify a use case that consists of handling a single message or event, you have probably actually identified a (rather small) piece of another use case. Remember that a use case typically represents many (possibly dozens or, in some cases, hundreds of) pages of textual requirements.

- *A low-level interface:* Low-level interfaces are the means by which use cases are realized. For example, if a hard disk is an actor, the low-level commands passing between the system and the actor, such as *move head* and *spin up,* are not use cases. Remember that the use case is *why* the actor communicates with the system not *how* it actually does it. Use cases should be expressed using the vocabulary of the user's problem domain not the engineering design domain.

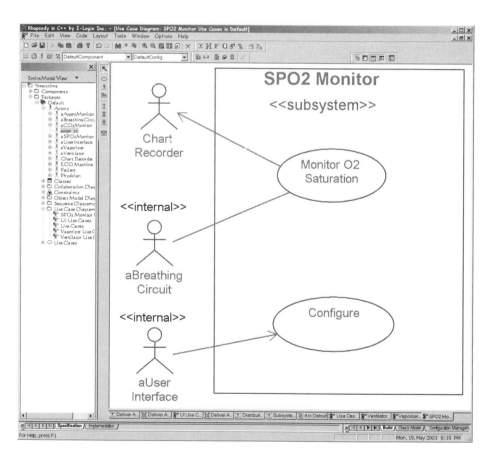

Figure 5-11: *SPO2 Monitor Use Cases*

- *A functional decomposition of the system design:* Later, we will see relations among use cases, such as generalization and dependency. The point of use case relations is *not* to decompose the system into a design that can be implemented directly in C! The purpose of use case relations is to allow a parsimonious description of the capabilities (i.e., requirements) of the system. Such relations can be useful but they are optional.

Figure 5-15 shows some of the unfortunately too-common ways to model use cases badly. A common problem is that as engineers we are primarily trained to design systems, and when first exposed to use cases, we may see them as design tools. The Make TCP Datagrams and Switch

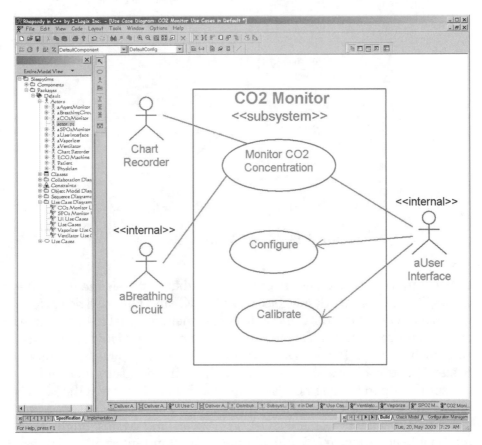

Figure 5-12: *CO2 Monitor Use Cases*

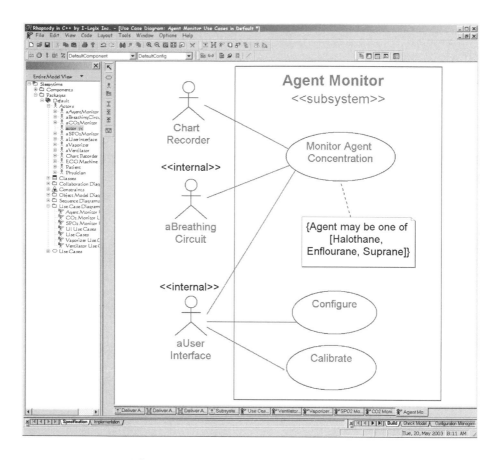

Figure 5-13: *Agent Monitor Use Cases*

to Backup Power use cases are examples of that, but so is the use of the actors Ethernet Network Interface Card (ENIC) and Battery. The ENIC is a both a low-level interface and a design element internal to our system, and is inappropriate as an actor. What would be better? How about a use case such as Store Patient Data with an actor of Hospital Information System? The use case should be something in the user's vocabulary, not something in the engineer's design vocabulary. Similarly, the Switch to Backup Power use case is both internal and over-decomposed. A better choice would be Reliably Deliver Power, and Mains might be a reasonable actor (since it *is* outside the system and internally a battery can provide backup as necessary).

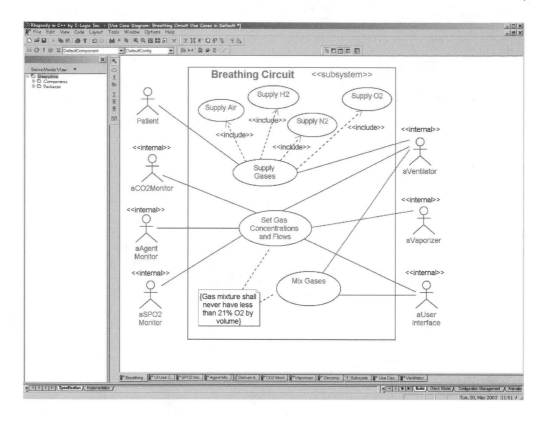

Figure 5-14: *Breathing Circuit Use Cases*

The Turn On Machine use case is probably not only a single scenario, it is probably a single message, "turn on." This is over-decomposed if this is the case. If the Turn On use case includes "perform POST" (power-on self-test), calibration, and configuration, and all of that is captured, then this would be a reasonable use case.

The delivered gas mixture's relative concentrations are set via Set O2 Concentration and Set Balance Gas use cases. However, while good use cases are highly independent, these are highly interdependent. When I set the O2 concentration to 30%, I am necessarily setting the balance gas concentration to 70%. These should be collapsed into a single Set Gas Concentration use case.

Perform Memory Test is a bad use case because it presumes a particular design (you can build an anesthesia machine without any

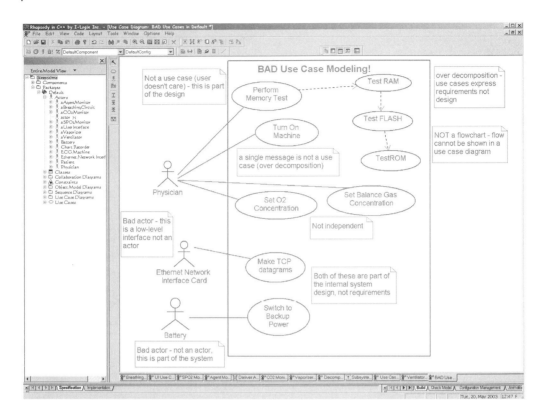

Figure 5-15: *Bad Use Case Modeling*

computer components!) and it is outside what the user cares about. That doesn't mean that performing memory tests is bad, nor that testing shouldn't be part of the system design—only that it *is* part of the system design and not part of the requirements. The Perform System Checkout use case is okay, though, because in typical usage the physician (or more likely, the technician) will perform periodic maintenance.

The Perform Memory Test use case is then decomposed into what looks like a flow of smaller use cases—Test RAM, Test FLASH, Test and ROM. Use cases do not show flow, although flow can be shown on more detailed views of requirements, including sequence diagrams, statecharts, and activity diagrams. Even if the dependency relations aren't depicting flows, they are over-decomposing the problem. Remember that a use case represents a coherent set of requirements that constitute a user-visible capability of a system without revealing or implying how that capability is achieved.

Different authors will tell you different things about use cases, not all of them useful. Some authors will say that all use cases are initiated by actors. This precludes systems that have autonomous behavior—a property of many real-time and embedded systems. Other authors will say that all use cases have a single primary scenario. Again, this is often—but not always—the case. In fact, some use cases have a number of equally important scenario variations.

5.2.2 Use Cases and Text

As developers we are all too familiar with the "Victorian novel" approach to capturing requirements—the generation of hundreds or thousands of pages of text specifying requirements of complex systems. Using text alone to capture requirements is problematic because text is difficult to make simultaneously precise, unambiguous, and understandable. Besides that, textual requirements commonly lack sufficient rigor to adequately capture exactly what is meant by the requirements, allowing different interpretations to arise. Further, requirements documents are often conflicting, having requirements mismatched in different parts of large documents. Nevertheless, text is useful because it is so expressive and flexible. It is possible to employ a use case approach and specify requirements entirely in text—it is simply a matter of using use cases to specify organizational units (e.g., chapters) within the Victorian novel. This approach, while having some merit, still suffers from the problems identified previously.

The UML provides more formal languages (notably, statecharts, activity diagrams, and sequence diagrams) for capturing the details of requirements, as we shall see later. However, text is still useful in conjunction with these more formal approaches. It is common, for example, to provide textual information to characterize the use case. Different authors have defined different contents and formats for such textual characterizations. What I have found most useful appears in Figure 5-16.

The figure shows several fields of information that can be entered into the use case description provided by most UML tools. The Name field is optional and need only be entered if it is otherwise impossible to disambiguate the use case in question. The Purpose field provides a location for a high-level statement as to the user purpose for the

Name: Alarm on Critical Event

Purpose
The purpose is to identify when the patient is at imminent risk and identify this to the attending anesthesiologist so that appropriate action can be taken.

Description
ACE-1: When an alarming condition occurs, it shall be annunciated—that is, a meaningful alarm message (including the time of occurrence, the type of alarm, the source of the alarm, and the likely cause of the alarm) shall be displayed and an alarming tone shall be sounded.
ACE-2: When multiple alarms are being annunciated, they shall be displayed in order of severity first, then in order of occurrence, newest first.
ACE-3: If an annunciated alarm isn't displayed (because higher criticality alarms are being displayed and there is insufficient space to display the alarm in question), then it cannot be acknowledged without first being displayed on the screen.
ACE-4: Alarms must be explicitly acknowledged by the user pressing the Alarm Ack button after they have occurred even if the originating alarming condition has been corrected.
ACE-5: If the originating condition of an alarm has been corrected but the alarm has not yet been acknowledged, then the display of the alarm message shall be greyed out. All other alarm messages shall be displayed in the normal color.
ACE-6: The Alarm Ack button shall cause the audible alarm sound to be silenced but does not affect the visual display of the alarm message. The silence shall hold for 2 minutes. If the alarm condition ceases after the acknowledgement but before the silence period times out, then the alarm shall be dismissed. If, after the silence period has elapsed, the originating condition is still valid or if it has reasserted itself during the silence period, then the alarm shall be reannunciated.

Preconditions
1. System is properly configured and has been initialized.
2. Alarming parameters have been set.
3. Alarming is enabled.

Postconditions
1. Alarming conditions are displayed and audibly announced.

Other Constraints
1. Alarms shall be filtered so that each patient condition results in a single annunciated alarm.
2. Alarms shall be detected within 9 seconds of their occurrence.
3. Alarms shall be annunciated within 1 second of the detection of the alarming condition.
...

Figure 5-16: *Textual Characterization of Use Cases*

capability of the use case. The Description field is where detailed textual requirements may be stated. The Preconditions, Postconditions, and Other Constraints fields hold explicit constraints about the execution of the use case. Preconditions are conditions that must be true before the use case begins, while postconditions are conditions that are guaranteed to be true by the system after the use case is finished. The Other Constraints field is commonly used to hold (QoS requirements for the use case, such as worst-case execution time, average-case execution time, reliability, maintainability, and so on. If the description field can contain hyperlinks,[5] as they can in Rhapsody from I-Logix, then text, mathematical models, or other navigable references can be made in the UML tool. Hyperlinks are very useful in this context because clicking on them invokes the external tool to bring up the referenced document or, if an internal hyperlink, the document or referenced model elements are brought to the fore.

5.2.3 Use Case Relations

The UML defines three distinct relationships among use cases. *Generalization* means that one use case is a more specialized or refined version of another. For example, the Validate User use case can be specialized into Check Password, Check Fingerprint Scan, and Check Retinal Scan use cases. Each of these subuse cases is a specialized version of the base use case.

The other two kinds of use case relations are stereotypes of dependency. «include» is used when the capability described in the client use case uses the capability described in another use case. «include» should only be used when the behavior is shared among two or more use cases or is mapping the "part" use case to a system architectural component and is required for all of the client use case scenarios.

The third kind of relation is «extend». «extend» is used when one use case provides an optional additional capability within a client use case. This optional capability is inserted at a named extension point. Figure 5-17 shows the syntax of the use case relations. Remember that the

---

[5] A hyperlink, as used here, is a reference either to a document managed by an external tool (an *external* hyperlink) or to some diagram or description somewhere else in the model (an *internal* hyperlink). Typical use of a hyperlink involves selection of the hyperlink to invoke the referenced document or model element in its native tool and format.

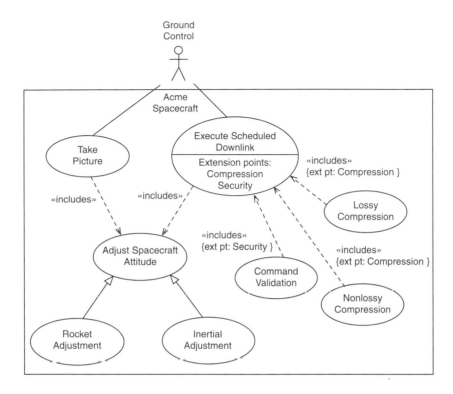

Figure 5-17: *Use Case Relations*

closed arrowhead indicates generalization with the arrow pointing toward the more general use case. Dependency is shown with an open
arrowhead and a dashed line. For an «include» relation, the arrow points
to the part use case. "The Take Picture use case includes the Adjust
Spacecraft Attitude use case." Perhaps confusing, but the arrowhead on
the «extend» relation points in the opposite direction! "The Lossy Compression use case extends the Execute Scheduled Downlink use case."

In Figure 5-17, the spacecraft turns in order to achieve two
capabilities—taking a picture (under the premise that you must point
at something to take its picture) and executing a scheduled downlink of
information. Because this common capability is required for both these
use cases, it is extracted out and put into its own use case. The two
means by which the spacecraft can be turned are specialized use cases
of the Adjust Attitude base use case. In one case, rockets can be fired to

turn the spacecraft, and in the other, reaction wheels are activated. Finally, the scheduled downlink can optionally compress images, either using lossy or non-lossy compression algorithms. Because this is an option, it is shown as an «extends» relation. Also, for risky command sequences, a high-level security clearance may be required. Note that the extension points are identified in the base use case and then referred to by the extending use cases.

A caution: Too often, beginners overuse the use case relations and use them to capture the wrong things. Remember that you can model the requirements of systems without using generalization, «extends», or «includes». Their use can make a requirements model a little simpler, but not if they are misused.

5.2.4 Using Use Cases

Use cases can provide a unifying strategy for the entire project development. They are an embodiment of what the customer wants and expects to see when the dust settles[6] and the product ships. Use cases group together scenarios related to the system capability described by the use and provide valuable information into all phases, as shown in Table 5-1.

5.2.5 Identifying Use Cases

There are four primary approaches to identifying use cases:

- List the primary capabilities of the system, then identify the actors and scenarios within each use case.

- Identify the actors to the system and the messages they send or receive (the scenarios), and then group them into use cases.

- Start with system scenarios, identify the actors that participate in them, and then lump them into use cases.

- Identify a system workflow with an activity diagram at the highest level and from there determine how these might be mapped into use cases.

---

[6] That is, when the customer finally stops changing the requirements long enough for you to actually *build* the darn thing.

Table 5-1: *Using Use Cases in Development*

Phase	Application of Use Cases
Analysis	• Suggest large-scale partitioning of the domain • Provide structuring of analysis objects • Clarify system and object responsibilities • Capture and clarify new features as they are added during development • Validate analysis model
Design	• Validate the elaboration of analysis models in the presence of design objects
Coding	• Clarify purpose and role of classes for coders • Focus coding efforts
Testing	• Provide primary and secondary test scenarios for system validation
Deployment	• Suggest iterative prototypes for spiral development

All of these approaches can work well.

How does the analyst extract the primary capabilities of the system? Although some domain experts may think in abstract terms, the vast majority will be more comfortable identifying specific scenarios or specific system workflows rather than use cases. The analyst must identify the dozens (or hundreds) of scenarios that map the important system aspects and from these deduce the use cases. A number of approaches to identifying the scenarios are possible.

The analyst can sit with the customer and ask probing questions, such as these:

- What are the primary functions of the system?
- What are the secondary functions of the system?
- Why is this system being built? What is it replacing and why?

The analyst must then identify the following for each use case:

- The role the actors and system play in each scenario

- The interactions (flows) necessary to complete the scenario
- The sequence of events and data needed to realize the scenario
- The variations on the scenario that are possible (other related scenarios)

For example, the primary functions of an ECG monitor are to display waveforms for the physician, provide discrete patient numeric values (such as heart rate), and sound an alarm when the patient is at risk. Secondary functions might be to provide a remote display for the surgeon, provide a reliable software upgrade facility, allow configuration, and even support a demonstration mode of operation for the sales reps. Why is the system being built? Perhaps it provides better arrhythmia detection, color displays for better differentiation of lead configurations, or faster response times, or it interfaces to the hospital network

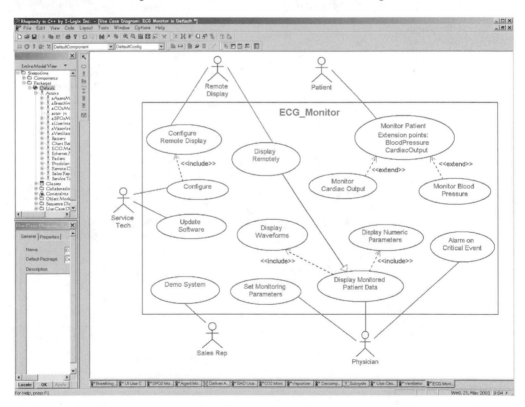

Figure 5-18: *ECG Use Cases*

and the operating room anesthesia machines. Figure 5-18 shows a reasonable use case model for an ECG monitor. Note that this use case diagram uses all three kinds of relations among use cases—includes, extends, and generalization.

Use cases are used primarily during requirements analysis, but Figure 5-19 shows that use cases have a role in other phases of the ROPES process as well. Once the system is broken down into its primary subsystems (in the systems analysis phase), use cases may be applied

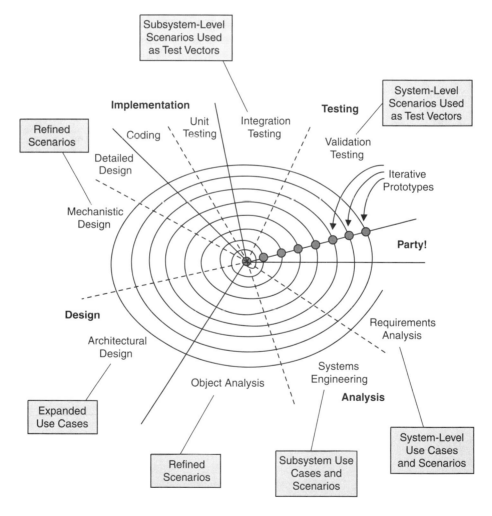

Figure 5-19: *Use Cases in Development*

to each of the subsystems in turn to define its requirements with respect to the other elements of the system. As the object model becomes fleshed out, the system- and subsystem- level use cases may be refined in more detail, replacing the system with the objects collaborating within the system to realize the specific use case. The need for additional use cases having to do with the concurrency and component models is normally uncovered during architectural design as well. Even in testing, the use cases and their associated scenarios form the key set of tests to be applied to the system.

Use cases are a powerful tool for capturing requirements and for binding those requirements into design and testing as development continues.

5.3 Detailing the Use Cases

So far, we've identified what a use case is: a named system operational capability. We've also noted that use cases organize functional and quality of service requirements. However, a name alone isn't enough to understand what a use case means. For example, consider the use case Set Ventilator Tidal Volume[7]—the user turns a knob and sets the amount of mixed breathing gas pumped out per breath for the ventilator. That's not enough detail to understand how it actually works. For example:

- What is the maximum value that can be selected? What is the minimum value that can be selected?
- What is the accuracy of the delivery of tidal volume with respect to its set value? +/- 10 ml? +/- 5%?
- Are there different ranges, such as one range for adults, another for pediatrics, and another for neonates?
- What happens if the knob is turned accidentally—does tidal volume change directly or is an explicit confirmation required?
- If there is a confirmation, can the user cancel the operation?
- What happens if the user tries to set a different value, say respiration rate, before confirmation?

---

[7] *Tidal volume* is the amount of gas delivered per breath.

- How does the user know whether a value is currently being set (waiting for confirmation)?
- Does anything have to either precede or come after setting tidal volume, such as setting patient age or weight?

In requirements analysis, the devil is in the details and answering these questions is crucial. The process of identifying the dozens or perhaps hundreds of detailed, specific requirements is known as "detailing the use case" in the ROPES process. Two categories of approaches are possible. A specification can be written for the requirements. This specification can be either informal (text) or formal using a formal or semi-formal language such as statecharts or activity diagrams. The other approach is to provide examples of operational usage. Remember that in Section 5.1, we identified three kinds of requirements. Functional requirements are best captured in specifications. Operational requirements are best captured in scenarios or activity diagram workflows. QoS requirements are added to both representations as modifiers of the primary requirements. It should be noted that functional requirements can be defined in scenarios just as operational requirements can be defined in specifications. However, the general rule is that functional requirements are most often captured in specifications and operational requirements are most often captured in scenarios.

5.3.1 Scenarios for Use Cases

A *scenario* is a particular actor-system interaction corresponding to a use case—it is a specific example of a use case execution in the system's operational environment. Scenarios model order-dependent message sequences among object roles collaborating to produce system behavior in its operational environment. Different scenarios within a given use case show permutations of object interactions. Even early in analysis, the advantage of scenarios is that domain experts and users can usually quite easily walk the analyst through dozens of typical system usage scenarios. The domain expert can explain why each step is taken, who initiates it, what the appropriate responses are, and what kinds of things can go awry. In going through this process, the analyst will uncover many important facets of the system behavior not mentioned within the problem statement. Scenarios provide an invaluable tool for validating the problem statement against the user's expectations as well as uncovering the less obvious requirements. Late in analysis, they can be used to test the object structure by ensuring the appropriate participation by each object in each scenario.

Generally, a medium-sized system will have a few to a few dozen use cases. Each use case will have anywhere from a few to a few dozen scenarios of interest. There are an infinite set of scenarios, but it is only necessary to capture the ones that are interestingly different—that is, the ones that capture operational, functional, or QoS requirements, including exceptions and error identification, isolation and recovery, as appropriate. The scenario set is said to be complete when all of the operational requirements are covered in at least one scenario. This, of course, is a small subset of all possible scenarios. Some use cases have a "sunny day" or *primary* scenario. In this case, most or all of the other scenarios for the use case are variants on the primary scenario.

Every scenario has an underlying structural context. This structural context is the set of object roles that may appear in the interactions. Early in analysis, the structural context is the use case diagram; the objects available for scenarios are the system (or the use case, which isn't an object, but *is* a classifier and may be used for a lifeline in a sequence diagram) and the actors identified on use case diagram. The structural context is shown on the use case diagram, but if desired, a Context Diagram (i.e., a class diagram with the actors and the system) can be drawn. In most cases, I have found the system use case diagram sufficient for this purpose.

Use cases are *realized* by collaborations of objects inside the system working together. Later analysis decomposes the system into such objects, and the use case scenarios can be refined by adding these additional levels of detail. It is important that you only use objects in the scenario that appear in the structural context. That means that if the use case diagram has two actors and the system, only three objects can appear in the scenario. Later, once the system is opened up and is under design, internal objects are identified. At that time, these internal objects may then appear in the scenarios as well, but to do so too early is a common and fundamental mistake in requirements analysis. Requirements should be as free of design as is possible. This means not mixing in design elements too early—that is, the purpose of the identification of the structural context for the scenario. It is crucial to make sure you *always* know the structural context. Otherwise, you'll be making stuff up on the fly with only a vague notion as to the underlying structural model. If you have a number of people doing this, the chances the models will all play together later is vanishingly small because each designer will be making up different (and incompatible) pieces. At the end, the system requirements will be specified in terms of mutually incompatible design decisions and must be thrown away and redone. By drawing and agreeing on the structural context before beginning the scenario analysis, the scenarios from use cases elaborated by different analysts will all play together when it comes time to decompose or implement the model.

It is important to stress that building and analyzing scenarios is a creative process of discovery. It is not simply a matter of starting with postulates and applying mathematical deduction to derive all possible behavior paths. Deep within the crevices of the domain experts' minds are hidden requirements that may never be explicitly identified.[8] These cannot be deduced from the problem statement per se. The process of scenario modeling brings these hidden requirements to the surface so they can be added to the system features.

Three primary scenario representations exist within the UML: sequence, communication (formerly collaboration), and timing diagrams. Sequence diagrams, the most commonly used, emphasize messages and their sequence. Communication diagrams are less popular and tend to stress the system object structure. Timing diagrams are best applied when the requirements are highly time-sensitive. All of these diagram types show scenarios but differ in what they emphasize. Almost exclusively, in use case analysis, sequence diagrams are preferred over communication diagrams. Communication diagrams are not used until the object model of the system stabilizes (and even then, many people prefer sequence diagrams anyway). Timing diagrams are less applied, but are useful when timing is crucial. In this chapter, we will primarily focus on sequence diagrams.

5.3.1.1 Sequence Diagrams for Requirements Capture

Sequence diagrams represent scenarios. A scenario is a specific interaction of object roles consisting of a potentially large number of scenario steps. Each scenario step may be a message, stimulus, event reception,

---

[8] At least not until *after* the product is delivered!

or action. In requirements analysis, scenarios are used to capture operational requirements; that is, requirements around the interaction of the system with its environment. This means that the operational requirements include not only the specification of the services provided by the object roles, but also the allowed and disallowed sequences of those services and their QoS requirements.

Most development organizations have a history of using textual specifications for capturing requirements. Even after adopting the UML, many organizations continue using text as an adjunct to scenarios and statecharts to capture requirements in a more formal way. Figure 5-20

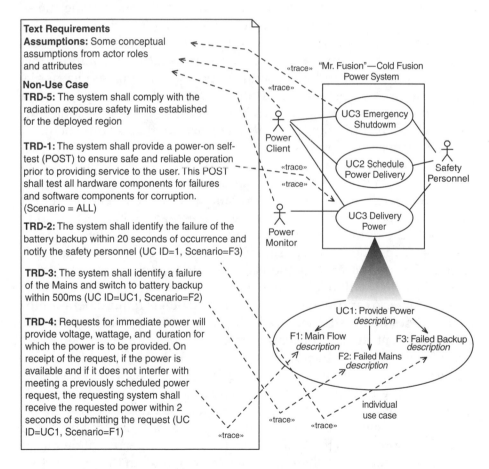

Figure 5-20: *Relating Text and Scenarios*

illustrates the trace relationships between textual requirements and use cases and their scenarios. If the requirements are captured entirely, or mostly, in the UML model, then internal «trace» stereotyped dependency relations can provide traceability inside the model. If extensive external textual documents are used, then requirements traceability tools can provide the link to navigate between model elements and the requirements that they represent or realize.

An example sequence diagram from the anesthesia machine is shown in Figure 5-21. This diagram has several aspects worthy of note. First, the diagram has a descriptive note in the upper right corner that names the sequence diagram (not required if you're using the sd operator for UML 2.0 sequence diagrams), a brief description, and the preconditions and postconditions. While every use case has pre- and postconditions, use case sequence diagrams usually have a more constrained set of them and it is useful to specify it. In this sequence diagram, the use case is used as a lifeline rather than the system. The appropriate interpretation for this lifeline is "the system executing the use case." If you prefer the System object instead, that is equivalent.

The sequence diagram shows one particular path through the execution of the use case, that is, it represents one of many scenarios. This scenario was captured because it was both a reasonable use of the system and because it showed an important operational interaction of the system, as specified by the sequence of message exchanges. In addition, note the use of constraints to add functional and QoS specifications, such as the allowed set of anesthetic agents, the allowable settings for concentration of these agents, and the accuracy of the delivery of the drugs with respect to those settings.

Of course, to capture the operational (and other) requirements of the Deliver Anesthesia use case, several dozen scenarios would be provided, using different drugs, concentrations, and operational sequences. A non-trivial number of these would capture the exceptional scenarios— the scenarios that involve something going wrong, such as system misuse, failures, errors, or unexpected events. The scenario in Figure 5-21 gives an example of what might happen if the drug reservoir runs low— the system triggers an alarm, and the physician silences the alarm and adds more drugs to the reservoir. Other scenarios might detail the operational sequences when the system can't maintain the proper drug concentration, there is a failure in one or more of the gas supplies, the

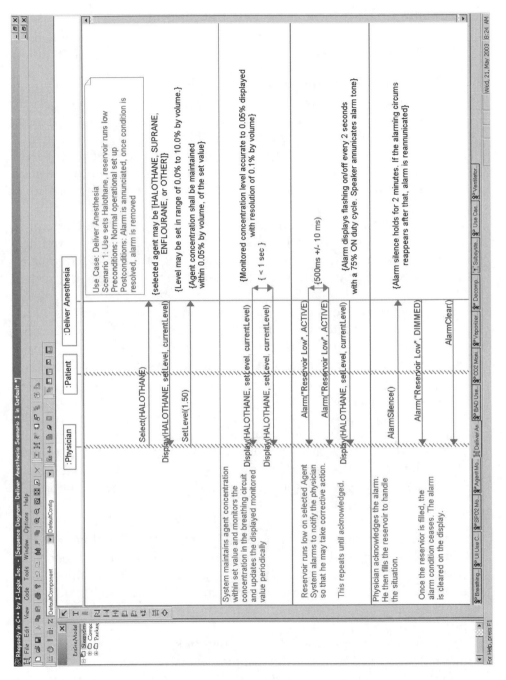

Figure 5-21: *Use Case Sequence Diagram*

ventilator (shaping the breaths) fails, there is a breathing circuit discon-
nection, there is a kink in the gas delivery line to the patient, the agent
monitor reports an internal failure, the delivered agent is different than
the commanded agent, and so on.

As we've seen, it is important to only use elements on the sequence
diagram that appear in the problem context. At the systems level for
the anesthesia machine, that means that only the system actors (e.g.,
the Patient or Physician) and either the System or the relevant use case.
What about moving forward into the subsystem architecture or even
the semantic object model? How do we know that we've done a good
job of the subsystem architecture or specifying the semantic objects of
the system?

Remember that we've captured the requirements at least in part in
sequence diagrams. Therefore a measure of goodness of the architecture or object model is that the design (at the level of abstraction being
considered) can realize the operational scenarios defined at the system
level. If it can realize all of the scenarios defined at the system level,
then the architecture or object model is good and if not, then it is inadequate. To demonstrate this is true, we *elaborate* the scenarios by adding
the level of detail from the architecture or the object model and then we
execute the system to demonstrate that the elaborated scenario executes
properties.

Consider the object model in Figure 5-22. This shows three subsystems working together to realize the Deliver Anesthesia use case, with
the internal structure of the Vaporizer subsystem detailed (with respect
to this collaboration—it may well contain other elements not used in
this collaboration). A very relevant question to ask of this collaboration
is "Is this good?" That is the same as asking, "Does this collaboration
meet its requirements?"

To find out, we can elaborate the system-level scenario in Figure 5-21
with these semantic elements to see. The elaboration is shown in Figures 5-23 and 5-24. The lifeline elements for the semantic objects are
taken from the class diagram shown in Figure 5-22 and are added to the
elements shown on the original sequence diagram. To highlight the
original elements, the arrows from the original scenario are made with
heavier lines.

As a matter of personal preference, when I elaborate scenarios
in this way, I like to leave the original scenario exactly the same and
add the more detailed elements to it. This greatly facilitates tracing the

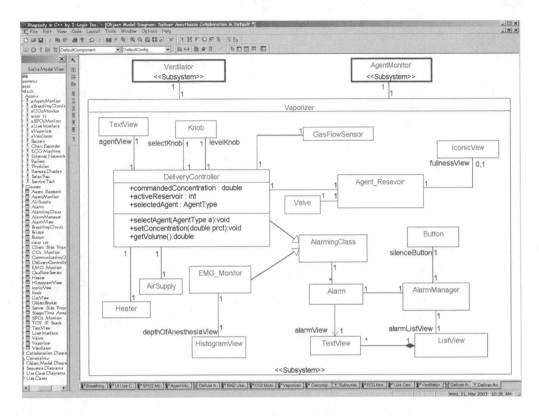

Figure 5-22: *Deliver Anesthesia Collaboration*

elaborated scenario back to the original system scenario and helps ensure that the elaborated scenario is in fact an elaboration of the original. If elements are removed in the elaboration, then demonstrating the equivalence is much more difficult. Thus the elaborated scenario shows the use case from the original as the mediator of messages into the system. Because some developers find this odd, they prefer to use the System object there instead, which is equivalent. The point is to demonstrate that the design elements of the system collaborate together to realize the set of scenarios used to capture the requirements for the system.

In UML 2.0, this elaboration can be done by decomposing the Use Case or System lifeline, representing its internal structure on a separate (referenced) sequence diagram. The primary advantages of this approach are that it keeps the original sequence diagram the same and

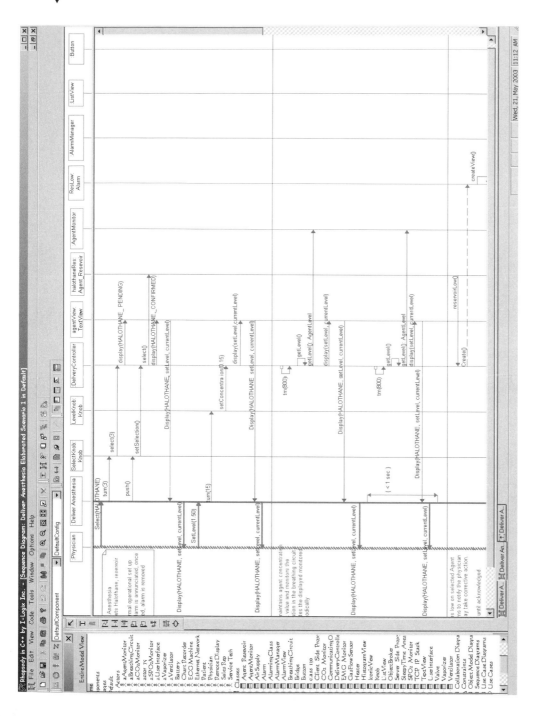

Figure 5-23: *Elaborated Scenario Part 1*

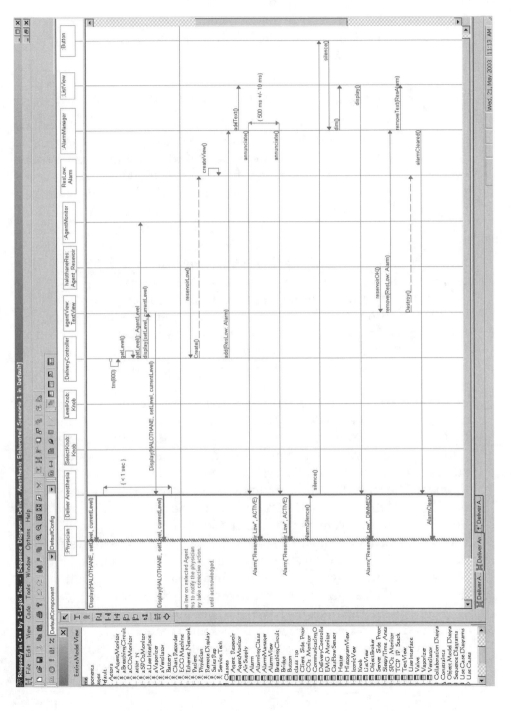

Figure 5-24: *Elaborated Scenario Part 2*

scales up to possibly many levels of decomposition as the system design progresses. The disadvantage is that the more detailed interaction cannot be seen on a single diagram.

5.3.1.2 *Capturing QoS Requirements on Sequence Diagrams*

The single most differentiating characteristic of real-time systems is their concern and treatment of time, as discussed in the previous chapters. In the realm of real-time systems, defining the external timeliness requirements is crucial to understanding the problem. However, most timing requirements are derived rather than primary requirements. That is, a specific timing constraint may arise from a need for accuracy or fault tolerance. Because these requirements are derived, it is all too common for them to be missed by systems designers, leading to unstable system performance. Thus, it is vital that these time constraints be captured as part of the system model so that they can be treated appropriately.

A number of time values can be captured. Those time values that are QoS requirements can be captured as constraints applied against the actions or messages. Those time values that are estimates, used for the purpose of analysis, can be captured as tagged values (user-added properties of model elements). Tagged values are shown as *{property − value}* pairs in constraints.

A number of parameters are required to specify the timing requirements for real-time systems. Naturally, incoming messages must have their timing characterized. If they are periodic, then their periods and jitter must be identified. If they are aperiodic, then appropriate values, such as their minimum interarrival times and averages rate, must be defined. The system response timing is commonly defined in terms of deadlines. If the response has a hard deadline, then missing the deadline constitutes a systems failure. In a soft deadline response, the response performance must be stochastically specified. Soft systems are permitted to lag in their response but are expected to maintain an average throughput or system response. Firm deadlines have both a hard deadline as well as an average throughput requirement.

Response performance may be further specified into a worst-case hard deadline and an average response time when appropriate. Some performance requirements must be met only in the long run, and occasionally missing a deadline creates no difficulties. These soft deadlines may be defined as average response time requirements or a bounded mean lateness. Firm deadlines have both a hard deadline and a shorter average response time.

More complex timing behavior requires more complex modeling, as noted in Chapter 4. In some cases, scalars cannot adequately specify the timing of behavioral responses. Many actions require relatively long periods of time to perform and intermediate responses may be important. For example, an emergency shutdown of a nuclear reactor is implemented by insertion of control rods into the core. This may be initiated by an event such as a coolant leak or an explosive temperature and pressure buildup. This takes time. To avert an incident, it is preferable to insert the rods 90% of the way as soon as possible even if the remaining 10% takes much longer. Control loops are another example. Quick, if incomplete, responses stabilize PID control loops, even if the system response asymptotically converges much later.

These issues are domain- and system-specific. For many situations, the only concerns are service time and latency. Modeling 50% or 80% response times may be important in some special applications. In other applications, several points from a stimulus-response curve may be required to adequately characterize the performance requirements.

In most real-time systems, the time-response requirements are crucial because they define a performance budget for the system. As objects and classes are defined, this performance budget propagates through the analysis and design phases. Ultimately, they define a performance (sub)budget for each and every operation and function call in the thread of execution responding to the event. The sum of the (sub)budgets must meet the specified overall system performance requirement. For example, a message and the completion of its reaction may have a hard deadline at 500 ms. The overall response may be implemented via a chain of six operations. Each of these operations must be allocated some portion of the overall performance budget.

5.3.2 Statecharts

Statecharts are a formal behavioral language that lends itself to the specification of use case behavior. The use case formal language has a number of advantages over text:

- It is verifiable, through mathematical analysis or execution.
- It is precise, and not nearly as likely to be misinterpreted.

- It is generative, meaning that creation of an executable requirements model is possible.

The primary disadvantage of using statecharts is that because they are a precise formal language, most customers and marketers will not understand them and will not be able to assist directly in validation or verification. However, this limitation can be addressed very easily by generating scenarios traversing the various paths in the statechart. Customers and marketers *can* understand scenarios very easily. I have found it very useful to generate both statecharts and sets of sequence (or timing) diagrams that traverse the statecharts. This topic will be discussed later in this section.

The semantics and syntax of statecharts was described in some detail in Chapter 3. We will concern ourselves here with their application in the capture and analysis of requirements. Statecharts are particularly effective when the use case is reactive; that is, it has inherent states (conditions) and remains in those conditions until an event of interest has occurred. Events and messages from the actors are modeled as events in the statechart while messages to the actors are modeled as actions on the state machine.

Consider the requirements for the Alarm On Critical Event, shown in Figure 5-25. We see a relatively small number of requirements, but they are still nonetheless nontrivial to understand. One can envision a number of scenarios traversing different paths through that textual specification, some with the alarm ceasing before the acknowledgment, some after, and some never ceasing. A statechart shows the interaction of the requirements more clearly, as shown in Figure 5-26.

The and-states show the independent aspects of the processing of the incoming events—the silence, the acknowledgement semantics, the display, and the sounding of the tone. The GEN() operation generates events that are consumed by the other and-states. For example, when the use case is in the state AlarmToneInactive (because the alarm silence button was pressed), and the silence time elapses, then a stopSilence event is produced which is consumed by each active and-state that needs it.[9]

---

[9] Remember that the entire use case receives each event. When the use case has and-states, each and-state receives every event sent to the use case and may act on it or discard it as appropriate, independently from the other and-states.

Name: Alarm on Critical Event

Purpose
The purpose is to identify when the patient is at imminent risk and identify this to the attending anesthesiologist so that appropriate action can be taken.

Description
ACE-1: When an alarming condition occurs, it shall be annunciated—that is, a meaningful alarm message (including the time of occurrence, the type of alarm, the source of the alarm, and the likely cause of the alarm) shall be displayed and an alarming tone shall be sounded.
ACE-2: When multiple alarms are being annunciated, they shall be displayed in order of severity first, then in order of occurrence, newest first.
ACE-3: If an annunicated alarm isn't displayed (because higher criticality alarms are being displayed and there is insufficient space to display the alarm in question), then it cannot be acknowledged without first being displayed on the screen.
ACE-4: Alarms must be explicitly acknowledged by the user pressing the Alarm Ack button after they have occurred even if the originating alarming condition has been corrected.
ACE-5: If the originating condition of an alarm has been corrected but the alarm has not yet been acknowledged, then the display of the alarm message shall be greyed out. All other alarm messages shall be displayed in the normal color.
ACE-6: The Alarm Ack button shall cause the audible alarm sound to be silenced but does not affect the visual display of the alarm message. The silence shall hold for 2 minutes. If the alarm condition ceases after the acknowledgement but before the silence period times out, then the alarm shall be dismissed. If, after the silence period has elapsed, the originating condition is still valid or if it has reasserted itself during the silence period, then the alarm shall be reannunicated.

Preconditions
1. System is properly configured and has been initialized.

Postconditions
1. Alarming conditions are displayed and audibly announced.

Other Constraints
1. Alarms shall be filtered so that each patient condition results in a single annunciated alarm.
2. Alarms shall be detected within 9 seconds of their occurrence.
3. Alarms shall be annunciated within 1 second of the detection of the alarming condition.
...

Figure 5-25: *Alarm On Critical Event Requirements*

Statecharts can be related to the text in a straightforward fashion, as was shown with sequence diagrams. Figure 5-27 uses trace dependencies to show where the alarming requirements are represented in the statechart.

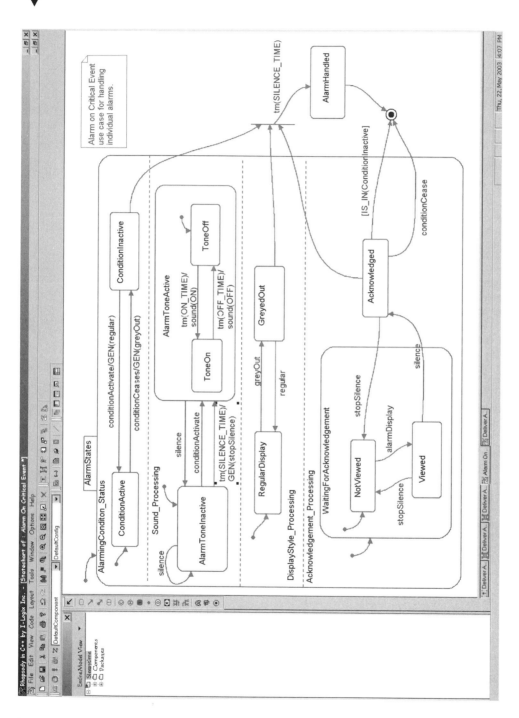

Figure 5-26: *Alarm On Critical Event Statechart*

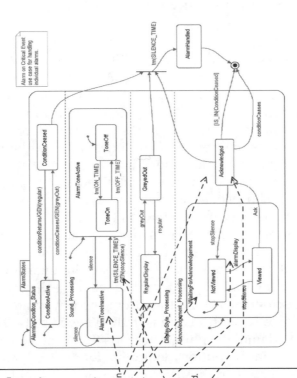

Name: Alarm on Critical Event

Purpose

The purpose is to identify when the patient is at imminent risk and identify this to the attending anesthesiologist so that appropriate action can be taken.

Description

ACE-1: When an alarming condition occurs, it shall be annunciated—that is, a meaningful alarm message (including the time of occurrence, the type of alarm, the source of the alarm, and the likely cause of the alarm) shall be displayed and an alarming tone shall be sounded.

ACE-2: When multiple alarms are being annunciated, they shall be displayed in order of severity first, then in order of occurrence, newest first.

ACE-3: If an annunciated alarm isn't displayed (because higher criticality alarms are being displayed and there is insufficient space to display the alarm in question), then it cannot be acknowledged without first being displayed on the screen.

ACE-4: Alarms must be explicitly acknowledged by the user pressing the Alarm Ack button after they have occurred even if the originating alarming condition has been corrected.

ACE-5: If the originating condition of an alarm has been corrected but the alarm has not yet been acknowledged, then the display of the alarm message shall be greyed out. All other alarm messages shall be displayed in the normal color.

ACE-6: The Alarm Ack button shall cause the audible alarm sound to be silenced but does not affect the visual display of the alarm message. The silence shall hold for 2 minutes. If the alarm condition ceases after the acknowledgement but before the silence period times out, then the alarm shall be dismissed. If, after the silence period has elapsed, the originating condition is still valid or if it has reasserted itself during the silence period, then the alarm shall be reannunciated.

Preconditions

1. System is properly configured and has been initialized.

Postconditions

1. Alarming conditions are displayed and audibly announced.

Other Constraints

1. Alarms shall be filtered so that each patient condition results in a single annunciated alarm.
2. Alarms shall be detected within 9 seconds of their occurrence.
3. Alarms shall be annunciated within 1 second of the detection of the alarming condition.

…

Figure 5-27: *Statecharts and Text*

As mentioned previously, statecharts can be related to scenarios as well. Different operational scenarios take different paths through the statechart, allowing us to easily relate to two notational forms. How many scenarios are represented by the statechart in Figure 5-26? The answer is infinitely many—not only do we have loops (and one time through a loop is different than 10 times through the loop), we also have concurrent and-state regions in which the relative processes of each with respect to each other is not defined.

Figure 5-28 shows one such path through the statechart, but we can see that there are very many more. In this scenario, the ECG machine actor detects that the patient goes into asystole (i.e., the patient's heart stops beating). The system then prints an alarm message to the Chart Recorder and begins annunciating the tone. Simultaneously (hence the use of the par or parallel operator in the sequence diagram), the display accepts the scrollDown() message from the physician and scrolls the alarm into view. Now the alarm is in the Viewed state. The alarm continues to sound until the physician sends the silence() message (mostly likely by pressing a button dedicated for that purpose). Now the alarms are silenced and the alarm display is grayed out. The physician gets the patient's heart to beat (perhaps he shows him the bill), and the ECG machine detects that the alarm condition has ceased and sends a message to that effect to the system. The system responds as specified by the use case statechart, transitioning to the AlarmHandled state.

5.3.3 Activity Diagrams

In UML 1.x, activity diagrams are isomorphic with statecharts. In UML 2.0 they are a superset, since their semantic basis is now token flow semantics, which represent Turing machines. However, the most common use of activity diagrams in the development of real-time and embedded systems will still most likely be in their use as concurrent flowcharts. Activity diagrams are most commonly used when a behavior can be specified as a set of control flows with operators (sequence, alternative, loop, fork, and join), and progress is made primarily on the completion of actions rather than waiting in a state until an external event is received. That is, activity diagrams are most commonly used to represent algorithms that, once initiated, proceed inexorably to their conclusion. Statecharts can represent algorithms as well by using

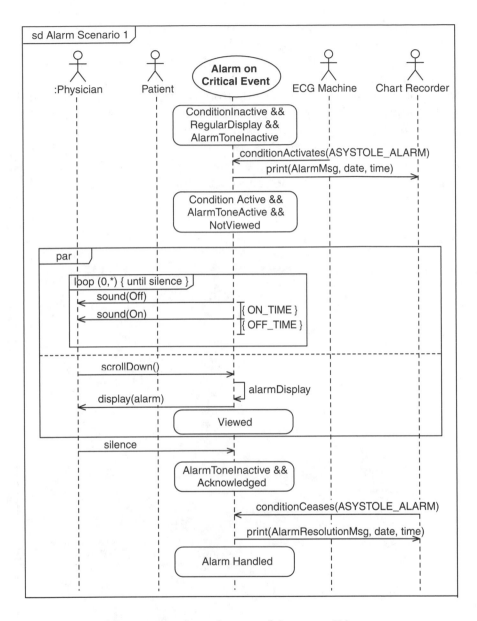

Figure 5-28: *Statecharts and Sequence Diagrams*

null-triggered (anonymous) events connecting states although their most common use is with explicit triggering events.

For example, consider the control algorithm for processing incoming waveforms shown in Figure 5-29. This activity diagram includes the acquisition of the waveform data from the ECG acquisition module. The first transition, in fact, is triggered by an incoming event from that module, perhaps implemented as an interrupt, indicating that some data samples are ready (probably somewhere between two and 10, depending on a number of factors). The subsequent processing proceeds from activity to activity as the actions within the activities complete.

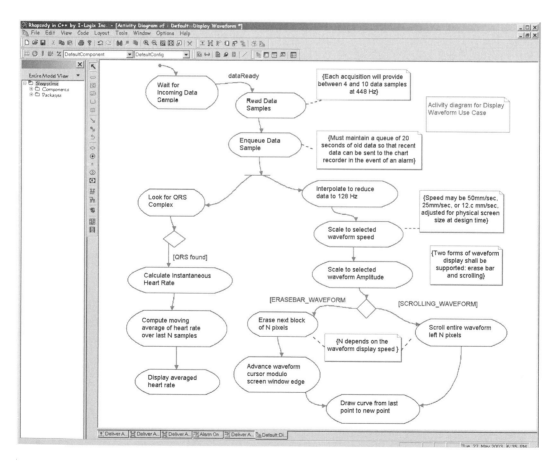

Figure 5-29: *Display Waveform Activity Diagram*

After the data is enqueued, two independent processing threads (these are *logical* threads and do not necessarily imply OS threads or tasks) proceed independently. One of them scans the data stream for evidence of a QRS complex indicating a ventricular contraction (heartbeat), and if found, uses this information to calculate the instantaneous heart rate (the reciprocal of the time between this and the last beat). Since individual heartbeats vary based on many factors—such as pressure on the chest, the presence of an inspiration or expiration, blood gas concentration, and so on—the physician is actually interested in the average heart rate, so a moving average filter is applied to reduce the high-frequency variance artifacts in the heart rate. The second logical thread performs a data reduction because it is typically sampled four times or more faster than it needs to be for display purposes. The physician scales the waveform display in time (displaying the waveform at 50 mm/sec, 25 mm/sec, or 12.5 mm/sec) and in amplitude to adjust for variances in electrode placement, subcutaneous adipose tissue, and other factors. Finally, a curve is drawn from the last displayed point to the new point to display.

The physician can select either of two waveform display styles. The first, called the *erase bar style*, advances a cursor with each new displayed data point and erases the area from the last data point to the cursor (as it is currently displaying old data there) and then draws the new data as a curve from the old data point to the new. The cursor advancement is done modulo the screen edge so that when the cursor advances past the right edge of the screen, the cursor snaps to the left edge of the screen. The other style is called *scrolling waveforms* and is often done with hardware support. While in the first form the position of new data changes constantly, with scrolling waveforms new data always appears at the right edge of the waveform window. When the next data is ready to be displayed, the old data is scrolled left (data at the left edge of the window being discarded) and the new data is drawn. The qualities of service required for this algorithm are provided in constraints in the figure.

5.3.4 Timing Diagrams

Similar in some ways to sequence diagrams, timing diagrams also represent scenarios. The essential difference between sequence and timing diagrams is that the latter emphasize change in value or state over time while the former emphasize sequences of message exchange. They are, approximately at least, isomorphic and able to represent the same information, but their purpose is different. Sequence diagrams used in requirements analysis focus primarily on the sequences of messages in operational scenarios. Timing diagrams focus on the qualities of service having to do with time, such as execution time, jitter, deadlines, periodicity, and so on, and how they affect the state of the system (or, more precisely, of the use case) or an important value held by the system.

Use cases, being classifiers, can have operations and attributes. The use case operations will be realized by services offered by the system to actors in its environment. Attributes will ultimately be realized by object (or attributes of objects) held within the system. Use case behavior can also be specified by statecharts and activity diagrams. In requirements analysis, timing diagrams are best applied to use cases when there are significant timeliness qualities of service of either some attribute or the state of the use case.

It is important to remember that timing diagrams show *scenarios* with an emphasis on their time properties. Scenarios represent very particular runs of the system, and different runs of the system may result in different timing. For example, suppose in one case an event comes in at t_0+20ms[10]; the next time the scenario is run, the event might occur at t_0+22ms. Is one of them wrong? No, but they may differ. To *specify* the timing requirement, you will use a constraint such as { $t = t_0 + 21$ ms +/- 2 ms }. This can be done using the RT profile properties as well, if desired, as described in Chapter 4, but this requires a level of expertise that most customers may not possess.

The activity diagram from Figure 5-29 is used as the basis for the scenario, shown in Figure 5-30. The comment box in the upper right corner gives the preconditions for the particular scenario (waveform display speed is 25 mm/sec and the erase bar waveform style is used). The scenario then shows the change of state (activity state in this case) as processing progresses from the dataReady event until processing is complete. Since this is a scenario, the durations spent in the various activities are not specifications but *examples*. In several places, timing specifications are given using constraints.

---

[10] t_0 here represents the time of the start of the scenario.

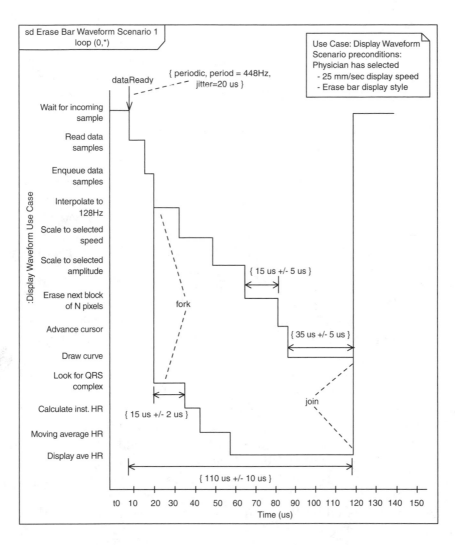

Figure 5-30: *Use Case Timing Diagram*

5.4 Looking Ahead

One of the first things done on any project is to determine the detailed requirements of the system. These requirements may either be capabilities of the system or how well those capabilities are to be achieved. The

UML provides use cases, scenarios, and statecharts to capture these requirements. Use cases identify the primary capabilities of a system. The details of how those capabilities are achieved—at least from an outside, black-box view—is captured in the scenarios or specifications associated with the use cases. A use case is normally detailed by a few up to several dozen scenarios, shown on sequence or timing diagrams. Alternatively, or in combination, a single statechart or activity diagram can provide the behavioral details of the entire use case.

This is crucial in order to understanding *what* system is to be built—its capabilities and required characteristics. None of this, however, has anything (directly) to do with *how* it's built. Use cases are realized by collaborations of objects working together for a common purpose (to implement the use case). It is, at best, less than obvious, to go from a set of requirements *regardless of how they are modeled* to a set of objects. Many objects may work together to realize a use case, but the same object may participate in multiple use cases as well.

The identification of objects and their classes is done in two phases. *Object analysis* identifies the key, essential set of objects necessary to realize the set of identified use cases. That is the subject of the next two chapters. Chapter 6 deals with how to open the box and identify the key concepts required to construct the essential logical object model of the system. Chapter 7 focuses on how to define the behavior of those logical elements, and map them back to the use case behavioral details.

Chapters 8 through 10 go on to discuss *design*. While object analysis identifies the set of objects required for *any* reasonably resolution of the requirements, design is all about *optimization*. Design selects one particular solution that optimizes total system quality with respect to all of its quality criteria.

Armed with that understanding, let's go open up the box and peer inside.

5.5 Exercises

1. What are the three kinds of requirements defined in this chapter?

2. Map each of the following requirements types (from the "UML for Systems Engineering" work-in-progress) into requirements types identified in question 1: operational, design constraint, functional,

interface, performance, physical, storage, stakeholder need, and specialized. Be prepared to defend your mapping!

3. Define the term *use case*.

4. Compare and contrast use cases, specifications, and scenarios.

5. What are the primary representational forms (in the UML) for specification? What are the pros and cons of each, and under what conditions might each be applied?

6. What are the primary representational forms (in the UML) for scenario depiction? What are the pros and cons of each?

7. What is an actor? What kinds of objects may be actors?

8. How does the ROPES process map system requirements down to subsystems?

9. Should use cases be independent or interdependent? Why?

10. How are the use case relations generalization, «extends», and «includes»different in their usage?

11. What is the realization of a use case in your systems design?

12. How do you validate that your use case realization is good?

13. Scenarios best capture what kind of requirements?

14. In each of the diagrams used in requirements capture, where and how are QoS requirements captured?

15. How do activity diagrams and statecharts differ semantically? How do they differ in usage?

5.6 References

[1] *UML for Systems Engineering Request For Proposal.* Document ad/03-31-41. Needham, MA: OMG, 2003.

[2] Laplante, Philip A. *Real-Time Systems Design and Analysis: An Engineer's Handbook.* New York: IEEE Computer Society Press, 1992.

[3] Gomaa, Hassan. *Designing Concurrent, Distributed, and Real-Time Applications with UML.* Reading, MA: Addison-Wesley, 2000.

[4] Ward, Paul, and Steve Mellor. *Structured Development for Real-Time Systems.* 4 vols. Englewood Cliffs, NJ: Prentice Hall, 1985.

[5] Booch, Grady. *Object-Oriented Analysis and Design with Applications.* 2nd ed. Redwood City, CA: Benjamin/Cummings, 1994.

[6] Booch, Grady. *Object Solutions: Managing the Object-Oriented Project.* Menlo Park, CA: Addison-Wesley, 1996.

[7] Harel, David. "Statecharts: A Visual Formalism for Complex Systems," *Science of Computer Programming* 8 (1987): 231–274.

[8] *Unified Modeling Language: Superstructure, Version 2.0* ptc/03-08-02 Needham, MA: OMG, 2003, *www.omg.org.*

[9] Douglass, Bruce Powel. *Doing Hard Time: Developing Real-Time Systems Using UML, Objects, Frameworks, and Patterns.* Reading, MA: Addison-Wesley, 1999.

Chapter 6

Analysis: Object Domain Analysis

Once the system's external environment is defined, the analyst must identify the key objects and classes and their relationships within the system itself. This chapter presents several strategies that have proven effective in real-time systems development for the identification of the key objects and classes. These strategies may be used alone or in combination. Relationships and associations among classes and objects enable higher-level behaviors. This chapter goes on to identify some rules for uncovering and testing these relationships.

Notation and Concepts Discussed

Object Identification Strategies	Class Relationships	Sequence Diagrams
Object Associations	Class Diagrams	

6.1 The Object Discovery Process

In this chapter, we discuss object and class identification and how to infer relationships and associations among them. Chapter 7 deals with the definition and elaboration of object behavior and state. The topics covered in the two chapters form the basis of all object-oriented analysis.

The use case and context diagrams constructed in the previous step provide a starting point for object-oriented analysis *per se.* The end result will be a structural model of the system that includes the objects and classes identified within the system, their relationships, and generalization hierarchies. This structural model will be complemented by the behavioral model (see Chapter 7) and the entire analysis model will be elaborated in design.

Chapter 1 discussed, among other things, the lifecycles of the ROPES process. Remember that the ROPES process exists simultaneously on three timescales—macro (the entire project), micro (the production of a single prototype or system "increment") and nano (the minute-to-minute development steps). The nanocycle is very akin to the Extreme Programming or Agile Methods approach[1]—the idea is to construct aspects of the system with a philosophy of continual testing and validation. Object collaborations are constructed to realize the use cases, but these collaborations themselves are constructed iteratively in very rapid cycles of object identification–class specification–collaboration validation. This is the essence of the nanocycle shown in Figure 6-1.

This chapter focuses on the microcycle phase of object domain analysis. The task is to take the requirements (captured in the requirements phase of the microcycle), possibly in the context of the systems architecture (specified in the optional systems engineering phase of the microcycle), and construct the essential or *domain model.* The domain model identifies the key concepts from the application domain necessary to realize the use case requirements and refine them in various ways. Figure 6-1 shows how the nanocycle proceeds. Object domain analysis is a process of discovery that works as much by free association as by sequential processes, but the key is *continual validation.* If a use case will ultimately be realized by a collaboration of 50 objects instantiated from a

---

[1] The usage of the nanocycle in the context of larger-scoped timeframes is why I consider XP or AM to be "one third of a good process."

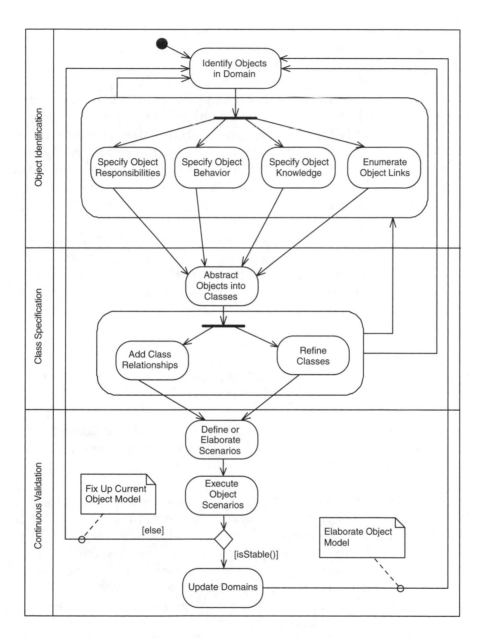

Figure 6-1: *ROPES Nanocycle for Domain Analysis*

set of 35 classes, what we do *not* want to do is put down 50 objects or 35 classes and then beat on them until it more or less works.[2] Instead we want to construct the collaboration in very small pieces, validating each portion of the collaboration before we move on to the next.

It has been said that the best way not to have defects in a system is to not put them in the system in the first place. The nanocycle typically proceeds by identifying one or two objects, getting them to work in isolation, refactoring and refining them as necessary through testing and debugging, then moving on and adding the next object or class, validating the expanded collaboration, refactoring and refining as necessary, then adding the *next* object or two, and so on. In this way, we construct a system from pieces that are known (and demonstrated!) early to be of high quality and with few, if any, defects. By the time the entire collaboration is constructed, it typically works very well. Compare that with the more common approach of drawing a diagram with the 50 objects and then beating on it for days or weeks until it seems to work, only to discover later all the defects that had not been uncovered.

6.2 Connecting the Object Model with the Use Case Model

Now let's look at a number of strategies for identifying the objects and, subsequently, the classes inherent in a system. It's important to connect the object model with the preceding use case model for a couple of reasons.

First, the use case model *drives* the object model. Each use case will be realized by a set of objects working together. In the UML, this is called a *collaboration*. As a model element, a collaboration is represented as an oval, similar to a use case but with a dashed line (see Figure 6-2). The collaboration represents a set of objects, assuming specific roles in order to achieve the use case. By concentrating on a use case at a time, we can have help guide our analytic efforts in fruitful directions.

Second, if we make sure to connect the identified objects to the use case model, we are more likely to build the best system that actually meets the requirements. Some developers ignore the requirements of a

---

[2] Or, even worse, let the customers beat on it until you fix it.

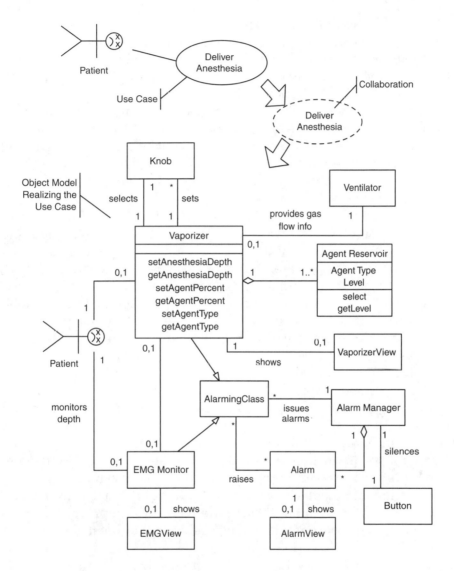

Figure 6-2: *Use Cases, Collaborations, and Objects*

system, but they do so at their own peril. It is unfortunately too common to add features to a system so that it does more than is actually required while at the same time failing to meet the specified requirements. Both of these problems can be avoided by letting the use case model drive the object analysis.

Once the object model has been created for the use case, the system-level use cases can be *refined* to take into account the identified objects and their relations. This allows checking that the object model actually does meet the requirements specified in the use cases as well as illustrating *how* the objects work together to do it.

In object domain analysis, we want to avoid introducing design, because we want to construct a model of the underlying application domain first. If we are constructing a model of an ECG system Display Waveforms use case, first we want to focus on the *essential* concepts of that use case, things that are meaningful to the physicians and nurses who will use the system: the heart rate, arrhythmias, scaling in time in (12.5, 25, or 50 mm/sec display speeds are common), scaling in amplitude, and so on. We *don't* want to worry yet about internal queues to hold data, whether we will use spinlocks or mutex semaphores, how many task threads there are, and so on. The users of the system don't care about those things, but if the system doesn't allow scaling in those two dimensions, if it doesn't understand or produce a heart rate, then the system is fundamentally *wrong*. The essential or domain model is the construction of an object (and class) model that includes these key concepts and their essential relationships. Later, in design, we will refine the domain model into a design model, but first we need to get the domain model correct.

Every application domain has its own specialized vocabulary and concepts. In actuality, a system is always constructed from elements taken from a large number of domains. Some of these domains are closely related to the problem space while others are closely related to the solution space. For example, in our anesthesia system, the problem-domain domains might be Cardiology, Physiology, and Anesthesiology, as shown in Figure 6-3. These are realized in terms of the more concrete domains of computer science, which are ultimately realized in terms of hardware of various kinds.

The domain diagram[3] in Figure 6-3 shows several things of interest. First, domains implemented in the UML as a stereotype of Package, and as such hold types and classes. In the UML, packages are used to organize models and have no existence at runtime. The UML does not provide guidance as to how the packages should be organized or how elements should be partitioned into packages.

---

[3] Which is nothing more than a class diagram showing the domains as packages.

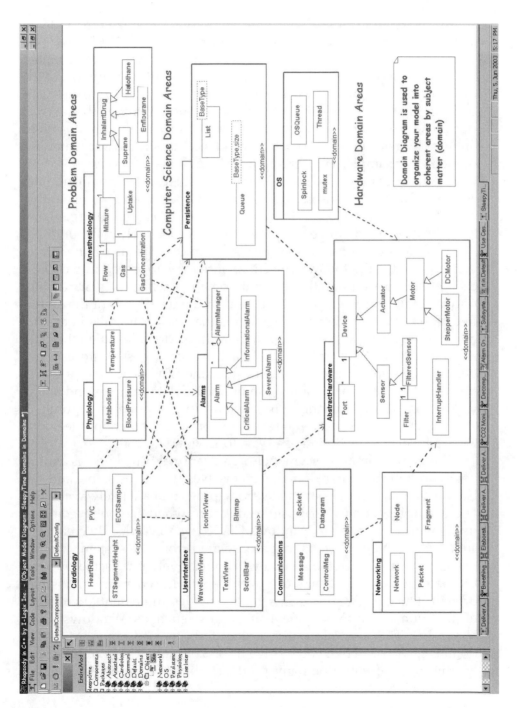

Figure 6-3: *Domains*

In the ROPES process, packages are used to organize the model in specific ways by providing specific guidance. In the ROPES process, a domain is a stereotype of Package that adds a criterion for element inclusion—the element falls within the subject matter of concern of the domain. Thus, domains serve to represent what the ROPES process calls the logical architecture—that is, the organization of things that exist at design time. We can see that each of these packages only contains types and classes relevant to that particular subject matter; the User Interface domain, for example, has user interface things—WaveforView, TextView, IconicView, Scrollbar, and so on—while the Abstract Hardware domain contains things like sensors and actuators. Other types of organization are, of course, possible, but this one has been successful at organizing systems from tiny to huge, allowing teams to effectively collaborate.

In object domain analysis, objects are uncovered using the strategies outlined in the following section; once they are typed into classes, each class is placed into the relevant domain. Each class is placed into only a single domain—in fact, one test for the usefulness of the identified classes and the domain selection is that each class falls in exactly one domain. If a class seems to fall in multiple domains, then the class is probably overly complex and should be decomposed into its independent concepts. For example, consider the ECG concept of a waveform—this is both the organization of a set of data samples and a way to visualize this information on a display. In the model in Figure 6-3, "Waveform" is broken up into the notion of the information (the waveform per se) and the notion of a WaveformView.

The use of domains as a model-organizational principle has a number of advantages. First, domains themselves tend to be stable and can isolate the majority of your model from things that are likely to change. For example, suppose that you're not sure whether you're going to implement the system in Windows CE, XP, or VxWorks. By creating a set of OS domain concepts that are isolated from the system, you are ensuring that most of the system will be relatively unaffected by your ultimate decision. Domains can even be subclassed from an abstract domain (such as AbstractOS), which provides the essential concepts of the domain, into specific realizations (such as WindowsCE or VxWorks). This also allows the system to be ported among different domains, such as when you change the OS or networking architecture. Furthermore, if your company produces different products that will work on the same platform environment, then domains help by providing a reusable infrastructure onto which different application or problem domains can sit.

6.3 Key Strategies for Object Identification

Over the years, I've consulted in an extremely varied set of problem domains, from medical systems to factory automation to avionics and fire control (weapons control systems). The *good* part about consulting in such a broad range of fields is that it is extraordinarily interesting and one gets to learn daily.[4] The *bad* part about that is that one is expected to sound intelligent about the problem almost immediately.[5] For any consultant to be successful in that kind of environment, he or she must have some effective strategies for working with engineers and managers who understand their problem domain very well but who are often neophytes when it comes to the application of the UML to their problems. Table 6-1 outlines what I have found to be the most effective of these object-identification strategies.

This chapter discusses all these strategies, but note that the analyst need not use them all on any specific project. These approaches are not orthogonal and the objects they find will overlap to a significant degree. In fact, many subsets of the strategies will find the exactly the same set of objects. Some methods will fit some analysts' approaches better than others. It is common to select three or four strategies on a given project and apply them more or less simultaneously. As with all modeling strategies, use those that work well for you and discard the ones that do not.

6.3.1 Underline the Noun Strategy

The first strategy works directly with the written problem or mission statement. Underline each noun or noun phrase in the statement and

---

[4] Which has dropped me square in the middle of what I call the *knowledge paradox*: The more I *learn*, the less I *know*. I figure by the time I'm 60, I'll have learned so much that I will actually *know* nothing whatsoever! So far, I'm on target ;-)

[5] Good looks and charm only get you so far when they actually want to *fly* the thing!

Table 6-1: *Object Discovery Strategies*

Strategy	Description
Underline the noun	Used to gain a first-cut object list, the analyst underlines each noun or noun phrase in the problem statement and evaluates it as a potential object.
Identify causal objects	Identify the sources of actions, events, and messages; includes the coordinators of actions.
Identify services (passive contributors)	Identify the targets of actions, events, and messages as well as entities that passively provide services when requested.
Identify messages and information flow	Messages must have an object that sends them and an object that receives them as well as, possibly, another object that processes the information contained in the messages.
Identify real-world items	Real-world items are entities that exist in the real world, but that are not necessarily electronic devices. Examples include respiratory gases, air pressures, forces, anatomical organs, and chemicals.
Identify physical devices	Physical devices include the sensors and actuators provided by the system as well as the electronic devices they monitor or control. In the internal architecture, they are processors or ancillary electronic widgets.
Identify key concepts	Key concepts may be modeled as objects. Bank accounts exist only conceptually, but are important objects in a banking domain. Frequency bins for an on-line autocorrelator may also be objects.
Identify transactions	Transactions are finite instances of associations between objects that persist for some significant period of time. Examples include bus messages and queued data.

Table 6-1: (*cont.*)

Strategy	Description
Identify persistent information	Information that must persist for significant periods of time may be objects or attributes. This persistence may extend beyond the power cycling of the device.
Identify visual elements	User interface elements that display data are objects within the user interface domain such as windows, buttons, scroll bars, menus, histograms, waveforms, icons, bitmaps, and fonts.
Identify control elements	Control elements are objects that provide the interface for the user (or some external device) to control system behavior.
Apply scenarios	Walk through scenarios using the identified objects. Missing objects will become apparent when required actions cannot be achieved with existing objects.

treat it as a potential object. Objects identified in this way can be put into four categories:

- Objects of interest or their classes
- Actors
- Uninteresting objects
- Attributes of objects

The point of the exercise is to find objects within the first category—objects of interest or their classes. Actors have usually already been identified in the use case model, but occasionally some new ones are identified here. Uninteresting objects are objects that have no direct relevance to your system. Attributes also show up as nouns in the problem statement. Sometimes an attribute is clearly just a property of an object. When in doubt, tentatively classify the noun as an object. If subsequent analysis shows the object is insufficiently interesting, it can be included as an attribute of some other object.

Let's see how this works by looking at an elevator, a real-time system familiar to everyone. We begin with a problem statement for an elevator system with the noun phrases emphasized:

> *A software* system *must control a* set of eight Acme elevators *for a* building *with 20* floors. *Each* elevator *contains a* set of buttons, *each corresponding to a desired* floor. *These are called* floor request buttons, *since they indicate a* request *to go to a specific* floor. *Each* elevator *as well has a* current floor indicator *above the* door. *Each* floor *has two* buttons *for requesting* elevators *called* elevator request buttons, *because* they *request an* elevator.
>
> *Each* floor *has a sliding* door *for each* shaft *arranged so that two* door halves *meet in the center when closed. When the* elevator *arrives at the* floor, *the* door *opens at the same time the* door *on the* elevator *opens. The* floor *does have both* pressure and optical sensors *to prevent closing when an* obstacle *is between the two* door halves. *If an* obstruction *is detected by either* sensor, *the* door *shall open. The* door *shall automatically close after a* timeout period *of 5 seconds after the* door *opens. The detection of an* obstruction *shall restart the* door closure time *after an* obstruction *is removed. There is a* speaker *on each* floor *that pings in response to the arrival of an* elevator.
>
> *On each* floor (except the highest and lowest), *there are two* elevator request buttons, one for UP *and* one for DOWN. *On each* floor, *above each* elevator door, *there is an* indicator *specifying the* floor *that the* elevator *is currently at and another* indicator *for its current* direction. *The* system *shall respond to an* elevator request *by sending the nearest elevator that is either idle or already going in the requested* direction. *If no elevators are currently available, the* request *shall pend until an* elevator *meets the above-mentioned* criterion. *Once pressed, the* request buttons *are backlit to indicate that a* request *is pending. Pressing an* elevator request button *when a* request *for that* direction *is already pending shall have no* effect. *When an* elevator *arrives to handle the* request, *the* backlight *shall be removed. If the* button *is pressed when an* elevator *is on the* floor *to*

handle the request *(i.e.,* it *is slated to go in the selected* direction*), then the door shall stop closing and the* door closure timer *shall be reset.*

To enhance safety, a cable tension sensor *monitors the* tension *on the* cable *controlling the* elevator. *In the event of* a failure *in which the* measured tension *falls below a* critical value, *then four external* locking clamps *connected to running* tracks *in the* shaft *stop the* elevator *and hold* it *in place.*

Many of these are clearly redundant references to the same object (synonyms). Others are not of interest. The elevator cable, for example, is not nearly as interesting to the safety system as the cable tension sensor.[6] Likewise, the passengers (clearly actors) are not as interesting as the buttons they push and the indicators they read, which are likely to be inside the scope of the system under development. Other objects clearly need not be modeled at all.

A list can be constructed from the emphasized noun phrases of the likely candidate objects by this kind of analysis. Table 6-2 shows object quantities, where specified, with parentheses.

Some likely attributes of a couple of these objects are shown in Table 6-3.

You can see that this strategy quickly identified many objects but also identified nouns that are clearly not interesting to the analyst.

6.3.2 Identify the Causal Objects

Once the potential objects are identified, look for the most behaviorally active ones. These are objects that

- Produce or control actions
- Produce or analyze data
- Provide interfaces to people or devices
- Store information
- Provide services to people or devices
- Contain other types of fundamental objects

---

[6] That is, it need not be modeled within the system. The cable tension sensor, however, must be modeled.

Table 6-2: *Candidate Objects*

system (1)	elevator (8)	building (1)
floor (20)	request	button
floor request button (8*20)	elevator request button (20*2)	current floor indicator (8)
door (20*8 + 8)	optical sensor	obstruction
pressure sensor	speaker	UP button
door half	elevator door	indicator
DOWN button	floor door	secondary pressure sensor
internal door set	OPEN button	CLOSE button
elevator control panel	alarm	central station
EMERGENCY CALL button	elevator request	door closure timer
electrical power	telephone	elevator occupants
Stop-Run Switch	switch	message
emergency locks	alarm area	mechanical locking clamp
pressure sensor	tracks	electrical power source

Table 6-3: *Object Attributes*

Object	Attribute
Elevator	Direction Status Location
Button	Backlight
Alarm	Status
Cable tensor sensor	Cable tension Critical tension

The first two categories are commonly lumped together as *causal objects*. A causal object is an object that autonomously performs actions, coordinates the activities of component objects, or generates events. Many causal objects eventually become *active objects* and serve as the root composite object of a thread.[7] Their components execute within the context of the thread of the owner composite.

Clearly, the most behaviorally active objects are few in number:

- Floor
- Elevator
- Door
- Button
- Request
- Indicator
- Cable tension sensor
- Mechanical locking clamp

6.3.3 Identify Services (Passive Contributors)

Passive objects are less obvious than causal objects. They may provide passive control, data storage, or both. A simple switch is a passive control object. It provides a service to the causal objects (it turns the light on or off on request), but does not initiate actions by itself. Passive objects are also known as servers because they provide services to client objects.

Simple sensors are passive data objects. An A/D converter might acquire data on command and return it to an actor, or as the result of an event initiated by an active object. Printers and chart recorders are common passive service providers because they print text and graphics on command. A hardware passive service provider might be a chip that performs a cyclic redundancy check computation over a block of data.

---

[7] Although the thread model for the system isn't determined until architectural design, as discussed in Chapter 8.

6.3.4 Identify Messages and Information Flows

For each message, there is an object that sends it, an object that receives it, and potentially, another object that processes it. Messages are the realization of information flows. Information flows, taken from older data flow diagram techniques, specify information flowing from one object to another. Information flow is usually applied in early analysis, while later analysis takes into account the packaging of these flows into messages and service calls. This strategy is very similar to the strategy of identifying service calls, but it can be applied earlier in analysis or at a higher level of abstraction. The UML 2.0 specification allows for information flows to be drawn on class diagrams; these will become associations among the classes of those objects acting as conduits for the specific messages derived from the flows.

Figure 6-4 shows an example of information flows in UML 2.0. This diagram captures, at a high level of abstraction, the information flowing from one class to another. Flows are classifiers in UML and so they can be defined using standard classifier techniques—statecharts, activity diagrams, operations, and attributes. These flows can be described by showing a class box stereotyped «flow» somewhere on the diagram, usually close to the flow between the objects. Notice that the flow between objects is shown as a stereotype of dependency.

6.3.5 Identify Real-World Items

Embedded systems need to model the information or behavior of real-world objects even though they are not part of the system per se. For example, an anesthesia system must model the relevant properties of patients, even though customers are clearly outside the anesthesia system. Typical customer objects will contain attributes such as

- Name
- Social Security number
- Address
- Phone number
- Insurance reference
- Weight
- Sex
- Height

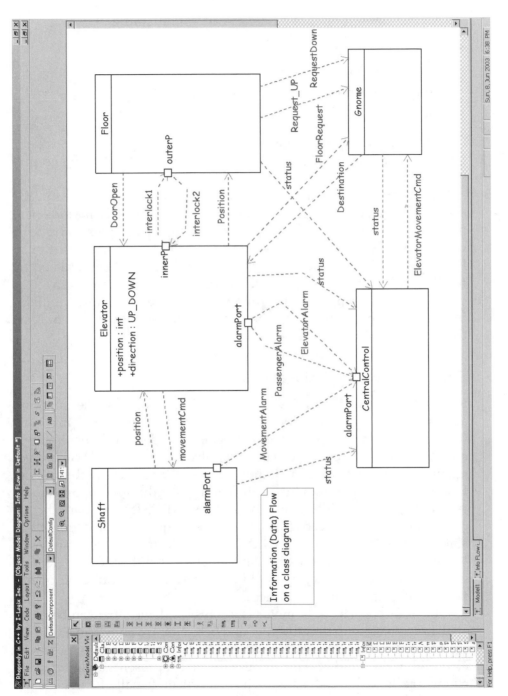

Figure 6-4: *Information Flows*

An ECG monitor might model a heart as containing

- Heart rate
- Cardiac output
- Frequency of preventricular contractions
- Electrical axis

In anesthesia systems, modeling organs as "sinks" for anesthetic agent uptake can aid in closed loop control of agent delivery and prevent toxemia.

This strategy looks at things in the real world that interact in the system. Not all of the aspects of these real-world objects are modeled, only the ones relevant to the system. For example, the color of the heart or its neural control properties won't typically be modeled within an ECG system. Those aspects are irrelevant to the use cases realized by the ECG monitor. However, modeling its beat and PVC rate, as well as cardiac output *is* appropriate and relevant. If the system manipulates information about its actors, then the system should model at least their relevant aspects as objects.

6.3.6 Identify Physical Devices

Real-time systems interact with their environment using sensors and actuators in a hardware domain. The system controls and monitors these physical devices inside and outside the system and these objects are modeled as objects. Devices must also be configured, calibrated, enabled, and controlled so that they can provide services to the system. For example, deep within the inner workings of the system, processors typically perform initial power-on self-tests (POSTs) and periodic (or continuous) built-in tests (BITs). Devices frequently have nontrivial state machines and must provide status information on command. When device information and state must be maintained, the devices may be modeled as objects to hold the information about their operational status and available services.

For example, a stepper motor is a physical device that can be modeled as an object with the attributes and behaviors, as shown in Table 6-4.

Normally, only the interfaces to physical devices are actually modeled within this kind of class because the object presents an interface to client objects within the system. The object itself usually focuses on the

Table 6-4: *Stepper Model Object*

Attributes	Position
Operations	Step(nSteps) GetPos Zero

communication with the device to achieve its client's purposes and not how the device actually works. The only exception to this rule is in constructing simulation systems, in which case modeling the internal behavior of the device is the point of the object.

6.3.7 Identify Key Concepts

Key concepts are important abstractions within the domain that have interesting attributes and behaviors. These abstractions often do not have physical realizations, but must nevertheless be modeled by the system. Within the User Interface domain, a window is a key concept. In the banking domain, an account is a key concept. In an autonomous manufacturing robot, a task plan is the set of steps required to implement the desired manufacturing process. In the design of a C compiler, functions, data types, and pointers are key concepts. Each of these objects has no physical manifestation. They exist only as abstractions modeled within the appropriate domains as objects or classes.

6.3.8 Identify Transactions

Transactions are objects that must persist for a finite period of time and that represent the interactions of other objects. Some example transaction objects are outlined in Table 6-5.

In the elevator case study, an elevator request is clearly a transaction. It has a relatively short life span, either

- Beginning when the (future) passenger pushes the elevator request button and ending when the elevator arrives and opens its doors, or

- Beginning when the passenger pushes the floor request button and ending when the elevator arrives at its destination and opens its doors.

Table 6-5: *Example Transaction Objects*

Object 1	Object 2	Association	Transaction Object
Woman	Man	Marriage	Marriage object: • wedding date • wedding location • prenuptial agreement • witnesses
Woman	Man	Marriage	Divorce object: • filing date • decree date • maintenance schedule • amount paid to lawyers
Controller	Actuator	Controls	Control message over bus
Alarming Class	Alarm Manager	Issues alarms	Silence Alarm
Customer	Store	Buys things at	Order Return
Display System	Sensor	Displays values for	Alarm Error
Elevator Request Button	Elevator	Issues request to	Request for elevator
Floor Request Button	Elevator	Issues request to	Request for floor
Task Plan	Robot Arm	Controls	Command

Other examples of transactions are alarms and (reliable) bus messages. Alarms must persist as long as the dangerous condition is true or until explicitly handled, depending on the system. Alarms will typically have attributes such as

• Alarm condition
• Alarm priority

- Alarm severity[8]
- Time of occurrence
- Duration of condition

Reliable message transfer requires that a message persist at the site of the sender until an explicit acknowledgement is received. This allows the sender to retransmit if the original message is lost. Bus messages typically have attributes such as

- Message type
- Priority
- Source address
- Target address
- Message data
- Cyclic redundancy check

6.3.9 Identify Persistent Information

Persistent information is typically held within passive objects such as stacks, queues, trees, and databases. Either volatile memory (RAM or SRAM) or long-term storage (FLASH, EPROM, EEPROM, or disk) may store persistent data.

A robot must store and recall task plans. Subsequent analysis of the system may reveal other persistent data. For example, the information in Table 6-6 may be persistent.

Such data can be used for scheduling equipment maintenance, and may appear in monthly or yearly reports.

6.3.10 Identify Visual Elements

Many real-time systems interact directly or indirectly with human users. Real-time system displays may be as simple as a single blinking LED to indicate power status or as elaborate as a full GUI with buttons,

---

[8] Priority and severity are orthogonal concepts. *Priority* refers to how a scheduler will resolve execution order when multiple events are waiting to be handled (and is a combination of importance and urgency); the *severity* refers to how bad the outcome of the fault condition may be if unhandled. These concepts are discussed in more detail in [5].

Table 6-6: *Persistent Information Objects*

Information	Storage Period	Description
Task plans	Unlimited	Programs for the robotic system must be constructed, stored, recalled for editing, and recalled for execution.
Errors	Between service calls	An error log holding the error identifier, severity, location, and time/date of occurrence will facilitate maintenance of the system.
Equipment alarms	Until next service call	Equipment alarms indicate conditions that must be brought to the attention of the user, even though they may not be errors. Tracking them between service calls allows analysis of the reliability of the system.
Hours of operation	Between service calls	Hours of operation aid in tracking costs and scheduling service calls.
Security access	Unlimited	Stores valid users, their identifiers, and passwords to permit different levels of access.
Service information	Unlimited	Service calls and updates performed can be tracked, including when, what, and by whom.

windows, scroll bars, icons, and text. *Visual elements* used to convey information to the user are objects within the user interface domain.

In many environments, user interface (UI) designers specialize in the construction of visual interaction models or prototypes that the developers implement.

For example, consider the sample screens for the elevator central control station shown in Figures 6-5 through 6-7.

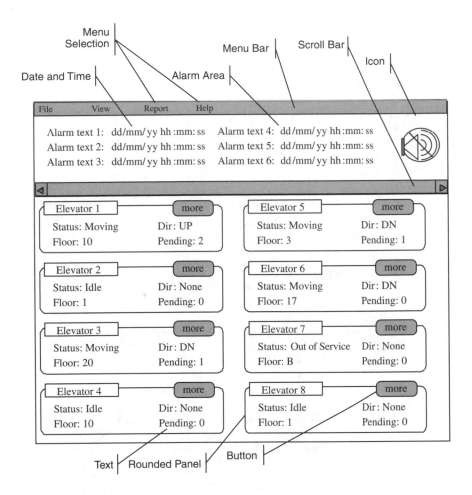

Figure 6-5: *Elevator Central Station Main View*

We see a number of common visual elements:

- Window
- Rectangle
- Rounded panel
- Horizontal scroll bar
- Scroll button (left, right, up, down)

- Button
- Menu bar
- Menu selection
- Drop-down menu
- Menu item
- List box
- Text
- Icon (for alarm silence)

Each of these is an object within the UI domain for the elevator central station. These UI objects are depicted in an object message diagram later in this chapter.

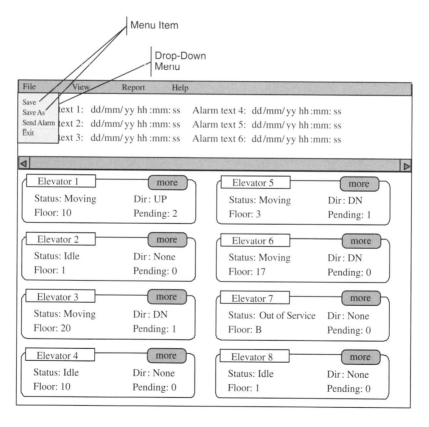

Figure 6-6: *Elevator Central Station Menu View*

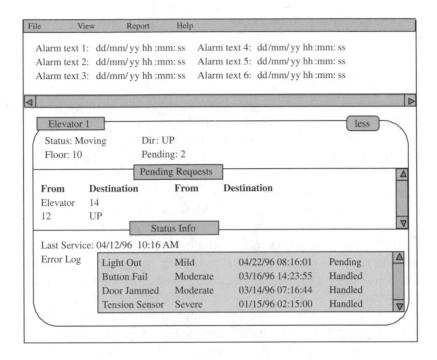

Figure 6-7: *Elevator Central Station Zoom View*

6.3.11 Identify Control Elements

Control elements are entities that control other objects. These are specific types of causal objects. Some objects, called *composites*, often orchestrate the behaviors of their part objects. These may be simple objects or may be elaborate control systems, such as

- PID control loops
- Fuzzy logic inference engines
- Expert system inference engines
- Neural network simulators

Some control elements are physical interface devices that allow users to enter commands. The elevator case study has only a few:

- Button (elevator and floor)
- Switch (elevator and floor)

- Keyboard (central station only)
- Mouse (central station only)

6.3.12 Apply Scenarios

The application of use case scenarios is another strategy to identify missing objects as well as to test that an object collaboration adequately realizes a use case. Using only known objects, step through the messages to implement the scenario. When "you can't get there from here," you've probably identified one or more missing objects.

In mechanical terms, this is done by *refining* the use case scenario. Remember from Chapter 5 that the structural context for a use case scenario is the system and the actors participating in the scenario. This means that a use case scenario cannot show objects internal to the system *because they are not yet known.* However, once you have identified and captured the set of objects in the collaboration, you can replace the single System object with the set of objects in the collaboration. This provides a more detailed or refined view of the scenario and ensures that the collaboration does, in fact, realize the use case.

For example, consider the use case scenario in Figure 6-8. It shows the black-box behavior of the pacemaker with respect to the actors Pacing Engine and Heart (and the Communications Subsystem). Using the

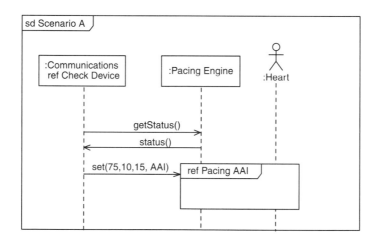

Figure 6-8: *Pace the Heart in AAI Mode (Use Case Level)*

object identification strategies previously mentioned, let's assume we can construct the model in Figure 6-9. We can now refine the scenario by elaborating the scenario with the set of identified objects, as shown in Figure 6-10. This is now a white-box view that we can relate directly to our black-box use case view. This more refined view of the same scenario, shown in Figure 6-8, shows how the objects in the collaboration work together. Note, for example, that when the Programmer instructs the pacemaker to go into AAI pacing mode, the Pacing Engine tells the Atrial Model to go to Inhibited model and the Ventricular Model to go to Idle mode. Figure 6-10 even shows the relationship between the scenario and the state models (not shown) of the Atrial Model and Ventricular Model objects.

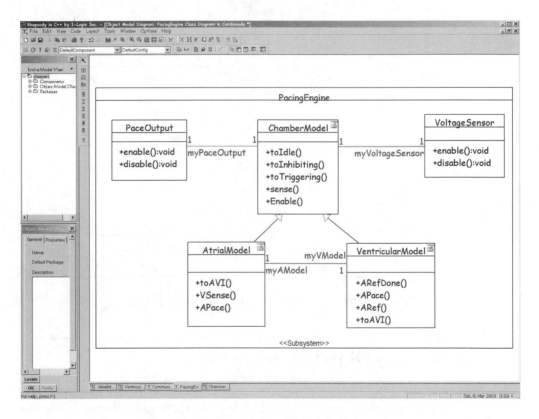

Figure 6-9: *Pacemaker Object Collaboration*

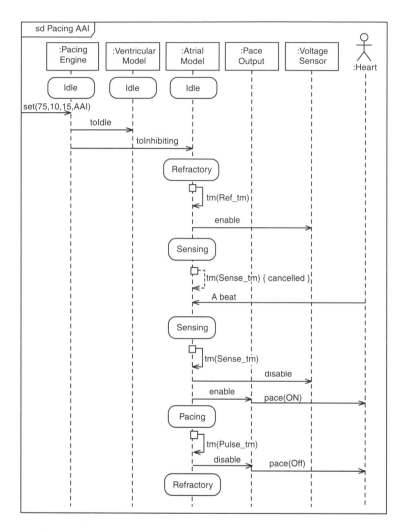

Figure 6-10: *Pace the Heart in AAI Mode (Object Level)*

6.4 Identify Object Associations

Early in the analysis, some objects seem to relate to others even though it is not always clear exactly how. The first step is to identify the existence of such associations. We discuss the characterization of associations later in this chapter.

There are a few strategies for the identification of object relationships. Each relies on the fact that objects send messages to other objects and every message implies an association. Table 6-7 shows the most common strategies used to identify associations.

In our elevator example, there are a number of associations, shown in Table 6-8.

Class and object diagrams capture these associations. A line drawn between two objects represents a link (instance of an association) between those objects, supporting the transmission of a message from one to the other.

The object diagram in Figure 6-11 shows the general structure of the identified objects and their neighbors. The system consists of 38 high-level objects: 8 shafts, 8 elevators, 20 floors, and one central station and one elevator gnome. The numbers at the upper lefthand corner of the object represents the instance count, that is, the number of instances of the object in the enclosing context. The shaft, elevator, and floor are all

Table 6-7: *Object Association Strategies*

Strategy	Description
Identify messages	Each message implies an association between the participating objects.
Identify message sources	The sensors that detect information or events and the creators of information or events are all message sources. They pass information on to other objects for handling and storage.
Identify message storage depots	Message storage depots store information for archival purposes or provide a central repository of information for other objects. The depots have associations with the message sources as well as the users of that information.
Identify message handlers	Some objects centralize message dispatching and handling. They form connections to either or both message sources and message storage depots.
Identify whole/ part structures	Whole/part relations will become aggregation or composition relationships among objects. Wholes often send messages to their parts. *(continued)*

Table 6-7: (*cont.*)

Strategy	Description
Identify more/less abstract structures	Some objects are related to each other by differences in levels of abstraction. It is not uncommon for a single higher-level abstraction to be implemented by a tightly knit set of objects at a more concrete level of abstraction. The larger object in this case will become a composite object and the smaller objects, its component parts. The relationship among them will become a composition relation.
Apply scenarios	Walk through scenarios using the identified objects. The scenarios explicitly show how the messages are sent between objects.

Table 6-8: *Elevator Object Associations*

Message Source	Message Target	Message
Elevator request button	Elevator gnome	Requests an elevator
Elevator gnome	Elevator	Request status
Elevator gnome	Elevator	Add destination for elevator
Elevator	Elevator gnome	Accept destination
Elevator	Floor speaker	Arrival event beep
Elevator floor sensor	Elevator	Location
Cable tension sensor	Locking clamps	Engage
Central station	Locking clamps	Release
Cable tension sensor	Central station	Alarm condition
Elevator	Central station	Status
Floor request button	Elevator	Add destination
Run-stop switch	Elevator	Stop/run
Run-stop switch	Central station	Stop/run
Alarm button	Central station	Alarm condition
Elevator	Door	Open/close

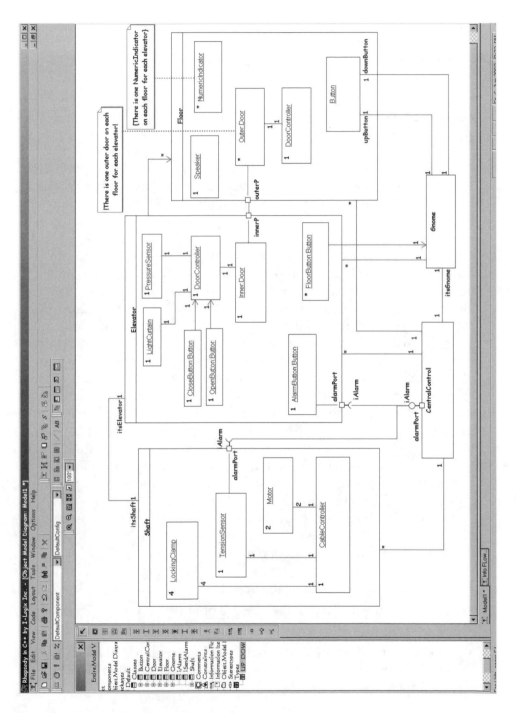

Figure 6-11: *First-Cut Elevator Object Diagram*

composites that strongly aggregate their components. The instance counts of their components as per instance of their context. That is, each Elevator has 20 instances of Floor Request Button.

6.5 Object Attributes

The UML defines an attribute to be "a named property of a type." In this sense, attributes are "smaller" than objects—they have only a primitive structure and, of themselves, no operations other than *get_* and *set_*. Practically speaking, attributes are the data portion of an object. A sensor object might include attributes such as a calibration constant and a measured value. Attributes are almost always primitive and cannot productively be broken down into smaller pieces. If you find attributes to be structurally nonprimitive or behaviorally rich, then they should usually be modeled as objects owned (via composition) by the main object, rather than as attributes of that main object. For example, if a sensor has a simple scalar calibration constant, then it would be appropriate to model it as an attribute of the sensor object. If, however, the sensor object has an entire set of calibration constants, the calibration constants should be each be modeled as an object aggregated unidirectionally by the sensor object with a 1-* multiplicity. The set of constants would probably be managed by a container class (added in design), as shown in Figure 6-12. It is important to remember that modeling the table in this way does not necessarily entail any additional overhead in terms of performance or memory usage but does provide superior encapsulation of concerns and easier maintenance.

Sometimes the primary attributes of an object are obvious, but not always. Developers can ask themselves some key questions to identify the most important attributes of objects:

- What information defines the object?
- On what information do the object's operations act?
- What does the object know?
- Are the identified attributes rich in either structure or behavior? (If so, they are probably objects in their own right rather than simple attributes.)

Not this . . .

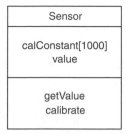

but this . . .

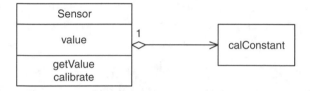

which will become (in mechanistic design) this...

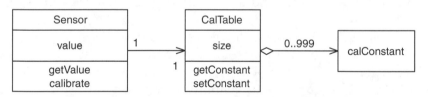

Figure 6-12: *Modeling Nonprimitive Attributes*

- What are the responsibilities of the object? What information is necessary to fulfill these responsibilities?

The Elevator class provides a good example of a real-time class with attributes. Let's ask these questions about this class:

- *What information defines the object?* The Elevator is a physical thing that must be controlled. To fulfill its function it must know where it is, where it is going (destination list), its current direction, its operational status, and its error history.

- *On what information do the object's operations act?* It has a goto() operation, which must act on where it is, its current direction, and its state (moving, stopped, etc.).

- *What does the object know?* It knows where it is, where it is going, and what it is doing right now.

- *Are the identified attributes rich in either structure or behavior?* If so, they are probably objects rather than attributes. The Elevator has a door that has state (open, closed, opening, closing), interlocks with the floor door, and operations. The door is probably a separate object.

- *What are the responsibilities of the object? What information is necessary to fulfill these responsibilities?* The Elevator's primary responsibility is to transport passengers from one floor to another safely. It needs the attributes of where it is, in which direction it is traveling, a list of current destinations, and its current state.

There are cases in which an object with no attributes is valid within the domain. A button is a reasonable class, but what attributes does it have? Probably none. Some composite objects are only aggregates of many objects with no data specific in and of themselves. Other objects contain only functions and so are often called *functoids* or (in UML-speak) *class utilities.*

In object domain analysis, we are not particularly concerned with the visibility of the attributes (or of the operations). Later, in design, we will mark them as public (+'), private (-) or protected (#). If you'd like to mark your best guess as to visibility when you enter these features, that's fine, but it isn't a primary focus.

6.6 Discovering Candidate Classes

Of all the objects identified in the problem statement, many are structurally identical. In the elevator case study, for example, there are eight elevators, all the same. Similarly, there are scads[9] of buttons, but they all appear to be structurally identical. Each is activated by depression, acknowledges with a backlight, and so on. Objects that are identical in structure are said to be of the same *class.* The next analysis activity is to propose candidate classes for the identified objects.

---

[9] *Scad:* A technical term meaning "a lot." Antonym: *scootch.*

Classes are abstractions of objects. Objects that are identical in type (even if different in specific value) are abstracted into a class. In the elevator example, buttons differ by purpose. Floor request buttons reside within the elevator and request a destination for that specific elevator. Elevator request buttons reside on the floor and request any elevator to come to the floor and take passengers in a specific direction. Each button is structurally identical and differs only in its context. It depresses when pushed and issues a message when released. When the message is accepted, the button is backlit. The *button* appears to be a good choice for a candidate class.

Similarly, other objects can be abstracted into candidate classes:

- Elevator
- Door
- Floor
- Speaker
- Floor indicator
- Elevator indicator

and so on. From these classes, specific objects, such as "Elevator #2 Request Button for Floor #8," may be instantiated. Classes so identified can be put in a class diagram for a simpler structural view than the object diagram, especially since the object model of a system changes over time (as objects are created and destroyed).

6.7 Class Diagrams

Class diagrams are the single most important diagrams in object-oriented analysis and design. They show the structure of the system in terms of classes and objects, including how the objects and classes relate to each other. Class diagrams are the primary road map of the system and its object-oriented decomposition. They are similar to object diagrams except they show primarily classes rather than instances. Object diagrams are inherently snapshots of the system at some point in time, showing the objects and the links among them that exist at that instant in time. Class diagrams represent, in an important sense, all possible such snapshots and are therefore more "universal." For this reason, almost all structural modeling of systems is done with class diagrams rather than object diagrams.

So far in this book, we've already seen plenty of class diagrams. One of the disadvantages of building real systems (as opposed to constructing examples for books) is that in real systems you always come up with more classes than you can conveniently put on a single diagram even if you go to 2-point font and E-size plotter paper. Developers need criteria for dividing up their class structures into different diagrams that make the system understandable, accessible, and modifiable in the various ways that the stakeholders need. Different methodologies have different solutions for this. The ROPES process has a simple process rule: *Every* diagram should have a single important concept it is trying to show. This is called the *mission* of the diagram. Common missions for a class diagram include these:

- Show the context of an architectural class or object (a context diagram)
- Show the architectural elements within a system and how they relate (a *subsystem* diagram or *component* diagram)
- Show the parts within a structured class (a *class structure* diagram)
- Show the architectural elements that work together to provide redundancy, replication, or fault tolerance (a *structure reliability* or *structure safety* diagram)
- Show how the architectural or collaborating elements distribute across multiple address spaces (a *deployment* diagram)
- Show how instances distribute themselves across multiple address spaces with respect to their communication (a *distribution* diagram)
- Show the classes within a collaboration realizing a use case at an object-domain level of abstraction (a *essential object* diagram or *essential class* diagram)
- Show the classes within a collaboration, including the design refactoring and inclusion of design elements (a *class design* diagram)
- Show the information flow among types or instances (a *data flow* or *information flow* diagram
- Show the classes within a package or domain
- Show the package organization of the model (a *package* diagram)
- Show the classes within a single generalization taxonomy (an *inheritance* diagram)

- Show the classes related to the concurrency or resource model (a *task* diagram)
- Show the classes related to access of a single resource of particular significance (a *resource* diagram)
- Show a view of structural elements bound together by a coupled set of constraints (a *constraint* diagram)
- Show a set of instances and their links for a typical or exception condition or state of the system (an *object* diagram)
- Show the abstraction of a set of design elements into a design pattern (a *design pattern* diagram)

With a little thought, I'm sure you can come up with even more specific missions for class diagrams. Note that many of these missions are common enough to be given specific names, such as *task diagram*, but this doesn't mean that the diagram *type* is different, only its *usage*. The mission of a diagram focuses on why we want to construct a particular diagram and how it helps us, but the same set of elements (class, object, package, component, node) may all appear on the same diagram type. So these aren't fundamentally different diagrams. Systems are organized this way to help us understand all their relevant aspects. Organizing the diagrams by missions makes sense aids comprehension and defect-identification. A common complaint about the UML is that there are too many different diagrams, but really there are only a handful. There are, however, just a few diagram types, but many *missions* or purposes to which these few diagrams may be applied.

6.7.1 Associative Classes

In the UML 1.x, an associative class clarified associations that had interesting structure or behavior. In the UML 2.0, all associations are classifiers and so may be shown as a stereotyped class where useful. In distributed systems, the classic example of an associative class is a bus message class. In addition to the information being sent from one object to another, the message object may contain additional information specific to the relationship and even the link instance. For example:

- Message priority
- Message route

- Session identifiers
- Sequence numbers
- Flow control information
- Data format information
- Data packaging information
- Time-to-live information for the message
- Protocol revision number
- Data integrity check information

In a transaction-oriented system, associative classes also contain information specific to the transaction.

An associative class is used when information does not seem to belong to either object in the association or belongs to both equally. Marriage is an association between two people objects. Where do the following attributes belong?

- Date of marriage
- Location of marriage
- Prenuptial agreement

Clearly, these are attributes of the marriage and not the participants.

Figure 6-13 shows a case of an associative class. In this distributed system model, one subsystem contains the sensor class and acts as a server for the data from the sensors. The client subsystem displays this data to the user. The association between the measurement server and measurement client is of interest here.

One way to implement the association is to have the client explicitly ask whenever it wants data to display. Another is to have the server provide the data whenever it becomes available. However, neither option may be the best use of a finite-bandwidth bus. Additionally, what if another client wants to be added to the recipient list for the data? Some buses provide the ability to broadcast such data, but most target a specific recipient.

The associative class solution provided here uses a *session*. A session is a negotiated agreement between two communicating objects. Sessions save bandwidth because they negotiate some information up front so

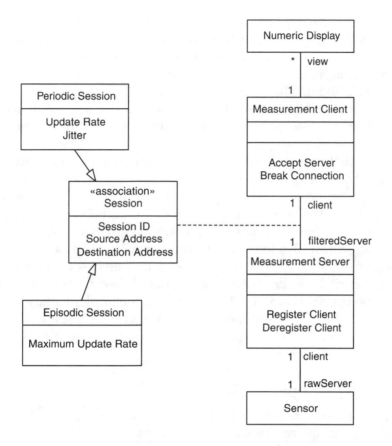

Figure 6-13: *Session Associative Class*

that it need not be passed within each message. Nonsessioned (*connec-tionless*) communications are similar to postcards. Each and every time a postcard is mailed, it must contain the complete destination and source addresses. A session is more like a phone call. Once the destination is dialed and the connection established, the communication can be any length or complexity without resending or reconnecting.

In this case, the session contains two important pieces of information: the source and the target addresses. Two session subtypes are defined based on the update policy. The update policy can be either *episodic* or *periodic. Episodic,* in this context, means that the server sends data when it changes—that is, when an episode occurs. *Periodic* means that the server must send the data at a fixed interval. Episodic sessions in this example have a maximum update rate to make sure that a bursty system does not overload the bus. Periodic sessions have a defined update rate.

The measurement server contains two operations to assist in session management. The first is Register Client. This operation accepts the registration of a new client and participates in the negotiated construction of a session object. The Deregister Client operation removes a registered client.

The measurement client contains two operations to support its role in negotiating the session: Accept Server and Break Connection.

Who owns the session? Arguments can be made for both the server and the client. The server must track information about the session so that it knows when and how to issue updates. The client initiates the session and must also know about update policy and rates. The solution shown in Figure 6-13 is that the session is an associative class and contains attributes about the relationship between the two primary classes. Because this is a distributed system, the implementation would involve creating two coordinating session objects (or a single *distributed object*), one on each processor node, providing session information to the local client or server.

6.7.2 Generalization Relationships

Generalization is a taxonomic relationship between classes. The class higher in the taxonomic hierarchy is sometimes called the *parent, generalized, base,* or *superclass.* The class inheriting properties from the base class is called the *child, specialized, derived,* or *subclass.* Derived classes have all the properties of their parents, but may extend and specialize them.

Using Aristotelian logic and standard set theory, generalizing along a single characteristic guarantees that the classes are *disjoint*.[10] When the set of subclasses enumerates all possible subclasses along the characteristic, the subclassing is said to be *complete.*

Consider our elevator example. An elevator has many buttons— ones to go to a floor, one to open the door, one to close the door, one to send an alarm, and so on. An elevator might have 30 different button

---

[10] By *disjoint* we mean that the classes represent nonoverlapping or orthogonal alternatives. Male and female, for example, are disjoint sets. Fuzzy sets are inherently nondisjoint and allow partial membership. Object subclasses are assumed to be crisp sets (all-or-none membership) rather than fuzzy.

instances in it, but how many *classes* do we have? Are the buttons different in terms of their structure or behavior? No—they all work the same way—you push them and they report a press event; when you release them, they report a release event; when selected, they will be backlit, and so on. They only differ in their *usage* not in their *type*, and should be modeled as different instances of a single class. In other environments, there may be buttons that differ in their structure and behavior.

The button subclasses in Figure 6-14 are specialized along the lines of behavior. Simple buttons issue an event message when pressed, but have no state memory. Toggle buttons jump back and forth between two states on sequential depressions. Multistate buttons run through a (possibly elaborate) state machine with each depression. Group buttons deselect all other buttons within the group when depressed.

In the UML, generalization implies two things: *inheritance* and *substitutability*. Inheritance means that (almost) everything that is true of a superclass is also true of all of its subclasses. This means that a subclass has all of its parent's attributes, operations, associations, and dependencies. If the superclass has a statechart to define its behavior, then the subclass will inherit that statechart. The subclass is free to both specialize and extend the inherited properties. *Specialization* means that the subclass may polymorphically redefine an operation (or statechart) to be

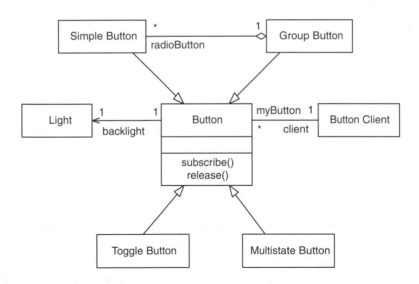

Figure 6-14: *Button Subclasses*

more semantically appropriate for the subclass. Extension means that the subclass may add new attributes, operations, associations, and so on.

Substitutability means that an instance of a subclass may always be substituted for an instance of its superclass without breaking the semantics of the model. This is known as the *Liskov Substitution Principle* (LSP) [3]. The LSP states that a subclass must obey polymorphic rules in exactly the same manner as its superclass. For example,

```
class Animal {
public:
    virtual void speak(void) = 0;    // virtual base
        class
};
class dog: public Animal {
public:
    void speak(void) { cout << "Arf!" << endl; };
};
class fish: public Animal {
public:
    void speak(void) { cout << "Blub! " << endl; };
};
class cat: public Animal {
public:
    void speak(void) {
        cout << "<Aloof disdain>" << endl; };
};
void main(void) {
    Animal *A;
    dog d;
    fish f;
    cat c;
    A = &d;
    A->speak();
    A = &c;
    A->speak();
    A = &f;
    A->speak();
};
```

The base class (Animal) accesses the three subtypes through a pointer (A). Nonetheless, the access to the speak() method for each is identical, satisfying the LSP.

For the LSP to work, the relationship between the superclass and subclass must be one of specialization or extension. Whatever is true of the superclass must also be true of the subclass because the subclass is a type of its superclass. A dog *is* an animal, so all of the things true about *all* animals are also true about dogs. All of the behaviors common to all animals can also be performed by dogs. If the abstraction *animal* had an attribute or behavior that was not true of dogs (such as being able to produce free oxygen via photosynthesis), a dog would not be a type of animal.

That being said, a subclass is free to specialize the behavior of a superclass. The speak() method defined within animal is an example. Each subclass does a different thing while still meeting the requirement of supporting the behavior speak(). Locomote() is another example. Dogs, cats, fish, and birds all locomote, but they implement it differently. This is what is meant by *specialization*.

Subclasses are also free to extend their inherited structure by adding new behaviors or attributes. We can add some new behaviors to the dog and cat classes that are not true of animals in general.

```
class dog: public Animal {
public:
    void speak(void) { cout << "Arf!" << endl; };
    void slobber(float slobberIndex);
    void AttackJogger(int fearLevel);
};

class cat: public Animal {
public:
    void speak(void) {
        cout << "<Aloof disdain>" << endl; };
    void ClawFurniture(long ClawLength);
    void SnubOwner(void);
};
```

Now dogs can slobber() and AttackJogger() while cats can Claw-Furniture() and SnubOwner(). Animals in general (and fish for that matter) can perform none of these charming behaviors.

Frequently, base classes cannot be instantiated without being first specialized. *Animal* might not do anything interesting, but dogs, cats, and fish do. When a class is not directly instantiated, it is called an *abstract class*. C++ classes are made abstract by the inclusion of a *pure virtual function*. A C++ virtual function is a class method that is denoted by the keyword *virtual*. It need only be so indicated in one class in the inheritance tree, and it will be virtual for all derived classes. A virtual .

function is made pure virtual with the peculiar syntax of assigning the function declaration the value zero. For example,

```
class widget {
public:
    virtual void doSomething() = 0;
};
```

Note that in C++, constructors and destructors cannot be made pure virtual. Furthermore, if a C++ class contains a virtual function, it is a logical error not to define the destructor as virtual.[11] C++ does not allow virtual constructors.

6.7.2.1 Positioning Features in the Inheritance Tree

Generalization relationships form class hierarchies with the most general classes at the top and the most specialized classes at the bottom. Structuring these hierarchies is done by using three complementary approaches:

- *Extension*: Derived classes extend the capabilities of the parent class (top-down).

- *Specialization*: Derived classes specialize the capabilities of a parent (top-down).

- *Bubbling up*: Attributes and behaviors that are common in peer children become attributes and behaviors of the parent class (bottom up).[12]

The first strategy, extension, means that a subclass can add behaviors and attributes to those it inherits from its parents. This is an example of the Open-Closed Principle (OCP) [4]. The OCP states that for maximum reusability, a class should be open for extension but not modification. The focus of the OCP is that changes in a well-designed class hierarchy should be made by subclassing rather than modifying the hierarchy itself. Another term for this concept is *programming by difference*. The developer finds a class in the hierarchy that is close to what

---

[11] Just one of many such opportunities provided by the C++ language.

[12] Note that restriction of the parent class is not included. All popular object-oriented languages allow the *augmentation* or *extension* of a class, but not *restriction* (removal of a behavior or attribute). To do so breaks the fundamental tenet of inheritance—that the child *is a type of* its parent—and therefore violates the LSP.

is needed, subclasses it, and extends the subclass to meet the particular needs. The OCP focuses on reuse, but it applies equally well to the construction of class hierarchies. Subclasses may extend the capabilities of their parents without modifying the parents.

LSP applies not only to features such as attributes, operations, and states. It also applies to constraints. Following the generalization principle of "any subclass must be at least able to do what the parent class can," constraints should be loosened in subclasses not tightened. This makes sense if you look at a feature or quality of service of a superclass and ask the question, "Can the subclass do this?" Put another way, a subclass inherits all of the features (and constraints) of the superclass, although it may be some additional ones. The rule is *substitutability*. That is, a constraint in a subclass must be consistent with constraints in the superclass. For example,

- If an *offered interface* has a timing requirements, such as "worst-case execution time = 18 ms +/– 2 ms," then any subclass must meet this, but it may do *better*, such as "worst case execution time = 16 ms +/– 1.5ms"; but it cannot fail to meet those constraints without violating substitutability. For example, a subclass of the previously mentioned class can't use the constraint "25 ms +/– 1ms" or even "17ms +/– 5ms."

- *Required interfaces* have similar restrictions. If a class B meets the required interface of the superclass, then it should also meet the required interface for any subclass.

- *Subranges for values being sent to the class* realizing the interface may be extended in the subclass, but not further constrained; this is because every value sent to the superclass must be valid while being sent to the subclass.

- *Subranges for values being returned from the class* realizing the interface may be constrained but not extended; this is because every value returned by the subclass in this case may also be returned by the superclass and so maintains substitutability. The fact that it doesn't return all possible values isn't a problem. However, if the subclass returned a value beyond what the superclass could do, this could break a client.

Figure 6-15 shows how constraints are properly propagated to subclasses. It is, perhaps, counterintuitive that an InfraredDopplerLight is

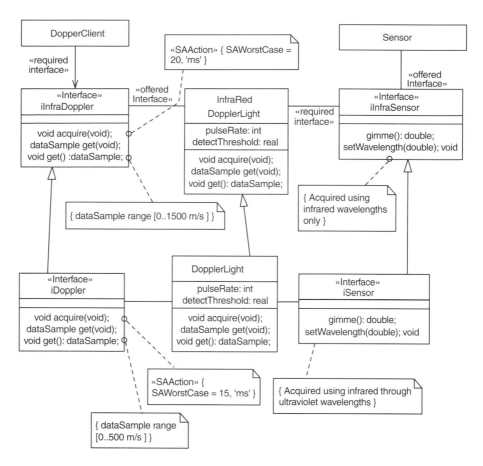

Figure 6-15: *Generalization and Constraints*

the superclass and DopplerLight is the subclass, but the Infrared-DopplerLight allows sensing wavelengths to be set only in the infrared range, while the DopplerLight can use a wider range of light wavelengths. In this example, this arrangement of generalization allows substitutability to preserved:

- The iInfraDopplerLight interface provides an operation acquire() with a specified worst-case execution time of 20ms. The subclass interface iDoppler provides the same operation with a specified worst-case execution of 15ms. The subclass can be substituted for the superclass and meet the interface requirements

- The iInfraDopplerLight interface has an operation get(), which returns a data sample in the range of 0..1500. The subclassed interface iDoppler::get() returns a data sample in the range of 0..500. This is likewise consistent since every value returnable from the subclass is valid for the superclass (and therefore for its clients) so any client usage of the iDopper in the role of an iInfraDoppler is correct.

- The iInfraSensor interface has a setWavelength() operation that accepts parameters only in the infrared range. The subclass interface iSensor::setWavelength() allows all the parameters that can be passed to it from an iInfraSensor client as well as more, since it can also take wavelengths in the visible and ultraviolet range.

As an exercise, decide how to arrange the following in a generalization taxonomy: shape, square, rectangle. This simple problem has caused more debate than you might think!

Generalization is useful because of the substitutability of the subclass whenever a superclass is used. Consider Figure 6-16. A client needs to use the Queue superclass to store strings (OMString is a type provided by the Rhapsody tool and so is used here).[13] Sometimes, a client might need to store more elements that there is main memory available for storage, so a CachedQueue (a subclass of Queue) can be substituted, to cache elements out to disk as necessary.

Figure 6-16 shows a simple example of extending a subclass. The Queue superclass provides several methods—insert(), remove(), nElements(), isFull(), and isEmpty()—as well as some attributes—head, tail, and size (all of type int). It also has a composition relation to OMString (the type of elements that it stores). The source code for this class is shown in Code Listing 6-1 (Queue.h, the c++ header file) and Code Listing 6-2 (Queue.cpp, the implementation file). This code is generated from the I-Logix Rhapsody tool, so it contains some macros (such as GUARD_OPERATION, which allocates a mutex to protect the Queue class from mutual exclusion problems) and other aspects that are autogenerated and may be pretty much be ignored. You can see by

---

[13] Note that in a properly defined container class we would probably use parameterized classes to isolate the container functionality from the type being contained, but that would only muddy the waters of this particular example so we use a specific type with a specific size for simplicity.

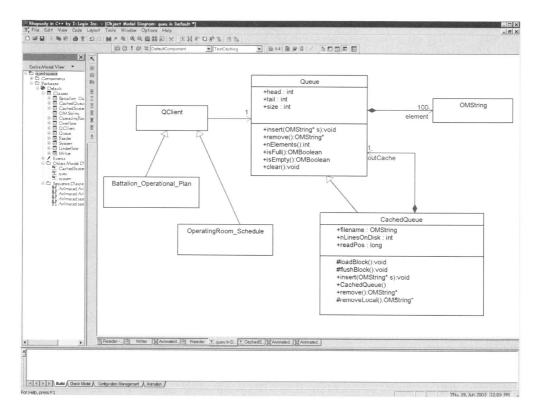

Figure 6-16: *Extending and Specializing*

looking at the model in Figure 6-16 and the source code that the Queue class is fairly straightforward.

```
/* * * * * * * * * * * * * * * * * * * * * * * * * * * * * * * * * * * * * * * * * * * *
       Rhapsody      : 5.0
       Login         : Bruce
       Component     : DefaultComponent
       Configuration    : TestCaching
       Model Element    : Queue
//!    Generated Date   : Wed, 18, Jun 2003
       File Path     : DefaultComponent\TestCaching\
                       Queue.h
* * * * * * * * * * * * * * * * * * * * * * * * * * * * * * * * * * * * * * * * * * * * */

#ifndef Queue_H
#define Queue_H
```

```
//#[ ignore
#define _OMFLAT_IMPLEMENTATION 1
//#]
#include <oxf/oxf.h>
#include "fstream.h"
#include "stdio.h"
#include "Default.h"
#include <oxf/omreactive.h>
#include <oxf/state.h>
#include <oxf/event.h>
//## package Default
//- - - - - - - - - - - - - - - - - - - - - - - - - - - - - -
// Queue.h
//- - - - - - - - - - - - - - - - - - - - - - - - - - - - - -
class Overflow;
class Underflow;

//## class Queue
class Queue : public OMReactive {

////    Constructors and destructors    ////
public :

    //## operation Queue()
    Queue(OMThread*  p_thread = OMDefaultThread);

    //## auto_generated
    virtual ~Queue();

////    Operations    ////
public :

    //## operation clear()
    void clear();

    //## operation get(int)
    OMString get(int  index);

    //## operation insert(OMString*)
    virtual void insert(OMString*  s);

    //## operation isEmpty()
    virtual OMBoolean isEmpty();

    //## operation isFull()
    virtual OMBoolean isFull();
```

```
    //## operation nElements()
    virtual int nElements();

    //## operation remove()
    virtual OMString* remove();
////    Additional operations    ////
public :

    //## auto_generated
    int getHead() const;

    //## auto_generated
    void setHead(int  p_head);

    //## auto_generated
    int getSize() const;

    //## auto_generated
    void setSize(int  p_size);

    //## auto_generated
    int getTail() const;

    //## auto_generated
    void setTail(int  p_tail);

    //## auto_generated
    Overflow* getItsOverflow() const;

    //## auto_generated
    void setItsOverflow(Overflow*  p_Overflow);

    //## auto_generated
    Underflow* getItsUnderflow() const;

    //## auto_generated
    void setItsUnderflow(Underflow*  p_Underflow);
////    Framework operations    ////
public :

    //## auto_generated
    int getElement() const;

    //## auto_generated
```

```
    virtual OMBoolean startBehavior();
protected :

    //## auto_generated
    void cleanUpRelations();

////    Attributes    ////
protected :

    int head;            //## attribute head

    int size;            //## attribute size

    int tail;            //## attribute tail

////    Relations and components    ////
protected :

    OMString* element[100];           //## link
                                         element


    Overflow* itsOverflow;            //## link
                                         itsOverflow


    Underflow* itsUnderflow;          //## link
                                         itsUnderflow


};

#endif
/*****************************************************
     File Path    : DefaultComponent\TestCaching\
                    Queue.h
*****************************************************/
```

Code Listing 6-1: *Queue.h*

```
/*****************************************************
     Rhapsody    : 5.0
     Login       : Bruce
     Component   : DefaultComponent
```

```
        Configuration      : TestCaching
        Model Element      : Queue
//!     Generated Date     : Wed, 18, Jun 2003
        File Path    : DefaultComponent\TestCaching\
                       Queue.cpp
*****************************************************/
#include <oxf/omthread.h>
#include "Queue.h"
#include "Overflow.h"
#include "Underflow.h"
//## package Default
// - - - - - - - - - - - - - - - - - - - - - - - - - -
// Queue.cpp
// - - - - - - - - - - - - - - - - - - - - - - - - - -
//## class Queue

Queue::Queue(OMThread*  p_thread) {
    setThread(p_thread, FALSE);
    {
        for(int pos=0;pos<100;pos++)element[pos]=NULL;
    }
    itsOverflow = NULL;
    itsUnderflow = NULL;
    //#[ operation Queue()
    size=100;
    head=tail=0;

    //#]
}
Queue::~Queue () {
    cleanUpRelations();
}
void Queue::clear() {
    //#[ operation clear()
    head=tail=0;
    //#]
}
OMString Queue::get(int  index) {
    //#[ operation get(int)

    return *element[index];
    //#]
}
void Queue::insert(OMString*  s) {
    //#[ operation insert(OMString*)
        if (isFull())
```

```
            throw Overflow();
         else {
           element[head] = s;
           head = (head+1) % size;
           };
     //#]
}
OMBoolean Queue::isEmpty() {
     //#[ operation isEmpty()
      if ( head == tail) return TRUE;
       else return FALSE;

     //#]
}
OMBoolean Queue::isFull() {
     //#[ operation isFull()
        return ( (head+1) % size == tail);

     //#]
}
int Queue::nElements() {
     //#[ operation nElements()
        if (head >= tail) return head-tail;
        else return size-(tail-head)+1;

     //#]
}
OMString* Queue::remove() {
     //#[ operation remove()
      OMString* s;
       if (isEmpty())
         throw Underflow();

       else {
         // cout << "element[" << tail << "]=";
         s = element[tail];
         // cout << *s << "??" << s->GetLength()
         // << endl;
         tail = (tail+1) % size;
         return s;
       }

     //#]
}
int Queue::getHead() const {
     return head;
```

```cpp
}
void Queue::setHead(int  p_head) {
    head = p_head;
}
int Queue::getSize() const {
    return size;
}
void Queue::setSize(int  p_size) {
    size = p_size;
}
int Queue::getTail() const {
    return tail;
}
void Queue::setTail(int  p_tail) {
    tail = p_tail;
}
int Queue::getElement() const {
    int iter=0;
    return iter;
}
Overflow* Queue::getItsOverflow() const {
    return itsOverflow;
}
void Queue::setItsOverflow(Overflow*  p_Overflow) {
    itsOverflow = p_Overflow;
}
Underflow* Queue::getItsUnderflow() const {
    return itsUnderflow;
}
void Queue::setItsUnderflow(Underflow*  p_Underflow) {
    itsUnderflow = p_Underflow;
}
void Queue::cleanUpRelations() {
    if(itsOverflow != NULL)
        {
            itsOverflow = NULL;
        }
    if(itsUnderflow != NULL)
        {
            itsUnderflow = NULL;
        }
}
OMBoolean Queue::startBehavior() {
    OMBoolean done = FALSE;
    done = OMReactive::startBehavior();
    return done;
```

```
}

/*********************************************************
      File Path    : DefaultComponent\TestCaching\
                     Queue.cpp
*********************************************************/
```

Code Listing 6-2: *Queue.cpp*

The Queue class is subclassed by the CachedQueue class, which inherits these features. The CachedQueue class adds two some new methods—flushBlock(), loadBlock(), and removeLocal()—and some new attributes as well. The child class extends the functionality of the parent by providing new behaviors.

Note that the CachedQueue subclass internally contains two normal queues—one for the input cache and one for the output cache. The input cache is strongly aggregated by the CachedQueue already because it *is* a kind of Queue, and the Queue class has a strong aggregation to an array of OMStrings. The other is done by aggregating a separate Queue subclass with the role name outCache for storing things as they come *off* the disk. Thus, data is inserted by a client into the input cache (directly aggregated by CachedQueue), or data may be written out to disk when that cache gets full, or the oldest data may reside in the indirectly aggregated output cache via the composition relation to the Queue class (role name outCache).

Specializing the CachedQueue as a subclass of Queue redefines some of the class's (virtual) behaviors, particularly, insert() and remove(). The code for the insert() and remove() operations of the Queue class is relatively simple, but more complex than Queue::insert() and Queue:: remove, as shown in Code Listings 6-3 and 6-4.

In the simple Queue class, the insert() operation checks to see whether there is room and, if so, sticks it in, doing the necessary math on the head pointer. In the CachedQueue, if there isn't room, then the input cache must be flushed out to disk, the input cache cleared, and the data inserted.

Similarly, the Queue::remove() operation is very simple—if there is any data, return it, otherwise throw an exception. The CachedQueue:: remove() operation is more complex: If the data is in the output cache, then get it from there; if the output cache is empty and there is data on disk, then load the next block from the disk and then get it from there. If there is no data in the output cache or on disk but there is data in the input cache, then get it from there. Lastly, if there is no data anywhere, throw an underflow exception.

```
/***************************************************
        Rhapsody    : 5.0
        Login       : Bruce
        Component   : DefaultComponent
        Configuration    : TestCaching
        Model Element    : CachedQueue
//!     Generated Date   : Wed, 18, Jun 2003
        File Path   : DefaultComponent\TestCaching\
                      CachedQueue.h
 ***************************************************/

#ifndef CachedQueue_H
#define CachedQueue_H

//#[ ignore
#define _OMFLAT_IMPLEMENTATION 1
//#]
#include <oxf/oxf.h>
#include "fstream.h"
#include "stdio.h"
#include "Default.h"
#include <oxf/omprotected.h>
#include "Queue.h"
//## package Default
// - - - - - - - - - - - - - - - - - - - - - - - - -
// CachedQueue.h
// - - - - - - - - - - - - - - - - - - - - - - - - -
class Overflow;
class Underflow;

//## class CachedQueue
class CachedQueue : public Queue {
    OMDECLARE_GUARDED


////    Constructors and destructors    ////
public :

    //## operation CachedQueue()
    CachedQueue(OMThread*  p_thread =
      OMDefaultThread);
```

```
    //## auto_generated
    ~CachedQueue();

////    Operations    ////
public :

    //## operation insert(OMString*)
    void insert(OMString*  s);

    //## operation remove()
    OMString* remove();

    //## operation removeLocal()
    OMString* removeLocal();
protected :

    // write out the input cache to disk. Writing will
    // append at the end of the file
    //## operation flushBlock()
    void flushBlock();

    // loadBlock reads the next block off disk -
    // loading occurs at the FRONT of the file.
    //## operation loadBlock()
    void loadBlock();

////    Additional operations    ////
public :

    //## auto_generated
    OMString getFilename() const;

    //## auto_generated
    void setFilename(OMString  p_filename);

    //## auto_generated
    int getNLinesOnDisk() const;

    //## auto_generated
    void setNLinesOnDisk(int  p_nLinesOnDisk);

    //## auto_generated
    long getReadPos() const;

    //## auto_generated
    void setReadPos(long  p_readPos);
```

```
        //## auto_generated
        Queue* getOutCache() const;

        //## auto_generated
        Queue* newOutCache();

        //## auto_generated
        void deleteOutCache();

////    Framework operations    ////
public :

        //## auto_generated
        virtual OMBoolean startBehavior();
protected :

        //## auto_generated
        void initRelations();

        //## auto_generated
        void cleanUpRelations();

////    Attributes    ////
protected :

    OMString filename;          //## attribute filename

    int nLinesOnDisk;           //## attribute
                                     nLinesOnDisk

    long readPos;          //## attribute readPos

////    Relations and components    ////
protected :

    Queue* outCache;            //## link outCache


};

#endif
/***********************************************
        File Path   : DefaultComponent\TestCaching\
                      CachedQueue.h
 ***********************************************/
```

Code Listing 6-3: *CachedQueue.h*

```
/********************************************************
      Rhapsody     : 5.0
      Login        : Bruce
      Component    : DefaultComponent
      Configuration    : TestCaching
      Model Element    : CachedQueue
//!   Generated Date    : Wed, 18, Jun 2003
      File Path    : DefaultComponent\TestCaching\
                       CachedQueue.cpp
********************************************************/
#include <oxf/omthread.h>
#include "CachedQueue.h"
#include "Overflow.h"
#include "Underflow.h"
//## package Default
//- - - - - - - - - - - - - - - - - - - - - - - - - - -
// CachedQueue.cpp
//- - - - - - - - - - - - - - - - - - - - - - - - - - -
//## class CachedQueue

CachedQueue::CachedQueue(OMThread*  p_thread) {
    setThread(p_thread, FALSE);
    initRelations();
    //#[ operation CachedQueue()
    // constructor must clear any debris in the
    // cache file.
    filename = "C:\\cachefile.txt";
    nLinesOnDisk = 0;
    readPos = 0; // start of file

    // ios::trunc clears out the file when the
    // CachedQueue is constructed
    ofstream cacheFile(filename, ios::trunc);

    //#]
}
CachedQueue::~CachedQueue() {
    cleanUpRelations();
}
void CachedQueue::flushBlock() {
    GUARD_OPERATION
    //#[ operation flushBlock()
    // open file for writing, appending at the end
    // write out the strings in the buffer
```

```cpp
        // then clear the local buffer
        OMString* s;
        ofstream cacheFile (filename, ios::in|ios::app);

        cout << " --> OPENED " << filename << " for
          Writing" << endl;

        while (!isEmpty()) {
          s = removeLocal();
          // get the data from the input side
          cacheFile << *s << endl;
          // write it to disk
          // cout << "W<- " << *s << endl;
          // show it ++nLinesOnDisk;
          };
        cacheFile.close();
        cout << "Write file closed" << endl;

        clear();

        //#]
}
void CachedQueue::insert(OMString*  s) {
        GUARD_OPERATION
        //#[ operation insert(OMString*)
        // check if there is room in the local store.
        // if not, then write the buffer to disk
(appending)
        // clear it, then insert the new string
        // using the superclass's insert();
        if (isFull())
          flushBlock();
        Queue::insert(s);


        //#]
}
void CachedQueue::loadBlock() {
        GUARD_OPERATION
        //#[ operation loadBlock()
        // preconditions, there is at least one block
        // in the cacheFile
        // (checked by examining nBlocksOnDisk
        // prior to calling this
```

```
#define MAXLENGTH 100
char buf[MAXLENGTH]; // buffer for input
OMString* s;
int j=1;

ifstream cacheFile(filename);
cout << " --> OPENED " << filename << " for
reading" << endl;
cacheFile.seekg(readPos);

while (!cacheFile.eof() && !outCache->isFull() &&
nLinesOnDisk>0) {
    cacheFile.getline(buf, MAXLENGTH);
    s = new OMString((char*) buf);
    outCache->insert(s);
    // cout << "Loading string < -" << *s << endl;
    --nLinesOnDisk;
    }; // end while
readPos = cacheFile.tellg();

cacheFile.close();
cout << "Read file closed" << endl;

/*
// check on the outcache
int n = outCache->nElements();
int t = outCache->getTail();
// cout << "LoadBlock done. OutCache now has "
// << n << " elements" << endl;
for (j=0; j < n; j++) {
  cout << "[" << t << "]" << outCache->get(t)
    << endl;
  t = (t+1) % outCache->getSize();
};
cout << "done showing the elements" << endl;
*/

//#]
}
OMString* CachedQueue::remove() {
    GUARD_OPERATION
    //#[ operation remove()
    // if there is stuff in the output cache, return
        that
```

```
    // else if there's stuff on disk, pull it off and
        return the first
    // else if there's stuff in the input buffer,
        then return that
    // else through an exception OMString* s;
    if (outCache->nElements()>0) {
        //cout << "CachedQueue.remove path 1 "
            << endl;
      s = outCache->remove();
      }
    else if (nLinesOnDisk>0) {
        //cout << "CachedQueue.remove path 2 "
            << endl;
      loadBlock();
      s = outCache->remove();
      }
    else if (nElements()>0) {
        //cout << "CachedQueue.remove path 3 " << endl;
      s = removeLocal();
      }
    else {
      //cout << "CachedQueue.remove path 4 " << endl;
      throw Underflow();
      }

    // cout << "CachedQueue::remove got string: "
        << *s << endl;

    return s;
    //#]
}
OMString* CachedQueue::removeLocal() {
    GUARD_OPERATION
    //#[ operation removeLocal()
    return Queue::remove();
    //#]
}
OMString CachedQueue::getFilename() const {
    return filename;
}
void CachedQueue::setFilename(OMString  p_filename) {
    filename = p_filename;
}
int CachedQueue::getNLinesOnDisk() const {
    return nLinesOnDisk;
}
```

```
void CachedQueue::setNLinesOnDisk(int  p_nLinesOnDisk)
{
    nLinesOnDisk = p_nLinesOnDisk;
}
long CachedQueue::getReadPos() const {
    return readPos;
}
void CachedQueue::setReadPos(long  p_readPos) {
    readPos = p_readPos;
}
Queue* CachedQueue::getOutCache() const {
    return outCache;
}
Queue* CachedQueue::newOutCache() {
    outCache = new Queue(getThread());
    return outCache;
}
void CachedQueue::deleteOutCache() {
    delete outCache;
}
void CachedQueue::initRelations() {
    outCache = newOutCache();
}
void CachedQueue::cleanUpRelations() {
    {
        deleteOutCache();
        outCache = NULL;
    }
}
OMBoolean CachedQueue::startBehavior() {
    OMBoolean done = FALSE;
    done = Queue::startBehavior();
    outCache->startBehavior();
    return done;
}

/*******************************************************
     File Path   : DefaultComponent\TestCaching\
                   CachedQueue.cpp
********************************************************/
```

Code Listing 6-4: *CachedQueue.cpp*

The last strategy for constructing generalization hierarchies works from the leaves of the inheritance tree. After structuring the hierarchy, siblings subclassed from the same parent are examined for attributes and behaviors in common. If all siblings have the same property, it belongs to the parent rather than being replicated in each sibling. If the characteristic is common to some, but not all, of the siblings, then it may indicate a class is needed between the parent and the similar siblings.

Figure 6-17 shows an inheritance tree for bus messages. Each child class inherits the attributes Priority, Source Address, and Destination Address. We see, however, that each message has a Contents attribute. Event Report and Sequenced Event Report messages must identify the event in their Contents field. ACKs and NAKs must identify the message to which they are responding in their Contents field. Since all siblings have the Contents attribute, it can be moved up into the parent class, Bus Message.

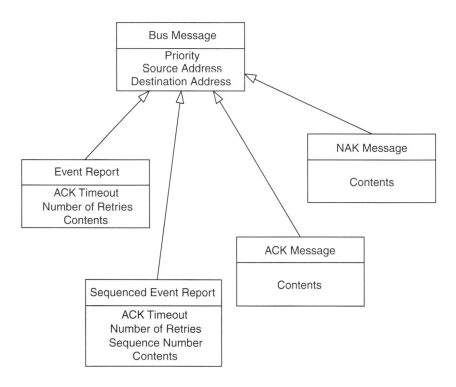

Figure 6-17: *Positioning Attributes in the Generalization Hierarchy*

Event Report and Sequenced Event Report messages share ACK Timeout and Number of Retries attributes. These do not appear in the ACK and NAK messages. Therefore, these may be abstracted into a class between Event Report and Bus Message and Sequenced Event Report and Bus Message. This is called Reliable Message because protocol mechanisms exist to support retransmission if no response to them is received. Figure 6-18 shows the resulting reorganization.

Of course, the astute analyst may mix all three strategies. It is possible to extend, specialize, and bubble up all at the same time.

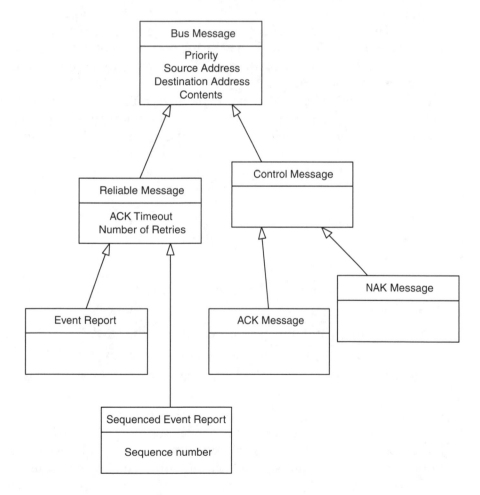

Figure 6-18: *Repositioned Attributes*

6.8 Looking Ahead

This chapter discussed the first half of analysis—the identification of objects, classes, and relationships. Many strategies can be used to identify objects and classes—underlining the nouns, identifying the physical devices, looking for persistent data, and so on. These objects have attributes and behaviors that allow them to fulfill their responsibilities. Classes are abstractions of objects so that all objects instantiated from a particular class are structurally identical.

To support collaboration of objects, classes have relationships to each other. These may be associations among class instances, such as association or aggregation, or they may be relationships between classes, such as generalization. Objects use these associations to communicate by sending messages to each other.

The other half of analysis is concerned with defining the behavior of the classes. As we shall see in Chapter 7, class behaviors may be classified in three different ways—simple, state, and continuous. The dynamic properties of these classes allows them to use their structure to meet the system responsibilities in real time.

6.9 Exercises

1. What are the three primary activities in the ROPES nanocycle?
2. Summarize, in one sentence, the intent of the nanocycle.
3. What is a domain and how is it represented in the UML?
4. Identify a possible set of domains for a microwave oven.
5. Identify the five object-identification strategies you are most likely to use.
6. Use these five strategies to identify the objects in a Cook Food use case for a microwave oven. Draw at least one object diagram for these objects with information flows showing, at a high level, the information sources and sinks. A simple problem statement might look like this:

The NukeOMatic microwave oven allows the user to cook food by setting a single time-to-completion with a power amplitude (settings from 1 to 10, equally dividing power output from 0 to 700 watts). In addition, the microwave can be programmed to remember "recipes," which consist of sequences of (power value, time value) pairs, with programmable pauses (including optional stops for user to do something and hit the Continue button to move on to the next phase. During cooking, an internal plate rotates at the rate of 3 rpm. At the end of the cooking cycle (or the recipe sequence) an alarm may optionally sound.

7. Are there any transactional or persistent objects identified?

8. Construct some scenarios of the Cook Food use case showing how your collaboration of objects works.

9. What are your favorite association identification strategies? Identify the classes of the objects on the diagrams and redraw your class diagram showing associations, attributes, and operations.

10. What is an attribute?

11. How does one identify attributes?

12. What is meant by *diagram mission*? Give some examples for class diagrams.

13. When is it appropriate to use associative classes? Give an example of an associative class not mentioned in this chapter.

14. What are the two important aspects of generalization?

15. How does one decide where in a generalization taxonomy to place attributes and operations?

16. Explain the Open-Closed Principle (OCP).

17. Draw a generalization taxonomy for the following shapes: shape, square, and rectangle. If we follow the rule that a subclass can only expand constraints, which class is at the top of the generalization taxonomy?

18. What are the two things that can be done to make a subclass different from its base class?

6.10 References

[1] Cook, Rick. *The Wizardry Compiled.* Riverdale, NY: Baen Books, 1990.

[2] Booch, Grady. *Object-Oriented Analysis and Design with Applications.* 2nd ed. Redwood City, CA: Benjamin/Cummings, 1994.

[3] Liskov, Barbara. "Data Abstraction and Hierarchy." *SIGPLAN Notices 23,* no. 5 (May, 1988).

[4] Martin, Robert. "The Open-Closed Principle." *C++ Report 8,* no. 1 (1996).

[5] Douglass, Bruce Powel. *Doing Hard Time: Developing Real-Time Systems with UML, Objects, Frameworks, and Patterns.* Reading, MA: Addison-Wesley, 1998.

[6] Neumann, Peter G. *Computer Related Risks.* Reading, MA: Addison-Wesley, 1995.

Chapter 7

Analysis: Defining Object Behavior

Chapter 6 showed how to define the system structure by identifying the fundamental objects and classes and their relationships. In this chapter, we define and refine operations and behaviors. There are a number of means for specifying overall object behavior, the most important of these being modeling the object as a finite state machine. Scenario modeling helps you test your behavioral models to ensure that the objects can collaborate to achieve the system responsibilities. The state and scenario models lead to the definitions of class operations required to process the incoming messages and events.

Notation and Concepts Discussed

Simple Behavior	Or-state	Action
Continuous Behavior	And-state	Pseudostate
State Behavior	Event	Statechart
State	Transition	Operation

7.1 Object Behavior

Chapter 6 presented the analysis and decomposition of systems into their object structure and relationships. The other pillar of object-oriented analysis is the specification of *dynamic behavior*. Behavior binds the structure of objects to their attributes and relationships so that objects can meet their responsibilities. Ultimately, an object's operations implement its behavior. There are means for constraining and controlling these primitive operations into permissible sequences. The most important of these is the finite state machine. The behavioral notations and semantics of the UML were introduced in Chapter 3; this chapter focuses on how to effectively apply these notations and semantics to solve our real-world problems.

7.1.1 Simple Behavior

We define three types of behavior: *simple, state,* and *continuous*. The object with simple behavior performs services on request and keeps no memory of previous services. A simple object always responds to a given input in exactly the same way regardless of its history. Some examples of simple behaviors are

- Simple mathematical functions, such as cosine or square root
- A search operation of a static data structure that always starts from the same point, such as the search of a static binary tree
- Sort operations
- A knob that returns the number of clicks for a given user action

    For example,

$$\cos\frac{\pi}{2} = 0$$

returns the same value regardless of what value can call the COS() function with previously. In other cases, the distinction is not as clear. Is the search of a binary tree simple or state-driven? If the behavior changes due to previous input, then it cannot by definition be simple. If the binary tree provides methods like next() and previous(), then it must maintain an internal state between calls. If the tree only provides calls such as find(), then at least to its clients it exhibits stateless behavior.

Activity diagrams provide token-flow semantics. That is, an activity is decomposed into subactivities, until at the bottom we find actions. Actions execute when they receive a control token from each of their predecessor activities. In the case of simple sequential actions within an activity, this is just a statement that an activity (or action) begins to execute when the activity (or action) that comes before it completes. In the case of concurrency, an activity (or action) can have multiple predecessors, and so must receive a control token from *every* one of its predecessors before it is allowed to execute.

Figure 7-1 shows an activity diagram for computing net worth. The forks and joins show activities that may be allowed to execute in parallel. Token flow semantics are simple to explain in the figure:

- For a sequential flow (simple arrow between lines) a control token is passed when the previous activity completes; the subsequent activity begins once it receives the control token.

- For a fork, a control token is passed to *every* subsequent activity, meaning that they are all free to execute, and the order of execution of its concurrent peer activities is not defined.

- For a join, a control token must be passed by *every* predecessor activity before the subsequent activity is allowed to run. Thus, all of the following activities must complete before the "print Assets" activity is allowed to run:

  - ▼ Assets += Get Property Assets

  - ▼ Assets += Get Bank Assets

  - ▼ Assets += Get Investment Assets

- For branches (the diamond), only a *single* control token is passed. The active branch is selected on the basis of guard conditions; if a guard is TRUE then that branch may be passed the control token when the predecessor activity completes. If multiple guards evaluate to TRUE, then any of the true branches may be selected, but only one will receive the control token (however, it is impossible to say which one will be selected).

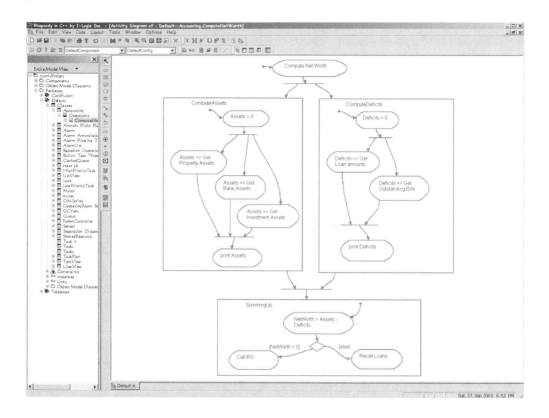

Figure 7-1: *Token-Flow Semantics*

7.1.2 State Behavior

The second type of object behavior is called *state, state-driven,* or *reactive.* Our definition of a state is as follows:

> *A state is an ontological condition that persists for a significant period of time that is distinguishable from other such conditions and is disjoint from them. A distinguishable state means that it differs from other states in the events it accepts, the transitions it takes as a result of accepting those events, or the actions it performs. A transition is a response to an event that causes a change in state.*

Modeling an object as a finite state machine (FSM) attempts to reduce the behavioral complexity by making some simplifying assumption. Specifically, it assumes the following:

- The system being modeled can assume only a finite number of existence conditions, called *states*.

- The system behavior within a given state is essentially identical and is defined by

  ▾ The messages and events accepted

  ▾ The actions associated entering or leaving the state

  ▾ The activities performed while in the state

  ▾ The reachability graph of subsequent states

  ▾ The complete set of transition-target state pairs

- The system resides in states for significant periods of time.

- The system may change these conditions only in a finite number of well-defined ways, called *transitions*.

- Transitions run to completion, including the action execution, whether they are associated directly with the transition itself, or entry or exit actions for the state entered or exited.

The set of all possible behaviors of an object is bounded by the set of operations defined on the object. An FSM adds constraints regarding when and under what conditions those operations will execute.

7.1.3 Continuous Behavior

The third kind of object behavior is called *continuous*. Many objects show continuous behavior, including digital filters and PID[1] control loops. All that is required is that the current output depend on the previous history in a smooth way. An object with continuous behavior is one with an infinite, or at least unbounded, set of existence conditions. PID control systems, fuzzy sets, and neural networks all display continuous behavior.

---

[1] Proportional integral-differential, a common type of control theoretic system using feedback, integration, and differentiation to smoothly control continuous systems.

The UML is very expressly a discrete modeling language, and provides no direct means for modeling continuous system behavior.[2] However, many kinds of continuous behavior can be defined using token flow semantics. This is normally done by expressing the algorithm as difference equations (derived from the differential equations). Thus, activity diagrams can be used to express behavior that is continuous in value but discrete in execution. A PID control loop, for example, implemented with a difference equation, is executed periodically, and the object uses attributes to remember the previous value(s) necessary for the computations. However, activity diagrams cannot, without extension, model behavior that is continuous in *time*, such as the continuously executing mixing of gases, or combustion of fuel. It is often sufficient to use a difference equation approach for the behavioral modeling, but not always.

It is even sometimes appropriate to mix state and continuous behavior. For example, different sets of trajectory differential equations may be used, depending on whether a spacecraft is undergoing launch, achieving orbit, in orbit, or cruising. The sets of equations used in this case depend on the state (in this case, phase of flight) of the trajectory object. This is accomplished by modeling the overall behavior of the object as a state machine; the set of difference or differential equations is modeled as a "do activity" within the states. As the object enters a new state, a different set of differential equations governs the execution of the activity within the state.

Since the UML relies so heavily on finite state machines to represent discrete behavior, let's now explore what than means in more detail.

7.2 Defining Object State Behavior

In state machines designed by traditional structured methods, the portion of the system exhibiting the state behavior is not clearly defined. Some set of functions and data collaborate in a way that lends itself to finite state modeling, but generally this set is only vaguely defined. In

---

[2] The UML for Systems Engineering specification effort, currently underway, is extending the UML activity model to include continuous behavior, such as that of a gas mixer that continuously mixes multiple gases to produce a mixed output gas. In this case, the notion of execution tokens, required by activity diagrams, doesn't make any sense. This effort should be available for vote in the OMG sometime in mid to late 2004.

object-oriented methods, the programmatic unit exhibiting state behavior is clear—only classifiers, such as classes and use cases, can define state models, and only objects execute state machines.[3]

Consider a simple, retriggerable, one-shot timer. Such a timer is generally in one of two possible states: idle and counting down. When the timeout event occurs, the timer issues an event to a client object, (implicitly) resets, and returns to the counting-down state. This model is shown in Figure 7-2.

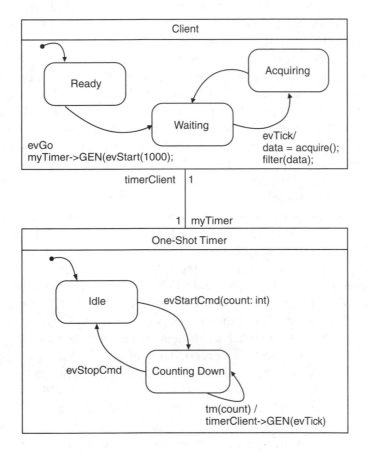

Figure 7-2: *Retriggerable One-Shot Timer FSM*

---

[3] We use the term *state model* to mean the definition of a state machine, which, when used, must defined within a class. The term *state machine* is an instance of a state model and therefore must belong to an object.

Remember that the UML does not define an action language, although it does define the set of things you can specify with actions—the *action semantics*. We will use C++ and the occasional macro (such as GEN() to generate an event) as the action language here, but any computer or formal language can be used.

The example state machine for the OneShotTimer class shown in Figure 7-2 consists of two states and three transitions. In the Idle state, the timer isn't counting down—it sits patiently waiting for the evStart Cmd. The evStartCmd event carries with it a single value, the length of time between timeouts. When the event occurs, the object transitions to the counting-down state. As soon this state is entered, an implicit timer is started because the state has an exiting timeout transition (shown using the common tm() event trigger[4]). When the timeout occurs, the tm() transition is taken, and the actions in its action list are executed. Actions are shown in an action list, which is separated from the transition label with a slash (/). The action in the tm() transition's action list is to send a signal to a client object. The actions in the action list are normally short, but in any case they will run to completion before the transition completes. The counting-down state is then re-entered. This restarts the timer associated with the timeout transition.

In the counting-down state, the object can respond to two events: a timeout and an evStopCmd. In the latter case, the object enters the Idle state. The timer corresponding to the tm() transition is (implicitly) stopped as soon as its source state (counting down) is exited.

Another example of object state behavior is demonstrated by the model shown in Figure 7-3. In this model, objects that either send or receive such messages have the class CommunicatingObjects; such objects know how to construct messages to be sent or how to extract information from messages received. They associate with a Communicator class that knows how to orchestrate their transmission or reception. Note that the Communicator class has two associations with the CommunicatingObject, as indicated by the *sender* role and the *receiver* role. When one object (in the sender role) sends a bus message to a remote object (playing the receiver role) using a reliable communication protocol, an object is temporarily created until it can be verified that the receiver has received the message properly. Such an object is

---

[4] Note that some other tools use after() rather than tm().

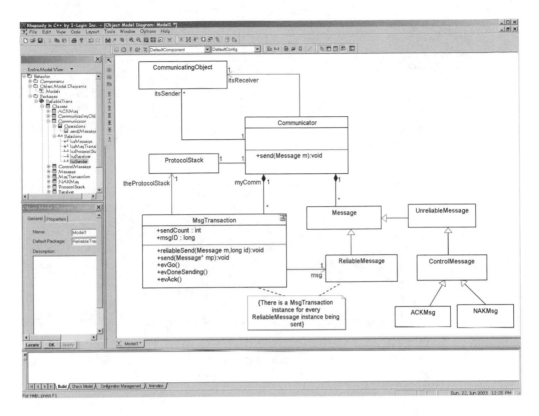

Figure 7-3: *Message Transaction Structure*

called a *transactional object* because it only exists for the duration of an interaction, or transaction, between other objects.

The transactional object in Figure 7-3 is called *MsgTransaction*. Its behavior is specified with the statechart in Figure 7-4. Instances of Msg Transaction begin life in the ReadyToSend state. When commanded (via the evGo event), they enter the sending state and invoke a method in the protocol stack called *send*. Because MsgTransaction objects mediate reliable message delivery, once done sending the message, they wait for an acknowledgement (an ACKMsg) for that specific message (as specified with a message identifier). If an acknowledgement message for the transmitted message is received, then we're done. If not, the MsgTransaction object, after waiting an appropriate length of time, retransmits the same message and resumes waiting. If after some

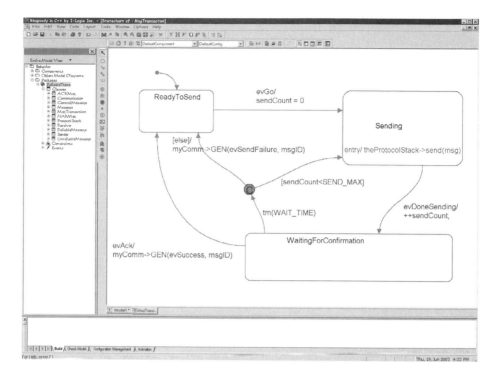

Figure 7-4: *Message Transaction Behavior*

number of attempts, the acknowledgement is not received, the Msg Transaction object gives up and sends a failure event to the Communicator, which will in turn inform the sender. Either way, the MsgTransaction object is eventually discarded and destroyed.

As a brief aside, the astute reader will notice that the Communicator knows how to send using both reliable and unreliable means. It is important, for example, that ACKMsgs and NAKMsgs are *not* sent reliably or the system will enter an infinite recursion.

Also notice the © symbol on the statechart. As discussed in Chapter 3, this is a notation for the conditional pseudostate, a type of junction pseudostate in which a single event triggers the transition and at most one exiting transition branch will be taken, on the basis of the evaluation of the guard conditions. Guards are side effect–free Boolean conditions placed in square brackets that are evaluated before any actions are executed.

7.2.1 Cardiac Pacemaker Example

A cardiac pacemaker is an excellent example of a predominantly reactive system in which many objects use finite state machines to specify their behavior. The following problem statement will be developed into a class model that will allow us to see how the various statechart features can be used in a real system.

Problem Statement: A Cardiac Pacemaker

The human heart is a marvelous four-chambered pump made up of two atrial chambers that contract slightly before the two larger ventricular chambers, and an electrical conduction system that, in the healthy heart, ensures the heart beats in an efficient, timely, and effective way. The atrial contraction preloads the larger and more powerful ventricular chamber by pumping extra blood into it, stretching its muscle fibers. The one-way a-v valves then close, and the ventricles contract strongly, sending unoxygenated blood in the right ventricle into the lungs to bind with oxygen and oxygenated blood from the lungs into the arterial system of the body. Myocardial cells contract autonomously because they have leaky membranes with ionic pumps that maintain a charge across the membrane. When the charge reaches a certain level, a set of ionic pores open up in the membrane causing a rapid depolarization of the muscle cell, causing it to contract. Different cells have different rates at which this contraction occurs. The fastest contracting cells are located in the sinoatrial (SA) node; because this area contracts first, and the depolarization spreads from cell to cell electrically, this area is said to be the "pacemaker" of the heart. The upper part of the heart, housing the atria, is separated electrically from the lower part, housing the ventricles. This separation (called the AV node) causes a slight delay in the contraction of the ventricles. This is hemodynamically important because it allows the ventricles to more completely fill before they contract and adds 20% or so to the volume of the blood pumped per beat. That's in the healthy heart. Sometimes the electrical control system fails

(continued)

continued from previous page

and this can lead to any number of problems, the most common of which is a heart beat that is too slow to allow normal activity, a condition known as bradycardia.

A cardiac pacemaker is an implanted device that assists cardiac function when underlying pathologies make the intrinsic heart rate too low or absent[5] by taking over the initiation of a cardiac contraction. Pacemakers operate in quite a number of behavioral modes, each indicated by a three-letter acronym. The first letter is either A, V, or D depending on whether the atrium or the ventricle or both (dual) is being paced (i.e., induced to contract via the delivery of a well-quantified electric shock). The second letter is also A, V, or D, depending on which heart chamber is being monitored for intrinsic heart beats. The last letter is I, T, or D, indicating inhibited, triggered, or dual pacing modes. In an inhibited mode, a sensed heartbeat will inhibit the delivery of a pace from the pacemaker. In triggered mode, a sensed heart event will immediately trigger a pace from the pacemaker. For example, VVI mode means that the ventricle is paced (the first *V*) if a ventricular sense (the second *V*) does not occur. A ventricular sense event is generated when the ventricle of the heart contracts. If a ventricular sense does occur, then the pace is inhibited (the *I*). Dual modes are more complex and will not be discussed here.

Most of the time, a pacing pacemaker waits for a sense event. When it decides to pace, the pacemaker first shuts off the sensing hardware to prevent electrical damage, and then delivers an electric current of a programmable voltage (called the *pulse amplitude*) for a programmable period of time (called the *pulse width*). Following a pace, the pacemaker is put into a refractory state for a set period of time, during which all cardiac activity is ignored. Following the refractory period the pacemaker resumes monitoring for the next cardiac event. The rate of pacing is determined by the

---

[5] Other kinds of pacemakers address other pathologies, such as the heart beating too fast (tachycardia) and as well as extra ventricular beats (preventricular contractions or PVCs) and uncoordinated muscular contractions (fibrillations).

continued from previous page

programmable pacing rate. The period of time the pacemaker will remain in the waiting state is based on the pacing rate and the pulse width. The refractory period is usually fixed. Our problem is to create a pacemaker that operates in VVI, AAI, VVT, AAT, and AVI pacing modes as programmed by the physician.

Pacemaker parameters are programmed via a telemetric interface to an external programmer. Telemetry is sent by pulsing an electromagnetic coil a certain number of times to indicate a 0 bit and a different number of times to indicate a 1 bit. To avoid inadvertent programming by electrical noise, a reed switch must be closed with a magnet before programming is enabled and must remain closed as long as communication is ongoing. Removal of the magnet disables communications. In this particular pacemaker, commands are of the form

```
[CD][Command ID] [Length][Data][CRC]
```

The command is an 8-bit value that specifies the command to be executed; the length is an 8-bit value that specifies the number of bytes in the data field, plus the size, plus 4 (to account for the command ID byte, the length byte, and the 16-bit CRC). Table 7-1 lists the messages for the pacemaker.

The commands constructed from the bits must be checked with the 16-bit CRC before they can be acted on. If the command validates properly, then an ACK message is returned. Communications occur between two devices: the pacemaker and a device used by the physician called a *programmer*. The communications protocol between the two devices requires the programmer to receive an ACK before sending the next command. If the pacemaker doesn't respond within 5 seconds or if a NAK is received, the programmer will resend the message. This occurs automatically. After five successive transmission failures, the programmer notifies the physician (this can occur if the programming wand is too far from the pacemaker resulting in a weak telemetry signal). Note that communications cannot affect pacing other than as the result of processing a command that affects pacing; that is, they must occur in parallel.

Table 7-1: *Pacemaker Messages*

Command ID	Value	Description
Get parameters	0	Request programmable settings in pacemaker.
Get serial number	1	Request manufacturers information from the pacemaker.
Set pacing mode	3	Sets the pacing mode to one of AAI=0, VVI=1, AAT=2, VVT=3, AVI=4. Data is 8 bits in length.
Set parameters	4	Sets the three pacing parameters, each of which is 8 bits long: pulse amplitude in mV from 0 (off) to 15 mV in integral units of mV. Pulse width is specified from 0ms to 30ms. Rate is set in beats per minute in the range of 30 .. 120, inclusive.
Exit low power Mode	32	Command the pacemaker to power the electronics for normal operation.
Enter low power Mode	33	Commands the pacemaker to disable all electronics except as necessary to perform communications.
Parameters	128	Data consists of four values plus 32-bit numbers: pacing mode (1 byte), pulse amplitude (1 byte), pulse width (1 byte), pacing rate (1 byte), and battery voltage (fixed point integer for range of 0.00 to 5.00 volts) (returned from the pacemaker).
Serial number	129	Data consists of four ASCII characters, "ACME," followed by three 32-bit numbers: the serial number, the hardware version number, and the software version number (returned from the pacemaker).
ACK	254	Acknowledgement of last message.
NAK	255	Last command failed validation.

A typical pacemaker-programmer interaction might be

Programmer:	Get Parameters
Pacemaker:	ACK
Pacemaker:	Parameters (AAI, 12mV, 15mS, 70ppm, 3.66V)

Programmer:	Set Pacing Mode (AVI)
Pacemaker:	ACK
Programmer:	Set Pacing mode (AVI)
Programmer:	Set Parameters (10mV, 20ms, 60 ppm)
Pacemaker:	ACK

Figure 7-5 shows the primary use cases for the CardioNada pacemaker. Three use cases are shown: set pacing parameters, retrieve current pacemaker settings, and pace the heart. Figure 7-6 shows the class model for the pacemaker. There are two packages in this system, each containing a single subsystem and the parts of those subsystems used to achieve the use cases. The Comm_Subsystem contains the classes necessary to send and receive, validate, and process those commands.

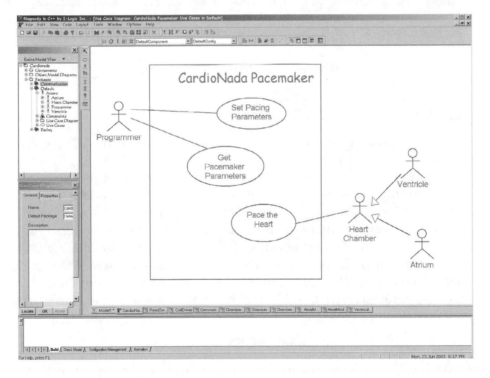

Figure 7-5: *Pacemaker Use Cases*

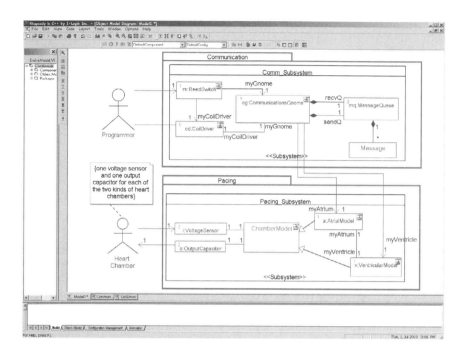

Figure 7-6: *Pacemaker Class Diagram*

7.2.1.1 How Communications Work

The first package contains the classes for communications. These are briefly described in Table 7-2.

Communications is achieved with the collaboration of the elements in the Communications_Subsystem. The *ReedSwitch* has simple On-Off state behavior. It propagates events to other classes in the communication subsystem to enable and disable communications—specifically the CoilDriver and CommunicationsGnome. This prevents inadvertent reprogramming of the pacemaker by ambient radiation, arc welders, and microwave ovens. The GEN() macro sends the named event (and any specified parameters) to the object with the named role. For example, the ReedSwitch knows the CommunicationsGnome as myGnome. Using

$$myGnome\text{->}GEN(RS\_Close)$$

sends the RS_Close event to the CommunicationsGnome. The Reed Switch has simple On-Off state behavior, as shown in Figure 7-7.

The CoilDriver class has more elaborate state behavior, as shown in Figure 7-8. At the highest level, the CoilDriver has two or-states: Disabled (the default) and Enabled. When the ReedSwitch closes, it propagates an RS_Open event to the CoilDriver and the CoilDriver enters the Enabled states.

Inside of the Enabled state, there are three nested or-states: Idle, Receiving, and Transmitting. Since these are or-states, communication proceeds in a half-duplex fashion.

Table 7-2: *Communication Package Classes*

Class	Description
Comm_Subsystem	This is a subsystem that manages communications and command processing.
ReedSwitch	Interfaces with the magnetic reed switch and sends events to the CoilDriver and Communications Gnome when the switch opens or closes. Communications is disabled unless the reed switch is closed.
CoilDriver	The CoilDriver pulses the magnetic coil 15 times to produce a 0 bit and 8 times to produce a 1 bit, with a programmed time interval between bits and a longer time interval between bytes and a still longer period between messages. Telemetry is half-duplex; that is, messages can be sent or received at any given time.
Communications gnome	The gnome processes receives income bytes, constructs messages from them, and validates them. If valid, the gnome sends out an ACKMsg (or a NAKMsg if not valid) as well as processes valid commands.
MessageQueue	There are two message queue objects in the Comm_Subsystem, one for holding bytes as them are received (until an EOM—End Of Message—event is received), and the other for holding messages ready to be transmitted.
Message	A set of bytes defined by the protocol.

When the CoilDriver is in the Idle state, an incoming pulse causes it to go into the receiving state. The CoilDriver hardware contains an internal one-shot timer that determines pulse widths and issues an interrupt to the CoilDriver when a pulse is detected that is within the proper time window that results in the evPulse event shown in the statechart.

The ReceivingBit state counts the pulses that occur within the bit window. As long as a pulse is received before the timeout occurs, the timer is restarted. The number of pulses is tracked in the *count* attribute of the CoilDriver class. When the tm(BIT_WAIT) occurs, the decode() operation determines that it is either a 0 (in the range of 13 to 17 pulses) or a 1 (in the range of 5 to 10 pulses). This decoded bit is then shifted into a value that will hold the transmitted byte. Once all 8 bits have been shifted in, the completed byte is sent over to the Communications Gnome and the CoilDriver enters the WaitingForBit state. In this state, either an evPulse can be received (indicating the start of the next bit) or a timeout (indicating the end of the message) occurs. If the end of the message is found, the end of message (EOM) event is sent to the CommunicationsGnome so that it can process the now completely received message.

The other possibility from the Idle state is that the Communications Gnome sends a byte to be transmitted. For each bit in the byte to be transmitted, the CoilDriver shifts out the next bit, determines the number of pulses needed to send the bit (held in the pulstCt attribute), and sends pulses the coil that many times. Once all the bits have been sent out, the CoilDriver sends a DoneSending event to the CoilDriver to get the next byte to transmit.

The Communications Gnome oversees the communication process for the pacemaker (see Figure 7-9). It is enabled and disabled by the RS_Close and RS_Open events propagated from the Reed Switch. When enabled, but in the absence of incoming or outgoing messages, the Communications Gnome spends its time in its Idle state. The message level is almost completely decoupled from the strict timing requirements of the CoilDriver. In the Receiving state, the Communications Gnome adds the incoming bytes into the message until the EOM event is received. Then the message is validated (to be valid, the command must have a valid command byte, be of the correct length, and must pass the CRC check). If it is validated, an ACKMsg is queued to send and the command is processed. If the command fails validation, a NAKMsg is sent instead.

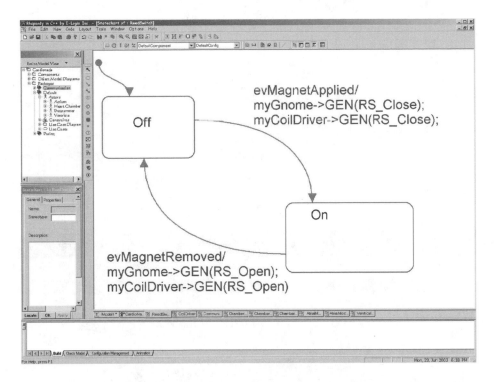

Figure 7-7: *ReedSwitch State Model*

In terms of setting pacing modes, the Communications Gnome sends commands to the instances of the AtrialModel and Ventricular-Model. When the Communications Gnome receives a command to put the pacemaker in AAI mode, for example, it sends a toIdle event to the VentricularModel instance and a toSelfInhibited event to the Atrial Model instance. The effects of the system pacing mode on the Atrial Model and VentricularModel objects are shown in Table 7-3.

For setting pulse width and pulse amplitude and heart rate, these are sent to both the AtrialModel and VentricularModel instances.

7.2.1.2 How Pacing Works

The Pacing package contains classes, shown in Table 7-4, used in monitoring and pacing the heart.

The Chamber Model specifies most of the pacing behavior (see Figure 7-10). Pacing the ventricle works largely in the same fashion as

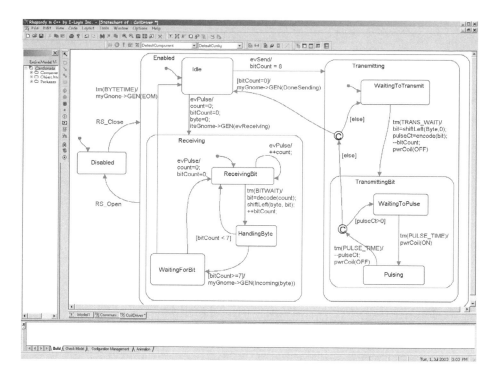

Figure 7-8: *CoilDriver State Model*

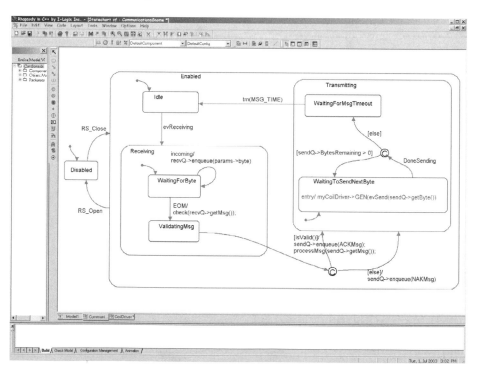

Figure 7-9: *Communications Gnome State Model*

Table 7-3: *Pacing Modes and States*

Pacing Mode	AtrialModel State	VentricularModel State
Off	Idle	Idle
AAI	SelfInhibited	Idle
VVI	Idle	SelfInhibited
AAT	SelfTriggered	Idle
VVT	Idle	SelfTriggered
AVI	DualMode	DualMode

Table 7-4: *Pacing Subsystem Classes*

Class	Description
Pacing_Subsystem	This subsystem manages the monitoring and pacing of the heart through delegation to its internal pieces.
Chamber Model	This abstract base class defines the basic functionality for monitoring and pacing a cardiac chamber, including associations to a voltage sensor and an output capacitor.
Atrial Model	A concrete subclass of the Chamber Model class that uses the basic behavior defined in the Chamber Model class and that specializes the behavior of AVI (dual mode) pacing. This class monitors and/or paces the atrium of the heart via its associations to its own voltage sensor and output capacitor.
Ventricular Model	A concrete subclass of the Chamber Model class that uses the basic behavior defined in the Chamber Model class and that specializes the behavior of AVI (dual mode) pacing. This class monitors and/or paces the ventricle of the heart via its associations to its own voltage sensor and output capacitor.
Voltage Sensor	This class drives the hardware voltage sensor with operations that enable it (turn it on) and disable it (turn it off). When a contraction of the associated heart chamber is detected, it issues a Sense event to its associated Atrial_Model or Ventricular_Model instance.
Output Capacitor	This class controls the release of current stored in the output capacitor. The voltage is controlled by setting the voltage level in the enable() operation. The pulse width is the length of time the voltage is delivered.

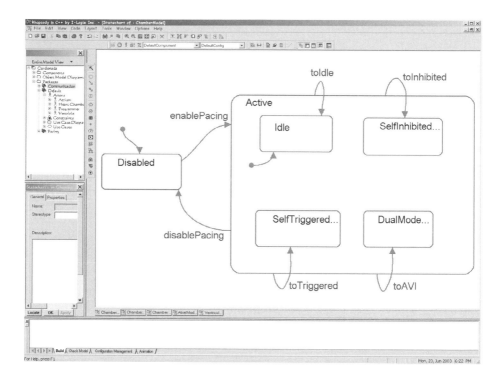

Figure 7-10: *Chamber Model State Model*

pacing the atrium. The On state contains four nested or-states corresponding to idle, inhibited, triggered, and dual modes. For all but the last, there is no need for specialization in the subclasses. In the last (dual mode) however, the AtrialModel and VentricularModel play different roles in the interaction and specialization is a natural way to capture those differences.

The statechart in Figure 7-10 references three submachines. A submachine, you will remember, is a specification for the internals of a state when it is shown in a separate diagram. Figure 7-11 shows the internal structure of the SelfInhibited state and Figure 7-12 shows the internal structure for the SelfTriggered state. Note that the actions in these submachines invoke operations of the associated voltage sensor and output capacitor. The Dual state is decomposed as well, but it was left empty and so isn't shown here.

For the most part, the AtrialModel and VentricularModel state behavior is identical to that specified by the Chamber Model superclass.

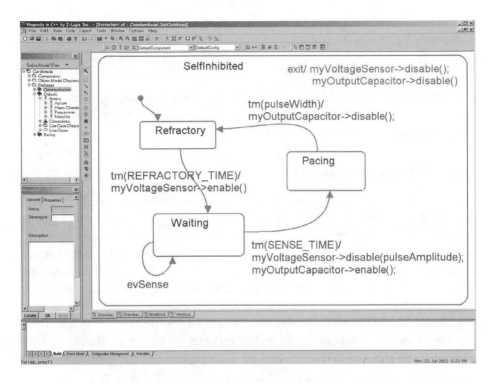

Figure 7-11: *Chamber Model SelfInhibited Statechart*

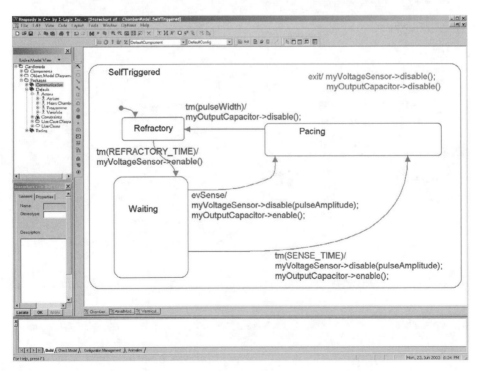

Figure 7-12: *Chamber Model SelfTriggered Statechart*

However, in AVI mode, the atrial model does the pacing and signals the VentricularModel when it should and should not pace. Those statecharts are shown in Figure 7-13 and Figure 7-14.

7.2.2 Calculator Example

Another highly reactive system, although admittedly one not normally considered either embedded or real-time, is a calculator. A calculator is an almost ideal example: It is conceptually simple yet complex enough to be difficult to implement in handwritten source code; it is highly reactive with rich state behavior; it has a well-understood behavioral model; and test examples to validate the model's correctness are easy to come up with.

Figure 7-15 shows the calculator's use cases. Because it is a simple device, there is only a single primary use case—to evaluate an expression. In this case, that means to take an input string of characters

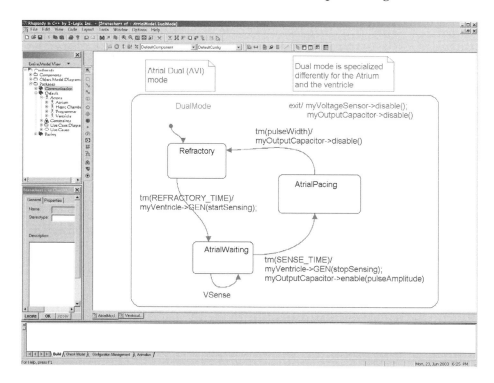

Figure 7-13: *AtrialModel Dual Mode Statechart*

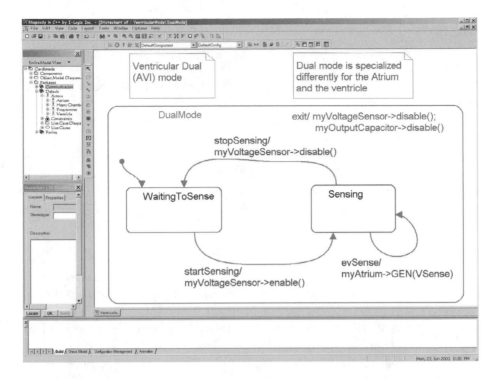

Figure 7-14: *VentricularModel Dual Mode Statechart*

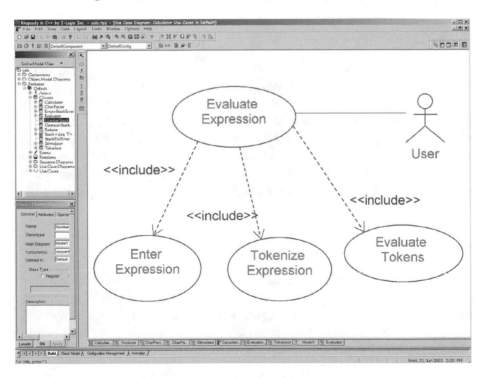

Figure 7-15: *Calculator Use Cases*

representing a mathematical expression using real numbers and the arithmetic operators +, –, *, /, (and), and to return a string representing the arithmetic result. The calculator should observe the normal operator precedence rules:

- Parentheses have the strongest binding.
- The next strongest binding is the unary + or – operator.
- The next strongest binding is for the multiplicative operators * and /.
- The weakest binding is for the binary additive operators + and –.

For example, the expression 6 + –3/4 should be evaluated as –3 divided by 4; the result of that subexpression should then be added to 6.

While it is possible to construct a monolithic (and complex) object to read in the string and spit out the answer, the solution provided in the class diagram is shown in Figure 7-16. The system is shown as a composite class named Calculator. It contains a number of parts, each of which fulfills some responsibilities to achieve the use case. Table 7-5 lists the general responsibilities of the various classes.

7.2.2.1 Calculator Class

The Calculator class is the composite class that represents the entire system. As a composite, it has the responsibility to construct and destroy the part instances. This makes it a convenient way to create the entire system—we simply create a single Calculator instance and it in turn creates all of the parts and links them together as specified. Notice that all of the parts have single instances—if the multiplicity was specified as *, the Calculator class wouldn't have enough information to do its job in its constructor, because the number of part instances and links wouldn't have been specified.

7.2.2.2 CharParser Class

The CharParser class takes a string, decomposes it into an ordered set of characters, identifies the types of each of these characters, and for each character, generates an event for the Tokenizer of the appropriate character type and passes the character. The types of characters are white space, digits (0 through 9), dot (.), or operators. These are computed via

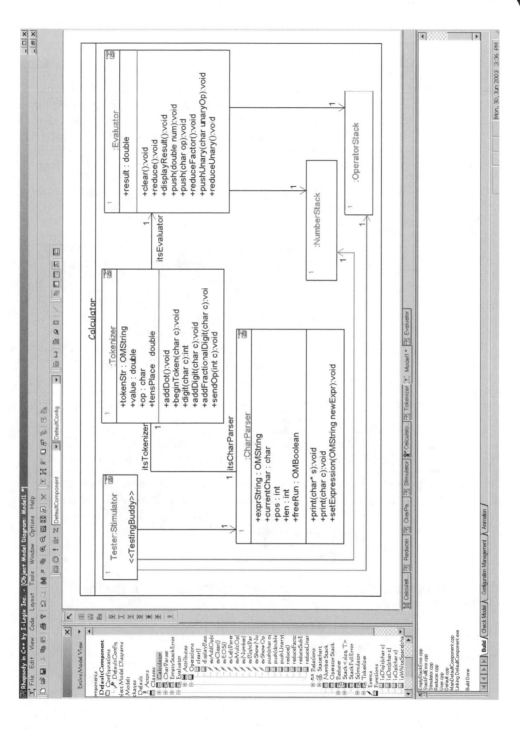

Figure 7-16: *Calculator Classes*

Table 7-5: *Calculator Class Responsibilities*

Class	Responsibility
Calculator	A System class, Calculator is composed of all of the parts of the internal system. As a composite, it is responsible for the creation and destruction of the parts it owns, as well as for wiring them together by instantiating the links between the parts with fixed multiplicities (in this case, all of them).
CharParser	Takes the input string and reads out a character at a time, identifies the type of the character (number, operator, or white space), then sends an appropriate event (along with the character) to the Tokenizer.
Tokenizer	Takes the input characters and constructs tokens—either operators or numbers—to be evaluated. Once a token is parsed, the token is sent to the Evaluator for evaluation.
Evaluator	The Evaluator takes in numeric and operator tokens and processes them using the operator precedence rules. Numbers are pushed onto the number stack, and operators are pushed onto the operator stack. The numbers and operators are reduced according with the rules of arithmetic and operator precedence.
NumberStack	An instantiation of a parameterized Stack class, this stack holds objects of type double.
OperatorStack	An instantiation of a parameterized Stack class, this stack holds objects of type char, representing the operators.
Stimulator	An object whose only purpose is to provide test vectors and force the calculator through its paces. The stereotype «TestingBuddy» indicates that it is part of the testing and debugging structures.

the set of utility functions define in the package, as shown in Code Listing 7-1.

```
//## operation isDigit(char)
OMBoolean isDigit(char  c) {
    //#[ operation isDigit(char)
    return (c>='0' && c<='9');
    //#]
```

```
}
//## operation isDot(char)
OMBoolean isDot(char   c) {
    //#[ operation isDot(char)
    return c == '.';
    //#]
}
//## operation isOp(char)
OMBoolean isOp(char   c) {
    //#[ operation isOp(char)
    return (c=='-' || c=='+' ||
        c=='*' || c=='/' || c == '^' ||
        c == '(' || c == ')');
    //#]
}
//## operation isWhiteSpace(char)
OMBoolean isWhiteSpace(char   c) {
    //#[ operation isWhiteSpace(char)
    return (c==' ' || c== '/t');
    //#]
}
```

Code Listing 7-1: *Calculator Utility Functions*

The CharParser has the list of attributes shown in Table 7-6.

The behavior of the CharParser is highly state dependent. The statechart for this class is shown in Figure 7-17. The statechart could be simplified somewhat, but allows for both single-stepped operation and for free-run operation. The CharParser statechart begins parsing the expression once it receives an evGo event. Then it extracts the first character and types it, using the utility functions mentioned previously. Once the character has been typed, the CharParser GENs an event for the Tokenizer, passing the character with the event. The CharParser then continues with the next character until all characters have been read. As mentioned in , the freeRun attribute determines whether it will single-step or wait for the evGetNextChar event after each character is read and processed. Note that a special token end of string (EOS) is sent once all the characters have been processed.

7.2.2.3 Tokenizer Class

The Tokenizer class receives the events from the CharParser that correspond to the sequence of characters of the string to be evaluated. These

Table 7-6: *CharParser Attributes*

Attribute	Type	Description
currentChar	char	Holds the current character extracted from exprString.
exprString	OMString	OMString is a basic string type provided by the Rhapsody tool. The exprString contains the expression to be evaluated.
freeRun	OMBoolean	OMBoolean is a basic Boolean type. This attribute is set to TRUE when you do not want to single step the execution; when set to FALSE, the characters are extracted, typed, and sent to the Tokenizer and the CharParser waits for the evGetNextChar event one at a time.
len	int	Length of exprString.
pos	int	Position of currentChar within exprString.

events are evDigit, evDot (for a decimal place), evOp (for an operator), and evWhiteSpace (for a character to be ignored). For operators, the processing is very straightforward—it constructs a single character token from the operator (since all operators are a single token), then calls sendOp(op) to send the operator to the Evaluator.

The Tokenizer has a number of attributes, shown in Table 7-7.

Table 7-7: *Tokenizer Attributes*

Attribute	Type	Description
op	char	The operator currently being tokenized
tensPlace	int	The decimal place for the current digit being processed
tokenStr	OMString	A string constructed of the incoming characters (used only for debugging)
value	double	The value of the number being tokenized

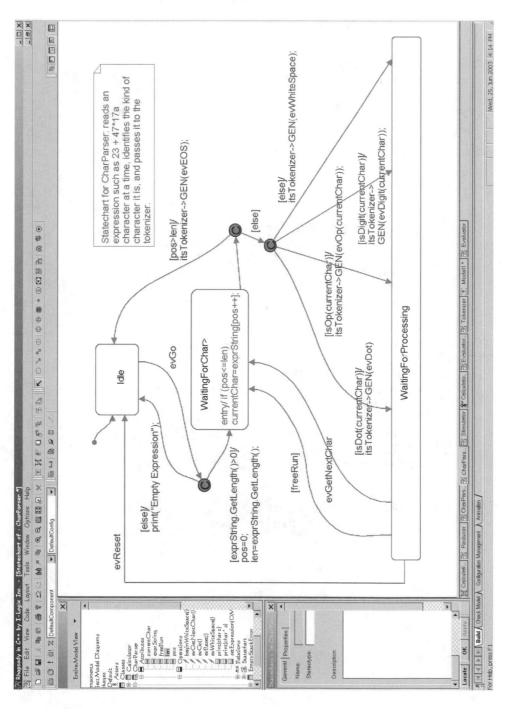

Figure 7-17: *CharParser Statechart*

The code for the important operators is shown in Code Listing 7-2.

```
void Tokenizer::addDigit(char  c) {
    //#[ operation addDigit(char)
    tokenStr = tokenStr + c; // build up string
    value = value*10 + digit(c);
    //#]
}
void Tokenizer::addDot() {
    //#[ operation addDot()
    tokenStr = tokenStr + '.';
    tensPlace = 10;
    //#]
}
void Tokenizer::addFractionalDigit(char  c) {
    //#[ operation addFractionalDigit(char)
    tokenStr = tokenStr + c;
    value = value + digit(c)/tensPlace;
    tensPlace *= 10; // get next decimal position
    //#]
}
void Tokenizer::beginToken(char  c) {
    //#[ operation beginToken(char)
    tokenStr = c;
    if (isDigit(c))
      value = digit(c); // value of the number so far
    else {
      value = 0;
      if (isOp(c)) op = c;
      };
    tensPlace = 10; // digit position
    //#]
}
int Tokenizer::digit(char  c) {
    //#[ operation digit(char)
    return c-'0';

    //#]
}
void Tokenizer::sendOp(int  c) {
    //#[ operation sendOp(int)
    switch (op) {
      case '-':
      case '+': itsEvaluator->GEN(evAddOp(op)); break;
      case '*':
      case '/':
```

```
        case '^': itsEvaluator->GEN(evMultOp(op));
          break;
        case '(': itsEvaluator->GEN(evLeftParen(op));
          break;
        case ')': itsEvaluator->GEN(evRightParen(op));
          break;
        default: throw "Unknown operator";
        };

    //#]
}
```

Code Listing 7-2: *Tokenizer Operations*

The processing for numbers is more complex. Because we need to properly interpret numbers such as 12, 12.4, 0.4, and .56789, the Tokenizer statechart (Figure 7-18) separates the processing of the whole part of the number from the fractional part. In addition, it uses its operations, shown in Listing 7-2, to compute a value, held in attribute value. As digits are read in, the tensPlace attribute holds the decimal place; this is used to multiply the current value by 10 before adding the next digit. Once we've found a decimal point (dot), we use this to divide the digit by $10^{tensPlace}$ to add that fraction to the value. The management of the execution of these operations is controlled by the Tokenizer statechart.

Note that the sendOp(op) operation further types the operator tokens into AddOp (+ or -) or MultOp (*, /) before sending them to the Evaluator. This simplifies the job for the Evaluator, as we shall see next.

7.2.2.4 Evaluator Class

So far, we've been getting ready to evaluate the string. The CharParser sends typed characters one at a time to the Tokenizer. The Tokenizer, in turn, constructs arithmetic tokens—numbers or operators—from these characters. The Evaluator actually does the mechanics of evaluating the string of tokens. As you might expect, it has the most complex statechart (see Figure 7-19).

Let's walk through this statechart so that we understand how it works. Remember that the Evaluator gets tokens—either operators (which are addition operators (+ or −), multiplicative operators (* or /), numbers, or a special token called EOS (end of string)).

LIVERPOOL JOHN MOORES UNIVERSITY
LEARNING SERVICES

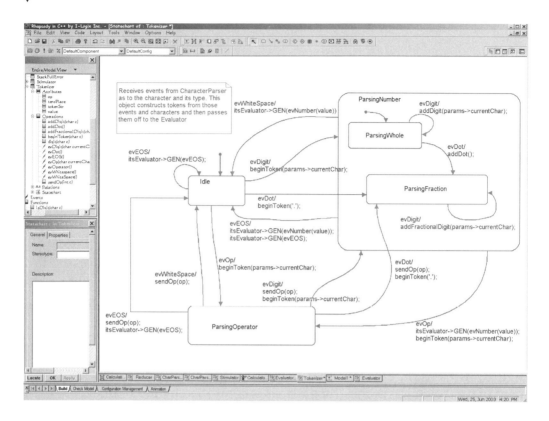

Figure 7-18: *Tokenizer Statechart*

Expressions that can be evaluated are of the form

```
[ "signed number" operator "signed number" ]
```

where the elements inside the square brackets may repeat. *Signed number* is a number with an optional additive operator preceding it. Thus, the following are acceptable expression for the evaluator:

–16

+8 – 45/89+19 – 1

White space is, as you might expect, discarded as the elements of the expression are tokenized so the Evaluator never "sees" white space.

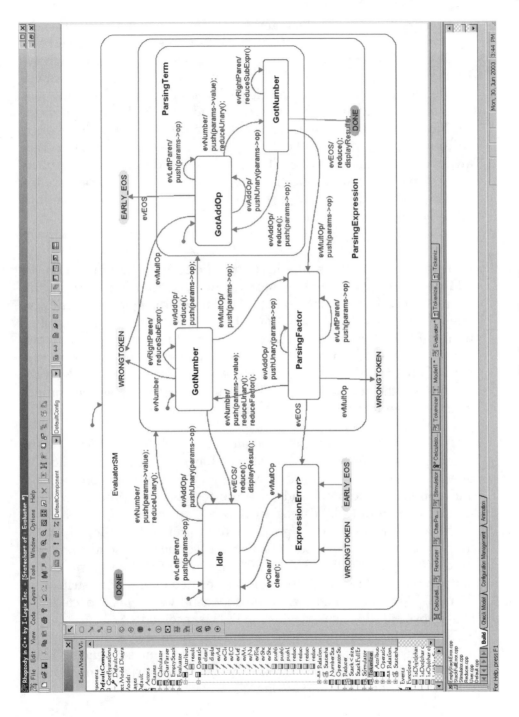

Figure 7-19: *Evaluator Statechart*

The first thing the Evaluator expects to find is either a number (via an evNumber event) or a sign (via an AddOp event). In the case of an AddOp, the pushUnary(op) pushes a special token # to signify when a leading minus sign occurs; if a leading plus sign occurs, then it can be ignored (since while syntactically legal, it doesn't change the value).

Eventually, a number is received and the Evaluator enters the GotNumber state. Now it expects either an operator or an EOS token. Additive operators have the same precedence—that is, because they are inverse operations, it doesn't matter in which order they are applied. In the same sense, multiplicative operators have the same precedence. However, the multiplicative operators have a higher precedence than additive ones. For example,

```
1 + 2*4
```

returns 9 because the multiplication is performed first and then the addition. If operators were simply evaluated from left to right, this expression would evaluate to 12 (=3*4). Therefore, if we see an additive operator we need to save it for later because we don't want to apply it until we know whether or not there is a multiplicative operator coming. That's why when the Evaluator is in the GotNumber state and we receive an additive operator (via the AddOp(op) event), we push the number on the operator stack. This is also why, when we see a multiplicative operator, we can immediately apply it (okay, not *immediately*, as we have to get the second number first).

As long as we get additive operators we push the numbers and the operators onto the appropriate stacks. Once we see a multiplicative operator followed by a number, we can pop the numbers off the stack and apply the operators and push the results. This process is called *reduction* and is done by calling the reduce() operation.

Most of the rest of the transitions are for error handling. To make the statechart less ugly, several diagram connector pseudostates are used (WRONG TOKEN, EARLY EOS, and DONE) when special things happen. The first two of these are for ill-formed expressions such as 5.6 7.7 or 6 + * 8, where the token received wasn't what was expected. The DONE pseudostate is used when an EOS is received.

The methods defined for the Evaluator class are relatively simple, as the complexity of the Evaluator behavior is in the sequencing of the method calls, and that is controlled by the statechart. The methods of interest are shown in Code Listing 7-3.

```
void Evaluator::clear() {
    //#[ operation clear()
    itsNumberStack->clear();
    itsOperatorStack->clear();
    //#]
}
void Evaluator::displayResult() {
    //#[ operation displayResult()
    try {
      result = itsNumberStack->pop();
      cout << "Result = " << result << endl;
    }
    catch (EmptyStackError){
      cout << "Found Empty stack in
Evaluator.displayResult()" << endl;
      };


    //#]
}
void Evaluator::push(double  num) {
    //#[ operation push(double)
    itsNumberStack->push(num);
    //#]
}
void Evaluator::push(char  op) {
    //#[ operation push(char)
    itsOperatorStack->push(op);
    //#]
}
void Evaluator::pushUnary(char  unaryOp) {
    //#[ operation pushUnary(char)
    // '#' is pushed to indicate a unary minus
    // if a unary plus is found (the other option)
    // if can just be ignored and tossed away
    if (unaryOp == '-')
        itsOperatorStack->push('#');

    //#]
}
void Evaluator::reduce() {
    //#[ operation reduce()
    OMBoolean done = FALSE;

    while (!done) {
     if (itsNumberStack->getTopOfStack()>1)
```

```
            if (itsOperatorStack->elementAtTop() != '(')
                    reduceFactor();
            else
                    done = TRUE; // done if left
                      parenthesis
         else
          done = TRUE; // done if no numbers are left
        }; // end while


    //#]
}
void Evaluator::reduceFactor() {
    //#[ operation reduceFactor()
    char opToApply;
    double num1,num2;
    if (itsOperatorStack->elementAtTop() != '(') {
      opToApply = itsOperatorStack->pop();
      num1 = itsNumberStack->pop();
      num2 = itsNumberStack->pop();
      switch (opToApply) {
            case '+': result = num1 + num2; break;
            case '-': result = num2 - num1; break;
            case '/': if (num1 == 0) throw "Divide by
              Zero";
                      else result = num2 / num1;
                      break;
            case '*': result = num2 * num1; break;
            case '(': throw "Unmatched Left
              Parenthesis";
            case ')': throw "Parsing Error: Found
              Right Parenthesis";
            };
      itsNumberStack->push(result);
    };


    //#]
}
void Evaluator::reduceSubExpr() {
    //#[ operation reduceSubExpr()
    char op;
    OMBoolean done = FALSE;

    // reduce stack until left parenthesis found
    while (!done) {
```

```
        if (itsOperatorStack->getTopOfStack()>0) {
            op=itsOperatorStack->elementAtTop();
            switch (op) {
                case '#': reduceUnary(); break;
                case '(': op = itsOperatorStack->pop();
                          done = TRUE;
                          break;
                case '+':
                case '-':
                case '*':
                case '/': reduceFactor(); break;
                }
            }
        else // didn't find matching left parenthesis
            throw "Unmatched Right parenthesis";
        };


    //#]
}
void Evaluator::reduceUnary() {
    //#[ operation reduceUnary()
    char opToApply;
    double num;
    OMBoolean done = FALSE;

    // reduce all leading signs as in
    // 1 - - - - - -6 to 1 + 6
    while (!done) {
      if (itsOperatorStack->getTop()>0) {
        if (itsOperatorStack->elementAtTop() == '#') {
            opToApply = itsOperatorStack->pop();
            num = itsNumberStack->pop();
            result = -num;
            itsNumberStack->push(result);
            }  // end if
        else
          done = TRUE;
      } // end if
        else
            done = TRUE;
    }; // end while
    //#]
}
```

Code Listing 7-3: *Evaluator Methods*

7.2.2.5 NumberStack and OperatorStack Classes

The NumberStack and OperatorStack are instantiations of a parametric class called Stack. C++ and Ada support the notion of *parametric classes.* A parametric class (called a *template class* in C++) is simply a class that is incompletely specified. Parametric classes are extremely useful for defining various kinds of containers, such as queues, stacks, lists, and trees, in which the containment behavior is fundamentally independent from the types of the elements being contained. In the definition of a parametric class, these undefined elements are given symbolic names and referred to by those names. Because part of the definition of the parametric class is missing, parametric classes cannot be directly instantiated into objects—the missing information must first be provided.

The Stack class defers the specification of two important features— the type of element being stored and the maximum number of elements being stored. The code for the stack is standard C++ code, as shown in Code Listing 7-4. The UML representation (not shown) is a class box named Stack with a dashed box in the upper righthand corner listing the parameters (size and T).

```
//## class Stack
template <int size = 100, class T> class Stack  {
public :

    #ifdef _OMINSTRUMENT
        //## ignore
        typedef OMAnimatedStack<size, T>
OMAnimatedStackType;

    #endif // _OMINSTRUMENT

//## class Stack

////    Friends    ////
public :


#ifdef _OMINSTRUMENT
    friend  class OMAnimatedStack<size, T> ;
#endif // _OMINSTRUMENT
```

```
////    Constructors and destructors    ////
public :

    //## auto_generated
    Stack();

    //## auto_generated
    ~Stack();

////    Operations    ////
public :

    //## operation clear()
    void clear();

    //## operation isEmpty()
    OMBoolean isEmpty();

    //## operation isFull()
    OMBoolean isFull();

    //## operation pop()
    T pop();

    //## operation push(T)
    void push(T  element);

    //## operation show()
    void show();

////    Additional operations    ////
public :

    //## auto_generated
    T getStk(int  i1) const;

    //## auto_generated
    void setStk(int  i1, T  p_stk);

    //## auto_generated
    int getTop() const;

    //## auto_generated
    void setTop(int  p_top);

////    Attributes    ////
protected :
```

```
    T stk[size];        //## attribute stk

    // top of stack - the index into the array
    int top;            //## attribute top
};
//## class Stack
```

Code Listing 7-4: *Stack Parameterized Class*

A NumberStack is simply a Stack for doubles and an OperatorStack is a stack for operators (base type char).

```
//## class NumberStack
typedef Stack<50, double> NumberStack;
//## class OperatorStack
typedef Stack<100, char> OperatorStack;
```

Code Listing 7-5: *NumberStack and OperatorStack Classes*

In Code Listing 7-5, we see that the NumberStack can handle up to 50 doubles, while the OperatorStack can store 100 operators. If you want to show that the NumberStack is a parametric instantiation of Stack, you can represent NumberStack as a class with a solid-line rectangle in the upper righthand corner, with the values assigned to the parameters.

The purpose of the stack is to remember the numbers and operators until the rules of evaluation allow them to be processed. When a finite-state machine is combined with one or more stacks, it is called a *stack machine*. A stack machine is often used in parsing applications such as compiler front ends.

7.2.2.6 Stimulator Class

The Stimulator class is there as a debugging aid; it has the stereotype «TestingBuddy», which indicates it is part of the testing harness for the system. You can see from its statechart (Figure 7-20) that when it receives events such as test1, it sets a specific expression string to be evaluated and then kicks off the evaluation process by sending an evGo to the CharParser. Additionally, the stimulator can set whether the evaluation is done as a free-run process or requires single-stepping through the expression, a character at a time. The TestInput event is used when you want to just type characters into standard input.

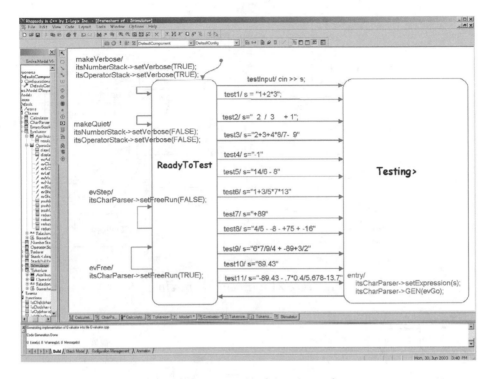

Figure 7-20: *Stimulator Statechart*

7.2.3 Event Hierarchies

Because some events may be specialized versions of other events, it is possible to build event-class generalization hierarchies. Event hierarchies are useful because they allow polymorphic event receptions. This means that different objects (or states within the same object) can accept events at different levels in the hierarchy as appropriate.

Figure 7-21a shows a simple hierarchy for user input events. A user input active object accepting InputEvent objects would also accept any subclass of InputEvent, such as LeftMouseClick or KeyboardEvent, because a LeftMouseClick is a kind of InputEvent.

Figure 7-21b illustrates how one object might use the event hierarchy. The object has four and-states. A key thing to remember is that when the object receives an event, each active and-state logically receives its own copy of the event and is free to act independently on it, or discard it, as appropriate. For example, suppose the user moves the

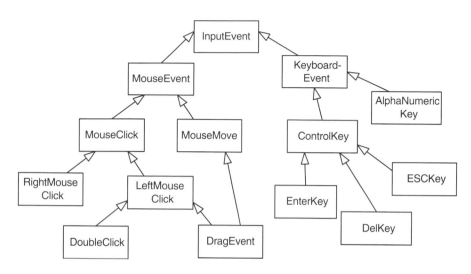

Figure 7-21a: *Event Hierarchy*

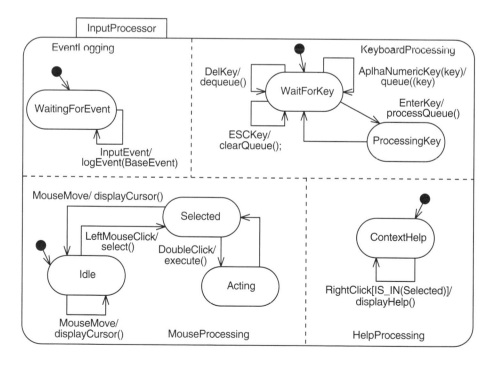

Figure 7-21b: *Event Reception*

mouse over an element on the screen, selects it with a left mouse click, then double clicks to activate editing of that element, types in the name "Robotoothbrush," and hits the Enter key. The MouseProcessing and-state processes the mouse events while the KeyboardProcessing and-state processes the keystrokes. The EventLogging and-state accepts and logs every input event, because MouseMove, AlphNumeric, Left Click, and so on events are all InputEvents and as such, activate the transition in the EventLogging and-state.

7.3 Interactions

A state diagram provides a static view of the entire state space of an object at some level of abstraction, from the complete system down to simple primitive objects. Because the complete behavior of a state-driven object can be represented by a sufficiently detailed state model, state models are said to be *constructive.* This means that they can be used to fully generate executable code for the object.[6]

What state diagrams do not show are typical paths through the state space as the system is used, nor are they effective at showing how collaborations of objects interact. Such interactions are captured as *scenarios.* Scenarios may not visit all states in all the participant objects nor activate all transitions, but they provide an order-dependent view of how the set of objects is expected to behave under some set of conditions with a specific ordering of external and internal stimuli. Because a scenario does not have enough information to fully define the complete behavioral model of an object, scenarios are said to be *partially constructive.* They can add operations and event handling to a state model, but they do not fully define the model.

There are two methods for showing scenarios that are particularly useful in real-time systems. The primary notational form for scenarios is the sequence diagram, which shows order but not strict timing. The second is the timing diagram, which is best used when strict timing must be shown. There is a third, the diagram formerly known as a collaboration diagram but in UML 2.0 called a *communication diagram.* A communication diagram is basically an object diagram showing the message sequences as being attached to the links between the objects

---

[6] Activity models are also constructive.

and indicating ordering with numbers on the messages. This last form is used rather infrequently and so will not be discussed here.

7.3.1 Sequence Diagrams

Sequence diagrams are (by far) the more common way to show scenarios, as discussed earlier in this book. Sequence diagrams use vertical lines to represent the objects participating in the scenario and horizontal directed lines to represent the messages sent from one object to another. Time flows from top to bottom; that is, messages shown lower on the page take place later than ones above it. The basic syntax and semantics of sequence diagrams have been discussed in Chapter 3. The focus in this section is to discuss how sequence diagrams may be usefully employed in the constructions of analysis object models.

Sequence diagrams are representations of specific interactions among the elements of a collaboration. They only tell a part of the story (what happened in this particular case) and not what always must happen (a specification). As such, sequence diagrams are a way to detail a use case. The sequence diagram helps to capture the operational perspective of a set of elements, such as a system, and the actors with which it interacts, or a set of elements inside a system. As we construct our object analysis model, we can use sequence diagrams to capture how the elements in the object analysis model interact to achieve the higher-level interaction described in the use case scenario.

The other use of sequence diagrams has to do with validation, the use of sequence diagrams as either a debugging tool or as a test vector.

7.3.1.1 CardioNada Scenarios Example

It would be useful to look at the interaction of the instances in the pacemaker model. In a real development project we would create many sequence diagrams. Some of these sequence diagrams would be for the communications with sending and receiving messages, with and without errors. Other sequence diagrams would show the interactions necessary to achieve the pacing behavior, most likely several in each of the pacing modes. Still other sequence diagrams would depict the interaction of the communications and the pacing system to show how the programmer sets and queries the pacing modes and parameters. In this chapter, we are going to focus on pacing in AAI.

In this case, I am going to use the executability characteristics of the Rhapsody tool to both drive and monitor the execution of the model. First, to help drive the model, I will create a statechart for the Heart Chamber actor. We call this "instrumenting the actor" because we are creating executable behavior for the actor to help us explore how the objects inside the system interact to make sure that we got it right. This is almost exactly the same process as creating the «test buddy» class we saw previously in the calculator example. It differs in a couple of important ways. First, the actor is outside the scope of the pacing subsystem so we can't rely on the pacing subsystem to connect the actor with the parts of the subsystem automatically—we'll have to do that ourselves. Secondly, instrumenting the actor is less obtrusive in the model of the system, since the actor must use the specified interfaces and services. The statechart for the actor is shown in Figure 7-22.

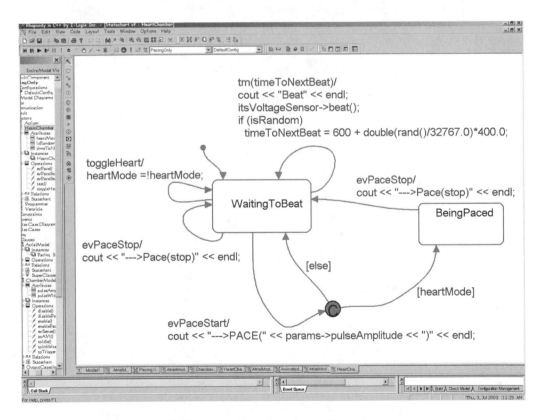

Figure 7-22: *HeartChamber Actor Statechart*

We can see that the HeartChamber actor primarily acts like a heart. It beats at the rate held in the attribute timeToNextBeat. It can have randomness if we set the local attribute isRandom to TRUE. When it beats, it invokes the beat() method on the VoltageSensor to which it connects (which in turn sends an evSense event to the AtrialModel in this case). It accepts evPaceStart and evPaceStop events sent to it from the OutputCapacitor to which it connects. Code Listing 7-6 shows the code used to create the pacing subsystem and heart chamber instances. All but the sections between //#[and //#] are generated automatically by Rhapsody. The two lines of code between those marks were added to allow the heart chamber to send events to the voltage sensor, and to allow it to receive events from the output capacitor. The Object Execution Framework (OXF) code starts up the framework so it can begin processing events and executing the state machines.

```
int main(int  argc, char*  argv[]) {
    if(OXF::init(argc, argv, 6423))
        {
                HeartChamber * p_HeartChamber;
                Pacing_Subsystem * p_Pacing_Subsystem;
                p_HeartChamber = new HeartChamber;
                p_HeartChamber->startBehavior(),
                p_Pacing_Subsystem = new Pacing_Subsystem;
                p_Pacing_Subsystem->startBehavior();
                //#[ configuration
PacingOnly::DefaultConfig
                // set the heart chamber to send events
// to first voltage sensor
                // set first output capacitor to send
// its pace events to the heart chamber
                p_HeartChamber->setItsVoltageSensor(
p_Pacing_Subsystem->getSensorInput());
                p_Pacing_Subsystem->setPaceOutput
(p_HeartChamber);

                //#]
                OXF::start();
                delete p_HeartChamber;
                delete p_Pacing_Subsystem;
                return 0;
        }
    else
        {
```

```
        return 1;
    }
}
```

Code Listing 7-6: *CardioNada main()*

A word about debugging and testing: When I build systems using the UML, I want to debug and test at the *same level of abstraction* at which I design—that is, I want to test and debug in UML, not in the underlying source language or the even-more underlying assembly language. While I may, at times, find it necessary to drill down to those levels of detail, the vast majority of my testing and debugging ought be at the model level, not the code level. For this reason, Rhapsody provides a rich set of debugging and testing tools that we'll use here. I bring this up now because once we begin to look at the sequence diagrams it is important to know how they were created mechanically (via the insertion of events, for example) as well as to understand that these sequence diagrams were generated automatically by Rhapsody as the system was executed.

When testing or debugging state-based objects, one of the basic things you need to be able to do is to insert events. Rhapsody provides a number of means to do this. Figure 7-23 shows one way—a dialog box that can be opened that allows the user to select the object and event to be inserted into the running model. It should be noted that Rhapsody also provides a means to call operations as well (not shown here). Figure 7-24 shows a different way. Rhapsody allows you to "webify" a model; that is, mark which elements you wish to monitor and/or control via a standard Web browser and then automatically generate such a Web page and to insert a Web server in your application. This is an extremely useful feature because it allows you to monitor and control a system via the Internet even while it is running on the actual target hardware (provided, of course, that it supports TCP/IP and can connect to the Internet). In the figure, we see two panes in the browser—the left identifies the elements that I've specified that I want to monitor or control, and the right presents the elements that I can use. We see that I can view (and set) the value for timeToNextBeat, set the heartMode, and isRandom Boolean attributes, and even send events such as evPace and evPaceStart (which takes a single int parameter). I can also construct custom views, picking among the elements I want to view together.

Figure 7-23: *Inserting Events*

Lastly, I also want to be able to see various features of the objects in the running system. Figure 7-25 shows the debugging view for the HeartMonitor. We see all the current attributes and even the links connecting the HeartMonitor to the VoltageSensor. The instance is identified by its name rather than by its memory address, making it much more useful. With these basic tools, I can control and monitor the execution of my system, whether it runs on my desktop, on the actual target hardware connected to the desktop, or on a machine thousands of miles away. Pretty cool, huh?

The ability to debug systems is a crucial one, so even if you're not going to generate the system from the UML model,[7] you must still be able to answer the question "Is this right???" about the model you've constructed. These debugging tools allow you to run your system and validate that it is doing the right thing.

---

[7] Although I highly recommend it.

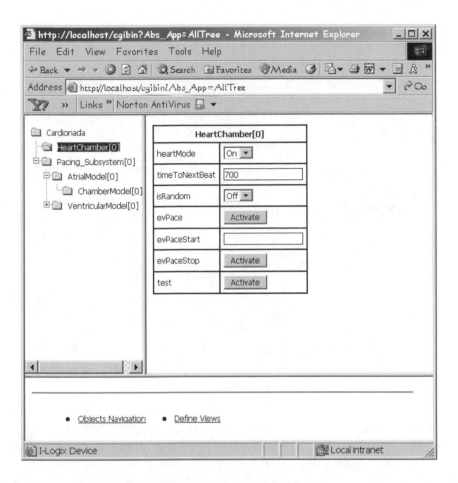

Figure 7-24: *Debugging with a Web Browser*

Now, back to our main subject—the sequences of interaction of the pacing subsystem parts. The first sequence, shown in Figure 7-26, captures the creation of the two primary objects, the HeartMonitor and the Pacing_Subsystem, and how, in turn, the Pacing_Subsystem creates its internal parts. The ones shown are the instances of the AtrialModel, VoltageSensor, and OutputCapacitor. Note that there are other instances created as well, such as the VentricularModel instance and another instance each of the VoltageSensor and OutputCapacitor. Since we're not using them in this scenario, I didn't draw those instance lines and the creation messages to those instances are therefore not shown.

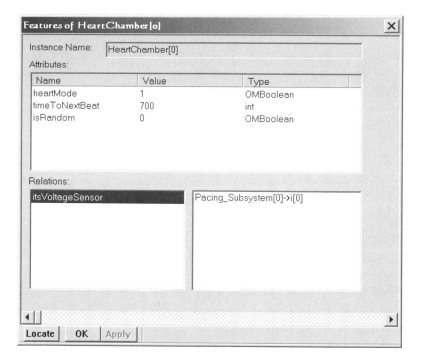

Figure 7-25: *Debugging View*

The calls we entered into the main() shown in Code Listing 7-6 appear in the sequence diagram right after the construction of the system objects; we see getSensorInput() and setPaceChamberOutput() sent from the main() (as represented by the collaboration boundary) and the Pacing_Subsystem instance.

Since the statechart of the HeartChamber begins immediately we see the timeout events on the HeartChamber lifeline and the invocation of the VoltageSensor::beat() operation. Then from the debugger, we enter the enablePacing and toInhibited events.

Figure 7-27 shows an example of pacing. Notes were manually added to the automatically generated sequence to aid understanding. This figure is, in fact, a continuation of the scenario shown in Figure 7-26. In Figure 7-27 we can look at the interaction among the instances. At the top of the figure we see the timeout that causes the transition of the AtrialModel from its Refractory to its Waiting state. The transition

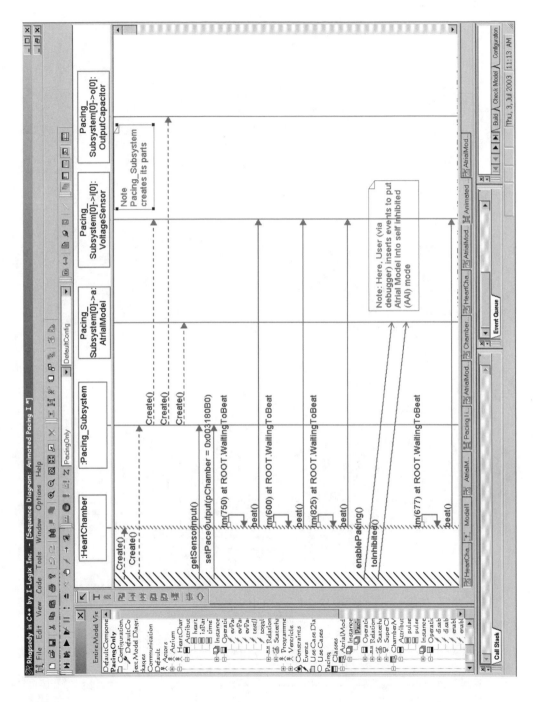

Figure 7-26: *CardioNada Sequence 1—Creation and Initialization*

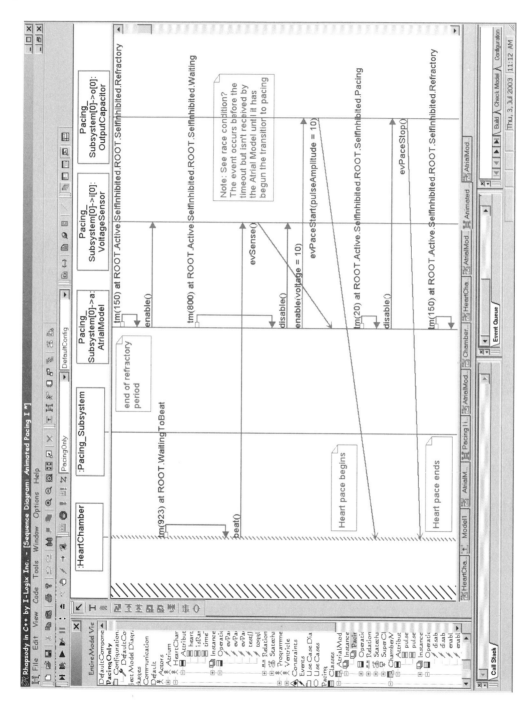

Figure 7-27: *CardioNada Sequence 2—Pacing*

action, a call to VoltageSensor::enable() lets the VoltageSensor turn on the hardware to listen (in the real system).

Next we see something interesting. The HeartChamber times out and sends a beat to the VoltageSensor, which in turn sends an evSense event to the AtrialModel. Even as that happens, though, the Atrial Model state machine times out before it receives the evSense event. Therefore it proceeds to pace the heart even though the heart just completed a pace.[8] Such race conditions occur frequently in real-time systems and it is good to see that the evSense event is appropriate discarded when that occurred.

The pacing of the heart is accomplished by first disabling the Voltage-Sensor and then invoking the OutputCapacitor::enable() method (which passes the amplitude of voltage pulse to be delivered). The pace is completed with the OutputCapacitor::disable() call. Then the Atrial model waits for a period of time (its refractory period) to allow the electrical charge in the heart to dissipate before reenabling the VoltageSensor.

The next sequence diagram, Figure 7-28, is a continuation of the previous one. In this case, the HeartChamber "beats" and invokes the

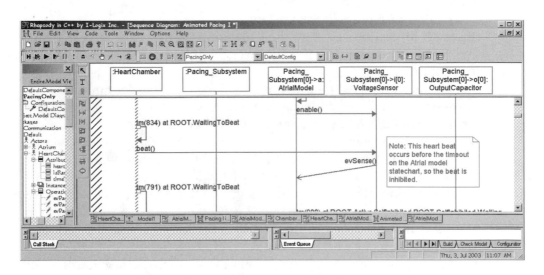

Figure 7-28: *CardioNada Sequence 3—Inhibiting*

---

[8] This is hemodynamically fine as the cardiac muscle fibers will not be recovered enough to respond to the pace in this case.

VoltageSensor::beat() method. This method then sends an evSense event to the AtrialModel. It is received, causing the Atrial model to exit and then reenter its Waiting state. This causes the timeout that will invoke the pacing behavior to retrigger and start over. This is exactly what was desired in the SelfInihibited mode of operation.

7.3.1.2 Calculator Scenario Example

In the previous section, we saw how the scenarios allowed us to examine and ensure that the pacemaker was pacing properly. In this section, we'll use scenarios to make sure that the Calculator is doing the same.

At the black-box level of testing, we can just pump mathematical expressions in one end of the Calculator and look at standard output to see if the value is correct. However, unit testing is all about the white-box view: making sure that the internal pieces of the system are doing what they are supposed to be doing. Scenario-based testing can allow us to insert events, change values, and invoke behaviors to actually demonstrate that objects are doing so and the interactions are what we expect.

In this case we can take a few simple expressions and run them through the various parts of the Calculator. In this way, we can examine them and see if we are convinced that the parts are all doing the right thing.

In this effort, we'll take advantage of the multiple configuration features of the Rhapsody tool, just as we've taken advantage of the model-level execution, debugging, and code-generation features previously. We'll create another configuration of the system, called *Debug*, that generates instrumentation in the code, allowing the generated application to talk back to Rhapsody. This feedback lets Rhapsody animate, via dynamic color-coding, the various states of the objects and dynamically construct the sequence diagrams during the execution of the system. We used these features in the previous section to create the sequence diagrams we looked at, but now we'll create a debug configuration of the Calculator as a separate item. This allows us to, at the click of a button, generate either a production version of the application, which we could ship off to a customer, or a debug version. The underlying model is the same either way, which greatly facilitates the testing of our model, since changes to the model we make as a result of testing and debugging automatically appear in the production version.

Figure 7-29 shows the Setting pane of the features of the Debug configuration of our calculator. The difference between this and the default (production) configuration is that instrumentation mode is set to Animation. This tells Rhapsody to insert macros in the generated code that send information back to the Rhapsody tool when events are processed, method calls are invoked, and attributes are changed. This allows Rhapsody to construct the dynamic visualizations of the application execution. Note that both configurations have Web Enabling

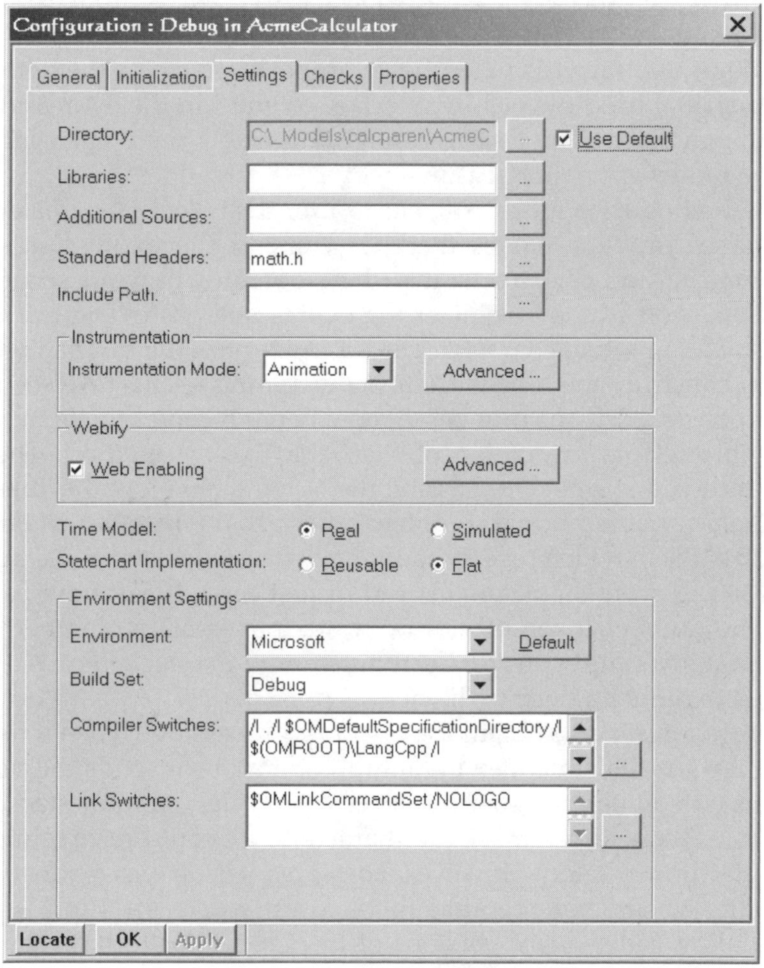

Figure 7-29: *Debug Configuration*

checked. The Advanced button allows us to set which things are webi-fied in the generated system, and so control whether this configuration has monitoring and control of internal portions of the system or just to enter expressions and see results.

It is common to have multiple such configurations. Some will have debugging capabilities enabled while others won't; some will be tar-geted at desktop systems such as Windows or Solaris, while others will be targeted at embedded RTOSes, such as VxWorks or OSE.

For the purpose of this debugging effort, let's examine what hap-pens when we process the expression 2*(3+4). This simple expression allows us to ensure that we process both the addition and multiplica-tion operators as well as parentheses properly. To create the figures for the scenario, I used the webify interface to enter in the expression and start things going. The Debug configuration sets the webify interface and the model animation features active.

The first figure (Figure 7-30) starts after the objects are created. The CharParser instance parses the characters in the expression string, identifies the kind of character it is (digit, operator, or white space), and sends them off to the Tokenizer via events such as evDigit or evOp, along with the actual character. The Tokenizer has the more interesting job—to construct the tokens from the incoming events. We see that it begins constructing the number token when it receives the first evDigit event through its invocation of the beginToken() method. The next event received is an evOp, passing the * character. Now the Tokenizer knows that the number is complete (after all, the number could have been 2345.78, in which case it would have had to construct the number token from seven characters instead of just one). It can now pass the complete number token off to the Evaluator via an evNumber event. The Evaluator simply pushes the number onto the stack. It calls reduce-Unary() to reduce a unary −, if one was present.

The Tokenizer also begins the operator processing. When it receives the next character (the open paragraph operator), it sends the * opera-tor off to the Evaluator, which pushes it onto the operator stack. Note that since all operators are single characters, we could have sent off the * operator immediately. However, a design decision was made to allow for multiple character operators in the future, such as ++ and +='. This would allow subsequent versions of the Calculator to have variables and more elaborate behavior.

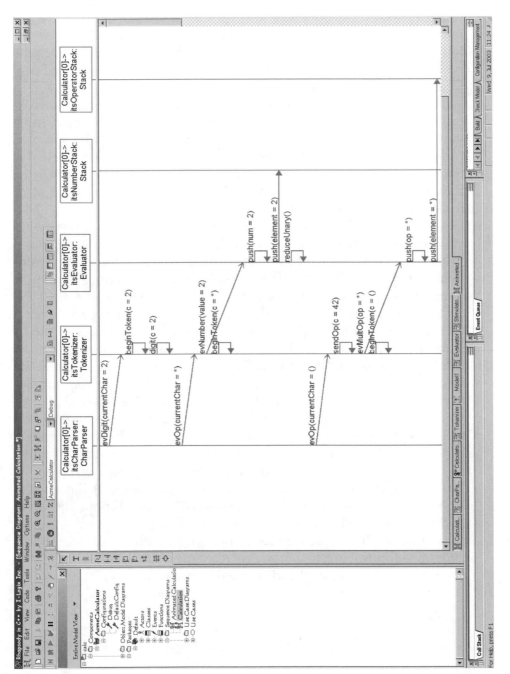

Figure 7-30: *Calculator Scenario 2*(3+4) page 1*

Figure 7-31 picks up where the previous figure leaves off. The Evaluator pushes the * operator. The CharParser meanwhile sends the digit 3 to the Tokenizer. The latter now sends the (operator off to the Evaluator, which pushes it onto the operator stack. The processing continues with the + operator inside the parenthesis.

Figure 7-32 continues the scenario with the digit 4. Now the Tokenizer can send the operator + to the Evaluator. The Evaluator now wants to see if it can apply the operator, so it calls reduce(). It cannot, as it happens, so it pushes the operator onto the operator stack. At this point, the number stack has the value 3 at the top, followed by 2 (the number 4 hasn't been pushed onto the stack yet). The operator stack has + at the top, followed by (and then *.

The next character is the) operator. The processing continues in Figure 7-33. We see that the last number, 4, is pushed on the stack. The last token is a special one, called end of string (EOS). That forces the evaluation of the last operator,). This calls the operation reduceSubExpr(), which does a reduction until a left parenthesis operator is found. We see that the Evaluator checks to ensure that the next operator is not a left parenthesis (after all (5) is a perfectly legal subexpression). Since it is not, the Evaluator pops the operator (a +) and two operands off the number stack, does the math (actually performed in the body of the reduceFactor() method), and pushes the result (7) onto the number stack. Then the (is popped from the operator stack and discarded.

The final reduction is done by processing the EOS event in the Evaluator. This is shown in the last of these figures, Figure 7-34. The reduceFactor() method is called (since we're processing a multiplicative operator) and we pop the operator from the stack (*), the two operands (7 and 2), do the math, and push the result on the stack (14). Since we're at the end of the string, we call displayResult(), which pops the value off the number stack and sends it to standard output.

In a book, this sequence seems long and involved, as it is spread across five figures. In a tool, however, the entire scenario is a single diagram, and may be scrolled and zoomed as necessary.

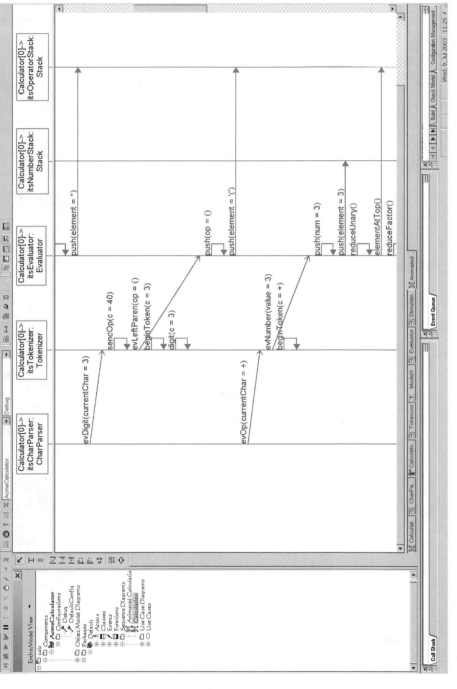

Figure 7-31: *Calculator Scenario 2*(3+4) page 2*

LIVERPOOL
JOHN MOORES UNIVERSITY
AVRIL ROBARTS LRC
TEL. 0151 231 4022

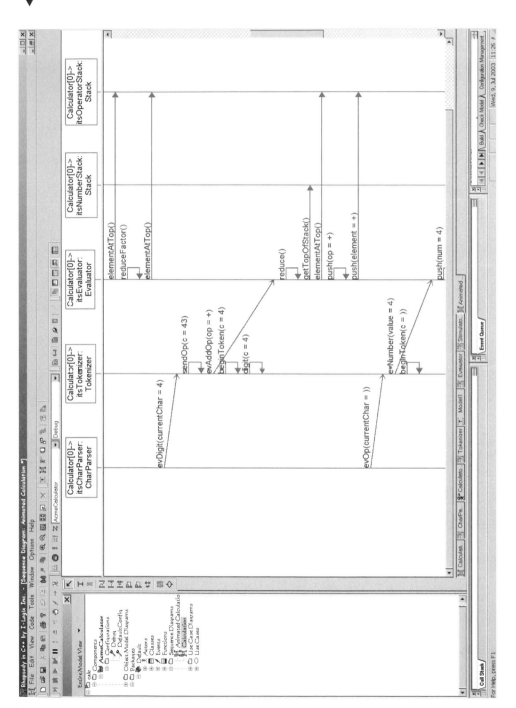

Figure 7-32: *Calculator Scenario 2*(3+4) page 3*

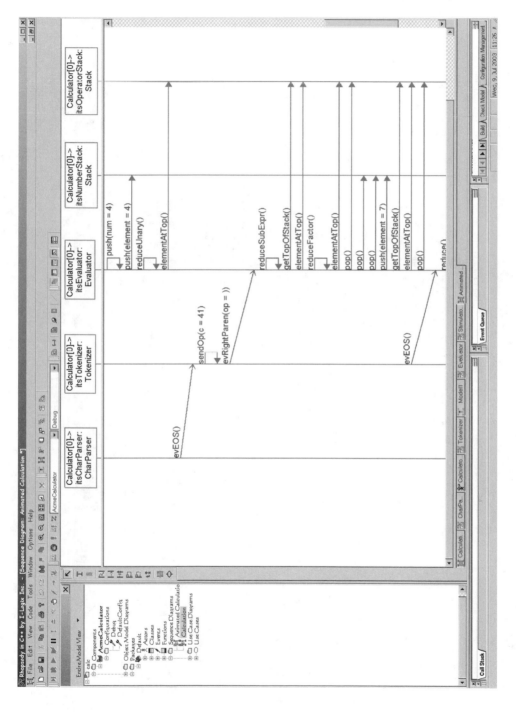

Figure 7-33: *Calculator Scenario 2*(3+4) page 4*

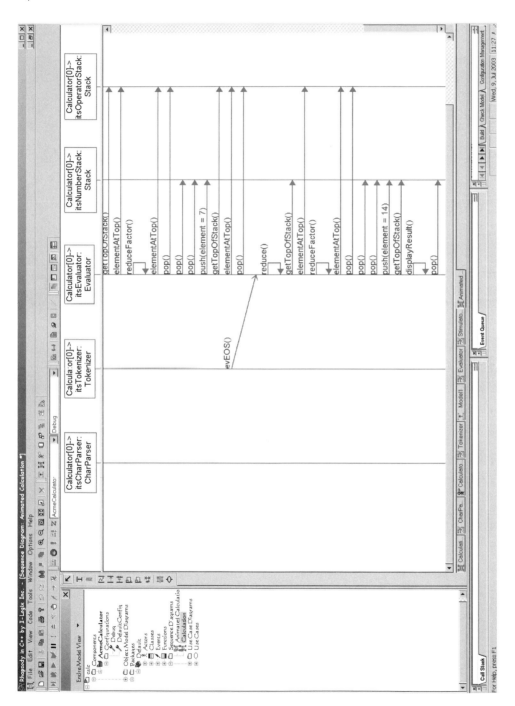

Figure 7-34: *Calculator Scenario 2*(3+4) page 5*

7.4 Defining Operations

All class operations either handle messages or assist in their handling. This means that once a class's state machine is defined and important scenarios elucidated, the messages and events shown on those diagrams become class operations.

In the UML, an *operation* is the specification of a behavior. This is distinct from a *method*, which is the realization of an operation. An operation is the fundamental unit of object behavior. The overall behavior of the object is decomposed into a set of operations, some of which are within the interface of the class and some of which are internal and hidden. Naturally, all objects of the same class provide the same set of operations to their clients. An object's operations must directly support its required functionality and its responsibilities. Often behaviors are decomposed into more primitive operations to produce the overall class behavior. This is similar to the functional decomposition in structured system design.

Operations have a protocol for correct usage consisting of the following:

- Preconditional invariants, that is, assumptions about the environment that must be satisfied before the operation is invoked
- A signature containing an ordered formal list of parameters and their types and the return type of the operation
- Postconditional invariants that are guaranteed to be satisfied when the operations are complete
- Rules for thread-reliable interaction, including synchronization behavior

The responsibility for ensuring that preconditional invariants are met falls primarily in the client's realm. That is, the user of the operation is required to guarantee that the preconditional invariants are satisfied. However, the server operation should check as many of these as possible. Interfaces are hotbeds for common errors and the inclusion of preconditional invariant checking in acceptor operations makes objects much more robust and reliable.

In strongly typed languages, the compiler itself will check the number and types of parameters for synchronous operation calls. However, some language type checking is stronger than others. For example, enumerated values are freely and automatically converted to integer types in C++. A caller can pass an out-of-range integer value when an enumerated type is expected and the compiler typing system will not detect it. Ada's stronger type checking[9] flags this as an error and will not allow it unless an explicit unchecked_conversion type cast is performed. Even in Ada, however, not all range violations can be caught at compile time. In such cases, the operation itself must check for violations of its preconditional invariants.

For example, consider an array class. Because C++ is backwardly compatible with C, array indices are not checked.[10] Thus, it is possible (even *likely*) that an array will be accessed with an out-of-range index, returning garbage or overwriting some unknown portion of memory. In C++, however, it is possible to construct a reliable array class, as shown in Code Listing 7-7.

```cpp
#include <iostream.h>
template<class T, int size>
class ReliableArray {
T arr[size];
public:
    ReliableArray(void) { };
    T &operator[](int j) {
        if (j<0 || j >=size)
            throw "Index range Error";
            return arr[j];
    };
    const T *operator&() { return arr; };
    T operator*() { return arr[0]; };
};
int main(void) {
    ReliableArray<int, 10> iArray;
    iArray[1] = 16;
    cout << iArray[1] << endl;
    iArray[19] = 0; // INDEX OUT OF RANGE!
    return 0;
};
```

Code Listing 7-7: *Reliable Array*

---

[9] It has been said "C treats you like a consenting adult. Pascal treats you like a naughty child. Ada treats you like a criminal."

[10] It is well documented that "the major problem with C++ is C."

Classes instantiated from the ReliableArray template overload the bracket ("[]") operator and prevent inappropriate access to the array. This kind of assertion of the preconditional invariant ("Don't access beyond the array boundaries") should be checked by the client,[11] but nevertheless is guaranteed by the server (array class).

7.4.1 Types of Operations

Operations are the manifestations of behavior. This behavior is normally specified on state diagrams (for state-driven classes) and/or scenario diagrams. These operations may be divided up into several types. Booch[2] identifies five types of operations:

- Constructor
- Destructor
- Modifier
- Selector
- Iterator

Constructors and *destructors* create and destroy objects of a class, respectively. Well-written constructors ensure the consistent creation of valid objects. This normally means that an object begins in the correct initial state, its variables are initialized to known, reasonable values, and required links to other objects are properly initialized. Object creation involves the allocation of memory, both implicitly on the stack, as well as possibly dynamically on the heap. The constructor must allocate memory for any internal objects or attributes that use heap storage. The constructor must guarantee its postconditional invariants; specifically, a client using the object once it is created must be assured that the object is properly created and in a valid state.

Sometimes the construction of an object is done in a two-step process. The constructor does the initial job of building the object infrastructure, while a subsequent call to an initialization operation completes the process. This is done when concerns for creation and initialization of the object are clearly distinct and not all information is known at creation time to fully initialize the object.

---

[11] If known—clearly a negative index into an array is probably nonsensical, but the client may not know the upper bounds of the array. If you always put range checking in the server array class, you can be assured that even if the client forgets, the array integrity will be maintained.

Destructors reverse the construction process. They must deallocate memory when appropriate and perform other cleanup activities. In real-time systems, this often means commanding hardware components to known, reasonable states. Valves may be closed, hard disks parked, lasers deenergized, and so forth.

Modifiers change values within the object while *selectors* read values or request services from an object without modifying them. *Iterators* provide orderly access to the components of an object. Iterators are most common with objects maintaining collections of other objects. Such objects are called *collections* or *containers*. It is important that these three types of operations hide the internal object structure and reveal instead the externally visible semantics. Consider the simple collection class in Code Listing 7-8.

```
class Bunch_O_Objects {
    node* p;
    node* current_node;
public:
    void insert(node n);
    node* go_left(void);
    node* go_right(void);
};
```

Code Listing 7-8: *Simple Collection Class*

The interface forces clients of this class to be aware of its internal structure (a binary tree). The current position in the tree is maintained by the current_node pointer. The implementation structure is made visible by the iterator methods go_left() and go_right(). What if the design changes to an n-way tree? A linked list? A hash table? The externally visible interface ensures that any such internal change to the class will force a change to the interface and therefore changes to all the clients of the class. Clearly, a better approach would be to provide the fundamental semantics (the concept of a next and a previous node), as in Code Listing 7-9.

```
class Bunch_O_Objects {
    node* p;
    node* current_node;
public:
    void insert(node n);
```

```
    node* next(void);
    node* previous(void);
};
```

Code Listing 7-9: *Better Simple Collection Class*

However, even this approach has problems. This interface works fine provided that marching through the objects in the collection will always be in a sequential manner and only a single reader is active.

The first problem can be resolved by adding some additional operations to meet the needs of the clients. Perhaps some clients must be able to restart the search or easily retrieve the last object. Perhaps having the ability to quickly locate a specific object in the list is important. Considering the client needs produces a more elaborate interface, shown in Code Listing 7-10.

```
class Bunch_O_Objects {
    node* p;
    node* current_node;
public:
    void insert(node n);
    node* next(void);
    node* previous(void);
    node* first(void);
    node* last(void);
    node* find(node &n);
};
```

Code Listing 7-10: *Even Better Simple Collection Class*

This interface isn't primitive or orthogonal, but it does provide common-usage access methods to the clients.

Providing support for multiple readers is slightly more problematic. If two readers march through the list using next() at the same time, neither will get the entire list; some items will go to the first reader, while others will go to the second. The most common solution is to create separate iterator objects, one for each of the various readers. Each iterator maintains its own current_node pointer to track its position within the collection, as shown in Code Listing 7-11.

```
class Bunch_O_Objects {
    node* p;
public:
```

```
    void insert(node n);
    node *next(node *p);
    node *previous(node *p);
    friend class BOO_Iterator;
};
class BOO_Iterator {
    node* current_node;
    Bunch_O_Objects& BOO;
public:
    BOO_Iterator(Bunch_O_Objects& B) : BOO(B) {
        current_node = BOO.p; };
    node* next(void);
    node* previous(void);
    node* first(void);
    node* last(void);
    node* find(node &n);
};
```

Code Listing 7-11: *Simple Collection Class with Iterator*

7.4.2 Strategies for Defining Operations

Defining a good set of operations for a class interface can be difficult. There are a number of heuristics that can help you decide on the operations:

- Provide a set of orthogonal primitive interface operations.
- Hide the internal class structure with interface operations that show only essential class semantics.
- Provide a set of nonprimitive operations to
    - ▼ Enforce protocol rules
    - ▼ Capture frequently used combinations of operations
- Operations within a class and class hierarchy should use a consistent set of parameter types where possible.
- A common parent class should provide operations shared by sibling classes.
- Each responsibility to be met by a class or object must be represented by some combination of the operations, attributes, and associations.
- All messages directed toward an object must be accepted and result in a defined action.

▼ Events handled by a class's state model must have corresponding acceptor operations.

▼ Messages shown in scenarios must have corresponding acceptor operations.

▼ Get and set operations provide access to object attributes when appropriate.

- Actions and activities identified on statecharts must result in operations defined on the classes providing those actions.

- Operations should check their preconditional invariants.

Just as with strategies for identifying objects, classes, and relationships, these strategies may be mixed freely to meet the specific requirements of a system.

By providing the complete elemental operations on the class, clients can combine these to provide all nonprimitive complex behaviors of which the class is capable. Consider a Set class, which provides set operations. The class in Code Listing 7-12 maintains a set of integers. In actual implementation, a template would most likely be used, but the use of the template syntax obscures the purpose of the class so it won't be used here.

```
class Set {
    int size;
    SetElement *bag;
    class SetElement {
    public:
        int Element;
        SetElement *NextPtr;
        SetElement(): NextPtr(NULL); {};
        SetElement(int initial): Element(initial),
NextPtr(NULL) { };
    };
public:
    Set(): size(0), bag(NULL) { };
    Set union(set a);
    Set intersection(set a);
    void clear(void);
    void operator +(int x); // insert into set
    void operator -(int x); // remove from set
    int numElements(void);
    bool operator ==(set a);
```

```
    bool operator !=(set a);
    bool inSet(int x); // test for membership
    bool inSet(Set a); // test for subsethood
};
```

Code Listing 7-12: *Set Class*

This simple class provides a set type and all the common set operations. Elements can be inserted or removed. Sets can be compared for equality, inequality, and whether they are subsets of other sets. Set unions and intersections can be computed.

Often a series of operations must be performed in a specific order to get the correct result. Such a required sequence is part of the protocol for the correct use of that object. Whenever possible, the operations should be structured to reduce the amount of information the clients of an object must have in order to use the object properly. These protocol-enforcing operations are clearly not primitive, but they help ensure the correct use of an object.

A sensor that must first be zeroed before being used is a simple example. The sensor class can simply provide the primitive operations doZero() and get(), or it can provide an acquire() operation that combines them, as shown in Code Listing 7-13.

```
class Sensor {
    void doZero();
    int get();
public:
    int acquire(void) {
        doZero();
        return get();
    };
};
```

Code Listing 7-13: *Sensor Class*

The acquire() operation enforces the protocol of zeroing the sensor before reading the value. Not only does this enforce the preconditions of the get() operation, but it also simplifies the use of the class. Since the doZero() and get() operations are always invoked in succession, combining them into a single operation creates a common-use nonprimitive.

Polymorphic operations are operations of the same name that perform different actions. Depending on the implementation language, polymorphism may be static, dynamic, or both. Static polymorphism is resolved at compile time and requires that the compiler have enough context to unambiguously determine which operation is intended. Dynamic polymorphism occurs when the binding of the executable code to the operator invocation is done as the program executes. Both static and dynamic polymorphism are resolved on the basis of the type and number of parameters passed to the operation.[12] Ada 83 operator overloading is purely static. C++ polymorphism may be either static or dynamic. Smalltalk polymorphism is always dynamic.

7.5 Looking Ahead

We have now seen both parts of analysis. Chapter 6 covered identifying the object structure of a system, finding the classes of those objects, and linking them with relationships and associations. This chapter covered the dynamic aspects of objects—the definition of behavior, with special attention given to state-driven objects, and the operations necessary to implement those behaviors.

The task of analysis is to find the object structure required of all acceptable solutions to the problem. Put another way, analysis finds the essential objects, classes, and relationships inherent in the system under study. Analysis defines the *what* of the system. The next process step, design, will add the *how*. We have deferred many questions about implementation strategies and structures, such as the number of tasks running, how messages will be implemented, and the internal design of the objects themselves. Let's continue with the large-scale architectural design in Chapter 8.

---

[12] C++ class operations have an invisible *this* pointer in their parameter lists. Thus, even an operation with otherwise identical parameter list can be polymorphic if a subclass redefines the operation, since the *this* pointer is a pointer to a different type.

7.6 Exercises

1. What are the three fundamental kinds of behavior and how do they differ?

2. What is meant by the term *token flow semantics*?

3. Define the terms *state, transition,* and *action.*

4. What is a guard? Where is it found in a statechart? What are its special semantics?

5. What modifications would be required to the Calculator model in this chapter to add ^ as an exponentiation operator, as it 2^7?

6. In what way do sequence diagrams assist as a debugging tool when a system is specified with state machines?

7. Create a sequence diagram that explores the behavior of the CardioNada pacemaker in AVI (dual) operational mode.

8. Discuss the pros and cons of using model-based debugging and testing versus code-based debugging and testing.

9. What is the difference between an operation and a method?

10. What are Booch's five kinds of operations?

11. What is the advantage of an iterator?

7.7 References

[1] Harel, David. "Statecharts: a Visual Formalism for Complex Systems." *Science of Computer Programming* 8 (1987): 231–274.

[2] Booch, Grady. *Object-Oriented Analysis and Design with Applications.* 2nd ed. Redwood City, CA: Benjamin/Cummings, 1994.

[3] Douglass, Bruce Powel. *Doing Hard Time: Developing Real-Time Systems with UML, Objects, Frameworks, and Patterns.* Reading, MA: Addison-Wesley, 1999.

[4] Klein, Mark, Thomas Ralya, Bill Pollak, Ray Obenza, and Michael Gonzalez Harbour. *A Practitioner's Handbook for Real-Time Analysis: Guide to Rate Monotonic Analysis for Real-Time Systems.* Boston: Kluwer Academic Publishers, 1993.

Chapter 8

Architectural Design

The last three chapters have dealt with analysis of the system. Chapter 5 looked at ways of capturing requirements using context diagrams and use cases. Chapters 6 and 7 presented approaches for identifying and characterizing classes and objects inherent in the problem. Analysis looks at key concepts and structures in the system that are independent of how the solution is implemented.

Now we're ready for design. Design specifies a particular solution that is based on the analysis model in a way that optimizes the system. The ROPES process divides design into three categories according to the scope of decisions made: architectural, mechanistic, and detailed. This chapter discusses the first: architectural design.

Architectural design identifies the key strategies for the large-scale organization of the system under development. The ROPES process identifies five important views of architecture: subsystem and component, concurrency and resource, distribution, safety and reliability, and deployment. This chapter presents the features available in the UML for architectural design and shows how they can be applied to real-time systems.

Notation and Concepts Discussed

Design Phases	Component	Component Diagram
Architectural Design	Multiprocessor Systems	Task Diagram
Active Object	Deployment Diagram	
Node		

8.1 Overview of Design

By now you should have a good grasp of the process and products of analysis. Analysis identifies the criteria of acceptance of any solution. The first part of analysis studies system-environment interaction and explores and captures this interaction with context and use case diagrams. The second part of analysis drills down inside the system to identify the fundamental concepts that must be represented in the system's structure and dynamics. These concepts are captured as classes and objects.

Design is the process of specifying a specific solution that is consistent with the analysis model. Design is all about *optimization* and therefore is driven by the set of required quality of service properties of the system, such as reusability, timeliness, schedulability, throughput, memory usage, safety, reliability, and so on. The ROPES process divides design into three categories—architectural, mechanistic, and detailed design—as shown in Figure 8-1. *Architectural design* details the largest software structures, such as subsystems, packages, and tasks. The *mechanistic design* includes classes working together to achieve common goals. *Detailed design* specifies the internal primitive data structures and algorithms within individual classes. The three categories are described in greater detail in Table 8-1.

For simple systems, most of the design effort may be spent in the mechanistic and detailed levels. For larger systems, including avionics and other distributed real-time systems, the architectural level is crucial to project success. This chapter focuses on architectural design.

The design process can be either *translative* or *elaborative*. Translative design takes the analysis model and, using a translator, produces an

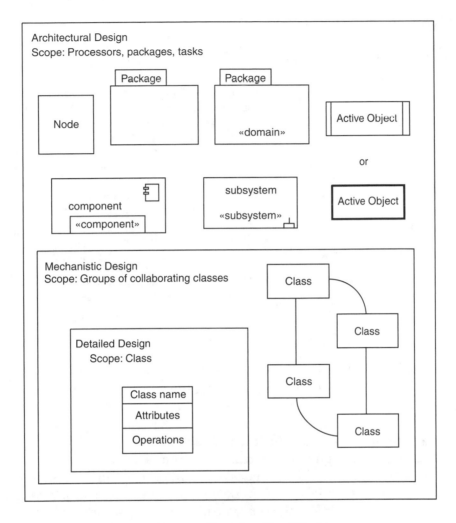

Figure 8-1: *Three Levels of Design*

executable system more or less autonomously. Great care must be put into the design of the translator, which is often highly customized for a particular problem domain and business environment. Translation is the focus of the model-driven architecture (MDA) and query/view/translate (QVT) initiatives within the OMG. As with any approach, there are benefits and detriments to translation. On the one hand, these approaches separate the realization details from the logical aspects, facilitating the portability

Table 8-1: *Phases of Design*

Design Phase	Scope	What Is Specified
Architectural	System-wide Processor-wide	• Subsystems and components • Concurrency and resource management • Distribution across multiple address spaces • Safety and reliability management • Deployment of software onto hardware elements
Mechanistic	Collaboration-wide	• Instances of design patterns of multiple objects collaborating together • Containers and design-level classes and objects • Medium-level error handling policies
Detailed	Intra-object	• Algorithmic detail within an object • Details of data members (types, ranges, structure) • Details of function members (arguments, internal structure)

and reuse of the intellectual property held in the models. On the other hand, the applications may have lowered performance and increased complexity. Nonetheless, the MDA approach is popular, particularly for designs that are expected to have a long lifetime.

Elaborative design adds increasing amounts of design detail until the system is fully specified. This is done either by adding detail to the analysis model, maintaining a single model of the system of increasing detail, or by maintaining two separate models. Each approach has pros and cons. Maintaining a single model is less work and less error prone than maintaining two models, but the design information "pollutes" the analysis model. On the other hand, maintaining two models by hand is error-prone but has the advantage of separation of concerns.

In practice, I recommend a combination of elaborative and translative design. Certain aspects are easy to add via translation (such as target source language and OS targeting), while others, such as the application of architectural design patterns, as most easily applied via elaboration. The UML is process-independent and applies equally to whatever design is selected.

8.2 What Is Architectural Design?

The analysis model identifies objects, classes, and relationships but does not specify how they are organized into large-scale structures. As shown in Table 8-1, architectural design is concerned with large-scale design decisions involving collaborations of packages, tasks, or processors.

The ROPES process defines two fundamental kinds of architecture—logical and physical.[1] *Logical architecture* refers to the organization of things that exist only at design time—that is, the organization of classes and data types. Logical architecture is concerned with how models are themselves organized; this organization can be simple or very complex, depending on the needs and structure of the team(s) using it. The logical architecture is unrelated to the organization of the system at runtime, although one logical architecture pattern is to mirror the physical architectural structure. Figure 8-2 shows the roles of logical and physical architectures.

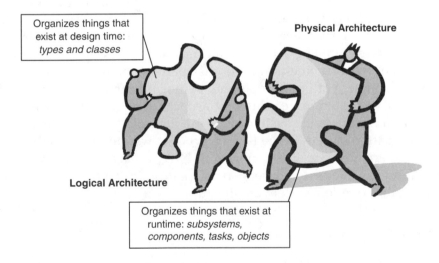

Organizes things that exist at design time: *types and classes*

Physical Architecture

Logical Architecture

Organizes things that exist at runtime: *subsystems, components, tasks, objects*

Figure 8-2: *Logical and Physical Architecture*

---

[1] Some authors use the terms *logical* and *physical* differently; in some methodologists' views, a logical model is one devoid of physical constraints (e.g., memory or speed) and a physical model is one with such constraints added. I find this unsatisfying because until the system is completely specified, the models are almost always partially logical and partially physical so that this distinction becomes more a shade of gray than a true dichotomy.

The primary place that architectural design work is done is, naturally enough, the architectural design part of the design phase. Here, strategic design decisions are made in each of the five views (or four views, if the subsystem architecture is already defined in the systems engineering part). These views will be detailed in the next section.

For the most part, architecture is done through the application of architectural design patterns. A *design pattern* is a generalized solution to a commonly occurring problem. Design patterns have three primary parts: a problem to be solved, the solution (the pattern), and a set of consequences. With architectural design patterns, the problem to be solved is always based in optimizing some small set of system QoS properties at the expense of others. Certain patterns optimize safety but by increasing recurring cost or complexity. Other patterns enhance reusability but at the expense of average execution time. Still others optimize predictability of execution time at the expense of optimal worst-case execution time (see [9] for many different architectural patterns for real-time systems).

Patterns can be mixed and matched as necessary, although clearly some mixes won't make any sense. It is common, for example, to mix a pattern for primary subsystem organization with another pattern for allowing distributed objects to communication and another pattern for concurrency management and another pattern for fault management and still another pattern for mapping to the underlying hardware. This gives rise to the notion of different aspects of architecture. The complete architecture of the system is the melding together of all the architectural patterns used. In the ROPES process, we identify five different views of architecture. It is common to have at least one pattern from each (and in some cases, more than one pattern in each) mixed together to form the complete system architecture.

8.2.1 Logical Architecture

There are many ways to organize a design model. The ROPES process recommends a logical architecture based on the concept of *domains*. A domain is an independent subject area that generally has its own vocabulary. Domains provide a means by which your model can be organized; or partitioned into its various subjects, such as User Interface, Hardware, Alarm Management, Communications, Operating

System, Data Management, Medical Diagnostics, Guidance and Navigation, Avionics, Image Reconstruction, Task Planning, and so on.

This way, a domain is just a UML package used in a particular way. UML packages contain model elements, but, other than providing a namespace, packages have no semantics and are not instantiable.[2] The UML does not provide a criterion for what should go in one package versus another, but domains do. For this reason, we represent domain as a «domain» stereotyped package that includes a mission, specifically "hold classes and types around the common subject matter." The use of domains does not dictate how objects will be organized and deployed at runtime however; that is what the physical architecture is all about.

Figure 8-3 shows a typical domain diagram—a package diagram that shows the relations of the domains themselves and the classes within the domains. In the figure, we see that the Alarm domain contains classes around the concept of alarm management—a couple of types of alarms, an alarm manager, and an alarm filter policy class. The alarms must be displayed in a list, so the Alarm Manager associates with a Text List class that is a user interface element and so is found in the User Interface domain. Alarms themselves are displayed as text, so the Alarm class (in the Alarm domain) associates with the Text class in the User Interface domain. Alarms must also be annunciated, so the Alarm Manager associates with the Speaker class in the Hardware domain. Also, the user needs to be able to acknowledge and silence the alarm and so the Alarm Manager associates with a Button class from the Hardware domain.

Physical architecture is concerned with the organization of things that exist at runtime. Although packages (and therefore domains) don't exist at runtime (being solely design-time concepts), they provide a place for the definition of the classes that will be used via instantiation in the various subsystems.

Domain structure usually does not completely reflect the physical architecture. For example, the physical architecture may have the notion of a Power Subsystem, which is constructed from instances of the classes defined in various domains. For example, the Power Subsystem may contain instances of many classes from a number of different domains, as shown in Figure 8-4. Using the standard name-scoping operator (::),

---

[2] Meaning that you cannot create an instance of a package at runtime. Packages are a purely design-time organizational concept.

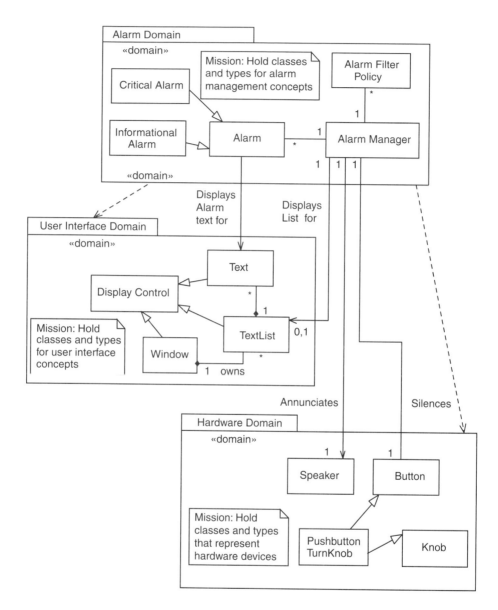

Figure 8-3: *Logical Domain Architecture*

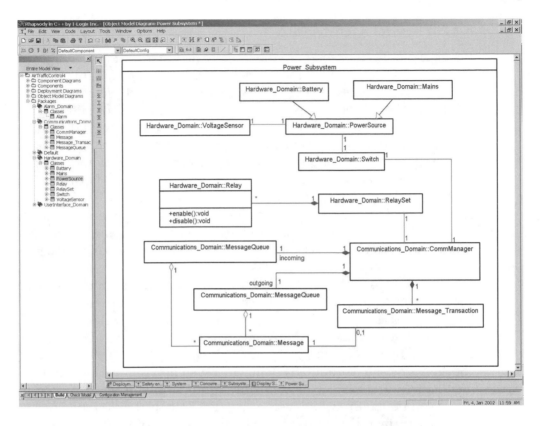

Figure 8-4: *Relating Logical and Physical Architecture*

the name of the domain package precedes the name of the class. So, for example, Hardware_Domain::Switch is the class Switch in the Hardware_Domain package, while Communications_Domain:: Message_Transaction is the Message_Transaction class in the Communications_Domain package.[3]

That being said, often there may be specialized domains containing classes only instantiated in one subsystem. For example, classes from a Guidance and Navigation domain will be likely instantiated solely in a Navigation subsystem. Most domains are more general than that, however, and are represented in many, if not all, subsystems.

---

[3] We could also have nested the package inside the subsystem as a notational alternative.

8.2.2 Physical Architecture

Physical architecture refers to the large-scale organization elements of the system at runtime, so these elements must be instantiable things. The typical elements are subsystems, components, and «active» objects, but other specialized forms, such as a channel (a kind of subsystem) may be used. These large-scale organizational elements don't do much, in and of themselves, but they organize the more primitive instances that do the real work and provide management oversight and delegation of requests and messages to the appropriate objects. They allow us to view and understand the system at different levels of abstraction. This is crucial for the construction and understanding of large complex systems. We need to look at assemblies of parts and refer to them as a single, albeit more abstract, element. Figure 8-5 shows a common set of abstraction levels.

The most abstract level in the figure is the complete system (Level 0), such as "Mars Sample Return Mission." The next level down is the systems engineering level (Level 1), where subsystems are defined and their interfaces specified. In the Mars project example, subsystems might be "Deep Space Network," "Launch Vehicle," "Orbiter," "Lander," "Spacecraft," and "Ground System." In a systems engineering environment, these are not yet broken down into software and hardware. There can be multiple sublevels at this level of abstraction, before the system is further decomposed into hardware and software aspects. For example, the "Spacecraft" could be decomposed into (sub)subsystems such as "Guidance and Navigation," "Avionics," "Attitude Control," "Communications," and "Power Management."

Next, we've decomposed the system into the engineering disciplines (Level 2): electronic, mechanical, chemical, and software. If a system uses commercial, off-the-shelf (COTS) hardware, then this step may be skipped, but if you are developing custom hardware it may be very important. Notice that hardware/software decomposition is done primarily at the subsystem level rather than at the system level. For example, a jet's attitude control subsystem can be thought of as being composed of electronic aspects (processors, relays, motors, valve controls, a variety of sensors and serial connections), mechanical parts (reaction wheels, thruster assemblies, fuel lines and mixers, and enclosures), chemicals (fuel mixture and oxygen), and, of course, software

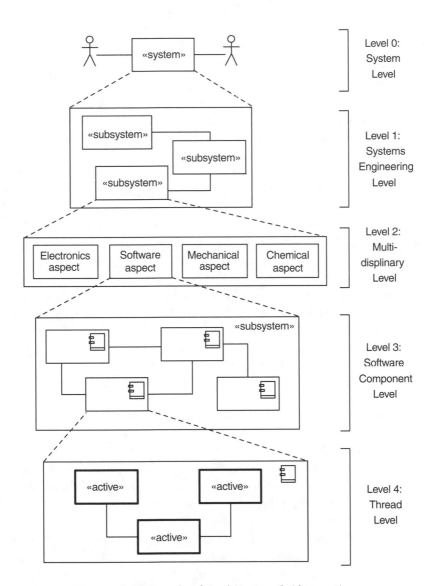

Figure 8-5: *Levels of Architectural Abstraction*

(the "smarts" to receive and interpret commands, control electronic parts that control mechanical parts that work with chemicals).

The software for the subsystem may then be decomposed into its major architectural units, components, or software subsystems (Level 3).

These are the major replaceable pieces of software that comprise the subsystem. For example, the components for the attitude control subsystem might include a TCP/IP communications protocol stack, math library, PID control loops for reaction wheels and thrusters, fuel management component, reaction wheel control component, and so on.

Lastly, we see the thread level (Level 4). This is the level at which concurrency is managed. Some components may be passive in the sense that they execute in the thread of the caller. However, there will be at least one component (or software subsystem) that creates and executes at least one thread. These threads will be owned by design-level «active» objects that also aggregate, via composition, the so-called primitive objects that ultimately perform application services. Here, if desired, the different kinds of concurrency units (processes, threads, fibers, and so on) may be specified, if that level of detail is required.

The last level is the object level (not shown). These are the primitive objects that do the real work of the system. In any particular system, there may be either a greater or fewer number of these abstraction levels depending on the complexity and scale of the system. For a cardiac pacemaker, you might represent only the system level and the thread level of architecture, while in our Mars project example, you might ultimately have as many as 8 or 10 levels. Not all of these levels need to be visible to all developers, of course.

The physical architecture may be constructed from virtually any model organization and so is thought of as distinct from the organization of the model per se, although it is possible to organize your model around the physical architecture. The high-level physical architecture is usually constructed in with systems engineering phase of the ROPES spiral but may be deferred to the architectural design phase if the systems engineering phase is omitted.

The ROPES process identifies the five views of (physical) architecture. These focus on more-or-less independent aspects of the large-scale runtime structure of the system. Of course, ultimately there is only one system. Limiting our perspective of the system to a single aspect allows us to focus on that aspect. The term view, used in this way, refers to showing a subset of the system model to allow a keener examination of some particular aspect.

These aspects are not completely independent and in a well-formed model certainly should not conflict with one another. The best way to

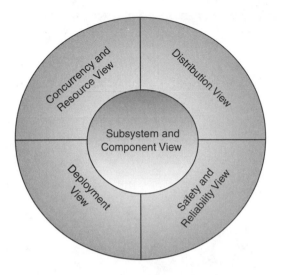

Figure 8-6: *The Five Views of Architecture*

think about this is to understand that there is a single model underlying the system that includes the architecture. The views just look at parts of the single model that are related to each other in specific ways. So these are not independent aspects, but a filtered view that only shows certain aspects at a time.

The five views of architecture defined in the ROPES process are shown in Figure 8-6.

These views of architecture capture structure aspects and so are typically described with UML structural diagrams. A concurrency task diagram, for example, is nothing more than a class diagram showing the structural elements related to the concurrency view—things like «active» objects, message queues, semaphores, and the like. When architectural behavior is being described, it is usually the interaction of the architectural elements that is of primary concern, so primarily sequence diagrams are used. To show the behavior of the architectural element in isolation, the functionality is usually divided up into use cases for the element and then each of these may be detailed with a statechart or activity chart.

Figure 8-7 shows a system view for an air traffic control system, using Rhapsody.

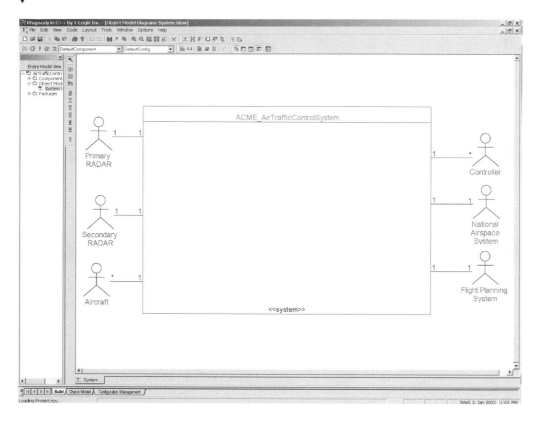

Figure 8-7: *System View*

We see in Figure 8-7 the System object ACME_AirTrafficControlSystem and its environmental context. This consists of the actors[4] with which the system interacts.

8.2.3 Subsystem and Component View

The subsystem and component view (or subsystem view for short) identifies the large-scale pieces of the system and how they fit together. As previously mentioned, this is usually created during the systems engineering phase, but it may also be done later in the architectural design phase for projects not using a systems engineering phase. Sub-

---

[4] An actor is an object outside the scope of the system that has interactions of interest with the system as the system executes.

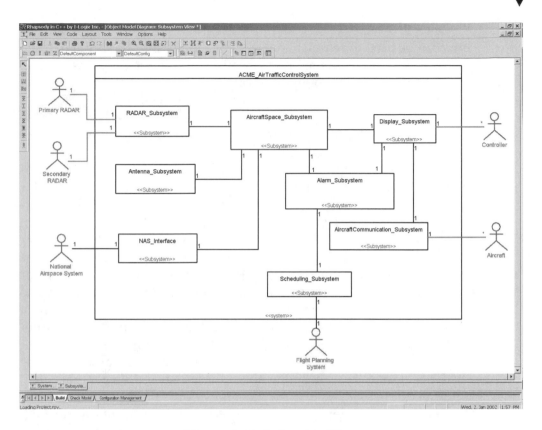

Figure 8-8: *Subsystem View*

system architecture is captured using a subsystem diagram, which is really a class diagram that shows primarily the subsystems and their relations.

In a software-only development in which we are not concerned about the underlying hardware (or at least not very concerned), a subsystem is a runtime organization of software. It is a large-scale object that contains, via composition, part objects that do the real work of the subsystem. The criteria for inclusion in the subsystem is common behavioral purpose, that is, the objects included in the subsystem are there because they contribute to the subsystem's use case realization. Software subsystems give us a way to think about systems at different levels of decomposition rather than just as a flat sea of relatively undifferentiated objects.

The subsystem concept can be used in a couple of ways. Subsystems can be used to reason about systems before they are broken down into hardware and software parts, as discussed in the previous section. You may also use subsystems as a software-only concept. In either case, a subsystem is a really big object that provides well-defined interfaces and delegate service requests to internal hidden parts. How you use these UML building blocks is up to you. UML provides a vocabulary but it's up to you to write the story.

If you use a component-based development approach, the components are also architectural elements. The UML has a different icon for components, although UML 1.x is not prescriptive about the differences between a component and a subsystem. In the UML, a subsystem is basically a big object that contains part objects that do the real work of the subsystem. A component, on the other hand, is a replaceable part of the system. Typically, components use a component framework for loading and unloading components, component identification, and so on. In the UML 2.0, a component is a kind of structured classifier, and a subsystem is a kind of component. This doesn't address how components and subsystems should be used. Is a component bigger or smaller than a subsystem? How should they be mixed and matched? The UML does not say anything about these issues. As a general rule, I recommend that subsystems be the largest-scale parts of a system and that these may be internally decomposed into components, as desired.

The UML component diagram is just another structural diagram, one that emphasizes the component aspects of the system. An example of a component diagram is given in Figure 8-9, which shows the components for the Display_Subsystem of the ACME_AirTrafficControl System.

There are patterns that can help you effectively use these elements to architecturally structure your system. [9] provides a number of the ones that have particular relevance to real-time and embedded systems.

8.2.4 Concurrency and Resource View

The concurrency and resource view of the system architecture focuses on the management of resources and the concurrent aspects of system execution. Because of the importance of this aspect, it is the subject of several chapters in [9].

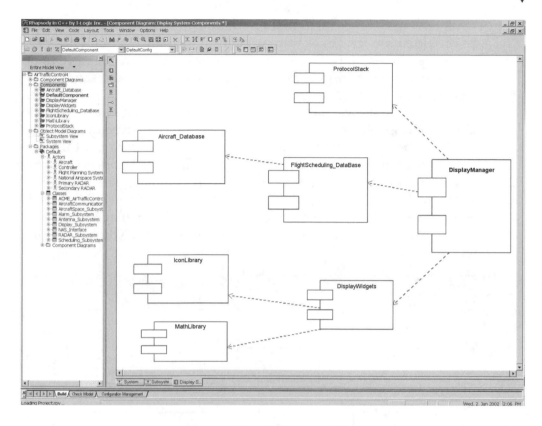

Figure 8-9: *Component View*

By *concurrent,* we mean that objects may execute in parallel rather than sequentially. We are stating that we neither know nor care about the relative order of execution of actions between the threads[5] except where specifically mentioned. These points of synchronization are often called *rendezvous* and are the hard parts of concurrency modeling. Sharing data and information is a common reason for threads to rendezvous and synchronize. Another is the need to control and coordinate asynchronously executing system elements.

---

[5] In this book *thread* and *task* are treated identically. There are some detailed design differences, but both are units of concurrency and may be treated the same at the architectural level. If, in your design, that distinction becomes important, you can make it clear by using appropriate stereotypes, such as «process», «thread», «task», or «fiber».

A *resource* is an element that has a finite and quantifiable aspect to its provided service. For example, it may allow only one actor at a time access its internal data. Since the hard parts of concurrency have to do with the sharing of resources, resources are treated in the same architectural view as concurrency.

Figure 8-10 shows a task diagram for the Alarm_Subsystem done in UML—a class diagram that emphasizes the task structure. All the «active» objects are shown with a heavy border (standard UML). Additionally, they may have «task» stereotype. Some of the classes show the stereotype as text while others use an icon. Similarly, the figure contains two «resource» objects—AlarmList and ListView. The first is associated with a semaphore (shown to its left) that manages the serialization of requests. The second is managed by its owning thread, Alarm_

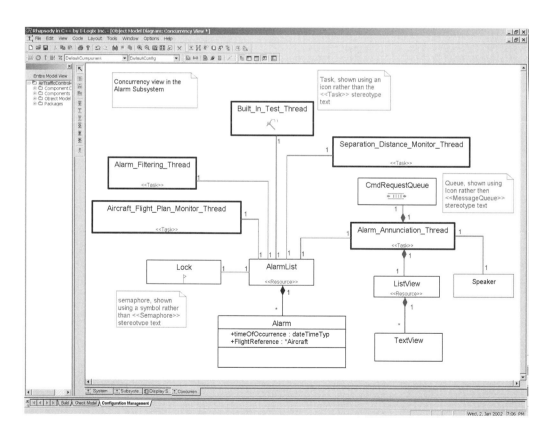

Figure 8-10: *Concurrency and Resource View*

Annunciation_Thread, which, incidentally, has a «MessageQueue» object to manage information sharing.

«Active» objects are the primary means for modeling concurrency in the UML. An «active» object owns the root of a thread and manages the execution of the thread and delegation of messages from the thread message queue to the appropriate objects.

There are a number of common strategies for identifying threads that will be later reified as «active» objects:

- Single event groups
- Event source
- Related information
- Interface device
- Recurrence properties
- Target object
- Safety level

The single event groups strategy creates a separate thread for every event, and that event pends on its occurrence. This strategy is useful for simple systems but doesn't scale up to large complex systems well.

The event source strategy creates a thread for each source of an event and pends on any event from that source. It is useful when you have a small number of event sources and relatively simple designs.

The related information strategy creates a thread that manages all data within a topic or subject matter, such as all information related to cardiac health. In an anesthesia machine, this information might include pulse rate (from a blood pressure monitor), heart rate (from an ECG monitor), preventricular contraction count, cardiac output, stroke volume, temperature of the blood coming from the superior vena cava and emptying in the right atrium, and so on. This information comes from a variety of sources and a single thread could manage it. This strategy is effective for sensor fusion applications that require significant processing of data from disparate sources. Further, this strategy tends to reduce the number of thread rendezvous, which can be a source of significant overhead.

The interface device strategy is a specialized form of event source strategy that is used for systems with multiple data and command buses. One or more threads are spawned to manage the bus traffic and related processing.

The recurrent properties strategy is a demonstrably optimal strategy for thread selection when schedulability of the threads is an important concern. The recurrence properties include whether or not the event set processed by the thread is periodic (time-based) or aperiodic (event-based). Periodic tasks execute and do work every so often with a defined frequency of execution. It is common to have several periodic tasks, each handling events that occur in a common time frame, such as one for the 10 ms-based events, one for the 100 ms-based events, and another for the 250 ms-based events. Aperiodic events can either be handled by a general aperiodic event handler, or you can introduce a separate thread for each aperiodic event (as in the single event group strategy). Most systems must process a combination of periodic and aperiodic events.

The target object strategy creates a thread for a few special objects that are the target of events from disparate sources. For example, database or data manager objects sometimes have threads assigned to them so they can do appropriate processing when processing cycles are available.

The safety level strategy creates threads for managing safety and reliability functionality, such as the execution of periodic built-in tests (BITs), stroking watchdogs, monitoring actuation to ensure that it is proceeding correctly, and so on.

No matter how you come up with the set of threads you decide you want to use, the common development approach is to first construct the *collaborations*—sets of objects working together to realize a use case—then identify the set of threads and create an «active» object for each thread. Each primitive object from the collaboration is aggregated via composition by the appropriate «active» object allowing it to execute in the appropriate thread.

8.2.5 Distribution View

The distribution view deals with how objects find and collaborate with each other even though they may be in different address spaces. The distribution view includes policies for how the objects communicate, including the selection and use of communication protocols. In *asymmetric distribution architectures*, an object is dedicated to a particular address space at design time. This makes finding that object simple during runtime because the other objects can be granted a priori knowledge about how to locate and contact the object in question. In *symmetric distribution architectures*, the location of an object isn't decided until runtime. Symmetric architectures are useful for a complex system that must dynamically balance processing load over multiple processors. When objects become ready to run, the distributed OS runs the object in an optimal locale, based on the current loadings on the various processors. This improves overall performance but at a cost—increased complexity. How, for example, can objects find each other during runtime? This is the subject of the distribution patterns in [9].

The broker architecture in Figure 8-11 is used to mediate communication among distributed objects. In this case, the objects are to participate in a possibly distributed communications subclass of the Communicating Object class. We see that this class has the stereotype «CORBAInterface». Rhapsody produces the CORBA interface descrip-

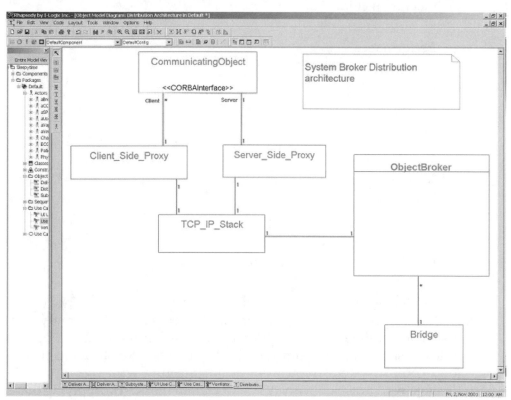

Figure 8-11: *Distribution View*

tion language (IDL) automatically for you; for other tools, you will probably have to write the IDL manually. The IDL generates code that produces the Client_Side_Proxy and Server_Side_Proxy classes. These encapsulate information on how to serialize the data and contact the broker. The Broker object is typically purchased from an object request broker (ORB) vendor and provides connection and naming (and a whole host of other) distribution services. The Bridge object allows ORBs to communicate across multiple networks. In a sufficiently capable tool, you will only have to write the classes you want to communicate and specify that they have the «CORBAInterface» interface, and the tool will generate all the rest of the code for the distribution. In less capable tools, each of these classes will need to be generated by hand.

Selecting a distribution architecture is highly driven by the QoS of the collaboration. The most relevant QoS to drive the distribution architecture include

- Performance
  - ▾ Worst case
  - ▾ Average case
  - ▾ Predictability
- Throughput
  - ▾ Average
  - ▾ Burst
- Reliability
  - ▾ Of message delivery
  - ▾ Of message integrity
- Recurring (e.g., hardware) cost

Of course, in real-time and embedded systems performance can be crucial to success. In hard real-time and safety-critical systems, worst-case delivery time is the most important. For example, control loops are notoriously sensitive to time delays. To implement distributed closed-loop control systems, you want an architecture with short and predictable worst-case delivery times for certain messages, implying that a priority-based message delivery scheme might be the most appropriate. In such a case, using an asymmetric architecture (or some variant of the observer pattern) with a predictable priority-based transport protocol might fit the system performance needs—for example, an asymmetric distribution on top of a bit-dominance protocol, such as the CAN bus protocol. Ethernet is a common, but less-than-optimal choice in such cases, as it is based on a Collision-Detect Multiple Access (CDMA) protocol, meaning that while the bus is multimastered, collisions (multiple sources attempting to transmit at the same time) can occur. When they occur with the Ethernet protocol, the senders stop trying to transmit and retry later at random times. This means that Ethernet networks saturate at about 30% utilization. Above that point, Ethernet spends an inordinate amount of time resolving transmission collisions and little time actually sending information. Ethernet can be used for hard real-time distribution when very lightly loaded (meaning that collisions are rare) or when the message delivery time is a small part of the overall execution budget.

In so-called soft real-time systems, the average performance is a more important criterion that worst-case performance. Average performance may be measured in terms of average length of time for message delivery or in "mean-lateness" of the messages. Such systems usually don't care if a small set of the messages is late when the system is under load, as long as the average response is sufficient. It may even, in some case, be permissible to drop some messages altogether when the system is under stress. For example, a broker pattern with a CDMA transport protocol such as UDP transport protocol on top of an Ethernet network protocol will serve this purpose well if the average load is low. For systems in which peak loads are few and far between, and individual message delivery times are not crucial, CDMA can be a good choice. Interestingly, many systems are built on TCP/IP even when it is a demonstrably poor choice given the quality of service requirements for the system.

Time Division Multiple Access (TDMA) protocols work by dividing up available communication time among the devices on the bus. Each device gets to transmit for a certain period of time and then passes along a master token to the next device on the bus. TDMA protocols have low communication arbitration overhead but don't scale up to large numbers of devices well. Further, like a round robin approach to task scheduling, such a system is not responsive in an event-driven application because an event requiring transmission must wait until the owning device has the master token.

Priority-based protocols typically have more overhead on a per-message basis, but allow higher-priority messages through first at the expense of lower-priority messages, making it a natural fit for systems in which scheduling is primarily priority-driven. Bit-dominance protocols are a common way to achieve priority-based messaging. In a bit-dominance protocol, each sender listens to what appears on the bus while it's transmitting; low-priority bits are the passive state of the bus and high-priority bits are the active state. If a higher-priority bit occurs in the bus when it sent out a lower-priority bit, then it assumes that it is in conflict with a device trying to send out a higher-priority message, and it drops out to retry later. The device sending out the higher-priority message wins and keeps transmitting. For example, this is how the CAN bus protocol works. Each message contains a priority sequence called a *message identifier*, followed by the message contents. If each message has a unique identifier, then it has a unique position in the priority scheme.

An issue with the CAN bus protocol is that it allows only 8 bytes of data per message, requiring larger messages to be fragmented into multiple bus messages during transmission and reassembled at the receiver end. The SCSI bus is another example of a priority-based transmission protocol, but the SCSI bus is also a parallel bus meaning that it can achieve greater bandwidth. Complicating its use as a general message passing bus, however, is the fact that the priority is not based on the message but on the device transmitting the message.

Reliability for distribution means the reliability of correct message delivery. There are many reasons why messages might not be properly delivered, such as attenuation due to distance, interference with electrical noise, temporary or permanent failure of the media or associated device, and software or hardware design flaws. These things may be handled by adding complexity into the communications protocol to check the integrity of messages and to retry transmission if the message is either corrupted or not delivered. Of course, redundant buses are a solution as well, with the advantage of improved reliable and timeliness in the presence of errors, but at a higher recurring cost.[6]

Software solutions for message integrity usually require the addition of some level of redundancy, such as a parity bit (very light-

---

[6] Recurring cost is the cost per shipped item.

weight), checksum (lightweight), or cyclic redundancy check (CRC). Of these, the best is CRC because it will identify all single and dual bit errors as well as a very high percentage of multiple-bit errors. CRCs are somewhat more complex to compute than a checksum, but a table-driven CRC computation can be very fast and hardware chips are available that can compute a CRC from a serial bit stream.

Another approach is the use of Hamming codes. Hamming codes are codes that are differentiated by what is called a Hamming distance—the minimum number of bit errors necessary to come up with an incorrect, but valid code. For example, in an 8-bit byte, the codes in Table 8-2 have a Hamming distance of 2 because they require two bits to be modified before you can come up with another valid code.

The use of Hamming codes provides some protection against bit errors because it requires multiple bit errors to construct another valid possibility.

It is even possible to send the message multiple times (usually twice, if error detection is required, and thrice if error correction is needed). If the message data is sent twice, then the second copy can be sent as a ones-complement of the original so that stuck-at bit errors can be detected.

8.2.6 Safety and Reliability View

The safety and reliability view examines how system redundancy is defined and managed, in order to raise system reliability and safety. The safety and reliability architecture is concerned with correct functioning in the presence of faults and errors. Redundancy may be used in many ways to get different degrees and types of safety and reliability.

Table 8-2: *Hamming Codes*

Binary	Decimal	Hexadecimal
00000000	0	0H
00000011	3	3H
00010100	20	14
10001000	136	88

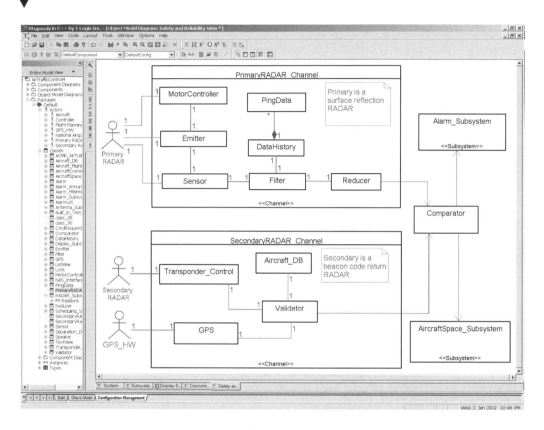

Figure 8-12: *Safety and Reliability View*

In Figure 8-12, *heterogeneous redundancy* (also known as *diverse redundancy*) is used to provide protection from failures and errors. The Primary Radar channel processing surface reflection RADAR information produces three-dimensional position (in terms of direction, range, and azimuth) as well as velocity using the Doppler effect. The Secondary channel uses the beacon return codes to get a transponder code from the aircraft and the aircraft's position and velocity information.

Reliability is a measure of the up-time or availability of a system—specifically, it is the probability that a computation will successfully complete before the system fails. It is normally estimated with mean time between failure (MTBF). MTBF is a statistical estimate of the probability of failure and applies to stochastic failure modes.

Reducing the system downtime increases reliability by increasing the MTBF. Redundancy is one design approach that increases availability because if one component fails, another takes its place. Of course, redundancy only improves reliability when the failures of the redundant components are independent.[7] The reliability of a component does not depend on what happens after the component fails. Whether the system fails safely or not, the reliability of the system remains the same. Clearly the primary concern relative to the reliability of a system is the availability of its functions to the user.

Safety is distinct from reliability. A safe system is one that does not incur too much risk to persons or equipment. A *risk* is an event or condition that can occur but is undesirable. Risk is the product of the severity of the incident and its probability. The failure of a jet engine is unlikely, but the consequences can be very high. Thus the risk of flying in a plane is tolerable; even though it is unlikely that you would survive a crash from 30,000 feet, such an incident is an extremely rare occurrence. At the other end of the spectrum, there are events that are common, but are of lesser concern. There is a risk that you can get an electric shock from putting a 9-volt battery in a transistor radio. It could easily occur, but the consequences are small. Again, this is a tolerable risk.

The key to managing both safety and reliability is *redundancy.* For improving reliability, redundancy allows the system to continue to work in the presence of faults because other system elements can take up the work of the broken one. For improving safety, additional elements are needed to monitor the system to ensure that it is operating properly; other elements may be needed to either shut down the system in a safe way or take over the required functionality.

8.2.7 Deployment View

The deployment view focuses on how the software architecture maps onto the physical devices such as processors, disk drives, displays, and so on. The UML uses the concept of a *node* to represent physical devices. Nodes are often stereotyped to indicate the kind of hardware they represent. Some developers may only differentiate between processors

---

[7] Strict independence isn't required to achieve a beneficial effect. Weakly correlated failure modes still offer improved tolerance to faults over tightly correlated failure modes.

(devices that execute code that you write) and devices (ones that don't), while others prefer to identify more detail such as whether a device is a stepper motor, DC motor, thermometer, IR sensor, and so on.

Figure 8-13 is a typical UML deployment diagram. Most stereotypes are shown using icons, but text in guillemots (e.g., «Bus») can be used as easily; it is a matter of personal preference. This deployment diagram shows two «Bus» devices, several different processors, redundant flight recorder devices, and redundant display controllers. The diagram also indicates some of the components executing on selected processors.

The primary use for the deployment view is to represent asymmetric deployment architectures. Then the hardware platform can be schematically represented and the mapping of software subsystems

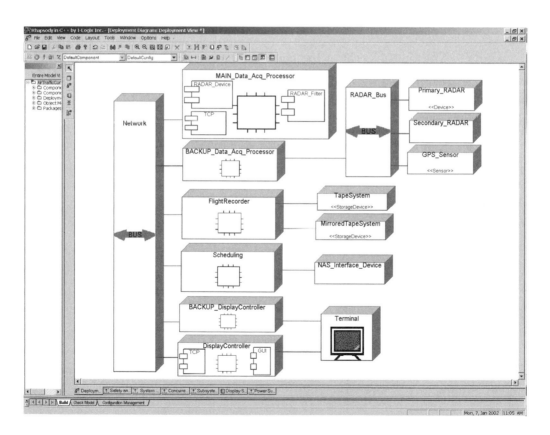

Figure 8-13: *Deployment View*

and components can be detailed. For asymmetric systems this is particularly important to understanding how the software on the different processors will collaborate and permits performance analysis. You can either nest the software components inside the system or use a dependency from the component or software subsystem to indicate that the node supports or executes that software element. Figure 8-13 shows a couple of nodes with components nested inside them. Any software element can be shown in this way, but showing components and subsystems this way makes the most sense.

For symmetric architectures, the deployment diagram is perhaps less interesting, but only marginally so. The underlying hardware is even then a mixture of symmetric and asymmetric aspects. The interesting part, the execution of software elements on the nodes, is in principle not known when the deployment diagram is drawn at design time. In some cases, a software element might even migrate from one node to another. The UML provides the «becomes» stereotype of the dependency relation to indicate that an element might move from one node to another, such as might happen in the event of a fault on the original processor.

8.2.8 Physical Architecture Issues

System architectural design is broader in scope than just software and involves the hardware architecture as well, including electronic and mechanical design. Naturally, hardware architecture has a great impact on the software architecture. Together, hardware and software architectures combine to form the *system architecture.* In most embedded systems, the system architecture is by necessity a collaborative effort among engineers from a wide variety of disciplines, including software, electronics, mechanics, safety, and reliability. The system design must ensure that all the pieces will ultimate fit together and achieve the system objectives in terms of functionality, performance, safety, reliability, and cost.

The software must ultimately map to the electronic, mechanical, and chemical aspects of the system. This mapping occurs primarily at the architectural and detailed levels of design. The detailed design level deals with the physical characteristics of the individual hardware components and ensures that low-level interface protocols are followed. The architectural level maps the large-scale software components such as subsystems, packages, and tasks onto the various processors and devices. Mechanistic design is insulated away from most aspects of physical architecture.

It is crucial to the success of the system that the electrical and software engineers collaborate on these decisions. If the electrical engineers don't understand the software needs, they are less able to adequately accommodate them. Similarly, if the software engineers don't have a sufficient understanding of the electronic design, their architectural decisions will be at best sub-optimal, and at worst unworkable. For this reason, both disciplines must be involved in device specification, particularly processors, memory maps, and communication buses. It is an unfortunate truth that many systems do not meet their functional or performance requirements when this collaboration is missing in the development process.

The software concerns for each processor are as follows:

- Envisioned purpose and scope of the software executing on the processor
- The computational horsepower of the processor
- Availability of development tools such as compilers for the selected language, debuggers, and in-circuit emulators
- Availability of third-party components, including operating systems, container libraries, communication protocols, and user interfaces
- Previous experience and internal knowledge with the processor

How the processors are linked together is another far-reaching set of electronic design decisions. Should the communication media be arranged in a bus or star topology? Should it be bus-mastered or master-slave? Should it arbitrate on the basis of priority or fairness? Point-to-point or multidrop? How fast must the transmission rate be? These are the requirements of just the physical communications media. The software must layer appropriate communications protocols on top of that to ensure timely and reliable message exchange.

Naturally, these electronic design decisions can have a tremendous impact on the software architecture. Smaller processors can be used if there are more of them and they are linked together appropriately, or a smaller number of larger processors can do the same work. If the bus mastering is not arbitrated in hardware, it becomes more difficult to implement a peer-to-peer communications protocol required for distributed processing. Only by working together can the electronic and software engineers find an optimal solution given the system constraints. The optimal solution itself is specific to both the application domain and the business goals and approaches.

8.2.9 Software Architecture Issues

Within the confines of the physical architecture, the software itself has large-scale structures. The UML defines a subsystem as a subordinate system within a larger system [1]. In the embedded world, it is useful to further constrain our use of the term to mean *an integrated set of software components residing on a single physical processor.*[8] These components will typically be packages that contain other packages, tasks, objects, and classes. Software architecture then becomes the process of designing subsystems, packages, and tasks and their interconnections.

UML 2.0, as discussed previously, has elaborated the concept of a subsystem to be a kind of structured class with internal parts, which may connect to other elements via ports. Ports and interfaces aren't required to use subsystems, but they do aid in the encapsulation of the subsystem internal structure and its isolation of the subsystem internals from the environment. Figure 8-14 shows an example that has ports with and without required and offered interfaces and associations between subsystems that are not mediated by ports.

Subsystems are often organized as a set of layered elements, each of which may itself be decomposed into smaller parts. Many complex systems have several layers ordered hierarchically from the most abstract (closest to the system problem domain) down to the most concrete (closest to the underlying hardware). For example,

- Application
- User interface
- Communication
- OS
- Hardware abstraction

---

[8] Many other people use the notion of subsystem to refer to a more loosely-associated set of objects that work to achieve a common set of use cases, even though they may appear within multiple processors. This is also a reasonable perspective.

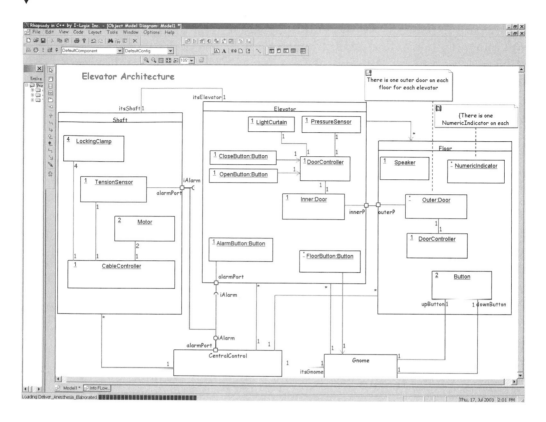

Figure 8-14: *Elevator Architecture*

The OSI seven-layer reference model is a common layered architecture for communications protocols, as shown in Figure 8-15. The lollipop at the left of each subsystem represents its *interface*, a set of classes and objects that may be externally accessed via its ports.[9]

In the layered architecture pattern [9], the basic organization is a set of client-server relationships among the layers. The more abstract layers are the clients that invoke the services of the more concrete layers. This one-way dependency makes it possible to use the same lower-level server layers in different contexts because they know nothing of their clients. Similarly, since the lower layers offer a well-defined set of interfaces, they can be replaced with different lower layers, making the entire subsystem easily portable to other physical environments.

---

[9] These are service access points (SAPs) in OSI nomenclature.

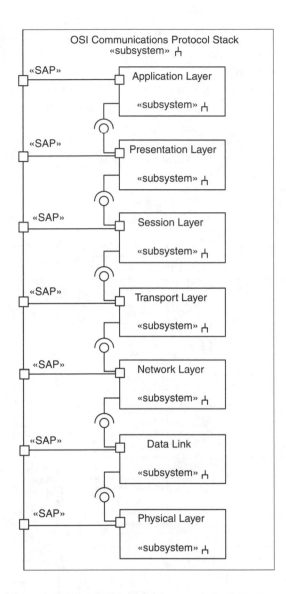

Figure 8-15: *OSI Model Layered Architecture*

A layered implementation strategy would build each layer independently and link them together as they are completed. However, this approach has been proven to be risky and expensive in practice because fundamental (i.e., architectural and requirement) flaws that affect the overall subsystem functionality are not caught until post-integration. A better implementation strategy is to implement vertical slices, as shown in Figure 8-16.

Each vertical slice implements only the portion of each layer relevant to the purpose of the slice. This approach to implementation is

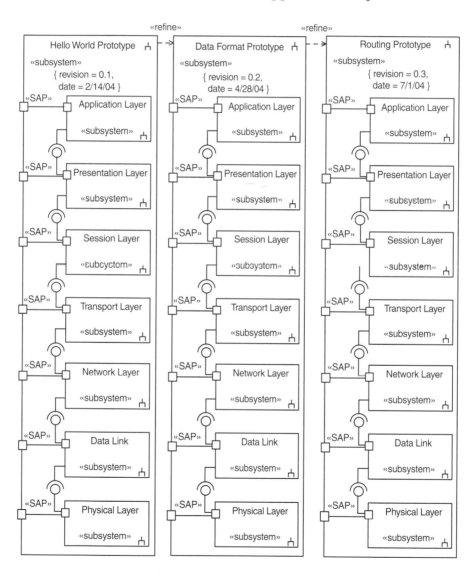

Figure 8-16: *Vertical Slices*

called *iterative prototyping* and each slice is called a *prototype.* The prototypes are implemented so that each prototype builds on the features implemented in its predecessors. The sequence of prototypes is decided based on which features logically come first as well as which represent the highest risk. With risk-based development, higher-risk items are explored and resolved as early as possible. This typically results in less rework and a more integrated, reliable system.

Figure 8-16 shows a set of *subsystems* with a *refinement* relation between successive versions. The refinement relation is a stereotyped dependency in which one model element represents a more refined version of another. Also note that two tagged property values are used to indicate the version and date using the normal {tag = value} syntax.

A more complete set of prototypes for Figure 8-16 might include those shown in Table 8-3.

Note how the later prototypes build on the services implemented in their predecessors. This is the essence of the iterative prototyping development philosophy—gradually adding capability until the entire sys-

Table 8-3: *Vertical Slice Prototypes*

#	Prototype Name	Description
1	Hello World	Implement enough of each layer (and stub the remainder) to send a message from one node to another.
2	Data Format	Mostly presentation layer—implement data encode, decode and network data format conversions. Also include timed ACK/NAK transport layer protocol.
3	Routing	Mostly network and data link layers to control routing of messages.
4	Flow Control	Data link Xon/Xoff flow control, and message CRCs to implement data integrity checks with automatic retry on message failure.
5	Connections	Connections and sessions (transport, data link, session layers).
6	Performance	Performance tuning of all layers to optimize throughput.

tem is complete. Naturally, iterative prototyping applies to more than just communication protocol design. Any sufficiently complex piece of software can be broken down into a set of hierarchical layers in a client-server topology.[10]

It is common for these components to contain one or more threads. The concurrency model is another piece of architectural design that can greatly impact system performance. In a soft real-time environment, average throughput must be ensured, but individual deadlines are not crucial to system correctness. In hard real-time environments, however, each deadline must be met and the concurrency model must ensure the ability of the system to meet all deadlines. For most multitasking systems, this is a nontrival problem because the exact arrival patterns are not periodic and synchronous. Commonly, the system must respond to periodic events with vastly different periods as well as aperiodic events that may be bursty. Concurrency design is the subject of the latter half of this chapter.

The last primary architectural goal is to design the global error handling policies to ensure correct system performance in the presence of faults.[11] Many strategies are possible, ranging from each object assuming full responsibility for all errors to a single global error handler that decides the correct action to take in all error conditions. Most systems are a hybrid of such approaches. One popular strategy is to have multiple levels of error handling with the general rule that each error will be handled at the point at which enough context is available to make the correct decision. An object with enough redundancy of its data members (such as triple storage for important data) might process an invalid data value by reconstructing the appropriate data value or assigning a default value in the event of an error. A subsystem might reboot itself and let the remainder of the system function when it discovers some particular error. Some errors may require a global handler to intervene and coordinate a correct system shutdown, such as in the event of a failure in a nuclear power plant.

Error handling policies are usually at least as complex as the primary software functionality and may result in systems three times as large and an order of magnitude more complex. Complicating error

---

[10] The formal inductive proof of this statement is left as an exercise.
[11] Note that a requirement for fault tolerance almost always translates to a hard deadline for fault detection and handling, even in otherwise soft real-time systems.

handling is the fact that it is highly system dependent, yet only through clear error handling policies can safety-critical systems be deployed safely.[12] This is an important aspect of the software architecture. [7] discusses the fundamental concepts of safety and reliability in the context of embedded system and [9] provides set of architectural design patterns for optimizing various aspects of system safety and reliability.

8.3 Software Meets Hardware: Deployment Architecture in UML

The UML represents hardware/software mapping with deployment diagrams. There are a number of important diagrammatic elements, as shown in Figure 8-17. The icon of primary importance on deployment diagrams is the *node*. Nodes represent processors, sensors, actuators, routers, displays, input devices, memory, custom PLAs, or any physical object of importance to the software. Typically, nodes are stereotyped to indicate the type of node. Interconnects represent physical interconnections among nodes. They are most commonly electronic, but can as easily be optical or telemetric.

Classes are part of the *logical* architecture of the system. That it, the represent the logical concepts of the system and low they are inherently linked together. Subsystems, *components, tasks,* and *objects* are part of the *physical* architecture. A component is an artifact of development that exists at runtime. Typical components are executables, libraries, files, configuration tables, and so on. Such software artifacts end up deployed on hardware—this is represented by the node and may communicate across physical linkages. See Figure 8-17.

Nodes are often divided into two fundamental kinds—those that run software that we produce (processors) and those that do not (devices). These are often stereotyped into more specific kinds of hardware, such as DC motors, stepper motors, laser ranger finders, displays, buttons, keyboards, pressure sensors, and the like. You don't have to stereotype the nodes, but many people do and like to use special icons to represent the various hardware devices.

---

[12] Something for you to think about the next time you fly off to visit grandma.

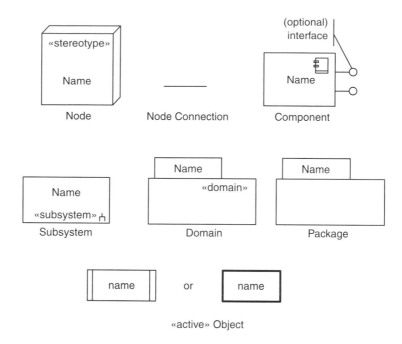

Figure 8-17: *Deployment Diagram Notation*

There are always many ways that a logical architecture can be mapped to a physical architecture. In fact, the same logical architectural elements may end up instantiated in multiple components. For example, many components may have to communicate with each other across a bus. They may all contain classes to assist the marshalling and unmarshalling of resources for bus transfer.

Processor nodes are occasionally shown containing classes or objects, but usually processor nodes contain components that may be broken down into subcomponents and tasks (represented as «active» objects). To show tasks, include the «active» objects in the component on the diagram. Of course, these components are the realization of objects and classes, but classes and objects usually only appear on class and object, not deployment, diagrams.

Figure 8-18 shows a simple deployment diagram for a telescope position control system. The user interface consists of an LCD display and two rotary encoder knobs, which are tied to the same processor. The positioning subsystem consists of two independent subsystems,

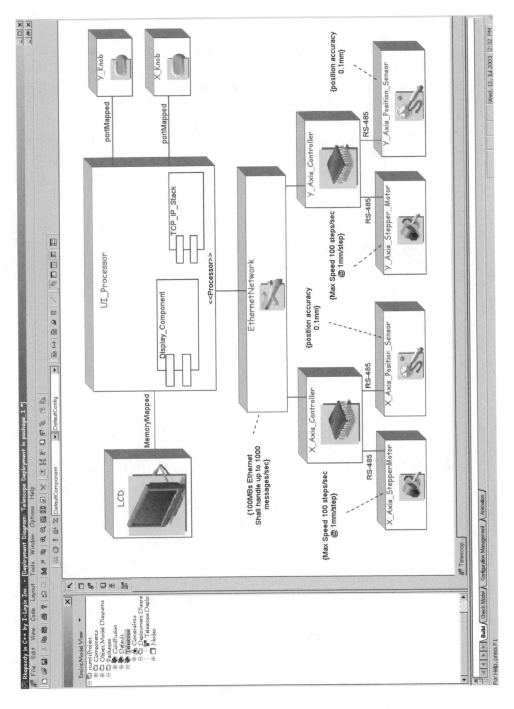

Figure 8-18: *Telescope Position Controller Deployment Diagram*

each containing a stepper motor and an independent sensor. The processors are linked across an Ethernet network, and both use Ethernet controller boards to access the network.

This figure shows two methods for specifying the software running on the processors. The first is shown in the *UI Processor* node. This node contains software components; in this case, a Display component and a TCP/IP protocol stack. The stereotype «processor» is shown textually. The other two notation processors, controllers for the *x* and *y* axes, use the iconic form to show their stereotype. The devices are also shown using iconic stereotype forms.

8.4 Concurrency and Resource Design

Real-time systems typically have multiple threads of control executing simultaneously. A *thread* can be defined as a set of *actions* that execute sequentially, independent from the execution of action in other threads. *Actions* are statements executing at the same priority in a particular sequence or perform some cohesive function. These statements can belong to many different objects. The entirety of a thread is also known as a *task*. Multiple objects typically participate within a single task. Commonly, a distinction is made between *heavyweight* and *lightweight* threads. Heavyweight threads use different data address spaces and must resort to expensive messaging to communicate data among themselves. Such threads have relatively strong encapsulation and protection from other threads. Lightweight threads coexist within an enclosing data address space. Lightweight threads provide faster inter-task communication via this shared global space, but offer weaker encapsulation. Some authors use the terms *thread* or *task* to refer to lightweight threads and *process* to refer to heavyweight threads. We use *thread*, *task*, and *process* as synonyms in this book, with the understanding that if these distinctions are important, the «active» object would be more specifically stereotyped as «process», «task», or «thread».

8.4.1 Representing Threads

The UML can show concurrency models in a several ways. The primary way is to stereotype classes as «active»; other ways include orthogonal regions (and-states) in statecharts, forks and joins in activity diagrams, and the par operator in UML 2.0 sequence diagrams.

Class and object diagrams can use the stereotype «active» or the active object stereotype icon to represent threads. By including only classes and objects with this stereotype, we can clearly show the task structure. A task diagram is nothing more than a class diagram showing only active objects, the classes and objects associated with concurrency management such as semaphores and queues, and the relations among these classes and objects.

8.4.2 System Task Diagram

Class and object models are fundamentally concurrent. Objects are themselves inherently concurrent and it is conceivable that each object could execute in its own thread.[13] During the course of architectural design, the objects are aligned into a smaller set of concurrent threads solely for efficiency reasons. Thus the partitioning of a system into threads is always a design decision.

In UML, each thread is rooted in a single active object. The active object is a structured class that aggregates the objects participating within the thread. It has the general responsibility to coordinate internal execution by the dispatching of messages to its constituent parts and providing information to the underlying operating system so that the latter can schedule the thread. By only showing the classes with the «active» stereotype on a single diagram, you can create a system task diagram.

The appropriate packaging of objects into nodes and threads is vital for system performance. The relationships among the threads are fundamental architectural decisions that have great impact on the performance and hardware requirements of the system. Besides just identifying the threads and their relationships to other threads, the characteristics of the messages must themselves be defined. These characteristics include

- Message arrival patterns and frequencies
- Event response deadlines

---

[13] This is, after all, how biological neural systems work. Neural structures are massively parallel systems that operate independently but collaborate by sending molecular messages (in the form of neurotransmitters) across synapses (the neural analog of interfaces). See [6].

- Synchronization protocols for inter-task communication
- "Hardness" of deadlines

Answering these questions is at the very heart of multithreaded systems design.

The greatest advantage of a task diagram is that the entire set of threads for the system can be shown on a single diagram, albeit at a high conceptual level. It is easy to trace back from the diagram into the requirements specification and vice versa. Elaborating each thread symbol on the task diagram into either a lightweight task diagram or an object diagram means that the threads can be efficiently decomposed and related to the class, object, and behavioral models.

Figure 8-19 shows a task diagram for an elevator model; the primitive objects—the ones that do the actual management of the elevator

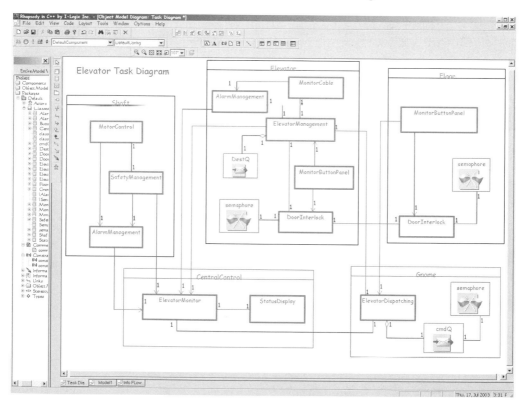

Figure 8-19: *Elevator Task Diagram*

system—are subsumed within the shown «active» classes. The diagram shows a number of useful things. First, notice that the structured classes for the various subsystems (Floor, Elevator, Shaft, Central Station, and Gnome) contain the task threads, and the task threads will internally contain the primitive objects. The tasks are shown with the heavy border. Some of the tasks show that they associate with semaphores and queues, which can be identified with the icons (or could be identified with textual stereotypes).

Within each processor, objects are busy collaborating to achieve the goals of that subsystem. However, on the system task diagram, only the threads and concurrency management classes are shown. Remember that each thread is rooted in a single «active» composite object that receives the events for that thread and dispatches them to the appropriate object within the thread.

The associations among the threads are shown using conventional association notation. These associations indicate that the threads must communicate in some fashion to pass messages.

8.4.3 Concurrent State Diagrams

Rumbaugh [2] has suggested a means by which concurrent threads can be diagrammed using the statecharts. He notes that concurrency with objects generally arises by aggregation; that is, a composite object is composed of component objects, some of which may execute in separate threads. In this case, a single state of the composite object may be composed multiple states of these components.

«active» objects respond to events and dispatch them to their aggregate parts. This process can be modeled as a finite state machine. The other orthogonal component is due to the thread itself having a number of states. Since the active object represents the thread characteristics to the system, it is very natural to make this an orthogonal component of the active object.

Figure 8-20 shows the two orthogonal components of a typical «active» object class. The dashed line separates the orthogonal components of the *running* superstate. Each transition in the event processing component can only take place while the «active» object is in one of the substates of the running superstate of the thread component. After all, that is the only time it actual consumes CPU cycles. On the other hand, if the running thread becomes preempted or suspended, the event process-

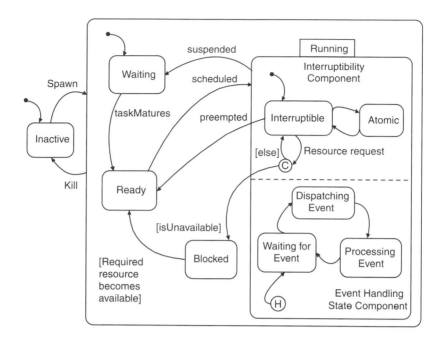

Figure 8-20: *Concurrency in Active Objects*

ing component will resume where it left off, as indicated by the history connector.

Table 8-4 provides a brief description of the states.

8.4.4 Defining Threads

During analysis, classes and objects were identified and characterized and their associations defined. In a multitasking system, the objects must be placed into threads for actual execution. This process of task thread definition is two-fold:

1. Identify the threads.
2. Populate the threads with classes and objects from the analysis and design process.

There are a number of strategies that can help you define the threads based on the external events and the system context. They fall into the general approach of grouping events in the system so that a thread handles one or more events and each event is handled by a single thread.

Table 8-4: *States of the Active Object Thread Component*

State	Description
Inactive	Thread is not yet created.
Waiting	Thread is not ready to run, but is waiting for some event to put it in the ready state.
Ready	Thread is ready to run and is waiting to execute. It is normally stored in a priority FIFO queue.
Running	Thread is running and chewing up CPU cycles. This superstate contains two orthogonal, concurrent components.
Interruptible	The thread is running and may be preempted. This is substate of the interruptibility component of the running state.
Atomic	The thread is running but may not be preempted. Specifically, task switching has been disabled. This is substate of the interruptibility component of the running state.
Blocked	Thread is waiting for a required resource to become available so that it may continue its processing.
Waiting for event	The thread is waiting for an event to handle. This is substate of the Event Handling state component of the running state.
Dispatching Event	The object is handling an incoming event and deciding which aggregates should process it. This is substate of the Event Handling state component of the running state.
Processing Event	The designated aggregate of the active object composite is responding to the event. This is substate of the *Event Handling* state component of the running state.

There are conditions under which an event may be handled by more than one thread. One event may generate other *propagated* events, which may be handled by other threads. For example, the appearance of waveform data may itself generate an event to signal another thread to scale the incoming data asynchronously. Occasionally, events may be multicast to more than one thread. This may happen when a number of threads are waiting on a shared resource or are waiting for a common event that permits them all to move forward independently.

8.4.5 Identifying Threads

Internal and external events can be grouped in a variety of ways into threads. The following are some common event grouping strategies.

- *Single Event Groups:* In a simple system, it may be possible to create a separate thread for each external and internal event. This is usually not feasible in complex systems with dozens or even hundreds of possible events or when thread switch time is significant relative to the event response timing.

- *Sequential Processing:* When it is clear that a series of steps must be performed in a sequential fashion, they may be grouped within a single thread.

- *Event Source:* This strategy groups events from a common source. For example, all the events related to ECG numerics may be grouped into one thread (such as HR Available, ECG Alarms, etc.), all the noninvasive blood pressure (NIBP) data in another, the ventilator data in another, the anesthetic agent in another, and the gas mixing data in yet another. In an automobile, sources of events might be the ignition, braking, and engine control systems. In systems with clearly defined subsystems producing events that have roughly the same period, this may be the simplest approach.

- *Interface Device (Port):* This grouping strategy encapsulates control of a specific interface within a single thread. For example, the (periodic) SDLC data can be handled in one thread, the (episodic) RS232 data to the external models by another, and the (episodic) user buttons and knobs by another. This strategy is a specialization of the event source grouping strategy.

- *Related Information:* Consider grouping all waveforms to be handled by a single thread, and all measured numeric parameters within another thread. Or all information related to airfoil control surfaces in each wing and tail section might be manipulated by separate threads. This grouping may be appropriate when related data is used together in the user problem domain. Another name for this grouping is *functional cohesion.*

- *Arrival Pattern:* If data arrives at a given rate, a single periodic thread could handle receiving all the relevant data and dispatching it to different objects as necessary. Aperiodic events might be handled by a single interrupt handler and similarly dispatch control to appropriate objects. Generally, this grouping may be most useful with internal events, such as timer interrupts, or when the periods of events naturally cluster around a small set of periods. Note that this is the primary strategy for identifying threads that have deadlines—use of other policies with time-constrained event responses can lead to priority inversion unless the designers are especially careful.

- *Target Object/Computationally Intense Processing:* One of the purposes of rendezvous objects is to encapsulate and provide access to data. As such, they are targets for events, both to insert and remove data. A waveform queue object server might have its own thread for background scaling and manipulation, while at the same time participating in threads depositing data within the queue object and removing data for display.

- *Purpose:* Alarms serve one purpose—to notify the system user of anomalies, so that he or she can take corrective action or vacate the premises, whichever seems more appropriate. This might form one event group. Safety checks within a watchdog thread, such as checking for stack overflow or code corruption, might form another. This purpose might map well to a use case.

- *Safety Concerns:* The system hazard analysis may suggest threads. One common rule in safety-critical systems is to separate monitoring from actuation. In terms of thread identification, this means that a thread that controls a safety-relevant process should be checked by an independent thread. From a safety perspective, it is preferable to run safety checks on a separate processor, so that common-mode hardware and software faults do not affect both the primary and the safety processing simultaneously.

During concurrency design, you must add events to groups where appropriate so that each event is represented in at least one group. Any events remaining after the initial grouping can each be considered independently. As mentioned earlier, it is recommended that thread actions with hard deadlines use the arrival-pattern strategy to ensure a schedulable set of threads. Create a task diagram in which the processing of each group is represented by a separate thread. Most events will only occur within a single thread, but sometimes events must be dispatched to multiple threads.

Frequently, one or more of these groupings will emerge as the primary decomposition strategy of the event space, but it is also common to mix grouping strategies. When the grouping seems complete and stable, you have identified an initial set of threads that handle all events in your system. As the product development evolves, events may be added to or removed from groups, new groups may suggest themselves, or alternative grouping strategies may present themselves. This will lead the astute designer to alternative designs worth consideration.

8.4.6 Assigning Objects to Threads

Once you have identified a good set of threads, you may start populating the groups with objects. Note that I said "objects" and not "classes. "Objects are specific instances of classes that may appear in different threads or as an interface between threads. There are classes that only create a single instance in an application (*singletons*), and there are classes that instantiate to multiple objects residing within a single thread, but generally, classes instantiate a number of objects that may appear in any number of threads. For example, there may be queues of threads, queues of waveform data, queues of numeric data, queues of network messages, command queues, error queues, alarm queues, and so on. These might appear in a great many threads, even though they are instances of the same class (queue).

8.4.7 Defining Thread Rendezvous

So far, we have looked at what constitutes a thread, some strategies to select a set of threads, and how to populate threads with objects. The remainder of this chapter provides ways to define how the threads communicate with each other.

There are a number of strategies for inter-task communication. The simplest by far is to use the OS to send messages from one thread to another. While this approach maintains encapsulation and limits coupling among threads, it is expensive in terms of compute cycles and is relatively slow. Lightweight expeditious communication is required in many real-time systems in order for the threads to meet their performance requirements. In this chapter, we consider some methods for inter-task communication that are both lightweight and robust. [9] details the rendezvous pattern as a means of specifying arbitrarily complex rules for synchronizing tasks.

The two main reasons for thread communication are to share information and to synchronize control. The acquisition, manipulation, and display of information may occur in different threads with different periods, and may not even take place on the same processor, necessitating some means of sharing the information among these threads. Synchronization of control is also very common in real-time systems. In asynchronous threads that control physical processes, one thread's completion (such as emptying a chemical vat) may form a precondition for another process (such as adding a new volatile chemical to the vat). The thread synchronization strategy must ensure that such preconditions are satisfied.

When threads communicate, the rendezvous itself has attributes and behavior, which makes it reasonable to model it as an associative class. The important questions to ask about thread synchronization are these:

- Are there any preconditions for the threads to communicate? A precondition is generally a data value that must be set, or some object must be in a particular state. If a precondition for thread synchronization exists, it should be checked by a guarding condition before the rendezvous is allowed to continue.

- What should happen if the preconditions are not met, as when the collaborating thread is not available? The rendezvous can

  - Wait indefinitely until the other thread is ready (a *waiting rendezvous*)

  - Wait until either the required thread is ready or a specified period has elapsed (*timed rendezvous*)

  - Return immediately (*balking rendezvous*) and ignore the attempt at thread communication

  - Raise an exception and handle the thread communication failure as an error (*protected rendezvous*)

- If data is to be shared via the rendezvous class, what is the relationship of the rendezvous object with the object containing the required information? Options include
  - ▼ The rendezvous object contains the information directly.
  - ▼ The rendezvous object holds a reference to the object containing the information, or a reference to an object serving as an interface for the information.
  - ▼ The rendezvous object can temporarily hold the information until it is passed to the target thread.

Remember that objects must ensure the integrity of their internal data. If the possibility exists that shared data can be simultaneously *write* or *write-read* accessed by more than a single thread, then it must be protected by some mechanism, such as a mutual-exclusion semaphore, as is done in Figure 8-19. In general, synchronization objects must handle

- Preconditions
- Access control
- Data access

8.4.8 Sharing Resources

Rendezvous objects control access to resources and classical methods exist to handle resource usage in a multitasking environment. In the simplest case, resources can be simultaneously accessed—that is, access is nonatomic. Many devices use predetermined configuration tables burned into FLASH or EPROM memory. Since processes can only read the configuration table, many threads can access the resource simultaneously without bad effects.

Data access that involves writing requires some form of access control to ensure data integrity. Clearly, if multiple internal attributes must be simultaneously updated, another reader thread cannot be permitted to read these values while only some of them are updated.

In large collections of objects, it may be necessary to allow read accesses in one or more portions of the database even while other sections are being updated. Large airline reservation databases must function in this fashion, for example. Algorithms to control these processes are well defined and available in texts on relational and object databases.

8.4.9 Assigning Priorities

Thread *priority* is distinct from the importance of the actions executed by the thread. Priority in a preemptive priority scheme determines the *required timeliness* of the response to the event or precondition. For example, in an ECG monitor, waveform threads must have a high priority to ensure that they run often enough to avoid a jerky appearance. ECG waveforms have tight timeliness requirements. On the other hand, a jerky waveform is not as important to patient outcome as sounding an alarm when the patient is at risk. An asystole alarm is activated when the monitor detects that the heart is no longer beating. Clearly, bringing this to the attention of the physician is very important, but if the alarm took an extra second to be annunciated, it would not affect patient outcome. Such an alarm is very important, but does not have a very high urgency, as compared with some other events.

In rate monotonic scheduling (RMS), the assignment of priorities is simple: The priority of all threads is inversely proportional to their periods. The shorter the period, the higher the priority. The original RMS scheme assumed that the deadline is equal to the period. When this is not true, the priority should be assigned based on the deadline, rather than the period. In general, the RMS scheduling makes intuitive sense—threads with short deadlines must be dealt with more promptly than those with longer deadlines. It is not uncommon to find a few exceptions to the rule, however. RMS scheduling and the associated mathematics of proving schedulability are beyond the scope of this book. For a more detailed look, see [7,8].

8.5 Looking Ahead

Analysis is all about the development of a consistent logical model that describes all possible acceptable solutions to a problem. Design is about *optimization*—selecting a particular solution that optimizes some set of design criteria in a way that is consistent with the analysis model.

Architectural design consists of the specification of the kind and quantity of devices, the media and rules they use to communicate, and the large-scale software components mapping to the physical architecture. The units of software architecture are subsystems and threads. Subsystems are typically layered sets of packages arranged in a hierarchical fashion. Threads cut through all layers, although they are rooted in a single active object.

The software architecture must map to the set of physical devices. The UML shows this mapping with the deployment diagram. This diagram shows not only nodes and communication paths, but also large-scale software components.

The iterative refinement implementation strategy builds these layered subsystems using vertical slices passing through all layers as well. Each vertical slice constitutes an iterative prototype. Prototypes build on the services defined in the previous prototypes. The order of prototypes is determined by the required services as well as the level of risk. Elaborating high-risk prototypes early lowers overall project risk with a minimum of rework.

The specification of the concurrency model is very important to performance in real-time systems. The concurrency model identifies a relatively small number of threads and populates these threads with the objects identified in the analysis model. Inter-task communication allows threads to share information and to synchronize control. This is often accomplished using a rendezvous pattern to ensure robust exchange of information.

The next step is to specify the middle layer of design, known as mechanistic design. This level of design focuses on the collaboration of small groups of classes and objects. In the process of mechanistic design we add classes to optimize information or control flow and to specify details that have been so far ignored.

8.6 Exercises

1. What are the two types of architectures defined in the ROPES process? How do they differ?

2. What are the primary organizational elements in each of the two types of architecture?

3. What is a domain? How is it modeled in the UML?

4. Identify and define the five aspects of physical architecture.

5. What is the relationship between components and subsystems?

6. How are concurrency units modeled in the UML?

7. What are the seven task/thread identification strategies?

8. Distinguish between symmetric and asymmetric distribution. What are the advantages of each?

9. Define the term *recurring cost* and relate it to hardware/software tradeoff decisions.

10. What is a Hamming distance? How is it useful in communication protocols?

11. Describe the difference between safety and reliability.

12. What are the advantages and disadvantages of heterogeneous versus homogeneous redundancy?

13. Explain the concept of vertical slices and its application to the construction of prototypes.

14. What are the two primary kinds of nodes to be found on deployment diagrams?

15. What is a resource in the UML?

16. Contrast the terms *importance, urgency,* and *priority.*

17. How are priorities assigned with the RMS strategy?

8.7 References

[1] *Unified Modeling Language: Superstructure, Version 2.0* ptc/03-08-02. Needham, MA: OMG, 2003 *www.omg.org.*

[2] Rumbaugh, James, Michael Blaha, William Premerlani, Frederick Eddy, and William Lorensen. *Object-Oriented Modeling and Design.* Englewood Cliffs, NJ: Prentice Hall, 1991.

[3] Buschmann, Frank, Regine Meunier, Hans Rohnert, Peter Sommerlad, and Michael Stal. *A System of Patterns: Pattern-Oriented Software Architecture.* New York: John Wiley & Sons, 1996.

[4] Alexander, C., S. Ishikawa, and M. Silverstain. *A Pattern Language.* New York: Oxford University Press, 1977.

[5] Gamma, Erich, Richard Helm, Ralph Johnson, and John Vlissides. *Design Patterns: Elements of Reusable Software.* Reading, MA: Addison-Wesley, 1995.

[6] Douglass, Bruce Powel. *Statistical Analysis of Simulated Multinerve Networks: Use of Factor Analytical Methods.* Ph.D. Dissertation. Vermillion, SD: USD Medical School, 1984.

[7] Douglass, Bruce Powel, *Doing Hard Time: Developing Real-Time Systems Using UML, Objects, Frameworks, and Patterns.* Reading, MA: Addison-Wesley, 1998.

[8] Klein, Mark, Thomas Ralya, Bill Pollak, Ray Obenza, and Michael Gonzalez Harbour. *A Practitioner's Handbook for Real-Time Analysis: Guide to Rate Monotonic Analysis for Real-Time Systems.* Boston: Kluwer Academic Publishers, 1993.

[9] Douglass, Bruce Powel. *Real-Time Design Patterns: Robust Scalable Architecture for Real-Time Systems.* Reading, MA: Addison-Wesley, 2002.

Chapter 9

Mechanistic Design

This chapter explains the middle level of design, called *mechanistic design*. Mechanistic design deals with how collaborations (relatively small sets of classes and objects that collaborate to achieve common goals) can be optimized. Mechanistic design is primarily organized around the discovery and use of patterns of object collaboration and its scope tends to be an order of magnitude smaller than that of architectural design. The mechanistic design patterns are reified solutions to structurally similar problems. This chapter will identify several smaller-scale patterns useful in real-time embedded systems.

Notation and Concepts Discussed

Design Patterns	Smart Pointer Pattern	Rendezvous Pattern
Observer Pattern	Proxy Pattern	Container Pattern
Reliable Transaction Pattern	Guarded Call Pattern	Policy Pattern

9.1 What Is Mechanistic Design?

Mechanistic design is concerned with adding and organizing classes to optimize a single collaboration. The mechanistic design process elaborates the analysis model and iterates it by adding objects to facilitate a particular design. As mentioned in Chapter 8, a set of classes and objects working together is called a *collaboration*. A collaboration is specified in terms of specific classes playing named roles (called *classifier roles*). When the collaborators may be replaced with others that can fulfill those roles, the collaboration is called a *pattern.* The roles define, in an abstract sense, the formal parameter list for the pattern. When bound with an actual parameter list (the classes whose instances will actually play the part of those roles at runtime), the pattern may be instantiated into a collaboration. A *mechanism* [1] is a type of pattern that is limited in scope to a few classes (i.e., it does not have architectural scope), but is generally applicable in many circumstances.

A typical real-time system may have dozens or even hundreds of mechanisms operating concurrently. While the analysis model identifies the classes and objects fundamental to the problem domain, mechanistic design reorganizes and optimizes the interaction of these entities to facilitate their collaboration. A common example is the addition of container classes to handle multivalued roles[1] in associations.

In the analysis model, many associations will have multivalued roles. For example:

- A customer can have many bank accounts.
- An autopilot can use many sensors and actuators.
- A physiological parameter can be shown in many different views simultaneously.

The most common implementation of a one-to-one association is a pointer or reference in the client allowing the client to send messages to the server (i.e., to call one of the server's member functions), such as that shown in Code Listing 9-1.

---

[1] A *multivalued role* of an association is defined to be an association role with a nonunity multiplicity, such as (0,1) or *.

```
class Actuator {
     int value;
public:
     int gimme(void) { return value; };
     void set(int v) { value = v; };
};
class Autopilot {
     Actuator *s;
public:
     void AutoPilot(Server *YourActuator):
       s(YourActuator) { };
     void setIt(int a) { s->set(a); } // send msg to
       Server object s
     void IncIt(void) {
         int a = s->gimme();
         s->set(++a);
     };
};
```

Code Listing 9-1: *A Sample Pointer*

The class Autopilot uses pointer *s* to locate its Actuator object. It can then send the object messages like s->set(a) and s->gimmc(). The use of a simple pointer is appropriate because the multiplicity of the association is one-to-one. But what if the association is one-to-many?

It is entirely possible to build the ability to manage collections of Actuator objects directly into the Autopilot class. A strategy could be used, such as using a vector, linked list, or binary tree to manage the collection by adding operations into the class Autopilot for adding, finding, sorting, and deleting these objects in the collection.

This simple approach has a number of drawbacks. First of all, the machinery to manage the collection is entirely unrelated to the primary purpose of the class Autopilot. Inserting such methods would obscure this purpose. Second, depending on the nature of the collection itself, the management of the collection may be quite complex, such as balancing AVL or red-black trees. Adding this behavior would make the class larger and more complex. Further, managing collections is a subject domain of its own and such collection class packages may be purchased. Indeed, C++ provides one called the Standard Template Library (STL); the Rhapsody tool provides another or can automatically use the STL. Building the behavior directly into the Autopilot class makes reuse of these libraries impossible. If the system has 20 classes with multivalued roles, this behavior must be rewritten for each such class. Building the behavior directly into each class that uses it makes changing to a different kind of collection much more difficult.

The more common approach is to introduce a new class during mechanistic design, one to handle the vagaries of managing the contained objects. Such a class is called a *collection* or *container* class. This allows third-party libraries to be used, separates out unrelated concerns of container management, and allows the type of collection to be changed fairly easily. The analysis model identified the association and its multiplicity, but the use of a container class is a design decision because it is a specific way to implement the analysis model. The use of collection classes is so common that it can be reified into a design pattern:

> *When a class must manage a number of objects of the same class, a useful design approach is to add a container class between the primary class and the set of multiple objects.*

The rest of mechanistic design proceeds in a similar vein. Classes are added to facilitate the implementation of the analysis model. When generalized solutions can be applied to the specifics of a particular design, this is called *applying the design pattern*. This is nothing more than the classic elaborative or iterative development method—repeated refinement of the model via reorganization and addition.

In the following section, we will present a number of design patterns that can be profitably applied in the design of real-time systems. The use of these patterns simplifies the system's design and allows reuse on a grander scale than the reuse of individual objects and classes.

9.2 Mechanistic Design Patterns

Design patterns consist of at least three aspects:

- A common problem, including a common problem context
- A general approach to a solution
- Consequences of the pattern

The problem statement describes the general characteristics of the problem at hand. This description may include context and preconditions. For example:

> *Problem: When exception handling is used, raw pointers can lead to memory leaks when exceptions are thrown. The use of temporary pointers within normal C++ functions or class member functions may not be properly cleaned up if an exception is thrown because the inline delete operator may be bypassed. This does not apply to objects created on the stack because when objects go out of scope, their destructors are called. Raw pointers do not have destructors.*

It should be noted, that this problem—as with all problems addressed by design patterns—specifies an optimization concern. Design is all about optimization and so is driven by the required or desired quality of service properties of the collaboration. In this case, we are trying to optimize robustness by noting that there is a problem with using standard pointers.

This statement identifies a problem common to many designs within many domains. The context is broad—programs using C++ with exception handling. Since a generally applicable solution to this problem is available, it can be reified into a design pattern:

> *Solution: Rather than use a raw pointer, a "smart" pointer object can be used when a temporary pointer is needed. The smart pointer is responsible for identifying whether a memory must be deallocated when the pointer is destroyed.[2] This requires an internal mechanism, such as reference counting, to determine whether other smart pointers are referring to the same object in memory.*

---

[2] There may be other pointers to the memory, so it is not always clear whether the memory being pointed to can be safely deleted along with the pointer.

Table 9-1: *Mechanistic Patterns*

Category	Pattern Name	Purpose
Simple patterns	Observer	Allows multiple clients to effectively share a server and be autonomously updated.
	Proxy	Provides an observer pattern in a distributed environment.
	Reliable transaction	Controls communication between objects with various levels of reliability.
	Smart pointer	Avoids problems associated with standard pointers.
	Guarded call	Allows robust and timely access to services and data across thread boundaries.
Reuse	Container	Abstracts away data structuring concepts from application domain classes to simply model and facilitate reuse.
	Interface	Abstracts away the type of an object from its implementation to support multiple implementations of a given type and to support multiple types with a common internal structure.
	Rendezvous	Provides a flexible mechanism for lightweight inter-task communication.

Naturally, design patterns have pros and cons. These are the consequences of the design pattern:

> *Consequences: The smart pointer makes the design more robust in the presence of thrown exceptions, but it increases the code complexity somewhat and requires an additional level of indirection for each pointer reference. Although this can be made syntactically invisible to the user, it involves a small runtime overhead. Enforcement of the smart pointer policy cannot be automated, but must be ensured by consensus and review. Further, if smart and raw pointers are both applied against the same object, reference counting should be disabled.*

Mechanistic design patterns are medium scale, involving as few as two or as many as a dozen classes. Several patterns are provided in this chapter, but this is a rich area of active research. See the references at the end of this chapter for more patterns.[3]

As specified, you may find these patterns too specific or too general. Feel free to adapt these patterns to the particular needs of your system.

This chapter presents the mechanistic patterns listed in Table 9-1.

9.3 The Observer Pattern

The observer pattern is used when there are potentially many clients of a service or information flow from a single server. These clients may not even be known at design time. The pattern provides a simple way to dynamically wire clients with the server so that the clients can receive timely updates from the server.

9.3.1 Abstract

The observer pattern (sometimes called the publish-subscribe pattern) addresses the specific issue of how to notify a set of clients in a timely way that a value they care about has changed, especially when the notification process is to be repeated over a relatively long period of time. The basic solution offered by the observer pattern is to have the clients subscribe to the server to be notified about the value in question according to some policy. This policy can be "when the value changes," "at least every so often," "at most every so often," and so on. This minimizes computational effort for notification of clients, and across a communications bus minimizes the bus bandwidth required for notification of the appropriate clients.

9.3.2 Problem

The problem addressed by the observer pattern is how to notify some number of clients, in a timely fashion, of a data value according to some

---

[3] Another good source of patterns is the patterns home page at *http://hillside.net/patterns/ patterns.html.* Other interesting Web pages can be found by looking for design patterns using your favorite Web search engine.

abstract policy, such as "when it changes," "every so often," "at most every so often," and "at least every so often." One approach is for every client to query the data value, but this can be computationally wasteful, especially when a client wants to be notified only when the data value changes. Another solution is for the server of this information to be designed to know its clients. However, we don't want to break the classic client-server model by giving the server knowledge about its clients. Doing so makes the addition of new clients a design change, which would be difficult to do dynamically at runtime.

9.3.3 Pattern Structure

Figure 9-1 shows the structure of the observer pattern. The structure expresses a very simple idea—that the client should be dynamically coupled to the server with a subscription mechanism. Clients register

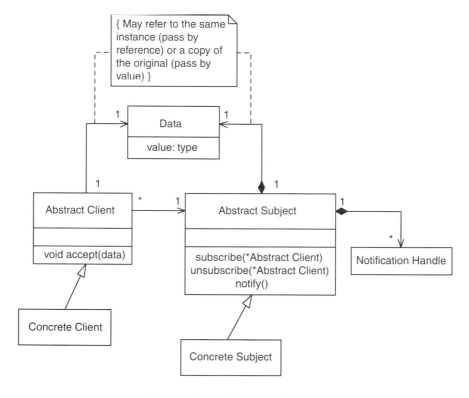

Figure 9-1: *Observer Pattern*

or deregister for the data they want. When a client registers, it supplies the server with a way to send that information. Classically, this is a *call-back* (method address), but it can also be an object ID or some other means to pass the value back to the client. When the policy indicates the data should be sent to the clients, the server looks up all the registered clients and sends them the data.

The observer pattern is deemed a mechanistic design pattern because the scope of the application of the pattern is collaboration-wide rather than system-wide. The observer pattern can be used as a basis for more elaborate patterns that employ its principle across distributed architectures as well [9].

9.3.4 Collaboration Roles

- *Abstract Client:* The AbstractClient class associates with the Abstract-Subject class so that it can invoke subscribe() and unsubscribe() as necessary. It contains an accept() operation called to accept the information required by the subscription, the address (as a *notification handle instance*) to be passed to the AbstractSubject instance to which it connects. There are many different ways to specify how to notify the client when new or updated information is available, but callbacks (pointers to an accept() operation of the client) are the most common.

- *AbstractSubject:* The AbstractSubject class acts as a server of information desired by the AbstractClients. It accepts subscribe and unsubscribe requests from its clients. When the policy dictates that the AbstractSubject needs to notify its clients, it walks the client list to notify each. As noted in Section 9.3.6, a number of implementation means may be used to notify the subscribed clients.

- *NotificationHandle:* The NotificationHandle class stores information for each client so that the Abstract Subject can notify the Abstract Client of the value stored in the Data class. The most common implementation strategy for object communication is to use a pointer (or a reference) to the AbstractClient::accept() operation. However, there are other means to implement NotificationHandles, such as local object identifiers, URLs, protocol-specific remote object IDs, network node port numbers, or even URLs.

- *ConcreteClient:* The ConcreteClient is an application-specific subclass of the AbstractClient class. The pattern is applied by subclassing the

AbstractClient and adding application-specific semantics into the new subclass.

- *ConcreteSubject:* The ConcreteSubject is an application-specific subclass of the Abstract Subject class. The pattern is applied by subclassing the Abstract Subject and adding application-specific semantics to the subclass.

- *Data:* The Data class contains the information that the Abstract Subject class knows and the AbstractClient class wants to know. The Data object containing the appropriate value may be shared with the clients either by reference (such as by passing a pointer to the single instance of the Data object) or by value (by copying the Data object for each of the subscribing clients). Such implementations are known as *callbacks.*

9.3.5 Consequences

The observer pattern simplifies the process of managing the sharing of values among a single server with possibly many clients. The simplification occurs in a number of ways. First, the observer pattern has runtime flexibility. It is easy at runtime to change the number of subscribers as well as the identity of the subscribers, because the Abstract Subject class does not need to have any information about its clients prior to their subscription. Further, all the information the AbstractSubject class needs can be provided by the clients during the subscription process. Second, a single policy regarding the timely or efficient updating of the clients can be centralized in the server and need not be replicated in the (potentially many) clients. This means the code that implements the notification policy needs to be running in only a single place (the server) rather than in many places (the individual clients).

9.3.6 Implementation Strategies

The primary points of variation in implementing the observer pattern are in the formulation of the NotificationHandle class, the implementation of the notification policy, and the type of data sharing.

The most common means for implementing object associations is a pointer (in C or C++) or a reference (in C++ or Java). A callback is a virtualized association and may use the same implementation. In this case, the one-to-many composition relation between the Abstract Subject and the NotificationHandle classes is implemented using an array or list of function pointers. When the server and the clients are not in the same address space, we use a proxy pattern.

The notification policy may be built into the AbstractSubject class and potentially overridden in the ConcreteSubject subclasses, or the strategy pattern may be employed. To use the strategy pattern, we reify the notification policy as a separate class that instructs the Abstract Subject when it is appropriate to notify the registered clients. The most common notification policies are

- When the relevant data (data value) changes
- Periodically
- Both on change and periodically

The last primary implementation issue is how to pass the information around. The two primary approaches are by reference and by value. When data is passed by reference, the most common implementation is to pass a pointer or reference to the single Data object owned by the server. In this pattern it is important to ensure that the clients only read the information; the data should only be modified by the AbstractSubject instance. Further, if the data is to be shared among clients that may reside in different threads, care must be taken to protect the data from corruption due to mutual exclusion problems. The guarded call pattern can be used to ensure that the resource's integrity is maintained when data is shared across thread boundaries. When the data is shared by value, a copy of the Data object is made for each subscriber, which then has the explicit responsibility for destroying that object when it is no longer needed. This approach has the advantage that data protection issues go away but the disadvantage that more memory is needed and the issues around dynamic allocation, such as lack of timeliness predictability and memory fragmentation, must be dealt with.

9.3.7 Sample Model

Figure 9-2 shows a straightforward example of this simple pattern. Figure 9-2a shows the class structure of the model. Central to that structure is the WheelSensor, which acts as the «concrete subject» and the

CruiseControl, Speedometer, and the AntispinController, which act as «concrete clients».

Figure 9-2b shows an example scenario of the execution of the structure shown in Figure 9-2a. In this scenario, each of the clients registers with the server by calling its subscribe operation. Later, when an evGetData event is sent to the server, the server walks the Callback List to find all the registered clients and sends them the data. It does this by calling the Callbacklist::getFirst and CallbackList::getNext() operations; these return a pointer to a client, which may then be dereferenced and the target object's accept() function called. When the CallbackList::get Next() operation returns NULL, the walk-through of the list is complete. At the end of the scenario, the Antispin Controller is sent an evDisable event and so it unsubscribes from the server.

9.4 The Proxy Pattern

The proxy pattern abstracts the true server from the client by means of a stand-in or surrogate class, providing a separation of a client and a server, and allowing specified properties of the server to be hidden from the clients.

9.4.1 Abstract

The proxy pattern decouples the true server from the client by means of a stand-in or surrogate class. There are a number of reasons why this may be useful, such as to hide some particular implementation properties from the clients and thus allow them to vary transparently to the client. For our purposes, the primary reason to use the proxy pattern is to hide from its client the fact that a server may be actually located in another address space. This allows the server to be located in any accessible location and the clients need not concern themselves with how to contact the true server to access required information or services.

9.4.2 Problem

The design of modern embedded systems must often be deployed across multiple address spaces, such as different processors. Many

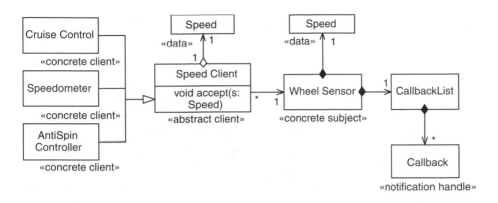

Figure 9-2a: *Observer Pattern Example Structure*

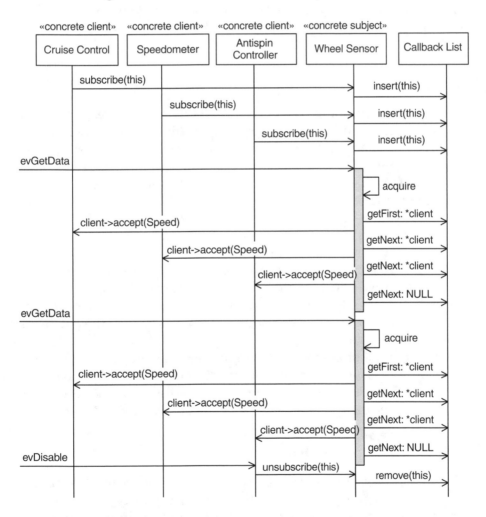

Figure 9-2b: *Observer Pattern Example Scenario*

times such details are subject to change during the design process, or even worse, during the implementation of the system. It is difficult to hard-code the knowledge that a server may be remote because this may change many times as the design progresses. Further, the clients and servers may be redeployed in other physical architectures, using different communications media, and if the clients are intimately aware of these design details then porting the clients to the new platforms is made more difficult.

The two primary problems addressed by the proxy pattern are the transparency of the potential remoteness of the servers and the hiding and encapsulation of the means by which to contact such remote servers.

9.4.3 Pattern Structure

The proxy pattern, shown in Figure 9-3, clearly gets its lineage from the observer pattern. Indeed, the proxy pattern differs primarily in that it adds a proxy between the Abstract Client and the Abstract Subject classes.

The pattern has two sides. In the first side, the Client-side Proxies subscribe to the Server-side Proxies, which publish the data under the command of the Concrete Servers. When the Concrete Servers call the send() operation, all the remote Client-side Proxies are notified of the new data.

On the other side, the Concrete Clients subscribe in turn to the Client-side Proxies, just as in the observer pattern the Concrete Clients subscribe to Concrete Servers. When these Client-side Proxies are notified of new data, they walk their notification lists to send the data to all their local subscribers.

Although the structure of the pattern emphasizes the exchange of Data objects, this is only one kind of service that can be performed via the proxy pattern. In fact, any service may be published by the server and accessed via the proxy classes, even if no data is actually exchanged.

9.4.4 Collaboration Roles

- *AbstractClient:* The AbstractClient associates with the Client-side Proxy so that it can invoke the latter's subscribe() and unsubscribe() operations as necessary. It contains an accept() operation

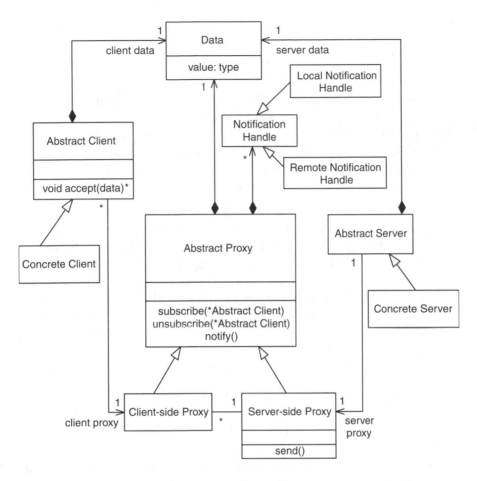

Figure 9-3: *Proxy Pattern*

called to accept the information required by the subscription, the address (as a NotificationHandle), which is passed to the Client-side Proxy instance to which it connects.

- *AbstractProxy:* The AbstractProxy class provides the general mechanisms to handle client subscriptions and data delivery. It aggregates, via composition, zero-to-many NotificationHandle objects (to notify the instances of its clients) and Data objects. It has two subclasses, one to service the application clients and one to service the application server. On the client side, the proxy acts in the same fashion as the AbstractSubject class in the observer pattern—clients subscribe to receive the data that is subsequently pushed to them. On the server side, the Client-side Proxy subclass acts as a client to the Server-side Proxy subclass.

- *AbstractServer:* The AbstractServer acts as a server of information desired by the AbstractClients. When appropriate, it pushes the data object to the Server-side Proxy by calling the latter's send() operation. There is only a single Server-side Proxy object for each AbstractServer. The AbstractServer is subclassed into Concrete-Server for the specific application classes.

- *Client-side Proxy:* The Client-side Proxy is a specialized proxy that serves as the local stand-in for the ultimate server. Because its clients are local, it uses localized NotificationHandles so that when it receives updated information from its associated Server-side Proxy, it can notify its local clients. It must unmarshal the data messages and reformat the Data object into a local format from network format. It subscribes to the Server-side Proxy that ultimately provides the marshalled data from the AbstractServer. The Client-side Proxy usually subscribes to the Server-side Proxy immediately on its creation or as soon as its first client subscribes.

- *ConcreteClient:* The ConcreteClient is an application-specific subclass of the AbstractClient. The pattern is applied by subclassing the AbstractClient and adding application-specific semantics into the new subclass.

- *ConcreteServer:* The ConcreteSubject is an application-specific subclass of the AbstractServer class. The pattern is applied by subclassing the AbstractServer and adding application-specific semantics to the subclass.

- *Data:* The Data class contains the information that the Abstract Server knows and the AbstractClient wants to know. The Data object containing the appropriate value may be shared with the clients by value since it must be at least potentially delivered to different address spaces.

- *LocalNotificationHandle:* This subclass of the NotificationHandle class is used by the Client-side Proxy class. Most commonly, callbacks (pointers to the accept() method of the Client-side Proxy class) are used for the LocalNotificationHandle.

- *NotificationHandle:* The NotificationHandle class stores information for each client so that the Abstract Proxy can notify its clients of the value stored in the Data class.

- *RemoteNotificationHandle:* This subclass of the NotificationHandle class is used by the Server-side Proxy class to store the required information to contact its remote clients, instances of the Client-side Proxy class.

- *Server-side Proxy:* The Server-side Proxy provides encapsulation of the AbstractServer from the communications media and protocols. It manages remote subscriptions from Client-side Proxy objects and notifies them when data is pushed to it by the AbstractServer. It is responsible for marshalling the information into a network or bus message and converting the data values into network format. The Server-side Proxy usually subscribes to the AbstractSubject immediately on its creation.

9.4.5 Consequences

The proxy pattern does a good job of isolating the subject from knowledge that the server may be remote. The advantage to this is that the clients are simplified, not having to deal differently with remote and local clients. The proxy pattern also encapsulates the knowledge of how to contact the servers into the proxy classes so that should the communications media change, fewer classes must be updated.

Because there are usually many fewer client proxy instances (one per data type per address space) than client instances, the traffic on the communications media is minimized. One message is sent across the bus or network for each proxy, rather than one per client. This reduces bus traffic, a common bottleneck in embedded and real-time systems. Bus traffic is reduced even further because of the use of a subscription policy, resulting in transmission of the data only when necessary, as opposed to polling for the data.

9.4.6 Implementation Strategies

On the local (client-proxy) side, the same implementation strategies used for the observer pattern apply here. The AbstractClient objects subscribe to the Client-side Proxies in the same way as in the observer pattern. For the remote (server) side, the implementation is generally highly protocol-specific. The Server-side Proxy marshals the messages from the AbstractServer and invokes the communications system to transmit them to its clients, the remote Client-side Proxy objects. The Server-side Proxy can do this because the Client-side Proxy objects subscribe to the Server-side Proxy.

Note that in this case, the Client-side Proxy objects must know a priori how to contact the Server-side Proxy for the desired information. Thus, this pattern is especially useful on asymmetric distribution architectures, that is, architectures in which the locations of objects are known at design time.

Note also that both the Client-side Proxy and the Server-side Proxy classes aggregate Notification Handle objects via composition. This latter class will typically be subclassed into "local" and "remote" flavors as an optimization. LocalNotificationHandles may be simple function pointers to the accept() method of the ConcreteClient class. Remote NotificationHandles must rely on the underlying transport protocol for message delivery.

9.4.7 Sample Model

The example for the proxy pattern is shown in Figures 9-4 and 9-5. The first figure shows the structure of the collaboration and the mapping of the objects onto the physical architecture. The latter figure gives an example of how such a system behaves.

Figure 9-4 shows four nodes: the GasMixer, Safety, MedicalDelivery, and UserControl processors. The GasMixer contains the server, an object of class O2FlowSensor. This connects with a server-side proxy class O2 FlowServerProxy. This proxy aggregates Object IDs to use as addresses on the bus connecting the nodes running a custom communications protocol. This bus (shown as the heavy lines connecting the nodes) provides the physical means to deliver the messages among the objects running on different processors.

The GasMixerProcessor contains the O2FlowSensor, which acts as a server for the data. The O2FlowSensor invokes O2ServerProxy::send() to send the data to all the registered clients. This is done by walking the notification handle list (which holds Object IDs that the lower-level communications protocol uses for message delivery) and sending a message to each registered client (the O2FlowClientProxies).

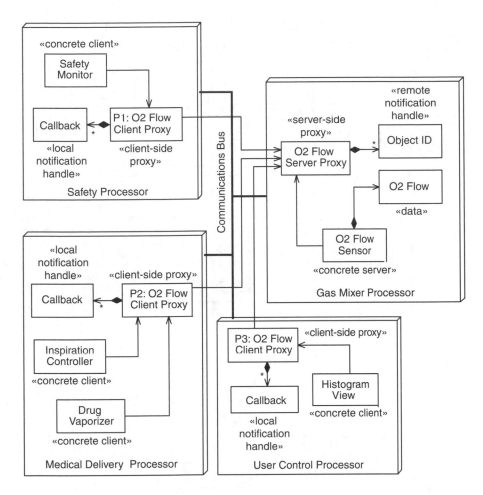

Figure 9-4: *Proxy Example Structure*

There are four clients of the Flow data object: the SafetyMonitor running on the SafetyProcessor, the InspirationController and the Vaporizer running on the MedicalDeliveryProcessor, and the HistogramView running on the UserControlProcessor. Each processor containing at least one client also has a single O2FlowClientProxy instance to obtain the value from the O2FlowServerProxy.

The scenario in Figure 9-5 shows the clients subscribing to their client proxies and the client proxies subscribing to the server proxy.

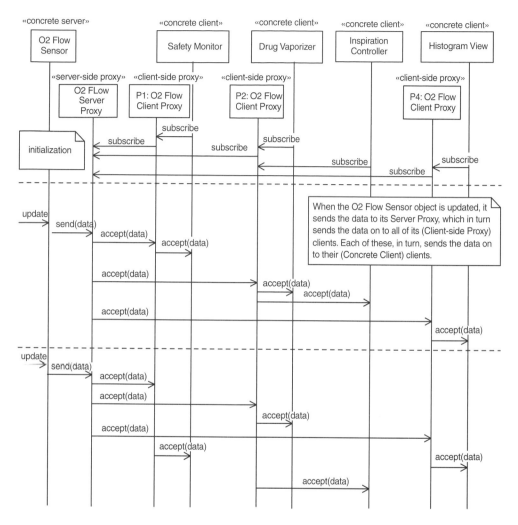

Figure 9-5: *Proxy Example Scenario*

Later, when the O2FlowSensor receives an update, it invokes the O2FlowServerProxy::send() operation, which walks the Notification-Handle list (not shown to save space) and for each registered client proxy sends the data. In turn, the receiving client proxy walks its client list, for the ultimate delivery of the data.

Note: Although the send() operation walks the list of subscribers (RemoteNotificationHandles) in a serial fashion, the delivery of the messages is generally asynchronous, and you cannot determine the arrival order of the messages from the sending order. This is because the objects in different addresses usually operate in different threads, so relative order cannot be determined. That is why in the second update, a different deliver order is shown with respect to the delivery of the data to the concrete clients.

9.5 Reliable Transaction Pattern

Real-time systems use communication protocols to send and receive critical information, both among internal processors, and with external actors in the environment. Within the same system, different messages may have different levels of criticality and so may have different requirements for the reliability of message transfer. Further, different media have different reliability, as do different environments.

The transaction is used when communication reliability is required over unreliable media or when extraordinary reliability is required. For example, suppose the system needs three distinct levels of communications reliability:

- *At Most Once* (AMO): A message is transmitted only once. If the message is lost or corrupted, it is lost. This is used when lightweight transfer is required and the reliability of message transfer is high compared to the probability of message loss.

- *At Least Once* (ALO): A message is transmitted repeatedly until either an explicit acknowledgement is received by the sender or a maximum retry count is exceeded. This is used when the reliability of message transfer is relatively low compared to the probability of message loss, but receipt of the same message multiple times is OK.

- *Exactly Once* (EO): A message is treated as an ALO transaction except that, should a message be received more than once due to retries, only the first message instance will be acted on. This is used when message transfer reliability is relatively low but it is important that a message is acted on only once. Increment or toggle messages, for example, must only be acted on once.

9.5.1 Abstract

The transaction pattern is particularly suited to real-time systems that use a general communication protocol with a rich grammar when different levels of reliability of message transfer are required. It allows the application designers flexibility in their choice of communications method so that they may optimize for speed or reliability.

9.5.2 Problem

The basic problem addressed by this pattern is to support three levels of reliability in the transmission of messages over unreliable communications media.

9.5.3 Pattern Structure

Figure 9-6 shows the structure of the reliable transaction pattern. Ultimately, the sender wants to send a message to the receiver—these are object roles played by instances of the class CommunicatingObject. This is mediated by CommStack, which represents a protocol stack. Notice that in the usual case, there are two instances of CommStack—for any given message, one is mediating the sending of the message and the other is mediating the reception of the message. The sender and receiver roles are usually connected to different instances of the CommStack class. Each CommStack may, at any time, be sending and receiving dozens or hundreds of messages. Each message may, if at the appropriate level of reliability, be associated with a SendTransaction instance (for ALO and EO protocols) and a ReceiveTransaction instance (for EO protocol).

The important classes in the pattern are the SendTransaction and the ReceiveTransaction instances, as they actually mediate the reliable delivery of the messages. Their statecharts are shown in Figure 9-7.

The AMO semantics are the simplest to implement because no transaction objects are required. The reliability of the communications medium and protocol are sufficiently high, and the consequences of a lost message are sufficiently low, so that no extra measures are needed. Transferring messages using AMO semantics is fast and requires the fewest computation resources.

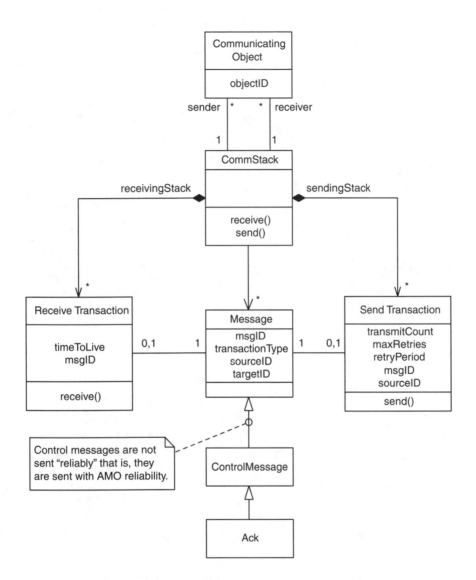

Figure 9-6: *Transaction Pattern*

ALO semantics require that the sending CommStack maintain a transaction object until an explicit acknowledgment is received back from the receiver. If an acknowledgment is received, the transaction object is destroyed. If no acknowledgment is received within the retry

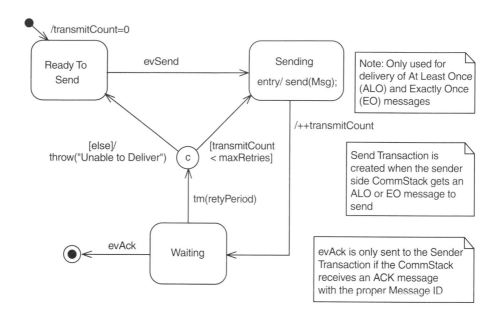

Figure 9-7a: *Sender Transaction Statechart*

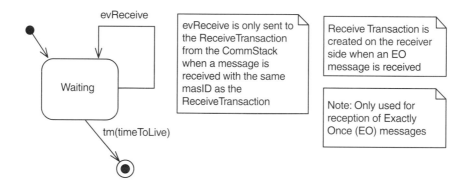

Figure 9-7b: *Receiver Transaction Statechart*

period, then the SendTransaction automatically retransmits the message to the receiving CommStack. If the SendTransaction fails to successfully get the message to the receiver (i.e., the MaxRetries count is exceeded), the message originator is notified so that corrective measures can be initiated.

The sending CommunicatingObject cannot distinguish between a loss of the message and a loss of the acknowledgement, so the Receiver object may receive the message more than once. This is normally not a problem for operations like set() when setting an absolute value, but it becomes problematic when the operation is something like increment(). ALO semantics are incompatible with incremental operations.

EO semantics require transaction objects on both sides. The objects on the sending side function exactly as they do to support ALO semantics. What is different is that the receiving CommStack object must now create a ReceiveTransaction. When the receiving CommStack receives a message with an EO transaction type, it creates a ReceiveTransaction object and sets its timeToLive and msgID attributes. The timeToLive attribute is used for a timeout; once this timeout occurs, the Receive-Transaction object is destroyed. If a duplicate message is received before that occurs, the receiving CommStack sends an evReceive event to the ReceiveTransaction, causing it to reenter the waiting state, restarting its timeout period from zero.

9.5.4 Collaboration Roles

The following objects participate in this pattern.

- *ACK:* An ACK is a kind of ControlMessage, sent back to the sending CommStack when a message is received by a target CommStack and it has passed whatever integrity tests the protocol defines, such as checksum or CRC.

- *CommunicatingObject:* A CommunicatingObject knows how to create messages and how to invoke the CommStack::send() service. It can also receive messages from the CommStack.

- *CommStack:* The CommStack object manages the sending of messages, creating instances of SendTransaction as necessary, and the reception of messages and their delivery to the target objects, creating ReceiveTransaction objects as necessary. When sending, the CommStack object creates a SendTransaction instance to mediate the reliable delivery of the message only for ALO and EO reliabilities. AMO can be sent (and immediately forgotten) without using a SendTransaction. The CommStack creates a ReceiveTransaction only when it receives a message with the EO reliability; messages received with AMO or ALO reliabilities do not require a Receive-Transaction.

- *ControlMessage:* A ControlMessage assists in the delivery of other messages. An ACK, or acknowledgement message, is one of these. ControlMessages are never delivered "reliably"—that is, they are always transmitted with the AMO level of reliability.

- *Message:* The Message contains the data of interest to the Source and Target, as well as metadata,[4] such as a MsgID and Transaction Type. The MsgID must be unique within the lifespan of the transaction object so that it uniquely identifies the message. The Transaction Type tells the Sender and Receiver whether or not transaction objects are required for this message.

- *ReceiveTransaction:* This object tracks the receipt of messages using EO semantics. It is created when the Receiver gets a message with the EO transaction type. The purpose of the ReceiverTransaction is to discard extra copies of a received message, which can occur if ACK responses to an ALO or EO message are lost. The statechart for this class is shown in . Note that the timeToLive timeout transition is retriggered (restarts from zero) each time an evReceive event is received from the local CommStack in response to receiving a message with the proper msgID. When no evReceive event has occurred for the timeToLive period, the ReceiveTransaction is destroyed.

- *SendTransaction:* This is the transaction created (and destroyed) by the CommStack in the sendingStack role. Each transaction corresponds to a single ALO or EO message. It tracks the number of times the message has been transmitted as well as its retry period. If an acknowledgement specifying the original MsgID is not received within the retry period, the message is retransmitted and the transmit count is incremented. If the count exceeds maxRetries, the originating CommunicatingObject source is notified.

---

[4] Metadata is information about information; for example, a field that tells the size of a message can be considered metadata.

9.5.5 Consequences

The reliable transaction pattern simplifies the delivery of messages with three distinct levels of reliability: AMO, ALO, and EO. This is particularly true when many messages may be in transit at any given time, such as when peer-to-peer communications are occurring across a multimastered bus. In a master-slave communications environment, in which a master is in charge of initiating and managing all communications, this pattern is overly complex. The pattern as it is can handle any number of simultaneously active messages.

9.5.6 Implementation Strategies

The implementation of these classes is straightforward. The CommStack is highly protocol specific, of course, but the SendTransaction and ReceiveTransaction objects have simple statecharts.

9.5.7 Sample Model

Figure 9-8a shows the structure of a simple example. In a medical device, the AnesthesiaControl is remote from the Vaporizer. It needs to send an Increment Dose command to the Vaporizer. Because an "increment" style command is one that should be sent with EO semantics, it creates the message with the transactionType attribute set to EO. It adds the source objectID (99) and the target object (54) as needed by the message. Since the CommunicatingObjects don't have anything to do with the actual message transmission, it leaves the msgID attribute of the Message blank for the CommStack to fill in. Because the EO semantics demand both a SendTransaction and a ReceiveTransaction, those are part of the class diagram.

Figure 9-8b shows a scenario for sending the Increment Dose message. In this scenario, the returning ACK is lost (indicated by the X) so the sending transaction, not knowing whether the original message or the responding ACK was lost, must retransmit after its timeout. The receiving side, meanwhile, has received the message and forwarded it on to the Vaporizer. It has also created a ReceiveTransaction, which waits and receives (and discards) the second command, before eventually timing out and being destroyed.

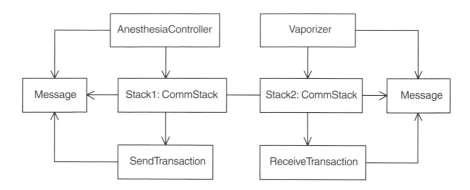

Figure 9-8a: *Reliable Transaction Example Structure*

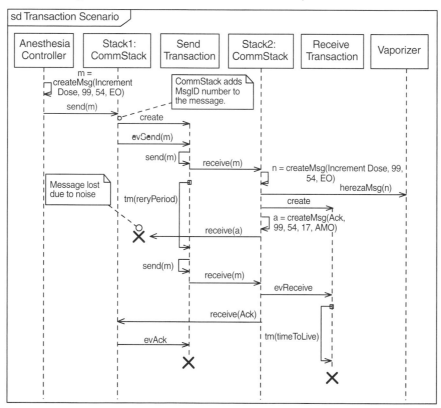

Figure 9-8b: *Reliable Transaction Example Scenario*

9.6 Smart Pointer Pattern

In my experience over the last couple of decades leading and managing development projects implemented in C and C++, pointer problems are by far the most common and hardest to identify kinds of defects. They are common because the pointer metaphor is very low level and requires precise management, but it is easy to forget about when you are dealing with all possible execution paths. Inevitably, it seems, a pointer is destroyed (or goes out of scope) but the memory is not properly freed (a memory leak), memory is released but nevertheless accessed (dangling pointer), or memory is accessed but not properly allocated (uninitialized pointer). These problems are notoriously difficult to identify using standard means of testing, and peer reviews and tools such as Purify[5] and LINT[6] that can identify "questionable practices" sometimes flag so many things it is virtually impossible to use the results. The smart pointer pattern is a mechanistic approach that has produced excellent results.

9.6.1 Abstract

Pointers are by far the most common way to realize an association between objects. The common implementation approach is whenever there is a navigable association, the object uses an attribute of type pointer, and this pointer is dereferenced as necessary to send messages to (i.e., invoke member functions on) the target object. The problem with pointers is that they are not objects; they are just data. Because they are not objects, the primitive operations you can perform on them are not checked for validity. Thus, we are free to access a pointer that has never been initialized or after the memory to which it points has been freed; we are also free to destroy the pointer without releasing the memory, resulting in the loss of the now no-longer-referenceable memory to the system.

The smart pointer pattern solves these problems by making the pointer an object. A Smart Pointer object can have constructors and

---

[5] See *http://www.rational.com/products/purify_nt/index.jsp* for a commercial product description.
[6] See *http://www.gimpel.com/* for a commercial product description.

destructors and operations that can ensure that its preconditional invariants (rules of proper usage) are maintained.

9.6.2 Problem

In many ways, pointers are the bane of the programmer's existence. If they weren't so dang useful, we would have discarded them long ago. Because they allow us to dynamically allocate, deallocate, and reference memory dynamically, they form an important part of the programmer's toolkit. However, their use commonly results in a number of kinds of defects:

- *Memory Leaks:* Destroying a pointer before the memory they reference is released. This means that the memory block is never put back in the heap free store, so its loss is permanent, at least until the system is rebooted. Over time, the available memory in the heap free store (i.e., memory that can now be allocated by request) shrinks and eventually the system fails because it cannot satisfy memory requests, even though it ought to be able to.

- *Uninitialized Pointers:* Using a pointer as if it were pointing to a valid object (or memory block) but neglecting to properly allocate the memory. This can also occur if the memory request is made but refused.

- *Dangling Pointers:* Using a pointer as if it were pointing to a valid object (or memory block) but *after* the memory to which it points has been freed.

- *Pointer Arithmetic Defects:* Using a pointer as an iterator over an array of values, but inappropriately. This can be because the pointer goes beyond the bounds of the array (in either direction), possibly stepping on memory allocated to other objects, or becoming misaligned, pointing into the middle of a data value rather than at its beginning.

These problems arise because pointers are inherently stupid. They are only data values (addresses) and the operations defined on them are primitive and without checks on their correct use. If only they were objects, their operations could be extended to include validity checks and they could identify or prevent inappropriate use.

9.6.3 Pattern Structure

The basic solution of the smart pointer pattern is to reify the pointer into an object. Once a pointer comes smart, or potentially smart, its operations can ensure that the preconditions of the pointer (i.e., it points to valid memory) are met. Figure 9-9a shows the simple structure of this pattern and Figure 9-9b shows a common variant.

9.6.4 Collaboration Roles

- *Client:* The Client is the object that at the analysis level simply has an association to the Target object. If this is a bi-directional association, then both these objects have smart pointers to the other.

- *SmartPointer:* The Smart Pointer object contains the actual pointer (rawPtr) as an attribute, as well as constructor, destructor, and access operations. The access operations will usually be realized by overriding pointer dereference operators ([] and ->) in C++, to hide the fact that a smart pointer is being used. The Target::referenceCount attribute keeps track of the number of smart pointers that are referring to the specific target object. This is necessary to know when to destroy the dynamically created Target.

  The Smart Pointer object has two constructors. The default constructor creates a corresponding Target object and sets referenceCount to the value 1. The second constructor initializes the rawPtr attribute to the value of the address passed in and increments the Target::referenceCount. The destructor decrements the Target::referenceCount; if it decrements to 0, the Target is destroyed. In principle, the Target::referenceCount must be referred to by all Smart Pointer objects that point to the *same* object.

- *Target:* The Target object provides the services that the Context object wishes to access. In the basic form of the pattern (a), the Target object also has a reference count attribute that tracks the number of Smart Pointer objects currently referencing it.

- *TargetWrapper:* In the smart pointer pattern variant b, the Target object is not at all aware of Smart Pointers or reference counts. The TargetWrapper object contains, by composition, the Target object, and owns the referenceCount attribute.

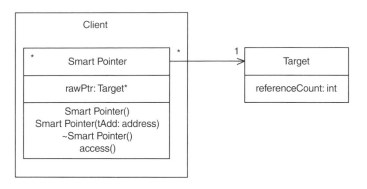

Figure 9-9a: *Basic Smart Pointer Pattern*

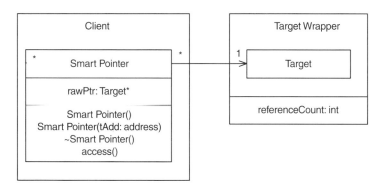

Figure 9-9b: *Wrapper Variant*

9.6.5 Consequences

The advantages of the application of this pattern is that it is a simple way to ensure that objects are destroyed when they are no longer accessible—that is, when all references to them have been (or are being) destroyed. This requires some discipline on the part of the programmers. If the Target object is being referenced by *both* smart and raw pointers, then this pattern will break, with potential catastrophic consequences. On the other hand, the pattern can be codified into an easily checked rule: Use no raw pointers, and validate during code reviews.

To ensure robustness in the presence of multithreaded access to an object (i.e., Smart Pointers exist in multiple threads that reference the same Target), care must be taken in the constructors and destructor. The simplest way to handle them is to make them atomic (i.e., prevent task-switching during the construction or destruction of a Smart Pointer). You can easily do this by making the first operation in the constructor a call to the OS to prevent task-switching (just don't forget to turn it back on when you're done!). The destructor must be similarly protected. Otherwise, there is a possibility that the object may be destroyed *after* you checked that it was valid and thus that a Smart Pointer is now pointing to a Target that no longer exists.

Finally, there is one situation in which Smart Pointers may be correctly implemented but still may result in memory leakage. The Smart Pointer logic ensures that whenever there is no Smart Pointer pointing to a Target, the Target will be deleted. However, it is possible to define small cycles of objects that contain Smart Pointers, but the entire cycle cannot be accessed by the rest of the application. In other words, it is still possible to get a memory leak if the collaboration of objects has cycles in it. Figure 9-10 shows how this can happen.

In Figure 9-10, object Obj3 and Obj5 form a cycle. If Obj2 and Obj4 are destroyed, the reference counts associated with Obj3 and Obj5 decrement down to 1 rather than 0, and these two objects are unable to be referenced by the remainder of the application. Since their reference

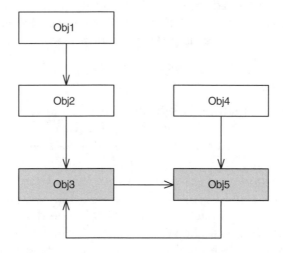

Figure 9-10: *Smart Pointer Cycles*

counts are greater than 1, they cannot be destroyed, but neither can the application invoke services of these objects because there are no references to these objects outside the cycle itself.

The easiest way to handle the problem is to ensure than no Target itself references another object that could even reference the original. This can usually be deduced from drawing class diagrams of the collaborations and some object diagrams resulting from the execution of the class diagram. If cycles cannot be avoid, then it might be better to avoid using the smart pointer pattern for those cycles specifically.

9.6.6 Implementation Strategies

This pattern is simple and straightforward to implement and should create no problems. If you desire a smart pointer pattern that can handle cyclic object structures, then this can be solved at the cost of increased complexity and processing resource usage. A good discussion of these methods is provided in [9], Chapter 3.

9.6.7 Related Patterns

More elaborate forms of the Smart Pointer object are described in [9], although they are expressed as algorithms defined on the Smart Pointer rather than as patterns per se, as is done here. When cycles are present but the benefits of the smart pointer pattern (protection against pointer defects) are strongly desired, the garbage collector or compacting garbage collector patterns [8] may be indicated.

9.6.8 Sample Model

Figure 9-11 shows a simple application of this pattern. Two clients of the HR Sensor object exist: One object that displays the values and another that tracks values to do trending analysis. When the HR Display object runs, it creates an HR Sensor object via a Wrapped Sensor object. The HR Display object also notifies the HR Trend object to begin tracking the heart rate information (via the Wrapped Sensor object).

Later, the HR Display is destroyed. It calls the delete operation on the WrappedSensor class. The WrappedSensor decrements its reference count but does not delete the HR Sensor because the reference count is

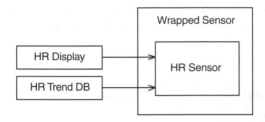

Figure 9-11a: *Smart Pointer Pattern Structure*

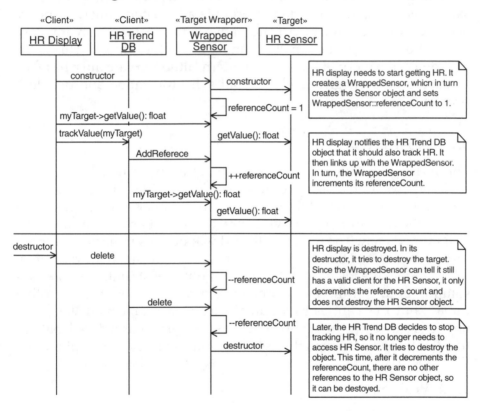

Figure 9-11b: *Smart Pointer Pattern Scenario*

greater than zero (the HRTrendDB still has a valid reference to it). Later on, when the HRTrendDB removes the last pointer to the HR Sensor object, the HR Sensor object is finally deleted.

9.7 Guarded Call Pattern

Sometimes asynchronous communication schemes, such as the message queuing pattern [8], do not provide adequately timely response across a thread boundary. An alternative is to synchronously invoke a method of an object nominally running in another thread. This is the guarded call pattern. It is a simple pattern, although care must be taken to ensure data integrity and to avoid synchronization and deadlock problems.

9.7.1 Abstract

The message queuing pattern enforces an asynchronous rendezvous between two threads, modeled as «active» objects. In general, this approach works very well, but it means a rather slow exchange of information because the receiving thread does not process the information immediately. The receiving thread will process it the next time the thread executes. This can be problematic when the synchronization between the threads is urgent (e.g., tight time constraints). An obvious solution is to call the method of the appropriate object in the other thread, but this can lead to mutual exclusion problems if the called object is currently doing something else. The guarded call pattern handles this case through the use of a mutual exclusion semaphore.

9.7.2 Problem

The problem this pattern addresses is the need for a timely synchronization or data exchange between threads. In such cases, it may not be possible to wait for an asynchronous rendezvous. A synchronous rendezvous can be made more timely, but this must be done carefully to avoid data corruption and erroneous computation.

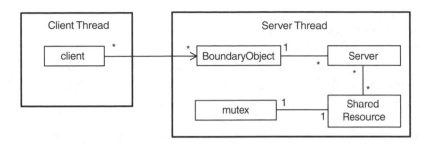

Figure 9-12: *Guarded Call Pattern Structure*

9.7.3 Pattern Structure

The guarded call pattern solves this problem by using a semaphore to guard access to the resource across the thread boundary. If another thread attempts to access the resource while it is locked, the latter thread is blocked and must allow the previous thread to complete its execution of the operation. This simple solution is to guard all the relevant operations (*relevant* as defined to be accessing the resource) with a single mutual exclusion semaphore. The structure of the pattern is shown in Figure 9-12.

9.7.4 Collaboration Roles

- *ServerThread:* This «active» object contains the Server objects that share the SharedResource and protect them with the Mutex.

- *ClientThread:* This «active» object contains (via the composition relation) the Client object that synchronously invokes the method, ultimately, on the Server objects. The Client runs in the thread of the ClientThread.

- *BoundaryObject:* The BoundaryObject provides the protected interface to the Server objects; that is, it presents the operations the servers wish to provide across the thread boundary for a guarded call rendezvous. The BoundaryObject combines all the operations (because they may all affect the SharedResource). If multiple shared resources are to be protected, then the Server Thread can provide multiple BoundaryObjects. The important concept is that the Mutex associated with the SharedResource blocks any operation that attempts to use the SharedResource.

- *Mutex:* The Mutex is a mutual exclusion semaphore object that permits only a single caller through at a time. It can be explicitly locked and unlocked by the caller, but it is safer if the operations of the SharedResource invoke it whenever a relevant service is called, locking it prior to starting the service and unlocking it once the service is complete. ClientThreads that attempt to invoke a service when the services are already locked become blocked until the Mutex is in its unlocked state.

- *Server:* Each Server object (and there may be many) has two relevant properties. First, it uses the Shared Resource object, and second, it may provide a service useable to a Client across the thread boundary that may use the SharedResource.

- *SharedResource:* The SharedResource object is any object that provides data or a service that is shared among multiple Servers in such a way that its integrity must be protected by the serialization of access. For objects that protect data in this way, it means that the Servers may write to or in some way affect its value. For service objects, it usually means that they provide an interface to some physical device or process that is changed by execution of the process, often in a nonreversible way.

9.7.5 Consequences

The guarded call pattern provides a means by which a set of services may be safely provided across a thread boundary. This is done in such a way that even if several internal objects within the called thread share a common resource, that resource remains protected from corruption due to mutual exclusion problems. This is a synchronous rendezvous, providing a timely response, unless the services are currently locked. If the services are currently locked, the resource is protected, but timely response cannot be guaranteed unless analysis is done to show that the service is schedulable [6,7].

The situation may be even simpler than required for this pattern. If the Server objects don't interact with respect to the SharedResource, the SharedResource itself may be contained directly within the Server object. In this case, the Server objects themselves can be the Boundary Objects or the BoundaryObjects can participate in a façade pattern (also called an *interface pattern*). Then there is simply one Mutex object for every Server object. This is a simpler case of this more general pattern.

9.7.6 Implementation Strategies

Both the ClientThread and ServerThread are «active» objects. It is typical to create an OS thread in which they run in their constructors and destroy that thread in their destructors. They both contain objects via the composition relationship. For the most part, this means that the «active» objects execute an event or message loop, looking for events or messages that have been queued for later asynchronous processing. Once an event or message is taken out of queue, it is dispatched to objects contained within it via composition, calling the appropriate operations on those objects to handle the event or message.

For the synchronous rendezvous, the «active» object allows other objects visibility to the BoundaryObjects (i.e., they are in its public interface) and their public operations. When a BoundaryObject is created, it creates a Mutex object.

Ports can be used to delegate the services of internal parts and make them explicitly visible across the thread boundary, but the technique works and is implemented in exactly the same way.

9.7.7 Sample Model

Figure 9-13a shows the model structure for the example. Three active objects encapsulate the semantic objects in this system. The View Thread object contains a view of the reactor temperature on the user interface. The Alarming Thread manages alarms in a different thread. And the Processing Thread manages the acquisition and filtering of the data itself. Stereotypes indicate the pattern roles.

Figure 9-13b walks through a scenario. Note that the messages use a thread prefix ("A:" or "B:") and the activation lines on the sequence diagram are coded with different fill patterns to indicate in which thread they belong. This is an alternative way to show concurrent message threads, other than the PAR sequence diagram operator. This form is used because we want to clearly see the synchronization points

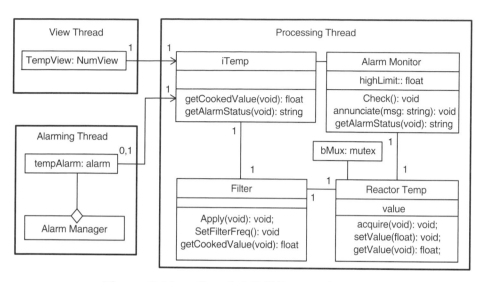

Figure 9-13a: *Guarded Call Pattern Structure*

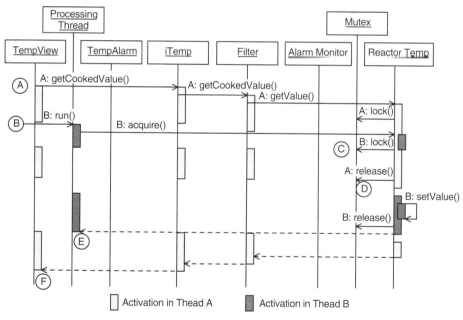

Figure 9-13b: *Guarded Call Pattern Scenario*

between the threads. Points of special interest are annotated with circled letters.

The scenario shows how the collision of two threads is managed in a thread-safe fashion. The first thread (A) starts up to get the value of the reactor temperature for display on the user interface. While that thread is being processed, the higher-priority thread (B) begins to acquire the data. However, it finds the ReactorTemp object locked, and so it is suspended from execution until the Mutex is released. Once the Mutex is released, the higher-priority thread can now continue—the lock() operation succeeds and the B thread continues until completion. Once thread B has completed, thread A can now continue, returning the (old) value to the TempView object for display. The points of interest for the scenario are as follows:

A. Thread A starts in View Thread to get the reactor temperature for display.

B. Thread B starts in Processing Thread to acquire and set a new value for the reactor temperature.

C. Because Mutex is already locked, thread B suspends and thread A continues.

D. Now that the Mutex is released, the higher-priority thread B can continue.

E. Thread B has completed, and now thread A can complete and return the (old) value for display.

F. Thread A is now complete.

9.8 Container Pattern

Analysis models the *what* of a system—what it is, what fundamental concepts are involved, and what the important relations and associations among them are. Design specifies the *how* of all the unspecified portions of the system. One of the important hows of design is how message transport for each and every message will be implemented— is it a function call, an OS mail message, a bus message, an RPC, or something even more exotic? Another important how is the resolution of associations with multivalued roles.

When an object has a one-to-many association, the question arises as to the exact mechanism the "one" class will use to access the "many" objects. One solution is to build features into the "one" class to manage the set of contained objects. These facilities typically manifest themselves as operations such as add(), remove(), first(), next(), last(), and find(). Often the semantics of the associate dictate elaborate operations, such as maintaining the set of objects in a specific order or balancing the tree. Building these features into each and every class that must maintain a one-to-many association is repugnant for several reasons outlined in Section 9.1. The common solution to these problems is to insert a container object (also called a *collection object*) between the "one" and the "many."

Adding a container object to manage the aggregated objects doesn't entirely solve the problem because often the container must be accessed from several clients. If the container keeps track of the client position, it will become confused in a multiclient environment. To get around this, iterators are used in conjunction with the containers. An iterator keeps track of where the client is in the container. Different clients use different iterators, so the separate concerns of managing the collection and tracking position within the container are abstracted away from each other. A single client may use several different iterators. The Standard Template Library (STL), a part of the ANSI C++ standard, provides many different containers with a variety of iterators, such as first, last, and so on.

9.8.1 Abstract

The container pattern reifies the association itself as a class dedicated to the management of multiple instances. This solution can easily take advantage of container libraries that offer various containers that are optimal under different conditions, and can be done by some UML tools automatically.

9.8.2 Problem

The obvious form of association realization—pointers and references—only work in their naïve form for multiplicities of 1–1 or (0,1) – (0,1). Their implementation for multivalued roles (e.g., *) isn't obvious.

Simply adding containment management to one of the existing classes complicates that class with a set of semantics unrelated to its normal purpose. Further, it is important in many circumstances that the same collection of objects be used by multiple clients without the access by one client affecting any of the others.

9.8.3 Pattern Structure

The container pattern addresses the realization of multivalued association multiplicities by inserting a class between the classes in question, one charged with the management of collection management. Different kinds of collection classes can be used to optimize different qualities of service, such as memory space, read access time, write access time, searching, and so on. Additionally, the use of iterators allows the collection to be used by multiple clients without the access of one client affecting the access of another.

Like the guarded call pattern, the container pattern is very simple, although the container itself may be quite complex internally. This pattern will be elaborated more in the next pattern (the Rendezvous Pattern).

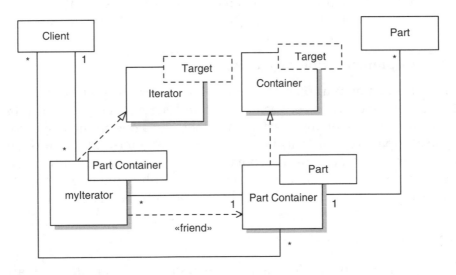

Figure 9-14: *Container Pattern*

9.8.4 Collaboration Roles

The following objects participate in the container pattern:

- *Container:* The Container object manages the collection and provides accessor operations.
- *Iterator:* The Iterator acts like a smart pointer and mediates access to the parts for the client. An iterator query access, such as first() or next(), typically returns a pointer to a Part object. Insertion and deletion of parts may also be mediated through the iterator.
- *Client:* The Client is the object needing access to the Part objects managed by the Container.
- *Part:* The Part objects are the objects managed by the Container object. In a system managing bank accounts, for example, the Part objects might be individual accounts or transactions within those accounts.

9.8.5 Consequences

The container pattern provides good isolation of the techniques and complexities of part management by abstracting the container into a separate class to manage the (possibly) many contained parts. The use of iterators allows the same Container to be used by several clients as well, at the cost of some complexity due to the use of such iterators.

9.8.6 Implementation Strategies

The most common implementation of this pattern is to elaborate one-to-many relationships between a client and parts to a one-to-one relationship to the client and the part container, and a one-to-many relation from the part container to the parts. The container and iterators are most commonly taken from a container library, such as STL. Rhapsody does the elaboration and implementation of the containers directly, either with their built-in container library or with the STL (C++ only).

9.8.7 Sample Model

The example of this pattern, shown in Figure 9-15, is an aircraft flight planning system. A flight plan consists of a set of waypoints. Each waypoint contains a name, an altitude, and a position in terms of latitude and longitude. The flight plan must manage arbitrary number of waypoints. This includes operations such as these:

- nWaypoints(), which returns the number of waypoints in the flight plan
- mininumAltitude(), which searches the set of waypoints and returns the lowest altitude of any of the waypoints
- pathDistance(), which computes the distance along a path, assuming a minimum flight distance between waypoints

Each of these operations, as well as the facility to add and remove waypoints in the flight plan, requires the FlightPlan class to manipulate the set of waypoints. In this case, this is via the application of the container pattern, implemented, in this case, with the vector template. Code Listing 9-2 shows the FlightPlan.h file and 9-3 shows the corresponding FlightPlan.cpp file. The operation implementation is shown

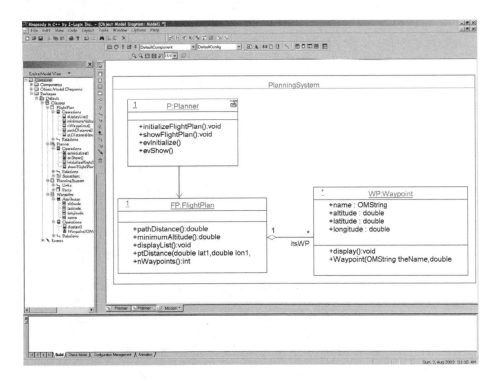

Figure 9-15a: *Container Pattern Example*

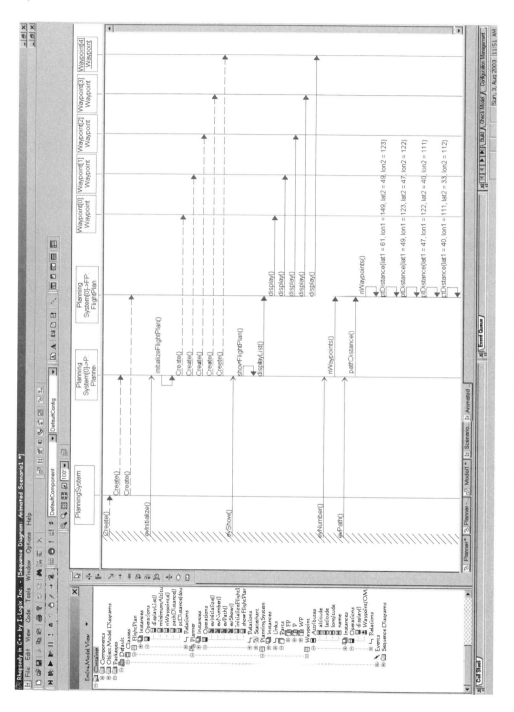

Figure 9-15b: *Container Pattern Example*

in this latter file. An iterator is used to scan the list of waypoints. The iterator starts at the beginning of the list using the special begin() iterator and terminates at the end of the list with the special end() iterator. The use of this is illustrated by the body of the nWaypoints() operation, which simply counts the number of waypoints.

```
int n = 0;
    vector<Waypoint*>::const_iterator trailBlazer;

    for (trailBlazer = itsWP.begin(); trailBlazer !=
        itsWP.end(); ++trailBlazer) {
        ++n;
      };

    return n;

/************************************************************
    Rhapsody : 5.0
    Login      : Bruce
    Component    : DefaultComponent
    Configuration  : DefaultConfig
    Model Element  : FlightPlan
//!   Generated Date  : Sun, 3, Aug 2003
    File Path    : DefaultComponent\DefaultConfig\
                   FlightPlan.h
************************************************************/

#ifndef FlightPlan_H
#define FlightPlan_H

#include <oxf/oxf.h>
#include <string>
#include <algorithm>
#include "math.h"
#include "Default.h"
#include <vector>
#include <iterator>
#include "Waypoint.h"
//## package Default
// - - - - - - - - - - - - - - - - - - - - - - - - - - - - -
// FlightPlan.h
// - - - - - - - - - - - - - - - - - - - - - - - - - - - - -
#ifdef _MSC_VER
// disable Microsoft compiler warning (debug
// information truncated)
```

```cpp
#pragma warning(disable: 4786)
#endif
//## class FlightPlan
class FlightPlan  {

////     Constructors and destructors     ////
public :

    //## auto_generated
    FlightPlan();

    //## auto_generated
    ~FlightPlan();

////     Operations     ////
public :

    //## operation displayList()
    void displayList();

    // Returns the minimum altitude in the flight plan
    //## operation minimumAltitude()
    double minimumAltitude();

    //## operation nWaypoints()
    int nWaypoints();

    //## operation pathDistance()
    double pathDistance();

// Distance calculation in miles is sqrt(x^2 + y^2)
// where x= 69.1*(lat2 -lat1) and y = 69.1*(lon2 -
// lon1)*cos(lat1/57.3).
// More accurate conversion can be done by using the
   greater distance
// formula.
//## operation ptDistance(double,double,double,double)
double ptDistance(double lat1, double lon1, double
  lat2, double lon2);

////     Additional operations     ////
public :

    //## auto_generated
```

```
    std::vector<Waypoint*>::const_iterator getItsWP()
      const;

    //## auto_generated
    std::vector<Waypoint*>::const_iterator
      getItsWPEnd() const;

    //## auto_generated
    void addItsWP(Waypoint* p_Waypoint);

    //## auto_generated
    void removeItsWP(Waypoint* p_Waypoint);

    //## auto_generated
    void clearItsWP();

////     Framework operations     ////
public :

    //## auto_generated
    void _addItsWP(Waypoint* p_Waypoint);

    //## auto_generated
    void _removeItsWP(Waypoint* p_Waypoint);

    //## auto_generated
    void _clearItsWP();
protected :

    //## auto_generated
    void cleanUpRelations();

////     Relations and components     ////
protected :

    std::vector<Waypoint*> itsWP;          //## link itsWP

};

#endif
/********************************************************
   File Path    : DefaultComponent\DefaultConfig\
                  FlightPlan.h
 ********************************************************/
```

Code Listing 9-2: *FlightPlan.h*

```
/*****************************************************
    Rhapsody : 5.0
    Login    : Bruce
    Component    : DefaultComponent
    Configuration  : DefaultConfig
    Model Element  : FlightPlan
//!   Generated Date : Sun, 3, Aug 2003
    File Path    : DefaultComponent\DefaultConfig\
                    FlightPlan.cpp
*****************************************************/
#include "FlightPlan.h"
//## package Default
// - - - - - - - - - - - - - - - - - - - - - - - - - -
// FlightPlan.cpp
// - - - - - - - - - - - - - - - - - - - - - - - - - -
//## class FlightPlan

FlightPlan::FlightPlan() {
}
FlightPlan::~FlightPlan() {
    cleanUpRelations();
}
void FlightPlan::displayList() {
    //#[ operation displayList()
    vector<Waypoint*>::const_iterator trailBlazer;
    for (trailBlazer = itsWP.begin(); trailBlazer !=
      itsWP.end(); ++trailBlazer) {
        (*trailBlazer)->display();
    };
    cout << "DONE" << endl;

    //#]
}
double FlightPlan::minimumAltitude() {
    //#[ operation minimumAltitude()
    double minAlt= 1E06;
    double altitude;
    vector<Waypoint*>::const_iterator trailBlazer;

    for (trailBlazer = itsWP.begin(); trailBlazer !=
      itsWP.end(); ++trailBlazer) {
        altitude = (*trailBlazer)->getAltitude();
      if (minAlt > altitude) minAlt = altitude;
      };

     return minAlt;
```

```
        //#]
}
int FlightPlan::nWaypoints() {
    //#[ operation nWaypoints()
    int n = 0;
    vector<Waypoint*>::const_iterator trailBlazer;

    for (trailBlazer = itsWP.begin(); trailBlazer !=
itsWP.end(); ++trailBlazer) {
        ++n;
      };

     return n;
    //#]
}
double FlightPlan::pathDistance() {
    //#[ operation pathDistance()
    double distance = 0;
    double lat1,lon1,lat2,lon2;

    vector<Waypoint*>::const_iterator trailBlazer;
    if (nWaypoints() > 1) {
      trailBlazer = itsWP.begin();
      lat1 = (*trailBlazer)->getLatitude();
      lon1 = (*trailBlazer)->getLongitude();

      for (trailBlazer = itsWP.begin()+1; trailBlazer
          != itsWP.end(); ++trailBlazer) {
            lat2 = (*trailBlazer)->getLatitude();
            lon2 = (*trailBlazer)->getLongitude();

            distance += ptDistance(lat1, lon1, lat2,
              lon2);
            lat1=lat2;
            lon1=lon2;
            };
    };

    return distance;
    //#]
}
double FlightPlan::ptDistance(double lat1, double
  lon1, double lat2, double lon2) {
    //#[ operation
ptDistance(double,double,double,double)
    double x,y, distance;
```

```
    x = 69.1*(lat2 -lat1);
    y = 69.1*(lon2 -lon1)*cos(lat1/57.3);
    distance = sqrt(x*x + y*y);

    return distance;

    //#]
}
std::vector<Waypoint*>::const_iterator
  FlightPlan::getItsWP() const {
    std::vector<Waypoint*>::const_iterator iter;
    iter = itsWP.begin();
    return iter;
}
std::vector<Waypoint*>::const_iterator
  FlightPlan::getItsWPEnd() const {
    return itsWP.end();
}
void FlightPlan::_addItsWP(Waypoint* p_Waypoint) {
    itsWP.push_back(p_Waypoint);
}
void FlightPlan::addItsWP(Waypoint* p_Waypoint) {
    if(p_Waypoint != NULL)
        {
            p_Waypoint->_setItsFlightPlan(this);
        }
    _addItsWP(p_Waypoint);
}
void FlightPlan::_removeItsWP(Waypoint* p_Waypoint) {
    std::vector<Waypoint*>::iterator pos =
      std::find(itsWP.begin(),
      itsWP.end(),p_Waypoint);
    if (pos != itsWP.end()) {
      itsWP.erase(pos);
    };
}
void FlightPlan::removeItsWP(Waypoint* p_Waypoint) {
    if(p_Waypoint != NULL)
        {
            p_Waypoint->__setItsFlightPlan(NULL);
        }
    _removeItsWP(p_Waypoint);
}
void FlightPlan::_clearItsWP() {
    itsWP.clear();
```

```
}
void FlightPlan::clearItsWP() {
    std::vector<Waypoint*>::const_iterator iter;
    iter = itsWP.begin();
    while (iter != itsWP.end()){
        (*iter)->_clearItsFlightPlan();
        iter++;
    }
    _clearItsWP();
}
void FlightPlan::cleanUpRelations() {
    {
        std::vector<Waypoint*>::const_iterator iter;
        iter = itsWP.begin();
        while (iter != itsWP.end()){
            FlightPlan* p_FlightPlan = (*iter)->
              getItsFlightPlan();
            if(p_FlightPlan != NULL)
                {
                    (*iter)->__setItsFlightPlan(NULL);
                }
            iter++;
        }
        itsWP.clear();
    }
}
/**********************************************************
    File Path    : DefaultComponent\DefaultConfig\
                   FlightPlan.cpp
 **********************************************************/
```

Code Listing 9-3: *FlightPlan.cpp*

9.9 The Rendezvous Pattern

The rendezvous pattern is a simplified form of the guarded call pattern and is used to synchronize a set of threads or permit data sharing among a set of threads. It reifies the synchronization of two threads as an object itself. There are many subtle variants of this pattern. The Rendezvous object may contain data to be shared as the threads synchronize, or it may simply provide a means for synchronizing an arbitrary number of threads at a synchronization point with some synchronization policy or precondition before allowing them all to continue independently. The simplest of these preconditions is that a certain number of threads have registered at their synchronization points. This special case is called the *thread barrier pattern.*

9.9.1 Abstract

A precondition is something that is specified to be true prior to an action or activity. Preconditions are a type of constraint that is usually generative; that is, they can be used to generate code either to force the precondition to be true or to check that a precondition is true. In fact, the most common way to ensure preconditions in UML or virtually any design language is through the use of state machines. A state is a precondition for the transitions exiting it.

The rendezvous pattern is concerned with modeling the preconditions for synchronization or rendezvous of threads. It is a general pattern and easy to apply to ensure that arbitrarily complex sets of preconditions can be met at runtime. The basic behavioral model is that as each thread becomes ready to rendezvous, it registers with the Rendezvous class and blocks until the Rendezvous class releases it to run. Once the set of preconditions is met, the registered tasks are released to run using whatever scheduling policy is currently in force.

9.9.2 Problem

The problem addressed by this pattern is to codify a collaboration structure that allows any arbitrary set of precondition invariants to be met for thread synchronization, independent of task phasings, scheduling policies, and priorities.

9.9.3 Pattern Structure

The basic behavioral model, shown in Figure 9-16, is that as each thread becomes ready to rendezvous, it registers with the Rendezvous class and then blocks until the Rendezvous class releases it to run. Once the set of preconditions is met, the registered tasks are released to run using whatever scheduling policy is currently in force. The rendezvous itself is abstracted into a class, as is the set of preconditions. This approach

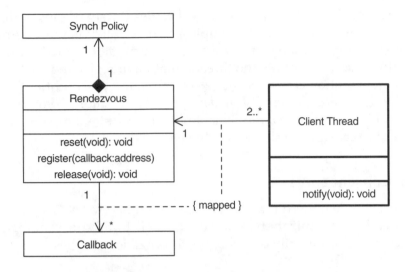

Figure 9-16: *Rendezvous Pattern Structure*

provides a great deal of flexibility in modeling arbitrarily complex pre-condition invariants.

9.9.4 Collaboration Roles

- *Callback:* The Callback object holds the address of the ClientThread object. This is so the Rendezvous object can notify all the threads that have registered when the preconditions are met. This callback may be an object address, a URL, or any other means that enables the Rendezvous object to unambiguously signal the ClientThread when the preconditions are met.

- *ClientThread:* There are at least two ClientThread objects. When they reach their synchronization point, they register with the Rendezvous object and pass their callback. The notify() operation is called by dereferencing the callback; this signals the Client Thread that the pre-conditions have been met and thus it is now free to continue.

- *Rendezvous:* The Rendezvous object manages the ThreadSynchro-nization object. It has a register(callback: address) operation that the ClientThreads invoke to indicate that they have reached their synchronization point.

- *SynchPolicy:* The SynchPolicy object reifies the set of preconditions into a single concept. The simplest Synch Policy is nothing more than the registration count reaching some predetermined, expected value; that is, it counts the threads that have registered, and when the registration count reaches a set value, the precondition is met. This is called the *thread boundary pattern.* For more complex synchronization policies, the SynchPolicy object may employ a statechart to capture the richness of the required policy.

9.9.5 Consequences

This is a simple pattern that can be widely applied for various policies for thread synchronization. It scales up well to arbitrary number of threads and to arbitrarily complex synchronization policies.

9.9.6 Implementation Strategies

The SynchPolicy and Rendezvous classes are stateful, and most likely be implemented as statecharts. In the case of the thread barrier pattern specialization, it is enough simply to implement a counting machine. Figure 9-17 shows a simple counting machine statechart that counts object registrations. It begins to synch (i.e., to process evSynch events) in its Counting state. After each event, it increments its Count attribute. If it equals or exceeds the expected number of threads waiting to rendezvous, then the else clause is taken, and the Synch Policy object sends a evReleaseAll event to the Rendezvous object.

The Rendezvous class accepts register messages from the associated ClientThread objects; when it receives a register message, it sends an evSynch event to the SynchPolicy object. When the Rendezvous object receives an evReleaseAll event, it iterates over the list of Callback objects, sending each a notify message, informing it that the synchronization is complete, and the thread is free to continue.

The Callback class is little more than that the storage of an address of some kind. In some cases, it will literally be the address of the notify operation, to be called directly, or in a thread-safe way, using the guarded call pattern. In other cases, the notify message will be sent to that thread's event queue to be processed when the thread is scheduled to run by the operating system. In still other cases, such as when a com-

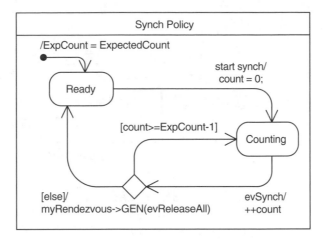

Figure 9-17: *Thread Barrier Synch Policy Statechart*

ponent infrastructure is used, perhaps COM or CORBA, the Callback will contain the object ID which the component infrastructure will dereference to locate the proper object.

9.9.7 Related Patterns

This pattern can be mixed with the other thread management patterns, such as the message queue and guarded call patterns, as well as the other nonconcurrency model architectural patterns, such as the component and layered patterns.

9.9.8 Sample Model

Figure 9-18a shows an example with three threads, each of which controls a different aspect of a robot arm: two joints and a manipulator. When each of the three threads is ready, they are all allowed to proceed. Figure 9-18b shows the flow of a scenario. Note how each thread (other than the last) is blocked until the Rendezvous object releases them all. Then they will be scheduled by the OS according to its scheduling policy.

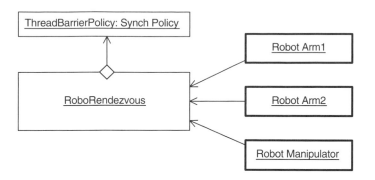

Figure 9-18a: *Rendezvous*

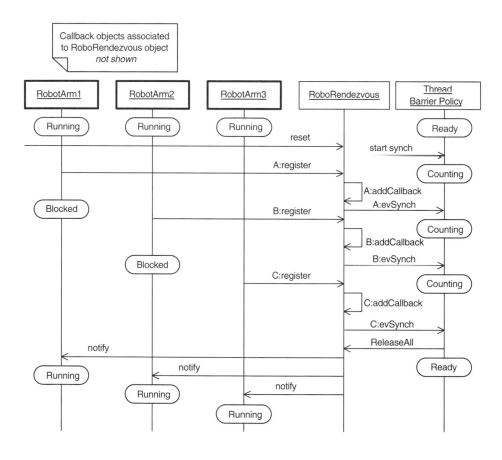

Figure 9-18b: *Rendezvous Pattern Scenario Example*

9.10 Looking Ahead

Mechanistic design is concerned with specifying the details of inter-object collaboration. Parameterized patterns for small groups of objects acting together within collaborations are referred to as mechanisms. Mechanistic design takes the collaborative groups of objects identified in analysis and adds design-level objects to facilitate and optimize their implementation. For example, containers and iterators are added to manage associations consisting of multiple objects. Smart Pointer objects glue associations together in such a way as to eliminate memory leaks and inappropriate pointer dereferencing. Policy objects abstract away strategies and algorithms from their context so that they can be easily modified or replaced, even while the system executes.

Many of the objects added during mechanistic design reappear in many designs because they solve problems common to many systems. These collaborations are reified into mechanistic design patterns. These patterns are templates of object interaction consisting of a problem, context, and a structural solution. The reification of the patterns allows them to be cataloged and studied systematically so they can be used again in future projects. This chapter presented a number of patterns useful in mechanistic design. You are invited to explore the references at the end of the chapter for more patterns.

Chapter 10 discusses the detailed design of object-oriented systems in a real-time context. Detailed design is concerned with the implementation of data structures and algorithms within the scope of a single class. Space and time complexity tradeoffs are made during detailed design in order to achieve the performance requirements specified for your system.

9.11 Exercises

1. What does *reify* mean?
2. What is the scope of design decisions made in mechanistic design?
3. What are the three fundamental elements of a design pattern?

4. What aspect of a collaboration does the observer pattern attempt to optimize?

5. What pattern does the proxy pattern specialize?

6. When should a proxy pattern be employed?

7. What three kinds of reliability does the reliable transaction pattern optimize? How do they differ?

8. Why would someone use the smart pointer pattern?

9. How does the use of dynamic memory deallocation cause memory fragmentation?

10. What are some of the cons of the smart pointer pattern?

11. Why would someone use the guarded call pattern rather than queue messages for a target task?

12. What is the purpose of an iterator in the container pattern?

13. What is the primary strategy of the rendezvous pattern?

14. How does the thread barrier pattern work?

9.12 References

[1] Booch, Grady, James Rumbaugh, and Ivar Jacobson. *The Unified Modeling Language User's Guide.* Reading, MA: Addison-Wesley, 1999.

[2] Gamma, Erich, Richard Helm, Ralph Johnson, and John Vlissides. *Design Patterns: Elements of Reusable Software.* Reading, MA: Addison-Wesley, 1995.

[3] Buschmann, Frank, Regine Meunier, Hans Rohnert, Peter Sommerlad, and Michael Stal. *A System of Patterns: Pattern-Oriented Software Architecture.* New York: John Wiley & Sons, 1996.

[4] Coplien, James, and Douglas Schmidt, eds. *Pattern Languages of Program Design.* Reading, MA: Addison-Wesley, 1995.

[5] Vlissides, John, James Coplien, and Norman Kerth, eds. *Pattern Languages of Program Design 2.* Reading, MA: Addison-Wesley, 1996.

[6] Douglass, Bruce. *Doing Hard Time: Developing Real-Time Systems with UML, Objects, Frameworks, and Patterns.* Reading, MA: Addison-Wesley, 1999.

[7] Klein, Mark, Thomas Ralya, Bill Pollak, Ray Obenza, and Michael Gonzalez Harbour. *A Practitioner's Handbook for Real-Time Analysis: Guide to Rate*

Monotonic Analysis for Real-Time Systems. Boston: Kluwer Academic Publishers, 1993.

[8] Douglass, Bruce Powel. *Real-Time Design Patterns: Robust Scalable Architecture for Real-Time Systems.* Boston: Addison-Wesley, 2002.

[9] Jones, R., and Lins, R. *Garbage Collection: Algorithms for Automatic Dynamic Memory Management.* West Sussex, England: John Wiley & Sons, 1996.

Chapter 10

Detailed Design

In the preceding chapters, we've seen how architectural design defines the largest-scale strategic design decisions and that mechanistic design specifies exactly how groups of objects collaborate together. Now it is time to peer inside the objects themselves and learn how to design their internal structure. Detailed design specifies details such as the storage format used for attributes, the implementation of associations, the set of operations the object provides, the selection of internal algorithms, and the specification of exception handling within the object.

Notation and Concepts Discussed

Data Collections	Visibility	Data Structure
Realizing Associations	Algorithms	Derived Attributes
Operations	Exceptions	

10.1 What Is Detailed Design?

You're just about at the point where you can actually run code on that pile of wires and chips cluttering up your Geekosphere,[1] so if you're like me, you're getting pretty excited. If architectural design is deciding which planet to fly to and mechanistic design is the flight path to the selected planet, then detailed design is deciding on which rock you want to eat your "tube of salami" sandwich once you arrive.[2] It is the smallest level of decomposition before you start pounding code.

The fundamental unit of decomposition in object-oriented systems is the *object*. As we have seen, the object is a natural unit from which systems can be specified and implemented. We have also seen that it is necessary but insufficient for large-scale design. Mechanistic design deals with mechanisms (groups of collaborating objects) and architectural design is concerned with an even larger scale—domains, tasks, and subsystems. At the root of it all remains the object itself, the atom from which the complex chemistry of systems is built.

Although most objects are structurally and behaviorally simple, this is certainly not universal. Every nontrivial system contains a significant proportional of "interesting" objects that require further examination and specification. The detailed design of these objects allows the objects to be correctly implemented, of course, but also permits designers to make tradeoff decisions to optimize the system.

One definition of an object is "data tightly bound to its operations forming a cohesive entity." Detailed design must consider both the structure of information and its manipulation. In general, the decisions made in detailed design will be these:

- Data structure
- Class refactoring
- Implementation of associations
- Set of operations defined on the data

---

[1] Geekosphere (n): the area surrounding one's computer ("Jargon Watch," *Hardwired*, 1997)

[2] My personal choice would be the Yogi rock on Mars (see http://www.jpl.nasa.gov, a public mirror site for the Mars Pathfinder mission).

- Visibility of data and operations
- Algorithms used to implement those operations
- Exceptions handled and thrown

10.2 Data Structure

Data format in objects is generally simple because if it were not, a separate object would be constructed to hold just the data. However, not only must the structure of the data be defined, the valid ranges of data, accuracy, preconditions, and initial values must also be specified during detailed design. This is part of what Bertrand Meyer calls "design by contract" [7]. Detailed data design applies to "simple" numeric data just as much as of user-defined data types. After all, aircraft, spacecraft, and missile systems must perform significant numeric computation without introducing round-off and accuracy errors or bad things are likely to happen.[3] Consider a simple complex number class. Complex numbers may be stored in polar coordinates, but let's stick to rectilinear coordinates for now. Most of the applications using complex numbers require fractional values, so that using ints for the real and imaginary parts wouldn't meet the need. What about using floats, as in

```
class complex_1 {
public:
    float iPart, rPart;
    // operations omitted
};
```

That looks like a reasonable start. Is the range sufficient? Most floating-point implementations have a range of 10^{-40} to 10^{+40} or more, so that is probably OK. What about round-off error? Because the infinite continuous set of possible values are stored and manipulated as a finite set of machine numbers, just representing a continuous value using floating-point format incurs some error. Numerical analysis identifies two forms of numerical error—absolute error and relative error [1]. For

---

[3] Having one's F-16 flip upside down when crossing the equator is an example of such a "bad thing." Fortunately, this defect was discovered during simulation and not during actual flight.

example, consider adding two numbers, 123456 and 4.567891, using six-digit-precision floating-point arithmetic:

123456.000000

+000004.567891

123460.567891 = 0.123460567891 × 10^6

Because this must be stored in six-digit precision, the value will be stored as 0.123460 × 10^6, which is an absolute error of 0.567891. Relative error is computed as

$$\frac{(A–B)—[m(A)—m(B)]}{A - B}$$

where m(x) is the machine number representation of the value x. This gives us a relative error of 4.59977 × 10^{-8} for this calculation. Although this error is tiny, errors can propagate and build during repeated calculation to the point of making your computations meaningless.

Subtraction of two values is a common source of significant error. For example,

0.991012312

−0.991009987

0.000002325 = 0.2325 × 10^{-5}

But truncating these numbers to six digits of precision yields

0.991012

−0.991010

0.000002 = 0.20 × 10^{-5}

which is an absolute error of 0.325 × 10^{-6} and a relative error of 14%. This means that we may have to change our format to include more significant digits, change our format entirely to use infinite precision arithmetic,[4] or change our algorithms to equivalent forms when a loss

---

[4] Infinite precision arithmetic is available in some Lisp-based symbolic mathematics systems, such as Derive and MacSyma.

of precision is likely, such as computing $1 - \cos(x)$ when the angle close to zero can result in the loss of precision. You can use the trigonometric relation

$$1 - \cos(\phi) = 2 \sin(\tfrac{\phi}{2})$$

to avoid round-off error.[5]

Data is often constrained beyond its representation limit by the problem domain. Planes shouldn't pull a 7g acceleration curve, array indices shouldn't be negative, ECG patients rarely weigh 500 Kg, and automobiles don't go 300 miles per hour. Attributes have a range of valid values and when they are set unreasonably, these faults must be detected and corrective actions must be taken. Mutator operations (operations that set attribute values) should ensure that the values are within range. These constraints on the data can be specified on class diagrams using the standard UML constraint syntax, such as {range 0..15}.

Subclasses may constrain their data ranges differently than their superclasses. Many designers feel that data constraints should be monotonically decreasing with subclass depth, that is, that a subclass might constrain a data range further than its superclass. Although system can be built this way, this violates the Liskov Substitution Principle (LSP):

> *An instance of a subclass must be freely substitutable for an instance of its superclass.*

If a superclass declares a color attribute with a range of {white, yellow, blue, green, red, black} and a subclass restricts it to {white, black} then what happens if the client has a superclass pointer and sets the color to red, as in

```
enum color {white, yellow, blue, green, red, black};
class super {
protected:
    color c;
public:
    virtual void setColor(color temp); // all colors
valid
};
```

---

[5] Widely different computational results of algebraically equivalent formulations can lead to hazardous situations. See [5].

```
class sub: public super {
public:
    virtual void setColor(color temp); // only white
and black now valid
};
```

Increasing constraints down the superclass hierarchy is a danger-ous policy if the subclass will be used in a polymorphic fashion.

Aside from normal attributes identified in the analysis model, detailed design may add *derived attributes* as well. Derived attributes are values that can in principle be reconstructed from other attributes within the class, but are added to optimize performance. They can be indicated on class diagrams with a «derived» stereotype, and defining the derivation formula within an associated constraint, such as {age = currentDate − startDate}.

For example, a sensor class may provide a 10-sample history, with a get(index) accessor method. If the clients often want to know the aver-age measurement value, they can compute this from the history, but it is more convenient to add an average( ) operation like so:

```
class sensor {
    float valuc[10],
    int nMeasurements, currentMeasurment;
public:
    sensor(void): nMeasurements(0),
            currentMeasurement(0) {
            for (int j = 0; j<10; j++) value[10] = 0;
    };
      void accept(float tValue) {
            value[currentMeasurement] = tValue;
            currentMeasurement = (++currentMeasurement)
              \ 10;
            if (nMeasurements < 10) ++nMeasurements;
            };
        float get(int index=0) {
            int cIndex;
            if (nMeasurements > index) {
                cIndex = currentMeasurement-index-1; //
                last valid one
                if (cIndex < 0) cIndex += 10;
                return value[cIndex];
            else
                throw "No valid measurement at that
                    index";
```

```
        };
    float average(void) {
        float sum = 0.0;
        if (nMeasurements > 0) {
            for (int j=0; j < nMeasurements-1; j++)
                sum += value[j];
            return sum / nMeasurements;
            }
        else
            throw "No measurements to average";
    };
};
```

The average() operation only exists to optimize the computational path. If the average value was needed more frequently than the data was monitored, the average could be computed as the data was read:

```
class sensor {
    float value[10];
    float averageValue;
    int nMeasurements, currentMeasurment;
public:
    sensor(void): averageValue(0), nMeasurements(0),
            currentMeasurement(0) {
        for (int j = 0; j<10; j++) value[10] = 0;
    };
  void accept(float tValue) {
        value[currentMeasurement] = tValue;
        currentMeasurement = (++currentMeasurement)
          \ 10;
        if (nMeasurements < 10) ++nMeasurements;
            // compute average
        averageValue = 0;
        for (int j=0; j < nMeasurements-1; j++)
            averageValue += value[j];
            averageValue /= nMeasurements;
        };
    float get(int index=0) {
        int cIndex;
        if (nMeasurements > index) {
            cIndex = currentMeasurement-index-1; //
                    last valid one
            if (cIndex < 0) cIndex += 10;
            return value[cIndex];
        else
```

```
            throw "No valid measurement at that
                index";
        };
    float average(void) {
        if (nMeasurements > 0)
            return averageValue;
        else
            throw "No measurements to average";
    };
};
```

In this case, the derived attribute averageValue is added to min-imize the required computation when the average value is needed frequently.

Collections of primitive data attributes may be structured in myriad ways, including stacks, queues, lists, vectors, and a forest of trees. The layout of data collections is the subject of hundreds of volumes of research and practical applications. The UML provides a role constraint notation to indicate different kinds of collections that may be inherent in the analysis model. Common role constraints for multivalued roles include

{ordered}	Collection is maintained in a sorted manner.
{bag}	Collection may have multiple copies of a single item.
{set}	Collection may have at most a single copy of a given item.
{hashed}	Collection is referenced via a keyed hash.

Some constraints may be combined, such as {ordered set}. Another common design scheme is to use a key value to retrieve an item from a collection. This is called a *qualified association* and the key value is called a *qualifier.*

Figure 10-1 shows examples of constraints and qualified associa-tions. The association between Patron and Airline is qualified with Fre-quent Flyer Num. This qualifier will be ultimately implemented as an attribute within the Patron class and will be used to identify the patron to the Airline class. Similarly, the Patron has a qualified association with Library using the qualifier Library Card Num. The associations between Airline and Flight and between Library and Book have con-strained multivalued roles. The former set must be maintained as an

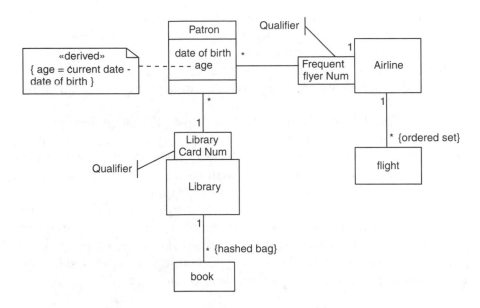

Figure 10-1: *Role Constraints and Qualified Associations*

ordered set while the latter is a hashed bag. Note also the use of a text note to constrain the Patron's age attribute. The stereotype indicates that it is a derived attribute and the constraint shows how it is computed. Other constraints can be added as necessary to indicate valid ranges of data and other representational invariants.

Selection of a collection structure depends on what characteristics should be optimized. Balanced trees, for example, can be searched quickly, but inserting new elements is complex and costly because of the need to rotate the tree to maintain balance. Linked lists are simple to maintain, but searching takes relatively long.

10.3 Associations

Associations among objects allow client objects to invoke the operations provided by server objects. There are many ways to implement associations, appropriate to the nature and locality of the objects and their association. Implementations appropriate for objects within the same thread will fail when used across thread or processor boundaries. Accessing objects with multivalued roles must be done differently than with a 1-to-1 association. Some implementation strategies that work for composition don't work for client-server associations. One of the purposes of detailed design is to resolve the management of associations within the objects.

The simplest cases are the 1-to-1 or 1-to-(0,1) association between objects within the same thread. The 1-to-(0,1) is best done with a pointer to the server object, since there are times when the role multiplicity will be zero (i.e., the pointer will be null). A 1-to-1 association may also be implemented with a reference (in the C++ sense) because the association link is always valid.[6] A 1-to-1 composition association may also be used in inline class declaration, which would be inappropriate for the more loosely coupled client-server association. Normal aggregation is implemented in exactly the same way as an association. The following class shows these simple approaches.

```
class testAssoc {
    T myT;      // appropriate only for 1-to-1
                   composition
    T* myT2;    // ok for 1-to-1 or 1-to-(0,1)
                   association or composition
    T& myT3;    // ok for 1-1 association or composition
};
```

As discussed in Chapter 9, multivalued roles are most often resolved using the container pattern. This involves inserting a container class between the two classes with the multivalued role, and possibly iterators as well, as shown in Figure 10-2. Review Chapter 9 for more detail on the container pattern.

Crossing thread boundaries complicates the resolution of associations somewhat. Simply calling an operation across a thread boundary is not normally a good idea because of mutual exclusion and reentrancy problems. It can be done if sufficient care is taken: The target operation can implemented using mutual exclusion guards and both sides must agree on the appropriate behavior if access cannot be immediately granted. Should the caller be blocked? Should the caller be returned to immediately with an indication of failure? Should the caller be blocked,

---

[6] C++ requires that references always be valid; that is, a null reference is semantically illegal.

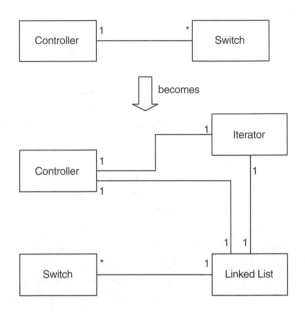

Figure 10-2: *Detailed Design of Multivalued Roles*

but only for a maximum specified period of time? All of these kinds of rendezvous are possible and appropriate in different circumstances.

Although directly calling an operation across a thread boundary is lightweight, it is not always the best way. If the underlying operating system or hardware enforces segmented address spaces for threads, it may not even be possible. Operating systems provide additional means for inter-task communication, such as OS message queues and OS pipes.

An OS message queue is the most dominant approach for requesting services across a thread boundary. The receiver thread's active object reads the message queue and dispatches the message to the appropriate component object. This approach has a fairly heavy run-time cost, but maintains the inherent asychronicity of the threads.

OS pipes are an alternative to message queues. They are opened by both client and server objects and are a slightly more direct way for the client to invoke the services of the server.

When the service request must cross processor boundaries, the objects must be more decoupled. Common operating services to meet intra-processor communications include sockets and remote procedure calls (RPCs). Sockets usually implement a specified TCP/IP protocol across a network. The common protocols are the Transmission Control Protocol (TCP) and User Datagram Protocol (UDP). The TCP/IP protocol suite does not make any guarantees about timing, but it can be placed on top of a data link layer that does. TCP supports reliable transmission using acknowledgements; it also supports what are called *stream sockets*. UDP is simpler and makes no guarantees about reliable transmission.

Lastly, some systems use RPCs. Normally, RPCs are implemented using a blocking protocol so that the client is blocked until the remote procedure completes. This maintains the function call–like semantics of the RPC, but may be inappropriate in some cases.

Using any of the approaches that cross the thread boundary (with the exception of the direct guarded call), requires a different implementation in the client class. The client must now know the thread ID and a logical object ID to invoke the services. So rather than a C++ pointer or reference, ad hoc operating system–dependent means must be used.

These methods can be implemented using the broker pattern from [9] or the observer pattern described in Chapter 9. The observer pattern allows the server to be remote from the client, but requires that the client know the location of the server. The broker pattern adds one more level of indirection, requiring only that the client know a logical name for the target object, which allows the Broker to identify and locate the server.

Note that this discussion has been independent of the underlying physical medium of inter-processor communication. It can be implemented using shared memory, Ethernet networks, or various kinds of buses, as appropriate. Reusable protocols are built using the layered architecture pattern, so that the data link layer can be replaced with one suitable for the physical medium with a minimum of fuss.

10.4 Operations

The operations defined by a class specify how the data may be manipulated. Generally speaking, a complete set of primitive operations maximizes reusability. A *set* class template typically provides operators such as add item or set, remove item or subset, and test for item or subset membership. Even if the current application doesn't use all these operations, adding the complete list of primitives makes it more likely to meet the needs of the next system.

Analysis models abstract class operations into object messages (class, object, sequence, and collaboration diagrams), state event acceptors (statecharts), and state actions (statecharts). The great majority of the time, these messages will be directly implemented as operations in the server class using the implementation strategy for the association supporting the message passing (see the previous section).

Analysis and early design models only specify the public operations. Detailed design often adds operations that are only used internally. These operations are due to the functional decomposition of the public operations. For example, a queue might provide the following set of public operations:

```
template <class T, int size>
class queue {
protected:
    T q[size];
    int head, tail;
public:
    queue(void): head(0), tail(0);
    virtual void put(T  myT);
    virtual T get(void);
};
```

A cached queue caches data locally but stores most of it on a more remote, but larger data store, such as a hard disk. Operations can be added to implement the caching so that it is invisible to the client, maintaining LSP:

```
template <class T, int size>
class cachedQueue : public queue<T, size> {
protected:
    void writeToDisk(void);
    void readFromDisk(void);
public:
    cachedQueue(void): head(0), tail(0);
    virtual void put(T  myT);      // new version uses
                                   // writeToDisk
                            // when cache fills
    virtual T get(void);           // new version uses
                                   // readFromDisk
```

```
                                      // when data is not
                                      cached
};
```

These operations are added to support the additional functionality of the cachedQueue subclass.

Functional decomposition of operations is shown in structured methods using structure charts. Since the UML does not provide structure charts, activity diagrams should be used instead.

10.5 Visibility

Visibility in the UML refers to *accessibility* of internal object elements by other objects. Visibility is always a design concern. There are four general guidelines of visibility:

1. **If clients need it, make it visible, otherwise make it inaccessible.** This first guideline is pretty obvious. Once you are down in the depths of detailed design, you should have a pretty good idea which messages are being sent to an object. If other clients are depending on the service, then they must be able to call it. This is none other than the old data-hiding principle in vogue since the 1970s.

2. **Only make semantically appropriate operations visible.** This guideline seeks to avoid pathological coupling among classes. For example, suppose a class is using a container class. Should the operations be GetLeft() and GetRight() or Prev() and Next()? The first pair makes the implementation visible (binary tree) while the latter pair captures the essential semantics (ordered list).

3. **Attributes should never be directly visible to clients.** This guideline is similar to the previous one in that it wants to avoid tight coupling whenever possible. If clients have direct access to attributes, they fundamentally depend on the structure of that attribute. Should the structure change, the clients all become instantly broken and must be modified as well. Additionally, accessor and mutator operations applied to that attribute can ensure that preconditions are met, such as valid ranges or consistency with other class attributes. Direct

access to the attribute circumvents these safeguards. The "Hungarian" naming convention uses the type of the variable or attribute in the name. I recommend that this highly questionable practice be avoided precisely because it introduces an artificial and unnecessary tight coupling attribute and its type.

4.   **When different levels of visibility are required to support various levels of coupling, use the interface pattern to provide the sets of interfaces.** Sometimes a class must present different levels of access to different clients. When this is true, the interface pattern is an obvious solution. A class can have many interfaces, each semantically appropriate to its clients.

The UML provides a simple, if peculiar, syntax for specifying visibility on the class diagram: A visibility attribute is prepended to the class member. The UML defines the following visibility attributes:

#	Private—accessible only within the class itself
−	Protected—accessible only by the class and its subclasses
+	Public—generally accessible by other classes
~	Package—accessible to other member of the same package

Some theorists are adamant that attributes should be private (as opposed to protected) and even subclasses should go through accessor methods to manipulate them. Personally, I find that view somewhat draconian because subclasses are already tightly coupled with their superclasses, but to each his or her own.

Another approach to providing different levels of access is through the use of friend classes.[7] Friend classes are often used as iterators in the container pattern, discussed in Chapter 9. Another use is the facilitation of unit testing by making unit testing objects friends of the class under test.

---

[7] The use of friend classes results in a kind of "clothing-optional" design, which, although it can be fun, may make some designers nervous.

10.6 Algorithms

An algorithm is a step-by-step procedure for computing a desired result. The complexity of algorithms may be defined in many ways, but the most common is *time complexity*, the amount of execution time required to compute the desired result. Algorithmic complexity is expressed using the "order of" notation. Common algorithmic complexities are

- $O(c)$
- $O(\log_2 n)$
- $O(n)$
- $O(n \log_2 n)$
- $O(n^2)$
- $O(n^3)$

where c is a constant and n is the number of elements participating in the algorithmic computation.

All algorithms with the same complexity differ from each other only by a multiplicative and additive constant. Thus, it is possible for one $O(n)$ algorithm to perform 100 times faster than another $O(n)$ algorithm and be considered of equal time complexity. It is even possible for an $O(n^2)$ algorithm to outperform an $O(c)$ algorithm for sufficiently small n. The algorithmic complexity is most useful when the number of entities being manipulated is large (as in "asymptomatically approaching infinity") because then these constants become insignificant and the complexity order dictates performance. For small n, they can only given rules of thumb.

Execution time is not the only optimization criteria applied to systems. Objects may be designed to optimize

- Runtime performance
  - ▼ Average performance
  - ▼ Worst-case performance
  - ▼ Deterministic (predictable) performance
- Runtime memory requirements
- Simplicity and correctness

- Development time and effort
- Reusability
- Extensibility
- Reliability
- Safety
- Security

Of course, to some degree these are conflicting goals.[8] For example, some objects must maintain their elements in sorted order. A Bubble sort is very simple, so it requires a minimum of development time. Although it has a worst-case runtime performance of $O(n^2)$, it can actually have better performance than more efficient algorithms if n is small. Quicksort is generally much faster—$O(\log_2 n)$ in the normal case, and $O(n^2)$ in the worst case—but is more complicated to implement. It is not always best to use a Quicksort and it is not always worst to use a Bubble sort even if the Quicksort is demonstrably faster for the data set. Most systems spend most of their time executing a small portion of the code. If the sorting effort is tiny compared to other system functions, the additional time necessary to correctly implement the Quicksort might be more profitably spent elsewhere.

Some algorithms have good average performance but their worst-case performance may be unacceptable. In real-time systems, raw performance is usually not an appropriate criterion—deterministic performance is more crucial. Often, embedded systems must run in a minimum of memory, so that efficient use of existing resources may be very important. The job of the designer is to make the set of design choices that results in the best overall system, and this includes its overall characteristics.

Classes with rich behavior must not only perform correctly, they must also be optimal in some sense. Most often, average execution speed is the criterion used for algorithm selection, but as we saw in Section 10.1, many other criteria may be used. Once the appropriate algorithm is selected, the operations and attributes of the class must be designed to implement the algorithm. This will often result in new attributes and operations that assist in the execution of the algorithm.

---

[8] Which is why they are called *tradeoffs*.

For example, suppose you are using the container pattern and decide that a balanced AVL tree container is best.[9] An AVL tree, named after its inventors Adelson, Velskii, and Landis, takes advantage of the fact that the search performance of a balanced tree is $O(\log_2 n)$. A balanced binary tree is one in which all subtrees are the same height ±1. Each node in an AVL tree has a balance attribute,[10] which must be in the range [−1, 0, +1] for the tree to be balanced. The problem with simple trees is that their balance depends on the order in which elements are added. In fact, adding items in a sorted order to an ordinary binary tree results in a linked list, with search properties of $O(n)$. By balancing the tree during the addition and removal of items, we can improve its balance and optimize its search performance.

Let's assume that we want an in-order tree—that is a tree in which a node is always "greater than" its left child and "less than" its right child, such as the one shown in Figure 10-3. Note that node 10 is greater than its left child (6) and less than its right child (12). If we now add a 9 to the tree, we could make it the left child of node 10 and the parent of node 6. But this would unbalance the tree, as shown in Figure 10-4. If we then balance the tree we might end up with a tree such as the one in Figure 10-5.

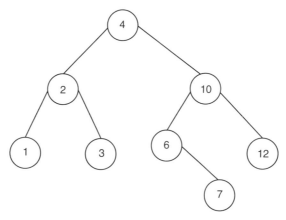

Figure 10-3: *Balanced In-Order Tree*

---

[9] An AVL tree is not a specifically real-time example, but the algorithm is well known in the computer science literature and is quite straightforward. Thus, we will use it here for our discussion.
[10] This is a derived attribute. It can be explicitly stored and maintained during addition and deletion, or it can be recomputed as necessary.

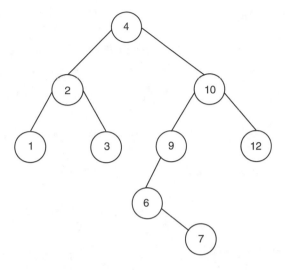

Figure 10-4: *Unbalanced Tree after Adding Node 9*

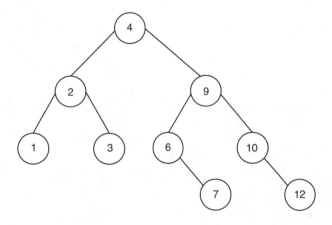

Figure 10-5: *Rebalanced Tree*

AVL trees remain balanced because whenever a node is inserted or removed that unbalances the tree, nodes are moved around using techniques called *tree rotations* to regain balance. The algorithm for adding a node to an AVL tree looks like this:

1. Create the new node with NULL child pointers, set the attribute Balance to 0.
2. If the tree is empty, set the root to point to this new node and return.
3. Locate the proper place for the node insertion and insert.
4. Recompute the balance attribute for each node from the root to the newly inserted node.
5. Locate an unbalanced node (balance factor is ±2). This is called the *pivot node*. If there is no unbalanced node, then return.
6. Rebalance the tree so that it is now balanced. There are several situations:

   a. Pivot has a balance of +2. Rotate the subtree based at the Pivot left.

   b. Pivot has a balance of –2. Rotate the subtree based at the Pivot right.
7. Continue balancing subtrees on the search path until they are all in the set [-1, 0 +1].

Rotating left means replacing the right child of the pivot as the root of the subtree, as shown in Figure 10-6. Right rotations work similarly and are applied when the balance of the pivot is –2. Many times, double rotations are required to achieve a balanced tree, such as a left-right or a right-left rotation set.

The set of operations necessary to meet this algorithm are

```
typedef class node {
public:
    data d; // whatever data is held in the tree nodes
    int balance; // valid values are -1, 0 , 1
    node* leftPtr;
    node* rightPtr;
} * nodePtr;
class avlTree {
    nodePtr root;
    void rotateLeft(nodePtr n);
    void rotateRight(nodePtr n);
public:
    void add(data a);
    void delete(data a);
    nodePtr find(data a);
};
```

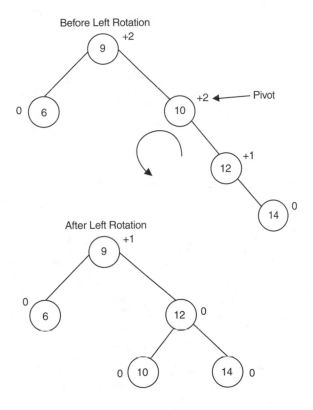

Figure 10-6: *Left Rotation*

Structured English and pseudocode, as shown above, work perfectly well in most circumstances to capture the essential semantics of algorithms. The UML does define a special kind of state diagram, called an *activity diagram*, which may be helpful in some cases.

Activity diagrams depict systems that may be decomposed into activities—roughly corresponding to states that mostly terminate upon completion of the activity rather than as a result of an externally generated event. Activity diagrams may be thought of as a kind of flowchart where diagrammatic elements are member function calls. Figure 10-7 shows the activity diagram for the addNode() operation of our AVL tree class.

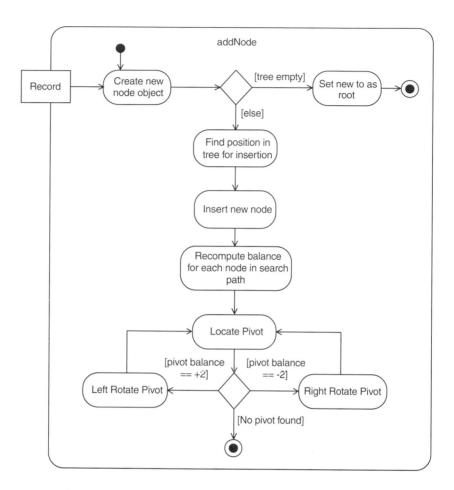

Figure 10-7: *Activity Diagram for Add Node Operation*

10.7 Exceptions

In reactive classes, exception handling is straightforward—exceptions are signals (associated with events) specified in the class state model that result in transitions being taken and actions being executed. In nonreactive classes, the specification means is less clear. The minimum requirements are to identify the exceptions raised by the class and the exceptions handled by the class.

Exception handling is a powerful addition to programming languages. Language-based exception handling provides two primary benefits. The first is that exceptions cannot be ignored. The C idiom for exception handling is to pass back a return value from a function, but this is generally ignored by the clients of the service. When was the last time you saw the return value for print checked?

The correct usage for the C fopen function is something like this

```
FILE *fp;
if ( (fp = fopen("filename", "w")) == NULL) {
    /* do some corrective action */
    exit(1); /* pass error indicator up a level */
    };
```

Many programmers, to their credit, always do just that. However, there is no enforcement that the errors be identified or handled. It is up to the programmer and the code peer review process to ensure this is done. With exceptions, the error condition cannot be ignored. Unhandled exceptions are passed to each preceding caller until they are handled—a process called *unwinding the stack*. The terminate-on-exception approach has been successfully applied to programs in Ada and C++ for many years.

The other benefit of exception handling is that it separates the exception handling itself from the normal execution path. This simplifies both the normal processing code and the exception handling code. For example, consider the following standard C code segment:

```
if ( (fp = ftest1(x,y,z))) == NULL) {
    /* do some corrective action */
    printf("Failure on ftest1");
    exit(1); /* pass error indicator up a level */
    };
if (!ftest2()) {
    /* do some corrective action */
    printf("failure on ftest2");
    exit(1);
    };
if (ftest3() == 0) {
    /* do some corrective action */
    printf("failure on ftest3");
    exit(1);
    };
```

This is arguably more difficult to understand than the following code:

```
// main code is simplified
try {
    ftest1(x,y,z);
    ftest2();
    ftest3();
}
// exception handling code is simplified
catch (test1Failure& t1) {
    cout << "Failure on test1";
    throw; // rethrow same exception as in code
             above
}
catch (test2Failure& t2) {
    cout << "Failure on test2";
    throw;
};
catch (test3Failure& t3) {
    cout << Failure on test3";
    throw;
};
```

The second code segment separates the normal code processing from the exception processing, making both clearer.

Each operation should define the exceptions that it throws as well as the exceptions that it handles. There are reasons to avoid using formal C++ exceptions specifications [2] but the information should be captured nonetheless. Exceptions should never be used as an alternative way to terminate a function, in much the same way that a crowbar should not be used as an alternative key for your front door. Exceptions indicate that a serious fault requiring explicit handling has occurred.

Throwing exceptions is computationally expensive because the stack must be unwound and objects destroyed. The presence of exception handling in your code adds a small overhead to your executing code (usually around 3%) even when exceptions are not thrown. Most compiler vendors offer nonstandard library versions that don't throw exceptions and so this overhead can be avoided if exceptions are not used. Destructors should *never* throw exceptions or call operations that can throw exceptions nor should the constructors of exception classes throw exceptions.[11]

Exception handling applies to operations (i.e., functions) and is a complicating factor in the design of algorithms. In my experience, writing *correct* programs (i.e., those that include complete and proper exception handling) is two to three times more difficult than writing code that merely "is supposed to work."[12]

Capturing the exception handling is fundamentally a part of the algorithm design and so can be represented along with the "normal" aspects of the algorithms. Exceptions can be explicitly shown as events on either statecharts or activity diagrams.

That still leaves two unanswered questions:

- What exceptions should I catch?
- What exceptions should I throw?

The general answer to the first question is that an operation should catch all exceptions that it has enough context to handle or that will make no sense to the current operation's caller.

The answer to the second is "all others." If an object does not have enough context to decide how to handle an exception, then its caller might. Perhaps the caller can retry a set of operations or execute an alternative algorithm.

At some point exception handling will run out of stack to unwind, so at some global level, an exception policy must be implemented. The actions at this level will depend on the severity of the exception, its impact on system safety, and the context of the system. In some cases, a severe error with safety ramifications should result in a system shutdown, because the system has a fail-safe state. Drill presses or robotic assembly systems normally shut down in the presence of faults because that is their fail-safe state. Other systems, such as medical monitoring

---

[11] In C++, if an exception is thrown while an unhandled exception is active, the program calls the internal function terminate() to exit the program. As the stack is unwound during exception handling, local objects are destroyed by calling their destructors. Thus destructors are called as part of the exception handling process. If a destructor is called because its object is being destroyed due to an exception, any exception it throws will terminate the program immediately.

[12] In contrast to prevailing opinion, I don't *think* this is solely due to my recently hitting 40 and the associated loss of neural cells.

systems, may continue by providing diminished functionality or reset and retry, because that is their safest course of action. Of course, some systems have no fail-safe state. For such systems, architectural means must be provided as an alternative to in-line fault correction.

Exceptions can be modeled in several ways in the UML. In the absence of state machines and activity diagrams, throw, try, and catch statements are simply added to the methods directly. This works well within a single thread, but fails thread boundaries. For reactive objects—those with state machines—the best way is simply to model the exceptions as events. If the event handling is asynchronous, then this approach will work across thread boundaries. However, virtually all state machines use FIFO queues for unhandled events. Since the UML does not assign priorities to events, exception events are treated as normal events and will be handled in a FIFO way. This may not be what is desired.

For activities, exceptions are modeled as *interrupting edges* applied to an interruptible segment of an activity diagram. This causes the activity to terminate and control flow proceeds along the interrupting edge.

10.8 Summary

One definition of an object is "a set of tightly coupled attributes and the operations that act on them." Detailed design takes this microscopic view to fully specify the characteristics of objects than have been hitherto abstracted away and ignored. These characteristics include the structuring of the attributes and identification of their representational invariants, resolution of abstract message passing into object operations, selection and definition of algorithms, including the handling of exceptional conditions.

Attributes are the data values subsumed within the objects. They must be represented in some fashion supported by the implementation language, but that is not enough. Most often, the underlying representation is larger than the valid ranges of the attribute, so the valid set of values of the attributes must be defined. Operations can then include checking the representational invariants to ensure that the object remains in a valid state.

Analysis models use the concept of message-passing to represent the myriad of ways that objects can communicate. Detailed design must decide the exact implementation of each message. Most often, messages are isomorphic with operations, but that is only true when the message source is always in the same thread of execution. When this is not true, other means, such as OS message queues, must be employed to provide inter-object communication.

Many objects are themselves algorithmically trivial and do not require a detailed specification of the interaction of the operations and attributes. However, in every system, a significant proportion of objects have "rich" behavior. Although this requires additional work, it also provides the designer with an opportunity to optimize the system performance along some set of criteria. Algorithms include the handling of exceptions and this is usually at least as complex as the primary algorithm itself. Algorithms can be expressed using state charts or activity diagrams. Other representations, such as mathematical equations, pseudocode, or text can be used as well.

10.9 Exercises

1. What is round-off error? How does it accumulate?
2. What is a derived attribute?
3. What is the most common implementation of an association?
4. What are some other possible implementations of associations?
5. What are the rules used to determine visibility?
6. What are they four kinds of visibility and how are the denoted?
7. What does «friend» dependency indicate? What is a reasonable use of it?
8. What is the difference between an $O(n)$ and $O(\log n)$ algorithm?
9. What is the common way of indicating error conditions in C? What are the problems with it?
10. What is the common way of indicating error conditions in C++? What are the advantages and problems with that?

LIVERPOOL
JOHN MOORES UNIVERSITY
AVRIL ROBARTS LRC
TEL. 0151 231 4022

10.10 References

[1] Douglass, Bruce Powel. *Numerical Basic.* Indianapolis: Howard Sams Press, 1983.

[2] Meyers, Scott. *More Effective C++.* Reading, MA: Addison-Wesley, 1996.

[3] Harel, David. *Algorithmics.* Reading, MA: Addison-Wesley, 1993.

[4] Barry, Dave. *Dave Barry's Complete Guide to Guys.* New York: Fawcett Columbine Books, 1995.

[5] Neumann, Peter. *Computer Related Risks.* Reading, MA: Addison-Wesley, 1995.

[6] Douglass, Bruce Powel. *Real-Time Design Patterns: Robust Scalable Architecture for Real-Time Systems.* Boston: Addison-Wesley, 2002.

[7] Meyer, Bertrand. *Object-Oriented Software Construction.* Englewood Cliffs, NJ: Prentice-Hall PRT, 2000.

Chapter 11

Special Topic: C⁴ISR Architecture and the UML

In the Department of Defense (DoD) world, the Command, Communications, Control, Computers, Intelligence, and Reconnaissance Architecture Framework (C⁴ISR-AF) specifies a unifying set of views of architecture. However, this architecture was published about the same time as the original UML specification and so did not use the UML notations or semantics. This chapter shows you how to represent the C⁴ISR products using the UML.

Notations and Topics Discussed

C⁴ISR	Operational View	Systems View
Technical View	Required Products	Supporting Products

617

11.1 Introduction

The UML is particularly adept at clearly showing architectures, system structures, and behavior—all vital aspects of any C[4]ISR-compliant product. Besides being useful and appropriate for creating C[4]ISR products, the UML has a number of other significant advantages for architectural description. First, it is a widely used standard that is taught in many universities. There are over a hundred books available about the UML, and there are easily over a dozen different commercial tools available. The UML is in widespread use by systems and software engineers in the real-time and embedded domain. The UML can be used all the way through the development process, from specifying the operational architecture (via C[4]ISR products) to systems engineering and software development—they can all use the same language for specification and design. This minimizes confusion and error-prone translation among discipline-specific languages.

11.2 What Is C[4]ISR?

The C[4]ISR Architecture Framework (C[4]ISR-AF) is a semantic framework for representing architectures in a consistent way [1]. It was conceived as a way of providing a common means to specify systems for the Department of Defense (DoD) in its many facets and programs. It is being updated by the DoD Architecture Framework Working Group (AFWG) into a new standard called the DoD Architecture Framework (DAF) [3,4]. As stated in the C[4]ISR-AF specification:

> *Architectures provide a mechanism for understanding and managing complexity. The purpose of C[4]ISR architectures is to improve capabilities by enabling the quick synthesis of "go-to-war" requirements with sound investments leading to the rapid employment of improved operational capabilities, and enabling the efficient engineering of warrior systems. The ability to compare, analyze, and integrate architectures developed by the geographical and functional, unified Commands, Military Services, and Defense Agencies (hereinafter also*

referred to as Commands, Services, and Agencies, or C/S/As) from a cross-organizational perspective is critical to achieving these objectives.

The C⁴ISR Architecture Framework is intended to ensure that the architecture descriptions developed by the Commands, Services, and Agencies are interrelatable between and among each organization's operational, systems, and technical architecture views, and are comparable and integratable across Joint and combined organizational boundaries.

The purpose of the C⁴ISR-AF is to provide assistance in the specification of architectures. Architecture itself has a number of definitions. The C⁴ISR-AF uses the definition of IEEE 610.12 [2]:

The structure of components, their relationships, and the principles and guidelines governing their design and evolution over time.

Architectures in the C⁴ISR-AF have three fundamental views: operational, systems, and technical. The emphasis in each of these views is, of course, different and distinct, but they overlap to a significant degree.

The *operational view* is a description of the tasks and activities, operational elements, and information flows required to accomplish or support a military operation. This view includes doctrine (which in another environment might be called business rules), activities, and assignment of these activities to operational elements and the sequences and time frames of the execution of the activities. Operational architectures are usually independent of the systems used to implement them.

The *systems view* is a description of the systems and their interconnections providing for, or supporting, war-fighting functions. The systems view includes the large-scale elements and objects that interact to achieve the operational goals as well as their locations, interconnections, and so on. The systems involved may include key nodes (including materiel), networks (as well as interconnections and interfaces), war-fighting platforms, weapons systems, and so on, as well as their various qualities of service such as mean time between failures (MTBF), maintainability, speed, capacity, and availability. Systems described in the systems view can be used to achieve many different operational architectures, organizations, and missions. The systems view does depend on the underlying technology described in the technical view and is constrained by its limitations.

The *technical view* provides the minimal set of rules governing the arrangement, interaction, and interdependence of system parts or elements, whose purpose is to ensure that a conformant system satisfies a specified set of requirements. The technical view provides the basis for engineering specification of the systems in the systems view and includes technical standards. Put another way, the technical view is the engineering infrastructure that supports the systems view.

Within each of these architectural areas, the standard defines work products. The list of these products is given in Table 11-1. Each of these products will be discussed and in most cases a UML view that meets both the needs and intent of the product will be shown.

Table 11-1: *DAF (C4ISR) Work Products[1]*

Applicable View	Framework Product	UML Views	Framework Product Name	General Description
All Views	AV-1	Descriptions, notes, text	Overview and Summary Information	Scope, purpose, intended users, environment depicted, analytical findings.
All Views	AV-2	Model repository, reports	Integrated Dictionary	Data repository with definitions of all terms used in all products.
Operational	OV-1	Class diagram, deployment diagram	High-Level Operational Concept Graphic	High-level graphical/ textual description of operational concept.

---

[1] There are a number of ways to map C4ISR products to the UML. This table represents one way proposed by the author.

Table 11-1: (*cont.*)

Applicable View	Framework Product	UML Views	Framework Product Name	General Description
Operational	OV-2	Class diagram, deployment diagram	Operational Node Connectivity Description	Operational nodes, operational activities performed at each node, connectivity and information exchange need lines between nodes.
Operational	OV-3	Report from model repository	Operational Information Exchange Matrix	Information exchanged between nodes and the relevant attributes of that exchange.
Operational	OV-4	Class diagram	Command Relationships Chart	Organizational, role, or other relationships among organizations.
Operational	OV-5	Activity diagram, statechart, class diagram with flows	Operational Activity Model	Operational activities, relationships among activities, inputs and outputs. Overlays can show cost, performing nodes, or other pertinent information.
Operational	OV-6a	Sequence diagram, activity diagram, statechart	Operational Rules Model	One of the three products used to describe operational activity sequence and timing. Identifies business rules that constrain operation.

(*continued*)

Table 11-1: (*cont.*)

Applicable View	Framework Product	UML Views	Framework Product Name	General Description
Operational	OV-6b	Statechart, activity diagram	Operational State Transition Description	One of three products used to describe operational activity sequence and timing. Identifies business process responses to events.
Operational	OV-6c	Sequence diagram, statechart, activity diagram	Operational Event-Trace Description	One of three products used to describe operational activity sequence and timing. Traces actions in a scenario or sequence of events and specifies timing of events.
Operational	OV-7	Class diagram	Logical Data Model	Documentation of the data requirements and structural business process rules of the operational view.
Systems	SV-1	Class diagram Text in descriptions	Systems Interface Description	Identification of systems and system components and their interconnections, within and between nodes.
Systems	SV-2	Class diagram	Systems Communications Description	Systems nodes and their related communications lay-downs.

Table 11-1: *(cont.)*

Applicable View	Framework Product	UML Views	Framework Product Name	General Description
Systems	SV-3	Class diagram, report on model	Systems-Systems Matrix	Relationships among systems in a given architecture; can be designed to show relationships of interest, e.g., system-type interfaces, planned vs. existing interfaces, etc.
Systems	SV-4	Use case diagram, class diagram with flows	Systems Functionality Description	Functions performed by systems and the information flow among system functions.
Systems	SV-5	Class diagram with dependencies, DOORS traceability matrix	Operational Activity to Systems Function Traceability Matrix	Mapping of systems back to operational capabilities or of system functions back to operational activities.
Systems	SV-6	Data flow on class diagram	Systems Data Exchange Matrix	Provides details of systems data being exchanged between systems.
Systems	SV-7	Class diagram with constraints for performance quality of service	Systems Performance Parameters Matrix	Performance characteristics of each system(s) hardware and software elements, for the appropriate timeframe(s).

(continued) |

Table 11-1: *(cont.)*

Applicable View	Framework Product	UML Views	Framework Product Name	General Description
Systems	SV-8	Activity diagram	Systems Evolution Description	Planned incremental steps toward migrating a suite of systems to a more efficient suite or toward evolving a current system to a future implementation.
Systems	SV-9	Text	Systems Technology Forecast	Emerging technologies and software/hardware products that are expected to be available in a given set of timeframes and that will affect future development of the architecture.
Systems	SV-10a	Statechart, activity diagram, sequence diagram	Systems Rules Model	One of three products used to describe systems activity sequence and timing. Constraints that are imposed on systems functionality due to some aspect of systems design or implementation.
Systems	SV-10b	Statechart	Systems State Transition Description	One of three products used to describe systems activity sequence and timing. Responses of a system to events.

Table 11-1: *(cont.)*

Applicable View	Framework Product	UML Views	Framework Product Name	General Description
Systems	SV-10c	Sequence diagram	Systems Event-Trace Description	One of three products used to describe systems activity sequence and timing. System-specific refinements of critical sequences of events and the timing of these events.
Systems	SV-11	Deployment diagram, class diagram	Physical Schema	Physical implementation of the information of the logical data model, e.g., message formats, file structures, physical schema.
Technical	TV-1	Hyperlinks in model, text	Technical Standards Profile	Extraction of standards that apply to the given architecture.
Technical	TV-2	Text	Technical Standards Forecast	Description of emerging standards that are expected to apply to the given architecture, within an appropriate set of timeframes.

11.3 Required Products of C⁴ISR

The C⁴ISR-AF identifies a large number of artifacts, called *products*, that are used in the description of the various architecture views. Some of these are required for compliance to the C⁴ISR-AF, but most are optional and can be used when appropriate. These are referred to as *supporting products.* In this section, we discuss the required products listed in Table 11-1.

11.3.1 AV-1 Overview and Summary Information

The Overview and Summary Information product is an essential artifact for making projects compliant with C4ISR-AF. [1] provides a list of the required contents of this artifact as well as a sample format. This information may be directly entered into the model in the model description field, as shown in Figure 11-1, or it may be created in a separate textual document and hyperlinked in the Rhapsody model.

11.3.2 The AV-2 Integrated Dictionary

The Integrated Dictionary product defines the metadata of the product and is normally provided in a textual output. This metadata is maintained for you automatically by Rhapsody and may be viewed in the Rhapsody browser or used to generate reports and details as desired. This is illustrated in Figure 11-2. Besides the built-in report-on model, which can generate reports, Rhapsody has a powerful reporting facility known as ReporterPLUS, which allows you to generate reports in customizable formats and templates.

11.3.3 OV-1 High-Level Operational Concept Graphic

This is a very general architectural picture of the architecture-description products. It is used to facilitate human-human communication, especially among high-level decision makers. Commonly, it graphically depicts the coordinated deployment of systems to achieve the operational objectives. This is easily done in a class or deployment diagram, using stereotypes to identify the various kinds of systems involved in the operational concept. Figure 11-3 shows an example operational concept diagram as a class diagram using standard UML elements—classes with appropriate stereotypes and dependency relations.

Figure 11-4 shows the same diagram using meaningful bitmap icons to represent the operational elements. This is very simple to do with Rhapsody and simplifies the interpretation of the graphic.

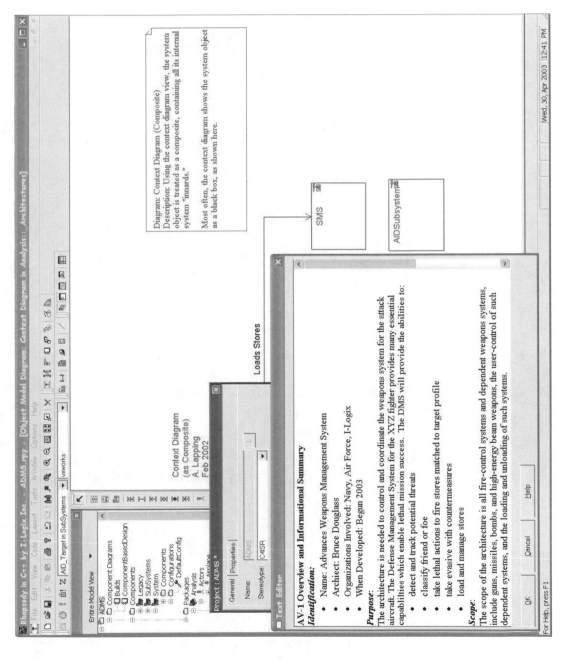

Figure 11-1: *Report on Model for AV-1 Overview*

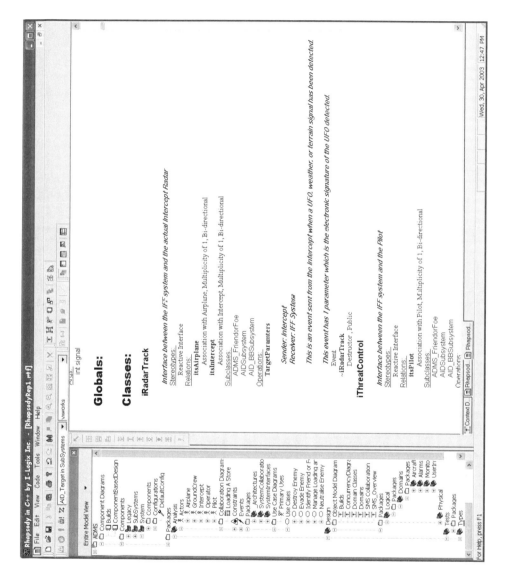

Figure 11-2: *AV-2 Integrated Dictionary*

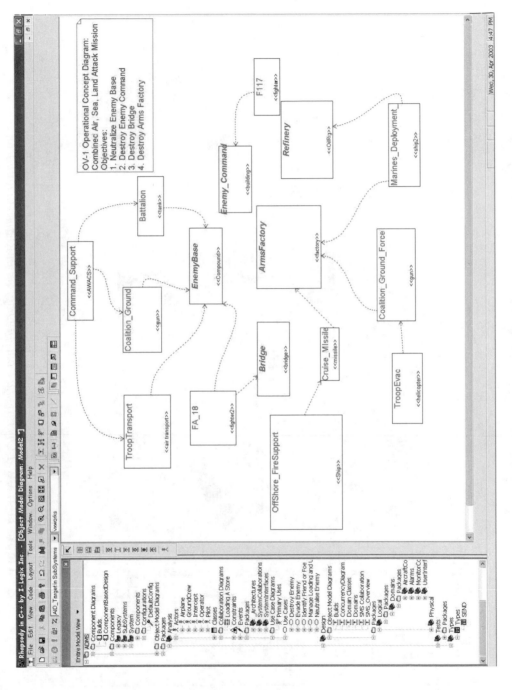

Figure 11-3: *OV-1 Operation Concept Diagram with Standard Notation*

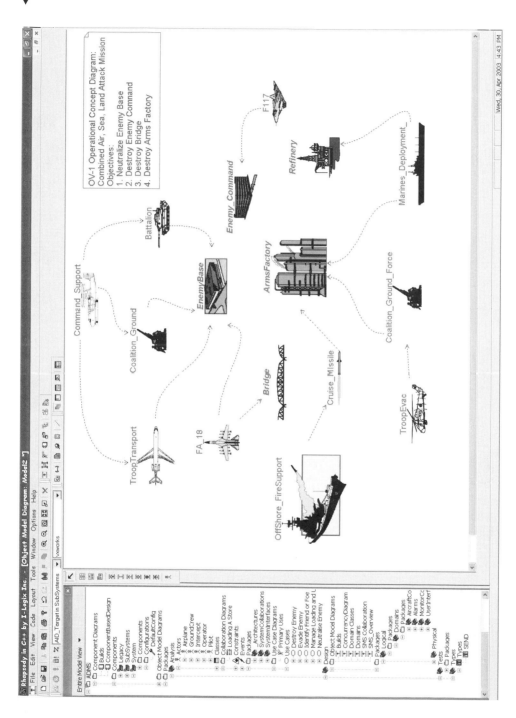

Figure 11-4: *OV-1 Operational Concept Diagram in Rhapsody with Icons*

11.3.4 OV-2 Operational Node Connectivity Description

The Operation Node Connectivity Description identifies the operational nodes, their connections, and the information shared among them. In the UML, operational nodes may be represented as classes on class diagrams or as nodes on deployment diagrams. In Figure 11-5,[2] operational nodes and subnodes are shown as classes; the interfaces among the operational nodes are mediated via the associations. The actual information content transmitted along these associations is captured in constraints (the notes with the curly braces), and supporting information is shown in either free text or comments within note boxes.

The same information is shown in the diagram in Figure 11-6, except that the operational nodes are shown as nodes on a deployment dia-

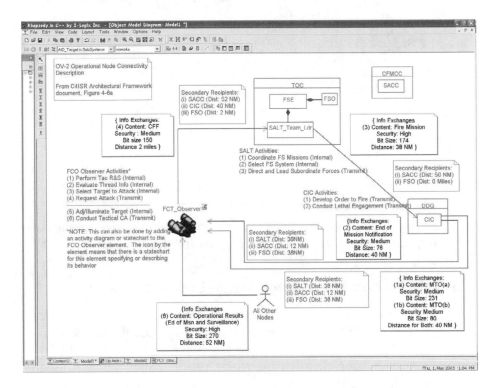

Figure 11-5: *OV-2 Operational Node Connectivity with Classes*

---

[2] The example is taken from [1] and recast into UML notation and semantics.

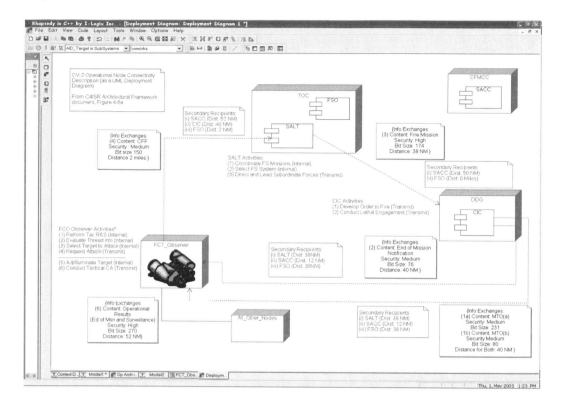

Figure 11-6: *OV-2 Operational Node Connectivity with Deployment Diagram*

gram. In general, classes have richer semantics than nodes on deployment diagrams and so are usually preferred for that reason.

11.3.5 OV-3 Operational Information Exchange Matrix

The Operational Information Exchange Matrix expresses the relationship between activities, operational elements, and information flow, focusing on the latter. The UML doesn't have a matrix notation, but this can be cast as a specialized format of a report constructed from the model repository held by Rhapsody.

Alternatively, the data flow notation of the UML 2.0 can easily depict the information exchange among operational elements. In the UML diagram in Figure 11-7, icons are used to represent operational

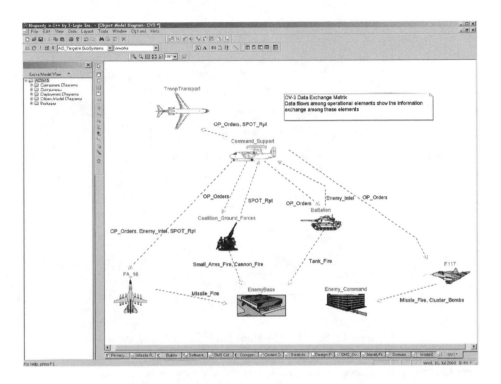

Figure 11-7: *OV-3 Data Information Exchange*

elements (modeled with UML classes) with information flows among these elements.

11.3.6 SV-1 System Interface Description

The System Interface Description shows the structural elements of the systems architecture and the informational interfaces among them.

Sometimes it is important to show the large-scale deployment of the elements into the systems rather than their categories, as is shown in Figure 11-8. Figure 11-9 shows the deployed systems as structured classes with the internal subsystems as classes. These elements may have stereotypes attached, if desired. This more detailed view shows the subsystems and their interconnections within the systems as well as between systems.

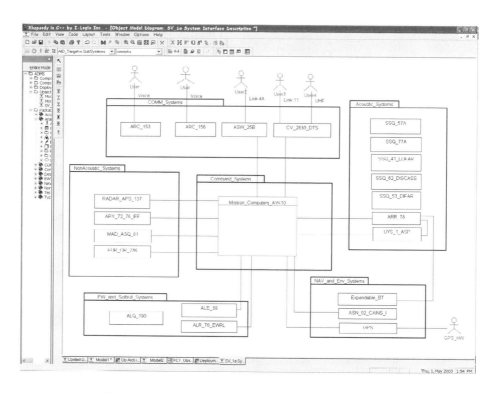

Figure 11-8: *SV-1 System Interface Description*

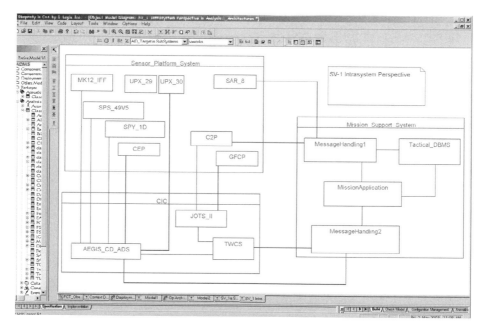

Figure 11-9: *SV-1 Intrasystem Perspective*

11.3.7 TV-1 Technical Architecture Profile

The Technical Architecture Profile is a description of the technologies to be included in the system, normally as references to application standards documents, such as [1] or the POSIX standard. These may be specified in a textual document (most common) or they may be added as constraints to the model elements.

11.4 Supporting Products

There are a large number of optional supporting products defined in [1], [3], and [4], most of which can be easily and productively represented in the UML.

11.4.1 OV-4 Command Relationships Chart

The OV-4 diagram is used primarily for the command structure of some unit or units of battle. The UML view for this is a class diagram, using aggregation to show ownership. Other relations may be added; for significant communications between subunits or individuals, associations should be used. For less obvious relations, dependencies may be used. Figure 11-10 shows a relation set, including ownership and assignment relations, when a person is assigned to one unit or individual but commanded by another.

11.4.2 OV-5 Operational Activity Model

The Operational Activity Model specifies the flow of execution among activities, possibly with the generation of artifacts such as reports and OP orders. Figure 11-11 uses the UML activity diagram to show the primary activities and their subactivities to achieve a Joint Force Targeting activity. The nesting depicts the whole-part nature of the activities (i.e., activities may be divided into smaller subactivities). The arrows depict the flow of execution as the activities complete over time. The bars indicate forks or joins; a fork indicates a branching into concurrent (simultaneously executing) activities while a join indicates a merging together of previously concurrent activities.

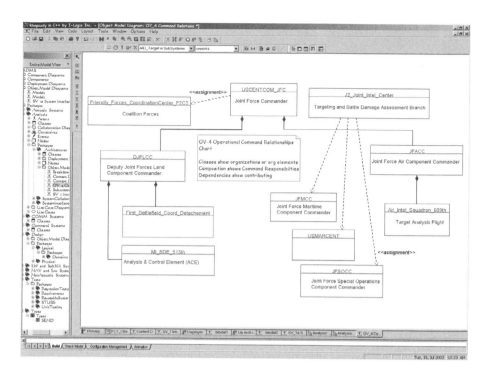

Figure 11-10: *OV-4 Command Relationship Chart*

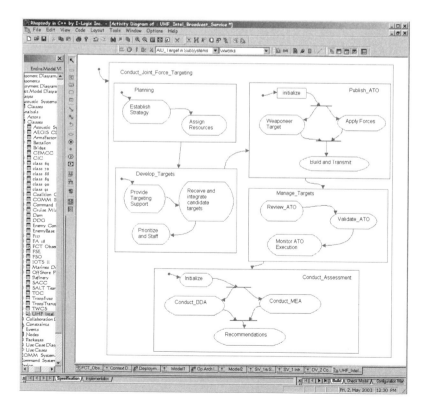

Figure 11-11: *OV-5 Operational Activity Model*

Often, activities are performed by a set of collaborating operational or system elements. This can be indicated using swim lanes to divide the activities into activities done by a single operational and those done by a systems entity. An abstract example is shown in Figure 11-12, with swim lanes for external elements, special OPs, CIC, battalion commander, and air support. This diagram shows forks and joins as well as branch points (indicated with a diamond). A fork differs from a branch in that all transitions from a fork become simultaneously active while only a single transition from a branch is taken.

Figure 11-13 shows a concrete example. Two entities, OTC CWC and FLTCINC, are shown executing a set of activities. The structure of their collaboration becomes clear in this diagram. Diagram connectors are used to beautify the diagram.

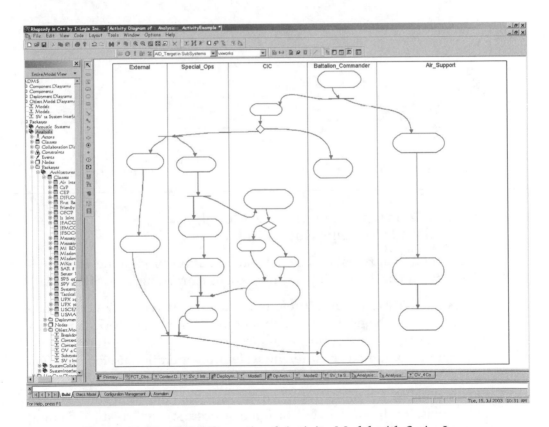

Figure 11-12: *OV-5 Operational Activity Model with Swim Lanes*

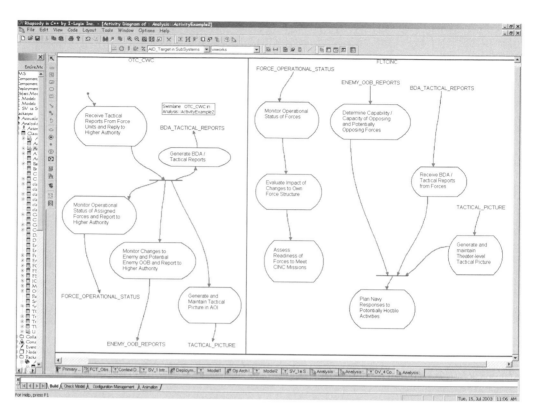

Figure 11-13: *OV-5 Operational Activity Model with Two Agencies*

11.4.3 OV-6a Operational Rules Model, SV-10a Systems Rules Model

The operational rules model shows the relationship among the activities. This can be done using any of the behavioral diagrams of the UML:

- An activity diagram is preferred when the activities flow from one activity to the next upon completion, but may have forks and joins (concurrently executing activities) or branching (alternatives), or may be assigned to different system or operational elements (via swim lanes).

- A statechart is preferred when the states or conditions of existence persist until some event of interest occurs, such as an incoming asynchronous event (e.g., a hostile missile launch), a synchronous service request (e.g., the requester waits until the service is completed before moving forward), or a timeout (e.g., a delayed launch). Behaviors are executed during the change of state or within a state when such an event is received.

- A sequence diagram is preferred when a particular operational scenario is to be shown, that is, a collaborative behavior of system or operational elements, beginning with specific preconditions and with a specific event sequence, ignoring other possibilities.

In this case (see Figure 11-14), we show only a class diagram for the logical data model and describe some business rules. In the later OV-6 diagrams we present a statechart for the OV-6b example and a sequence diagram for the OV-6c example.

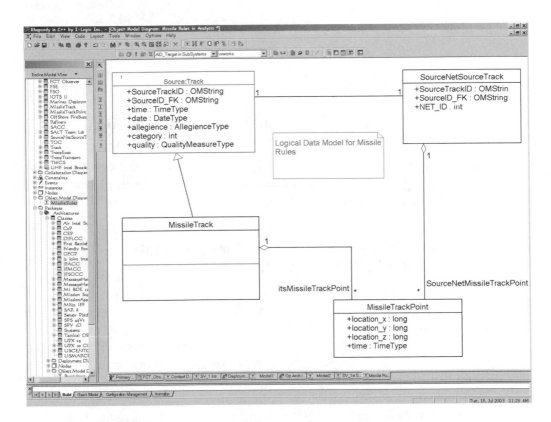

Figure 11-14: *OV-6a Logical Data Model for Operational Rules*

Business rules can be applied to the logical data model (taken from [1]):

```
For Each MISSILE TRACK entity instance
       If MISSILE TRACK boost phase code > 0,
              Then MISSILE TRACK acceleration rate is
              non-null
       Else MISSILE TRACK drag effect rate is non-null
              And
              There Exists a MISSILE TRACK POINT
                entity instance Such
              That
                     MISSILE TRACK.SOURCE TRACK
                       identifier =
                     MISSILE TRACK POINT.SOURCE TRACK
                     identifier
              And
                     MISSILE TRACK POINT.SOURCE
                       identifier
       End If
End For
```

11.4.4 OV-6b Operational State Transition Description, SV-10b Systems State Transition Description

The Operational State Transition Description is best described by a state chart. In Figure 11-15, the AIDSystem shows the states it goes through in selecting and destroying a target.

11.4.5 OV-6c Operational Event-Trace Description, SV-10c Systems Event Trace Description

OV-6c, the Event-Trace Description, is used to show the specific flow or sequence of messages and events during a very specific scenario or example execution of the system. Branch points are typically not shown. Emphasis is on a specific execution given a specific set of preconditions and a specific sequencing of incoming events and messages. It is common to produce dozens of such operational scenarios, each on a separate diagram, to explore variations of system behavior. Figure 11-16 shows a typical example of an event trace description shown with a UML sequence diagram.

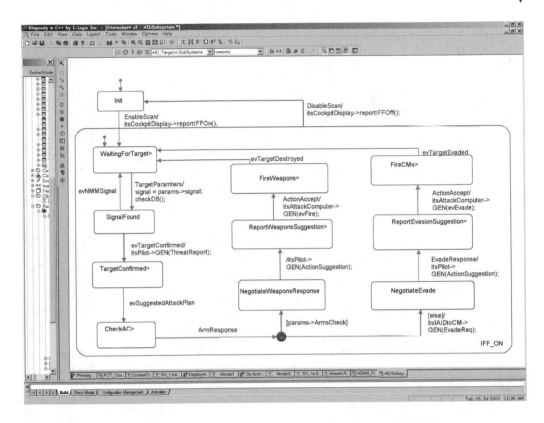

Figure 11-15: *OV-6b Statechart for Operation State Transition Description*

11.4.6 OV-7 Logical Data Model

The logical data model focuses on the information known to or processed by the system during its execution. In the UML, this is modeled with class diagrams. Class diagrams can depict system structure as well as information content, so to achieve the OV-7 goals, the class diagrams focus on the informational content of the system and the relationships among those data, and not on the processing of this information.

11.4.7 SV-3 Systems-Systems Matrix

The Systems-Systems Matrix shows the relationships among the set of large-scale entities (systems). As mentioned previously, the UML does

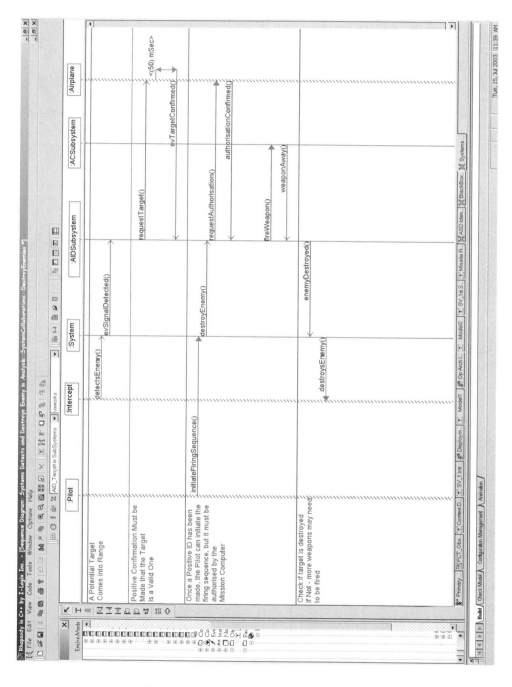

Figure 11-16: *OV-6c Event-Trace Description with Sequence Diagram*

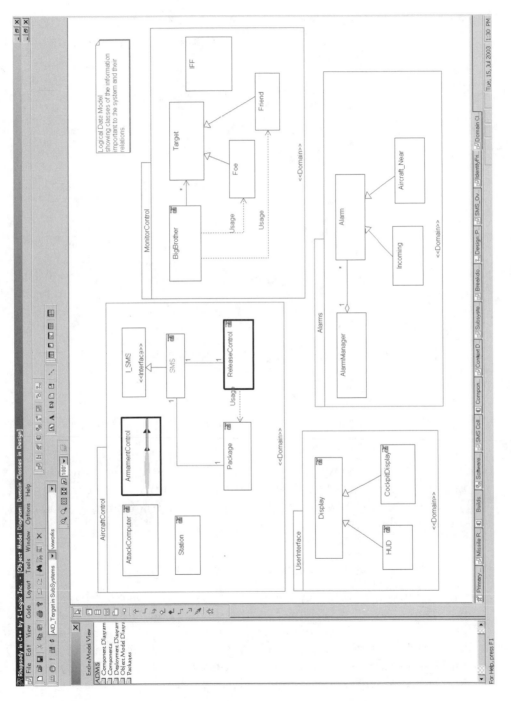

Figure 11-17: *OV-7 Logical Data Model*

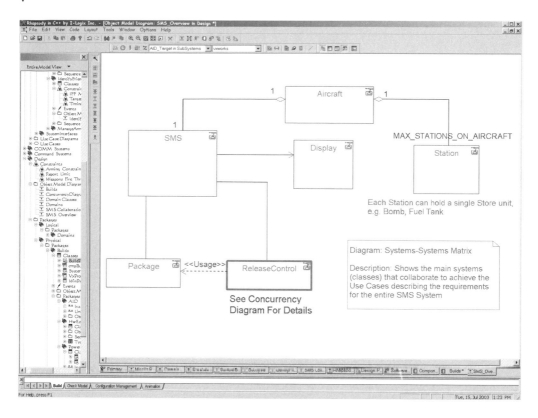

Figure 11-18: *SV-3 Systems-Systems Matrix with Class Diagram*

not have a matrix view. However, the information can be shown easily on a class diagram (also a two-dimensional view), as has been done in Figure 11-18. It is also possible to construct a matrix from the data held in the model repository.

11.4.8 SV-4 Systems Functionality Description

The Systems Functionality Description (SV-4) shows the functionality of a system or set of systems at a high-level view. The natural view in the UML is the use case diagram. Of course, using just the names of the use cases is insufficient, so Rhapsody has description fields that can hold text (and/or hyperlinks to other documents in other tools such as Word or Framemaker) to more fully explain the functionality repre-

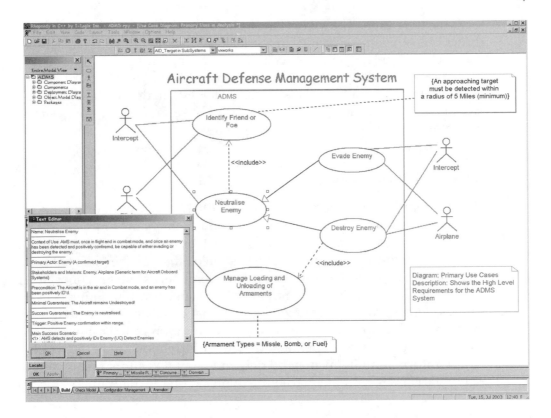

Figure 11-19: *SV-4 Systems Functionality Description*

sented by the use case. It is common to detail the use case with a combination of text, statecharts, activity diagrams, and sequence diagrams. Figure 11-19 shows a use case diagram with the description field for one of the use cases.

11.4.9 SV-5 Operational Activity to Systems Function Traceability Matrix

The purpose of the Operational Activity to Systems Function Traceability Matrix (SV-5) is to allow mapping from operational activities defined in OV-5, OV-6a, PV-6b, and OV-6c into systems functions. This can be done in UML using dependencies if desired, but the most common way in the UML to achieve this goal is with the swim lanes in the activity diagrams. The swim lanes can represent system elements or functions while the activities in the diagram are the operational activities. See Figure 11-12 and Figure 11-13 for examples.

Another common approach to traceability is to use third-party requirements traceability tools, such as DOORS, to define the mapping between the operational activities and the system use cases or system elements.

11.4.10 SV-6 Systems Data Exchange Matrix

The Systems Data Exchange Matrix (SV-6) shows how information is exchanged among system elements. Although the name of the product includes the word *matrix*, it may be met by any visualization that shows the information flow among system elements. The most natural view in the UML is to show the system elements as classes connected with data flows, as defined in the UML 2.0 specification. Figure 11-20 shows elements of an aircraft weapons management system with information flows among the elements. An information flow is shown as a «flow» stereotype of dependency, with information items attached. These information items may be rich and complex, and so may themselves be classes with their structure depicted on the diagram(s).

11.4.11 SV-7 Systems Performance Parameters Matrix

Performance is, of course, a crucial aspect of military and other real-time and embedded systems. In the UML, performance is a rather large subclass of the more general concept of QoS. Performance-related QoS properties include worst-case execution time, throughput, average execution time, capacity, and so on. The OMG provides a standard set of performance-related property tags in [5]. In the UML, QoS properties may be attached to just about any element. However, whether standard or custom properties are used, the usage model is the same. The system elements are stereotyped to have the appropriate properties (tags) and then these properties are assigned values in constraints. These constraints can be shown on the class diagrams with the elements they constrain, such as in Figure 11-21, or they may be view in the model browser and in reports, as shown in Figure 11-22.

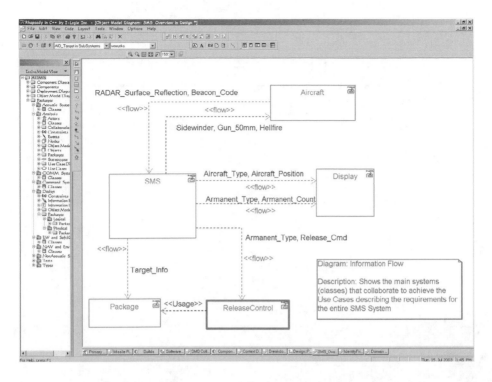

Figure 11-20: *SV-6 Data Flow on Class Diagram*

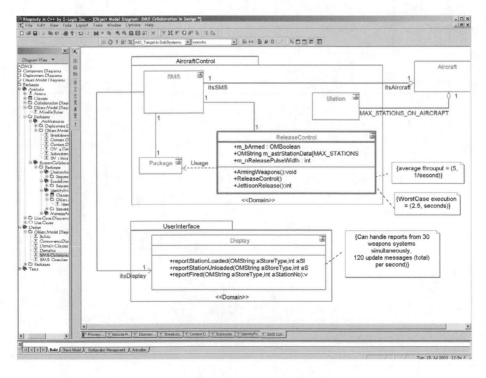

Figure 11-21: *SV-7 Systems Performance on Class Diagram*

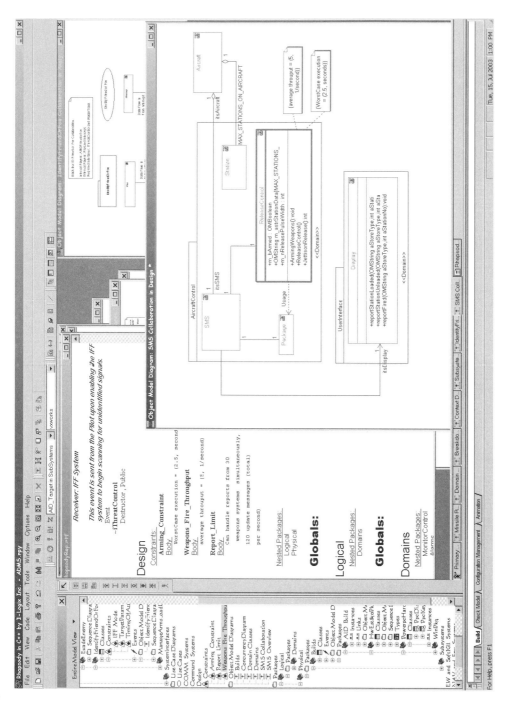

Figure 11-22: *SV-7 Systems Performance in Reports and Browser*

11.4.12 SV-8 Systems Evolution Description

The Systems Evolution Description (SV-8) is logically a map of development activities leading to successive releases and versions of one or more systems. The UML activity diagram represents such processes clearly and distinctly. In Figure 11-23, the development activities are shown in the rounded rectangles while the artifacts are shown in the rectangles. Such evolution descriptions may be as complex as needed to describe the development plans for any system element or set of system elements.

11.4.13 SV-9 Systems Technology Forecast

As with TV-2, Systems Technology Forecast (SV-9) is almost exclusively a textual document. There is no UML representation, although text can

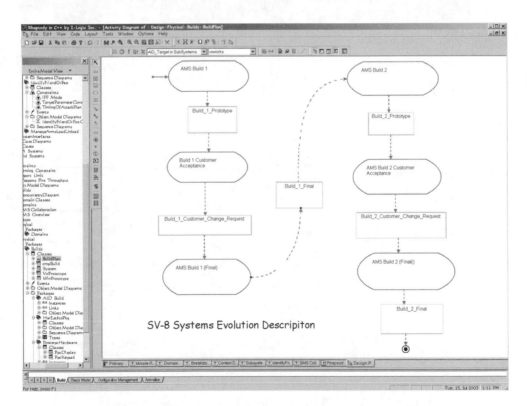

Figure 11-23: *SV-8 Systems Evolution Description*

be represented in the description fields of a tool such as Rhapsody. Additionally, external documents may be linked to with hyperlinks in Rhapsody so that selecting them executes the appropriate application to read, view, or modify the document.

11.4.14 SV-11 Physical Schema

The Physical Schema shows how the logical data model (OV-7) is to be physically realized—that is, how the information maps onto artifacts, devices, and other elements in the systems architecture view. This is most commonly done with a deployment diagram, where the nodes represent the hardware devices and the components represent the software

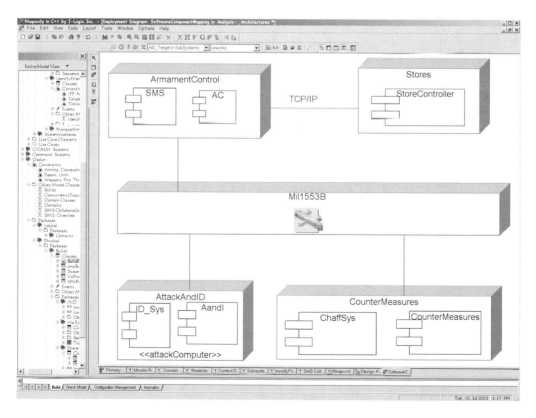

Figure 11-24: *SV-11 Physical Schema with Deployment*

or informational elements. It can also be done in a component diagram in which the logical elements (classes) are mapped into the components. A class diagram is yet another possibility, where some classes represent the physical items and others represent the logical elements.

Figure 11-24 shows the mapping of components onto the deployment nodes (hardware elements) using a standard UML deployment diagram.

Physical Schema may also refer entirely to the organization of software elements into component artifacts, such as documents, link libraries, executables, and so on. Figure 11-25 shows an example of this. The stereotypes «Executable», «Library», and «Hardware» show the kind of component being represented.

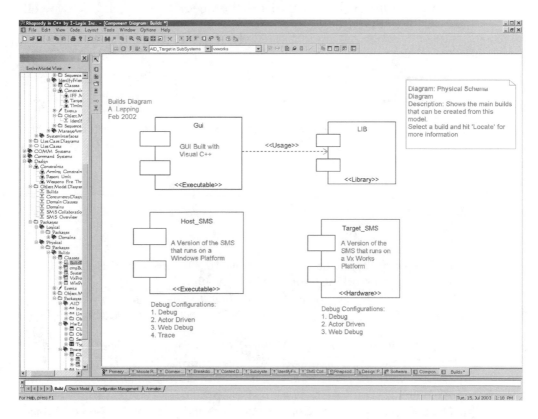

Figure 11-25: *SV-11 Physical Schema with Components*

11.5 Summary

The C⁴ISR (and the upcoming DAF) standard defines a number of work products, some of which are identified as required for a system to be compliant; others are identified as supporting and are recommended but not required. The 1997 standard [1] came out at about the same time as the UML standard and therefore doesn't take advantage of the rich semantics and clear notation provided by the UML. Since then, the UML has been widely adopted in the specification of software and systems within the DoD and other environments. This chapter discusses each product required by the C⁴ISR and shows how standard UML views and semantics can be used to represent them. Clearly, the unifying nature of the UML meets the needs of the C⁴ISR very well, now and into the future.

11.6 Acknowledgments

The aircraft weapon systems diagrams were taken or adapted from the ADMS model by Andy Lapping of I-Logix. Some of the other examples were adapted from [1].

11.7 References

[1] *C⁴ISR Architectural Framework, Version 2.0.* Department of Defense C⁴ISR Architectural Working Group. December 1997.

[2] *IEEE Standard Glossary of Software Engineering Terminology.* IEEE STD 610.12-1990. Piscataway, NJ: Institute of Electrical and Electronics Engineers, Inc., 1990.

[3] *DoD Architecture Framework: Volume I: Definitions and Guidelines, Version 1.0.* DoD Architecture Framework Working Group, 2003.

[4] *DoD Architecture Framework: Volume II: Product Description, Version 1.0.* DoD Architecture Framework Working Group, 2003.

[5] *UML Profile for Schedulability, Performance and Time,* ptc2003-03-02. Object Management Group, 2003.

Notational Summary

Class Diagram

Shows the existence of classes and
relationships in a logical view of a system

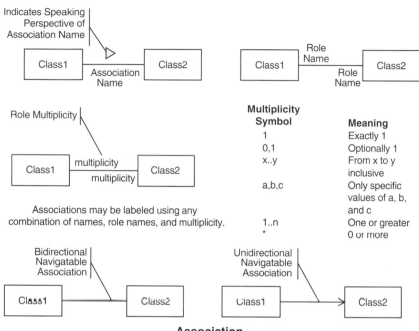

Multiplicity Symbol	Meaning
1	Exactly 1
0,1	Optionally 1
x..y	From x to y inclusive
a,b,c	Only specific values of a, b, and c
1..n	One or greater
*	0 or more

Associations may be labeled using any
combination of names, role names, and multiplicity.

Association

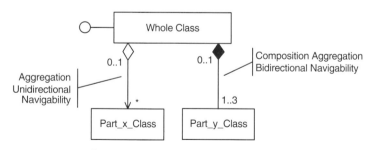

Aggregation and Composition

Class Diagram

Shows the existence of classes and
relationships in a logical view of a system

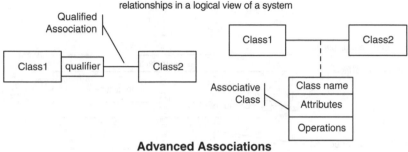

Advanced Associations

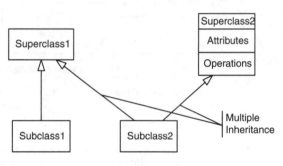

Generalization

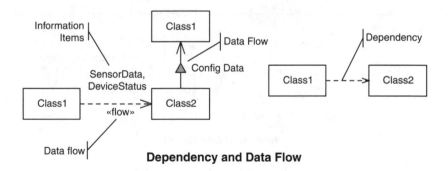

Dependency and Data Flow

Class Diagram

Shows the existence of classes and
relationships in a logical view of a system

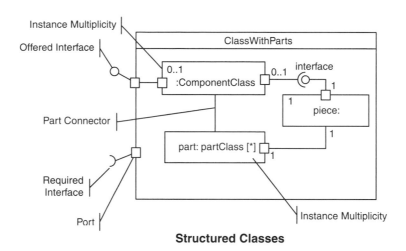

Structured Classes

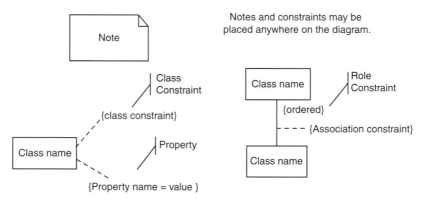

Notes and constraints may be
placed anywhere on the diagram.

Notes and Constraints

Class Diagram

Shows the existence of classes and
relationships in a logical view of a system.

«stereotype»

<<stereotype>>

Standard Stereotype
Indicators

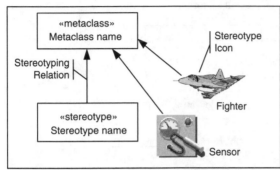

«metaclass»
Metaclass name

Stereotyping
Relation

«stereotype»
Stereotype name

Stereotype
Icon

Fighter

Sensor

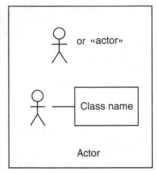

or «actor»

Class name

Actor

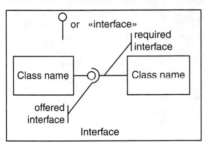

or «interface»

required
interface

Class name

Class name

offered
interface

Interface

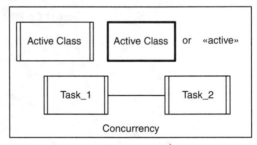

Active Class

Active Class

or   «active»

Task_1

Task_2

Concurrency

Stereotypes

Communication Diagram

Shows a sequenced set of messages illustrating a specific
example of object interaction.

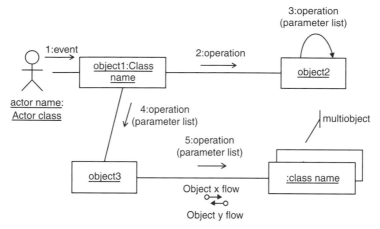

Object Collaboration

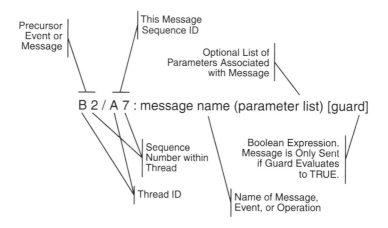

Message Syntax

Sequence Diagram

Shows a sequenced set of messages illustrating a specific
example of object interaction.

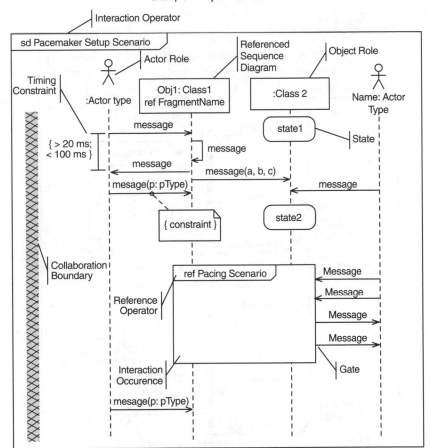

Sequence Diagram Elements

Sequence Diagram

Shows a sequenced set of messages illustrating a specific
example of object interaction.

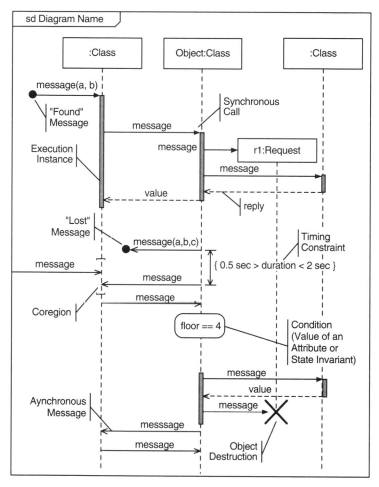

Sequence Diagram Annotations

Sequence Diagram

Shows a sequenced set of messages illustrating a specific example of object interaction.

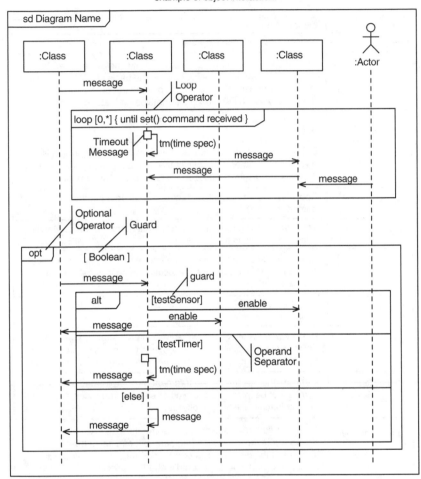

Interaction Operators

Sequence Diagram

Shows a sequenced set of messages illustrating a specific
example of object interaction.

Operator	Description
sd	Names an interaction fragment
alt	The alt operator provides alternatives, only one of which will be taken. The branches are evaluated on the basis of guards, similar to statecharts. An "else" guard is provided that evaluates to TRUE if and only if all other branch alternatives evaluate to FALSE.
opt	Defines an optional interaction segment, one that may or may not occur.
break	Break is a short hand for an alt operator where one operand is given and the other is the rest of the enclosing interaction fragment. A sequence diagram analogous to C++ "break" statement.
loop	Specifies that an interaction fragment shall be repeated some number of times.
seq	Weak sequencing (default). Specifies the normal weak sequencing rules are in force in the fragment.
strict	Specifies that the messages in the interaction fragment are fully ordered—that is, only a single execution trace is consistent with the fragment.
neg	Specifies a negative, or "not" condition. Useful for capturing negative requirements.
par	Defines parallel or concurrent regions in an interaction fragment. This is similar to alt in that subfragments are identified, but differs in that ALL such subfragments execute rather than just a single one.
criticalRegion	Identifies that the interaction fragment must be treated as atomic and cannot be interleaved with other event occurrences. It is useful in combination with the par operator.
ignore/consider	The ignore operator specifies that some message types are not shown within the interaction fragment, but can be ignored for the purpose of the diagram. The consider operator specifies which messages should be considered in the fragment.
assert	Specifies that the interaction fragment represents an assertion.

Interaction Operators

Use Cases

Use cases show primary areas of collaboration between the system and actors in its environment. Use cases are isomorphic with function points.

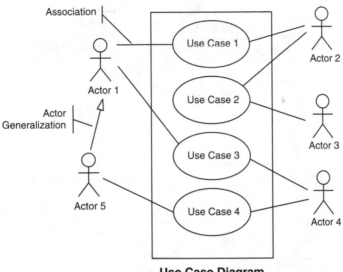

Use Case Diagram

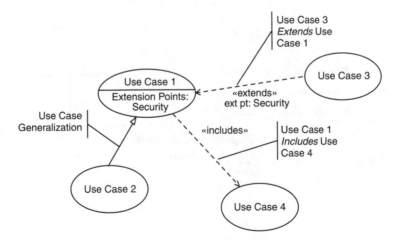

Use Case Relationships

Implementation Diagrams

Implementation diagrams show the runtime dependencies and packaging
structure of the deployed system.

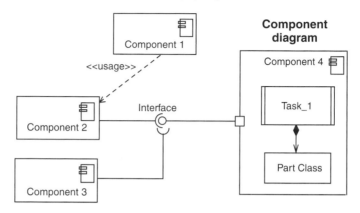

Component diagram

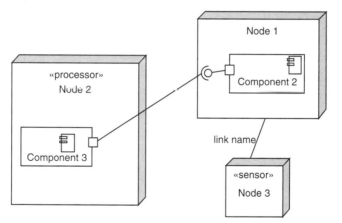

Deployment Diagram

Packages

Shows a grouping of model elements. Packages may appear within class and other diagrams.

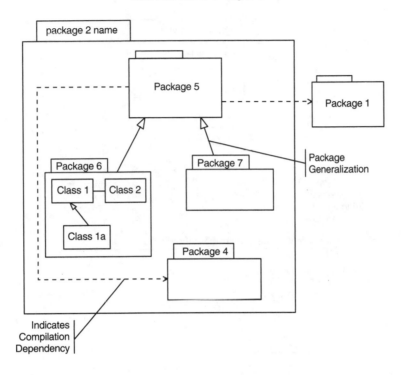

Statechart

Shows the sequences of states for a reactive class or interaction during its life in response to stimuli, together with its responses and actions.

State name

entry / action-list
event-name:action-list
do / activity-list
defer/ event-list
...
exit /action-list

State Icon

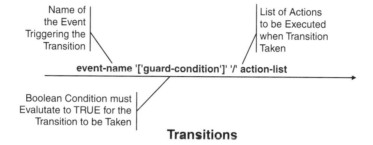

Name of
the Event
Triggering the
Transition

List of Actions
to be Executed
when Transition
Taken

event-name '['guard-condition']' '/' action-list

Boolean Condition must
Evalutate to TRUE for the
Transition to be Taken

Transitions

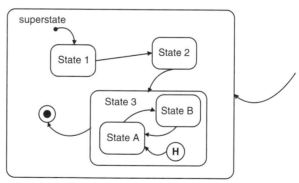

superstate

State 1 → State 2

State 3

State B

State A

H

Nested States

Statechart

Shows the sequences of states for a reactive class or interaction during its life in response to stimuli, together with its responses and actions.

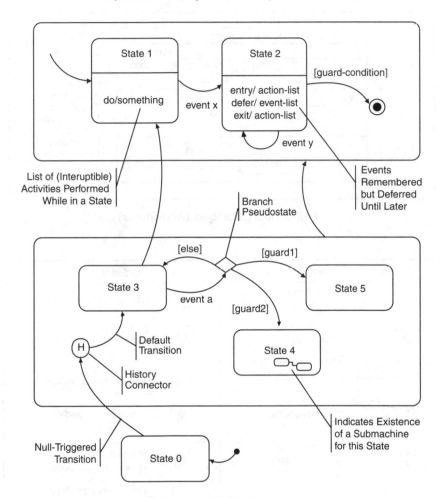

Sequential Substates

Statechart

Shows the sequences of states for a reactive class or interaction during its life in response to stimuli, together with its responses and actions.

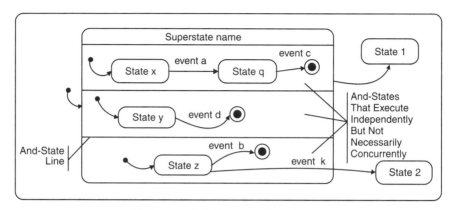

Orthogonal Substates (And-States)

Symbol	Symbol Name	Symbol	Symbol Name
ⓒ or ◇	Branch Pseudostate (*type of junction pseudostate*)	Ⓗ	(Shallow) History Pseudostate
Ⓣ or ◉	Terminal or Final Pseudostate	Ⓗ*	(Deep) History Pseudostate
⊛ or ⓝ	Synch Pseudostate		
		⌁	Initial or Default Pseudostate
↟	Fork Pseudostate	⬤	Junction Pseudostate
↡	Join Pseudostate	⬤	Merge Junction Pseudostate (*type of junction pseudostate*)
[g] ◯ [g]	Choice Point Pseudostate	◯ label	Entry Point Pseudostate
		⊗ label	Exit Point Pseudostate

Pseudostates

Statechart

Shows the sequences of states for a reactive class or interaction during its life in response to stimuli, together with its responses and actions.

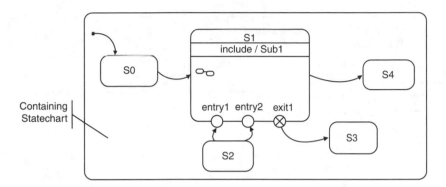

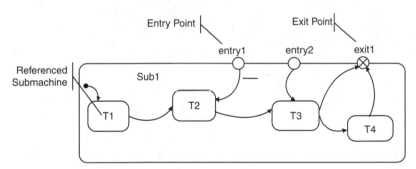

Submachines

Activity Diagrams

Activity diagrams are behavioral diagrams based on token flow semantics and that include branching, forks, and joins.

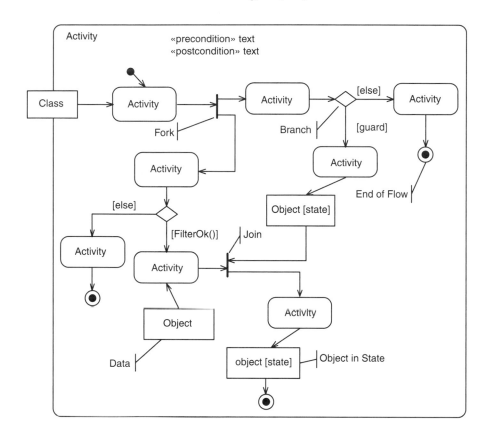

Activity Diagrams

Activity diagrams are behavioral diagrams based on token flow semantics and
that include branching, forks, and joins.

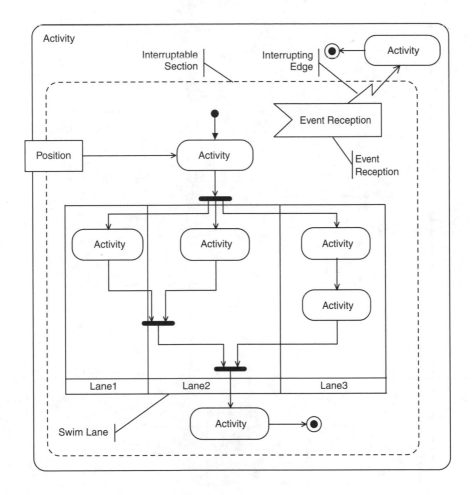

LIVERPOOL JOHN MOORES UNIVERSITY
LEARNING SERVICES

Timing Diagrams

Timing diagrams show the explicit change of state or value along a linear time axis.
(Timing diagrams are new in the UML 2.0 standard.)

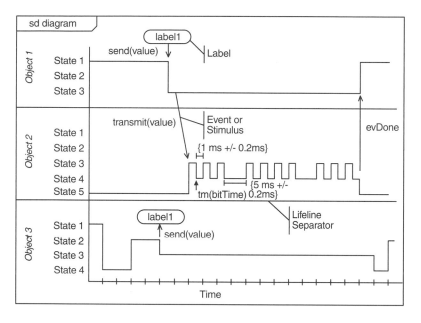

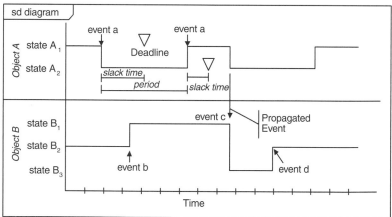

Timing Diagrams

Timing diagrams show the explicit change of state or value along a linear time axis.
(Timing diagrams are new in the UML 2.0 standard.)

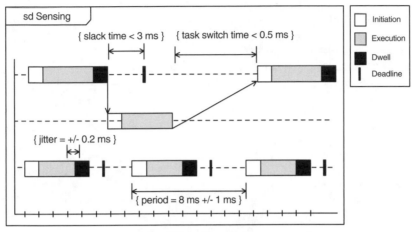

With Shading

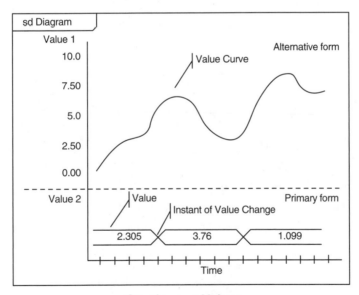

Continuous Values

Index

<> (angle brackets), 97
* (asterisk), 97, 198, 237–238
^ (caret), 97
{} (curly braces), 134
«» (guillemots), 90
- (hyphen), 364, 603
() (parentheses), 424
+ (plus sign), 88, 150, 364, 603
# (pound sign), 364, 603
[] (square brackets), 192, 408
~ (tilde), 603

Absolute Deadline attribute, 10
Abstract classes, 86, 90–91, 111–112,
    373. *See also* Abstraction
Abstraction. *See also* Abstract classes;
    ADTs (abstract data types)
  architectural hierarchy and,
      129–130
  debugging and, 35
  described, 82–83
  levels of, 130, 482–483
  model organization and, 64
  objects and, 82–83, 447
Action(s)
  architecture and, 513
  behavior and, 144–148
  blocking, 10
  concurrency and, 12
  described, 8–15, 145, 513
  execution order, 155–156
  importance of, 18
  language, 146

messages and, 92–94
nested, 243
priority of, 10
schedulable, 243
semantics, 406
specification of, 146–147
timeliness properties of, 9–11
types of, 145
urgency of, 18
Active
  classes, 134, 217
  resources, 13
Activities. *See also* Activity diagrams
  described, 144–148
  run-to-completion semantics and,
      147, 151
  statecharts and, 147
Activity diagrams. *See also* Activities
  behavior and, 140
  described, 184–189
  notation and, 670–671
  requirements analysis and,
      322–327
Actors
  described, 280, 282–297, 301
  identifying, 301
  naming, 282
Actual parameters, 107
Ada
  behavior and, 140
  definition object behavior and, 438,
      471
  exceptions, 611

Ada (*cont.*)
  generative tools and, 70
  generics and, 107, 438
  MDA and, 44, 45
  messages and, 92
  parametric classes and, 438
  PIM and, 44
ADTs (abstract data types),
    84, 187
Aggregation, 95, 98–99. *See also*
    Associations
Aircraft. *See* Flight control systems
Algorithms
  behavior and, 143–144
  complexity of, 6
  detailed design and, 604–610
  development costs and, 6
  requirements analysis and,
    322–324
  scheduling policy, 22
Algorithmic object, 143
alt operator, 196–199, 201, 662
Analysis microphase, 36, 37–38, 41
And-states
  described, 156–158
  requirements analysis and, 318
Angle brackets (< >), 97
Aperiodic arrival patterns, 11
Apply scenarios strategy, 341,
    356–358
Architecture, 71, 473–526. *See also*
    Design
  asymmetric distribution, 492
  deployment, 30–31, 509–512
  five primary aspects of, 30–31
  hierarchy, 129–130
  logical, 477, 478–481, 509
  metamodel language, 131–133
  model organization principles
    and, 57, 58
  physical, 477, 479, 481–486,
    501–503, 509

ROPES process and, 30–31, 38, 41,
    62, 473, 477–478, 484–486
  subdivisions of, 62
  use of the term, 30–31
Arithmetic operators in Calculator
    example, 424
Array classes, 465
Arrival patterns
  aperiodic, 11
  architecture and, 519
  described, 11
  periodic, 11
  UML profiles and, 237, 238
Arrowheads, 95, 97, 192
Artifacts
  components and, 122
  defect reports as, 71
  deployments and, 125
  described, 39
  high frequency, 325
  ROPES process and, 39–40
assert operator, 197, 199, 201, 202, 662
Associations. *See also* Relations
  bi-directional, 67
  classes and, 66–67
  described, 88, 95–98
  detailed design and, 596, 597–600
  labels, 97
  mechanistic design and, 529–530
  qualified, 596
  strategies for, 359–360
Associative classes, 98, 367–370
Asterisk (*), 97, 198, 237–238
Asych-asych transfers, 12
Asymmetric distribution
    architecture, 492
Atomic access, 22
Attributes
  behavior and, 428
  derived, 594
  described, 84, 85
  detailed design and, 594, 603

interfaces and, 90
nonprimitive, 362–363
object domain analysis and, 344–456, 362–364, 394–395
requirements analysis and, 326
virtualized, 90
visibility, 603
Average deadlines, 9
AVL trees, 606–610

Balking rendezvous, 12, 521
Ball-and-socket notation, 119
Base classes, 370
Basic Rate Monotonic analysis, 26
Behavior
    calculator examples, 422–441, 454–564
    cardiac pacemaker examples, 409–422, 444–454
    continuous, 143–144, 400, 403–404
    defining, 399–472, 404–441
    dynamic, 140
    event hierarchies and, 441–443
    functional, 142
    interactions and, 443–462
    operations and, 463–471
    primitives, 144–148
    requirements analysis and, 317–322
    sequence diagrams and, 444–462
    simple, 141–142, 400–402
    single objects and, 148–189
    state (reactive), 142–143, 186, 400, 402–441
    types of, 141–144
Bernoulli distribution, 238
BERT (Bruce's Evaluation and Review Technique) process, 48–50, 51
Binomial distribution, 238
BITs (built-in tests), 348
Black-box requirements. *See* Requirements analysis

Blocking, 10, 23, 26
    rate monotonic analysis with, 27
    rendezvous, 12–13
    RMA with, 254
Blocking Time attribute, 10
Boolean values, 155, 232, 243, 408
Bound arrival patterns, 237
bounded keyword, 237
branch pseudostate, 160, 161–163
Branches, 160, 161–163, 197–199
break operator, 196, 662
Builds model-based model organization, 62
Bursty arrival pattern, 11, 237

C (high-level language)
    attributes and, 85
    behavior and, 140
    detailed design and, 611
    generative tools and, 70
    MDA and, 44, 45
    mechanistic design and, 546, 555
    nodes and, 127
    PIM and, 44
C++ (high-level language)
    attributes and, 85
    behavior and, 140
    classes and, 86, 373–374, 438
    composition and, 102
    definition object behavior and, 406, 438, 464, 471
    detailed design and, 600, 611–612
    generalization and, 103
    generative tools and, 70
    hiding data members and, 94
    keywords and, 107
    mapping objects and, 110–113
    MDA and, 45
    mechanistic design and, 529, 531, 546, 555
    nodes and, 127
    templates, 107, 438

C⁴ISR Framework, 119, 617–652
  required products, 625–635
  supporting products, 635–637
Calculator examples, 422–441,
    454–564
Candidate classes, 364–365
Cardiac pacemaker(s), 3, 172–183.
    See also ECG
    (electrocardiography) machines
  definition object behavior and,
    409–422, 444–454
  messages, list of, 412
  object domain analysis and,
    356–358
  time constraints and, 8–9
  timing diagrams and, 206
Caret (^), 97
Causality loops, 229–230
CCM (CORBA Component Model),
    123
CDMA (collision-detect multiple
    access) protocol, 495
CDR (critical design review), 52
Central Limit Theorem, 52
CharParser class, 424–427
Child classes, 370
choice point pseudostate, 160, 163
CIs (configuration items), 56–59, 66
Class(es). *See also* Class diagrams;
    Subclasses; Superclasses
  abstract, 86, 90–91, 111–112, 373
  ADTs and, 84
  associative, 98, 367–370
  base, 370
  "boxes," 187, 217
  candidate, 364–365
  child, 370
  container, 529
  described, 83–86
  features of, 84
  hierarchy of, 370
  instantiable, 107, 112

  meta-, 43, 102–103, 217, 221
  nodes versus, 127–129
  notation and, 87–89
  parameterized, 107
  parametric, 438
  specialized, 370
  structured, 116–120
  transparent, 119
  utilities, 364
Class diagrams. *See also* Classes; Task
    diagrams
  cardiac pacemakers and, 174–175
  classification of, as structural
    diagrams, 108
  class structure diagrams, 366
  described, 43
  detailed design and, 603
  mission of, 366
  notation and, 88–89, 654–657
  object behavior and, 414
  object domain analysis and,
    365–395
Classifier(s)
  behavior and, 144–148
  requirements analysis and, 326
  roles and, 528
Client/resource model, 15
Clock(s)
  drift, 16
  interrupts, 17
  measurement of time by, 16–17
  offset, 16
  skew, 16–17
CM (configuration management),
    55–56, 66–67
Collaboration
  architecture and, 492
  described, 334–335
  mechanistic design and, 528,
    535–543, 551–552, 557–558,
    563–564, 570, 581–582
  pacemaker objects and, 357–358

roles, 535–536, 540–543, 551–552, 557–558, 563–564, 570, 581–582
Collections, 466–468, 529, 568
COM (Component Object Model)
  MDA and, 46
  mechanistic design and, 583
  PIM and, 44
Communication(s)
  connectionless (nonsessioned), 368–369
  diagrams, 308, 443–444, 658
  package classes and, 415
Compilers, 463–464
Component(s)
  architecture and, 129–130, 486–488, 509
  described, 113–130
  diagrams, 108, 366
  notation and, 122
  view, 486–488
Composites, 116–120
Composition, 95, 99, 100–103. *See also* Associations
Compound fragments, 197
Concurrency. *See also* Concurrent
  and-states and, 156
  architecture and, 30, 488–492, 508, 513–523
  described, 5, 8–15
  modeling subprofile, 240–243, 244
  partial ordering and, 194–195
  pseudostates and, 165
  ROPES process and, 41
  schedualability and, 17
Concurrent. *See also* Concurrency
  state diagrams, 515–516
  units, 13–14
Conditional pseudostate, 162, 408
Connection, use of the term, 127
Connectors, 116–120
consider operator, 197, 199–201, 202, 662

Constraint(s)
  described, 133–134
  detailed design and, 594, 596
  diagrams, 367
  generalization and, 375–376
  requirements analysis and, 278, 326
  tagged values and, 219–220
  UML profiles and, 219–221
Constructors
  C++ and, 374
  described, 86, 465
Container(s)
  classes, 529
  definition object behavior and, 466
  mechanistic design and, 529, 532
  pattern, 567–579, 598
Containment hierarchy, of systems, 119–120
Continual validation, 332
CORBA (Common Request Broker Architecture), 102, 493–494
  described, 268
  MDA and, 46
  mechanistic design and, 583
  PIM and, 44
  real-time CORBA subprofile and, 268–273
  standard, 268
  UML profiles and, 223, 226, 268–273
Coregion, 192–193
CPUs (central processing units)
  architecture and, 503, 510–512, 515–516
  detailed design and, 599–600
  manufacturing cost and, 5
  message transmission and, 12
  PIM and, 44
CRC (cyclic redundancy check), 411, 497, 551

Critical
    regions, 197, 199, 662
    sections, 22
criticalRegion operator, 197, 662
Curly braces ({}), 134
Cyclic
    Executive scheduling policy, 19
    redundancy check (CRC), 411, 497,
        551

Damm, Werner, 200
Data flow diagrams, 366
Deadline(s). *See also* Time constraints
    average, 9
    hard, 3, 8–10, 316–317
    monotonic analysis (DMA), 223
    Monotonic Scheduling (DMS)
        policy, 20
    soft, 8–10, 316–317
    timing diagrams and, 209
Debugging
    definition object behavior and,
        447–450, 454–464
    generative tools and, 70
    model-level, 70
    ROPES process and, 35, 42
    simulation and, 35
    tools, lack of sophisticated, 6
Decomposition, 117, 119
    requirements analysis and, 286,
        293, 296
    sequence diagrams and,
        201–204
deep history pseudostate, 160
Defect(s)
    reports, 71, 123
    ROPES process and, 33, 35
    strategic, 33
defer clause, 152
Delay Time attribute, 10
Department of Defense, 617.
        See also C⁴1SR Framework

Dependencies
    described, 106–108
    parameters and, 107
    requirements analysis and, 286,
        299–300, 310
Deployment, 125–127, 302
    architecture, 30–31, 509–512
    diagrams, 366, 664
    view, 499–501
Derived classes
    inheritance tree and, 374
    object domain analysis and, 370,
        374
Design. *See also* Architecture;
        Detailed design; Design
        patterns
    microphase, 36, 38, 41
    model organization principles
        and, 57
    phases, overview of, 476
    requirements analysis and, 302
    reviews, 52
    ROPES process and, 32–33, 35–36,
        41
Design pattern(s). *See also* Design
    applying, 530
    container pattern, 567–579, 598
    diagrams, 367
    guarded call pattern, 562–567
    mechanistic design and, 528,
        530–584
    model organization, 60–65
    observer pattern, 533–538
    proxy pattern, 538–547
    reliable transaction pattern,
        547–554
    rendezvous pattern, 579–584
    smart pointer pattern, 555–562
    thread boundary pattern,
        582
Destructor(s)
    C++ and, 374

definition object behavior and, 465–466

described, 86, 465

exceptions and, 612–613

Detailed design, 38, 41. *See also* Design

algorithms and, 604–610

associations and, 596, 597–600

data structure and, 591–597

described, 474, 476, 589–616

exceptions and, 610–614

operations and, 600–602

visibility and, 602–603

Device drivers, 4

Difference, programming by, 374

Distribution

architecture, 30

diagrams, 366

view, 492–497

Distributed objects, 370

DMA (deadline monotonic analysis), 223

DMS (Deadline Monotonic Scheduling) policy, 20

Domain(s), 63–65, 332. *See also* Object domain analysis

architecture and, 478–481

described, 58

packages and, 64–65, 114, 116

Duration

attribute, 10

described, 16

EC (estimate confidence) factor, 49, 50

ECG (electrocardiography) machines. *See also* Pacemakers

architecture and, 491, 518

classification of, as an embedded systems, 3

detailed design and, 593

environmental interaction and, 5

object domain analysis and, 336, 338

reactive nature of, 5

requirements analysis and, 284–289, 303–304, 322, 324–325

EDS (Earliest Deadline Scheduling) policy, 21, 27

EJB (Enterprise JavaBeans), 123

Elaborative design, 474

Embedded systems, described, 3

Emergency shutdowns, 317

EMI (electromagnetic interference), 7

Encapsulation, 117, 118–119

end attribute, 10

ENIC (Ethernet Network Interface Card), 294

entry point pseudostate, 160, 167

Episodic sessions, 369

EPROM memory, 522

ERNIE (Effect Review for Nanocycle Iterative Estimation) process, 48–51

Errors, 409, 592. *See also* Exceptions; GPF (General Protection Faults)

Essential

class diagrams, 366

object diagrams, 366

Estimation, 48–50. *See also* EWUs (estimable work units)

Ethernet

architecture and, 495, 512

nodes and, 127

PIM and, 44

requirements analysis and, 294

Evaluator class, 431–437

Event(s)

completion, 154

definition object behavior and, 441–443, 447–448

four kinds of, 153–155

groups, 518

hierarchies, 441–443

Event(s) (*cont.*)
  inserting, 447–448
  propagated, 517
  requirements analysis and,
    291–292
  signatures, 152–163
  sources, 518
  synchronous, 154
  time distributions, 238
EWUs (estimable work units),
  49–51, 54. *See also* Estimation
Exceptions, 610–614. *See also*
  Errors
Executable models, 35, 43
Execution instances, 192
Execution time. *See also* Time
  detailed design and, 604–605
  modeling resources and, 15
  worst-case, 10–11, 26–27, 134,
    604–605
exit point pseudostate, 160–161,
  167
Exit-transition-entry rule, 156
Exponential distribution, 238
Extensibility, 605

FIFO (first-in-first-out) scheduling,
  103–104, 257, 614
final pseudostate, 159
Fingerprint scans, 299
Finite state machine. *See* FSM
  (finite state machine)
FLASH memory, 522
Flight control systems
  classification of, as an embedded
    systems, 3
  GPFs and, 6
  objects and, 81–82
  resetting, 6
  scheduling policy and, 18
  structured classes and, 119–120

float data type, 85
fork pseudostate, 160, 164–167,
  186–187
Formal parameters, 107
Framework-based model
  organization, 61–62, 65
friend keyword, 107
FSM (finite state machine)
  cardiac pacemakers and,
    172–182
  definition object behavior and, 403,
    405–406
  described, 142–143
FTF (Finalization Task Force), 222
Functional cohesion, 519
Functoids, 364

Gamma distribution, 238
Gantt charts, 52
Gate, use of the term, 203
Gaussian distribution, 52, 256
Generalization, 103–106, 116.
  See also Relations
  object domain analysis and,
    370–394
  requirements analysis and,
    299–301
Generative tools
  described, 67, 68–70
  executability and, 68
Global RMA analysis, 253–254
GPF (General Protection Faults), 6.
  See also Errors
GRM (General Resource Model)
  subprofile, 227–240
Guards
  alternative branches and, 197
  definition object behavior
    and, 408
  described, 155
Guillemots («»), 90

Hamming codes, 497

Hard deadlines, 3, 8–10. *See also*
    Deadlines
  Laxity attribute and, 10
  requirements analysis and,
    316–317

Harel, David, 200

"Hello World" prototype, 52

Heterogeneous (diverse)
    redundancy, 498–499

Highest Locker Pattern, 24

Histogram distribution, 238

history pseudostate, 163–165

hyphen (-), 364, 603

Identify causal objects strategy, 340,
    343–345

Identify control elements strategy,
    341, 355–356

Identify key concepts strategy, 340,
    349

Identify messages and information
    flow strategy, 340, 346

Identify object associations strategy,
    358–361

Identify persistent information
    strategy, 341, 351–352

Identify physical devices strategy,
    340, 348–349

Identify real-world items strategy,
    340, 346–348

Identify services/passive
    contributors strategy, 340, 345

Identify transactions strategy, 340,
    349–351

Identify visual elements strategy,
    341, 351–355

IDL (interface definition language),
    493–494

IEEE (Institute of Electrical and
    Electronics Engineers), 619

ignore operator, 197, 199–201, 202,
    662

Implementation diagrams, 664

Importance, concept of, 18

Information flow diagrams, 366

Inheritance
  described, 103
  diagrams, 366
  generalization and, 103
  object domain analysis and, 366,
    371, 374–394
  tree, position features in, 374–394

Inheritance, state, 167–169

initial pseudostate, 159, 161

iNotion (I-Logix), 59

Instance(s)
  execution, 192
  model, 89
  multiplicity, 100, 118
  of classes, classification of objects
    as, 113
  port, 120

Instantiable classes, 107, 112

Institute of Electrical and Electronics
    Engineers (IEEE), 619

int data type, 83

Integration testing, 70–71

Intellectual property, 78

Interaction(s)
  definition object behavior and,
    443–462
  described, 140, 189–211
  fragments, 190, 192, 204, 206
  operators, 196–201
  partial ordering and, 194–195
  requirements analysis and, 278
  sequence diagrams and, 190–204

Interface(s)
  architecture and, 504, 518
  components and, 123
  described, 89–91

Interface(s) (*cont.*)
 low-level, 292
 mapping objects and, 111–113
 messages and, 92–94
 object domain analysis and, 375
 offered, 375
 realization of, 90
 required, 375
 requirements analysis and,
  290–292
 structured classes and, 118–119
 UML profiles and, 217–218
isAtomic attribute, 10
Iterative development
 described, 33
 MDD and, 33
 prototypes and, 507
 ROPES process and, 35, 39–40
 simulation and, 35
Iterators, 466
iUnknown interface, 123

Java
 behavior and, 140
 generative tools and, 70
 MDA and, 45
 mechanistic design and, 546
 nodes and, 127
 Virtual Machine (JVM), 127
join pseudostate, 160, 164–167
junction pseudostate, 159–160,
  161–163
JVM (Java Virtual Machine), 127

Laxity attribute, 10
Lifelines, 190, 192–193
 decomposition of, 201–204
 notation and, 192
 timing diagrams and, 207, 208
LIFO (last-in-first-out) scheduling,
  257
LINT, 555

Liskov Substitution Principle (LSP),
  167–169, 372–373, 375, 593
LL (Least Laxity) scheduling policy,
  21
Logical architecture. *See also*
  Architecture
 classes and, 509
 described, 477, 478–481
Logical model-based model
  organization, 62, 63–64
Lollipop notation, 90
loop operator, 196, 198–199, 662
LSP (Liskov Substitution Principle),
  167–169, 372–373, 375, 593

Macrocyles, 31–32, 33
Mainframes, 7
Maximum
 burst length, 11
 interarrival time, 11
MDA (model-driven architecture),
  43–46, 475–476
MDD (Model-Driven Development),
  33–36
Mean lateness, described, 11
Mechanism, use of the term, 529
Mechanistic design, 38, 41
 described, 474, 476, 527–587
 design patterns and, 530–538
Memory. *See also* RAM (random-
  access memory)
 architecture and, 522
 definition object behavior
  and, 464
 detailed design and, 604
 development environments and, 7
 EPROM, 522
 FLASH, 522
 mechanistic design and, 555,
  556
 objects and, 83
 testing, 296

Message(s)
  described, 12, 92–94
  identifiers, 496
  ignore operator and, 201
  interactions and, 192
  nodes and, 127
  overtaking, 195
  pacemaker, list of, 412
  requirements analysis and,
      291–292, 316
  synchronization patterns and
      12–13
Metaclasses
  described, 43
  stereotypes and, 102–103, 217
  UML profiles and, 217, 221
Metamodels, 131–133, 220–221
Methods
  described, 86, 89
  operations and, distinction
      between, 463
Meyer, Bertrand, 591
Microcycles, 31–32, 36–43, 52
Microphases, 36–52
Microwave ovens, 3, 156–158
Minimum
  arrival time, 26
  interarrival time, 11, 316
Mission(s)
  class diagrams and, 367
  common, 72–73
  described, 366
  prototypes and, 33
  ROPES process and, 72–73
  structural diagrams and,
      109–110
Model(s). *See also* Modeling
      languages
  -code bidirectional associativity, 35
  executability of, 68–70
  organization principles, 55–65
  use of the term, 43

Modeling languages. *See also* Models
  described, 43
  two parts of, 43
Modifiers, 466
Motivational schedules
  described, 47
  estimation and, 48
MTBF (mean time between failure),
      498–499, 619
MUF (Maximum Urgency First)
  policy, 20
Multiplicity
  instance, 100, 118
  property, 97–98
Mutex (mutual exclusion)
  semaphore, 23

Namespaces
  dependencies and, 107
  packages and, 116
Nanocycles, 31–33, 48–50
neg operator, 196, 662
.NET Framework (Microsoft), 123
Nodes
  architecture and, 509–512
  $C^4$1SR Framework and, 631–632
  classes versus, 127–129
  described, 125–127
  detailed design and, 606–610
  pivot, 608
  types of, 125–126
Normal distribution, 238
Notation
  activity diagrams and, 184–189,
      670–671
  additional, 133–136
  class diagrams and, 654–657
  communication diagrams and, 658
  components and, 122
  deployment diagrams and, 664
  events and, 154
  implementation diagrams and, 664

Notation (*cont.*)
  interfaces and, 119
  overview of, 87–89, 653–673
  packages and, 665
  ports and, 119
  sequence diagrams and, 659–663
  statecharts and, 666–669
  subsystems and, 124–125
  timing diagrams and, 672–673
  use cases and, 663
NumberStack class, 438–440

Object(s). *See also* Object domain
      analysis
  architectural hierarchy and,
      129–130
  behavior, defining, 399–472
  behavioral analysis, 38
  described, 80–83, 490
  diagrams, 108, 367
  mapping, to code, 110–113
  notation and, 87–89
  primitive, 141
  reactive, 142
  structural analysis, 38, 40
Object domain analysis, 38, 331–398.
      See also Domains
  attributes and, 344–456, 362–364,
      394–395
  candidate classes and, 364–365
  class diagrams and, 365–395
  connecting object models with
      use case models, 334–339
  generalization and, 370–394
  inheritance and, 366, 371,
      374–394
  object discovery process and,
      332–334
  strategies for, 339–358
OCP (Open-Closed Principle),
      374–375

OMG (Object Management Group),
      78, 475
  CORBA and, 268
  systems engineering and, 29
  UML profiles and, 7, 222
Open loop control systems, 4
Operational view, 619–622
Operations
  behavior and, 147, 463–471
  defined, 86, 463
  detailed design and, 600–602
  interactions and, 196–201
  interfaces and, 90–91
  pure virtual, 86
  strategies and, 468–471
  types of, 465–468
OperatorStack class, 438–440
opt operator, 196, 198, 662
OSI (Open Systems Interconnect)
      model, 504–505
OXF (Object Execution Framework),
      446

PA (Performance Analysis) package,
      226–227, 256–258
Pacemaker(s), 3, 172–183. *See also*
      ECG (electrocardiography)
      machines
  definition object behavior and,
      409–422, 444–454
  messages, list of, 412
  object domain analysis and,
      356–358
  time constraints and, 8–9
  timing diagrams and, 206
Package(s)
  described, 56, 113–130
  diagrams, 108, 366
  model organization and, 58, 60–65
  notation and, 665
  object behavior and, 415, 417

object domain analysis and, 336
UML profiles and, 224–225, 226
visibility, 88
par operator, 197, 201, 254, 662
Parallel regions, 199
Parameter(s)
events and, 153–154
ignore operator and, 201
lists, 107, 153
requirements analysis and, 316
Parameterized classes, 107
Parametric classes, 438
Parentheses, 424
Partial ordering, 194–195
Parts, described, 116–120
Party microphase, 36
Passive objects, 345
Passwords, 299
Patterns, design. *See also* Design
applying, 530
container pattern, 567–579, 598
diagrams, 367
guarded call pattern, 562–567
mechanistic design and, 528, 530–584
model organization, 60–65
observer pattern, 533–538
proxy pattern, 538–547
reliable transaction pattern, 547–554
rendezvous pattern, 579–584
smart pointer pattern, 555–562
thread boundary pattern, 582
PBX telephone systems, 148–156
PDF (probability density function)
burst length and, 11
time subprofile and, 238
PDR (preliminary design review), 52

Performance. *See also* RTP (UML Profile for Schedulability, Performance, and Time)
overview of, 7–28
requirements analysis and, 278, 316–317
workload and, 28
Period value, 238
Periodic
arrival patterns, 11, 238
sessions, 369
Permission relation, 107–108
Persistent information, 351
Petri nets, 186
Physical architecture. *See also* Architecture
described, 477, 479, 481–486
elements of, 509
issues, 501–503
Physical model-based model organization, 64
PID control systems, 144, 317, 403–404
Piece-wise continuous systems, 144
PIF (platform-independent framework), 46
PIM (platform-independent model), 43–46
Planning schedules, described, 47
Plus sign (+), 88, 150, 364, 603
Poisson distribution, 238, 256
Polymorphism, 103, 471
Port(s)
architecture and, 518
behavioral, 120
described, 116–120
instances, 120
interfaces and, 119
relay, 120
Post/pend pairs, 95
Postconditions, described, 93–94

POSTs (power-on self-tests),
348
Pound sign (#), 364, 603
Preconditions, 93–94
Preempted Time attribute, 10
Priorities, assigning, 523
Priority attribute, 10
Priority inversion model,
23–25, 27
Private visibility, 88
Process, use of the term, 512
Processors. *See* CPUs (central
processing units)
Profiles (UML). *See also* RTP (UML
Profile for Schedulability,
Performance, and Time)
adoption of, 7–8
described, 216–221
QoS and, 8
requirements analysis and, 278
stereotypes and, 217–218
tagged values and, 219–220
usage paradigm for, 225
Properties. *See* Tagged values
Property sheets, 219–221
Protected rendezvous, 521
Protected visibility, 88
Protocol state machines, 89, 182–184,
185
Prototypes
architecture and, 507–508
described, 36
iterative prototyping and, 507
mission of, 33
model organization principles
and, 59, 64
ROPES process and, 32–33, 36,
52–53
scheduling and, 51–53
Proxy pattern, 538–547
Pseudostates, 158–167
Public visibility, 88

Pure virtual
functions, 373
operations, 86
Purify, 555

QoS (Quality of Service)
architecture and, 494
constraints, 133–134
detailed design and, 605
modeling resources and, 15
overview of, 7–28
required/offered, 15
requirements analysis and,
278, 299, 307, 309–310, 316–317
UML profiles and, 8, 227, 229,
231, 241
Qualifiers, use of the term, 596
Quicksort, 605
QVT (query/view/translate), 475

RAM (random-access memory).
See also Memory
development costs and, 6
testing, 296
Rapid RMA (Tri-Pacific
Corporation), 79, 223
Ready Time attribute, 10
Real-time. *See also* RTP (UML
Profile for Schedulability,
Performance, and Time)
CORBA subprofile, 268–273
use of the term, 3
Receiver role, 406
Reduction, 434
ReedSwitch State Model, 177–178
ref operator, 196
Refactoring, 71
Relation(s). *See also specific types*
described, 94–113
requirements analysis and,
299–301
use cases, 299–301

Relative Deadline attribute, 10
Release Time attribute, 10
Reliability
    architecture and, 30, 497–499
    described, 498
    detailed design and, 605
    requirements analysis and, 278
    view, 497–499
Reliable transaction pattern, 547–554
Rendezvous
    architecture and, 489, 520–522
    described, 489
    mechanistic design and, 532,
        562–567, 579–584
    pattern, 579–584
    thread, 520–522
Requirements. *See also* Requirements
        analysis
    capture, sequence diagrams for,
        308–316
    described, 278–279
    taxonomy, 278–279
Requirements analysis. *See also*
        Requirements
    activity diagrams and, 322–327
    actors and, 280, 282–297, 301
    decomposition and, 286, 293, 296
    dependencies and, 286, 299–300,
        310
    described, 37, 277–330
    management (RM), 67–68
    model organization principles
        and, 57
    QoS and, 278, 299, 307, 309–310,
        316–317
    ROPES process and, 37–38, 40
    scenarios and, 306–317, 326
    statecharts and, 317–322, 323
    timing diagrams and, 308, 325–327
Resource(s)
    architecture and, 488–492, 513–523
    described, 490

diagrams, 367
histograms, 52–53, 54
scheduling and, 52–53, 54
sharing, 522–523
UML profiles and, 227–240
usage, 227
view, 488–492
Retinal scans, 299
Reusability, 605
Reviews, 52, 72. *See also* BERT
        (Bruce's Evaluation and Review
        Technique) process; ERNIE
        (Effect Review for Nanocycle
        Iterative Estimation) process
Rhapsody (I-Logix)
    architecture and, 485–486
    definition object behavior and, 445,
        447–448, 454–464
    executability and, 68
    MDA and, 44–46
    mechanistic design and, 529
    nanocycles and, 33
    ROPES process and, 40
    RTP and, 79
    Test Conductor, 46
    UML profiles and, 223
Risk, use of the term, 499
RM (requirements management),
        67–68. *See also* Requirements
RMA (rate monotonic analysis)
    with blocking, 27, 254
    UML profiles and, 223, 253–254
RMS (Rate Monotonic Scheduling)
        policy, 20, 21–22, 26, 523
RoC (rate of change), 81, 84
ROI (return on investment), 47
Role(s)
    detailed design and, 596–597
    mechanistic design and, 528
    names, 95–96, 101–102
ROM (read-only memory), 296. *See
        also* Memory

ROPES (Rapid Object-Oriented
    Process for Embedded System)
    process
    architecture and, 30–31, 38, 41, 62,
        473, 477–478, 484–486
    BERT (Bruce's Evaluation and
        Review Technique) process,
        48–50, 51
    described, 31–42
    Design microphase, 36, 38, 41
    ERNIE (Effect Review for
        Nanocycle Iterative Estimation)
        process, 48–51
    MDD and, 33–36
    microcycles, 31–32, 36–43, 52
    microphases, 36–52
    model organization principles
        and, 55–65
    object domain analysis and,
        332–334, 338, 366
    packages and, 114–116
    requirements analysis and, 286,
        304, 306
    rules for diagrams, 72
    SDP and, 66
    structural diagrams and, 109–110
Round Robin scheduling policy, 19
RPC (remote procedure call), 12, 92,
    567, 600
RS232 connections, 127
RS485 connections, 127
RSA (real-time CORBA
    schedulability analysis), 268
RTAD (Real-Time Analysis and
    Design Working Group),
    78, 222
RTOS, 92, 94, 46
RTP (UML Profile for Schedulability,
    Performance, and Time), 9–10,
    13, 16. See also UML profiles
    Concurrency subprofile, 225
    described, 7, 78–79, 215–275

GRM (General Resource Model)
    subprofile, 227–240
    Resource Modeling subprofile, 225
    stereotypes and, 134
    Time Modeling subprofile, 225

SA (Schedulability Analysis)
    package, 225, 226
Safety
    architecture and, 30, 497–499,
        519
    detailed design and, 605
    use of the term, 499
Safety and reliability view, 497–499
Scalability
    composition and, 102
    packages and, 113–114
    UML profiles and, 222–223
Scenario(s)
    analysis, 254–256
    described, 443
    identifying, 301
    PA subprofile and, 256–258
    partially constructive, 443
    primary, 307
    requirements analysis and,
        306–317, 326
    text for, 309
    use cases and, 306–317
Schedulability, 11, 17–28. See also
    Scheduling
    modeling subprofile, 242–256
    priority inversion model and,
        23–25, 27
    resources and, 15
    strong conditions for, 26
Scheduling. See also Schedulability;
    Scheduling policies
    estimation and, 48–50
    FIFO (first-in-first-out), 103–104,
        257, 614
    LIFO (last-in-first-out), 257

model-based projects, 46–55
reasons for, 46–55
Scheduling policies. *See also*
    Scheduling
categories of, 18–19
described, 5
fair, 18–19
importance of, 17–18
PA subprofile and, 257–258
priority, 18–21
responsive, 18–19
robust, 18–19
scheduling contexts and, 17
stable, 18
UML profiles and, 257–258, 268
unfair, 18–19
Scrolling waveforms, 325
SCSI (Small Computer Systems
    Interface) bus, 496
sd operator, 196, 662
SDP (software development plan), 66
Search operations, 142, 400
Security
    detailed design and, 605
    passwords, 299
    requirements analysis and, 278
Selectors, 466
Semantics
    additional, 133–136
    run-to-completion, 147
Semaphores, 14, 92, 219
SemiSpiral lifecycle, 33, 34
"Send-and-forget" rendezvous, 22
Sender role, 406
seq operator, 196, 662
Sequence diagrams
    decomposition of, 201–204
    definition object behavior and,
        444–462
    described, 190–204
    notation and, 659–663
    partial ordering and, 194–195

timing specifications and, 239–240
use cases and, 308–316
Serialization, accessing, 22–23
shallow history pseudostate, 160
Signatures, described, 93–94
Simulation, 35, 68, 257, 440–441
Simulator class, 440–441
Smalltalk, 471
Smart pointer pattern, 555–562
Soft deadlines, 8–10, 316–317. *See also*
    Deadlines
Soft real-time systems
    described, 3
    execution time and, 11
Software engineering
    nodes and, 127
    systems engineering versus, 29
Spacecraft, 6, 113–114
    architecture and, 482
    requirements analysis and, 300–301
Specialization, 270–371, 373, 374, 378
Specialized classes, 370
Square brackets ([]), 192, 408
Stack class, 438–440
Stacks, 438–440, 611–613
start attribute, 10
State(s). *See also* Statecharts
    described, 148, 403
    features of, 150–152
    models, inherited, 167–169
    nesting of, 149
Statecharts. *See also* States
    activity diagrams and, 186
    basic elements of, 148–156
    behavior and, 142–143, 147–156,
        420–423, 432–433
    ill-formed, 169–172
    model organization principles
        and, 57
    notation and, 666–669
    requirements analysis and,
        317–322, 323

Static model, analysis of, 254
Stereotype(s)
  components and, 122
  dependency and, 106–108
  described, 14, 90, 102–103, 134
  generalization and, 106
  interfaces and, 90
  nodes and, 125–126
  notation and, 14–15
  PA subprofile and, 257–260
  packages and, 114
  real-time CORBA, 270–271
  UML profiles and, 217–218,
    246–247
STL (Standard Template Library),
  529
Stochastic arrival pattern, 11
Strategic defects, 33
Stream sockets, 600
strict operator, 196, 662
Strong cohesion, 84
Structural diagrams, 108–110
Structured classifiers, 116–120
Structure reliability diagrams, 366
Structure safety diagrams, 366
Subclasses
  described, 370
  detailed design and, 593
  generalization and, 103, 105
  inherited state models and, 169
  LSP and, 375
Submachines, 167–168
Subprofiles, 224–227
Substitutability, 371–372
Subsystem(s)
  architectural hierarchy and,
    129–130
  described, 113–130, 123–125, 126
  diagrams, 366
  model-based model organization,
    62
  view, 486–488

Superclasses
  described, 370
  detailed design and, 593
  inherited state models and, 169
  LSP and, 372–373
Swim lanes, 140, 637
  activity diagrams and, 198
  described, 189
Symmetric distribution architecture,
    492–493
Synch-asynch pattern, 12
Synch-synch pattern, 12–13
System aspects, use of the term, 29
System architecture, 501–503. *See also*
    Architecture
System boundary, 280
System engineering
  described, 29
  nodes and, 127
  ROPES process and, 38
  software engineering versus, 29
System model-based model
    organization, 62
Systems view, 619, 622–625
System task diagram, 513–515

Tag definitions, 232, 235–236
Tagged values, 134, 219–221, 237
  described, 219–220
  PAclosedWorkload, 260
  PAhost, 260–261
  PAopenLoad, 261
  PAresource, 261–262
  PAstep, 262
  RSAclient, 271
  RSAconnection, 272
  RSAmutex, 272
  RSAorb, 273
  RSAserver, 273
  SAAction, 248–251
  SAResource, 251–252
  SATrigger, 252

Task(s)
  described, 513
  diagrams, 14, 366–367
  independence of, 27
  sets, sample, 27
TCP (Transmission Control
    Protocol), 293–294, 600. *See also*
    TCP/IP (Transmission Control
    Protocol/Internet Protocol)
TCP/IP (Transmission Control
    Protocol/Internet Protocol), 446,
    512. *See also* TCP (Transmission
    Control Protocol)
  architecture and, 484, 495, 512
  asych-asych transfers and, 12
  detailed design and, 600
  PIM and, 44
TDMA (Time Division Multiple
    Access) protocols, 495
Technical view, 620, 625
Template(s)
  classes, 438
  dependency and, 107
  detailed design and, 600–601
terminal pseudostate, 159
Testing. *See also* Debugging
  definition object behavior and,
    447–448, 454–464
  formal, 35
  model organization principles
    and, 57, 58–59
  requirements analysis and, 302,
    305
  ROPES process and, 35, 40, 70–71
  three levels of, 70–71
  unit, 59, 67, 70–71
Testing microphase, 36, 39, 42
Text node, 133. *See also* Nodes
Thread(s)
  assigning objects to, 520
  boundary pattern, 582
  defining, 516–518

  described, 513
  heavyweight/lightweight, 513
  identifying, 518–520
  rendezvous, 520–522
  representing, 513–514
  system task diagrams and, 513–515
Tilde (~), 603
Time. *See also* Constraints; Execution
    time; Timeliness
  complexity, 604
  concept of, 16–17
  constraints, described, 8–9
  events, two types of, 17
  modeling subprofile, 232–235
  subprofile stereotypes, 232
  subprofile tag definitions, 235–236
  timers and, 16–17
  worst-case execution, 10–11, 26–27,
    134, 604–605
Time-Division Round Robin
    scheduling policy, 19
Timed rendezvous, 521
Timed wait rendezvous, 12
timeInterval, 16
Timeliness. *See also* Time
  analysis, overview of, 7–28
  architecture and, 523
  assigning priorities and, 523
  modeling resources and, 15
  requirements analysis and, 278
Timeout events, 17
Timeout messages, 199
Timers, measurement of time by,
    16–17
Time-Triggered Cyclic Executive
    scheduling policy, 19
timeValue, 16
Timing diagrams, 204–211, 239, 308,
    325–327, 672–673
Token flow, 186
Tokenizer class, 427–431
Transactional objects, 406–408

Transactions, 349, 406–408
Transition(s)
    anonymous, 154
    C⁴ISR and, 640–641
    definition object behavior and, 403, 406
    described, 148, 152–153, 403
    execution order rules and, 156
    internal, 150–151
    legal, 155
    syntax, 152–153
Translation microphase, 36, 38–39, 42
Transparent classes, 119

U2P consortium, 79
UDP (User Datagram Protocol), 600
UML profiles. *See also* RTP (UML Profile for Schedulability, Performance, and Time)
    adoption of, 7–8
    described, 216–221
    QoS and, 8
    requirements analysis and, 278
    stereotypes and, 217–218
    tagged values and, 219–220
    usage paradigm for, 225
Unbounded
    arrival pattern, 238
    priority inversion, 23
Underline the noun strategy, 339–343
Uniform distribution, 238
Unit testing, 59, 67, 70–71. *See also* Testing
UNIX, 5–6
Urgency, concept of, 18
Use case(s)
    activity breakdown, 288–289
    -based model organization, 60–62
    definition object behavior and, 413, 422–423
    described, 280
    detailing, 305–328
    diagrams, described, 280–281
    identifying, 301–305
    notation and, 663
    object domain analysis and, 332–339
    realized, 280, 307
    relations, 299–301
    requirements analysis and, 280–305
    scenarios, 306–317
    textual characterizations of, 297–299
    user interface, 290–291
    using, 301
use keyword, 107
Utilization
    bound, 26–27
    use of the term, 26

Validation testing, 70–71. *See also* Testing
virtual keyword, 373
Virtual memory, 6. *See also* Memory
Visibility, 88, 602–603
VxWorks, 338, 456

Waiting rendezvous, 521
Waterfall lifecycle, 33, 51
Waveform display styles, 325
Windows (Microsoft), 102, 338, 456
Word (Microsoft), 123
Worst-Case Completion Time attribute, 10
Worst-case execution time, 10–11, 26–27, 134, 604–605. *See also* Execution time

Other Books by Bruce Powel Douglass

Doing Hard Time
Developing Real-Time Systems with UML, Objects, Frameworks, and Patterns

Doing Hard Time is written to facilitate the daunting process of developing real-time systems. It presents an embedded systems programming methodology that has been proven successful in practice. The process outlined in this book allows application developers to apply practical techniques—garnered from the mainstream areas of object-oriented software development—to meet the demanding qualifications of real-time programming.

ISBN 0-201-49837-5 • © 1999

Real-Time Design Patterns
Robust Scalable Architecture for Real-Time Systems

Sophisticated developers rely on design patterns—proven solutions to recurrent design challenges—for building fail-safe RTE systems. *Real-Time Design Patterns* is the foremost reference for developers seeking to employ this powerful technique. The text begins with a review of the Unified Modeling Language (UML) notation and then introduces the Rapid Object-Oriented Process for Embedded Systems (ROPES) and its key technologies. A catalog of design patterns and their applications follows. The book's extensive problem-solving templates, which draw on the author's years in the trenches, will help readers find faster, easier, and more effective design solutions.

ISBN 0-201-69956-7 • © 2003

For more information on these titles, visit www.awprofessional.com.

informIT

www.informit.com

YOUR GUIDE TO IT REFERENCE

Articles

Keep your edge with thousands of free articles, in-depth features, interviews, and IT reference recommendations – all written by experts you know and trust.

Online Books

Answers in an instant from **InformIT Online Book's** 600+ fully searchable on line books. For a limited time, you can get your first 14 days **free**.

POWERED BY
Safari
TECH BOOKS ONLINE

Catalog

Review online sample chapters, author biographies and customer rankings and choose exactly the right book from a selection of over 5,000 titles.

Wouldn't it be great

if the world's leading technical publishers joined forces to deliver their best tech books in a common digital reference platform?

They have. Introducing
InformIT Online Books
powered by Safari.

◾ Specific answers to specific questions.

InformIT Online Books' powerful search engine gives you relevance-ranked results in a matter of seconds.

◾ Immediate results.

With InformIT Online Books, you can select the book you want and view the chapter or section you need immediately.

◾ Cut, paste and annotate.

Paste code to save time and eliminate typographical errors. Make notes on the material you find useful and choose whether or not to share them with your work group.

◾ Customized for your enterprise.

Customize a library for you, your department or your entire organization. You only pay for what you need.

Get your first 14 days FREE!

For a limited time, InformIT Online Books is offering its members a 10 book subscription risk-free for 14 days. Visit **http://www.informit.com/onlinebooks** for details.

informit.com/onlinebooks

Register
Your Book

at www.awprofessional.com/register

You may be eligible to receive:
- Advance notice of forthcoming editions of the book
- Related book recommendations
- Chapter excerpts and supplements of forthcoming titles
- Information about special contests and promotions throughout the year
- Notices and reminders about author appearances, tradeshows, and online chats with special guests

Contact us

If you are interested in writing a book or reviewing manuscripts prior to publication, please write to us at:

Editorial Department
Addison-Wesley Professional
75 Arlington Street, Suite 300
Boston, MA 02116 USA
Email: AWPro@aw.com

Visit us on the Web: http://www.awprofessional.com

LIVERPOOL
JOHN MOORES UNIVERSITY
AVRIL ROBARTS LRC
TEL. 0151 231 4022